Sultz & Young's

HEALTH CARE USA

Understanding Its Organization and Delivery

Kristina M. Young, MS
Clinical Assistant Professor Emerita
School of Public Health and Health Professions
State University of New York at Buffalo
Buffalo, New York
President
Kristina M. Young & Associates, Inc.
Buffalo, New York

Philip J. Kroth, MD, MS
Director, Biomedical Informatics Research, Training and Scholarship
Health Sciences Library and Informatics Center
Associate Professor and Section Chief for Clinical Informatics
Divisions of Translation Informatics and General Internal Medicine
University of New Mexico School of Medicine
Albuquerque, New Mexico

D1709053

JONES & BARTLETT
LEARNING

World Headquarters
Jones & Bartlett Learning
5 Wall Street
Burlington, MA 01803
978-443-5000
info@jblearning.com
www.jblearning.com

Jones & Bartlett Learning books and products are available through most bookstores and online booksellers. To contact Jones & Bartlett Learning directly, call 800-832-0034, fax 978-443-8000, or visit our website, www.jblearning.com.

Substantial discounts on bulk quantities of Jones & Bartlett Learning publications are available to corporations, professional associations, and other qualified organizations. For details and specific discount information, contact the special sales department at Jones & Bartlett Learning via the above contact information or send an email to specialsales@jblearning.com.

11492-8

Production Credits

VP, Executive Publisher: David D. Cella
Publisher: Michael Brown
Associate Editor: Danielle Bessette
Production Editor: Vanessa Richards
Senior Marketing Manager: Sophie Fleck Teague
Manufacturing and Inventory Control Supervisor: Amy Bacus
Composition: Integra Software Services Pvt. Ltd.

Cover Design: Scott Moden
Rights & Media Specialist: Merideth Tumasz
Media Development Editor: Shannon Sheehan
Cover Image: © Lightix/Shutterstock
Printing and Binding: LSC Communications
Cover Printing: LSC Communications

Library of Congress Cataloging-in-Publication Data

Names: Young, Kristina M., author. | Kroth, Philip J., author. | Preceded by (work): Sultz, Harry A. Health care USA.
Title: Health care USA : understanding its organization and delivery / Kristina M. Young, Philip J. Kroth.
Description: Ninth edition. | Burlington, MA : Jones & Bartlett Learning, [2018] | Preceded by Health care USA : understanding its organization and delivery / Harry A. Sultz, Kristina M. Young. 8th ed. c2014. | Includes bibliographical references and index.
Identifiers: LCCN 2016044745 | ISBN 9781284114676 (paperback)
Subjects: | MESH: Delivery of Health Care | Health Policy | United States
Classification: LCC RA395.A3 | NLM W 84 AA1 | DDC 362.10973--dc23 LC record available at https://lccn.loc.gov/2016044745

6048

Printed in the United States of America
21 20 19 18 17   10 9 8 7 6 5 4 3 2 1

*This book is dedicated to our parents,
Jacob Jay and Marie Young, and Joseph R. Kroth and
Nathalie Baszczynski-Kroth. We owe each of them our
untold gratitude for the values they instilled and the
examples they provided.*

Contents

Foreword xi

Acknowledgments xiii

About the Authors xiv

About the Contributor xv

Introduction xvi

New to the Ninth Edition xxi

Chapter 1 Overview of Health Care: A Population Perspective 1

Problems of Health Care 2

Understanding Health Care 3

    Why Patients and Providers Behave the
Way They Do 3

    Indexes of Health and Disease 3

    Natural Histories of Disease and the Levels
of Prevention 4

Major Stakeholders in U.S. Healthcare
Industry 9

    The Public 9

    Employers 9

    Providers 11

    Hospitals and Other Healthcare
Facilities 11

    Governments 11

    Complementary and Alternative
Therapists 11

    Health Insurers 12

    Long-Term Care Industry 12

    Voluntary Facilities and Agencies 12

    Health Professions Education and Training
Institutions 13

    Professional Associations 13

    Other Health Industry Organizations 13

    Research Communities .13

Rural Health Networks 14

Priorities of Health Care 15

Tyranny of Technology 15

Social Choices of Health Care 16

Aging Population 16

Access to Health Care 17

Quality of Care 18

Conflicts of Interest 18

Health Care's Ethical Dilemmas 19

Continuing Challenges 20

Chapter 2 Benchmark Developments in U.S. Health Care 23

The Great Depression and the Birth of
Blue Cross 24

Dominant Influence of Government 25

Three Major Health Care Concerns 26

Efforts at Planning and Quality Control 27

Managed Care Organizations 28

The Reagan Administration: Cost Containment
and Prospective Hospital Reimbursement 28

Biomedical Advances: Evolution of
High-Technology Medicine 29

    Technical Advances Bring New
Problems 29

Roles of Medical Education and
Specialization 30

Influence of Interest Groups 31

    The American Medical Association 31

    Insurance Companies 31

    Consumer Groups 32

    Business and Labor 32

    Pharmaceutical Industry 32

    Public Health Focus on Prevention 33

Health Insurance Portability and
Accountability Act 33

The Balanced Budget Act of 1997 34

Oregon Death with Dignity Act and Other
End-of-Life Legislation 34

Health Information and Technology for
Economic and Clinical Health Act 35

The Internet and Health Care 36

The Patient Protection and Affordable Care
Act of 2010 36

    Judicial Challenges to the Affordable
    Care Act 37

The Affordable Care Act Implementation
Provisions 37

    New Consumer Protections 38

    Improving Quality and Lowering Costs 38

    Increasing Access to Affordable Care 39

    Holding Insurance Companies
    Accountable 40

**Chapter 3   Health Information
Technology 45**

Historical Overview 45

Historical Challenges in Implementing Health
Information Technology 46

The Federal Government's Response to Health
Information Technology Implementation
Challenges 50

HIT Opportunities: Improving Healthcare
Delivery Quality, Effectiveness, and
Efficiency 53

Health Information Exchanges 56

The Veterans Administration Health
Information System 62

Electronic Health Record Adoption Progress
in the United States 62

Future Challenges 65

✓**Chapter 4   Hospitals: Origin, Organization,
and Performance 71**

Historical Perspective 72

Effects of Insurance on the Hospital Industry 73

Health Insurance 73

Medicare and Medicaid 73

Growth and Decline in Numbers of Hospitals 74

Types of Hospitals 75

Financial Condition of Hospitals 76

Academic Health Centers, Medical Education,
and Specialization 76

Hospital System of the Department of
Veterans Affairs 77

Structure and Organization of Hospitals 78

    Medical Division 78

    Nursing Division 79

    Allied Health Professionals 80

    Diagnostic Services 80

    Rehabilitation Services 81

    Other Patient Support Services 81

    Nutritional Services 81

    Administrative Departments 82

    Hotel Services 82

Information Technology's Impact on
Hospitals 82

Complexity of the System 83

Types and Roles of Patients .83

    Rights and Responsibilities of
    Hospitalized Patients 84

    Informed Consent and Second
    Opinions 85

Diagnosis-Related Group Hospital
Reimbursement System 86

Discharge Planning 87

Post-Diagnosis-Related Group and Managed
Care 87

    Early Market Reforms 87

    Horizontal Integration 88

    Vertical Integration 89

Quality of Hospital Care 89

    Hazards of Hospitalization 89

    Variations in Medical Care 92

    Nurse Shortage Staffing Crisis 92

    Research Efforts in Quality
    Improvement 93

    Responsibility of Governing Boards for
    Quality of Care 93

Hospitalists 95

Forces of Reform. 96

    The Affordable Care Act 96

    Population Focus 96

    Market Consolidations: Hospital Mergers
        and Acquisitions 97

    Accountable Care Organizations 97

    Reimbursement and Payment Revisions 98

    Medicare Access & CHIP Reauthorization
        Act of 2015 102

Continuing Change. 103

Chapter 5   Ambulatory Care 109

Overview and Trends 109

Private Medical Office Practice 111

Integrated Ambulatory Care Models 114

    Patient-Centered Medical Homes 115

    Accountable Care Organizations 119

Other Ambulatory Care Practitioners 120

Ambulatory Care Services of Hospitals:
    History and Trends 120

Hospital Emergency Services 122

Non-hospital-Based (Freestanding) Facilities . . . 124

    Urgent Care Centers 124

    Retail Clinics 126

    Ambulatory Surgery Centers. 127

    Federally Qualified Health Centers 128

    Public Health Ambulatory Services. 130

    Not-for-Profit Agency Ambulatory Services 132

Telehealth 133

Continued Future Expansion and
    Experimentation 133

**Chapter 6   Medical Education and the
             Changing Practice of
             Medicine 141**

Medical Education: Colonial America to the
    1800s 141

Flexner Report and Medical School Reforms . . . 143

Transition from Academic Medical Centers to
    Academic Health Centers 144

Graduate Medical Education 145

Delineation and Growth of Medical
    Specialties 147

    Deficient Training of Medical
        Specialists 148

Certification of Physicians with Board
    Examinations 149

Accreditation of Graduate Physician Training . . . 150

Physician Workforce Supply and Distribution . . . 151

Ratios of Generalist to Specialist Physicians
    and the Changing Demand 152

Preventive Medicine 154

Changing Physician–Hospital Relationships 155

    Evidence-Based Clinical Practice
        Guidelines 156

Physician Report Cards and "Physician
    Compare" 157

Health Information Technology and Physician
    Practice 159

Escalating Costs of Malpractice Insurance 160

Ethical Issues 160

Physicians and the Internet 161

Future Perspectives 162

Chapter 7   The Healthcare Workforce . . . 169

Health Professions 169

    Credentialing and Regulating Health
        Professionals 170

Healthcare Occupations 172

    Physicians 172

    Nursing 173

    Registered Nurses 174

    Licensed Practical Nurses 177

    Nurse Practitioners 178

    Physician Assistants. 179

    Clinical Nurse Specialists. 180

    Dentistry 180

    Pharmacy 182

    Podiatric Medicine. 182

    Chiropractors. 183

    Optometry 183

    Healthcare Administrators 184

    Allied Health Personnel 184

Technicians and Technologists 185
  Laboratory Technologists and
    Technicians 185
  Radiologic and Magnetic Resonance
    Imaging Technologists 185
  Nuclear Medicine Technology 186
Therapeutic Science Practitioners 186
  Physical Therapy 186
  Occupational Therapy 187
  Speech-Language Pathology 187
Behavioral Scientists 187
  Social Work 188
  Rehabilitation Counselor 188
Support Services 188
  Health Information Administrators 189
  Complementary and Integrative
    Medicine Practitioners 189
  Medical Assistant 190
Factors That Influence Demand for Health
  Personnel 191
  Changing Nature of Disease, Disability,
    and Treatment 191
  Physician Supply 191
  Technology 191
  Expansion of Home Care 191
  Corporatization of Health Care 192
Healthcare Workforce Issues and the Patient
  Protection and Affordable Care Act 192
The Future: Complexities of National Healthcare
  Workforce Planning 193

Chapter 8 Financing Health Care 201

Healthcare Expenditures in Perspective 202
  Waste, Fraud, and Abuse 207
Drivers of Healthcare Expenditures 208
Evolution of Private Health Insurance 209
  The Rise of Blue Cross and Blue Shield
    and Commercial Health Insurance 209
Transformation of Health Insurance:
  Managed Care 210
  Managed Care Backlash 213
Managed Care Today 214
  MCOs and Quality 214

Private Health Insurance Cost Trends 216
Self-Funded Insurance Programs 217
Government as a Source of Payment:
  A System in Name Only 217
    Medicare 218
Medicaid and the Children's Health Insurance
  Program 228
    Children's Health Insurance Program 229
Medicaid Managed Care 230
Medicaid Quality Initiatives 230
Medicaid Expansion Under the Affordable
  Care Act 231
Disproportionate Share Hospital Payments 232
Healthcare-Financing Mandates of the
  Affordable Care Act for Individuals
  and Employers 232
    The Individual Mandate and Health
      Insurance Marketplaces 233
    The Employer Mandate 234
The Affordable Care Act: Insurance Coverage
  Progress and Costs 234
Continuing Challenges and Innovations 235

Chapter 9 Long-Term Care 245

Development of Long-Term Care Services 246
Modes of Long-Term Care Service
  Delivery 250
    Skilled Nursing Care 250
    Assisted-Living Facilities 252
    Home Care 254
    Hospice Care 258
    Respite Care 261
    Adult Day Care 263
Innovations in Long-Term Care 264
    Aging in Place 265
    Continuing Care Retirement and Life
      Care Communities 265
    Naturally Occurring Retirement
      Communities 267
    High-Technology Home Care: Hospitals
      Without Walls 267
Long-Term Care Insurance 267
Future of Long-Term Care 268

Chapter 10   Behavioral Health Services 277

Historical Overview 278

Recipients of Psychiatric and Behavioral
Health Services 281

Treatment Services 285

Barriers to Care 285

Children and Adolescents 285

Older Adults 286

The Organization of Psychiatric and Behavioral
Health Services 287

Paradigm Shifts 289

Recovery Oriented Systems of Care 289

Integration of Primary Care and
Behavioral Health Services 289

Financing Psychiatric and Behavioral Health
Services 291

Public Funding of Behavioral
Health Care 292

Cost Containment Mechanisms 293

The Future of Psychiatric and Behavioral
Health Services 295

**Chapter 11   Public Health and the Role
of Government in Health
Care 301**

Public Health Defined 301

Early History 302

Public Health in England 303

Development of U.S. Public Health and
Government-Supported Services 304

Government Responsibilities for Health and
Public Health 306

Federal Responsibilities 306

Veterans Health Administration 309

Department of Defense Military Health
System 309

State and Local Government
Responsibilities 310

State Roles 310

Local Roles 315

State and Local Health Department
Relationships 319

Voluntary National Public Health Department
Accreditation 320

Public Health Organization Challenges
and Responses 321

Public Health Accomplishments and
Resource Challenges of the 20th and
21st Centuries 323

Public Health Services of Voluntary
Organizations 327

Relationships of Public Health and Clinical
Medicine 327

Public Health Ethics 330

The ACA and Public Health 331

National Prevention, Health Promotion
and Public Health Council 331

Health Care Workforce Development 331

Current and Future: Enduring and Emerging
Public Health Challenges 332

Enduring Public Health Issues 332

Emergent Domestic Public Health
Issues 334

Emergent Global Public Health
Issues 338

The Future 341

**Chapter 12   Research: How Health Care
Advances 351**

Focus of Different Types of Research 352

Types of Research 352

Agency for Healthcare Research and
Quality 355

Health Services Research and Health
Policy 356

Quality Improvement 357

Medical Errors 359

Evidence-Based Medicine 360

Outcomes Research and the Patient-Centered
Outcomes Research Institute 363

The Patient-Centered Outcomes Research
Institute 364

Patient Satisfaction Surveys 365

Research Ethics and Conflicts of
Interest 366

Future Challenges 367

Chapter 13 Future of Health Care 371

Paradox of U.S. Health Care 372

Accountability for Quality and Costs 372

Health Information Technology 374

Hospitals 375

Changing Population Composition 376

Growth in Home Care and Ambulatory Care
    Services. 377

    Home Care Services 377

    Ambulatory Care Services 377

The Healthcare Workforce. 378

    Physician Supply and Distribution 378

    Emerging Physician Roles. 379

    Nurses. 380

    National Health Care Workforce
        Planning 380

Employer-Sponsored Health Insurance. 381

Medical Technology 382

ACA and MACRA: Reemergence of Population
    Health Principles 383

Ethical Challenges 384

Summary of Predictions and Future
    Questions. 385

Appendix A. 393

Glossary 397

Index. 411

Foreword

This ninth edition of *Health Care USA: Understanding Its Organization and Delivery* marks the end of an era and the beginning of a new one. In the early 1990s, I was invited to create a series of books on epidemiology, public health, and health care. For the volume on health care, I engaged my esteemed colleague and good friend Professor Harry Sultz, who, in turn, invited Professor Kristina Young to join him as coauthor. Having had unique and complementary experiences, they produced the first edition of this book in 1996, and it became a best seller.

Throughout his professional career, Professor Sultz was inspirational to his colleagues and students alike. He approached each new edition of the book with excitement. He always kept the reader in mind as he wrote clearly and succinctly. For each edition, he included the most up-to-date advances in health care with the comments and analyses of a seasoned researcher and author. Woven through the many subjects covered in the book, the reader can sense the special contribution of Professor Sultz, an author who indeed has "been there."

In 2014, after the eighth edition was published, Professor Sultz decided to retire from his coauthorship of the text, but his thoughts and contributions will continue to be evident in the ninth and succeeding editions. This ninth edition, under the able lead authorship of Kristina Young and with her new, highly credentialed coauthor, Dr. Philip Kroth, will continue the tradition of being on the cutting edge of understanding the complex issues of health care and its delivery—a fitting tribute to Professor Harry Sultz.

Now, almost 7 years since becoming law in 2010, the Patient Protection and Affordable Care Act (ACA) has survived an unprecedented number of Congressional challenges. Although the period since its implementation is very short in historical terms of system change, the ACA is beginning to yield results.

Through the ACA, more than 20 million Americans have gained access to health insurance through state-based marketplace exchanges and Medicaid expansion. Value-based payment reforms through patient-centered medical homes, accountable care organizations, and historic physician payment reforms are beginning to reign in cost growth and improve healthcare quality through increased transparency and accountability. It is certain that experimentation with new healthcare delivery models will continue to identify best practices as healthcare providers and organizations continue adapting to the ACA and marketplace changes.

The ninth edition of *Health Care USA* provides a clear overview of the technical, economic, political, and social forces that shape the healthcare industry and the public health enterprise. The authors have meticulously screened vast amounts of new information to include critical updates that make important contributions to students' knowledge of the current healthcare delivery system with a population focus.

Michel A. Ibrahim, MD, PhD
Professor of Epidemiology
Editor-in-Chief, Epidemiologic Reviews
Johns Hopkins Bloomberg School of
Public Health

and

Dean and Professor Emeritus
School of Public Health
University of North Carolina at
Chapel Hill

Acknowledgments

We acknowledge with our sincerest gratitude Susan V. McLeer, MD, MS, for her outstanding contribution of the chapter on behavioral health services. As a consummate clinician and academician, her expertise, effort, and enthusiastic participation has provided an exceptionally clear and insightful presentation of the complex issues and system responses in her field. Dr. McLeer's professional summary appears in the "About the Contributor" section. We are grateful to Michel Ibrahim, MD, PhD, professor, Johns Hopkins Bloomberg School of Public Health and Dean and professor emeritus of the School of Public Health at the University of North Carolina at Chapel Hill, who encouraged production of the first edition of this book in 1996 and has contributed the "Foreword" to each edition.

We also appreciate the invaluable help of experts who performed editing, literature searches, word processing, and other support services. This and earlier editions of this book benefited inestimably from the health care and library and information science research expertise of Karen Buchinger. Sharon Palisano reviewed and word processed all manuscripts of the nine editions of this book with meticulous attention to every detail of the publisher's requirements. We remain grateful for her unparalleled professional skill and patience with the complex details of these large texts. We also wish to recognize the important contributions of our publisher and publisher's staff for encouraging our efforts, helping shape the results, and motivating us to improve the book's utility to its users. To each of you we offer our profound thanks.

About the Authors

Kristina M. Young, MS, is a clinical assistant professor emerita who also served as the co-director of the health services administration concentration in the Department of Epidemiology and Environmental Health at the School of Public Health and Health Professions, State University of New York at Buffalo. For more than 20 years at the University at Buffalo, she taught graduate courses in healthcare organization and health policy for students in the fields of public health, law, and management. For several years, she also taught graduate courses on healthcare systems at Canisius College in Buffalo, New York. Ms. Young also is president and owner of Kristina M. Young & Associates Inc., a management consulting and training firm specializing in health and human services organizations. Her career has included administration of maternal and child health programs for a county health department; executive director of a multi-county public health alliance; executive vice-president of an organization dedicated to advancing the joint interests of a major teaching hospital and a health maintenance organization; and vice president for research and development for a teaching hospital system and executive director of its health, education, and research foundation. Ms. Young received her BA degree in biology from Canisius College in Buffalo, New York, and her M.S. degree in epidemiology from the State University of New York at Buffalo School of Medicine.

Philip J. Kroth, MD, MS, is an associate professor in the University of New Mexico (UNM) School of Medicine. He is also is the director of the Biomedical Informatics Research, Training, and Scholarship unit at the UNM Health Sciences Library and Informatics Center and Section Chief of Clinical Informatics in the UNM Department of Internal Medicine. Before joining UNM in 2004, Dr. Kroth received his B.S. in Computer Engineering from the Rochester Institute of Technology in 1987, his MD degree from the Medical College of Ohio in 1995, and completed his residency in internal medicine at the State University of New York at Buffalo in 1999. He completed a research fellowship in biomedical informatics at the Regenstrief Institute at the Indiana University Medical Center where he also earned an MS in clinical research in 2003. At UNM, in addition to practicing as a general internist, he directs a post-doctoral research fellowship in biomedical informatics and a new clinical informatics fellowship for physicians. Dr. Kroth was elected national chair of the American Medical Informatics Association Academic Forum for 2015. Dr. Kroth's areas of research focus include adapting clinical records for research, the promotion of open access publication, and assessing the impact of health information technology (HIT) on user burnout and fatigue. He is currently the principal investigator of an AHRQ-funded, multi-institutional research project focusing on clinician HIT stress. Dr. Kroth is board-certified in both internal medicine and clinical informatics.

About the Contributor

Susan V. McLeer, MD, MS, is professor and chair emerita of the Department of Psychiatry at the Drexel University College of Medicine and former professor and chair of the Department of Psychiatry at the State University of New York at Buffalo School of Medicine and Biomedical Sciences. Board-certified in both psychiatry and child and adolescent psychiatry and with a master's degree in psychiatric administration, she has extensive experience in managing and integrating services at all levels of care, both within public and private behavioral health systems. She continues as a fierce advocate for improvements in the public sector system of care and has taught multiple generations of medical students and residents aspiring to care for people who are in need of psychiatric and/or behavioral health services.

Dr. McLeer has more than 85 publications to her credit, including peer-reviewed journal articles, book chapters, and published abstracts. Combining her experience at the medical schools in Buffalo, New York, and Philadelphia, Pennsylvania, she has been the chair and chief clinical officer for an academic department of psychiatry for more than 19 years and served in academia for 40 years. She currently serves and provides expert consultation for the American Psychiatric Association's National Council on Healthcare Systems and Financing, a position she has held for more than 10 years. Additionally, she is an active member and contributor to the Council's Workgroup on Public Sector Psychiatry, a group that has been actively studying the impact of the U.S. economy on public sector behavioral health systems.

Introduction

The prior edition of this text devoted substantial material to outlining and explaining the new landmark Patient Protection and Affordable Care Act of 2010 (the ACA). At that point, work had just begun on enacting the ACA, and it had already survived U.S. Supreme Court challenges on the constitutionality of its core provisions for the "individual mandate" and Medicaid expansion.[1] The law survived another major challenge in 2015 when the Supreme Court deliberated a lawsuit alleging that federal tax subsidies to help offset health insurance costs for individuals in certain states were illegal.[1] Now, more than 6 years after its passage and approximately 3 years after its major provisions became effective, the impact of this young law is most evident by the fact that more than 21 million Americans have gained access to affordable health insurance through enrollment in private insurance and the public Medicaid program.[2,3] In 2015, for the first time in its 50-year history of conducting national surveys, the Centers for Disease Control and Prevention reported that the proportion of uninsured Americans had fallen below 10 percent.[4] While the historic reduction in the uninsured population is already well established, the provisions of the ACA designed to control the rising costs of health care and improve its quality are not yet fully implemented. To meet its cost-reduction goals, the ACA is now starting to make historic changes to the ways in which health care is delivered and how providers are compensated. In addition, the ACA embraces a population perspective on health and health care. This perspective shifts the system's longstanding focus from the care of individuals to health outcomes achieved for population groups. Increasingly, providers' compensation will be linked to quality of outcomes in populations under their care.

As the ACA achieves its intended effects over the coming years, the healthcare delivery system is expected to emerge from its old form of fragmented, piecemeal services and payments and opaque quality. The new system is expected to be one in which integrated systems of coordinated care reward providers for continuity of care and publicly disclosed outcomes. Along with the ACA, newer legislative initiatives such as the Medicare Access and Children's Health Insurance Program Reauthorization Act of 2015 (MACRA) will promote synergistic effects with the ACA and are discussed in detail in this new edition. In producing this edition, it was highly evident to the authors that prior lines of demarcation among delivery-system components are rapidly blurring as the population perspective gains traction. For example, the ACA continues experiments in which patients' illnesses are treated and paid for as single "episodes of care" by all involved providers—primary care physicians, specialists, hospitals, and others, in a seamless continuum rather than in a series of disconnected encounters.[5] While major system components remain largely intact, the ways in which they operate and interact with each other are changing dramatically. These are positive and challenging developments for healthcare providers and patients alike. They offer many opportunities for more efficient and effective use of U.S. healthcare resources and most importantly for the health of Americans.

We hope that our treatment of the subject matter provides a foundation for comprehending facts to encourage curiosity about continuing developments and the effects of legislation as its implementation proceeds. We also note that in just the first 2 years since its passage, proposed rules and regulations to implement the ACA underwent changes and revisions. As with any legislation, these changes and revisions can be expected to continue in what will be an ongoing and dynamic process.

The U.S. healthcare system remains a mystifying puzzle to many Americans, and ongoing changes will doubtless add additional complexity. Health care in the United States is an enormous $3 trillion industry. It includes thousands of independent medical practices, business partnerships, provider organizations, public and nonprofit institutions, hospitals, nursing homes, the pharmaceutical industry, and huge health insurance corporations. Health care is by far the largest service industry in the country. In fact, U.S. healthcare system expenditures rank it as the world's fifth largest economy, second only to that of the entire economy of Germany and larger than the entire economy of the United Kingdom.[6]

More intimidating than its size, however, is its complexity. Not only is health care a labor-intensive industry at all levels, but also the types and functions of its numerous personnel change periodically to adjust to new technology, knowledge, and ways of delivering services. As is frequently associated with progress, medical advances often create new problems while solving old ones. The explosion of medical knowledge that produced narrowly defined medical specialties compounded a longstanding shortcoming of American medical care. The delivery of sophisticated high-technology health care requires the support of a vastly complicated infrastructure that has resulted in disarray and allowed patients to fall between the cracks among its narrowly defined services and specialists. In addition, even at its enormous expense, the system proved inept in securing even a modicum of universal health insurance coverage for the general population.

The size and complexity of health care in the United States has contributed to its longstanding problems of limited access, inconsistent quality, and uncontrolled costs. The healthcare system remains challenged by disparities that result in wide variations in the access, availability, and quality of services for many of its citizens. These problems have concerned U.S. political and medical leaders for decades and motivated many legislative proposals aimed at reforms. Since World War II, attempts at major reforms were mounted by President Truman in the 1940s, President Johnson in the 1960s, President Nixon in the 1970s, and President Clinton in the 1990s.[7] Johnson's efforts resulted in the 1965 passage of Medicare, which provided universal health insurance to Americans beginning at 65 years of age, and Medicaid, which provided health insurance for qualifying low-income individuals of all ages. Nixon's legislation resulted in the HMO Act of 1973, which laid groundwork for development of the managed care insurance system of today. Truman's and Clinton's proposals failed. However, neither the Johnson nor Nixon successes resulted in comprehensive reforms, costs in line with other industrialized nations, or universal benefits for all Americans. Over years of implementation that will continue through 2019, the spectrum of the ACA provisions will vastly exceed the impacts of Medicare and Medicaid. Medicare and Medicaid affected specific populations of individuals qualified by program criteria; the ACA affects virtually all Americans.

Given the past history of failed attempts at comprehensive health reform, the ACA's development and passage within 14 months of President Obama's taking office in January 2009 is historically unprecedented and represents an unparalleled time trajectory for legislation of this magnitude, scope, and complexity. In fact, on the occasion of signing the new law, the President himself commented, "Our presence here today is remarkable and improbable."[8] The chronicle of rancorous partisan political debates, passionate outcries from a misinformed citizenry, negotiations with interest groups, and intervening events, such as the death of Democratic Senator Edward Kennedy and his replacement with a Republican, fills volumes in the history of the ACA.

The timing of the ACA's development, and ultimately its passage, represented the Obama administration's rapidly seizing a "policy window of opportunity" to put comprehensive health reform on the Congressional agenda. As described by a public policy expert, this "policy window of opportunity" for new or amended legislation arises when problems have reached a magnitude of scope and urgency that allows their survival in competition from other issues; potentially feasible solutions can be identified; and sufficient political will exists to drive the process forward.[9] In the case of the proposed ACA, problems included the widely acknowledged economic unsustainability of rising healthcare costs linked with the all-important issue of the rising federal deficit; the moral, social, and economic implications of more than 40 million uninsured citizens; and the system's well-documented shortcomings in quality. Proposals for potential solutions to these problems had a very lengthy and evidence-based research history. Political will to move comprehensive health reform onto the legislative agenda was established early by the highest-profile contenders for the 2008 Democratic party presidential nomination agreeing that they would support "universal coverage."[10] Also, in early 2008, the very powerful health-reform advocate Senator Edward Kennedy agreed to endorse Mr. Obama's candidacy with the pledge of Obama's commitment to make healthcare reform his top domestic priority, including a commitment to universal coverage.[8] Finally, with a new president elected on a platform of change and Democratic majorities in both houses of Congress, the "policy window of opportunity" allowed moving the comprehensive health reform agenda forward.

Over many past decades, healthcare reform as a market-driven, rather than a policy-driven, phenomenon began well in advance of the new healthcare reform legislation. Since the 1990s, in a world of accelerating consolidation to achieve ever-higher standards of effectiveness and economy, there have been surges of healthcare facility and service organization mergers and acquisitions, with new roles for individual and organizational providers.[11] In the past few years, the term "merger mania" describes rapid consolidations of hospital systems and insurers to prepare for the payment and delivery reforms of the ACA and other legislation.[12] Today, hospitals compete for patients and "market share," independently operated clinics are springing up in unprecedented numbers with convenient locations and venues, and physician group practices are forgoing their independence to embrace hospital employment to join with integrated systems of care that leverage population-based reimbursement schemes of the reformed system.[13] All of these factors will continue to interplay in highly dynamic professional, political, and economic landscapes as effects of legislative reforms continue unfolding.

The ninth edition coalesces the unique and congruent perspectives of its authors. Ms. Young is a career health services administrator, who trained as an epidemiologist and taught graduate courses for two decades in schools of medicine, public health, management, and law. Dr. Kroth is board-certified in both internal medicine and clinical informatics. He is an active clinician, researcher, informatics training program administrator, and medical school faculty member and mentor.

Collectively, the authors have worked in the academic, research, clinical, and health management spheres for decades and have assiduously studied and followed developments in the healthcare delivery system. In particular, their work with students always seeks ways to convey balanced perspectives on the outstanding features of the U.S. healthcare delivery system as well as its foibles.

As in the past eight editions, this edition intends to serve as a text for introductory courses on the organization of health care for students in schools of public health, medicine, nursing, dentistry, and pharmacy and in schools and colleges that prepare a host of other allied health professionals. It provides an introduction to the U.S. healthcare system and an overview of the professional, political, social, and economic forces that have shaped it and the provisions of new legislation that will continue to do so.

To facilitate its use as a teaching text, when read in sequence, chapters provide incremental additions of information to complete the reader's understanding of the entire healthcare system. As in prior editions, decisions about what subjects and material were essential to the book's content were relatively easy, but decisions about the topics and content to be left out were difficult. This was especially challenging as we researched the ACA and related legislation and made decisions about the breadth and depth of its subject matter to include. Thus, the authors acknowledge that information presented on the ACA and subsequent legislation is limited to what we believe most pertinent to the text's major subjects and note that the information is not exhaustive. Copious references are provided to lead interested readers to explore subjects in more detail and depth. Second, the authors respectfully acknowledge that certain categories of healthcare professionals may be disappointed that the text contains so little of the history that characterizes the evolution of their important professions. Given the centrality of those historical developments in students' educational preparation, the authors assumed that books written specifically for those purposes would be included in courses in those professional curricula. To be consistent with that assumption, the authors included only those elements in the history of public health, medicine, and hospitals that had a significant impact on how health care is delivered.

The authors made similar difficult decisions regarding the depth of information to include about other subjects. Topics such as epidemiology, the history of medicine, program planning and evaluation, quality of care, and the like each have their own libraries of in-depth texts and, in many schools, dedicated courses. Thus, the authors deemed it appropriate in this introductory text to provide only enough descriptive and interpretive detail about each topic to place it in the context of the overall subject of the book.

In this ninth edition, as in each previous edition, the authors have included important additions and updates to provide a current perspective on the healthcare industry's continuously evolving trends.

The authors hope that as this book's readers plan and expand their educational horizons and, later, their professional experiences, they will have the advantage of a comprehensive understanding of the complex and dynamically evolving system in which they practice.

▶ References

1. Obamacare Lawsuits. Updates on Obamacare related lawsuits: subsidies, NFIB, hobby lobby, John Boehner, and more. http://obamacarefacts.com /obamacare-lawsuit/. Accessed June 2, 2016.
2. Congressional Budget Office. Federal subsidies for health insurance coverage for people under age 65: 2016–2026. March 2016. https://www.cbo .gov/sites/default/files/114th-congress-2015-2016 /reports/51385-HealthInsuranceBaseline.pdf. Accessed May 25, 2016.

3. Department of Health and Human Services. Assistant Secretary for Planning and Evaluation. Health insurance marketplaces 2016 open enrollment period. January 7, 2016. https://aspe.hhs.gov/sites/default/files/pdf/167981/MarketPlaceEnrollJan2016.pdf. Accessed May 25, 2016.

4. Diamond D. Thanks, Obamacare: American's uninsured rate is below 10% for first time ever. *Forbes.* August 12, 2015. http://www.forbes.com/sites/dandiamond/2015/08/12/for-first-time-americas-uninsured-rate-is-below-10/#5ffdeff7741c. Accessed April 12, 2016.

5. Centers for Medicare & Medicaid. Center for Medicare & Medicaid Innovation. Bundled payments for care improvement (BPCI) initiative: general information. http://innovation.cms.gov/initiatives/bundled-payments/index.html. Accessed April 16, 2016.

6. The World Bank. Gross domestic product 2015 ranking table. July 22, 2016. http://databank.worldbank.org/data/download/GDP.pdf. Accessed April 16, 2016.

7. Blendon RJ, Benson JM. American's views on health policy: a fifty-year historical perspective. *Health Aff.* 2001;20:33–46. http://content.healthaffairs.org/content/20/2/33. Accessed May 27, 2016.

8. Staff of the Washington Post. Landmark. New York: Perseus Books Group; 2002:7.

9. Kingdon JW. *Agendas, Alternatives, and Public Policies.* 2nd ed. New York: HarperCollins College Publishers; 1995.

10. Bell, A. PPACA: a history. June 12, 2012. LifeHealthPro. http://www.lifehealthpro.com/2012/06/12/ppaca-a-history. Accessed May 27, 2016.

11. *Hospital Consolidations and Conversions: A Review of the Literature.* December 2014. Universal Health Care Foundation of Connecticut. http://universalhealthct.org/images/publications/Hospital_Consolidations_and_Conversions.pdf. Accessed June 2, 2016.

12. Terhune C. Obamacare cash fuels healthcare merger mania. *Los Angeles Times.* July 2, 2015. http://www.latimes.com/business/la-fi-health-net-centene-deal-20150702-story.html. Accessed May 27, 2016.

13. Gooch K. 6 forecasts for healthcare M&A in 2016. Becker's Hospital Review. February 24, 2016. http://www.beckershospitalreview.com/hospital-transactions-and-valuation/6-forecasts-for-healthcare-m-a-in-2016.html. Accessed May 27, 2016.

New to the Ninth Edition

The ninth edition updates all key financial, utilization, and other data with the latest available information. In addition, it conveys important, ongoing, and interrelated trends in the healthcare delivery system about costs, quality, U.S. demographics, personnel, technology, the political climate, and other factors that affect the system. Based on student feedback on the eighth edition, we have eliminated Appendix A and instead included pertinent acronyms following each chapter. Students repeatedly expressed that listing acronyms on a chapter-by-chapter basis rather than in a separate Appendix would be most valuable to their learning.

▶ Chapter 1: Overview of Health Care: A Population Perspective

- Current national health expenditure data
- New comparison of U.S. healthcare costs and health status with other developed countries
- Introduces the Medicare access and CHIP Reauthorization Act of 2015 (MACRA)
- Affordable Care Act tax provisions for insurance, pharmaceutical, and medical device companies.
- New estimates of the annual cost of addictive behaviors
- New report on the extent of medical errors
- Chapter acronyms

▶ Chapter 2: Benchmark Developments in U.S. Health Care

- Expanded discussion of the Health Insurance Portability and Accountability Act of 1996 (HIPAA) patient information privacy and security rules
- Discussion of discrete features of the Balanced Budget Act of 1997 relative to ongoing programs
- Updates on states' enactment of end-of-life legislation
- Addition of the Health Information and Technology for Economic and Clinical Health Act (HITECH) as a benchmark development in U.S. health care
- Updates on Affordable Care Act judicial challenges

▶ Chapter 3: Health Information Technology

- Update on the Medicare and Medicaid Electronic Health Record Incentive Program also known as the Meaningful Use Program including new information on Modified Stage 2 and updated statistics on physician and hospital participation rates
- Updated national electronic health record adoption statistics

- New discussion of information blocking and associated Congressional action
- New topic on national conversion to ICD-10 billing codes
- New key terms and chapter acronyms

Chapter 4: Hospitals: Origin, Organization, and Performance

- Added definition and the significance of the Triple Aim
- Added definition and the significance of the Two-Midnight Rule
- Added definition and the significance of the Choosing Wisely campaign
- Added information on certification of hospitalists
- Added a new section on the Medicare Access & CHIP Reauthorization Act of 2015 (MACRA) and how this will impact hospitals' quality reporting and charge capture activities
- New key terms and chapter acronyms

Chapter 5: Ambulatory Care

- Update of Patient Protection and Affordable Care Act primary care initiatives, programs, and demonstrations with latest data available on implementation and results, including federally qualified health centers and primary care workforce development
- Increasing hospital employment of physicians
- Research findings and trends on implementation of the patient-centered medical home and accountable care organizations
- Trends in emergency department use and emergence of clinical observation units

- Trends in increasing utilization of urgent care and retail clinics
- Discussion of telehealth
- New key terms and acronyms

Chapter 6: Medical Education and the Changing Practice of Medicine

- Description of the new Clinical Informatics Subspecialty
- Description and discussion on the American Board of Medical Specialty's (ABMS) Maintenance of Certification (MOC) Program
- Delineation of training program accreditation and individual physician board certification activities
- Delineation of the typical training pathway for U.S. physicians
- Update on physician work force training issues and the ratios of generalist to specialist physicians and the changing demand
- New description of the NIH Public Access Policy and discussion of the free and open access to the biomedical literature
- New discussion on the shortage of residency program slots relative to the increasing number of U. S. medical school graduates
- Update on Physician Compare
- New key terms and acronyms

Chapter 7: The Healthcare Workforce

- Addition of Maintenance of Certification (MOC) for physicians

- Addition of a description of Medical Assistants and the role they play in the modern healthcare system
- Update on all employment statistics and job outlook for the various healthcare occupations with the most recent U.S. Census data available
- Update on complementary and integrative health to reflect current definitions and terminology as well as updated complementary and integrative medicine use statistics for adults and children
- Update on the lack of Congressional funding for the National Health Care Workforce Commission in the Affordable Care Act
- Expanded key terms for review

▶ Chapter 8: Financing Health Care

- Most current national healthcare expenditure data with updated graphics
- Update on private health insurance coverage and costs
- Throughout the chapter, integration of ACA provisions in terms of system effects on payment and quality parameters for Medicare and Medicaid
- Current Medicare and Medicaid enrollment data
- Discussion of the federal financial impacts of the ACA implementation
- Organization of Medicare cost containment and quality initiatives by decade
- Introduction of Medicare and CHIP Reauthorization Act of 2015 (MACRA) into Medicare and Medicaid programs
- 2016 Medicaid managed care reform modernization legislation
- Parameters for Medicaid quality assessment of adult and children services
- Discussion of ACA Medicaid expansion results to date

- Addition of disproportionate share hospital payments in Medicaid section
- Update on health insurance marketplaces
- New key terms and acronyms

▶ Chapter 9: Long-Term Care

Updated:

- Projections of older American population
- Data on all forms of long-term care accommodations
- Data on long-term care resident characteristics, costs, and payment sources
- Data on nursing home ownership
- Data on number and dollar value of informal long-term caregivers
- Data on continuing care retirement and life care communities

Reports on:

- Ground-breaking 2012 National Study of Long-Term Care Providers (NSLTCP)
- Emerging states' initiatives to expand paid family medical leave

▶ Chapter 10: Behavioral Health Services

- New data and figures on the prevalence of all mental illness and serious mental illness by age groups, gender, and race/ethnicity
- Updated data and figures on types of neuropsychiatric disorders
- New cost data for behavioral health services
- New discussion of the impact of the Affordable Care Act insurance and Medicaid expansions on access to behavioral health services

- New review of homelessness and incarceration among mentally ill persons
- New discussion of behavioral health manpower shortages and evolving personnel changes in delivery of behavioral health treatment
- New discussion of the integration of psychiatric and primary care services through the evidence-based collaborative care model

▶ Chapter 11: Public Health and the Role of Government in Health Care

- Enhanced descriptions of federal, state, and local roles in U.S. health care and public health
- New figure on distribution of DHHS funds by program for FY 2017 budget
- New 2017 information on the Department of Health and Human Services programs and budgets
- Healthy People 2020 progress report
- New detailed discussion of the roles and responsibilities of state and local public health departments
- New tables outlining major state and local health department activities
- New discussion of research findings on state and local health department relationships
- Updated report on the deployment of the ACA Public Health Fund
- New discussions of domestic public health challenges: gun violence, opioid addiction, lead poisoning, and chronic disease management
- New discussion of recent and current U.S./global public health infectious disease

challenges and implications: Ebola, pandemic influenza, Severe Acute Respiratory Syndrome (SARS), and Zika virus
- Additional key terms and acronyms

▶ Chapter 12: Research: How Health Care Advances

- New and updated section on evidence-based medicine
  - The hierarchy of evidence
  - Detailed example using the Women's Health Initiative to describe the differences between observational studies and randomized controlled clinical trials
  - Definitions of systematic reviews, randomized controlled clinical trials, observational studies, case series, and expert opinion
  - Discussion of the ethics of randomized controlled clinical trials
- Clarification of the terms Big Data and Big Data Analytic for observational studies
- Discussion of the influence of the pharmaceutical industry over medical education and student-led push back
- Information on research ethics per the ACA Sunshine Act
- Updated Future Challenges section
- New key terms and acronyms

▶ Chapter 13: Future of Health Care

- Current overview of federal policies and regulations on population-based approaches to medical care and associated payment reforms including the Medicare Access and CHIP Reauthorization Act of 2015

- Update on healthcare technology trends and costs
- Updates on health system mergers and acquisitions and their effects

- Review of Congressional funding actions on ACA provisions
- Updated information on the future of employer-sponsored health insurance and the adoption of high-deductible health insurance plans

CHAPTER 1

Overview of Health Care: A Population Perspective

CHAPTER OVERVIEW

This chapter provides a broad overview of the U.S. healthcare industry—its policies, its values and priorities, and its responses to problems and changing conditions. It also provides a template for understanding the natural histories of diseases and the levels of medical intervention. Major influences in the advances and other changes to the health services system are described with pertinent references to the Patient Protection and Affordable Care Act of 2010 (ACA) and the Medicare Access and CHIP Reauthorization Act of 2015 (MACRA). Conflicts of interest and ethical dilemmas resulting from technologic advances in medicine are also noted.

Health care continuously captures the interest of the public, political leaders, and all forms of media. News of medical breakthroughs, health system deficiencies, high costs, and, most recently, federal healthcare reform through the Patient Protection and Affordable Care Act (ACA) attract high-profile attention. Consuming more than 17 percent of the nation's gross domestic product,[1] exceeding $3 trillion in costs,[1] and employing a workforce of more than 12 million,[2] health care occupies a central position in American popular and political discourse. In large measure, decades-long problems with rising costs, questionable quality, and lack of healthcare system access for large numbers of un- or underinsured Americans prompted the development and passage of the ACA. If the ACA is successful in accomplishing its intended goals by 2019, it will extend health insurance coverage to millions of uninsured people; the remaining uninsured will be illegal immigrants, low-income individuals who do not enroll in Medicaid, and others who choose to pay a penalty rather than purchase coverage.[3]

Based on 2013 data from the Organization for Economic Cooperation and Development (OECD) and other sources, a 2015 Commonwealth Fund report compared the United States with 12 other high-income OECD member countries throughout the world on healthcare spending, use of services, and prices. Compared with its high-income peer nations, U.S. population health outcomes are poor with the lowest life expectancy and the highest rates of infant mortality.[4]

These are startling outcomes given that the percentage of gross domestic product the United States devotes to health care is almost double the average of the other OECD member countries.[4] Although the ACA will provide vastly increased access to health care for millions of Americans, there are strong reasons why policy makers focus on whether increased access can result in measurable improvements in Americans' health status. "Health policy researchers are increasingly aware of the dangers of overstating the link between insurance and health."[5] As some suggest, improvements in population health will require success in merging the concepts of public health into the reformed system's approach to personal medical care.[3] With the ACA's emphasis on prevention and wellness and realigned financial incentives to support these, there is even reason for optimism that "over time, prevention and wellness could become a dominant aspect of primary care."[3]

For many, the fortunes and foibles of health care take on deeply serious meanings. There was a widespread sense of urgency among employers, insurers, consumer groups, and other policy makers about the seemingly unresolvable problems of inadequate access, rising costs, and questionable quality of care. Passionate debates about the ACA in healthcare reform focused many Americans on the role health care plays in their lives and about the strengths and deficiencies of the complex labyrinth of healthcare providers, facilities, programs, and services.

▶ Problems of Health Care

Although philosophical and political differences historically fueled the debates about healthcare policies and reforms, consensus finally emerged that the U.S. healthcare system is fraught with problems and dilemmas. Despite its decades-long series of impressive accomplishments, the healthcare system exhibits inexplicable contradictions in objectives; unwarranted variations in performance, effectiveness, and efficiency; and longstanding discord in its relationships with the public and with governments.

The strategies for addressing the problems of cost, quality and access over the eight decades since the passage of the Social Security Act reflected periodic changes in political philosophies. Government-sponsored programs of the 1960s were designed to improve access for older adults and low-income populations without considering the inflationary effects on costs. These programs were followed by regulatory attempts to address first the availability and price of health services, then the organization and distribution of health care, and then its quality. In the 1990s, the ineffective patchwork of government-sponsored health-system reforms was superseded by the emergence of market-oriented changes, competition, and privately organized managed care organizations (MCOs).

The failure of government-initiated reforms created a vacuum, which was filled quickly by the private sector. There is a difference, however, between goals for healthcare reform of the government and those of the market. Although the proposed government programs try to maintain some balance among costs, quality, and access, the primary goal of the market is to contain costs and realize profits. As a result, there remain serious concerns that market-driven reforms may not result in a healthcare system that equitably meets the needs of all Americans and may even drive up costs.[6]

▶ Understanding Health Care

Healthcare policy usually reflects public opinion. Finding acceptable solutions to the perplexing problems of health care depends on public understanding and acceptance of both the existing circumstances and the benefits and risks of proposed remedies. Many communication problems regarding health policy stem from the public's inadequate understanding of health care and its delivery system.

Early practitioners purposely fostered the mystique surrounding medical care as a means to set themselves apart from the patients they served. Endowing health care with a certain amount of mystery encouraged patients to maintain blind faith in the capability of their physicians even when the state of the science did not justify it. When advances in the understanding of the causes, processes, and cures of specific diseases revealed that previous therapies and methods of patient management were based on erroneous premises, new information remained opaque to the American public. Although the world's most advanced and proficient healthcare system provides a great deal of excellent care, the lack of public knowledge has allowed much care to be delivered that was less than beneficial and some that was inherently dangerous.

Now, however, the romantic naïveté with which health care and its practitioners were viewed has eroded significantly. Rather than a confidential contract between the provider and the consumer, the healthcare relationship now includes a voyeuristic collection of insurers, payers, managers, and quality assurers. Providers no longer have a monopoly on healthcare decisions and actions. Although the increasing scrutiny and accountability may be onerous and costly to physicians and other providers, it represents the concerns of those paying for health care—governments, insurers, employers, and patients—about the value received for their expenditures. That these questions have been raised reflects the prevailing opinion that those who now chafe under the scrutiny are, at least indirectly, responsible for generating the excesses in the system while neglecting the problems of limited access to health care for many.

Cynicism about the healthcare system grew with more information about the problems of costs, quality, and access becoming public. People who viewed medical care as a necessity provided by physicians who adhere to scientific standards based on tested and proven therapies have been disillusioned to learn that major knowledge gaps contribute to highly variable use rates for therapeutic and diagnostic procedures that have produced no measurable differences in outcomes. Nevertheless, as discussions about system-wide reforms demonstrated, enormously complex issues underlie the health industry's problems.

Why Patients and Providers Behave the Way They Do

Throughout the evolution of the U.S. hospital system, a long tradition of physicians and other healthcare providers behaving in an authoritarian manner toward patients prevailed. In the past, hospitalized patients, removed from their usual places in society, were expected to be compliant and grateful to be in the hands of professionals far more learned than they. More recently, however, recognizing the benefits of more proactive roles for patients and the improved outcomes that result, both healthcare providers and consumers encourage patient participation in healthcare decisions under the rubric of "shared decision making."[7]

Indexes of Health and Disease

The body of statistical data about health and disease has grown enormously since the late 1960s, when the government began analyzing the information obtained from Medicare and Medicaid claims and computerized hospital and insurance data allowed the retrieval and exploration of clinical information files. In addition, there have been continuing improvements in the collection, analysis, and reporting of vital statistics and communicable and malignant diseases by state and federal governments.

Data collected over time and international comparisons reveal common trends among developed countries. Birth rates have fallen and life expectancies have lengthened so that older people make up an increasing proportion of total populations. The percentage of disabled or dependent individuals has grown as healthcare professions have improved their capacity to rescue otherwise moribund individuals.

Infant mortality and maternal mortality, the international indicators of social and healthcare improvement, have continued to decline in the United States but have not reached the more-commendable levels of countries with more demographically homogeneous populations. In the United States, disparities in infant mortality rates between inner-city neighborhoods and suburban communities may be greater than those between developed and undeveloped countries. The continuing inability of the healthcare system to address those discrepancies effectively reflects the system's ambiguous priorities.

Natural Histories of Disease and the Levels of Prevention

For many years, epidemiologists and health-services planners have used a matrix for placing everything known about a particular disease or condition in the sequence of its origin and progression when untreated; this schema is called the natural history of disease. Many diseases, especially chronic diseases that may last for decades, have an irregular evolution and extend through a sequence of stages. When the causes and stages of a particular disease or condition are defined in its natural history, they can be matched against the healthcare interventions intended to prevent the condition's occurrence or to arrest its progress after its onset. Because these healthcare interventions are designed to prevent the condition from advancing to the next, and usually more serious, level in its natural history, the interventions are classified as the "levels of prevention."[8] **FIGURES 1-1, 1-2,** and **1-3** illustrate the concept of the natural history of disease and levels of prevention.

The first level of prevention is the period during which the individual is at risk for the disease but is not yet affected. Called the "pre-pathogenesis period," it identifies the behavioral, genetic, environmental, and other factors that increase the individual's likelihood of contracting the condition. Some risk factors, such as smoking, may be altered, whereas others, such as genetic factors, may not.

When such risk factors combine to produce a disease, the disease usually is not manifest until certain pathologic changes occur. This stage is a period of clinically undetectable, pre-symptomatic disease. Medical science is working diligently to improve its ability to diagnose disease earlier in this stage. Because many conditions evolve in irregular and subtle processes, it is often difficult to determine the point at which an individual may be designated "diseased" or "not diseased." Thus, each natural history has a "clinical horizon," defined as the point at which medical science becomes able to detect the presence of a particular condition.

Because the pathologic changes may become fixed and irreversible at each step in disease progression, preventing each succeeding step of the disease is therapeutically important. This concept emphasizes the preventive aspect of clinical interventions.

Primary prevention, or the prevention of disease occurrence, refers to measures designed to promote health (e.g., health education to encourage good nutrition, exercise, and genetic counseling) and specific protections (e.g., immunization and the use of seat belts).

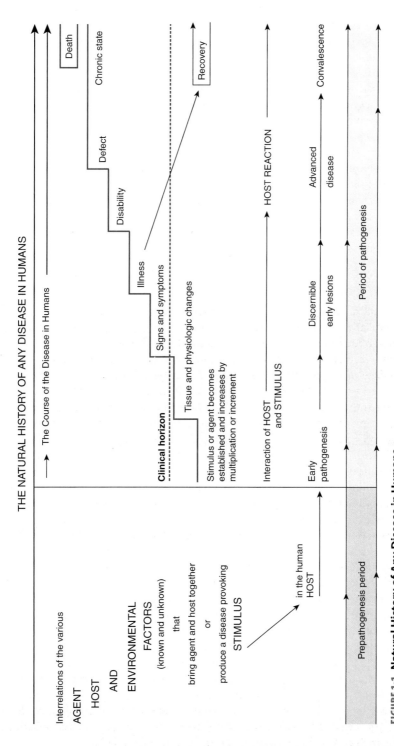

FIGURE 1-1 Natural History of Any Disease in Humans

Reprinted with permission from H.R. Leavell and E.G. Clark, Preventative Medicine for the Doctor in His Community: An Epidemiologic Approach. 3rd edition, p. 20, © 1965, The McGraw Hill Companies, Inc.

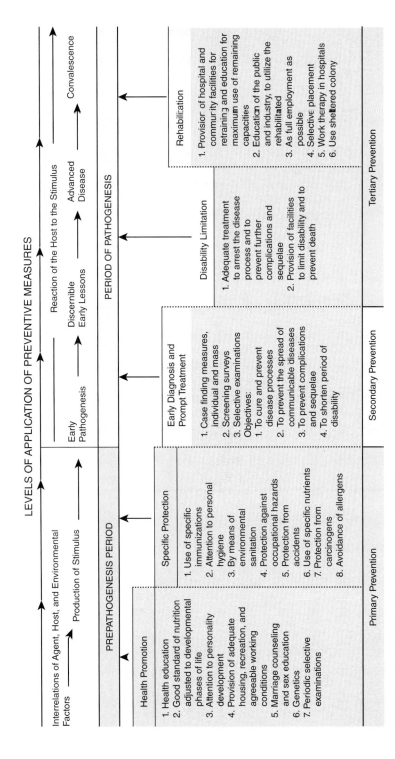

FIGURE 1-2 Levels of Application of Preventive Measures

Reprinted with permission from H.R. Leavell and E.G. Clark, Preventive Medicine for the Doctor in His Community: An Epidemiologic Approach. 3rd edition, p. 21, © 1965, The McGraw Hill Companies, Inc.

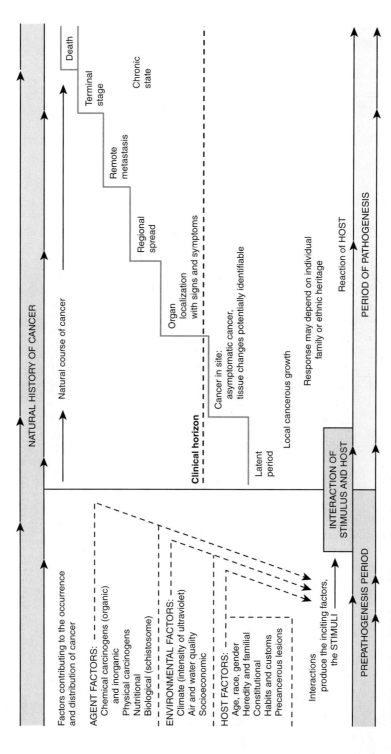

FIGURE 1-3 Natural History of Cancer (continues)

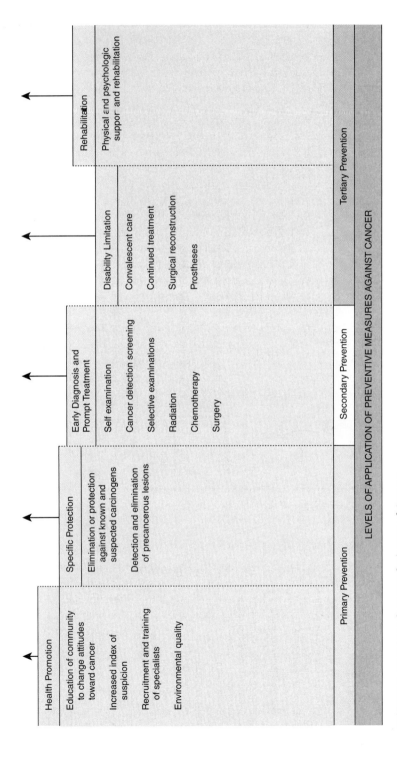

FIGURE 1-3 (continued) Natural History of Cancer

Reprinted with permission from H.R. Leavell and E.G. Clark, Preventative Medicine for the Doctor in His Community: An Epidemiologic Approach. 3rd edition, p. 272–273, © 1965, The McGraw Hill Companies, Inc.

Secondary prevention involves early detection and prompt treatment to achieve an early cure, if possible, or to slow progression, prevent complications, and limit disability. Most preventive health care is currently focused on this level.

Tertiary prevention consists of rehabilitation and maximizing remaining functional capacity when disease has occurred and left residual damage. This stage represents the most costly, labor-intensive aspect of medical care and depends heavily on effective teamwork by representatives of a number of healthcare disciplines.

FIGURE 1-4 illustrates the natural history and levels of prevention for the aging process. Although aging is not a disease, it is often accompanied by medical, mental, and functional problems that should be addressed by a range of healthcare services at each level of prevention.

The natural history of diseases and the levels of prevention are presented to illustrate two very important aspects of the U.S. healthcare system. First, in studying the natural history and levels of prevention for almost any of the common causes of disease and disability, it quickly becomes apparent that the focus of health care historically has been directed at the curative and rehabilitative side of the disease continuum. The serious attention paid to refocusing the system on population health and the health promotion/disease prevention side of those disease schemas is reflected by the National Prevention Strategy of the ACA.[9] This attention came about only after decades of relentlessly rising costs of diagnostic and remedial care and the lack of adequate insurance coverage for millions of Americans became a public and political embarrassment.

The second important aspect of the natural history concept is its value in planning community services. The illustration on aging provides a good example by suggesting health promotion and specific protection measures that could be applied to help maintain positive health status.

▶ Major Stakeholders in U.S. Healthcare Industry

To understand the healthcare industry, it is important to recognize the number and variety of the stakeholders involved. The sometimes shared and often-conflicting concerns, interests, and influences of these constituent groups cause them to shift alliances periodically to oppose or champion specific reform proposals or other changes in the industry.

The Public

First and foremost among healthcare stakeholders are the individuals who consume the services. Although all are concerned with the issues of cost and quality, those who are uninsured or underinsured have an overriding uncertainty about access. It remains uncertain as to whether the U.S. public will someday wish to treat health care like other inherent rights, such as education, but the passage of the ACA seems to suggest that there is agreement that some basic array of healthcare services should be available to all U.S. citizens.

Employers

Employers constitute an increasingly influential group of stakeholders in health care because they not only pay for a high proportion of the costs but also take proactive roles in determining what those costs should be. Large private employers, coalitions of smaller private employers, and public employers

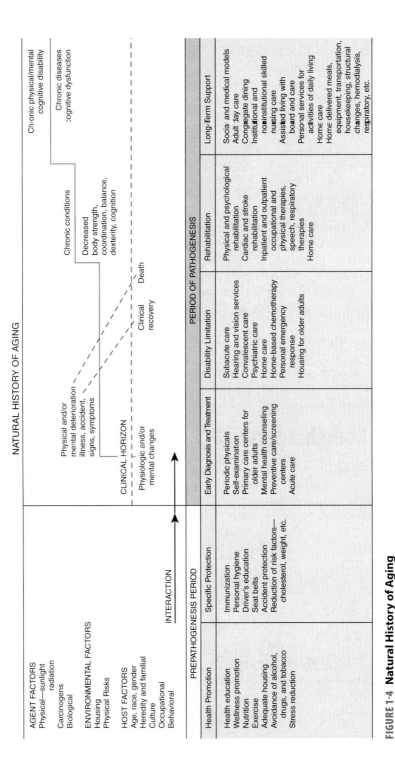

FIGURE 1-4 Natural History of Aging

Reprinted with permission from H.R. Leavell and E.G. Clark, Preventive Medicine for the Doctor in His Community: An Epidemiologic Approach. 3rd edition, p. 272–273, © 1965, The McGraw Hill Companies, Inc.

wield significant authority in insurance plan negotiations. In addition, employer organizations representing small and large businesses wield considerable political power in the halls of Congress.

Providers

Healthcare professionals form the core of the industry and have the most to do with the actual process and outcomes of the service provided. Physicians, dentists, nurses, nurse practitioners, physician assistants, pharmacists, podiatrists, chiropractors, and a large array of allied health providers working as individuals or in group practices and staffing healthcare institutions are responsible for the quality and, to a large extent, the cost of the healthcare system. Recognizing the centrality of individual providers to system reform, the ACA and the MACRA are now offering numerous opportunities for the participation of physicians and other healthcare professionals in innovative experimentation with integrated systems of care. The MACRA institutes performance-driven systems of patient care linked to the health outcomes of population groups.[10,11]

Hospitals and Other Healthcare Facilities

Much of the provider activity, however, is shaped by the availability and nature of the healthcare institutions in which providers work. Hospitals of different types—general, specialty, teaching, rural, profit or not-for-profit, and independent or multi-facility systems—are central to the healthcare system. However, they are becoming but one component of more complex integrated delivery system networks that also include nursing homes and other levels of care and various forms of medical practices.

Governments

Since the advent of Medicare and Medicaid in 1965, federal and state governments, already major stakeholders in health care, became the dominant authorities of the system. Governments serve not only as payers but also as regulators and providers through public hospitals, state and local health departments, veterans' affairs medical centers, and other facilities. In addition, of course, governments are the taxing authorities that generate the funds to support the system.

Complementary and Alternative Therapists

Unconventional health therapies—those not usually taught in established medical and other health professional schools—contribute significantly to the amount, frequency, and cost of health care. In spite of the scientific logic and documented effectiveness of traditional, academically based health care, it is estimated that one in three adults uses complementary forms of health interventions each year.[12] Complementary medicine consists of using modalities such as nutritional supplements, yoga, acupuncture, or meditation in conjunction with mainstream medical care.[13] Because of their popularity, state Medicaid programs, Medicare, and private health insurance plans provide benefits for some complementary therapies.[14] Alternative medicine uses non-mainstream treatments in place of conventional medicine. [13]

It is estimated that more than $9 billion per year is spent on complementary and alternative forms of health care such as Rolfing, yoga, spiritual healing, relaxation techniques, herbal remedies, energy healing, megavitamin therapy, chiropractic care, and a host of other mind–body healing techniques.[14]

The public's willingness to spend so much time and money on unconventional therapies suggests a substantial level of dissatisfaction with traditional scientific medicine. Thus, as a somewhat paradoxical development, some of the most ancient concepts of alternative health care are gaining broader recognition and acceptance in an era of the most innovative and advanced high-technology medicine. The National Institutes of Health operates a National Center for Complementary and Integrative Health (NCCIH) to fund studies on the efficacy of such therapies.

In recent years, a number of hospitals began offering forms of complementary and alternative medicine. According to an American Hospital Association survey, by 2000 more than 15 percent of U.S. hospitals had opened complementary or alternative medicine centers.[15] With a market estimated to be $34 billion and patients willing to pay cash for treatments, hospitals are willing to rationalize the provision of medically unproven services in response to patient demand.[16]

Health Insurers

The insurance industry has long been a major stakeholder in the healthcare industry. Today, MCO insurance plans are the predominant form of U.S. health insurance. MCOs may be owned by insurance companies, or they may be owned by hospitals, physicians, or consumer cooperatives. MCOs and the economic pressures they can apply through the negotiation of prepaid fees for healthcare services have produced much of the change occurring in the healthcare system during the past three decades. The insurance industry played a major role in the development of the ACA.[17] Under the ACA, between 2014 and 2018, the insurance industry will contribute annual fees to the federal government totaling $47.5 billion as a percent of premiums to help offset the ACA costs.[18] In subsequent years, the industry will pay fees based upon rates of premium increase.[18] This fee levy recognizes that the ACA will add millions of new insurance company customers.

Long-Term Care Industry

The aging of the U.S. population poses a formidable challenge to the country's systems of acute and long-term care. Nursing homes, home-care services, other adult-care facilities, and rehabilitation facilities will become increasingly important components of the nation's healthcare system. The ACA's creation of seamless systems of integrated care that permit patients to move back and forth among ambulatory care offices, acute care hospitals, home care, and nursing homes within a single network of facilities and services will provide a continuum of services required for the complex care of aging patients.

Voluntary Facilities and Agencies

Voluntary not-for-profit facilities and agencies, so called because they are governed by volunteer boards of directors, provide significant amounts of health counseling, health care, and research support and should be considered major stakeholders in the healthcare system. Although the voluntary sector traditionally has not received the recognition it deserves for its contribution to the nation's health care, it is often now viewed as the safety net to replace the services of government or other organizations eliminated by budgetary reductions.

Health Professions Education and Training Institutions

Schools of medicine, public health, nursing, dentistry, pharmacy, optometry, allied health, and other healthcare professions have a significant impact on the nature, quality, and costs of health care. As they prepare each generation of competent healthcare providers, these schools also inculcate the values, attitudes, and ethics that govern the practices and behaviors of those providers as they function in the healthcare system.

Professional Associations

National, state, and regional organizations representing healthcare professionals or institutions have considerable influence over legislative proposals, regulation, quality issues, and other political matters. The lobbying effectiveness of the American Medical Association, for example, is legendary. The national influence of the American Hospital Association and the regional power of its state and local affiliates are also impressive. Other organizations of healthcare professionals, such as the American Public Health Association, America's Health Insurance Plans, the American Nurses Association, and the American Dental Association, play significant roles in health policy decisions. The American insurance industry lobbyists from organizations such as America's Health Insurance Plans had major influences on the provisions of the ACA.

Other Health Industry Organizations

The size and complexity of the healthcare industry encourage the involvement of a great number of commercial entities. Several, such as the insurance industry noted above and the pharmaceutical and medical-device industries, have significant influence on the healthcare delivery enterprise. The ACA imposed annual fees on the pharmaceutical industry beginning in 2012 that will total $13.9 billion by 2018 and continue at $2.8 billion per year thereafter.[18] As with insurance companies, these fees acknowledged that the ACA would bring in much new business to the pharmaceutical industry from newly insured individuals. Medical supplies and equipment businesses and the various consulting, information, and management-system suppliers also are important players. Again recognizing that medical-device manufacturers would experience increased business from the ACA's newly insured, the law imposed a 2.3 percent excise tax on sales of taxable medical devices beginning in 2013.[18] Due to intense lobbying efforts, in late 2012 the ACA medical-device tax was suspended through the end of 2017.[19]

Research Communities

It is difficult to separate much of healthcare research from the educational institutions that provide for its implementation. Nevertheless, the national research enterprise must be included in any enumeration of stakeholders in the healthcare industry. Government entities, such as the National Institutes of Health and the Agency for Healthcare Research and Quality, and not-for-profit foundations, such as the Robert Wood Johnson Foundation, the Commonwealth Fund, the Henry J. Kaiser Family Foundation, and the Pew Charitable Trusts, exert tremendous influence over healthcare research, policy development, and practice by conducting research and widely disseminating findings and supporting and encouraging investigations that inform policy decision making.

▶ Rural Health Networks

Rural health systems often struggle with shortages of various services. Federal and state programs have addressed this situation by promoting rural health network development.[20]

Rural health networks may be formally organized as not-for-profit corporations or informally linked for a defined set of mutually beneficial purposes. Typically, they advocate at local and state levels on rural healthcare issues, cooperate in joint community outreach activities, and seek opportunities to negotiate with MCOs to provide services to enrolled populations. Most of these networks strive to provide local access to primary, acute, and emergency care and to provide efficient links to more distant regional specialists and tertiary care services. Ideally, rural health networks assemble and coordinate a comprehensive array of services that include dental, mental health, long-term care, and other health and human services.

With costs increasing and populations declining in many rural communities, it has been difficult for rural hospitals to continue their acute inpatient care services. Nevertheless, rural hospitals often are critically important to their communities. Because a hospital is usually one of the few major employers in rural communities, its closure has economic and healthcare consequences. Communities lacking alternative sources of health care within reasonable travel distance not only lose payroll and related business but also lose physicians, nurses, and other health personnel and suffer higher morbidity and mortality rates among those most vulnerable, such as infants and older adults.[21]

Some rural hospitals have remained viable by participating in some form of multi-institutional arrangement that permits them to benefit from the personnel, services, purchasing power, and financial stability of larger facilities. Many rural hospitals, however, have found it necessary to shift from inpatient to outpatient or ambulatory care. In many rural communities, the survival of a hospital has depended on how quickly and effectively it could replace its inpatient services with a productive constellation of ambulatory care, and sometimes long-term care, services.

Rural hospital initiatives have been supported by federal legislation since 1991.[21] Legislation provided funding to promote the essential access community hospital and the rural primary care hospital. Both were limited-service hospital models developed as alternatives for hospitals that were too small and geographically isolated to be full-service acute-care facilities. Regulations regarding staffing and other service requirements were relaxed in keeping with the rural settings[21] and included allowing physician's assistants, nurse practitioners, and clinical nurse specialists to provide primary or inpatient care without a physician in the facility if medical consultation is available by phone.

The Balanced Budget Act of 1997 included a Rural Hospital Flexibility Program that replaced the essential access community hospital/rural primary care hospital model with a critical access hospital (CAH) model.[22] Any state with at least one CAH may qualify for the program, which exempts CAHs from strict regulation and allows them the flexibility to meet small, rural community needs by developing criteria for establishing network relationships. Although the new program maintained many of the same features and requirements as its predecessor, it added more flexibility by increasing the number of allowed occupied inpatient beds and the maximum length of stay before required discharge or transfer. The new program also allowed a swing bed program to provide flexibility in their use. The goal of the CAH program is to enable small rural hospitals to maximize reimbursement and meet community needs with responsiveness and flexibility.

The Balanced Budget Act also served rural hospitals by providing Medicare reimbursement for telemedicine and other arrangements that link isolated facilities with clinical specialists at large hospitals. Telemedicine technology makes it possible for a specialist to be in direct visual and voice contact with a patient and provider at a remote location. The ACA contains significant support for the continued expansion of telemedicine programs that began with prior Medicare-supported pilot projects.[23]

▶ Priorities of Health Care

The historical priorities of America's healthcare system, which emphasize dramatic tertiary care and costly and intensive efforts to fend off the death of terminal patients for a few more days or weeks, have contributed to the obvious mismatch between the costs of health care and the failure to improve the measures of health status in the United States.

If health care were to be governed by rational policies, the benefits to society of investing in primary prevention that is unquestionably cost-effective would be compared with both the human and economic costs of salvaging individuals from preventable adverse outcomes. Unfortunately, priorities have favored heroic medicine over the more mundane and far less costly preventive care that results in measurable human and economic benefits. As noted previously, major tenets of the ACA are designed to shift the focus from curative to preventive priorities through the implementation of the National Prevention Strategy.[9]

▶ Tyranny of Technology

In many respects, as noted many times throughout this text, the healthcare system has accomplished remarkable work and continues to do so. Important advances have been made in medical science, bringing measurable improvements in the length and quality of life. The paradox is, however, that as technology grows in sophistication and costs, increasing numbers of people are deprived of its benefits. Healthcare providers can be so mesmerized by their own technologic ingenuity that things assume greater value than people. For example, hospital administrators and medical personnel commonly dedicate their most-competent practitioners and most-sophisticated technology to the care of terminal patients while allocating far fewer resources to primary and preventive services for ambulatory clinic patients and other community populations in need of basic medical services.

Some hospitals recognize this disparity by conducting outreach and education programs for the medically underserved. Now with the ACA aligning reimbursement with prevention and wellness efforts, more institutions likely will find it beneficial to initiate and maintain prevention initiatives and allocate more resources to the potentially more productive care of discharged patients and ambulatory clinic populations.

The recurring theme among health-services researchers assessing the value of technologic advances is a series of generally unanswered questions:

1. How does the new technology benefit the patient?
2. Is it worth the cost?
3. Are the new methods better than previous methods, and can they replace them?
4. Is treatment planning enhanced?
5. Is the outcome from disease better, or is the mortality rate improved?

Although many of the latest advances have gained great popularity and widespread acceptance, rigorous assessments that address these basic questions remain sorely needed.

Much of the philosophy underlying the values and priorities of the healthcare system today can be attributed to the unique culture of U.S. medicine. That philosophy owes much to the aggressive "can do" spirit of the frontier. Diseases are likened to enemies to be conquered. Physicians expect their patients to be aggressive, too. Those who undergo drastic treatments to "beat" cancer are held in higher regard than patients who resign themselves to the disease. Some physicians and nurses feel demoralized when dying patients refuse resuscitation or limit interventions to palliative care.

The treatment-oriented rather than prevention-oriented healthcare philosophy has been encouraged by an insurance system that, before managed care's prevention orientation and efforts to curb unnecessary interventions, rarely paid for any disease prevention other than immunizations. It also is understandable in a system prizing high-technology medicine and rewarding volume regardless of value that there has been much more satisfaction and remuneration from saving the lives of the injured and diseased than in preventing those occurrences from happening in the first place.

▶ Social Choices of Health Care

The American emphasis on cure over prevention disinclined the healthcare professions to address those situations over which they have had little control. Behavioral issues such as acquired dependence on tobacco, alcohol, and drugs must be counted among the significant causes of impaired health in the U.S. population with staggering human and economic costs. In 2014, the National Institute on Drug Abuse reported an estimated combined annual cost of $700 billion related to crime, lost work productivity, and health care due to these addictions.[24]

Nevertheless, outside of the public health disciplines, the considerable influence and prestige of the healthcare professions have been noticeably absent in steering public opinion and governmental action toward an emphasis on behavioral health. Similarly, in comparison with resources expended on treatment after illness occurs, relatively little attention had been given to changing high-risk behaviors even when the consequences are virtually certain and nearly always extreme.

▶ Aging Population

The aging of the U.S. population will have wide-ranging implications for the country. As the United States ages over the next several decades, its older population will become more racially and ethnically diverse. Projecting the size and structure in terms of age, sex, race, and ethnic origin of the older population is important to public and private interests, both socially and economically. Current estimates place the population 65 years of age and older at 44.7 million, 14.1 percent of the population, or about one in every seven Americans.[25] The number of persons aged 65 years or older is expected to grow to 21.7 percent of the population by 2040, totaling 82.3 million. A current U.S. Census projection estimates that the population 65 years or older will more than double in number between 2013 and 2060 reaching 98.2 million by year 2060.[25]

As medical advances find more ways to maintain life, the duration of chronic illness and the number of chronically ill individuals will increase with a concomitant increase in the need for personal support. The intensity of care required by frail older adults also has the potential of affecting worker productivity, as it is common for family members to leave the workforce or to work part time to care for frail relatives.

The increased number of older persons with chronic physical ailments and cognitive disorders raises significant questions about the capability and capacity of U.S. healthcare system. Healthcare professionals are just beginning to respond to the need to focus health care for older adults away from medications or other quick-fix remedies. The system is slowly acknowledging that the traditional medical service model is inappropriate to the care of those with multiple chronic conditions.

The growing number of older adults face serious gaps in financial coverage for long-term care needs. Unlike the broad Medicare program coverage for the acute healthcare problems of older Americans, the long-term care services needed to cope with the chronic disability and functional limitations of aging are largely unaddressed by either Medicare or private insurance plans. With the exception of the relatively small number of individuals with personal long-term care insurance, the costs of long-term care services are borne by individual older adults and their caregivers.

As a last resort, the Medicaid program became the major public source of financing for nursing home care. Medicaid eligibility, however, requires that persons "spend down" their personal resources to meet financial eligibility criteria. For those disabled older adults who seek care in the community outside of nursing homes, Medicaid offers very limited assistance. Provisions of the ACA make some progress in addressing these issues. The reform plan, called "Medicaid Money Follows the Person" (MFP), sets demonstration projects in motion by providing grants to states for additional federal matching funds for Medicaid beneficiaries making the transition from an institution back to their homes or to other community settings.[26] Grants enable state Medicaid programs to fund home- and community-based services for individuals' needs, such as personal care assistance to enable their safe residency in the community. Other long-term care provisions under the ACA include the "Community First Choice Option in Medicaid," which provides states with an increased federal Medicaid matching rate to support community-based attendant services for individuals who require an institutional level of care,[27] and a "State Balancing Incentive Program," which enhances federal matching funds to states to increase the proportion of Medicaid long-term services and support dollars allocated toward home- and community-based services.[28] It is hoped that these demonstrations will yield results that may be expanded to address the serious gaps that exist in services between home- and community-based and institutional care available for older Americans.

▶ Access to Health Care

Much attention has been paid to the economic problems of health care, and considerable investments of research funds have been made to address the issues of healthcare quality. However, the third major problem—that of limited access to health care among the uninsured or underinsured Americans—continues to confound decision makers and has evolved into both a moral and economic issue.

Polarized positions have been taken by those who have addressed the question of whether society in general or governments in particular have an obligation to ensure that everyone has the right to health care and whether the healthcare system has a corresponding obligation to make such care available. Consider these opposing viewpoints by P. H. Elias and R. M. Sade, respectively:

> Physicians who limit their office practice to insured and paying patients declare themselves openly to be merchants rather than professionals....

Physicians who value their professionalism should treat office patients on the basis of need, not remuneration.[29]

The concept of medical care as the patient's right is immoral because it denies the most fundamental of all rights, that of a man to his own life and the freedom of action to support it. Medical care is neither a right nor a privilege: it is a service that is provided by doctors to others who wish to purchase it.[30]

Although healthcare providers debate their individual and personal obligations to provide uncompensated care, the system itself finessed the problem for many years by shifting the costs of care from the uninsured to the insured. This unofficial but practical approach to indigent care was ethically tolerable as long as the reimbursement system for paying patients was so open ended that the cost of treating the uninsured could easily be passed on to paying patients. The cost shifting that worked under old reimbursement systems that paid for virtually everything after the fact was not feasible under pre-payment designs that began in the 1980s and vigorously continue today. Evolving insurance and reimbursement mechanisms recognize that a transparent approach to providing insurance coverage for low-income persons will help address the long-standing inequities in a cryptic system previously required to manage uncompensated care. In this regard, the ACA's health insurance provisions are a pointed example of the need for government intervention on behalf of its citizenry when markets are unable or unwilling to respond.

Ideally, U.S. health policy makers would have preferred to assure the public that the healthcare system would provide all citizens with comparable access to health care and to assure physicians and other healthcare providers that they would be free of government interference in decisions about service production and delivery. However, a very long history of failed attempts at free-market approaches has resulted in the indisputable conclusion that government intervention is needed to improve the access problem.

▶ Quality of Care

Another problem area in the delivery of health care is variations in the quality and appropriateness of medical care. The uncertainty that pervades current clinical practice is far greater than most people realize. Problems in the quality and appropriateness of many diagnostic and therapeutic procedures impact heavily on costs.

A 1999 report of the Institute of Medicine estimated that medical errors take from 44,000 to 98,000 lives per year, and it was widely acknowledged that the complexity of the healthcare system, the dangers inherent in surgical procedures, and the potential for error in the many information transfers that occur during hospital care combine to put patients at serious risk.[31] However, solutions have remained elusive. A 2016 *British Medical Journal* report aggregated research from several sources to conclude: "If medical error was a disease, it would rank as the third leading cause of death in the U.S."[32] In addition, while much attention is focused on the risk of errors in hospitals, serious concerns also exist in ambulatory care where treatment is episodic and there is significant discontinuity in communication among patients, physicians, and support service providers.[33]

▶ Conflicts of Interest

One of the greatest advantages of U.S. high-technology healthcare systems is the ability of physicians and patients to benefit from referrals to a broad range of highly specialized clinical, laboratory, rehabilitation, and other services.

In recent years, however, increasing numbers of physicians have begun to invest in laboratories, imaging centers, medical supply companies, and other healthcare businesses. In many cases, these are joint ventures with other institutions that conceal the identity of the investors. When healthcare providers refer patients for tests or other services to healthcare businesses that they own or in which they have a financial stake, there is a serious potential for conflicts of interest. For the last several years both federal and state governments and the American Medical Association have conducted studies confirming that physician-owned laboratories, for example, perform more tests per patient at higher charges than those in which physicians have no investment.[34] These conflicts of interest undermine the traditional professional role of physicians and significantly increase healthcare expenditures. In another dimension of conflicts of interest, the ACA includes "Sunshine" provisions that arose from activities related to enforcement of the federal kickback statute pertaining to financial relationships between health industry (pharmaceutical, biologics, and medical device companies) and healthcare providers.[35]

The ACA "requires reporting of all financial transactions and transfers of value between manufacturers of pharmaceutical/biologic products or medical devices and physicians, hospitals, and other covered recipients that are reimbursed by U.S. federal government."[35] In addition, the ACA requires the Centers for Medicare & Medicaid Services to establish a website to post information pertinent to these transactions in a searchable, downloadable database.[35] Fines for manufacturer noncompliance with reporting requirements can reach up to $1 million per reporting year.[35]

▶ Health Care's Ethical Dilemmas

Once almost an exclusive province of physicians and other healthcare providers, moral and ethical issues underlying provider–patient relationships are now in the domains of law, politics, journalism, health institution administrations, and the public. During the last few decades, the list of ethical issues has expanded as advances in areas such as genetic identification and engineering, a mounting armamentarium of highly specialized diagnostic and therapeutic interventions, and other technological advances have allowed the lives of otherwise terminal individuals to be prolonged. In addition, an energized healthcare consumer movement advocating more personal control over healthcare decisions, economic realities, and issues of appropriate use of limited resources are just some of the topics propelling values and ethics onto the healthcare agenda. There is a social dimension to health care that never existed before and that the health professions, their educational institutions, their organizations, and their philosophical leadership are now beginning to address.

Clearly, the rapid pace of change in health care and the resulting issues have outpaced U.S. society's ability to reform the thinking, values, and expectations that were more appropriate to a bygone era. Legislative initiatives are, correctly or not, attempting to fill the voids.

New York State's 1990 passage of healthcare proxy legislation that allows competent adults to appoint agents to make healthcare decisions on their behalf if they become incapacitated is one example. The 1997 decision of the U.S. 9th Circuit Court of Appeals permitting physician-assisted suicide for competent, terminally ill adults in the state of Oregon is another. And in 2016, California became the fourth state to enact physician-assisted suicide legislation.[36]

Issue by issue, the country is trying to come to grips with the ethical dilemmas that modern medicine has created. The pluralistic nature of this society, however, and the Judeo-Christian concepts about caring for the sick and disabled that served so well for so long, make sweeping reformation of the ethical precepts on which health care has been based very challenging.

▶ Continuing Challenges

As the United States pushes forward with the implementation of the ACA and other legislative initiatives, its experimentation to test strategies to reduce costs, improve quality, and increase access will likely be joined by other emerging concerns. How to improve Americans' health behaviors, how to involve consumers more effectively in healthcare decisions, and how to balance responsibilities and accountability between the government and private sectors remain among the looming challenges of this continuing era of health reform.

KEY TERMS FOR REVIEW

Natural History of Disease   Rural Health Networks   Tertiary Prevention
Primary Prevention   Secondary Prevention

CHAPTER ACRONYMS

ACA Patient Protection and Affordable Care
Act of 2010
CAH Critical Access Hospital
MACRA Medicare Access and CHIP
Reauthorization Act of 2015
MCO Managed Care Organization

MFP Medicaid Money Follows the Person
NCCIH National Center for Complementary and
Integrative Health
OECD Organization for Economic Cooperation
and Development

References

1. Centers for Medicare & Medicaid Services. Historical. Downloads. NHE summary including share of GDP CY 1980–2014. https://www.cms.gov /research-statistics-data-and-systems/statistics-trends -and-reports/nationalhealthexpenddata/national healthaccountshistorical.html. Accessed April 12, 2016.
2. United States Bureau of Labor Statistics. Occupational employment and wages summary. March 30, 2016. http://www.bls.gov/news.release/ocwage.nr0.htm. Accessed May 14, 2016.
3. Gostin LO, Jacobson PD, Record KL, Hardcastle LE. Restoring health to health reform: Integrating medicine and public health to advance the population's well-being. *U Pa L Rev*. 2011. http://scholarship.law.georgetown.edu /cgi/viewcontent.cgi?article=1608&context=facpub. Accessed June 4, 2016.
4. Squires D, Anderson C. U.S. health care from a global perspective: Spending, use of services, prices, and health in 13 countries. *The Commonwealth Fund*. http:// www.commonwealthfund.org/publications/issue -briefs/2015/oct/us-health-care-from-a-global -perspective. Accessed April 16, 2016.
5. Pollack H. Health reform and public health: Will good policies but bad politics combine to produce bad policy? *U Pa L Rev*. 2011;159:2061. http://scholarship .law.upenn.edu/cgi/viewcontent.cgi?article =1117&context=penn_law_review. Accessed June 4, 2016.
6. Melnick GA, Fonkych K. Hospital prices increase in California, especially among hospitals in the largest multi-hospital systems. *Inquiry*. 2026;53:2-7. http:// inq.sagepub.com/content/53/0046958016651555 .full.pdf+html. Accessed June 13, 2016.
7. Bernabeo E, Holmboe ES. Patients, providers and systems need to acquire a specific set of competencies to achieve truly patient-centered care. *Health Aff*. 2013;32:251-254. http://content.healthaffairs.org /content/32/2/250.full.html. Accessed June 4, 2016.
8. Leavell HR, Clark EG. *Preventive Medicine for the Doctor in His Community: An Epidemiologic Approach*.

3rd ed. New York: The McGraw Hill Companies, Inc.; 1965:20-21, 272-273.

9. Surgeon General. National prevention strategy. 2016. http://www.surgeongeneral.gov/priorities/prevention/strategy/. Accessed June 5, 2016.

10. Medicare.gov. Accountable care organizations. https://www.medicare.gov/manage-your-health/coordinating-your-care/accountable-care-organizations.html. Accessed April 11, 2016.

11. Centers for Medicare & Medicaid Services. The merit-based incentive payment system (MIPS) & alternative payment models (APMS): Delivery system reform, Medicare payment reform, & the MACRA. https://www.cms.gov/Medicare/Quality-Initiatives-Patient-Assessment-Instruments/Value-Based-Programs/MACRA-MIPS-and-APMs/MACRA-MIPS-and-APMs.html. Accessed March 10, 2016.

12. National Center for Complementary and Integrative Health. What complementary and integrative approaches do Americans use? Key findings from the 2012 national health interview survey. November 4, 2015. https://nccih.nih.gov/research/statistics/NHIS/2012/key-findings. Accessed May 13, 2016.

13. National Center for Complementary and Integrative Health. Complementary, alternative, or integrative health: What's in a name? March 29, 2016. https://nccih.nih.gov/health/integrative-health. Accessed May 13, 2016.

14. Davis MA, Martin BI, Coulter ID, Weeks WB. US spending on complementary and alternative medicine during 2002–08 plateaued, suggesting role in reformed health care system. *Health Aff.* 2013;32:45-47. http://content.healthaffairs.org/content/32/1/45.full.html. Accessed June 4, 2016.

15. Abelson R, Brown PL. Alternative medicine is finding its niche in nation's hospitals. *The New York Times.* April 13, 2002. http://www.nytimes.com/2002/04/13/business/alternative-medicine-is-finding-its-niche-in-nation-s-hospitals.html?pagewanted=all. Accessed June 5, 2016.

16. Andrews M. Hospitals are making room for alternative therapies. *Los Angeles Times.* January 2, 2012. http://articles.latimes.com/2012/jan/02/health/la-he-hospitals-alternative-medicine-20120102. Accessed June 5, 2016.

17. Speakout Now. Obamacare or corporate-care: The writing of the Affordable Care Act. http://speakout-now.org/obamacare-or-corporate-care-the-writing-of-the-affordable-care-act/. Accessed June 5, 2016.

18. The Henry J. Kaiser Family Foundation. Summary of the Affordable Care Act. April 25, 2013. http://kff.org/health-reform/fact-sheet/summary-of-the-affordable-care-act/. Accessed June 5, 2016.

19. Internal Revenue Service. Medical device excise tax: Frequently asked questions. https://www.irs.gov/uac/medical-device-excise-tax-frequently-asked-questions. Accessed June 5, 2016.

20. Health Resources and Services Administration. Rural health network development planning program. 2015. http://www.hrsa.gov/ruralhealth/programopportunities/fundingopportunities/?id=3bcf6a6e-aa56-4d34-8d79-90894f31ea24. Accessed May 26, 2016.

21. Fickenscher K, Voorman ML. An overview of rural health care. In: Shortell SM, Reinhardt UE, eds. *Improving Health Policy and Management: Nine Critical Research Issues for the 1990s.* Ann Arbor, MI: Health Administration Press; 1992:127, 133-134.

22. Centers for Medicare & Medicaid Services. Critical access hospital. February 9. 2016. https://www.cms.gov/Outreach-and-Education/Medicare-Learning-Network-MLN/MLNProducts/downloads/CritAccessHospfctsht.pdf. Accessed June 6, 2016.

23. Perna G. Supreme court ruling on ACA benefits telemedicine, says ATA. July 2, 2012. *Healthcare Informatics.* http://www.healthcare-informatics.com/news-item/supreme-court-ruling-aca-benefits-telemedicine-says-ata. Accessed May 19, 2016.

24. National Institute on Drug Abuse. Trends and statistics. https://www.drugabuse.gov/related-topics/trends-statistics. Accessed June 6, 2016.

25. U.S. Department of Health and Human Services, Administration on Aging. *A Profile of Older Americans: 2014.* http://www.aoa.acl.gov/aging_statistics/Profile/2014/docs/2014-Profile.pdf. Accessed February 1, 2016.

26. Medicaid.gov. Money follows the person (MFP). https://www.medicaid.gov/Medicaid-CHIP-Program-Information/By-Topics/Long-Term-Services-and-Supports/Balancing/Money-Follows-the-Person.html. Accessed June 3, 2016.

27. Medicaid.gov. Community first choice (CFC) 1915 (k). https://www.medicaid.gov/medicaid-chip-program-information/by-topics/long-term-services-and-supports/home-and-community-based-services/community-first-choice-1915-k.html. Accessed June 3, 2016.

28. Medicaid.gov. Balancing incentive program. https://www.medicaid.gov/medicaid-chip-program-information/by-topics/long-term-services-and-supports/balancing/balancing-incentive-program.html. Accessed June 3, 2016.

29. Elias PH. Letter to editor. *N Engl J Med.* 1986;314:314-391.

30. Sade RM. Medical care as a right: A refutation. *N Engl J Med.* 1971;285:1281, 1289.

31. The Lancet. Medical errors in the USA: Human or systemic? *The Lancet.* 2011;377:1289. http://www.thelancet.com/journals/lancet/article/PIIS0140-6736(11)60520-5/fulltext?rss=yes. Accessed June 4, 2016.

32. Makary MA, Daniel M. Medical error—The third leading cause of death in the U.S. *BMJ.*

2016;353:2139–2141. http://www.bmj.com/content/bmj/353/bmj.i2139.full.pdf. Accessed May 17, 2016.

33. Agency for Healthcare Research and Quality. Patient safety in ambulatory care. https://psnet.ahrq.gov/primers/primer/16/patient-safety-in-ambulatory-care. Accessed August 26, 2016.

34. Kirkner RM. The enduring temptation of physician self-referral. Managed Care Magazine Online. October 2011. http://www.managedcaremag.com/archives/2011/10/enduring-temptation-physician-self-referral. Accessed June 3, 2016.

35. Lauer K, Patel M, Pepitone K. Physician payment Sunshine Act: Potential implications for medical publication professionals. *AMWA Journal*. 2012; 27:7-8. http://www.amwa.org/Files/Publications/physicialpaymentssunshineact.pdf. Accessed June 3, 2016.

36. Medina J. Who may die? California patients and doctors wrestle with assisted suicide. *The New York Times*. June 9, 2016. http://nyti.ms/1WGoy06. Accessed June 11, 2016.

CHAPTER 2

Benchmark Developments in U.S. Health Care

CHAPTER OVERVIEW

This chapter describes important legislative, political, economic, organizational, and professional influences that transformed health care in the United States from a relatively simple professional service to a huge, complex, corporation-dominated industry. The effects of medical education, scientific advances, rising costs, and American values along with assumptions regarding health care are discussed. The chapter concludes with a brief discussion of the enactment of the Patient Protection and Affordable Care Act of 2010 (the ACA) and summaries of its major provisions.

From its earliest history, medical care was dominated by physicians and the hospitals they operated. In the 1800s and early 1900s, participation in U.S. medicine was generally limited to two parties—patients and physicians. Diagnosis, treatment, and fees for services were considered confidential between patients and physicians. Medical practice was relatively simple and usually involved longstanding relationships among physicians, patients, and their families. Physicians set and often adjusted their charges to estimates of patients' ability to pay and collect their own bills. This was an intimate physician–patient relationship that the profession held sacred.

Free from outside scrutiny or interference, individual physicians had complete control over where, when, what, and how they practiced. In 1934, the American Medical Association (AMA) published this statement: "No third party must be permitted to come between the patient and his physician in any medical matter."[1] The AMA was concerned about such issues as non-physician-controlled voluntary health insurance, compulsory health insurance, and the few prepaid contracts for medical services negotiated by remote lumber or mining companies and a few workers' guilds. For decades, organized medicine repeatedly battled against these and other outside influences that altered "the old relations of perfect freedom between physicians and patients, with separate compensation for each separate service."[1]

Flag: © Lightix/Shutterstock

As early as the 1800s, some Americans carried insurance against sickness through an employer, fraternal order, guild, trade union, or commercial insurance company. Most of the plans were simply designed to compensate for lost income during sickness or injury by providing a fixed cash payment.[1] Sickness insurance, as it was originally called, was the beginning of social insurance programs that mitigated the risks of income interruption by accident, sickness, or disability. Initially such insurance was provided only to wage earners. Later, it was extended to workers' dependents.[2]

About 1915, the drive for compulsory health insurance began to build in the United States, after most European countries had initiated either compulsory programs or subsidies for voluntary programs. The underlying concern was to protect workers against a loss of income resulting from industrial accidents that were common at the time. Families with only one wage earner, often already at the edge of poverty, could be devastated by loss of income caused by sickness or injury, even without the additional costs of medical care.

At the time, life insurance companies sold "industrial" policies that provided lump-sum payments at death, which amounted to $50 or $100 to pay for final medical expenses and funerals. Both Metropolitan Life and the Prudential Insurance Company rose to the top of the insurance industry by successfully marketing industrial policies that required premium payments of 10–25 cents per week.[2]

In 1917, World War I interrupted the campaign for compulsory health insurance in the United States. In 1919, the American Medical Association (AMA) House of Delegates officially condemned compulsory health insurance with the following resolution:[3]

> The American Medical Association declares its opposition to the institution of any plan embodying the system of compulsory contributory insurance against illness or any other plan of compulsory insurance which provides for medical service to be rendered to contributors or their dependents, provided, controlled, or regulated by any state or the federal government.

Most physician opposition to compulsory health insurance was attributed to an unfounded concern that insurance would decrease, rather than increase, physician incomes and to their negative experience with accident insurance that paid physicians according to arbitrary fee schedules.[1]

▶ The Great Depression and the Birth of Blue Cross

As the Depression of 1929 shook the nation, it also threatened the financial security of both physicians and hospitals. Physician incomes and hospital admission rates dropped precipitously as individuals were unable to pay out of pocket for medical care, and hospitals began experimenting with insurance plans. The Baylor University Hospital plan was not the first, but it became the most influential of those insurance experiments. By enrolling 1,250 public school teachers at 50 cents a month for a guaranteed 21 days of hospital care, Baylor created the model for, and is credited with the genesis of, Blue Cross hospital insurance. Baylor started a trend that developed into multihospital plans that included all hospitals in a given area. By 1937, there were 26 plans with more than 600,000 members, and the American Hospital Association began approving the plans.[4] Physicians were pleased with the increased availability of hospital care and the cooperative manner in which their bills were paid. The AMA, however, was hostile and called the plans "economically unsound, unethical, and inimical to the public interest."[5]

The AMA contended that urging people "to save for sickness" could solve the problem of financing health care.[2] Organized medicine's consistently antagonistic reaction to the concept of health insurance, whether compulsory or voluntary, is well illustrated by medicine's response to the 1932 report of the Committee on the Costs of Medical Care. The committee's establishment represented a shift from concern about lost wages to concern about medical expenses. Chaired by a former president of the AMA and financed by several philanthropic organizations, a group of prominent Americans from the medical, public health, and social science fields worked for five years to address the problem of financing medical care. After an exhaustive study, a moderate majority recommended adoption of group practice and voluntary health insurance as the best way of solving the nation's healthcare problems. However, even this relatively modest recommendation was rejected by some commission members who in a minority report denounced voluntary health insurance as more objectionable than compulsory insurance. Health insurance, predicted the minority, would lead to "destructive competition among professional groups, inferior medical service, loss of personal relationship of patient and physician, and demoralization of the profession."[6] In 1933, the AMA's House of Delegates again reiterated its longstanding opposition to health insurance of any kind by declaring that the minority report represented "the collective opinion of the medical profession."[7] The dissenting physicians did, however, favor government intervention to alleviate physicians' financial burden, resulting from their obligation to provide free care to low-income populations.

From the early 1900s to the present, there have been many efforts to enact various forms of compulsory health insurance. When the proponents of government-sponsored insurance limited their efforts to older adults and low-income populations, they finally were able to succeed in passing Medicaid and Medicare legislation in 1965. Voluntary insurance against hospital care costs became the predominant health insurance in the United States during those decades. The advocates of government-sponsored health insurance had little success in improving patient access to medical care, but the Blue Cross plans effectively improved hospitals' access to patients.

Following World War II, the federal government boosted the private health insurance industry by excluding health insurance benefits from wage and price controls and by excluding workers' contributions to health insurance from taxable income. The effect was to enable employees to take wage increases in the form of health insurance fringe benefits rather than cash. Also following World War II, the federal government began subsidizing the healthcare industry's expansion heavily through hospital construction and medical research, with physician compensation as an overriding policy objective.

Because insurance companies simply raised their premiums rather than exerting pressure on physicians and hospitals to contain costs, the post-World War II private health insurance system pumped an ever-increasing proportion of the national income into health care. There was little regard for cost growth, with attention focused on avoiding any infringement on physicians' or hospitals' prerogatives to set prices and costs. Medicare and Medicaid followed the same pattern.

▶ Dominant Influence of Government

Although the health insurance industry contributed significantly to the spiraling costs of health care in the decades after World War II, it was only one of several influences. The federal government's coverage of health care for special populations also played a prominent role. Over the years, the U.S. government developed, revised, and otherwise adjusted a host of categorical or disease-specific programs designed to address needs not otherwise met by state or local administrations or the private sector. Today, federally sponsored programs account for about 43 percent of U.S. personal healthcare expenditures.[8]

In the evolution of the U.S. healthcare delivery system, the policy implications of certain federal initiatives are very important. The government increased its support for biomedical research by establishing the National Institutes of Health in 1930 to support categorical programs that addressed heart disease, cancer, stroke, mental illness, mental retardation, maternal and infant care, and many other conditions. In 1935, by granting federal aid to the states for public health and welfare assistance, maternal and child health, and children with disabilities services, the Social Security Act became the most significant social policy ever passed by any Congress. The Social Security Act was the legislative foundation for many significant health and welfare programs, including the Medicare and Medicaid programs.

Programs such as direct aid to schools of medicine, dentistry, pharmacy, nursing, and other professions and their students along with support of health planning, healthcare regulation, and consumer protections, were all part of the Kennedy–Johnson presidential policy era called "Creative Federalism." The aggregate annual investment in those programs made the U.S. government the major player and payer in the healthcare field. Between 1964 and 1968, total grant awards to states excluding Social Security and Medicare nearly doubled, rising from $10.1 billion in 1964 to $18.6 billion in 1968.[9]

Several programs in addition to Medicare and Medicaid began during the Johnson administration to address mental illness and to support the healthcare professionals' role. The Health Professions Educational Assistance Act of 1963 provided direct federal aid to medical, dental, nursing, pharmacy, and other professional schools, as well as to their students. The Nurse Training Act supported special federal efforts for training professional nursing personnel. During the same period, the Maternal and Child Health and Mental Retardation Planning Amendments initiated comprehensive maternal and child health projects and centers to serve people with mental retardation. The Economic Opportunity Act supported the development of neighborhood health centers to serve low-income populations.[10]

In 1970, in a direction labeled "New Federalism," President Nixon expressed his intent to rescind the federal government's direct administration of several healthcare programs and shift revenues to state and local governments through block grants. Block grants are consolidated grants of federal funds, formerly allocated for specific programs, that a state or local government may use at its discretion. In the meantime, with no effective controls over expenditures, federal and state governments underwrote skyrocketing costs of Medicare and Medicaid. The planners of the Medicare legislation had made several misjudgments. They underestimated the growing number of U.S. older adults, the scope and burgeoning costs of new technology, and the public's rising expectations for use of advanced diagnostic and treatment modalities.

The Medicare and Medicaid programs provided access to many desperately needed healthcare services for older Americans, people with disabilities, and low-income populations. Because rising Medicare reimbursement rates set the standards for most insurance companies, however, their inflationary effect was momentous. In the mid-1960s, when Medicare and Medicaid were passed, the United States was spending about $42 billion on health care, or approximately 8.4 percent of the gross domestic product. The costs of U.S. health care now exceed $3 trillion and consume more than 17 percent of the gross domestic product.[11]

▶ Three Major Health Care Concerns

The three major healthcare concerns of cost, quality, and access have comprised a generations-long conundrum of the U.S. healthcare delivery system. Virtually, all attempts to control one or two of these concerns exacerbated the one or two remaining. The federal government's improvements in access to care by measures such as post-World War II hospital expansions and Medicare and Medicaid legislation were accompanied by skyrocketing expenditures and quality issues. These measures resulted in the healthcare system's expansions beyond actual need and, while virtually unchecked, funding improved access to competent and appropriate medical care for many; they also resulted in untold numbers of clinical interventions of questionable necessity.

Almost all the federal health legislation since the passage of Medicare and Medicaid and the Balanced Budget Act of 1997 was targeted at reducing costs but with little focus on the reciprocal effects of attenuating access and quality of healthcare issues. The ACA changed this trend by promoting and requiring value-based, rather than volume-based reimbursement.[12]

▶ Efforts at Planning and Quality Control

The federal government did not ignore the issues of cost and quality, but efforts to address those concerns were doomed to be ineffectual by their designs. Powerful medical and hospital lobbies exerted great influence over any legislation that might alter the existing constellation of healthcare services or that would scrutinize the quality of clinical practice. Bowing to powerful lobbyists, federal legislation required allowing physicians, hospital administrators, and other health professionals to maintain control over how the legislation was interpreted and enforced.

Two initiatives of the 1960s typified circumstances surrounding federal legislative efforts to address cost, quality, and access concerns. In 1965, the Public Health Service Act was amended to establish the Regional Medical Program initiative, a nationwide network of medical programs in designated geographic areas to address the leading causes of death: heart disease, cancer, and stroke.[13] Through regional medical programs, physicians, nurses, and other health professionals deliberated innovative ways to bring the latest in clinical services to patients. However, representatives of each constituency focused on advocating for funding in their respective disciplines. As a consequence, the regional medical programs added educational and clinical resources but did not materially improve prevention or cost reductions in the treatment of the target conditions. A parallel program, the Comprehensive Health Planning Act, was passed in 1966 to promote comprehensive planning for rational systems of healthcare personnel and facilities in designated regions. The legislation required federal, state, and local partnerships and also required a majority of consumers on every decision-making body.[14]

Almost all the Regional Medical Programs and Comprehensive Health Planning Act programs were dominated by medical and hospital leaders in their regions. Many productive outcomes resulted from the two programs, but conflicts of interest regarding the allocation of research and development funds were common. There was general agreement that the programs were ineffective in achieving their goals.

The Johnson-era programs of 1966–1969, especially Medicare and Medicaid, entrenched the federal government in the business of financing health care. President Johnson's ambitious creative federalism enriched the country's healthcare system and improved the access of many citizens, but it also fueled a persistent inflationary spiral of healthcare costs.

The National Health Planning and Resources Development Act of 1974 combined the Regional Medical Health Program and Comprehensive Health Planning Act programs with political rather than objective assessments. Congress apparently assumed that combining two ineffective programs would result in one successful program. Nevertheless, the legislation established new local organizations, Health Systems Agencies (HSAs), which required representation of healthcare providers and consumers on governing boards and committees to deliberate and recommend healthcare resource allocations to federal and state authorities.[15] HSAs were largely ineffective for many of the same reasons as their predecessor organizations and failed to develop meaningful strategies to address cost, quality, and access concerns. The ineffectiveness of HSAs in their regions was acknowledged by withdrawal of federal support.[15]

▶ Managed Care Organizations

In 1973, the Health Maintenance Organization Act supported the development of health maintenance organizations (HMOs) through grants for federal demonstration projects. An HMO is an organization responsible for the financing and delivery of comprehensive health services to an enrolled population for a prepaid, fixed fee. HMOs were expected to hold down costs by changing the profit incentive from fee-for-service to promoting health and preventing illness.

The concept was widely accepted, and between 1992 and 1999, HMOs and other types of managed care organizations experienced phenomenal growth, accounting for the majority of all privately insured persons. Subsequently, the fortunes of managed care organizations changed as both healthcare costs and consumer complaints increased. By the 1990s, a consumer and provider backlash resulted in all 50 states enacting protections against managed care access and cost restrictions.[16]

Beginning in 2001, a derivative of managed care organizations, preferred provider organizations (PPOs), gained in popularity. Although PPOs encompass important managed care characteristics, they were organized by physicians and hospitals to meet the needs of private, third-party, and self-insured firms. By 2002, PPOs had captured 52 percent of covered employees.[17] Today, PPOs remain the most popular form of employer-sponsored health insurance.[18]

▶ The Reagan Administration: Cost Containment and Prospective Hospital Reimbursement

The Reagan administration of the 1980s continued efforts to shrink federally supported programs begun in the 1960s and 1970s. One effort was decentralization of program responsibility to the states through block grants. Block grants consolidate grants of federal funds, formerly allocated for specific programs, so that states may use funding at their discretion and presumably more efficiently than the federal government.

One of the most significant health policy changes of the past decades occurred with the Reagan administration's implementation of the Medicare prospective payment system in hospitals. Based on diagnosis-related groups (DRGs), the system shifted hospital reimbursement from a fee-for-service retrospective mode to a pre-paid prospective mode based on patient diagnosis. Designed to encourage efficient use of resources, the DRG system put hospitals at financial risk for charges that exceeded per-case DRG limits. It also created an opportunity for hospitals to retain, if any, the portion of the unexpended predetermined case payment.[19] This unprecedented effort to contain healthcare costs was widely adopted as a standard by the health insurance industry.[19]

In an effort to reign in spiraling physician Medicare charges, the administration also created a new payment method, the resource-based relative value scale (RBRVS) to make physician payments equitable across various types of service, specialties, and geographic locations.[20]

▶ Biomedical Advances: Evolution of High-Technology Medicine

Health care in the United States dramatically improved during the 1900s. In the first half of the century, the greatest advances led to the prevention or cure of many infectious diseases. The development of vaccines to prevent a wide range of communicable diseases, from yellow fever to measles, and the discovery of antibiotics saved vast numbers of Americans from early death or disability.

In the second half of the century many technologic advances that characterize today's health care were developed, and the pace of technologic development accelerated rapidly. The following are a few of the seminal medical advances that took place during the 1960s:

- The Sabin and Salk vaccines ended annual epidemics of poliomyelitis.
- The tranquilizers Librium and Valium were introduced and widely prescribed, leading Americans to turn to medicine to cure their emotional as well as physical ills.
- The birth control pill was first prescribed and became the most widely used and effective contraceptive method.
- The heart–lung machine and major improvements in the efficacy and safety of general anesthesia techniques made possible the first successful heart bypass operation in 1964.

In addition, in 1972, computed tomography was invented. Computed tomography (CT), which unlike x-rays can distinguish one soft tissue from another, is installed widely in U.S. hospitals and ambulatory centers. This valuable and profitable diagnostic imaging device started an extravagant competition among hospitals to develop lucrative patient services through major capital investments in high-technology equipment. Noting the convenience and profit associated with diagnostic devices such as CT, and a few years later, magnetic resonance imaging (MRI), medical groups purchased the devices and placed them in their own facilities. The profit-driven competition and resulting redundant capacity continued to drive up utilization and costs for hospitals, insurers, and the public. Competition continued unabated with the introduction of even more sophisticated and expensive technology over succeeding years.[21]

New technology, new drugs, and new and creative surgical procedures have made possible a wide variety of life-enhancing and life-extending medical accomplishments. Operations that once were complex and hazardous, requiring hospitalization and intense follow-up care, have become common ambulatory surgical procedures. For example, the use of intraocular lens implants after the removal of cataracts has become one of the most popular surgical procedures. Previously requiring hospitalization, these implants are performed in outpatient settings on more than 3.6 million Americans annually.[22] The procedure takes less than one hour.

Technical Advances Bring New Problems

Almost every medical or technologic advance seems to be accompanied by new and vexing financial and ethical dilemmas. The increased ability to extend life raises questions about the quality of life and the right to die. New capabilities to use costly and limited resources to improve the quality of life for some and not others create other ethical problems.

Both the AMA and the federal government developed programs to explore these issues and to provide needed information for decision makers. The AMA established three programs to assess the ramifications of medical advancements: the Diagnostic and Therapeutic Technology Assessment Program, the Council on Scientific Affairs, and the AMA Drug Evaluations.[23]

In the Technology Assessment Act of 1972, Congress recognized that "it is essential that, to the fullest extent possible, the consequences of technologic applications be anticipated, understood, and considered in determination of public policy on existing and emerging national problems."[24] To address this goal, Congress created the Office of Technology Assessment (OTA), a nonpartisan support agency that worked directly with and for congressional committees. The OTA relied on the technical and professional resources of the private sector, including universities, research organizations, industry, and public interest groups, to produce their assessments and provide congressional committees with analyses of highly technical issues. Established by a Congress controlled by Democrats out of a distrust of the Nixon administration, it was intended to help officials sort out increasingly complex scientific information without advocating particular policies or actions. The OTA was shut down in 1995 as a result of political controversies adverse to the then Republican-controlled Congress.[25]

The Agency for Health Care Policy and Research, created by Congress in 1989 and now called the Agency for Healthcare Research and Quality, supports research to better understand the outcomes of health care at both clinical and systems levels. It has a challenging mission as technologic and scientific advances make it difficult to sort out the complexities of health care and determine what works, for whom, when, and at what cost.

▶ Roles of Medical Education and Specialization

Medical schools and teaching hospitals in the United States are the essential components of all academic health centers and are the principal architects of the medical care system. In addition to their research contributions to advancements in health care and their roles as major providers of health services, they are the principal places where physicians and other professional personnel are educated and trained.

From post-World War II to the mid-1970s, there were numerous projections of an impending shortage of physicians. The response at federal and state levels was to double the capacity of medical schools and to encourage the entry of foreign-trained physicians.[26]

The explosion of scientific knowledge in medicine and the technologic advances in diagnostic and treatment modalities encouraged specialization. In addition, the enhanced prestige and income of specialty practice attracted most medical school graduates to specialty residencies. It became evident that specialists were being produced in numbers that would lead to an oversupply. Also, because they wished to be close to their referring doctors and to associate with major hospitals, graduates tended to concentrate in urban areas. At the same time, the shortage of primary care physicians among rural and inner-city populations grew.

In response, medical schools and hospitals developed new physician workforce policies to maintain or increase their training capacities.[27] Schools erroneously assumed that producing more physicians would result in larger numbers of primary care physicians to work in underserved rural and inner-city areas. Unfortunately, this trickle-down workforce policy did little to change supply distribution problems and only added to the swelling ranks of specialists. Hospitals added to the problem by developing residencies that met their own service needs without regard for oversupply. Supplemental Medicare payments for teaching hospitals and indirect medical education adjustments for hospital-based residents were and still are strong incentives for specialty medicine.[28]

The rapid growth of managed care plans in the 1990s with their emphasis on prevention and primary care was expected to produce profound changes in the use of the physician workforce and cause a significant oversupply of specialists by the year 2000. To stave off the surplus, many medical schools and their teaching hospitals endeavored to produce equal numbers of primary care and specialist physicians instead of the one-third to two-thirds ratio that had existed for years. However, as soon as the effort produced a sizable increase in the number of primary care physicians, new medical workforce projections refuted the prior predictions and forecasted a shortage, rather than a surplus, of specialists. Clearly, estimating a future physician shortage or surplus is a tenuous endeavor.

▶ Influence of Interest Groups

Many problems associated with U.S. health care result from a system shared among federal and state governments and the private healthcare industry. The development of fully or partially tax-funded health service proposals initiated waves of lobbying efforts by interest groups for or against the initiatives. Federal and state executives and legislators receive intense pressure from supporters and opponents of healthcare system changes.[29] Lobbying efforts from special interest groups have become increasingly sophisticated and well financed. It is common for former congressional staffers to appear on the payrolls of private interest groups, and former lobbyists assume positions on Capitol Hill. This strong connection between politicians and healthcare lobbyists is evidenced by the record number of dollars spent to defeat the Clinton Health Security Act of 1993 and both "for" and "against" President Obama's healthcare reform plans.

Five major groups have played key roles in debates on tax-funded health services: providers, insurers, consumers, business, and labor. Historically, physicians, the group most directly affected by reforms, developed the most powerful lobbies. Although the physician lobby still is among the best financed and most effective, it is recognized as not representing the values of large numbers of physicians detached from the AMA. In fact, several different medical lobbies exist as a result of political differences among physicians.

The American Medical Association

The American Medical Association (AMA), founded in 1847, is the largest medical lobby, with a membership of 224,503 individuals, yet it represents only 25.6 percent of physicians and medical students.[30] At the height of its power from the 1940s to the 1970s, the AMA opposed government-provided insurance plans proposed by every president from Truman through Carter. Compromises gained in the final Medicare bill still affect today's program.

In 1989, the AMA changed its relationship with Congress. Initially locked out of White House discussions on the Clinton plan, the AMA was later included and supported, at least publicly, by the Obama plan for expanding healthcare access to all Americans. At the height of its power from the 1940s to the 1970s, the AMA opposed government provided insurance plans proposed by every President from Truman through Carter.[31]

Insurance Companies

Even more than physicians, nurses, or hospitals, insurers' political efforts have been viewed as self-serving. The efforts of insurance companies to eliminate high-risk consumers from the insurance pools and their frequent premium rate increases contributed significantly to the focus on cost containment and the plight of the uninsured and underinsured in the debate on healthcare reform.

Insurance companies played a strong role in the debates about President Obama's healthcare reform effort by appearing to support the general idea while vigorously opposing the idea of a public option that would severely limit their profits. The amount of dollars spent in lobbying efforts by insurers and others with vested interests in the status quo and in misinforming the public to raise unwarranted fears about the proposed healthcare reform legislation hit a new high in deception and a new low in political machinations.[32]

Consumer Groups

Although provider and insurance groups have been most effective in influencing healthcare legislation, the historically weak consumer movement gained strength. Much of the impetus for healthcare reform on the national scene was linked to pressure on politicians from consumers concerned about rising costs and lack of security in healthcare coverage. Despite widespread disagreement among groups about the extent to which government involvement was needed, all were concerned about the questions of cost, quality and access in the current healthcare system.

Better educated and more assertive citizens have become more cynical about the motives of leaders in both the political and the health arenas and have become more effective in influencing legislative decisions. A prominent example is the American Association of Retired Persons (AARP). Founded in 1958, the AARP is one of the most influential consumer groups in the healthcare reform movement. Because of its size and research capability, it wields considerable clout among legislators who are very aware that the AARP's 38 million older citizens are among the most determined voters.[33]

Business and Labor

The National Federation of Independent Businesses, founded in 1943, has 350,000 individual members and is the largest representative of small firms.[34] The National Association of Manufacturers founded in 1895 represents the interests of large employers and has a current membership of 11,000.[35] The U.S. Chamber of Commerce was founded in 1912 and represents 3 million businesses of all sizes.[36]

Whenever business groups are involved in an issue, and especially one of the magnitude of health reform, labor unions will have a strong presence to represent their members' interests. The American Federation of Labor and Congress of Industrial Organization (AFL-CIO), with 12.5 million members,[37] has had a tremendous influence on national health policy. Closely connected with the AFL-CIO is the Service Employees International Union, founded in 1921. It is the largest union representing healthcare workers, with a membership of 1.1 million.[38] During the mid-1940s, labor unions demanded and received healthcare benefits as an alternative to wage increases prohibited by postwar wage and price controls. The two major national unions, the AFL and the CIO, consolidated their power by merging in 1955. During the late 1960s, they were able to address the issues of occupational safety and health and achieved passage of the Occupational Safety and Health Act of 1970. Today, occupational safety and health hold prominent places on the national agenda.

Pharmaceutical Industry

In recent years, the highly profitable pharmaceutical industry increased its spending on lobbying tactics and campaign contributions to unprecedented levels. With prescription drug prices and pharmaceutical company profits at record highs, the industry correctly anticipated public and congressional pressure to legislate controls on drug prices and drug coverage for older adults on Medicare.

In 2003, as lawmakers moved to add a prescription drug benefit to Medicare that would include price controls, the pharmaceutical industry deployed more than 1,000 lobbyists.[39] The pharmaceutical industry played a major role in crafting the 2003 Medicare Part D prescription drug benefit plan. As a result, the final plan prohibited Medicare and the federal government from using its enormous purchasing power to negotiate prices with drug companies.[39]

Public Health Focus on Prevention

Although the groups discussed in the previous section are primarily concerned with the diagnostic and treatment services that constitute more than 95 percent of the U.S. healthcare system, there is an important public health lobby that speaks for health promotion and disease prevention. Often overlooked because of this country's historical emphasis on curative medicine, public health organizations have had to overcome several negative perceptions. Many health providers, politicians, and others associate public health with governmental bureaucracy or link the care of low-income populations with socialism. Nevertheless, the American Public Health Association, founded in 1872 and having an aggregate membership of approximately 25,000, has substantial influence on the national scene through its organized advocacy and educational efforts at the federal, state, and local levels.[40]

▶ Health Insurance Portability and Accountability Act

The Health Insurance Portability and Accountability Act (HIPAA) was enacted under the Clinton administration in 1996. It had two primary purposes. The first was to help ensure that workers could maintain uninterrupted health insurance coverage if they lost or changed jobs by enabling them to continue coverage through their prior employer's group health plan.[41] Employees using this provision reimburse their former employer directly without company subsidy for their premium costs. The law mandated the renewal of insurance coverage except for specific reasons, such as the nonpayment of premiums. The Act also regulated circumstances in which an insurance plan may limit benefits due to preexisting conditions and offered special enrollment periods for individuals who experience certain changes in family composition, such as divorce or the addition of a dependent.[41]

HIPAA's second primary purpose concerned the privacy of personal health information. Prior to HIPAA, no generally accepted set of security standards or general requirements for protecting health information existed in the healthcare industry. At the same time, new technologies were evolving, and the healthcare industry began to shift from paper processes to the use of electronic information systems to pay claims, answer eligibility questions, provide health information, and conduct many other administrative and clinically based functions.[42]

Known as the "Administrative Simplification" provisions of the law, they mandated the Department of Health and Human Services (DHHS) to establish national standards for regulations protecting the privacy and security of certain health information. To fulfill the mandate, DHHS published national standards known as the "Privacy Rule" and "Security Rule" applicable to virtually all organizations and providers with access to individuals' personal health information. The Security Rule particularly applies to certain health information that is held or transferred in electronic form.[42] In 2013 DHHS issued final rules under a 2009 law that significantly extended HIPAA's Privacy and Security provisions beyond healthcare organizations and providers to their subcontractors and other business entities which handle electronic patient information.[43] The DHHS Office of Civil Rights has responsibility for enforcing the Privacy and Security Rules with voluntary compliance activities and civil money penalties.[42]

▶ The Balanced Budget Act of 1997

The federal budget negotiations for 1997 reflected pressures to produce a balanced budget and to respond meaningfully to national health issues from consumer and cost-containment perspectives. The resulting Balanced Budget Act (BBA) created sweeping new policy directions for Medicare. The BBA proposed to reduce growth in Medicare spending through savings of $115 billion over five years and targeted hospitals for more than one-third of the savings.[44] The act increased cost sharing among Medicare beneficiaries and extended the prospective payment system introduced with DRGs to hospital outpatient services, home health agencies, skilled nursing facilities, and inpatient rehabilitation facilities.[45] The BBA also opened the Medicare program to private insurers through the Medicare + Choice Program (later renamed Medicare Advantage).

Declines in Medicare spending growth between 1998 and 2002 demonstrated the immediate impact of the BBA. After growing at an average annual rate of 11.1 percent for 15 years, the average annual rate of Medicare spending growth between 1998 and 2000 dropped to 1.7 percent, resulting in approximately $68 billion in savings.[46] Finally, the BBA included an initiative, the "State Children's Health Insurance Program" that complemented the Medicaid program by targeting uninsured children whose family income was too high to qualify for Medicaid and too low to afford private health insurance.[47] Subsequently renamed the "Children's Health Insurance Program" (CHIP) and with the goal of enrolling 10 million children, it was the largest expansion of health insurance coverage for children in the United States since Medicaid began. The CHIP has been continuously funded since inception and currently serves more than 8 million children.[45,48]

▶ Oregon Death with Dignity Act and Other End-of-Life Legislation

November 8, 1994, was a pivotal date in U.S. social legislation when Oregon voters approved the Oregon Death with Dignity Act.[49] The Act legalized physician-assisted suicide by allowing "an adult resident of Oregon, who is terminally ill to voluntarily request a prescription for medication to take his or her life."[50] The person must have "an incurable and irreversible disease that will, within reasonable medical judgment, produce death within six months."[50] The Death with Dignity Act was a response to the growing concern among medical professionals and the public about the extended, painful, and demeaning nature of terminal medical care for patients with certain conditions. An additional consideration was the worry that the extraordinary costs associated with lengthy and futile medical care would exhaust their estates and leave their families with substantial debts.

A survey of Oregon physicians showed that two-thirds of those responding believed that physician-assisted suicide is ethical in appropriate cases. Also, almost half of the responding physicians (46 percent) said they might assist in a suicide if the patient met the criteria outlined in the Act.[51]

The issue of euthanasia and physician-assisted suicide has been debated for years in other countries. Although among Westernized countries only Northern Australia has legalized physician-assisted suicide, the Netherlands has a long history of allowing euthanasia within the medical community.[52]

Oregon physicians must meet multiple requirements before they can write a prescription for a lethal combination of medications. The physician must ensure that the patient is fully informed about the diagnosis, the prognosis, the risks, and likely result of the medications and alternatives including comfort care, pain control, and hospice care. A consulting physician must then confirm that the patient's judgment is not impaired and that the decision is fully informed and voluntary. The patient is then asked to notify next of kin, although family notification is not mandatory. After a 15-day waiting period, the patient must again repeat the request. If the patient does so, the physician is then permitted to write the fatal prescription. Although it varies from year to year, not all patients requesting physician prescriptions opt to use them.[53] In Oregon as in other states which subsequently passed similar statutes, state departments of health are charged with tracking and reporting applications of the right-to-die laws.

In November 2008, the State of Washington initiated a Death with Dignity Act similar to Oregon's.[54] Effective in 2010, the Supreme Court of the State of Montana ruled to maintain the state law that protects doctors from prosecution for helping terminally ill patients die.[55] In 2013, Vermont enacted a "Patient Choice and Control at End-of-Life Act."[56] In June 2016, California became the fifth state to enact a death-with-dignity statute, the "End-of-Life Option Act.[57] In 2016, the New Mexico Supreme Court continued deliberations on a right-to-die statute.[58]

With the burgeoning aged U.S. population and this population group's increasing political strength in numbers, consumer pressure for more states to enact "right-to-die" legislation will be a subject of increasing interest. "Right-to-die" legislation does not only concern older Americans. In 2014, the case of a 29-year-old woman with terminal brain cancer brought national attention to this subject. A resident of California, the woman moved to Oregon to be able to control her end-of-life decisions.[59] As she intended, publicity surrounding her situation sparked much media attention and influenced passage of California's law in 2016.

▶ Health Information Technology for Economic and Clinical Health Act

The federal government took the most significant step in the history of health information technology on April 27, 2004, when President Bush created the Office of the National Coordinator for Health Information Technology (ONCHIT or "the ONC") by Executive Order.[60] The ONC was legislatively mandated in the American Recovery and Reinvestment Act (ARRA) when signed by President Obama on February 17, 2009.[61] Part of ARRA is the Health Information Technology for Economic and Clinical Health Act (HITECH) that designated $36.5 billion to promote the development of a nationwide network of electronic health records (EHRs). A law enacted in 2015 concerning providers' use of EHRs is presently in the federal rule-making process that may significantly alter the HITECH parameters for provider use of EHRs.

▶ The Internet and Health Care

Because data collection and information transfer are critical elements of the healthcare system, the Internet has become a major influence in U.S. health care. A 2012 Pew Foundation survey report noted that "one in three U.S. adults has gone online to diagnose a condition and about half consulted a medical professional about what they found."[62] The Internet provides consumers with access to vast resources of health and wellness information, the ability to communicate with others sharing similar health problems, and the ability to gain valuable data about medical institutions and providers that permit well-informed choices about services and procedures. Internet users are becoming more educated and participatory in clinical decision making, challenging physicians and other providers to participate with a more knowledgeable and involved patient population.

Physicians and other healthcare providers also are entering the online world of healthcare communication. After a slow start, provider-sponsored websites are proliferating at a rapid pace. In addition to information for consumers about providers' training, competencies, and experience, many encourage email exchanges that invite queries and provide opportunities to respond to consumers' informational needs.

A wide variety of other web-based entrepreneurial ventures have also begun to take advantage of the huge and growing market of smartphone users with apps that "give consumers access to health information wherever and whenever they need it."[62] Both professionally reliable and questionable entrepreneurs offer consumers opportunities to shop online for pharmaceuticals, insurance plans, medical supplies and equipment, physician services, and other health-related commodities, making the public well advised in exercising caution.

▶ The Patient Protection and Affordable Care Act of 2010

"The first promise Obama made as a presidential candidate was to enact a universal healthcare plan by the end of his first term."[63] Many months prior to his inauguration, senate Democrats—led by Senator Max Baucus, chair of the powerful Senate Finance Committee, and Senator Edward Kennedy—were collaborating with a diverse group of stakeholders to craft a plan.[63] Some in the new administration opposed advancing the cause of universal coverage at a time when the President also had to advance his pledges for an economic stimulus package, education reform, and bailouts for banks and the auto industry.[64] Nevertheless, believing "that rising medical costs were crippling average families, cutting into corporate profits, and consuming more and more of the federal budget,"[64] President Obama moved the healthcare agenda forward through a tortuous and rancorous maze of political machinations and public reactions.[65] Decades-long analyses and assessments by the most prestigious academic research and industry experts overwhelming noted that U.S. healthcare system focused on providing excellent care for the individuals with acute conditions, but virtually ignored the more basic health service needs of larger populations who could benefit from primary preventive care. The system continued to reward providers for the volume of services delivered with piecemeal reimbursement rather than with financial incentives to maintain or improve health status among populations of service recipients.

Given that a succession of federal administrations beginning in 1945 with President Truman had proposed and failed at enacting some form of universal healthcare coverage, the ACA was an achievement of historic proportion. The groundbreaking nature of the ACA resides in its addressing what were historically intractable systemic problems of cost, quality, and access.

The ACA intends to reverse incentives that drive up costs; to enact requirements that increase both accountability for, and transparency of, quality; and by 2019, to increase access by expanding health insurance coverage to several million Americans.[66,67] The ACA also adds consumer protections and enhances access to needed services for the nation's most vulnerable populations.[68]

Judicial Challenges to the Affordable Care Act

On the day the ACA was signed into law, the state of Florida filed a federal district court lawsuit challenging the constitutionality of the law's requirement for individual coverage and its expansion of the Medicaid program. Twenty-five additional states, the National Federation of Independent Businesses, and other plaintiffs also filed suit in Florida.[69] The Virginia state attorney general filed a separate lawsuit challenging the federal requirement for individuals to purchase health insurance.[70] The primary issues of contention were whether Congress had the authority to impose the individual coverage mandate with personal financial penalties for noncompliance under either its authority to regulate interstate commerce or its taxing power; and whether Congress had the authority to make all of a state's existing Medicaid funding contingent on compliance with the ACA's Medicaid expansion provisions.[69] The U.S. Supreme Court agreed to decide the two issues and heard oral arguments from proponents and detractors of the ACA provisions during the spring of 2012. On June 28, 2012, in a 5 to 4 decision, the Court upheld the constitutionality of the individual mandate with Chief Justice Roberts writing, "The mandate is not a legal command to buy insurance. Rather, it just makes going without insurance just another thing the government taxes."[71] The Court determined that the Medicaid expansion as described in the ACA was unconstitutionally coercive of states but remedied this violation of states' rights by prohibiting the federal government from making states' existing Medicaid funding contingent on participation in the expansion. The Court's decisions made no changes to the preexisting Medicaid law and the federal government's authority to require states' compliance with existing Medicaid program rules.[69] In 2015 the ACA survived another challenge when the Supreme Court negated a lawsuit alleging that federal tax subsidies to help offset health insurance costs for individuals in certain states were illegal.[72]

▶ The Affordable Care Act Implementation Provisions

The ACA is more than 900-pages long and written under 10 titles.[73] It is organized under four broad goals:

- Providing new consumer protections
- Improving quality and lowering costs
- Increasing access to affordable care
- Holding Insurance Companies Accountable

Following is a brief summary of the law's major provisions excerpted and edited from DHHS websites and categorized by the ACA's major goals listed above.[74,75] In addition, the Kaiser Family Foundation lists ACA implementation activities year-by-year with the status of the law's provisions.[76] For more detailed information, readers are encouraged to use this chapter's references and Internet links. The law's provisions are being implemented sequentially with all provisions expected to be in effect by 2019.

New Consumer Protections

- Establishes a website on which consumers can compare health insurance coverage options and choose their preference.
- Prohibits insurance companies from denying coverage of children based on preexisting conditions.
- Prohibits insurance companies from refusing to sell coverage or renew policies for adults because of preexisting conditions and prohibits insurance companies from charging higher rates because of gender or health status.
- Prohibits insurance companies from denying payments for a subscriber's illness because of technical or other errors discovered in a subscriber's original insurance application.
- Prohibits insurance companies from imposing lifetime dollar limits on essential benefits, such as hospital stays.
- Prohibits insurance companies' use of annual dollar limits on the amount of insurance coverage a patient may receive under new health plans in the individual market and all group plans.
- Provides consumers with a way to appeal coverage determinations or claims to their insurance company and establishes an external review process.
- Provides federal grants to states to establish or expand independent offices to help consumers navigate the private health insurance system.
- Prohibits insurers from dropping or limiting coverage because an individual chooses to participate in a clinical trial; applies to all clinical trials that treat cancer or other life-threatening diseases.

Improving Quality and Lowering Costs

- Provides small business health insurance tax credits to offset costs of employers' contribution to employees' health insurance premiums.
- Provides relief for older Americans' prescription drug costs.
- Requires that all new health plans cover certain preventive services, such as mammograms and colonoscopies without charging a deductible, co-pay, or coinsurance.
- Establishes a new $15 billion Prevention and Public Health Fund to invest in proven prevention and public health programs.
- Invests new resources and requires new screening procedures for healthcare providers to boost federal antifraud and waste initiatives in Medicare, Medicaid, and Children's Health Insurance Program.
- Provides certain free preventive services, such as annual wellness visits and personalized prevention plans for Medicare beneficiaries.
- Establishes a Center for Medicare & Medicaid Innovation to test new ways of delivering care to patients to improve the quality of care and reduce the rate of growth in costs for Medicare, Medicaid, and the Children's Health Insurance Program.
- Establishes a Community Care Transitions Program to help high-risk Medicare beneficiaries avoid unnecessary hospital readmissions by coordinating care and connecting patients to services in their communities.
- Establishes a new Independent Payment Advisory Board to develop and submit proposals to Congress and the President focused on ways to target waste in the system, recommend ways to reduce costs, improve health outcomes for patients, and expand access to high-quality care.

- Establishes a hospital Value-Based Purchasing program in traditional Medicare, offering financial incentives to hospitals to improve the quality of care; requires hospitals to publicly report performance for certain diagnoses and patients' perceptions of care.
- Provides incentives for physicians and hospitals to join together to form "Accountable Care Organizations" to better coordinate Medicare beneficiary patient care and improve the quality, help prevent disease and illness, and reduce unnecessary hospital admissions.
- Institutes a series of changes to standardize billing and requires health plans to begin adopting and implementing rules for the secure, confidential, electronic exchange of health information.
- Requires any ongoing or new federal health program to collect and report racial, ethnic, and language data to help identify and reduce disparities.
- Provides new funding to state Medicaid programs that choose to cover preventive services for patients at little or no cost to expand the number of Americans receiving preventive care.
- Establishes a national pilot program, Bundled Payments for Care Improvement (BPCI), to encourage hospitals, doctors, and other providers to work together to improve the coordination and quality of patient care by paying a flat rate for a total episode of care rather than billing Medicare for individual services.
- Pays physicians based on value not volume through a provision tying physician payments to the quality of care provided.
- Imposes an excise tax on high-cost insurance plans to limit the costs of health insurance plans to a tax-free amount with the intent to generate revenue to help pay for covering the uninsured.

Increasing Access to Affordable Care

- Provides a preexisting condition insurance plan with new coverage options for individuals who have been uninsured for at least six months because of a preexisting condition.
- Extends coverage for young adults who will be allowed to stay on their parents' plan until they turn 26 years of age.
- Expands coverage for early retirees through a $5 billion program to provide financial help for employment-based plans to continue providing health insurance coverage to people who retire between the ages of 55 and 65, as well as their spouses and dependents.
- Rebuilds the primary care workforce through new incentives to expand the number of primary care doctors, nurses, and physician assistants through scholarships and loan repayments for primary care doctors and nurses working in underserved areas.
- Provides eligibility for $250 million in new grants to states that have or will implement measures requiring insurance companies to justify premium increases; also may bar insurance companies with excessive or unjustified premium levels from participation in the new health insurance exchanges.
- Provides federal matching funds for states covering some additional low-income individuals and families under Medicaid for whom federal funds were not previously available.
- Provides increased payments to rural healthcare providers to help them attract and retain providers.
- Provides new funding to support the construction of and expand services at community health centers, allowing these centers to serve some 20 million new patients across the country.
- Allows states to offer home and community-based services to disabled individuals through Medicaid rather than institutional care in nursing homes through the Community First Choice Option.

- Requires states to pay primary care physicians no less than 100 percent of Medicare payment rates in 2013 and 2014 for primary care services, with full federal funding of the increase.
- Provides states with two additional years of CHIP funding to continue coverage for children not eligible for Medicaid.
- Makes tax credits available for middle-class individuals with incomes between 100 percent and 400 percent of the federal poverty level who are not eligible for other affordable coverage.
- Enables individuals to purchase health insurance directly in the health insurance marketplace if their employers do not offer health insurance.
- Enables Americans who earn less than 133 percent of the federal poverty level eligible to enroll in Medicaid; provides states with 100 percent federal funding for the first three years to support this expanded coverage, phasing to 90 percent federal funding in subsequent years.
- Requires most individuals who can afford it to obtain basic health insurance coverage or pay a fee to help offset the costs of caring for uninsured Americans; if affordable coverage is not available to an individual, he or she will be eligible for an exemption.
- Creates Health Care Choice Compacts that allow selling health insurance across state lines to increase competition among plans and give consumers more choices.

Holding Insurance Companies Accountable

- Ensures that premium dollars are spent primarily on health care by generally requiring that at least 85 percent of all premium dollars collected by insurance companies for large employer plans are spent on healthcare services and healthcare quality improvement; for plans sold to individuals and small employers, at least 80 percent of the premium must be spent on benefits and quality improvement; failing to meet these goals, insurance companies must provide rebates to subscribers.
- Eliminates additional Medicare costs from Medicare managed care plans (Medicare Advantage) and provides bonus payments to Medicare Advantage plans that provide high-quality care.

As noted above, all provisions of the ACA will become fully effective by 2019 and some have already undergone change as the implementation process has proceeded. However, centerpieces of the law such as the new availability of affordable insurance plans and the Medicaid expansion are yielding material results. At only six full years since its enactment, it remains early to speculate on the ACA's success in achieving its overall intended changes in the organization, delivery, efficiency, and effectiveness of a monstrously complex industry. Outcomes will unfold over the next several years. Regulatory and legal changes enacted by the ACA are indeed only two components of the equation. A multitude of other factors such as the nation's economy, the political environment, and provider and consumer reactions and behaviors, to name only a few, will determine the outcomes of this landmark legislation.

KEY TERMS FOR REVIEW

Block Grants
Diagnosis-Related Group (DRG)
Health Information Technology for Economic and Clinical Health Act of 2009 (HITECH)

Health Insurance Portability and Accountability Act of 1996 (HIPAA)
Health Maintenance Organization Act of 1973

Medicaid
Medicare
Oregon Death with Dignity Act of 1994
Social Security Act of 1935

CHAPTER ACRONYMS

AMA American Medical Association
HMO Health maintenance organization

CHIP Children's Health Insurance Program

References

1. Numbers RL. The third party: health insurance in America. In: Vogel MJ, Rosenburg CE, eds. *The Therapeutic Revolution: Essays in the Social History of American Medicine*. Philadelphia, PA: University of Pennsylvania Press; 1979.

2. Starr P. Transformation in defeat: the changing objectives of national health insurance, 1915–1980. In: Kindig DA, Sullivan RB, eds. *Understanding Universal Health Programs, Issues and Options*. Ann Arbor, MI: Health Administration Press; 1992.

3. American Medical Association. Minutes of the House of Delegates. *JAMA*. 1920;74:1317-1328.

4. Stevens R. *In Sickness and in Wealth: American Hospitals in the Twentieth Century*. New York, NY: Basic Books; 1989.

5. Leland RG. Prepayment plans for hospital care. *JAMA*. 1933;100:113-117.

6. American Medical Association Committee on the Costs of Medical Care. *Medical Care for the American People: The Final Report of the Committee on the Costs of Medical Care*. Chicago, IL: University of Chicago Press; 1932.

7. American Medical Association. Minutes of the Eighty-Fourth Session, 12-16. June 1933. *JAMA*. 1933; 100:44-53.

8. Centers for Medicare & Medicaid Services, Office of the Actuary, National Health Statistics Group. 2014. The health care dollar: where it went and where it came from. https://www.cms.gov/Research-Statistics-Data-and-Systems/Statistics-Trends-and-Reports/NationalHealthExpendData/Downloads/PieChartSourcesExpenditures2014.pdf. Accessed April 10, 2016.

9. Canada B. Report for Congress: federal grants to state and local governments: a brief history. February 19, 2003. Congressional Research Service. http://www.ait.org.tw/infousa/zhtw/DOCS/fedgrants.pdf. Accessed May 11, 2016.

10. Lee PR, Benjamin AE. Health policy and the politics of health care. In: Lee PR, Estes CL, eds. *The Nation's Health*. 4th ed. Sudbury, MA: Jones and Bartlett; 1994.

11. Centers for Medicare & Medicaid Services. Historical. Downloads. NHE summary including share of GDP CY 1980–2014. https://www.cms.gov/research-statistics-data-and-systems/statistics-trends-and-reports/nationalhealthexpenddata/nationalhealthaccountshistorical.html. Accessed April 12, 2016.

12. Nerney C. 5 steps for shifting to value-based reimbursement in healthcare. *Healthcare Finance*. August 27, 2015. http://www.healthcarefinancenews.com/news/5-steps-shifting-value-based-reimbursement-healthcare. Accessed June 3, 2016.

13. National Library of Medicine, Profiles in Science. The regional medical programs collection: brief history. Available from https://profiles.nlm.nih.gov/ps/retrieve/Narrative/RM/p-nid/94. Accessed May 19, 2016.

14. Melhado E. Health planning in the United States and the decline of public-interest policymaking. *Milbank Q*. 2006;84:359-440. http://www.ncbi.nlm.nih.gov/pmc/articles/PMC2690168/. Accessed May 19, 2016.

15. Brown LD. Political evolution of federal health regulation. *Health Aff*. 1992;11:17-37. http://content.healthaffairs.org/content/11/4/17.full.pdf±html. Accessed May 19, 2016.

16. Blendon RJ Brodie M Benson JM, et al. Understanding the managed care backlash. *Health Aff*. 1998;17:80-94. http://content.healthaffairs.org/content/17/4/80. Accessed February 19, 2013.

17. Hurley RE, Strunk BC, White JJ. The puzzling popularity of the PPO. *Health Aff*. 2004;23:56-68. http://content.healthaffairs.org/content/23/2/56.full.html. Accessed May 20, 2016.

18. Long M, Rae M, Claxton G. PPO enrollment: comparison of the availability and cost of coverage for workers in small firms and large firms: update from the 2015 employer health benefits survey. The Henry J. Kaiser Family Foundation. http://kff.org/private-insurance/issue-brief/a-comparison-of-the-availability-and-cost-of-coverage-for-workers-in-small-firms-and-large-firms-update-from-the-2015-employer-health-benefits-survey/. Accessed May 11, 2016.

19. Lee PR, Estes CL. *The Nation's Health*. 4th ed. Boston, MA: Jones and Bartlett; 1994.

20. McCormack LA, Burge RT. Diffusion of Medicare's RBRVS and related physician payment policies. Health Care Financ Rev. 1994;16:159-173. http://www.ncbi.nlm.nih.gov/pmc/articles/PMC4193488/. Accessed May 14, 2016.

21. Goozner M. High-tech medicine contributes to high-cost health care. *The Fiscal Times*. http://khn.org/news/

ft-health-care-high-tech-costs/. Accessed May 26, 2016.

22. Lindstrom R. Thoughts on cataract surgery: 2015. *Review of Ophthalmology*. http://www.reviewof ophthalmology.com/content/t/surgical_education /c/53422/. Accessed June 7, 2016.

23. McGivney WT, Hendee WR. Technology assessment in medicine: the role of the American Medical Association. *Archives of Pathology & Laboratory Medicine*. 1988;112:1181-1185.

24. Office of Technology Assessment. Assessing the Efficacy and Safety of Medical Technologies. Washington, DC: Government Printing Office; 1978.

25. Sadowski J. The much-needed and sane congressional office that Gingrich killed off and we need back. *The Atlantic*. http://www.theatlantic.com/technology/archive /2012/10/the-much-needed-and-sane-congressional -office-that-gingrich-killed-off-and-we-need -back/264160/#. Accessed February 20, 2013.

26. Reinhardt UE. Reinhardt on reform (interview done by Donna Vavala). *Physician Executive*. 1995;21:10-12.

27. American Association of Medical Colleges. 2015 state physician workforce data book. November 2015. http://members.aamc.org/eweb/upload/2015 StateDataBook%20(revised).pdf. Accessed June 6, 2016.

28. Eisenberg JM. If trickle-down physician workforce policy failed, is the choice now between the market and government regulation? *Inquiry*. 1994. 31:241-249.

29. Oberlander J. The politics of paying for health reform: zombies, payroll taxes, and the Holy Grail. *Health Aff*. 2008;27:w544-w555. http://content .healthaffairs.org/content/27/6/w544.full.html. Accessed June 6, 2016.

30. Robeznieks A. AMA saw membership rise 3.2% in 2012. *Mod Healthc*. http://www.modernhealthcare. com/article/20130509/NEWS/305099950. Accessed August 25, 2016.

31. Fuchs VR. Health reform: Getting the essentials right. *Health Aff*. 2009;28:w180-w183. http://content .healthaffairs.org/content/28/2/w180.full.html. Accessed June 3, 2016.

32. National Journal. Influence Alley. Exclusive: AHIP gave more than $100 million to Chamber's efforts to derail health care reform. 2012. https://www .healthcare-now.org/blog/ahip-gave-more-than-100 -million-to-chambers-efforts-to-derail-health-care -reform/. Accessed June 6, 2016.

33. AARP. About AARP. http://www.aarp.org/about -aarp/. Accessed June 6, 2016.

34. Pickert K. Is the NFIB really a voice for small businesses? Time.com. http://swampland.time.com/2010/05/14 /is-the-nfib-really-a-voice-for-small-businesses/. Accessed Jun 6, 2016.

35. National Association of Manufacturers. About the NAM-manufacturing in America. 2013. http://

www.nam.org/about-us/about-the-nam/US -manufacturers-association.aspx. Accessed June 7, 2016.

36. U.S. Chamber of Commerce. About the U.S. Chamber of Commerce. https://www.uschamber.com/about-us /about-the-us-chamber. Accessed June 6, 2016.

37. AFL-CIO. About the AFL-CIO. http://www.aflcio.org /About. Accessed June 7, 2016.

38. Service Employees International Union. What type of work do SEIU members do? http://www.seiu .org/cards/these-fast-facts-will-tell-you-how-were -organized/. Accessed June 7, 2016.

39. Singer M. Columbia Broadcasting System. Under the influence. 2009. http://www.cbsnews.com/8301 -18560_162-2625305.html. Accessed June 8, 2016.

40. American Public Health Association. Become a member. https://www.apha.org/become-a-member. Accessed June 9, 2016.

41. United States Department of Labor. The Health Insurance Portability and Accountability Act. https:// www.dol.gov/ebsa/newsroom/fshipaa.html. Accessed June 9, 2016.

42. HHS.gov. Summary of the HIPAA security rule. http://www.hhs.gov/hipaa/for-professionals/security /laws-regulations/. Accessed June 9, 2016.

43. American Health Information Management Association. HIPAA turns 10: Analyzing the past, present and future impact. http://library.ahima.org /doc?oid=106325#.V2MgR70uF51. Accessed June 9, 2016.

44. National Association of Social Workers. Balanced Budget Act of 1997, public law 105-33: Significant changes made in children's health, welfare, Medicaid and Medicare. http://www.socialworkers.org/archives /advocacy/updates/1997/grbudget.htm. Accessed May 14, 2016.

45. Shi L, Singh D. *Delivering Health Care in America: A Systems Approach*. Burlington, MA: Jones & Bartlett Learning; 2012.

46. Medicare Payment Advisory Commission. Report to the Congress: Medicare payment policy (March 2003), chapter 1, context for Medicare spending. http://www.medpac.gov/documents/reports/Mar03 _Entire_report.pdf?sfvrsn=0. Accessed May 15, 2016.

47. Lambrew JM. *The state children's health insurance program: past, present and future*. The Commonwealth Fund. February 2007. http://www.commonwealthfund .org/publications/fund-reports/2007/feb/the-state -childrens-health-insurance-program--past--present --and-future. Accessed May 9, 2016.

48. The Henry J. Kaiser Family Foundation. Total number of children ever enrolled in CHIP annually. http://kff .org/other/state-indicator/annual-chip-enrollment/. Accessed May 14, 2016.

49. Death with Dignity National Center. Oregon Death with Dignity Act: a history. https://www.deathwithdignity

.org/oregon-death-with-dignity-act-history/. Accessed June 2, 2016.

50. Emanuel EJ, Daniels E. Oregon's physician-assisted suicide law: Provisions and problems. *Archives of Internal Medicine*. 1996;156:46, 50.

51. Lee MA, Nelson HD, Triden UP, Ganzini L, Schmidt TA, Tolle SW. Legalizing assisted suicide: view of physicians in Oregon. *N Engl J Med*. 1996;334:310-315.

52. De Wachter MAM. Active euthanasia in the Netherlands. *JAMA*. 1989;262:3316-3319.

53. Hedberg K, Tolle S. Putting Oregon's Death with Dignity Act in perspective: Characteristics of decedents who did not participate. *J Clin Ethics*. Summer 2009;20(2):133-135.

54. Washington State Department of Health. Death with Dignity Act. 2011. http://www.doh.wa.gov/dwda/. Accessed June 2, 2016.

55. Johnson K. Montana ruling bolsters doctor-assisted suicide. December 31, 2009. *The New York Times*. http://www.nytimes.com/2010/01/01/us/01suicide.html?_r=0. Accessed June 2, 2016.

56. Vermont Department of Health. Patient choice and control at end of life. http://healthvermont.gov/family/end_of_life_care/patient_choice.aspx. Accessed June 2, 2016.

57. McGreevy P. Aid-in-dying law to take effect June 9 in California. *Los Angeles Times*. March 10, 2016. http://www.latimes.com/politics/la-pol-sac-assisted-suicide-law-can-take-effect-20160310-story.html. Accessed June 2, 2016.

58. Patients Rights Council. New Mexico. http://www.patientsrightscouncil.org/site/new-mexico/. Accessed June 2, 2016.

59. *People*. .Terminally ill 29-year-old woman: why I'm choosing to die on my own terms. http://www.people.com/article/Brittany-Maynard-death-with-dignity-compassion-choices. Accessed June 2, 2016.

60. Bush GW. Executive order: Incentives for the use of health information technology and establishing the position of the National Health Information Technology coordinator. April 27, 2004. http://georgewbush-whitehouse.archives.gov/news/releases/2004/04/20040427-4.html. Accessed March 8, 2016.

61. One Hundred Eleventh Congress of the United States of America. The American Recovery and Reinvestment Act. https://www.gpo.gov/fdsys/pkg/BILLS-111hr1enr/pdf/BILLS-111hr1enr.pdf. Accessed August 25, 2016.

62. Pew Research Center. Pew survey of Americans' online health habits. 2013. http://www.chcf.org/publications/2013/01/pew-survey-online-health. Accessed June 9, 2016.

63. Connolly C. Senators hurry to keep health care in forefront. 2008. *The Washington Post*. http://www.washingtonpost.com/wp-dyn/content/article/2008/11/11/AR2008111102511.html?sid=ST2008111200035. Accessed June 16, 2016.

64. Staff of the Washington Post. Landmark: *The Inside Story of America's New Health-Care Law and What It Means for Us All*. New York, NY: Perseus Books Group; 2002:13.

65. Frakes VL. Partisanship and (un)compromise: A study of the Patient Protection and Affordable Care Act. *Harvard Journal on Legislation*. 2012;49:135-149. http://harvardjol.wpengine.com/wp-content/uploads/2013/09/Frakes1.pdf. Accessed June 11, 2016.

66. Gotsin LO, Jacobson PD, Record KL, Hardcastle LE. Restoring health to health reform: integrating medicine and public health to advance the population's well-being. *U Pa L Rev*. https://www.pennlawreview.com/print/old/Gostin.pdf. Accessed June 14, 2016.

67. The Henry J. Kaiser Family Foundation. Summary of the Affordable Care Act. 2013. http://kff.org/health-reform/fact-sheet/summary-of-the-affordable-care-act/. Accessed May 11, 2016.

68. The Henry J. Kaiser Family Foundation. Summary of coverage provisions in the Patient Protection and Affordable Care Act and the Health Care and Education Reconciliation Act of 2010. http://kff.org/health-costs/issue-brief/summary-of-coverage-provisions-in-the-patient/. Accessed March 19, 2016.

69. The Henry J. Kaiser Family Foundation. A Guide to the Supreme Court's Affordable Care Act Decision. 2012. http://www.kff.org/healthreform/upload/8332.pdf. Accessed June 14, 2016.

70. Redhead SC, Chaikind H, Fernandez B, Staman J. PPACA: A brief overview of the law, implementation, and legal challenges. Congressional Research Service. 2011. https://www.fas.org/sgp/crs/misc/R41664.pdf. Accessed June 12, 2016.

71. Pazanowski MA. Split court upholds PPACA constitutionality, limits Medicaid. *Bloomberg BNA*. 2012. http://www.bna.com/split-supreme-court-n12884910401. Accessed June 14, 2016.

72. Obamacare Lawsuits. Updates on Obamacare related lawsuits: Subsidies, NFIB, hobby lobby, John Boehner, and more. http://obamacarefacts.com/obamacare-lawsuit/. Accessed June 2, 2016.

73. U.S. Government Printing Office. Patient Protection and Affordable Care Act of 2010. 2010. http://www.gpo.gov/fdsys/pkg/PLAW-111publ148/pdf/PLAW-111publ148.pdf. Accessed June 6, 2016.

74. HHS.gov. Key features of the Affordable Care Act. http://www.hhs.gov/healthcare/facts-and-features/key-features-of-aca/. Accessed August 26, 2016.

75. HHS.gov. Key features of the Affordable Care Act by year. http://www.hhs.gov/healthcare/facts-and-features/key-features-of-aca-by-year/index.html. Accessed August 26, 2016.

76. The Henry J. Kaiser Family Foundation. Health reform implementation timeline. http://kff.org/interactive/implementation-timeline/. Accessed August 26, 2016.

CHAPTER 3

Health Information Technology

CHAPTER OVERVIEW

This chapter outlines major historical developments in the evolution of health information technology and discusses government initiatives to support its implementation. It highlights both benefits and challenges of using this technology and the progress of its implementation to date.

▶ Historical Overview

The concept of using modern health information technology (HIT) to improve the quality and reduce the costs of health care is not new. In fact, the U.S. federal government has a half-century history of many HIT initiatives. One of the earliest is traceable back to the Kennedy Administration in the early 1960s. A report from the President's Science Advisory Committee, "Some New Technologies and their Promise for the Life Sciences," was optimistic about the benefits HIT would bring to biomedical research and the healthcare system.[1] Ironically, the report written more than a half century ago is still relevant to the HIT of today:

> The application of computer technology to the recording, storage, and analysis of data collected in the course of observing and treating large numbers of ill people promises to advance our understanding of the cause, course, and control of disease. The need for a general-purpose health information technology stems in large part from increasingly rapid changes in the pattern of illness in the United States and from equally significant changes in the way medicine is practiced. The acute infectious diseases from which the patient either recovered or died have largely given place to chronic disorders which run an extremely variable course dependent on many factors both in the environment and within the patient himself. . . . Within any sizable community there are numerous administrative

Flag: © Lightix/Shutterstock

organizations charged with providing health services. It is not uncommon for a single patient to be cared for by a large number of agencies in a single city, and workers in any one agency usually cannot find out about the activities of others; sometimes they even fail to learn that other agencies are active at all. . . . Modern data-processing techniques make it possible to assemble all the necessary information about all the patients in a given geographical or administrative area in one place with rapid access for all authorized health and welfare agencies. Such a system would produce an immediate and highly significant improvement in medical care with a simultaneous reduction in direct dollar costs of manual record processing and an even greater economy in professional time now wasted in duplicating tests and procedures.[1]

The federal government took the most significant step in the history of HIT on April 27, 2004, when President Bush created the Office of the National Coordinator for Health Information Technology (ONCHIT or "the ONC") by Executive Order.[2] It was then legislatively mandated in the American Recovery and Reinvestment Act (ARRA) when signed by President Obama on February 17, 2009.[3] Part of the ARRA is the Health Information Technology for Economic and Clinical Health Act (HITECH) that designated $36.5 billion to promote the development of a nationwide network of electronic health records (EHRs). EHRs are computerized patient records that are essentially replacing paper charts.

Surprisingly, despite this sizable investment and more than a half century of government incentives and technological advancements, the best scientific evidence today indicates that the benefits of HIT on the quality and cost of health care are, at best, mixed.[4] This chapter will explore the history of how HIT has evolved and the imprint HIT has made on the current healthcare system, and speculate on how HIT will likely influence the future healthcare system and health care in general.

▶ Historical Challenges in Implementing Health Information Technology

Using computers to improve health care in many ways parallels the development of the information technology industry. The late 1960s and early 1970s saw several pioneering efforts at a small number of universities to apply HIT to various aspects of the healthcare delivery process. Early systems were not the ubiquitous, web-based, interactive systems of today but were usually a hybrid of computer and paper integrated into a clinical work process.

One early example from the 1970s at Indiana University is where a small army of data entry clerks manually entered data into a computer on key parts of patients' medical records. The night before a patient's clinic appointment, a one-page, paper encounter form was printed for the next day's appointment listing the patients' name, record number, medical problem list (i.e., the known diagnoses and medical problems), medication list, medication allergies, and suggestions based on an analysis of the data in the computer system. "Suggestions" were calculated based on what patient information the computer had at the point in time the encounter form was printed the night before the patient's visit (e.g., laboratory results, prescription data, diagnoses, vital signs). The software detected any of 290 agreed-upon patient-care protocols or conditions defined by the biomedical literature and best medical practice. When a physician saw the patient in the clinic, they would handwrite notes on the paper encounter form and manually annotate the computer-printed problem list, medication list, and other items. Later, a team of data entry clerks would review the annotated encounter forms and update the computer system to reflect the physician's orders and updates to the patient's condition. The encounter form would then be filed to the patient's paper chart. The Indiana group conducted a study demonstrating a 29 percent improvement in adherence to agreed-upon treatment protocols in the group of physicians who received the computer "suggestions" for recommended treatments on the encounter forms versus those who did not.[5] Similar systems were designed and built during the same time period at a number of other U.S. universities, including The University of Pittsburgh,[6] The University of Utah,[7,8] Vanderbilt University,[9,10] Duke University,[11] and Harvard University/Massachusetts General Hospital.[12] These pioneering systems were custom designed, built, and maintained by in-house teams of computer programmers and systems engineers. Because of the custom designs, their great expense, and the fact they did not comprehensively implement the entire patient record, they were not practical for widespread use. Despite these limitations, the pioneering work done with these early systems laid the foundation for modern EHR design.

It was not until the 1990s that commercially produced EHR systems were mass marketed and sold to healthcare institutions in high volume. These commercially produced systems allowed hospitals to implement comprehensive EHRs without the prohibitive costs of designing and building custom systems. Instead, hospitals could buy an "off-the-shelf" system that although not completely customized to institutional work flows, could be configured to meet most of their perceived institutional needs. The "off the shelf," commercially produced EHRs of today still require extensive configuration to accommodate a hospital's unique and varying work processes. Also, commercial systems were not capable of easily exchanging patients' health information between systems and institutions. In fact, the configuration differences between institutions are often so significant that even institutions with the same commercial EHR systems cannot electronically exchange patients' records without customized software.

As the installed base of commercial systems expanded, many researchers at universities that pioneered early, customized systems began to study issues with implementation of new HIT in the healthcare setting.[13,14] Researchers learned there is a great deal more than just selecting the "right system" to insure a successful HIT implementation. **FIGURE 3-1** illustrates the three essential components required for successful HIT implementation.

The first essential component is the technology. However, organizations often focus solely on this first component with the mistaken belief that merely selecting the "right" technology or the "right EHR" is the most important aspect of HIT implementation.

The second component of successful implementation, work policies and procedures, makes implementing HIT systems in the clinical environment extremely challenging due to wide variations

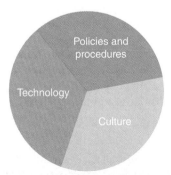

FIGURE 3-1 **The Three Essential Components of a Successful HIT Implementation**

in work policies and procedures among different organizations and institutions. An organization's policies and procedures describe and define the processes through which work is carried out. The process component is complex, because it requires HIT system implementers to understand fully all existing work processes. Many such processes are not written or formalized, having evolved over the years to accommodate the unique characteristics of a particular organization. Further, actual work processes may significantly differ from those officially documented or assumed to be in place, while many critical work processes are not documented at all. When a HIT system is implemented, it is common for many of the undocumented processes to become apparent for the first time.[15] Undocumented or unknown work processes have been the root cause for many HIT implementation failures.[16]

The third component is the most significant—the institutional and organizational culture—what people are willing to do.[14] This is the most critical, least studied, and least understood of the HIT implementation components.[17] Ash and Bates summarized the importance of organizational culture with regard to EHR adoption:[13]

> The organizational culture must be ready to support adoption by the individuals within it. There has been a period when clinicians have not experienced a sense of collaboration and trust between them and hospital administration. Consequently, if clinicians believe the administration wants to force them to use Computerized Physician Order Entry (CPOE), for example, they may dig in their heels. They may be more resistant to arguments based on safety and patient care benefit if the level of trust is not there. On the other hand, if the impetus comes from the clinical staff, other clinicians may be more apt to adopt sooner, and readiness will be at a higher level. One gauge of readiness is the extent to which certain categories of people hold positions within the organization. In particular, administrators at the highest level must offer both moral and financial support and demonstrate that they really believe in the patient care benefits of the systems. There must be clinical leaders, including a chief medical information officer if at all possible, who understand the fine points of implementation strategies, and opinion leaders among the clinical staff members. In addition, there need to be sufficiently skilled implementation, training, and support coordinators who understand both clinical and technical issues.*

There is a significant publication bias in the biomedical literature against revealing HIT implementation failures. Because of the human tendency to avoid publicizing an individual's mistakes, the body of literature is strongly skewed toward successful implementations and studies. This has made it more difficult to study and understand causes of HIT implementation failures. A significant advance for the HIT industry as a whole would be a shift in its culture toward not only reporting HIT failures, but also viewing them as valuable learning opportunities to be highlighted rather than embarrassing events to be downplayed and forgotten.

One major example of a HIT implementation failure occurred at the prestigious Cedars-Sinai Hospital in Los Angeles, California, in 2002. Three months after implementing a new $34 million HIT system, several hundred physicians refused to use it. Cedars-Sinai attempted to implement a new electronic medical record that changed the way physicians ordered patient treatments and

---

*Reproduced from Ash JS, Bates DW. Factors and forces affecting EHR system adoption: report of a 2004 ACMI discussion. *J Am Med Inform Assoc.* 2005;12:8-12. © 2005, with permission from BMJ Publishing Group Ltd.

tests in the hospital. Prior to implementing the new system, physicians wrote their orders on paper forms in the patients' paper charts. After new patient orders were written, physicians gave the chart to nurses or ward clerks to read and implement the orders. The new system required physicians to type orders directly into a computer workstation, where the software provided the physician with immediate feedback if they attempted to enter an order that the computer either did not understand or interpreted as a mistake. An article in the *Washington Post* reported:[18]

> A veteran physician at the prestigious Cedars-Sinai Medical Center here had been mixing up a certain drug dosage for decades. Every time he wrote the prescription for 10 times the proper amount, a nurse simply corrected it, recalled Paul Hackmeyer. The computers arrived—and when the doctor typed in his medication order, the machine barked at him and he barked back. . . . "What we discovered was that for 20 years he was writing the wrong dose."

This failure illustrates the three principal HIT implementation components described above:

- *Technology:* With physicians required to enter orders directly to the computer system, time required to enter orders became dependent on the computer's ordering input format and system response time.
- *Process:* Many undocumented processes in the old system were not carried to the new system. In this example, the nurse's automatic correction of an obvious dosage error was a critical, undocumented, process—a nursing check on the orders' accuracy. Although the new system caught the error, the physician user in this case could no longer rely on the nurse's checking and correcting his orders.
- *Culture:* The new system required physicians to interact with a computer, which took more time than writing orders on paper forms. The new system required physicians to change the way they practiced medicine in the hospital and as is common, people dislike change. This was a significant change in physicians' work culture in which nurses had routinely checked and corrected physician orders without communicating the corrections. Physicians also had to deal with a barrage of system alerts when they were imprecise or inaccurate in entering their orders. While potentially enhancing patient safety, responding to the system alerts increased the time (and physician irritation) required for physicians to place orders.

Another historical barrier to broad implementation of HIT is the gap between those who bear the costs of the technology and those who receive its benefits. The purchase and operation of an EHR system represents a major investment for large healthcare organizations and especially for small private physician groups. Not only must physician groups bear the costs of the hardware and software, but they also must support ongoing IT maintenance, staff training, and software upgrade costs. Because small practice groups often have no experience or expertise with IT issues, they also experience anxiety about making decisions necessary to convert from paper to electronic charting. While economies of scale make the marginal costs of adopting EHR technology somewhat lower for large healthcare organizations, these organizations often do not realize the costs savings from their investment. A good example of this is a healthcare system participating in a health information exchange (HIE). HIE systems share patient information across institutions and multiple EHR platforms. This allows patients and physicians access to a patient's comprehensive health record from multiple institutions, regardless of where the patient was seen. HIEs often reduce the number of duplicate laboratory and imaging tests, saving the patient and the payer significant expense.

However, the healthcare system may lose money by not receiving revenue for the duplicate tests not performed and for the expense they bear supporting the HIE. As with large healthcare systems, small practices that invest in EHR technology may not directly benefit from the technology. Patients may receive more age-appropriate screening[19,20] and preventive care[21], along with reduced duplicate testing, because physicians have access to HIEs and patient records from outside the practice group or health system.[22] However, from a practice's financial perspective, these factors actually may produce a significant disincentive for adopting EHRs.

▸ The Federal Government's Response to Health Information Technology Implementation Challenges

As mentioned previously, the U.S. government has sought ways to incentivize adoption of HIT for more than half a century. The largest incentive program to date has been the $36 billion in the HITECH Act that created the Medicare and Medicaid Electronic Health Record Incentive Program.[23] The Center for Medicare & Medicaid Services (CMS) used these funds to incentivize Eligible Professionals (individual physicians in solo or multi-physician practice groups) and Eligible Hospitals as they adopt, implement, upgrade, or demonstrate meaningful use of certified EHR technology to improve patient care. There were three progressive stages to the "Meaningful Use Program" with deadlines; the highest financial incentives were awarded to Eligible Professional or Eligible Hospitals for the earliest compliance with standards in each stage.[24] This program was in part an effort to address a portion of the gap between those that bear the costs of HIT implementation (physicians and hospitals) and those who receive most of its benefits (patients, public health agencies, and payers).

Eligible Professionals could receive up to $44,000 through the Medicare EHR Incentive Program and up to $63,750 through the Medicaid EHR Incentive Program. Eligible Professionals could participate in either the Medicare or Medicaid EHR Incentive Programs but not both. Eligible Hospitals could participate in both the Medicare and Medicaid incentive programs.[25] Each hospital incentive included a base payment of $2 million plus an additional amount determined by a formula based on the number of discharges per year.[26–28] **TABLE 3-1** compares the Medicare and Medicaid adoption incentive programs for Eligible Professionals and Eligible Hospitals.[23–25,29–35]

In 2009, the ONC was designated "the principal federal entity charged with coordination of nationwide efforts to implement and use the most advanced health information technology and the electronic exchange of health information."[36] In short, CMS provided the financial incentives for the meaningful use program and the ONC set the requirements. The ONC's mission, noted in its 2016 budget justification to Congress, is to "improve health, health care, and reduce costs through the use of information and technology."[37] **FIGURE 3-2** depicts the ONC's current organizational structure. The ONC had a budget of $60 million in fiscal year 2015.[38] The HITECH Act also created a HIT Policy Committee and the HIT Standards Committee under the auspices of the Federal Advisory Committee Act.[39] Both committees have multiple workgroups with representatives from payers, academia, and the healthcare industry. They address a variety of HIT-related issues including certification/adoption, governance, HIE, meaningful use, privacy and security, quality measures, implementation, and a HIT vocabulary standards committee.[39]

The Health IT Policy Committee makes recommendations to the National Coordinator for Health IT on a policy framework for the development and adoption of a nationwide health information infrastructure, including standards for the exchange of patient medical

TABLE 3-1 Comparison of Medicare and Medicaid Adoption Incentive Programs for Eligible Professionals (Individual Physicians in Solo and Group Practices) and Eligible Hospitals (Including Critical Access Hospitals)

	Medicare Program	Medicaid Program
Eligible Professionals	<ul><li>Administered by CMS</li><li>$44,000 Maximum per physician (over 5-year period)</li><li>90% or more of practice must be outpatient based</li><li>Cannot participate in Medicaid Program if enrolled in Medicare Program</li><li>Must apply for Stage 1 Meaningful Use by 2012 to obtain the maximum incentive</li><li>Medicare imposes payment penalty on those failing to demonstrate meaningful use beginning 2015</li></ul>	<ul><li>Administered by State Medicaid Agency</li><li>$63,750 Maximum per physician Participate (over 5 years)</li><li>Must have ≤ 30% Medicaid patient volume or ≤ 20% Medicaid patient volume and be a pediatrician or practice predominantly in a Federally Qualified Health Center or Rural Health Clinic and have ≤ 30% patient volume attributable to needy individuals</li><li>≤ 90% of practice must be outpatient based</li><li>Cannot participate in Medicare Program if enrolled in Medicaid Program</li><li>Can begin to certify for Meaningful Use by 2016 and still receive full incentive</li><li>Non-participants exempt from Medicaid payment reductions</li></ul>
Hospitals (Including Critical Access Hospitals)	<ul><li>Administered by CMS</li><li>Can begin receiving incentive FY 2011 to FY 2015, but payments will decrease for hospitals that start receiving payments in FY 2014 and later</li><li>Medicare and Medicaid Program eligible</li><li>Must apply for Stage 1 Meaningful Use by FY 2013 to receive maximum incentive</li><li>Hospitals that do not successfully demonstrate meaningful use will be subject to Medicare payment penalties beginning in FY 2015</li><li>Incentive payments are based on several factors, beginning with a $2 million base payment</li></ul>	<ul><li>Administered by State Medicaid Agency</li><li>Acute care hospitals (including critical access and cancer hospitals) with at least 10% Medicaid patient volume are eligible</li><li>Children's hospitals are eligible regardless of their Medicaid volume</li><li>Can apply for both Medicare and Medicaid Programs</li><li>Incentive payments are based on a number of factors, beginning with a $2 million base payment.</li></ul>

Data from the Centers for Medicare & Medicaid Services and the Office of the National Coordinator for Health Information Technology.

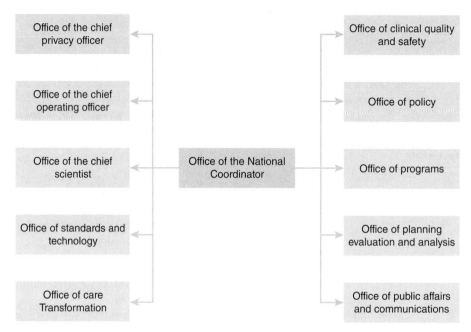

FIGURE 3-2 **Office of the National Coordinator for Health Information Technology Organizational Structure**

Modified from the Office of the National Coordinator of Health Information Technology: https://www.healthit.gov/newsroom/about-onc.

information. The American Recovery and Reinvestment Act of 2009 (ARRA) provides that the Health IT Policy Committee shall at least make recommendations on the areas in which standards, implementation specifications, and certification criteria are needed in eight specific areas.

The Health IT Standards Committee is charged with making recommendations to the National Coordinator for Health IT on standards, implementation specifications, and certification criteria for the electronic exchange and use of health information.

The meaningful use requirements were developed by these committees and the ONC. The evidence for the majority of meaningful use objectives was only at the expert opinion level. The science of HIT awaits rigorous research studies to validate the choices and designs of the meaningful use criteria.

To receive the maximum incentive payment under the meaningful use program, Eligible Professionals who chose to participate in the Medicare Program had to achieve stage 1 of Meaningful Use by 2012 or by 2014 for a reduced amount.[32] Eligible Professionals who chose to participate in the Medicaid Program had to achieve stage 1 by 2016 to receive the maximum payment.[40] Those eligible professionals who begin to certify under the Medicare Program in 2015 or later or under the Medicaid Program after 2016 will receive no incentive payments.

By the end of November 2014, only 25.2 percent of Eligible Professionals and 43.1 percent of Eligible Hospitals had met stage 2 requirements.[41,42] Many physicians and hospitals complained about the difficulty and complexity of the reporting requirements as well as the lack of HIT tools readiness to support these requirements from HIT vendors. On October 6, 2015, CMS published a fact sheet titled "EHR Incentive Programs in 2015 and Beyond" to communicate a simplification of the meaningful use requirements.[43] The criteria for Eligible Professional "modified stage 2" were simplified to 10 objectives, including one consolidated public health reporting objective. Previously, stage 2 required Eligible Professionals to meet 17 core objectives plus 3 of 6 menu objectives and to report electronically 9 out of 64 approved Clinical Quality Measures (CQM).[44] (These are standardized measures for healthcare providers and institutions to report on various aspects of the quality of care they provide.) For Eligible Hospitals, modified stage 2 objectives were reduced to 9, including one consolidated public health reporting objective. Previously, stage 2 required Eligible Hospitals to report on 16 core objectives plus 3 out of 6 menu objectives and to electronically report 16 out of 29 CQMs.[45] Under the same announcement, CMS finalized the requirements for stage 3 for 2017 and subsequent years. These included 8 objectives for Eligible Professionals and Eligible Hospitals, more requirements for interoperability, and improved quality reporting alignment with CMS quality reporting programs.[43]

Detailed information on the meaningful use requirements for modified stage 2 is available for Eligible Professionals[46] and Eligible Hospitals.[47] Some examples of meaningful use requirements for modified stage 2 for Eligible Professionals include:

- Performing a security risk analysis one time per year
- Using clinical decision support to improve performance on high-priority health conditions.
- Using Computerized Physician Order Entry (CPOE)
- Using an e-prescribing system for at least 50 percent of prescriptions
- Providing a summary care record when transferring patients from facility to facility
- Providing patient education with HIT
- Performing medication reconciliation at appropriate times
- Providing the capability for patients to view their electronic health information securely online or by downloading or transmitting it directly to a third party
- Using secure electronic messaging (email) to communicate with patients
- Transmitting required public health information electronically to the appropriate agencies

As noted previously, the ONC also has funded several programs to facilitate the adoption of EHRs. Examples include training programs to increase the number of professionals with IT skills required in the healthcare domain. Other programs fund the development of HIE standards across multiple EHR vendor platforms. The ONC also funds annual surveys to track HIT adoption and more recently HIT "developer contests" that incentivize innovation in ONC-targeted areas with monetary prizes.

▶ HIT Opportunities: Improving Healthcare Delivery Quality, Effectiveness, and Efficiency

With mediocre evidence to date for HIT goals to improve healthcare quality and reduce costs, the question looms: What is the driving force behind the United States' quest to implement HIT? The answer resides in understanding the limitations of the human brain and limited attention span. A healthy human's performance begins to measurably decrease in about 40 minutes while monitoring a continuous process.[48] These limitations explain regulations for work-time breaks for air traffic controllers and anesthesiologists, work-hour limitations for airplane pilots and commercial truck drivers, and more recently work-hour limitations for medical students and residents.[49] These regulations recognize that human performance is limited by innate biology and physiology and that fatigue degrades performance; no amount of training or willpower can overcome these biological and physiological limitations. These acknowledgements apply to healthcare delivery where a physician in a busy outpatient clinic or inpatient ward is much like an air traffic controller monitoring a continuous process. Patients are tightly scheduled with additional patients often "doubled-booked" at the last minute because of acute illness. Every patient must be seen and volumes of data accessed, processed, and synthesized to formulate a diagnosis and a plan of care. At the same time, the physician must document the encounter in detail, complete all required forms and insurance paperwork, respond to electronic pages and phone calls, speak with consultants, manage correspondence, and in many cases, also supervise midlevel providers, nurses, and office staff. Stead and Hammond have shown that the amount of data accessed and used by clinicians per medical decision is increasing exponentially despite the fact that physicians' ability to cope with the higher information load remains constant.[50] The driving concept behind EHRs' potential to improve the quality and reduce the cost of health care is represented in **FIGURE 3-3**.[51]

The ultimate goal is to combine the intuitive strengths of humans with the limitless data retention and recall speed of computers to create a hybrid system that is intuitive with a tireless data-processing capability. The physician's medical experience and communication and intuition abilities combine with the computer's ability to never tire or forget information. In other words, the computer provides the physician with a computerized decision support system (CDSS). The computer does not supplant the physician's role but enhances it by providing and managing the deluge of patient information to optimize the physician's performance beyond the brain's biological capability. However for CDSS to work, "the [computerized] interventions must deliver the right information, to the right person, in the right format, through the right channel, at the right point in workflow."[52] If any of these five requirements are missing, the system will tend to fail. With EHRs, the right place and the right point in the workflow often are when the physician is entering patient orders at a computer workstation, a process termed CPOE. At this place and time, the physician's mind is focused on the patient just seen or the patient they are currently thinking about. This also is the place and time at which it is easiest for the physician to take action, such as writing new orders that result in timely follow through for a patient's care.

For example, when a physician has completed a patient interview and examination and is using an EHR to enter e-prescriptions that will be sent securely over the Internet to the patient's pharmacy, the computer can present the physician with a pop-up "reminder" that the patient is allergic to the medication being prescribed. It can also indicate that the prescribed medication requires at least annual kidney function monitoring and that the last record of kidney function laboratory work is more than a year old. In this event, the system can present the physician with an option to order the appropriate laboratory work or to ignore the warning with a keystroke or mouse click. Most decision support is designed with these "soft stops" or interventions that allow the physician to heed or ignore the warning as he or she believes to be most appropriate. CDSS

FIGURE 3-3 Why EHRs Have Potential to Improve Quality and Reduce Costs

Adapted from Friedman CP. What informatics is and isn't. J Am Med Inform Assoc. 2012; 0: 1-3. Computer: © iStockphoto/Thinkstock. Head: © Lightspring/Shutterstock, Inc.

"The full extent of the information blocking problem is difficult to assess, primarily because health IT developers impose contractual restrictions that prohibit customers from reporting or even discussing costs, restrictions, and other relevant details. Still, from the evidence available, it is readily apparent that some providers and developers are engaging in information blocking."[62] The ONC has taken several actions to address this problem, including proposing new certification requirements for EHR systems.

These and other factors led to development of HIEs with their corresponding administering organizations, regional health information organizations (RHIOs). RHIOs attempt to create systems, agreements, processes, and technology to manage these factors in order to facilitate the appropriate exchange of healthcare information between institutions and across different vendor platforms. While most states and regions of the United States have RHIOs, the actual state of implementation and real data exchange varies widely. For example, some states have active RHIOs that are in the planning stages of establishing relationships with all key stakeholders, creating administration agreements, creating governance structures, securing funding, attempting to develop business models for sustained funding of the organization, etc. Other RHIOs have functioning HIEs where medical data are being exchanged between institutions and across disparate software EHR platforms. The ONC has funded many RHIOS to develop and test their national standards for HIE with the ultimate goal of creating the "Nationwide Health Information Network" that would be a network of regional networks across the whole country. Despite the testing and demonstration projects to date, actively functioning HIEs exist only at regional levels.

Each vendor's building toward one common standard would significantly reduce the technical complexity of data exchange. Unfortunately, vendors' products are still not being built toward one national standard to facilitate electronic HIE. Despite these limitations, there have been significant accomplishments in implementing the data and IT standards necessary to facilitate the exchange of health information among multiple EHR platforms. Today, most institutions participating in HIEs must build or configure "interface engines" that convert an institution's data format to the form used by the HIE. This is a major challenge as no single standard provides sufficient specification of data formats and communication protocols. Rather, a number of standards address various domains of data management. In addition, the voluminous scope of modern health care and continuous advancements in knowledge and technology make managing data in the healthcare domain extremely dynamic and complex.

As an example of this complexity, the Logical Observations Indexes Names and Codes (LOINC) standard was developed in the 1990s to solve a problem with an older health information communication protocol that specified how clinical data should be identified for transmission between computer systems. LOINC uniquely defines codes for information, such as blood chemistry laboratory tests, and clinical observations, such as patient blood pressure that can be recorded in many different formats. There are currently more than 70,000 LOINC-defined codes for uniquely reporting laboratory tests and clinical observations.[63] For example, there are 419 different codes for reporting blood pressure. With its unique codes for laboratory tests and clinical observations, LOINC enables computer systems receiving the data to generate exact interpretations. This is called semantic interoperability. Semantic interoperability is essential for patient record transmission from one EHR system to another so that the meaning of the critical data contained within the records is not at risk of erroneous interpretation.

Because new laboratory tests are constantly being developed and existing assays are being improved, LOINC creates and disseminates new codes so that semantic interoperability can be maintained. Old codes are not deleted from the system, ensuring that researchers using prior clinical databases can retrieve prior results comparable with new codes. LOINC is supported by the National Library of Medicine (NLM), one of the National Institutes of Health. The LOINC Committee publishes quarterly updates and holds twice-annual, national meetings to discuss proposed new clinical observations and laboratory tests for the assignment of new LOINC codes.

For an HIE to transfer information accurately, each EHR system must map its own internal code for each datum to a standard code to ensure that information passed from one EHR to another in the exchange is interpreted exactly the same by the receiver as by the sender's system. LOINC is one of the many HIT-related standards. The Systematic Nomenclature of Medicine (SNOMED) was originally developed by the College of American Pathologists (CAP) to specify tissue pathologic diagnoses. The same group also developed a standard for clinical observations called SNOMED Clinical Terms (SNOMED-CT). LOINC and SNOMED-CT domain standards somewhat overlap, but their design characteristics are valuable in different situations; for example, exchanging laboratory results (where LOINC works better) versus coding patient problem lists within EHRs (where SNOMED-CT works better). Similar to LOINC, CAP also provides periodic updates to SNOMED-CT codes.

To keep track of the many coding standards and the terms within, the NLM built and maintains the Unified Medical Language System (UMLS), which houses a massive "metathesaurus" and a variety of tools for mapping between and discovery of more than 200 biomedically related terminology standards.[64] Because LOINC, SNOMED-CT, and the 200 or so other standards are periodically updated, the UMLS also is updated regularly to keep the interstandard terminology mapping current and accurate.

Using HIEs, designated member groups of healthcare institutions exchange data in a standardized format using a combination of the previously described standards. This cooperation enables the access to a comprehensive clinical data set on individual patients across multiple institutions and multiple EHR vendor platforms.

There are two kinds of HIE architectures: "monolithic" and "federated." With the monolithic architecture design, all member institutions periodically send copies of their clinical data to one central repository where all the data reside together in one format. The advantage of this approach is that a patient's comprehensive data can be maintained in one place and in one format. However, this approach has several disadvantages. First, the frequency with which members contribute and update copies of institutional data can vary, making the comprehensive HIE medical record potentially out of date. Second, aggregating data from multiple institutions creates administrative complexity with regard to HIPAA regulations. HIPAA requires each healthcare institution to maintain security of its patients' data. If an institution's data are "mixed" in the HIE database with data from other institutions, the responsibility of ensuring patient privacy and data security reverts to all HIE member institutions. HIPAA requirements make fulfilling healthcare organization obligations to insure patient privacy more difficult and complex. Third, when data are aggregated by a third party or HIE, the ability of the source institution to assert control over data contributed to the collective HIE is limited. If, for example, an institution desires to stop participating in an HIE because of concern for patient privacy and data security, it may be technically difficult and time consuming to selectively delete all data from one institution from the HIE database. The monolithic model of health-information exchange is depicted in **FIGURE 3-4**.

The federated model of health information exchange is the most widely used, allowing contributing institutions to maintain control over data for which they are responsible under HIPAA. In this model, institutional data resides within each institution's system. The HIE database is small, containing only a master patient index (MPI) housing the identifiers for each patient in the form of each institution's unique patient record numbers along with patient

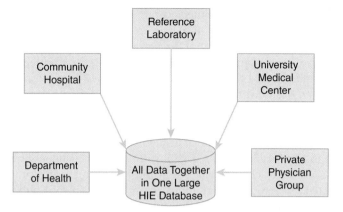

FIGURE 3-4 HIE Monolithic Model
Institutions periodically send copies of their clinical data to one central repository. Individual trans-institutional patient records are maintained in the central database where they can be accessed by authorized users.

demographic data sufficient to facilitate accurate identification of individual patients with the same or similar names. This information is mapped to all of the institutional-specific patient identifiers in the exchange. **FIGURE 3-5** depicts the federated model.

With the federated model, a patient who has medical records at more than one institution in the HIE would have all medical record numbers from the various institutions that store their clinical data linked together in the common MPI, along with basic demographics such as address, date of birth, and social security number. This allows for fast and accurate identification of patients named "John Smith" because the MPI maintains sufficient identifying information to ensure selection of the correct patient among all institutions in the exchange.

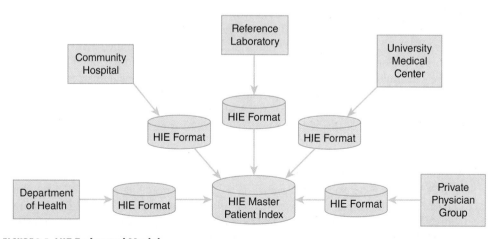

FIGURE 3-5 HIE Federated Model
Institutions maintain copies of their own data at their site in the format used by the HIE. Individual trans-institutional patient records are assembled in real time by searching all institutions' databases only when needed/requested by authorized users. Individual institutions can "opt-out" of the HIE at any time by disabling access to their database.

"John Smith" would be identified from others with the same name by parameters such as date of birth or social security number. No clinical data are stored in the MPI. Clinical data usually are maintained in the proprietary format of the particular EHR system used by each institution. Each institution also maintains a copy of the same data in the HIE standardized form. For example, all HIE members could agree to code all laboratory test results using the LOINC standard described earlier. Each institution would create and maintain a database of all patients' laboratory results coded with LOINC. When a user requests a comprehensive record from the HIE, the system would query all of its institutional members in real time to send all the data available on a particular patient as identified using the MPI. In this way, when an HIE receives a records request on a particular patient, each institution sends data on the requested patient from the database where all clinical data are in the HIE format. This process ensures that the data are collected securely, assembled into a comprehensive record, and made available to authorized users in real time. This comprehensive record is only accessible on a patient-by-patient basis for immediate patient care purposes; it is not copied to any institution's system. When the user logs out of the HIE, the comprehensive record assembled for that episode of patient care is deleted.

The federated model has several advantages over the monolithic model. With the federated model, each institution maintains complete control over its data, simplifying compliance with HIPAA regulations. If, for example, a data breach occurs in the database of an HIE that uses the monolithic model, responsibility for the data breach is not always clear. Data breaches in a federated system usually are attributable to a particular institution and not the HIE (unless there is a data breach of the MPI). Another benefit of the federated system is that trans-institutional data can be up-to-the-minute accurate because each time a user requests access, the clinical data from all institutions are assembled in real time. Institutional HIT administrators typically favor the federated model because they have the option of withdrawing from the HIE at any time in order to maintain control of patient privacy and data security under HIPAA guidelines.

While communities with HIEs generally appreciate the benefits of interoperability, the current reality is that most of the operating HIEs are heavily subsidized with federal research grant funding to keep them afloat. The RHIOs that administer the HIEs and seek funding have not developed a business model that can be used in all communities in order to sustain their HIEs independent of federal funding. Some HIEs require each participating institution to pay an annual amount based on their institution's size, the number of physicians, etc. Some have developed services for payers, charging them for access to the comprehensive records available in the HIE. These services allow payers to increase their claims-processing efficiency. Other HIEs have developed services to generate comprehensive quality reports to sell to payers desiring to track physician and health plan outcomes or to help them meet the meaningful use requirements for CMS financial eligibility incentives. Some communities are resistant to allowing payer access to a data resource they believe should be solely dedicated to improving patient care and quality.[65] An excellent example of this is the State of Vermont's 2006 law that prevented data miners from selling physicians' prescribing data to pharmaceutical companies who wanted the information to inform their marketing practices. In 2011, the law was struck down by the U.S. Supreme Court on a First Amendment basis.[66] Physicians may feel uncomfortable participating in an exchange they know government, payers, or pharmaceutical companies may use for monitoring individual practice outcomes and patterns. While the benefits of HIEs are documented and desirable, solving the cultural and business-model issues will be essential to obtaining the national goal of a network of regional exchanges that will span the entire country.

Another challenge to developing interoperability is the fact that many institutions' HIT resources are dedicated to keeping up with current quality reporting requirements, meaningful use adoption, and other mandated HIT issues. One recent example is the CMS-mandated conversion from using the International Classification of Disease Version 9 billing codes (ICD-9) to ICD-10. Originally designed to identify diagnoses for billing purposes only, ICD-9 codes have become valuable in performing automated chart reviews for quality control and research purposes. However, because of several deficiencies with ICD-9, the new ICD-10 standards have been mandated. A full discussion of the key differences between ICD-9 and ICD-10 is well beyond the scope of this book. A focus on just one issue illustrates the magnitude of the change—the impact on the complexity of physician documentation.

There are approximately 13,000 ICD-9 codes and more than 65,000 ICD-10 codes. The greater number of ICD-10 codes is due to the higher specificity of ICD-10. For example, ICD-9 codes did not include laterality (i.e., right and left side of body). ICD-9 has a grand total of two possible codes for a thumb fracture:

815.01	Closed Fracture of the Base of the Thumb (First) Metacarpal
815.11	Open Fracture of Base of Thumb (First) Metacarpal

Some of the codes for the same injury in ICD-10 include:

S62.511B	Displaced fracture of proximal phalanx of right thumb, initial encounter for open fracture
S62.511D	Displaced fracture of proximal phalanx of right thumb, subsequent encounter for fracture with routine healing
S62.511G	Displaced fracture of proximal phalanx of right thumb, subsequent encounter for fracture with delayed healing
S62.511K	Displaced fracture of proximal phalanx of right thumb, subsequent encounter for fracture with nonunion
S62.511P	Displaced fracture of proximal phalanx of right thumb, subsequent encounter for fracture with malunion
S62.511S	Displaced fracture of proximal phalanx of right thumb, sequela

In addition to the six ICD-10 codes listed above, there are 99 additional choices to account for various combinations of displaced/nondisplaced, open/closed, proximal/distal location, right/left, union/nonunion/mal-union of fracture, routine/delayed healing, initial/subsequent encounter, and so on. For decades, physicians have been writing their narratives in patient records supporting the billing process for the simpler ICD-9 code set. With ICD-10, the narrative in this example requires sufficient documentation to support the selection of the exact ICD-10 billing code; in other words, the narrative must include mention of displaced/nondisplaced, open/closed, proximal/distal phalanx location, right/left, etc. Failure to do so could result in not being reimbursed or even being fined if a CMS chart audit was performed. This requirement for added specificity has been the most significant change to the way in which physicians' document diagnoses in decades.

▶ The Veterans Administration Health Information System

No discussion of HIT, EHRs, and HIEs would be complete without noting the HIT system used by the Veterans Administration (VA). The VA is a model representing a single-payer healthcare system in the United States. Unlike other components of the healthcare delivery system, the VA HIT system supports only one payer, one pharmaceutical formulary, one provider group, and one supplier of laboratory testing. All VA physicians are employees of the same organization, so new policies and practices can be communicated, implemented, and monitored much more easily and efficiently than in the U.S. multi-payer, multi-formulary, siloed systems. Also, the VA has one universal EHR system with CPOE and CDSS. The VA EHR is able to code all data in one format that allows veterans who move from state to state to have their entire VA medical record seamlessly follow them. All these factors have allowed the VA to offer high-quality care at a relatively reasonable cost. Until the United States creates a single-payer system and uses the same EHR universally, the larger system will suffer from the enormous complexity and costs of developing and maintaining multiple data standards to support the exchange of health information among institutions and across vendor platforms.

▶ Electronic Health Record Adoption Progress in the United States

The National Center for Health Statistics (NCHS) has tracked the use of EHRs in the outpatient setting since 2006. The NCHS specifically defines two levels of adoption as "any" and "basic." This distinction is important because many other surveys report EHR adoption rates but do not define in any detail what "EHR adoption" actually means. This survey uses an exacting definition of "any" and "basic" EHR adoption that produces results that are much more valid than surveys where "adoption" is not well defined. **FIGURE 3-6**, "Percentage of office-based physicians with EHR systems: United States, 2001–2013,"[67] illustrates the adoption trends for the outpatient setting. This report indicated:

> In 2013, the National Ambulatory Medical Care EHR Survey showed that about 78 percent of office-based physicians used any EHR system. Since 2006 (first year for which data are available), the percentage of physicians who reported having an EHR system that met the criteria for a basic system increased 336 percent—from 11 percent in 2006 to 48 percent in 2013. Adoption of a basic EHR system varied greatly by state. Adoption ranged from 21 percent in New Jersey to 83 percent in North Dakota.

> The ONC has been tracking hospitals' adoption of EHRs since 2008 using standard definitions of "Certified" and "Basic" EHR systems. **FIGURE 3-7**, "Percent of non-federal acute care hospitals with adoption of at least a Basic EHR with notes system and possession of a certified EHR: 2008–2014" illustrates the hospital EHR adoption rates.[68] This report states:

> In 2008, hospital adoption of at least a Basic EHR system was above 20% in only 2 states (Connecticut and New Mexico). Three years later, hospital adoption of at least a Basic EHR system was above 20% in 32 states and above 40% in 7 states. In 2014, hospital adoption of at least a Basic EHR system was above 60% in all but 2 states (Hawaii and West Virginia), and above 80% in 17 states.[68]

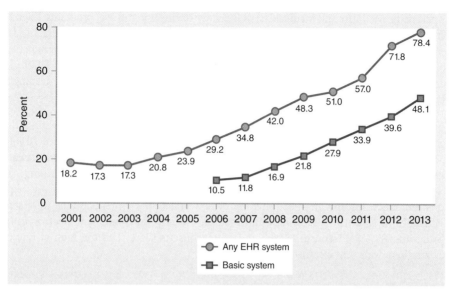

FIGURE 3-6 EHR Adoption Among U.S. Office-Based Physicians, 2001–2013

Reproduced from CDC/NCHS, National Ambulatory Medical Care Survey and National Ambulatory Medical Care Survey, Electronic Health Records Survey NCHS Data Brief No 143, http://www.cdc.gov/nchs/data/databriefs/db143.htm.

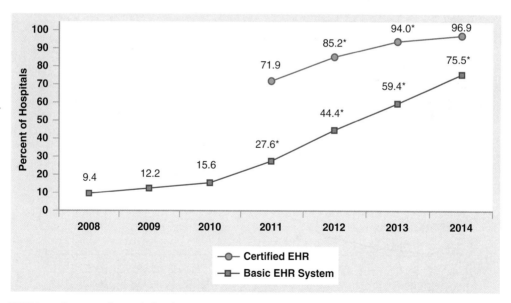

FIGURE 3-7 Percent of Non-federal Acute Care Hospitals with Adoption of at Least a Basic EHR with Notes System and Possession of a Certified EHR: 2008–2014

Reproduced from ONC/American Hospital Association (AHA), AHA Annual Survey Information Technology Supplement.

Note that EHR adoption rates are typically published every two to three years by the NCHS and the ONC. At the time of this printing, the most recent surveys published by NCHS and ONC were through 2013 and 2014, respectively.

As part of the Medicare and Medicaid EHR Incentive or "meaningful use" programs, Eligible Providers had to use their EHRs to meet several program objectives, including e-prescribing. In addition, the Medicare Improvements for Patients and Providers Act, or the "eRx incentive" program, began in 2008, offering financial incentives for providers to facilitate the use of e-prescribing.[69] **FIGURE 3-8** is a graph from an ONC Data Brief illustrating the e-prescribing rates in relation to the meaningful use and eRx incentive programs. From the data brief:[69]

> The growth in e-prescribing has not been limited to physicians. In the same period, the percent of community pharmacies enabled to accept e-prescriptions grew from 76% to 96%. Nearly all community pharmacies are enabled to accept e-prescriptions in Delaware (99%) and Maine (99%). The growth of physicians and pharmacies e-prescribing has corresponded with a thirteen-fold increase in the growth of new and renewal prescriptions sent electronically. In 2008, only 4% of new and renewal prescriptions were sent electronically. In 2013, 57% of new and renewal prescriptions were sent electronically. Minnesota (89%), Wisconsin (83%), and Massachusetts (77%) had the highest rate of new and renewals sent electronically.

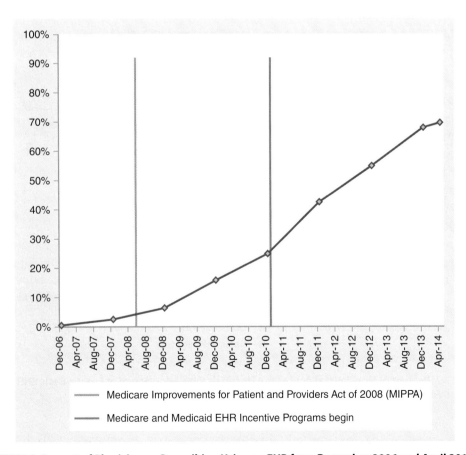

FIGURE 3-8 **Percent of Physicians e-Prescribing Using an EHR from December 2006 and April 2014**

▶ **Future Challenges**

Although there is mounting evidence supporting the value of EHRs with CPOE and CDSS in several well-defined areas such as improving preventive care delivery, extensive meta-analyses report combined average results. There have been several inconclusive and negative studies, and some have actually shown patient harm associated with the installation of CPOE. In one of the most extensively reported, the mortality rate in a neonatal intensive care unit more than doubled after a CPOE system was installed at the University of Pittsburgh.[70] Much has been written about the reasons for this negative result and despite the finger pointing, there is virtually universal agreement that HIT can be very disruptive to work processes and work cultures resulting in significant harm to patients.[71] Some have called for more HIT standards and regulation to prevent these negative consequences in the same way as the U.S. Food and Drug Administration regulates medical devices.[72,73]

Due to the administrative and technical difficulties of achieving the Nationwide Health Information Network, proprietary entities have offered alternate approaches to develop personal health records (PHRs) through which patients create their own records in a standardized format. In these approaches, patients may physically carry records or make them available to caregivers via the Internet. Microsoft, Google, and many other corporate entities have built such systems but with little marketing success. Google Health announced its shutdown on June 24, 2011, after only three years of operation. Google joins other lesser-known firms that have decided to close down PHR services.[74] Design of existing PHRs requires patients to have a high level of health literacy and computer savvy. A major reason analysts believed Google Health failed was the newness of the concept and the facts that PHRs are difficult to use and many people find the data-entry work necessary to complete their record too laborious.[75] One survey of patients found that only 7 percent had tried using a PHR and only about 3 percent continued to use them in 2011.[75] Other barriers to patient adoption include lack of personal health management tools, the difficulty in achieving semantic interoperability such that personal health management tools could be useful, problems vetting the identity of PHR users, patient privacy concerns, and perhaps, most importantly, the lack of a business model to support the long-term operation of PHRs.[74]

In addition to physicians and patients affected by development and implementation of HIT, there are many other healthcare professionals and venues affected by significant complexities and characteristics that make HIT implementation challenging. Many of the same issues previously discussed in this chapter apply to these venues, such as standardized data formats to facilitate data portability, work culture barriers, system costs, training issues, and other matters. For example, some emergency medical services (EMS) providers have begun to use a variety of portable EHRs to collect data at the scenes of patient incidents with systems designed to transmit data to receiving hospitals. The same issues that complicate the ease of universal HIE between healthcare institutions apply to the data exchange between EMS and hospital systems and will not be resolved easily.

To achieve the HIT goals of improving healthcare quality and reducing costs, extensive and rigorous work remains in the research and implementation arenas. After 50 years of efforts, most notably in the past five years, government, industry, and academia are only now recognizing the critically important and interdependent roles that standardization, administrative processes, and work cultures play in the achievement of HIT-desired outcomes.

KEY TERMS FOR REVIEW

Computerized Decision
  Support System (CDSS)
Computerized Physician Order
  Entry (CPOE)
Electronic Health Record (EHR)
Federated Model of Health
  Information Exchange
Health Information
  Exchange (HIE)

Health Information
  Technology for Economic
  and Clinical Health
  Act (HITECH Act)
Information Blocking
Meaningful Use
Monolithic Model of
  Health-Information
  Exchange

Office of the National
  Coordinator for Health
  Information Technology
  (ONCHIT or "the ONC")
Personal Health Record
  (PHR)
Regional Health Information
  Organization (RHIO)

CHAPTER ACRONYMS

ARRA American Recovery and
  Reinvestment Act
CAP College of American Pathologists
CDSS Computerized Decision Support
  System
CMS Centers for Medicare & Medicaid
  Services
CPOE Computerized Physician Order Entry
CQM Clinical Quality Measures
EHR Electronic health record
EMS Emergency medical services
HIE Health information exchange
HIPAA Health Insurance Portability and
  Accountability Act
HIT Health information technology
HITECH Health Information Technology for
  Economic and Clinical Health Act

LOINC Logical Observations Indexes Names
  and Codes
MPI Master patient index
NCHS National Center for Health Statistics
NLM National Library of Medicine
ONC Office of the National Coordinator (short
  for ONCHIT)
ONCHIT Office of the National Coordinator for
  Health Information Technology
PHR Personal health record
RHIO Regional Health Information
  Organizations
SNOMED Systematic Nomenclature
  of Medicine
SNOMED-CT Systematic Nomenclature
  of Medicine – Clinical Terms
UMLS Unified Medical Language System

References

1. The Life Sciences Panel of the President's Science Advisory Committee. *Some New Technologies and Their Promise for the Life Sciences.* Washington, DC: The White House; January 23, 1963.
2. Bush GW. Executive order: incentives for the use of health information technology and establishing the position of the national health information technology coordinator. April 27, 2004. http://georgewbush-whitehouse.archives.gov/news/releases/2004/04/20040427-4.html. Accessed March 8, 2016.
3. One Hundred Eleventh Congress of the United States of America. *The American Recovery and Reinvestment Act.* www.whitehouse.gov/recovery/about. Accessed March 8, 2016.
4. Lobach D, Sanders GD, Bright TJ, et al. Enabling health care decisionmaking through clinical decision support and knowledge management. April 2012. http://www.ncbi.nlm.nih.gov/books/NBK97318/. Accessed March 8, 2016.
5. McDonald CJ. Protocol-based computer reminders, the quality of care and the non-perfectability of man. *N Engl J Med.* 1976;295:1351-1355.
6. Yount RJ, Vries JK, Councill CD. The medical archival system: an information retrieval system based on

distributed parallel processing. *Inf Processing & Management*. 1991;27:1-11.

7. Gardner RM, Pryor TA, Warner HR. The HELP hospital information system: update 1998. *Int J Med Inform*. 1999;54:169-182.

8. Pryor TA, Gardner RM, Clayton PD, Warner HR. The HELP system. *J Med Syst*. 1983;7:87-102.

9. Higgins SB, Jiang K, Swindell BB, Bernard GR. A graphical ICU workstation. *Proc Annu Symp Comput Appl Med Care*. 1991:783-787.

10. Giuse DA, Mickish A. Increasing the availability of the computerized patient record. *Proc AMIA Annu Fall Symp*. 1996:633-637.

11. Stead WW, Hammond WE. Computer-based medical records: the centerpiece of TMR. *MD Comput*. 1988;5:48-62.

12. Greenes RA, Pappalardo AN, Marble CW, Barnett GO. Design and implementation of a clinical data management system. *Comput Biomed Res*. 1969;2:469-485.

13. Ash JS, Bates DW. Factors and forces affecting EHR system adoption: report of a 2004 ACMI discussion. *J Am Med Inform Assoc*. 2005;12:8-12.

14. Ash JS, Stavri PZ, Dykstra R, Fournier L. Implementing computerized physician order entry: The importance of special people. *Int J Med Inform*. 2003;69:235-250.

15. Campbell EM, Guappone KP, Sittig DF, Dykstra RH, Ash JS. Computerized provider order entry adoption: Implications for clinical workflow. *J Gen Intern Med*. 2009;24:21-26.

16. Bloomrosen M, Starren J, Lorenzi NM, Ash JS, Patel VL, Shortliffe EH. Anticipating and addressing the unintended consequences of health IT and policy: a report from the AMIA 2009 health policy meeting. *J Am Med Inform Assoc*. 2011;18:82-90.

17. Chaudhry B, Wang J, Wu S, et al. Systematic review: impact of health information technology on quality, efficiency, and costs of medical care. *Ann Intern Med*. 2006;144:742-752.

18. Connolly C. Cedars-Sinai doctors cling to pen and paper. *The Washington Post*. March 21, 2005. A01.

19. Dexter PR, Perkins S, Overhage JM, Maharry K, Kohler RB, McDonald CJ. A computerized reminder system to increase the use of preventive care for hospitalized patients. *N Engl J Med*. 2001;345:965-970.

20. Weiner M, Callahan CM, Tierney WM, et al. Using information technology to improve the health care of older adults. *Ann Intern Med*. 2003;139:430-436.

21. Dexter PR, Perkins SM, Maharry KS, Jones K, McDonald CJ. Inpatient computer-based standing orders vs. physician reminders to increase influenza and pneumococcal vaccination rates: a randomized trial. *JAMA*. 2004;292:2366-2371.

22. Overhage JM, Dexter PR, Perkins SM, et al. A randomized, controlled trial of clinical information shared from another institution. *Ann Emerg Med*. 2002;39:14-23.

23. Centers for Medicare & Medicaid Services. Medicare and Medicaid EHR incentive program basics. http://www.cms.gov/Regulations-and-Guidance /Legislation/EHRIncentivePrograms/Basics.html. Accessed March 8, 2016.

24. Office of the National Coordinator for Health Information Technology. How to attain meaningful use. https://www.healthit.gov/providers-professionals /how-attain-meaningful-use. Accessed March 8, 2016.

25. Centers for Medicare & Medicaid Services. EHR incentive programs for eligible hospitals & CAHs: what you need to know for 2015 tipsheet. https://www .cms.gov/Regulations-and-Guidance/Legislation /EHRIncentivePrograms/Downloads/2015_ NeedtoKnowEH.pdf. Accessed March 8, 2016.

26. Centers for Medicare and Medicaid Services. Medicare and Medicaid EHR incentive program basics. 2016. http://www.cms.gov/Regulations-and-Guidance /Legislation/EHRIncentivePrograms/Basics.html. Accessed January 25, 2016.

27. Centers for Medicare and Medicaid Services. Medicaid hospital incentive payments calculations. 2016. https://www.cms.gov/regulations-and-guidance /legislation/ehrincentiveprograms/downloads/mln _tipsheet_medicaidhospitals.pdf. Accessed January 25, 2016.

28. Office of the National Coordinator for Health Information Technology. How to attain meaningful use. 2013. https://www.healthit.gov/providers-professionals /how-attain-meaningful-use. Accessed January 25, 2016.

29. Centers for Medicare & Medicaid Services. Medicaid hospital incentive payments calculations. https:// www.cms.gov/regulations-and-guidance/legislation /ehrincentiveprograms/downloads/mln_tipsheet_ medicaidhospitals.pdf. Accessed March 8, 2016.

30. Centers for Medicare & Medicaid Services. An introduction to the Medicare EHR incentive program for eligible professionals. http://www.cms.gov/Regulations -and-Guidance/Legislation/EHRIncentivePrograms /Downloads/Beginners_Guide.pdf. Accessed March 8, 2016.

31. Centers for Medicare & Medicaid Services. Eligible hospital and CAH meaningful use table of contents core and menu set objectives. https://www .cms.gov/Regulations-and-Guidance/Legislation /EHRIncentivePrograms/downloads/Hosp_CAH _MU-TOC.pdf. Accessed March 8, 2016.

32. Centers for Medicare & Medicaid Services. Medicare electronic health record incentive payments for eligible professionals. https://www.cms.gov/regulations-and -guidance/legislation/ehrincentiveprograms /downloads/mln_medicareehrprogram_tipsheet _ep.pdf. Accessed March 8, 2016.

33. Centers for Medicare & Medicaid Services. Flow chart to help eligible professionals (EP) determine eligibility for the Medicare and Medicaid electronic health

record (EHR) incentive programs. https://www.cms
.gov/Regulations-and-Guidance/Legislation/EHR
IncentivePrograms/downloads/eligibility_flow
_chart.pdf. Accessed March 8, 2016.

34. Centers for Medicare & Medicaid Services.
Eligible hospital information. http://www.cms
.gov/Regulations-and-Guidance/Legislation
/EHRIncentivePrograms/Eligible_Hospital
_Information.html. Accessed March 8, 2016.

35. Centers for Medicare & Medicaid Services. Electronic
health record (EHR) incentive programs. http://www
.cms.gov/Regulations-and-Guidance/Legislation
/EHRIncentivePrograms/index.html?redirect=
/ehrincentiveprograms/. Accessed March 8, 2016.

36. Office of the National Coordinator for Health
Information Technology. About ONC. 2014. https://
www.healthit.gov/newsroom/about-onc. Accessed
January 25, 2016.

37. Office of the National Coordinator for Health
Information Technology. Justification of estimates for
appropriations committee fiscal year 2016. https://
www.healthit.gov/sites/default/files/ONC-FY2016
-budget-justification.pdf. Accessed March 8, 2016.

38. Office of the National Coordinator for Health
Information Technology. Justification of estimate
for appropriations committee fiscal year 2015.
https://www.healthit.gov/sites/default/files/onc_
fy2015justificationforappropriations.pdf. Accessed
March 8, 2016.

39. Office of the National Coordinator for Health
Information Technology. Federal Advisory Committees
Act (FACAs). https://www.healthit.gov/facas/. Accessed
March 8, 2016.

40. Centers for Medicare & Medicaid Services. Medicaid
electronic health record incentive payments for eligible
professionals. https://www.cms.gov/regulations
-and-guidance/legislation/ehrincentiveprograms
/downloads/mln_medicaidehrprogram_tipsheet_
ep.pdf. Accessed March 8, 2016.

41. Healthcare Information and Management Systems
Society. CMS and ONC provide MU data update
to health IT policy committee. http://www.himss
.org/News/NewsDetail.aspx?ItemNumber=37995.
Accessed March 9, 2016.

42. Office of the National Coordinator for Health
Information Technology. Health IT policy committee
meeting data analytics update. January 13, 2015. http://
www.healthit.gov/facas/sites/faca/files/HITPC_Data
_Analytics_update_2015-01-13_v3.pptx. Accessed
March 9, 2016.

43. Centers for Medicare & Medicaid Services. CMS fact
sheet: EHR incentive programs in 2015 and beyond.
https://www.cms.gov/Newsroom/MediaRelease
Database/Fact-sheets/2015-Fact-sheets-items
/2015-10-06-2.html. Accessed March 9, 2016.

44. United States Department of Health and Human
Services Office of the National Coordinator for Health
Information Technology. Eligible professional's guide
to: Stage 2 of the EHR incentive programs. https://
www.cms.gov/eHealth/downloads/eHealthU
_EPsGuideStage2EHR.pdf. Accessed March 8, 2016.

45. United States Department of Health and Human
Services Office of the National Coordinator for Health
Information Technology. Stage 2 overview tipsheet.
https://www.cms.gov/Regulations-and-Guidance
/Legislation/EHRIncentivePrograms/Downloads
/Stage2Overview_Tipsheet.pdf. Accessed February 3,
2016.

46. Centers for Medicare & Medicaid Services. Eligible
professional EHR incentive program objectives and
measures for 2015 table of contents. https://www
.cms.gov/Regulations-and-Guidance/Legislation
/EHRIncentivePrograms/Downloads/2015EP
_TableofContents.pdf. Accessed March 8, 2016.

47. Centers for Medicare & Medicaid Services. Eligible hospital
and critical access hospital EHR incentive program
objectives and measures for 2015 table of contents. https://
www.cms.gov/Regulations-and-Guidance/Legislation
/EHRIncentivePrograms/Downloads/2015EHCAH_
TableofContents.pdf. Accessed March 8, 2016.

48. Dukette D, Cornish D. *The Essential 20: Twenty
Components of an Excellent Health Care Team.* Pittsburgh,
PA: RoseDog Books; 2009:72-74.

49. Parthasarathy S. Sleep and the medical profession.
Curr Opin Pulm Med. 2005;11:507-512.

50. Institute of Medicine. *Free Executive Summary:
Beyond Expert-based Practice. IOM Annual Meeting
Summary: Evidence-Based Medicine and the Changing
Nature of Healthcare.* Washington, DC: The National
Academies Press; 2008:18-19.

51. Friedman CP. What informatics is and isn't. *J Am Med
Inform Assoc.* 2013;20:224-226.

52. Sirajuddin AM, Osheroff JA, Sittig DF, Chuo J, Velasco
F, Collins DA. Implementation pearls from a new
guidebook on improving medication use and outcomes
with clinical decision support. Effective CDS is essential
for addressing healthcare performance improvement
imperatives. *J Healthc Inf Manag.* 2009;23:38-45.

53. Evans RS, Pestotnik SL, Classen DC, et al. A
computer-assisted management program for
antibiotics and other antiinfective agents. *N Engl J
Med.* 1998;338:232-238.

54. Tierney WM, Dexter PR, Gramelspacher GP, Perkins
AJ, Zhou XH, Wolinsky FD. The effect of discussions
about advance directives on patients' satisfaction with
primary care. *J Gen Intern Med.* 2001;16:32-40.

55. Tierney WM, Miller ME, Overhage JM, McDonald CJ.
Physician inpatient order writing on microcomputer
workstations. Effects on resource utilization. *JAMA.*
1993;269:379-383.

56. Kho AN, Dexter P, Lemmon L, et al. Connecting the dots: Creation of an electronic regional infection control network. *Stud Health Technol Inform.* 2007;129:213-217.

57. Kho A, Dexter P, Warvel J, et al. Computerized reminders to improve isolation rates of patients with drug-resistant infections: design and preliminary results. *AMIA Annu Symp Proc.* 2005:390-394.

58. Rosenman M, Wang J, Dexter P, Overhage JM. Computerized reminders for syphilis screening in an urban emergency department. *AMIA Annu Symp Proc.* 2003:987.

59. Kroth PJ, Dexter PR, Overhage JM, et al. A computerized decision support system improves the accuracy of temperature capture from nursing personnel at the bedside. *AMIA Annu Symp Proc.* 2006:444-448.

60. Agency for Healthcare Research and Quality. Evidence report/technology assessment number 203: Enabling health care decisionmaking through clinical decision support and knowledge management. http://www.ncbi.nlm.nih.gov/books/NBK97318/pdf/Bookshelf_NBK97318.pdf. Accessed March 9, 2016.

61. Office of the National Coordinator for Health Information Technology. Report to congress on health information blocking. https://www.healthit.gov/sites/default/files/reports/info_blocking_040915.pdf. Accessed March 9, 2016.

62. DeSalvo KB, Daniel JG. Blocking of health information undermines health system interoperability and delivery reform. http://www.healthit.gov/buzz-blog/from-the-onc-desk/health-information-blocking-undermines-interoperability-delivery-reform/. Accessed March 9, 2016.

63. Lin MC, Vreeman DJ, McDonald CJ, Huff SM. Auditing consistency and usefulness of LOINC use among three large institutions–using version spaces for grouping LOINC codes. *J Biomed Inform.* 2012;45:658-666.

64. National Library of Medicine. UMLS quick start guide. http://www.nlm.nih.gov/research/umls/quickstart.html. Accessed March 9, 2016.

65. Sorrell WH. Supreme Court strikes down Vermont prescription privacy law. 2011. http://ago.vermont.gov/focus/news/supreme-court-strikes-down-vermont-prescription-privacy-law.php. Accessed March 9, 2016.

66. The Supreme Court of the United States. Sorrell, Attorney General of Vermont, et al. vs. IMS Health inc. et al. 2011. http://www.supremecourt.gov/opinions/10pdf/10-779.pdf. Accessed March 9, 2016.

67. Hsiao CJ, Hing E. Use and characteristics of electronic health record systems among office-based physician practices: United States, 2001–2013, NCHS data brief no. 143. 2015. http://www.cdc.gov/nchs/data/databriefs/db143.htm. Accessed March 9, 2016.

68. Charles D, Gabriel M, Searcy T. Adoption of electronic health record systems among U.S. nonfederal acute care hospitals: 2008–2014, ONC data brief no. 23. https://www.healthit.gov/sites/default/files/data-brief/2014HospitalAdoptionDataBrief.pdf. Accessed March 9, 2016.

69. Gabriel MH, Swain M. E-prescribing trends in the United States, ONC data brief no. 18. 2014. https://www.healthit.gov/sites/default/files/oncdatabriefe-prescribingincreases2014.pdf. Accessed March 9, 2016.

70. Han YY, Carcillo JA, Venkataraman ST, et al. Unexpected increased mortality after implementation of a commercially sold computerized physician order entry system. *Pediatrics.* 2005;116:1506-1512.

71. Sittig DF, Ash JS, Zhang J, Osheroff JA, Shabot MM. Lessons from "unexpected increased mortality after implementation of a commercially sold computerized physician order entry system." *Pediatrics.* 2006;118:797-801.

72. Miller RA, Gardner RM. Summary recommendations for responsible monitoring and regulation of clinical software systems. American Medical Informatics Association, the Computer-based Patient Record Institute, the Medical Library Association, the Association of Academic Health Science Libraries, the American Health Information Management Association, and the American Nurses Association. *Ann Intern Med.* 1997;127:842-845.

73. Miller RA, Gardner RM. Recommendations for responsible monitoring and regulation of clinical software systems. American Medical Informatics Association, Computer-based Patient Record Institute, Medical Library Association, Association of Academic Health Science Libraries, American Health Information Management Association, American Nurses Association. *J Am Med Inform Assoc.* 1997;4:442-457.

74. Rishel W, Booz RH. Google Health shutdown underscores uncertain future of PHRS. 2011. http://www.gartner.com/resources/214600/214682/google_health_shutdown_under_214682.pdf. Accessed March 9, 2016.

75. Lohr S. Google is closing its health records service. *The New York Times.* June 24, 2011.

CHAPTER 4

Hospitals: Origin, Organization, and Performance

CHAPTER OVERVIEW

This chapter's overview of the genesis of U.S. hospitals provides a basis for understanding their characteristics, organization, and major private and governmental insurance initiatives that contributed to their growth and centrality in the healthcare system. The chapter discusses the diverse functions of hospitals and their staff and management structures, along with important aspects of quality of care and the relationship between staff and patients. The chapter reviews and summarizes hospital marketplace activities in response to health reform and pertinent major elements of the Medicare Access & CHIP Reauthorization Act of 2015 (MACRA) as they directly affect hospitals.

Of all the institutions in U.S. society, the hospital is likely the most appreciated, most maligned, and least understood. In addition to serving as a place for the treatment of the sick and injured, it may function as a research laboratory, an educational institution, and a major employer within the community. In the era of healthcare reform, these core functions can be expected to remain intact. However, virtually everything about the way in which hospitals have operated—from their ownership structures and financing to their relationships with physicians, other healthcare providers, and their communities—will continue to undergo significant change. Hospitals are focal points in market reforms and for changes required by the Patient Protection and Affordable Care Act (ACA) and most recently the Medicare Access & CHIP Reauthorization Act of 2015 (MACRA). This chapter also discusses the significant challenges and opportunities created by reforms and efforts to improve the quality of care, increase patient satisfaction, improve the health of populations, and reduce costs.

Flag: © Lightix/Shutterstock

▶ Historical Perspective

The often-strained relationship between patients and hospital personnel dates back to the earliest history of health care in the United States. The indifference to patients' needs for information, comfort, and humane contact that is a common complaint about hospital care is rooted not only in the overall history of medical care but also—and especially—in the history of hospitals.

Hospitals in early America were founded to shelter older adults, the dying, orphans, and vagrants as well as to protect the community from the contagiously sick and the dangerously mentally ill.

During the 1700s, Boston was the largest city in the new democracy, with a population of about 7,000. Philadelphia and New York each had a population of about 4,000. Medical care in those days was provided in the home. It sometimes was necessary in these and other seaport towns to provide refuge for sailors and other shipboard victims of contagious diseases who often were unceremoniously left ashore when the ships departed. The town responded by organizing pest houses, quarantine stations, or isolation hospitals to segregate the sick from the town inhabitants and to prevent the spread of communicable disease. Because these facilities were not intended to be used by the local citizenry, they were usually located well outside the city limits.

As populations grew, mental illness became a more significant problem. Individuals whose behavior offended or frightened the community came to the attention of the town board. It was common in those days for the town board to order relatives or friends to build a small strong house, or cell, on their property to contain a person with mental illness. If the individual had no relatives or friends, the town might lease him or her at an auction to the lowest bidder, who would take responsibility for confining that individual for one year, usually in exchange for his or her labor.

The existence of pest houses, or isolation hospitals, also provided the towns with a solution for dealing with other individuals whose presence posed a risk to or offended its inhabitants. Over time, people with mental illness or those in poor health, the homeless, and the petty criminal joined the contagious ill that occupied those facilities.

Bellevue Hospital was originally the Poor House of New York City, established in 1736 to house the "poor, aged, insane, and disreputable." In 1789, the Public Hospital of Baltimore was established for low-income populations, people with mental or physical illness, and the seafaring of Maryland. One hundred years later, in 1889, it became the now-prestigious Johns Hopkins Hospital. Eventually, almost every city of any size in early America had a pest house to isolate patients during epidemics. Most cities also had an almshouse for low-income populations, sometimes with an added infirmary. Many of today's county or municipal hospitals were originally combinations of almshouses and infirmaries.

By the 1800s, hospitals began to reflect the early American concept of charity and public responsibility. This required that provision be made for low-income populations, people with physical or mental illness, vagrants, and criminals. Institutions originally classified as almshouses provided refuge for all of them. Physicians realized the value of separating the sick population from the rest of the needy and putting them in facilities more properly called hospitals. Despite this evolution in thinking, most hospitals that housed the sick and injured were still dirty, unventilated, and contaminated with infections. These early hospitals still focused on isolating the sick and mentally ill from the population at large as much as they focused on effectively treating patients. They were overcrowded, and the only nurses available were former prison inmates or women who could get no other work. The public knew little of these conditions because visiting was restricted. Patients were effectively cut off from the outside world. Persons with family or the means to obtain home medical or nursing care shunned hospitals.

Also during the 1800s, certain religious orders began to see the hospitals' clients as so helpless, so miserable with incurable disease, or so maimed by accident that they presented an opportunity for spiritual outlet for those seeking salvation through good works. So began the close relationships of the Protestant and Catholic religions with hospitals and hospital nursing. Catholic religious orders were the first groups responsible for kind and humane nursing performed by fairly well-educated, sincere, and devoted "sisters." The American branch of St. Vincent de Paul Sisters of Charity, founded by Mother Elizabeth Seton in 1809, established hospitals that still stand in cities across the United States. The Protestant nursing movement began in Germany and was brought to Pennsylvania in 1850. It was based on the formal training of nurses in religion, nursing, and nursing education. The nurse teachers were called deaconesses. The Protestant church hospital, or deaconess movement, had an important influence on nursing.

Ironically, it was the Civil War in the 1860s that brought about public appreciation of the work of women in nursing. When sick or wounded soldiers were returned to their hometowns attended by obviously dedicated and capable nurses, relatives of those soldiers encountered women as nurses for the first time. Nursing gained a much more positive image and came to be viewed as a respectable career option for women.

▶ Effects of Insurance on the Hospital Industry

Health Insurance

The transformation of hospitals from simple, charitable institutions to complex, technical organizations was accompanied by a parallel growth of private hospital insurance. In 1940, only 9 percent of U.S. population had hospital insurance. By the 1960s, billions of dollars were flowing into hospitals from insurance companies, such as Blue Cross/Blue Shield, medical society plans, and other plans sponsored by unions, industry, physicians, and cooperatives. The availability of hospital insurance removed an important cost constraint from hospital charges. The ability of insurers to cope with ever-rising hospital costs by distributing relatively small premium increases over large numbers of subscribers opened the floodgates to hospital admissions. Expanding hospital services and relatively unrestrained reimbursement rates created a rapid growth in hospital revenue that was to persist for decades.

In addition, technical and medical advances as well as medical specialization encouraged hospitalization, and the hospital industry expanded to meet the demand. After World War II, the American Hospital Association (AHA) convinced Senators Lister Hill and Harold Burton to sponsor legislation that provided federal monies to the states to survey hospitals and other health-care facilities and to plan and assist construction of additional facilities. The Hill–Burton Hospital Construction Act was signed as Public Law 79–75 in 1946 and became a major influence in the expansion of the hospital industry.[1] More than 4,600 projects to expand existing facilities or construct new ones were initiated within 20 years after its passage. That federal support of hospital construction was critically important to the location of hospitals in underserved rural areas.

Medicare and Medicaid

In 1966, Congress passed and the President signed into law Medicare, Title XVIII of the Social Security Act. This legislation provided the growing population of Americans over age 65 with significant hospital and medical benefits. With Medicare's creation, the large population of older

Americans, the group most likely to need hospitalization, was ensured hospital care and the hospitals were assured reimbursement on the basis of "reasonable costs."

The companion program, Medicaid, Title XIX of the Social Security Act, was established at the same time to support medical and hospital care for persons classified as medically indigent. Unlike Medicare, Medicaid required the states to establish joint federal–state programs that covered persons receiving public assistance and, if they wished, others of low income. Because the states had broad discretion over eligibility, benefits, and reimbursement rates, the programs that developed among the 50 states differed widely.

Medicare, and to a lesser extent Medicaid, had enormous impact on hospitalization rates in the United States. In a little more than 10 years after the implementation of Medicare, persons ages 65 years and older were spending more than twice as many days in the hospital as those ages 45–64.[1]

The Medicare and Medicaid programs also had another effect. Because these programs provided government funding for the hospital care of older adults and low-income populations, they altered the longstanding nature or mission of hospitals by diminishing the traditional charitable or social role of those voluntary institutions. Not long after the implementation of those programs, hospitals became increasingly focused on profit, maximizing the more lucrative activities and closing or reducing services that operated at a loss. In the 1980s, hospitals, along with most of the U.S. healthcare industry, became market oriented and aggressively enterprising. The monetary incentives built into the Medicare system favored entrepreneurial, short-term financial interests.

Rosemary Stevens, author of *In Sickness and in Wealth: American Hospitals in the Twentieth Century*, wrote, "One effect was to bring hospitals into prominence as enterprises motivated by organizational self-interest, by the excitement of the game, by greed."[1] She concluded with this statement:

> Medicare and Medicaid, supposedly designed to promote egalitarianism, fostered sharp inequities in the health-care system while disarming criticism from low-paid American workers and the poverty population. The stage was set for today's struggles to rethink, once again, the American health-care system—and to redefine the relative roles of voluntarism, government, and business for the last few years of the twentieth century.[1]

▶ Growth and Decline in Numbers of Hospitals

The number of hospitals in the United States increased from 178 in 1873 to 4,300 in 1909. In 1946, when the Hill–Burton Act was passed, there were 6,000 American hospitals, with 3.2 beds available for every 1,000 persons. The goal with the Act was to fund expansion of the hospital system to achieve the goal of 4.5 beds per 1,000 persons.[2] The system grew thereafter to reach a high of approximately 7,200 acute care hospitals.

During the 1980s, medical advances and cost-containment measures moved many procedures that once required inpatient hospitalization to outpatient settings. Outpatient hospital visits increased by 40 percent with a resultant decrease in hospital admissions. Fewer admissions and shortened lengths of stay for patients resulted in a significant reduction in the number of hospitals and hospital beds. Healthcare reform efforts and the emergence of managed care as the major form of insurance for U.S. health care resulted in hospital closings and mergers that reduced the number of governmental and community-based hospitals in the United States to approximately 5,700.

▶ Types of Hospitals

Acute care hospitals are distinguished from long-term care facilities such as nursing homes, rehabilitation centers, and psychiatric hospitals by the fact that the average length of stay for patients is less than 30 days. The following list indicates the types of hospital sponsorships and the number of each type as of January 2016.[3]

1. Nongovernment Not-for-Profit Community Hospitals (2,870)
2. Investor-Owned (For-Profit) Community Hospitals (1,053)
3. State and Local Government Community Hospitals (1,003)
4. Federal Government Hospitals or VA Hospitals (213)
5. Nonfederal Psychiatric Hospitals (403)
6. Other (e.g., prison hospitals, college infirmaries) (85)

Hospitals also may be classified as teaching and nonteaching hospitals. Approximately 7 percent of all 5,627 U.S. hospitals (about 400 hospitals) are teaching facilities affiliated with one or more of the allopathic or osteopathic medical schools in the United States.[3,4] Teaching hospitals provide clinical education for medical students and medical and dental residents. They, and many hospitals not affiliated with medical schools, also provide clinical education for nurses, allied health personnel, and a wide variety of technical specialists. Most teaching hospitals are voluntary, nongovernment, not-for-profit or government-sponsored public hospitals. Teaching hospitals provide 37 percent of all hospital charity care, 24 percent of all Medicaid hospitalizations, and 59 percent of all pediatric Intensive Care Unit beds.[4] The presence of medical school faculty with strong research interests and the availability of medical residents to assist in the collection of clinical data put teaching hospitals in the forefront of clinical research on medical conditions and treatments.

Public hospitals in many localities deliver the fiscally problematic, but essential, community services that other hospitals are reluctant to provide. These high-cost, low-fiscal-return services include sophisticated trauma centers, psychiatric emergency services, alcohol detoxification services, other substance abuse treatment, and burn treatment.

Investor-owned, for-profit hospitals grew from a few physician-owned facilities before the 1965 Medicare and Medicaid legislation to 1,053 in 2016.[4] Most for-profit hospitals belong to one of the large hospital management companies that dominate the for-profit hospital network. An increasing number, however, are physician-owned specialty hospitals. Such hospitals usually limit their services to treatments in one of three major specialty categories: orthopedics, surgery, or cardiology.

Although these new specialty hospitals are typically upscale facilities with many patient amenities, they usually operate with greater efficiency and provide excellent care because of the homogeneity of medical foci. Nevertheless, they have raised a series of concerns about their performance and their effect on community hospitals.

First, it is clear that specialty hospitals treat the less complex, more profitable cases, leaving the more difficult, less profitable, or uninsured patients to be served by community hospitals. Second, because physician-owners of specialty hospitals profit directly by the value of services provided by their hospitals, there are concerns that clinical decisions may be influenced by financial incentives.[5]

Supporters of physician-owned specialty hospitals point out that the physician-owners take great pride in the quality of care provided in their hospitals, that they also work in community hospitals, and that their facilities enhance their communities by paying taxes as for-profit companies.[6]

The number of beds in not-for-profit, state and local government, and federal hospitals decreased in the last decade, whereas the much smaller number of beds in for-profit facilities increased slightly. The most recent annual survey by the AHA counted 902,202 staffed beds among all U.S. registered hospitals in the United States.[3]

▶ Financial Condition of Hospitals

In the wake of pressures from managed care market penetration beginning in the 1990s, thousands of hospitals were involved in mergers, acquisitions, and other multihospital restructurings in an effort to capture and solidify market shares and gain economies of scale.

Hospitals' economic problems resulted from a combination of factors over which the hospitals had little control. The Balanced Budget Act of 1997, which reduced payments for Medicare patients below the costs of treating them, wreaked havoc on U.S. hospitals. At the same time, hospital charges were held in check by hard-bargaining managed care organizations. In this period, in contrast to the restraints on revenues, costs were rising at an unprecedented pace. Costly new technology, pharmaceuticals, and services, as well as inflation, combined with declining occupancy to significantly reduce operating margins. According to a survey by the AHA published in 2000, 90 percent of the responding hospitals reported serious financial problems that required cost-cutting measures, and many had reduced staff.[7] The development of private specialty hospitals and diagnostic centers owned by physicians, which compete with community hospitals only for their most profitable services, added to the continuing losses of community hospitals.

Market reforms of the 2000s and impacts of the ACA continue to press hospitals forward into altered patterns of ownership, operation, and reimbursement.

▶ Academic Health Centers, Medical Education, and Specialization

Medical, dental, nursing, pharmacy, and allied health schools and their teaching hospitals are the principal sources of education and training for most healthcare providers. An academic health center is an accredited, degree-granting institution that consists of a medical school, one or more other professional schools, or programs such as dentistry, nursing, pharmacy, public health, and allied health sciences that has an owned or affiliated relationship with a teaching hospital, health system, or other organized care provider.

Much of the basic and clinical research in medicine and other healthcare disciplines is conducted in these health centers and their related hospitals. The teaching hospitals usually provide the most technologically advanced care in their communities and also offer inpatient and ambulatory care for economically disadvantaged populations. Thus, the three objectives of academic health centers—education, research, and service—are fulfilled most adequately by teaching hospitals.

The influence of the academic health centers on health care during the last few decades has been extraordinary. The advances that occurred in the medical sciences and technology that resulted in the introduction of life-saving drugs, anesthetics, surgical procedures, and other therapies increased both the use and the costs of hospital services. This increased intervention resulted in increases in both the life expectancy of most Americans and the proportion of the gross national product devoted to health care. These advances also significantly expanded the knowledge base and performance skills required of physicians to practice up-to-date clinical medicine.

Academic health centers responded to advances in medical science and technology by increasing the number of physicians with in-depth expertise in increasingly narrow fields of clinical practice. Specialization and subspecialization grew, subdivided, and grew more. More and more physicians limited their activities to narrower and narrower fields of practice. In doing so, they greatly increased the overall technologic sophistication of hospital practice along with the number of costly consultations that take place among specialist hospital physicians. Specialists and subspecialists also drove increases in the amount of expensive equipment, supplies, and space maintained by hospitals to serve their needs and, in general, the complexity of patient care. The contributions of highly specialized clinical practice to the quality of hospital care have been both extraordinarily beneficial and regrettably negative. Although the superspecialists of U.S. medicine have given the profession its justified reputation for heroic medical and surgical achievements, specialization also has fragmented and depersonalized patient care and produced a plethora of often-questionable tests, procedures, and clinical interventions.

The addition of more subspecialists also created a communication problem between the increasing number of physicians and other healthcare professionals involved in the care of individual patients. As anyone with a complicated medical condition who tries to navigate through the system of multiple specialists knows, the easy and reliable transfer of patient records and test results between multiple specialists often is extremely problematic. Ironically, in an age with unprecedented communications and health information technology capabilities, communication of patient information still is a significant challenge for most patients. There is an extensive discussion on attempts to solve this important problem by creating health information exchanges in Chapter 3 of this book, "Health Information Technology."

While academic health centers have contributed admirably to the advancement of medicine, especially hospital-delivered medical and surgical care, they have not brought their impressive expertise to bear on solving health services delivery problems that have plagued their industry. Rather, the commitments of academic medicine to high-technology research and patient care and its adherence to traditional organizational structures and professional roles have prevented it from taking the lead in correcting healthcare system problems that emanate from fragmented and piecemeal approaches to care delivery. As vast reforms with a population health focus begin to take shape, academic medicine is faced with numerous challenges to prepare for ongoing changes.[8]

▶ Hospital System of the Department of Veterans Affairs

The tax-supported, centrally directed Veterans Health Administration (VHA) is a component of the United States Department of Veterans Affairs (VA). The VHA is the country's largest healthcare system and also is a significant component of America's medical education system. The VA owns and operates 150 hospitals, most of which are affiliated with medical schools and 819 community-based outpatient clinics throughout the United States. The VA serves approximately 22 million veterans with an annual budget of more than $182.3 billion proposed by the President for 2017.[9] Thirty-eight percent of the total proposed VA budget, or $69.3 billion, is dedicated to veterans' health services. Despite its large budget and large number of hospitals and other facilities with more than 12,000 full-time salaried physicians, more than 900 dentists, and 33,000 nurses, broad bipartisan political support for the VA generally has been unwavering.

However, in 2014 a major scandal broke at the VA Hospital in Phoenix, Arizona, where it was learned that hospital officials maintained a secret list of veterans waiting for appointments in order to deliberately falsify reports sent to Washington regarding appointment waiting times.[10] Subsequently in 2015, the VA Office of Inspector General released a scathing report entitled *Review of Alleged Mismanagement at the Health Eligibility Center*[11] that confirmed as of September 30, 2014, the VA had a system-wide backlog of 867,000 pending applications for initial care and entry into its system. The report estimated that approximately 47,000 veterans died while their healthcare applications were in a pending status during this backlog. The report had to estimate this number because the investigation also discovered the VA's "data system limitations" did not make it possible to accurately calculate the number who died while waiting. Many other problems found resulted in the resignation of the Secretary of Veteran's Affairs and the resignations or firing of several high level VA officials. Given the popularity of the VA among veterans and voters alike, the VA likely will go through several reorganizations in the wake of this scandal and continue on unabated.

▶ Structure and Organization of Hospitals

In addition to being a caring, people-oriented institution, a hospital also is a many-faceted, high-tech business. It operates just like any other large business, with a hierarchy of personnel, channels of authority and responsibility, constant concern about its bottom line, and a complex organizational structure. The people who work in hospitals exhibit the same range of human characteristics as their counterparts in other businesses. Patients and their families trying to obtain the best possible results from the services of a hospital should base their approach on the same principles they use in dealing with other service organizations. Hospital care consumers need to determine who is in charge, what services to expect from whom and when, with what results, and at what cost.

The following description of hospital structure and organization uses the voluntary not-for-profit community hospital as the example, because this type of institution historically has provided the model for hospital organization. The direction, control, and governance of the hospital are divided among three influential entities: the medical staff, the administration, and the board of directors or trustees. The major operating divisions of a hospital represent areas of the hospital's functions. Although they may use different names, typical divisions are medical, nursing, patient therapy, diagnosis, fiscal, human resources, hotel services, and community relations.

Medical Division

The medical staff is a formally organized unit within the larger hospital organization. The president or chief of staff is the liaison between the hospital administration and members of the medical staff. Typically, the medical staff consists primarily of medical physicians, but it also may include other doctoral-level professionals, such as dentists and psychologists and sometimes midlevel providers (e.g., nurse midwifes, physicians' assistants, nurse practitioners).

A major role of the medical staff organization is to recommend to the hospital board of directors the appointment of physicians to the medical staff. The board of directors approves and grants various levels of hospital privileges to physicians. Such privileges commonly include the right to admit patients to the hospital, to perform surgery, and to provide consultation to other physicians on the hospital staff. Another medical staff function is to provide oversight and peer review of the quality of medical care in the hospital. It performs this function through a number of medical staff committees, which coordinate their efforts closely with the hospital's administration and committees of the hospital's board of directors.

Members of the medical staff who have completed their training and are in practice are referred to as attending physicians. In addition, the hospital usually has a house staff of physicians who are engaged in residency training programs under the close supervision of attending physicians. These members of the house staff or residents rotate shifts to provide 24-hour coverage for the attending physicians' patients to which they are assigned.

There is no universal rule as to how a hospital's medical departments or divisions should be organized. Most often, the types of practice of the hospital's medical staff determine the specialty components within the medical division. Medicine, surgery, obstetrics and gynecology, and pediatrics usually are major departments. In larger hospitals and in most teaching hospitals, the subspecialty areas of medical practice are represented by departments or divisions of departments. In the internal medicine specialty, subspecialty divisions might include cardiology or cardiac care, nephrology, oncology, gastroenterology, pulmonary medicine, endocrinology, critical care, and a variety of others. In the surgical area, surgical divisions or departments might include orthopedics, thoracic, neurosurgery, cardiac surgery, and plastic and reconstructive surgery. Each department is headed by a physician department head or chairman and divisions are headed by a chief. These leaders are charged with overseeing the practice and quality of medical services delivered in their department or division. In a teaching hospital, an attending physician usually is appointed as a program director to coordinate the required educational experiences of medical students and residents in their department or division. Program directors also are responsible for maintaining their training program's accreditation, usually with the American College of Graduate Medical Education (ACGME). Training programs have to maintain extensive records documenting all trainees and their educational activities. They also undergo a formalized and periodic reaccreditation evaluation.

Nursing Division

The nursing division usually comprises the single-largest component of the hospital's organization. It is subdivided by the type of patient care delivered in the various medical specialties. Nursing units are composed of a number of patient beds grouped within a certain area to allow centralization of the special facilities, supplies, equipment, and personnel pertinent to the needs of patients with particular conditions. For example, the kinds of equipment and skills and the level of patient care needs vary considerably between an orthopedic unit and a medical intensive-care unit.

A head nurse, often with the title of "nurse manager," and who is usually a registered nurse, has overall responsibility for all nursing care in his or her unit. Such care includes carrying out the attending physician's and house staff physician's orders for medications, diet, and various types of therapy. In addition, the nurse manager supervises the unit's staff, which may include nurses' aides and orderlies. The nurse manager also is responsible for coordinating all aspects of patient care, which may include services provided by other hospital units, such as the dietary department, physical therapy department, pharmacy, and laboratories. The nurse manager also has the responsibility of coordinating the services of departments such as social work, discharge planning, and pastoral care for the patients in the unit. Increasingly, nurse managers are often extensively involved in compliance activities of the hospital as well, ensuring that all safety processes are followed and all exceptions to these processes are documented as required.

Because nursing services are required in the hospital at all times, staff usually is employed in three 8-hour shifts or two 12-hour shifts. Normally, the nurse manager of a unit works during the day shift, and two other members of the nursing staff assume what is referred to as "charge duty" on the other two shifts of the day. Charge nurses report to the nurse manager and take the leadership role when the nurse manager is not present on the unit.

A nurse manager may have responsibility for a number of nursing units and report to a member of the hospital's administration, who is usually a vice president for nursing, an assistant administrator, or the Chief Nursing Officer. It is also common to find an individual with the title of ward clerk or unit secretary on each nursing unit. The ward clerk acts as the nurse manager's administrative assistant and helps to schedule and coordinate the other hospital services related to patient care and administrative issues.

Allied Health Professionals

Not as well-known as the physicians and nurses who are central to the care and treatment of patients in hospitals is the wide array of personnel who provide other hospital services that support the work of the physicians and nurses and others who operate behind the scenes to make the facility run smoothly.

Staff members in an increasingly diverse array of healthcare disciplines are classified as allied health personnel. These professionals support, complement, or supplement the functions of physicians, dentists, nurses, and other professionals in delivering care to patients. They contribute to environmental management, health promotion, and disease prevention.

Allied health occupations encompass as many as 200 types of health careers within 80 different allied health professions. Advancing medical technology is likely to create the need for even more personnel with highly specialized training and relatively unique skills. Those who are responsible for highly specialized or technical services that have a significant impact on health care are prepared for practice through a wide variety of educational programs offered at colleges and universities. The range of allied health professions may be best understood by classifying them by the functions they serve in the delivery of health care. Some disciplines may serve more than one of these functions:

1. Laboratory technologists and technicians
2. Allied health practitioners of the therapeutic sciences
3. Behavioral scientists
4. Specialist support service personnel

Diagnostic Services

Every hospital either maintains or contracts with laboratories to perform a wide array of tests to help physicians diagnose illness or injury and monitor the progress of treatment. One such laboratory is the pathology laboratory, which examines and analyzes specimens of body tissues, fluids, and excretions to aid in diagnosis and treatment. These laboratories usually are supervised by the hospital's pathologist, who is a physician specialist.

Grouped under the rubric "diagnostic imaging services," in addition to basic radiographic images (x-rays), a wide array of more sophisticated imaging equipment that incorporates computer technology is found in these departments, including ultrasonography, computed tomography (CT), magnetic resonance imaging (MRI), and positron emission tomography (PET). Unlike radiograph technology, which is limited to providing images of the body's anatomic structures, these imaging advances have unique abilities to visualize structures in several planes and, with PET, even quantify complex physiologic processes occurring in the human body.

A variety of other diagnostic services also may be available through specific medical specialty or subspecialty departments, such as cardiology and neurology. For example, a noninvasive cardiac laboratory administers cardiac stress testing to assess a patient's heart function during exercise. Obstetricians commonly use an imaging capability called ultrasonography to visualize the unborn fetus.

Rehabilitation Services

Rehabilitation or patient-support departments provide specialized care to assist patients in achieving optimal physical, mental, and social functioning after resolution of an illness or injury. One such department is physical medicine, where diagnosis and treatment of patients with physical injuries or disabilities are conducted. This department is headed by a specialist physician called a physiatrist who usually works with a team of physical therapists, occupational therapists, and speech therapists. Other health-related specialists, such as social workers, may provide additional services to support the rehabilitation of patients with complex problems.

Other Patient Support Services

The hospital pharmacy purchases and dispenses all drugs used to treat hospitalized patients. The department is headed by a licensed pharmacist, who also is responsible for pharmacy technicians and others who work under his or her supervision.

Among other functions, the social services department helps patients about to be discharged to arrange financial support and coordinate needed community-based services. Generally, the social services department assists patients and their families to achieve the best possible social and domestic environment for the patients' care and recovery. Such services are available to all hospital patients and their families.

Discharge planning services (discussed in more detail later in this chapter) may or may not be a part of the social services department. Frequently, staffing includes both nurses and social workers who are responsible for planning post-hospital patient care in conjunction with the patients and their families. The discharge planning department becomes involved when the patient requires referral for one or more community services or placement in a special care facility after discharge.

Nutritional Services

The nutritional services department includes food-preparation facilities and personnel for the provision of inpatient meals, food storage, and purchasing and catering for hospital events. More than just a kitchen, the nutritional services department must be able to provide numerous special diets ordered for patients as part of their overall care in the hospital. Some examples include diabetic diets, soft diets, liquid diets, and a variety of others. In addition, the department must insure that all patients' meals are prepared taking into account patients' known food allergies. The department also may operate a cafeteria for employees and, in larger hospitals, may sponsor educational programs for student dietitians. An important function of this department's staff is educating patients on dietary needs and restrictions. This department usually is headed by a chief dietitian who has a degree in nutritional science, and it may be staffed by any number of other dietitians and clinical nutrition specialists with specific expertise in dietary assessment and food preparation.

Administrative Departments

Hospitals contain other professional units that provide a wide variety of nonmedical services essential to the management of the hospital's physical plant and business services. Patients are certainly aware of two of them: the admissions department, through which a hospital stay is initiated, and the business office, through which a hospital stay is terminated and patients' bills are generated. These units are two of the many components of the hospital's complex management structure.

The general administrative services of the hospital are headed by a chief executive officer (CEO) or president who has the day-to-day responsibility for managing all hospital business. He or she is the highest ranking administrative officer and oversees an array of administrative departments concerned with financial operations, public relations, and personnel. Larger hospitals have a chief operating officer (COO), who oversees the operation of specific departments, and a chief financial officer (CFO), who directs the many and varied fiscal activities of the hospital. Those key administrative officers are commonly positioned as corporate vice presidents. The large number of employees and the wide array of individual skills required to staff a hospital competently call for a personnel or human resources department with highly specialized labor expertise. That department usually is headed by a vice president for human resources. Because nursing is such a large component of the hospital's service operations, larger facilities also maintain a chief nursing officer (CNO) at the vice presidential level. Because of the increasing importance of health information technology (HIT) and electronic health records (EHRs) to hospital operations and business functions, chief information officers (CIOs) and chief medical information officers (CMIOs) are becoming more common in hospitals' management structures. CIOs are charged with the management of hospital IT infrastructure. CMIOs, who usually are physicians with background in clinical informatics, manage the functionality of the hospital's electronic health records system from the physicians' perspective.

Hotel Services

Hotel services include building maintenance, security, laundry, television, and telephone services.

▶ Information Technology's Impact on Hospitals

Hospitals typically adopted IT earlier than physicians because larger organizations could afford its high cost and benefit from the economies of scale of very large systems where the cost per user was low. Early on, hospitals used IT primarily for accounting and billing purposes. As technology advanced, again because of economies of scale, it was more feasible for larger hospitals to adopt EHRs before smaller hospitals, physician groups, and small practices. EHRs began to develop in hospitals in the 1970s and 1980s, but these were mostly at a handful of major academic health centers with research budgets sufficient to fund custom-tailored systems. Commercial EHRs began to appear in the 1990s. Because of the promise of better quality of care and lower costs and multiple federal incentive programs for both hospitals and smaller physician groups, adoption by smaller physician practices came about fairly rapidly in the last few years.[12] See Figure 3-7, Percent of

Non-federal Acute Care Hospitals with Adoption of at Least a Basic EHR, in Chapter 3 for the trend of hospital EHR adoption rates over the past several years. As the functionality of EHRs continued to advance, most of the early, pioneering academic health centers replaced their customized systems with commercial systems that are typically lower in maintenance costs. With EHR adoption basically a given, most hospital organizations now have their own IT departments headed by a CIO and/or a CMIO who works with one or more health information technology vendors to keep their systems functional and up to date.

▶ Complexity of the System

According to the Bureau of Labor Statistics, in January 2016 there were slightly more than 5 million hospital employees in the United States.[13] Major hospital systems may have thousands of employees and an accompanying maze of communication challenges. The newer diagnostic and therapeutic methods that are increasingly effective also are increasingly complex. Even this very limited description of the hospital's complex structure and organization should make it clear that with so many different kinds of employees and so many interrelated systems, functions, and regulations, it is a small wonder that hospitals function as well as they do. With the multitude of tasks performed every day by the hundreds of employees in a busy hospital, misunderstandings and information breakdowns in patient care are inevitable. In acknowledgment of this fact, the majority of this country's hospitals have patient representatives, sometimes called patient advocates, to serve as ombudspersons for the patients. They are prepared to intervene on behalf of the patients in a wide variety of situations. Contact information for those patient representatives usually is provided to patients in materials at admission or left conspicuously in patients' rooms.

▶ Types and Roles of Patients

In the early development of hospitals, the patient was considered an unavoidable burden to society. In its mercy, society provided the hospital as a refuge. Patients receiving this charity were expected to be grateful for the shelter and nursing care and even for the opportunity to lend their bodies and illnesses for medical students' instruction and practice.

By 1900 more advanced training in nursing, effective anesthetic agents, modern methods of antisepsis and sterilization, and other medical advances had revolutionized hospital practices. Hospitals changed from merely supplying food, shelter, and meager medical care to the unfortunate needy and contagious to providing skilled medical, surgical, and nursing care to everyone. However, the belief persisted that patients in the hospital, removed from their usual social environment, were in a dependent relationship with charitable authorities. Remnants of the idea that these professionals have the knowledge and authority to decide what is best for grateful and uncomplaining patients have persisted to this day, regardless of the expense to the patient or the merit of the services.

Unfortunately, the behavior of many patients and their families has been conditioned to reinforce this philosophy. While hospitalized, otherwise assertive, independent individuals tend to assume a passive and dependent "sick role." Numerous sociologic studies of patients' behavior have concluded that patients who behave in the traditional submissive sick role help to preserve the authoritarian attitude of healthcare providers that most healthcare consumers now consider patronizing and inappropriate.[14]

Rights and Responsibilities of Hospitalized Patients

Patients in hospitals have individual rights, many of which are protected by state statutes and regulations. The United States Constitution and, in particular, its Bill of Rights, is not suspended when a citizen enters a hospital. In fact, since 1972 and then revised in 1992, the AHA has published a "Statement on a Patient's Bill of Rights.[15] In 2003, the AHA replaced the Patient's Bill of Rights with brochure titled *The Patient Care Partnership*.[16] The brochure is free to all hospitals, published in eight languages, and made available to hospitals in paper form for a minor cost. The brochure contains six sections and is designed to explain a patient's rights and responsibilities in simple language:

- High quality hospital care
- A clean and safe environment
- Involvement in your care
- Protection of your privacy
- Help when leaving the hospital
- Help with your billing claims

In addition, hospitals are required by their accrediting body to make this information known to every patient admitted. Even though replaced by *The Patient Care Partnership* brochure, many hospitals continue to post and provide all patients with a copy or locally modified version of the AHA Patient's Bill of Rights. The Partnership brochure is an attempt to emphasize that although the ultimate responsibility for everything that happens within the hospital, including the medical care provided, lies with the hospital institution and its board of directors, patients also have an important and active role to play in their care. The Partnership brochure explains that patients are obligated to act responsibly toward physicians and hospitals by cooperating with all reasonable requests for personal and family information. It is to patients' benefit to inform medical or hospital personnel if they do not understand or do not wish to follow instructions. Patients are encouraged to identify to the physician and the hospital a family member or other advocate they wish to be involved in treatment decisions, and to provide contact information.

Patients also need to recognize that hospitals are highly stressful institutional settings and that other patients, as well as the hospital personnel, deserve consideration and respect. In no other institutional setting are individual rights at greater risk of being compromised than in a hospital. However, the risks do not arise from a purposeful disregard for patients by physicians or the hospital staff. The personal integrity of patients may be unintentionally violated as a result of certain institutional circumstances and factors unique to the hospital setting. These institutional circumstances arise from the fact that the hospital, like most complex organizations, has a life of its own, which pulses with an infinite array of daily scheduled events that pervade every aspect of its functioning. There are schedules for changing beds, bathing patients, serving meals, administering medications, obtaining specimens, providing therapy, checking vital signs, performing surgery, housekeeping, admitting, discharging, conducting patient rounds, receiving visitors, performing examinations, and, finally, preparing patients for the night.

The pressure of the daily schedule often makes it difficult for hospital personnel to pay attention to the special needs of individual patients. Even though a patient's particular schedule of tests, procedures, treatments, and examinations is uniquely related to his or her condition and the physician's orders, it also is influenced by the needs of fellow patients and the schedules of physicians and numerous others involved directly or indirectly in the patient's care.

A patient's treatment also may be modified by the schedule of institutional events unrelated to their care. Such institutional events may include inspections, safety drills, grand rounds, physician and nurse in-service training, unplanned staffing shortages, and an array of technical problems with any of the hundreds of the pieces of medical equipment required in a modern hospital.

A second reason why patient rights may be in jeopardy in the hospital setting is that physicians are likely to spend only a few minutes a day with each patient. This means that patients depend heavily on the nursing staff and other support personnel for medical and personal care. Ideally, nurses are able to continuously monitor each patient's condition and alert the physician to any change in a patient's status. However, the number of patients for whom a nurse is responsible and the number of tasks the nurse is required to perform during a single work shift make it extremely difficult, or sometimes impossible, to fulfill that obligation. In addition, the increasing number of caregivers involved with each patient provides additional opportunities for failures of communication and subsequent mistakes in the treatment programs for individual patients. Although hospitals continuously strive to develop fail-safe systems to protect patients against the possibility of human error in the delivery of their care, mistakes can and do happen. Medication errors, lost laboratory test results, and failures to implement physician orders are only a few examples.

As noted above, the "Patient Care Partnership" encourages patients to recognize their vulnerability during hospitalization and urges them or their family members to function as active participants in, rather than passive recipients or observers of, hospital care. In addition, state health departments, which license hospitals, ensure the right of patients to make complaints about hospital care and services. Hospitals are required by law to investigate patient complaints and respond to them. In fact, a hospital must provide a written response if a patient so requests.

Informed Consent and Second Opinions

No description of the structure and processes of hospitals is complete without mention of the very important personal decisions regarding medical care that patients are asked to make, often under stressful and intimidating circumstances. A cornerstone of the personal rights of hospitalized patients is the right to know:

- What is being done to them and why
- What the procedure entails
- How the procedure can be expected to benefit them
- What risks or consequences are associated with a procedure
- What is the probability of risks and consequences

In short, in almost all cases the doctrine of informed consent ensures that patients have ultimate control over their own bodies. This doctrine, first recognized legally in 1914, has been reaffirmed repeatedly over the years. It is now generally recognized to encompass not only the information mentioned above, but also the right to receive information about alternative forms of treatment to the one recommended.[17]

A physician has no legal right to substitute his or her judgment for the patient's in matters of consent. This principle means that the patient has the absolute right to reject or question a physician's recommendation. For these reasons, it is considered appropriate for patients to obtain second opinions to satisfy concerns about the necessity for various tests and other procedures. Many insurers now require a confirming second opinion before agreeing to pay for certain surgical or other procedures. Medicare and many private health plans cover most of the costs of second opinions.[18,19]

▶ Diagnosis-Related Group Hospital Reimbursement System

Until 1983, a patient stayed in the hospital until the physician decided that he or she was well enough for discharge. Each hospital monitored its own situation through a utilization review committee composed of physicians and administrators who reviewed the lengths of stay of hospitalized patients to ensure that neither the quality of care nor the efficiency of the hospital was being compromised by physicians' decisions.

During the 1970s and early 1980s, however, the cost of hospital care rose so fast that health insurance companies and corporations that paid huge insurance premiums to cover the hospitalization costs of their workers increased the pressure on federal agencies to find a way to stem the rising tide of hospital expenses. Two factors made change imperative.

First, hospitals were paid a set amount for each day that a patient stayed in the facility. That amount was determined retrospectively by determining the cost per day per bed to operate the hospital the year before. Under that arrangement, the hospital had no incentive to keep costs down. In fact, if it did, it would receive a smaller daily reimbursement rate the next year than if it spent freely. Furthermore, it became clear to the government and the insurance companies that they were paying not only for uncontrolled costs per hospital day but also for hospital days that were not necessary. On a national scale, hundreds of thousands of hospital days that did not benefit the patients, at a cost of several hundred dollars per day, amounted to a huge and valueless financial burden. Hospital costs were forcing the Medicare program to exceed all financial projections.

Second, payers recognized that not only were unnecessarily long hospital stays expensive, but they also could be dangerous to patients' health. Patients are exposed to infections in hospitals that they would not face at home. In addition, many older patients are at extreme risk of delirium and rapidly losing the ability to perform basic activities of daily living such as dressing, feeding, or toileting themselves during a long stay in a hospital. Patients' risk of falls and deadly hip fractures also is a significant concern. Often, older patients emerge from the hospital less able to function than when admitted. Shortened stays in hospitals, especially for older patients, often can be beneficial as well as less expensive.

In 1983, the federal government radically changed the way hospitals would be reimbursed for the costs of treating Medicare patients. The new payment system, referred to as diagnosis-related groups (DRGs), and discussed in more detail in Chapter 8, was designed to provide hospitals with a financial incentive to discharge patients as soon as possible. As a prospective payment system, the patient's diagnosis predetermines how much the hospital will be paid, and the hospital knows that amount in advance. The payment is a set amount based on the average cost of treating a particular illness at a certain level of severity. If the patient requires less care or fewer days in the hospital than the DRG average, the hospital is paid the average cost regardless, and the hospital makes money. If the patient requires a longer stay or more care than the DRG average, the hospital loses money.

This carrot-and-stick system was adopted quickly by almost all states and insurance companies and became the standard for insurance reimbursement of hospital costs. It quickly changed hospital behavior. In addition, medical staff became more conservative about ordering tests and procedures of marginal value in diagnosis and treatment. In most cases, the incentive to discharge patients as soon as safely possible did not result in negative consequences for patients.[20]

▶ Discharge Planning

As noted earlier in this chapter, hospitals are responsible for discharge planning functions to help patients arrange for safe and appropriate care after a hospital stay. Using information provided by the patient or the patient's family, a discharge planner must assure that the patient who needs follow-up services obtains them. The planner must then help make the necessary specific arrangements. If the patient requires a transfer to another level of institutional care, such as a nursing home, the discharge planner must arrange that transfer before the patient can be discharged from the hospital.

In implementing the DRG system, Medicare recognized that hospitals' financial incentives to discharge patients as soon as possible should never cause patients to be discharged before they are medically ready and before arrangements have been made to ensure they will receive the necessary post-hospital care. Medicare patients who believe that either of these two conditions will not be met by their discharge date have the right to appeal. A hospital's discharge notice must include instructions on how a Medicare-covered patient can have the hospital's decision reviewed by a Medicare quality improvement organization (QIO). A QIO's function under contract with the federal government is to ensure that hospitals and physicians follow Medicare rules. Every geographic area in the United States is covered by a federally designated QIO. A QIO may reverse a decision to discharge and require Medicare to cover the costs of additional hospital days with evidence that the patient is in need of continuing hospital care. Medicare also provides a mechanism to appeal the QIO's decision.[21]

▶ Post-Diagnosis-Related Group and Managed Care

Early Market Reforms

With consumers, employers, government, and commercial payers intensifying their demands for lower costs, higher quality, better access, and more information about outcomes, in the 1990s most hospitals undertook a series of competitive efforts to improve their market positions. Many engaged in mergers and consolidations intended to effect economies of scale and acquire stronger positions to negotiate with managed care organizations and other payers. Others, in communities with excess hospital capacity, either closed or converted to other uses, such as ambulatory or long-term care facilities.

Between the inception of DRGs in the mid-1980s and 2000s, approximately 2,000 U.S. hospitals closed, hospital inpatient days declined by one-third, and many hospitals consolidated into local, regional, or national multihospital systems. By 2001, more than half of U.S. hospitals operated as part of merged multihospital systems in contrast to 31 percent functioning within such multihospital systems in 1979.[22] Research on the effects of this early wave of mergers suggested that they resulted in cost and price reductions that varied across markets.[23]

One of the consequences of high-technology hospital care was the industrialization of patient care activities. Rather than being patient oriented, the care became task oriented, with every chore identified and delegated to the person at the lowest skill level who was capable of carrying it out. The result for patients was a succession of relatively anonymous caregivers, none of whom had a knowledgeable or holistic relationship with individual patients. Responsibility and accountability for the total care of patients became increasingly diffuse. Opportunities for patients to fall into the cracks between the many caregivers increased, and more midlevel managers were necessary to oversee operations.

Patient satisfaction studies reflected an increase in patient complaints about the loss of identity, dignity, and respect for individual needs. For most, the lack of communication between hospital staff, including physicians, patients, and their families was the most irritating aspect of the hospital experience. After an extensive survey of more than 6,000 hospital patients and 2,000 individuals who accompanied patients during their hospital stays, as well as research drawn from field visits and focus groups, the Picker/Commonwealth Program for Patient-Centered Care, established in 1987, was able to identify a series of patient care failings common among hospitals.[24] One devastating research finding was that as many as 20 percent of patients concluded that no one was in charge of their hospital care.[25] Clearly, advances in medical care and the industrialization of many, if not most, hospitals caused the medical system to lose touch with its essential constituency—its patients—and its essential mission to serve their needs.[26]

The trend has moved away from the industrial model of hospital care that eroded public trust and confidence in hospital care and toward small team responsibility for the quality of patient services. To attract patients who now have more options, hospitals focus on friendlier staff, better food, and more amenities. Many hospitals have eliminated visiting-hour restrictions and invite patients' visitors to stay as long as they like. Hospitals even accommodate visitors who stay the night with reclining chairs and breakfast.[27]

Horizontal Integration

Under the general business definition, horizontally integrated organizations are aggregations that produce the same goods or services. They may be separately or jointly owned and governed, operated as subsidiary corporations of a parent organization, or exist in a variety of other legal or quasi-legal relationships. According to Roger Kropf:[28]

> In the hospital industry, horizontal integration was viewed as potentially advantageous because it could benefit from economies of scale. Large groups of hospitals merged into one organization can purchase supplies and services at a volume discount, hire specialized staff at the corporate level to increase expertise, raise capital less expensively, and market hospital services under a single brand name in a number of communities.

In the 1980s, the horizontal integration strategy spawned large numbers of hospital mergers and acquisitions and significant growth in the number of multihospital systems. Both for-profit and not-for-profit hospitals engaged in horizontal integration in an effort to meet the economic imperatives of the changing industry climate. As the trend in inpatient utilization and lengths of stay continued to decline throughout the 1980s, managed care organizations and other large purchasers of health care increased demands for the availability of comprehensive, continuous care housed within discrete, accountable systems. For this and other reasons, horizontal integration as a primary strategic initiative declined in favor.

The initial wave of hospital consolidations crested in the mid-1990s, and a period of relative calm ensued over the next decade.[29] However, anticipating effects of new healthcare reform measures, the pace of both mergers and acquisitions has quickened rapidly since 2002.[29] As is discussed later in this chapter, in communities across the United States, consolidations of facilities, staff, and other resources of previously separate organizations are viewed as critical to survival in the reformed system.

Vertical Integration

Organizations that have vertical integration operate a variety of business entities, each of which is related to the other. In health care, a vertically integrated system includes several service components, each of which addresses some dimension of a population's healthcare needs. The system may be fully comprehensive, with a complete continuum of services ranging from prenatal to end-of-life care. Other systems may contain some, but not all, of the services required by a population. A fully vertically integrated system in its ideal form includes all facilities, personnel, and technologic resources to render the complete continuum of care, which comprises (1) all outpatient primary care and specialty diagnostic and therapeutic services, (2) inpatient medical and surgical services, (3) short- and long-term rehabilitative services, (4) long-term chronic institutional and in-home care, and (5) terminal care. Such a system also includes all required support services such as social work and health education. In theory, vertically integrated systems offer attractive benefits ("one-stop shopping") to their sponsoring organizations, patients, physicians, and other providers, as well as payers.

Vertically integrated organizations also gain the advantage of an increased market share across a mixture of high-profit, loss-generating, and break-even revenue sources. They benefit from an increased likelihood of retaining patients for many or all their service needs. In addition, they are advantageously positioned to negotiate with managed care organizations by ensuring the availability of comprehensive, continuous care for an insured population at competitive prices. For patients, the most obvious benefit is continuity of care throughout the various system components and improved case management. Physicians and other providers benefit from both greater certainty about the flow of patients to their practices and improved ease of referrals. Managed care organizations and other large purchasers view integrated organizations favorably because of the relative ease of negotiating pricing with one organization instead of several. In addition, quality monitoring, patient case management, and physician and other provider activity can be managed and monitored more efficiently when they are all part of the same organization. Vertical integration is a cornerstone of the seamless process of patient care sought in the reformed healthcare system.[30]

▸ Quality of Hospital Care

Hazards of Hospitalization

Medical errors have been a serious problem in hospitals for decades, but improving patient safety did not become a serious national concern until the late 1990s. Although those in the health professions and knowledgeable members of the public have long been aware of the error-prone nature of hospital care, it was not until the November 1999 release of a report of the prestigious National Academy of Science's Institute of Medicine (IOM) on medical mistakes that the magnitude of hospitalized patient risks gained public knowledge.

By extrapolating the findings of several well-conducted studies of adverse events occurring in hospitals to the 33.5 million hospital admissions in the United States during 1997, the IOM report concluded that at least 44,000 and as many as 98,000 deaths occur annually because of medical errors.[31] The report put the magnitude of the problem in the context of comparable concerns by noting that more people die from medical errors each year than motor vehicle accidents or breast cancer and that medication errors alone kill more people each year than workplace injuries.

Errors are defined as "the failure to complete a planned action as intended or the use of a wrong to achieve an aim."[31] Errors may be attributed to failures in diagnostic, treatment, or surgical procedures; selection or doses of medication; delays in diagnosis or treatment; and a host of other procedural lapses, including communication or equipment failures. There is general agreement that system deficiencies are the most important factor in the problem and not incompetent or negligent healthcare providers. As noted above, miscommunication among overstressed employees is common in busy hospitals. With so many steps and so many people involved in the care of hospital patients, the potential for error grows with every patient day, and small lapses develop into large tragedies.[31]

The 1999 IOM report presented recommendations to improve the quality of care over a 10-year period with a comprehensive strategy for reducing medical errors through a combination of technologic, policy, regulatory, and financial strategies intended to make health care safer. Better use of health information technology that included decision support, avoidance of similar-sounding and look-alike names and packages of medications, and standardization of treatment policies and protocols were suggested to help to avoid confusion and reliance on memory and handwritten communications. The most controversial of the recommendations was the call for a nationwide mandatory reporting system that would require states to report all "adverse events that result in death or serious harm."[31] The impact of the IOM report has been mixed.[32] According to one study published in 2013, the number of errors may actually be much higher than they were when the IOM report first came out with between 210,000 and 440,000 hospital-based medical errors annually.[33] Another more recent study published in 2015 showed that the number of hospital acquired conditions dropped 17 percent over three years and drug errors dropped by 19 percent.[34] No doubt medical errors is a topic that will garner continued study and controversy.

The healthcare system and its medical professionals need to make radical changes in cultural attitudes and individual prerogatives before the necessary system changes and reporting requirements can be institutionalized. The 1999 IOM report, which moved awareness of the magnitude of medical errors from the anonymity of hospitals to the nation's media and subsequently to the halls of Congress, produced vociferous debate over issues of mandatory or voluntary reporting. Questions of liability, confidentiality, and avoidance of punishment must be settled before any mandatory reporting legislation can be passed. In the meantime, other recommendations for more focus on patient safety by professional groups, medical societies, healthcare licensing organizations, and hospital administrations could be followed with more immediate benefits.

Historically, it has always been easier to evaluate the quality of the medical care provided in hospitals than that provided in medical offices or other delivery sites because of the availability of comprehensive medical records and other sources of clinical information, systematically collected and stored for later recovery. The definition of quality, however, is extremely complex as it derives from both operational factors and the measures or indicators of quality selected and the value judgments attached to them. For many years, quality was defined as "the degree of conformity with preset standards" and encompassed all the elements, procedures, and consequences of individual patient–provider encounters. Most often, however, the standards against which care was judged were implicit rather than explicit and existed only in the minds of peer evaluators.

The peer review technique commonly used in hospitals until the 1970s had both benefits and failings with the quality assurance process using chart audits. Periodically, an audit committee composed of several physicians appointed by the hospital medical staff would review a small sample of patient records and make judgments about the quality of care provided. Such audits were ineffective for several reasons. First, the evaluators used internalized or implicit standards to make qualitative judgments. Second, there was no rational basis for chart selection that would permit the evaluators to extrapolate the sample findings to the broader patient population. Third, when deficiencies were identified, physician auditors were reluctant to take corrective action because their deficient colleagues might be on the next audit committee reviewing their patient care.

Avedis Donabedian of the University of Michigan made a benchmark contribution to quality-of-care studies by defining the three basic components of medical care—structure, process, and outcome. He defined structural components as the qualifications of the providers, the physical facility, equipment, and other resources, and the characteristics of the organization and its financing.[35] Until the 1960s, the contribution of structure to quality was the primary, if not the only, quality assurance mechanism in health care. Traditionally, the healthcare system primarily relied on credentialing mechanisms, such as licensure, registration, and certification by professional societies and specialty boards, to ensure the quality of clinical care.

The past focus on structural criteria assumed erroneously that enough was known about the relationship of the structural aspects of health care to its processes and outcomes to identify the critical or appropriate structural indicators. Reviews for accreditation by The Joint Commission (TJC), the primary U.S. hospital accrediting body, were based almost exclusively on structural criteria. Judgments were made about physical facilities, the equipment, the ratios of professional staff to patients, and the qualifications of various personnel. The underlying assumption of structural quality reviews was that the better the facilities and the qualifications of the providers, the better the quality of the care rendered. It was much later that TJC hospital accreditation included process criteria and outcomes.

The process components identified by Donabedian are what occur during encounters between patients and providers. Process judgments include what was done, how appropriate it was, and how well performed, as well as what was omitted that should have been done. The assumption underlying the use of process criteria is that the quality of the actions taken during patient encounters determines or influences the outcomes.

The outcomes of care identified by Donabedian are all the activities that do or do not happen as a result of the medical intervention.

Only recently has hospital quality assurance and TJC criteria focused on the relationships among structure, process, and outcomes. In the past, providers always argued that so many different variables influence the outcomes of medical care that it is inappropriate and unfair to attribute patient outcomes solely to medical interventions. That argument was dismissed, and analytical techniques that collect and analyze data on most or all of potential intervening influences allow the findings to be adjusted for patient differences. Now, quality-of-care data are routinely standardized to account for age, gender, illness severity, accompanying conditions, and other variables that might influence outcomes.

Another quality framework for examining hospitals and the healthcare system is the Triple Aim Initiative developed by the Institute for Healthcare Improvement (IHI).[36] The premise of the IHI is that in order to optimize the healthcare system, three objectives must be addressed simultaneously:[36]

1. Improving the patient experience of care (including quality and satisfaction)
2. Improving the health of populations
3. Reducing the per capita cost of health care

The IHI believes that in the current structure of the U.S. healthcare system, no one entity is responsible for all three objectives. IHI contends that without such a structure, real reform is not likely possible. A complete description of the Triple Aim Initiative, its history, and implications is well beyond the scope of this text. Readers are directed to the IHI website on this topic as a starting place for more in-depth research.[36]

Variations in Medical Care

In 1973 two researchers, John Wennberg and Alan Gittlesohn, published the first of a series of papers documenting the variations in the amounts and types of medical care provided to patients with the same diagnoses living in different geographic areas.[37] Those publications emphasized that the utilization and costs of hospital treatment in a community had more to do with the number, physician specialties, and individual preferences of the physicians than the medical conditions of the patients.

With persistent concerns about improving the quality of hospital care and containing soaring costs, various groups formed to survey and report on the quality of hospital care. Chief among them has been the Leapfrog Group that was founded in 2000 by the Business Roundtable with support from the Robert Wood Johnson Foundation. Members include more than 160 Fortune 500 corporations and other large private and public sector health benefits purchasers who represent more than 36 million health insurance enrollees.

The Leapfrog Group fields the Leapfrog Hospital Quality and Safety Survey, a voluntary online survey that tracks hospitals' progress toward implementing all 30 of the safety practices endorsed by the National Quality Forum. Leapfrog's website displays each hospital's results and is updated each month with data from additional hospitals; anyone can review the results at no charge. Leapfrog also has compiled the first free online database of programs across the country that offer financial or nonfinancial rewards and incentives for improved performance.[38]

Nurse Shortage Staffing Crisis

Over the past two decades, three factors combined to drive a hospital nursing shortage to crisis proportions. First, increasing dissatisfaction with staffing reductions, overwork, and inadequate time to maintain the quality of patient care drove nurses out of hospitals into early retirement or into home or ambulatory care. Second, with the heavy work responsibilities of nursing as a career and many other more attractive options, fewer young people were entering the nursing field. Last, aging of the nurse workforce accelerated staffing losses. Because one-third of the employed nurses are over 50 years of age, only an increasing pool of new nurses entering the pipeline can rescue hospital nursing from this critical shortage.[39]

The consequences are serious. There is increasing evidence that nurse staffing is related to patient outcomes in both medical and surgical cases. Studies indicate a direct link between the number of registered nurses and the time they spend with patients and the number of serious complications and patient deaths. Low nurse staffing increases the likelihood that some patients will suffer pneumonia, shock and cardiac arrest, and gastrointestinal bleeding, and some patients will die as a result.[40]

The situation in nurse shortages has improved. In the last few years pay increases, relatively high national unemployment rates, along with private initiatives aimed at encouraging men and women to become nurses, have resulted in an increase in the supply of employable registered nurses. The period between 2002 and 2009 saw the number of full-time equivalent registered nurses increase by 62 percent.[41] In 2012, the Health Resources and Services Administration projected that by 2025, the number of nurses will have increased by 33 percent while the demand will have only increased by 21 percent.[42] Other analysts believe that variables such as the shortage of primary care physicians and the impact of the ACA will confound accurate predictions of whether future supply will be sufficient to meet future demand.[41,43]

Research Efforts in Quality Improvement

After the TJC recognized the development of multi-institutional hospital networks, it produced a new and quantitatively measurable definition of quality with a focus on results. The new definition characterizes the quality of a provider's care as the degree to which the care delivered increases the likelihood of desired patient outcomes and reduces the likelihood of undesired outcomes, given the current state of medical knowledge.

This objective and quantitative definition of quality contrasted sharply with the previous subjective, qualitative definition that required estimates of adherence to somewhat nebulous performance standards. It also left room for nonclinical outcomes, such as accessibility (the ease with which patients can avail themselves of services) and acceptability (the degree to which health care satisfies patients).

Hospitals now conduct regular patient satisfaction studies to obtain patients' views about the services they receive. Such studies encompass several aspects of care, including access, convenience, information received, financial coverage, and perceived quality. Patient satisfaction studies add a new dimension to the definition of quality. "Quality" becomes what the patient receives as judged by the patient rather than what the facility provides as judged by the providers.

Closely related to the cost and quality dilemma associated with high technology was the problem that some patients received too many procedures, tests, and/or medications that were inappropriate, useless, or even harmful. A large number of studies have examined the appropriateness of the use of various medical tests and procedures. Using similar methods, researchers compared medical records against well-established criteria for performing specific medical procedures. Those procedures were then rated as performed for "appropriate," "inappropriate," or "equivocal" reasons. The RAND Corporation summarized the findings of a number of RAND-supported research studies, as shown in **FIGURE 4-1**.[44]

In 2012, the Choosing Wisely Campaign was launched "with a goal of advancing a national dialogue on avoiding wasteful or unnecessary medical tests, treatments, and procedures."[45] This campaign was started by the American Board of Internal Medicine (ABIM) Foundation in partnership with Consumer Reports and more than 70 professional medical societies. The campaign tries to " ... promote conversations between clinicians and patients by helping patients choose care that is: supported by evidence, not duplicative of other tests or procedures already received, free from harm, and truly necessary."[45] The Choosing Wisely website maintains searchable evidence-based lists of recommendations for both patients and physicians that are shown by the evidence not to be of significant value. Some examples include recommendations to give the flu shot to most all patients even to those with allergy to eggs, to NOT get screened for cancer using whole body CT scanning, and to NOT get screened for cervical cancer with a Pap smear post-hysterectomy where the cervix was removed.[45]

Overall, it appears that a significant proportion of hospital procedures are performed for inappropriate reasons. The proportion of all procedures judged to be questionable or equivocal also shows wide-ranging variation. "On average, it appears that one-third or more of all procedures performed in the United States are of questionable benefit."[31]

Responsibility of Governing Boards for Quality of Care

Although medical staffs and other professional patient care providers in hospitals make the decisions and carry out the procedures that lead to the patient care outcomes, hospital governing

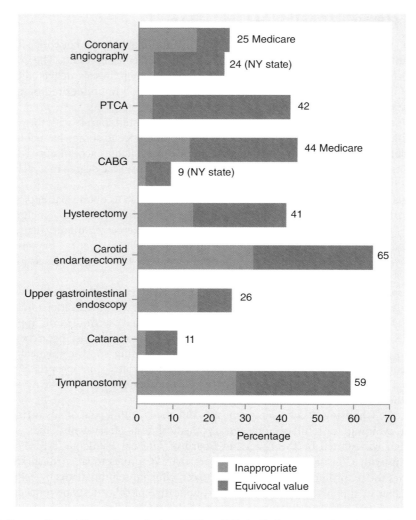

FIGURE 4-1 Proportion of Procedures Judged Either "Clinically Inappropriate" or "Of Equivocal Value": Summary of Selected Studies

Reprinted with permission from: RAND Health Research Highlights, "Assessing the Appropriateness of Care: How Much Is Too Much?" RB-4522, RAND.

boards ultimately are responsible for the quality of the care provided. The board is responsible for the hospital's quality assurance and risk management programs, all quality improvement programs, and the oversight of the medical staff. The latter responsibility is discharged primarily through its oversight of and final decisions regarding appointments and privilege delineations of medical staff members. Otherwise, oversight of the medical staff is delegated to the various committees of the medical staff organization.

The board oversees the hospital's quality assurance programs and related functions by monitoring specific information regarding program effectiveness in the identification and resolution of patient care problems and medical staff in quality assurance procedures. Some of the indicators that hospital boards regularly review are:

- Mortality rates by department or service
- Hospital-acquired infections
- Patient complaints
- Patient falls
- Adverse drug reactions
- Unplanned returns to surgery
- Hospital-incurred traumas

Needless to say, only the most diligent and dedicated lay board members are capable of interpreting these data and then formulating clear and understandable explanations for their occurrence. Healthcare reforms will refocus hospitals' quality-assessment criteria and as such can be expected to require a reorientation of hospital boards of directors' roles in what has been a historically important set of functions. Details of these changes for boards' quality-monitoring functions will await many future stages of healthcare reform implementation.

▶ **Hospitalists**

Physicians called hospitalists are rapidly taking over the care of inpatients in U.S. hospitals. Usually internists or family physicians by training, hospitalists assume responsibility for the care of inpatients from admission to discharge. They substitute for the patient's primary physician for the period of the hospital stay and provide and/or coordinate all patient care by staff and specialists. Hospitalists reduce the inherent costs of primary care physicians changing venues from the outpatient to the inpatient setting and back again by eliminating the need for daily primary care physician visits to inpatients. In addition, primary care physicians are less able to rush to a patient's bedside during emergencies, while hospitalists are available in house to attend to patients' emergent needs 24/7. Although hospitalists increase continuity of care for patients within the hospital setting, arguably, continuity of the inpatient care is lost when patients transition back to the outpatient setting and the primary care physician is less familiar with what transpired during the patient's hospital stay.

Because it is generally accepted that the presence of hospitalists shortens lengths of stay, improves the continuity and quality of hospital care, and has economic advantages to hospitals, hospitalist medicine is rapidly becoming the preferred model of inpatient care.[46]

While there is not yet a specific and distinct board certification available for hospitalists, in the early 1990s the ABIM created the Focused Practice in Hospital Medicine (FPHM) as part of its Maintenance of Certification (MOC) program for its Internal Medicine Board Certification. MOC is the program where board-certified physicians continue to maintain their board certification with required, yearly, documented educational activities. "While the FPHM MOC program is not a subspecialty, it is a variation of Internal Medicine [Board] certification. Diplomates cannot participate in both the FPHM and Internal Medicine MOC programs simultaneously. Completion of the program identifies diplomates as ABIM Board Certified in Internal Medicine with a Focused Practice in Hospital Medicine."[47] The American Board of Family Medicine soon followed with a focused Practice in Hospital Medicine for family medicine.[48] "Hospital Focused Practice Communities" in Orthopedics, Surgery/Post-Acute Surgery, Psychiatry, Oncology, OB/GYN and Neurosurgery have formally emerged in the Society of Hospital Medicine.[49] More recently in February of 2016, the Center for Medicare & Medicaid Services (CMS) created a set of dedicated billing codes for hospitalists.[50] Given that hospital medicine is the fastest growing medical specialty in the United States with more than 48,000 practitioners identifying as hospitalists,[50] the hospitalist "movement" will likely continue to evolve rapidly.

▶ Forces of Reform

The two most recent and major forces of reform are the implementation of the ACA and the soon-to-be-implemented MACRA. The provisions of these initiatives are or will soon radically alter virtually all dimensions of hospitals' institutional perceptions of themselves and their relationships with providers, payers, and patients. Details of the ACA and MACRA are provided in other chapters of this text. The following sections touch on the major components of both in general and explain the major impacts these initiatives have on hospitals.

The Affordable Care Act

The ACA was signed into law by President Obama on March 23, 2010. Many aspects of the ACA went into effect almost immediately, including the ability of parents to keep their young adult children on their insurance until the age of 26 and the regulation that prevents insurance plans from discriminating against patients with pre-existing conditions. Other aspects required more time to implement such as health insurance exchanges (2014) and penalties levied on individuals who do not have health insurance—also known as the individual mandate (2015). As originally planned, all ACA provisions will not take effect until 2018 and the five years since its passage are inadequate to assess the full impact of the program. Many aspects of the law's effects will take long-term studies to evaluate. However, the following sections review major elements of the ACA and provide some preliminary data on how the ACA is affecting health care in general and hospitals in particular.

The ACA addresses four foundational elements: (1) population focus, (2) market consolidations through mergers and acquisitions, (3) accountable care organizations (ACOs), and (4) reimbursement and payment revisions. For purposes of explanation, these elements are discussed separately. However, they are in fact interdependent and closely linked by the reformed system's overall goals of increasing the quality of care by encouraging improved coordination and better continuity of care that will result in reduced costs.

Population Focus

Perhaps the most enveloping changes of health reform for hospitals result from the new focus on outcomes rather than the number of patients served. Historically, medicine and public health have been two separate and distinct entities at most universities,[51] and "population health" was not embraced by hospitals or individual providers as they were both reimbursed on a piecemeal, procedure-by-procedure basis, with no accountability for the overall health status of the populations they treated. Health system reforms now require a population focus in which groups composed of many levels of healthcare providers including hospitals take responsibility for managing the total health spectrum of a group of patients "to achieve the best possible quality at minimum necessary cost."[51,52] This population focus is understandably foreign to hospitals accustomed to accountability for individual patient outcomes only within their institutions. As *Modern Health Care* noted in its January 21, 2013, edition, "Hospitals can no longer live in a four-walls, brick and mortar world. Community-based care will be the future metric against which providers will be measured. That is, their reimbursement will be based on performance of care rendered in multiple provider sites by various types of caregivers, including in-home settings."[53]

An example of how the new population focus manifests in the ACA is that hospitals now receive significant financial penalties if they incur higher-than-anticipated, 30-day Medicare readmission rates. Thirty-day readmissions were targeted because they are associated with high Medicare costs and usually poorer patient outcomes. Since this element of the ACA was enacted in 2012, the national 30-day readmission rate has declined from 19 to 18 percent, representing an approximate national reduction of 150,000 30-day readmissions per year.[54] Further discussion of this program appears in the Readmissions Reduction Program section later in this chapter.

Market Consolidations: Hospital Mergers and Acquisitions

In the past several years, both before and after the ACA, unprecedented numbers of hospitals joined with each other and with physician groups. This created new and larger integrated systems of care as the providers for larger population groups with expanded market share and more negotiating power with payers and suppliers.[55,56] Hospital merger and acquisition transactions increased by 18 percent in 2012 over 2011 with 109 deals affecting 352 facilities.[56] In 2014, the trend continued where "deal volume for the healthcare services sectors rose 18 percent, to 752 transactions versus 637 in 2013"[57]. Data from 2015 show the upward trend continues.[58] Between 2000 and 2010 the number of physicians employed directly by hospitals grew by 34 percent.[59] These transactions included one deal in which 10 not-for-profit hospitals agreed to change the ownership of 160 hospitals.[56] In 2014, Standard and Poor's Rating Service published the fact that 39 percent of its not-for-profit hospital financial ratings upgrades were due to merger and acquisition activity.[60] In certain markets, insurers are purchasing hospitals and physician practices with the goals of wielding greater control over the costs of care.[61] All these developments underscore that previously accepted tenets of competition and collaboration between providers and payers are changing significantly. As models of integrated care delivery continue gaining traction to align with reimbursement incentives for population-based health outcomes, forging of new and different relationships between and among components of the delivery and reimbursement systems can be expected to continue.

Accountable Care Organizations

The ACA provided financial incentives for healthcare providers to form new groups or organizations that leverage the integration and coordination of all aspects of health care to improve the quality and reduce the cost. These new organizations are called Accountable Care Organizations (ACOs). ACOs are intended to address the well-acknowledged fragmentation of the healthcare system by ensuring care coordination across multiple providers for the entire spectrum of needs so that all patients receive timely and appropriate care, avoiding unnecessary duplication of services, medical emergencies, and hospitalizations.[62] The intent under the ACA was to create a variety of ACO organizations with different incentive models to track and then to identify the models or organizational structures that worked best.

Under the ACA, ACOs are administered through Medicare and can be structured in several different ways:[62]

- *Medicare Shared Savings Program (MSSP)*: A program that helps Medicare fee-for-service program providers join together to become an ACO. Essentially Medicare provides financial incentives based on documented savings to Medicare.[63] A more expanded description of this program follows later in this chapter.

■ *Advance Payment ACO Model*: A supplementary incentive program designed for physician-based and rural providers who have come together voluntarily to provide coordinated high-quality care to the Medicare patients they serve. Through the Advance Payment ACO Model, selected participants will receive upfront and monthly payments, which they can use to make important investments in their care coordination infrastructure.[64] This provision was added to the law in response to protests from rural hospitals.[65]

■ *Pioneer ACO Model*: A program designed for early adopters of coordinated care where the member providers share the risk as well as the savings. This model is no longer accepting applications.[66]

Each ACO must be a legally constituted entity within its state and include healthcare providers, suppliers, and Medicare beneficiaries on its governing board. Each one must take responsibility for at least 5,000 Medicare beneficiaries for a period of three years.[67] To qualify for support under the ACA, ACOs also must meet Medicare-established quality measures of care appropriateness, coordination, timeliness, and safety.[67] Providers' participation in an ACO is voluntary, and Medicare recipients participating in ACOs are not restricted from using physicians outside of their ACO.[67]

In 2016, a total of 447 ACOs participated in the MSSP, serving more than 8.9 million beneficiaries since the MSSP and Pioneer ACO models began in 2012.[68] MSSP ACOs are evaluated on 33 quality indicators. In a study comparing patients' reports about timely access to care and their primary physicians being informed about specialty care, there were some improvements as reported by ACO Medicare beneficiaries as compared with Medicare patients who were not part of an ACO.[69] CMS reported an estimated $700 million in savings compared to the non-ACO controls over the study period. CMS also estimated a $385 million savings from the Pioneer Programs during the first two years of their operation, 2012 and 2013.[70] However, after paying bonuses, the program resulted in a net loss of $2.6 million.[65] Despite the net loss, Health and Human Services Secretary Sylvia Burwell has set a goal of tying 50 percent of all traditional Medicare payments to quality or value by 2018 through new payment models, including ACOs.[65]

Reimbursement and Payment Revisions

Various ACA provisions that affect hospitals use a combination of payment reforms to support the intentions of improving patient care quality, decreasing costs, and improving population health. This section summarizes major provisions.

Accountable Care Organizations

As mentioned previously, the ACA enables ACOs to share in the savings to the federal government based on ACO performance in improving quality and reducing healthcare costs.[65] Medicare provider participation in this program is voluntary, but if selected, participation requires a three-year commitment.[71] The basis for the shared savings incentive is an ACO's performance in reducing per-capita Medicare expenditures below a benchmark determined by the type of ACO as specified by CMS. Shared-savings payments equal the difference between the estimated per-capita Medicare expenditures and the benchmark.[72] Participating ACOs continue to receive the same fee-for-service payments as in the past, but they also can earn additional shared-savings amounts based on their quality performance.

The kind of ACO determines the level of financial risk (directly correlated with potential financial reward) it wishes to assume. The program offers providers a financially risk-free, "one-sided risk" option—the MSSP type ACO—that can earn a maximum of 50 percent of savings realized each year but not be penalized if losses should occur. The "two-sided risk" option—the Pioneer ACO Program—is one in which participants are at financial risk for shared losses for each of the three-year contract period but can earn up to 60 percent of savings realized each year.[71]

"ACOs may sound a lot like health maintenance organizations. But there are some critical differences—notably, an ACO patient is not required to stay in the network."[65] "In addition, unlike HMOs, the ACOs must meet a long list of quality measures to ensure they are not saving money by stinting on necessary care."[65]

Hospital Value-Based Purchasing Program

CMS began implementing pilot projects for the Value-Based Purchasing (VBP) Program in 2003. This model has been replicated by private insurers as well, structured to provide incentives to discourage inappropriate, unnecessary, and costly care.[73] Now mandated by the ACA, the VBP Program applies to more than 3,500 U.S. hospitals, enabling them to earn incentive payments based on clinical outcomes and patient satisfaction. "Participating hospitals are paid for inpatient acute care services based on the quality of care, not just quantity of the services they provide."[74] Hospitals with low case volumes and ones that offer only specific specialties such as psychiatry, long-term treatment, rehabilitation, and cancer treatment are exempted.[75] Quality is measured based on a hospital's Total Performance Score (TPS), which is based on how well they meet a number of specific patient care and outcome objectives. These objectives change from year to year as older objectives "top out" or when most hospitals are meeting them. New objectives are cycled in to address known cost or quality problems identified by CMS. The program is funded by an annual 1.75 percent (1.50 percent in FY 2015) reduction in the standard DRG reimbursement that Medicare pays all hospitals.[76]

In FY 2016 1,800 more hospitals will have a net positive change in their DRG payments than will have a net negative change. This is 600 more hospitals with a positive change than in FY 2015 (meaning more hospitals are exceeding the quality goals in the program.) The highest-performing hospital in FY 2016 will receive a net change in payments of slightly more than 3 percent while the worst-performing hospital will see the maximum net reduction of 1.75 percent.[76]

Readmissions Reduction Program

In 2009 prior to ACA enactment, 20 percent of all Medicare fee-for-service payments ($17 billion annually) were for unplanned readmissions.[77] Because of this substantial cost, the ACA instituted the Readmissions Reduction Program beginning with discharges on October 1, 2012. This program requires CMS to reduce payments to hospitals for the readmission of patients with specified diagnoses within 30 days of discharge from a prior hospitalization. The ACA also requires that readmission information be made public on the CMS "Hospital Compare" website.[78]

The intent of the program is to encourage hospitals to improve the quality and continuity of care beyond the acute episode that resulted in the initial hospitalization. Penalty determinations are based on three prior years' hospital discharge data.[78] Payment reductions were originally based on a CMS formula that assigned each hospital a benchmark for excess readmissions for heart attack, heart failure, and pneumonia. For FY 2014, diagnoses of acute exacerbation of chronic obstructive pulmonary disease, elective total hip replacement, and total knee replacement were added to the list of benchmarked conditions. In FY 2015, patients admitted for coronary artery bypass grafting and in FY 2016, patients admitted for certain types of pneumonia were also added to the list of conditions whose related 30-day readmissions would increase hospital penalties.

A recent analysis published in 2016 by the Department of Health and Human Services and Harvard Medical School reviewed admission rates before and after the Hospital Readmission Reduction Program went into effect. The study found that "from 2007 to 2015, readmission rates for targeted conditions declined from 21.5 to 17.8 percent, and rates for nontargeted conditions declined from 15.3 to 13.1 percent."[79] The reduction in the readmission rates for nontargeted conditions suggests that the measure hospitals are putting into place to avoid the CMS penalties for targeted conditions also is reducing the readmission rates for nontargeted conditions. See **FIGURE 4-2**.[80]

The study also reviewed readmission rates to clinical observation units (COUs) under the hypothesis that hospitals trying to avoid the CMS penalties for readmissions within the 30-day window would try to readmit these patients to COUs. (Discussed in Chapter 5, COUs are dedicated locations adjacent to hospital emergency departments or beds located in other areas of the hospital that use a period of 6–24 hours to triage, diagnose, treat, and monitor patient responses while common complaints are assessed and decisions whether to admit or discharge are made.) Although admissions to COUs increased from 2.6 to 4.7 percent during the study period, the authors concluded there was insufficient evidence to suggest that changes in COU stays accounted for the noted decrease in readmissions.[79] Based on the success of this program in reducing costly Medicare 30-day readmissions, CMS likely will continue to add more targeted conditions to the program or eventually include all readmissions.

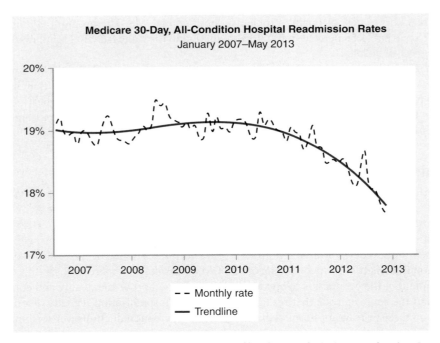

FIGURE 4-2 Hospital Readmissions Rates Before and After the Readmissions Reduction Program

Modified from Centers for Medicare and Medicaid Services. New data shows affordable care act reforms are leading to lower hospital readmission rates for Medicare beneficiaries. December 6, 2013; available from https://blog.cms.gov/2013/12/06/new-data-shows-affordable-care-act-reforms-are-leading-to-lower-hospital-readmission-rates-for-medicare-beneficiaries/. Accessed March 21, 2016.

Bundled Payments for Care Improvement Initiative

The Bundled Payments for Care Improvement Initiative (BPCI) was developed by the CMS Center for Medicare & Medicaid Innovation (CMMI) that was created by the ACA. The BPCI recognizes that separate Medicare fee-for-service payments for individual services provided during a beneficiary's single illness often result in fragmented care with minimal coordination across providers and settings and results in rewarding service quantity rather than quality. The BPCI is designed to test whether, as prior research has shown, bundled payments can align incentives for hospitals, post-acute care providers, physicians, and other healthcare personnel to work closely together across many settings to achieve improved patient outcomes at lower cost.[81] Approval for participation in the BPCI is determined through an application process administered by the CMMI. ACOs and other collaboratives of hospitals, physicians, and community-based providers are eligible to apply. The BPCI offers four broadly defined models of care linking payments for multiple services delivered to beneficiaries during an episode of care.[81] Model 1 defines an episode of care as an inpatient stay in an acute care hospital. In this model, Medicare pays the hospital an amount discounted from standard Medicare reimbursement and continues to pay physicians their usual fee-for-service amounts. Under defined circumstances, hospitals and physicians are permitted to share in Medicare savings that result from their redesigned care strategies.[81] In Models 2, 3, and 4, participants may select among 48 different clinically defined episodes of care. Models 2 and 3 use a retrospective bundled payment arrangement where expenditures are settled against a Medicare-determined discounted target price based on a participant's historical fee-for-service payments for the selected episode of care. Any reduction in expenditures beyond the discount reflected in the target price is paid to participants. Under Model 4, CMS makes a prospectively determined, single lump-sum payment to a hospital that encompasses all services furnished during an inpatient stay. Physicians and other practitioners are reimbursed by the hospital from the bundled, lump-sum payment.[81]

As of January 1, 2016, there were a total of 1,574 participants comprised of 337 BPCI "Awardees" (entities that assume financial liability for episodes of spending) and 1,237 "Episode Initiators" (healthcare providers that trigger BPCI episodes of care—they do not bear risk directly but participate in the model through an agreement with a BPCI Awardee).[81] An episode of care is defined by CMS and includes such diagnoses as "acute myocardial infarction" and "fractures of femur and hip/pelvis."[81] In February of 2015, the Lewin Group, a CMS contractor, conducted the first annual analysis of the CMS BPCI. The report stipulates that the amount of data available for analysis only allowed a quantitative analysis of Model 2 and only during the first quarter the BPCI was under operation. As a result, there were no significant conclusions the report could make on the program's effectiveness. The report states "As a result, this first Annual Report may be better thought of as the outline for future analyses as more participants enter BPCI and gain greater experience under the initiative."[82]

The foregoing descriptions of how the ACA affects hospital performance provide only a snapshot of initiatives. For more in-depth information, readers are strongly encouraged to access the websites included in the references to this chapter.

Two-Midnight Rule

Medicare reimburses hospitals for both inpatient and outpatient care. Inpatient care is paid under the Hospital Inpatient Prospective Payment System (IPPS) under the Medicare Part A Program. Outpatient care is paid under the Hospital Outpatient Prospective Payment System (OPPS) under the Medicare Part B Program.[83] The payment rate under these two very different programs usually are much higher for inpatient care than for outpatient care. Prior to 2013, CMS provided very little guidance on how to determine whether a particular patient should be treated on an inpatient or outpatient basis. In 2013, responding to audit findings indicating billing errors for inpatient services and an upsurge in COU use resulting in increased hospital billing for stays less than two-midnights long under Medicare Part A that could be appropriately managed in the outpatient setting, CMS announced the so-called Two-Midnight Rule.[83] This clarified when CMS expected a patient to be designated as an inpatient or outpatient. In other words, CMS thought hospitals were billing Medicare for Medicare Part A, inpatient care that should be billed under Medicare Part B, outpatient care, in order to increase the amount hospitals collected for outpatient services.

Hospitals' response to the new rule was robust and critical.[84] In response to the criticism, CMS released its finalized new rule to update the Two-Midnight Rule in October 2015. Under the new rule, CMS considers hospital stays of less than two-midnight's duration as outpatient visits, with a possible exception only on a case-by-case basis per the judgment of the admitting attending physician along with the appropriate supporting documentation. The new rule also changed CMS's auditing procedures. Hospital audits will now first be performed by Quality Improvement Organizations, independent organizations that work under the direction of CMS but that do not work on a contingency fee based on the funds recovered for CMS as a result of its audit. Previously, these reviews were conducted by Recovery Audit Contractors who were paid similar to "bounty hunters" on a contingency based on the amount of Medicare funds recovered by their audits.[85] Despite the clarifications in the new rule, more than 100 hospitals are participating in at least four lawsuits against CMS fighting against the decreased payment they are receiving under the Two-Midnight Rule.[86] Time will tell if the lawsuits are successful and whether CMS will have to update its new rule accordingly.

Medicare Access & CHIP Reauthorization Act of 2015

On April 16, 2015, President Obama signed into law the MACRA. The law contains several facets on payment reform including extending funding for Medicaid's Children's Health Insurance Program (CHIP) for four years and implementing the "Doc fix" to establish a schedule that predictably specifies the inflation rate for Medicare physician reimbursements rather than having Congress extend increases on a year-by-year basis.[87] Notably, MACRA contains two elements that are designed to help move the healthcare system toward paying more for value and better quality of care rather than quantity. Also, these elements will streamline the way physicians participate in quality reporting and various quality incentive programs.[87] These are:

- The Merit-Based Incentive Payment System (MIPS)
- The Alternative Payment Models (APMs)

Physicians will have the option to choose which of the two payment systems to participate in.

Option One: Merit-Based Incentive Payment System

Under the MACRA, three previous quality-reporting programs will be combined into one reporting system, scoring eligible professionals (EPs) on:

- Quality (30 percent of score)
- Resource Use (30 percent of score)
- Clinical Practice Improvement Activities (15 percent of score)
- Meaningful Use of Certified EHR Technology (25 percent of score)

The composite performance score will determine whether an EP will receive an upward, downward, or no payment adjustment.[88] Information about physicians' performance will be made available on Physician Compare.[89]

Option Two: Alternative Payment Models

Those who choose to participate in the APM program will not be subject to MIPS adjustments. Rather, those EPs will receive an annual lump sum payment based on 5 percent of the previous year's estimated aggregate expenditures under the fee schedule. The 5 percent incentive payment is available from 2019 to 2024, but beginning in 2026, the fee schedule growth rate will be higher for qualifying APM participants than for other practitioners.[88] Accountable Care Organizations (ACOs), Patient Centered Medical Homes, and bundled payment models are some examples of APMs.[87]

▶ Continuing Change

U.S. hospitals will retain their core roles as the purveyors of the most technologically sophisticated care in the world, the educational practice platforms of physicians and other health professionals, and the sites of clinical research. In the frenetic environment of health system reforms, hospitals now assume yet another role as one component of an integrated system and continuum of community-based care.

Debates and analyses will continue regarding hospitals' roles in the reformed system and healthcare marketplace. Results of government and private entity experiments with the reconfigured roles of hospitals in a new population-focused, value-driven delivery system will yield numerous opportunities for continued refinements that affect both the quality and costs of care. There are reasons for optimism in the prospect of ACOs, with hospitals as major participants, providing excellent patient-centered coordination of care that successfully addresses the negative hallmarks of the healthcare delivery system—fragmentation, duplication, medical errors, and excessive costs. Observers are expressing concern, however, that the newly established ACOs are combining healthcare organizations that otherwise would compete with each other, thus creating networks with dangerous market power.[90] Healthcare market analysts also have pointed out that the newly merged hospitals actually may increase the amounts they bill payers and the amounts they charge patients.[59]

Critical to the success of hospitals in the new era of reform will be a strong national health information infrastructure. This will require systems that not only will collect and store patients' health information, but also make that information available in many different ways, across traditional institutional and administrative boundaries, to enable the cost savings and quality improvement as part of the reform initiatives. The promise of the Health Information Technology for Economic and Clinical Health (HITECH) Act succeeded in getting hospitals to install EHRs—from 9.4 percent in 2008 to 75.5 percent in 2014. However, it failed to prioritize interoperability between EHR systems and vendors. In fact, some vendors, such as Epic, have been accused of actively making interoperability more difficult and expensive for its customers who want to connect with other vendors' systems so patient's health information can transfer seamlessly when appropriate.[91] Congressional hearings are now being held to determine why HITECH has not saved the promised $12.5 billion for Medicare through 2019.[91] There is also emerging concern that the current design of EHRs is inadequate to the task of providing the data needed to drive a variety of complex quality incentive programs as well as public health functions.[92,93]

Recent evidence bears out that there will be great variation in the capability of America's thousands of hospitals to adjust to radical reversals of form and function required by the ACA and other reforms. It is likely that the Darwinian law of nature—survival of the fittest—will determine which hospitals remain to serve the American public in the future.

KEY TERMS FOR REVIEW

Academic Health Center
Accountable Care
    Organization (ACO)
Alternative Payment Model
    (APM)
Bundled Payments for Care
    Improvement Initiative
    (BPCI)
Diagnosis-Related Group
    (DRG) Reimbursement

Hill–Burton Act
Health Information Technology
    for Economic and Clinical
    Health (HITECH) Act
Horizontal Integration
Hospitalist
Informed Consent
Medicare Access & CHIP
    Reauthorization Act of 2015
    (MACRA)

Merit-Based Incentive Payment
    System (MIPS)
Population Health Focus
Readmissions Reduction
    Program
Teaching Hospital
Two-Midnight Rule
Value-Based Purchasing (VBP)
Vertical Integration

CHAPTER ACRONYMS

ABIM American Board of Internal Medicine
ACA Affordable Care Act
ACO Accountable Care Organization
AHA American Hospital Association
APM Alternative Payment Models
BPCI Bundled Payments for Care Improvement
    Initiative
CEO Chief executive officer
CFO Chief financial officer
CHIP Children's Health Insurance Program
CIO Chief information officer
CMIO Chief medical information officer
CMS Centers for Medicare & Medicaid Services
CNO Chief nursing officer
CT Computed tomography
DRG Diagnosis-related group
EHR Electronic health record

EP Eligible professionals
FPHM Focused Practice in Hospital Medicine
HITECH Act Health Information Technology for
    Economic and Clinical Health Act
IHI Institute for Healthcare Improvement
IT Information technology
MACRA Medicare Access & CHIP
    Reauthorization Act of 2015
MIPS Merit-Based Incentive Payment System
MOC Maintenance of Certification
MRI Magnetic resonance imaging
MSSP Medicare Shared Savings Program
PET Positron emission tomography
QIO Quality improvement organization
VA United States Department of Veterans Affairs
VBP Value-based purchasing
VHA Veterans Health Administration

References

1. Stevens R. *In Sickness and in Wealth: American Hospitals in the Twentieth Century.* New York: Basic Books; 1989.
2. Teisberg E, Vayle E. *The Hospital Sector in 1992.* Boston, MA: Harvard Business School; 1991.
3. American Hospital Association. Fast facts on US hospitals. http://www.aha.org/research/rc/stat-studies/101207fastfacts.pdf. Accessed February 18, 2016.
4. American Association of Medical Colleges. Why teaching hospitals are important to all Americans.

https://www.aamc.org/newsroom/keyissues/teaching_hospitals/253374/teaching-hospitals.html. Accessed February 18, 2016.

5. Rohr R. Featured blog post: the paradox of specialty hospitals. http://www.hcpro.com/MSL-232887-3336/Featured-blog-post-The-paradox-of-specialty-hospitals.html. Accessed March 8, 2016.

6. Greenwald L, Cromwell J, Adamache W, et al. Specialty versus community hospitals: referrals, quality, and community benefits. *Health Aff.* 2006;25:106-118.

7. Bellandi D. Spinoffs, big deals dominate in '99. *Mod Healthc.* 2000;30:36-44.

8. Shomaker TS. Commentary: Preparing for health care reform: ten recommendations for academic health centers. *Acad Med.* 2011;86:555-558.

9. United States Department of Veterans Affairs. Budget in brief 2017. http://www.va.gov/budget/docs/summary/Fy2017-BudgetInBrief.pdf. Accessed March 21, 2016.

10. CNN. A fatal wait: veterans languish and die on a VA hospital's secret list. http://www.cnn.com/2014/04/23/health/veterans-dying-health-care-delays/index.html. Accessed March 8, 2016.

11. United States Department of Veterans Affairs Office of Inspector General: Office of Audits and Evaluation. Review of alleged mismanagement at the health eligibility center. 2015. http://www.va.gov/oig/pubs/VAOIG-14-01792-510.pdf. Accessed March 8, 2016.

12. Charles D, Gabriel M, Searcy T. Adoption of electronic health record systems among US nonfederal acute care hospitals: 2008-2014. ONC data brief no. 23. https://www.healthit.gov/sites/default/files/data-brief/2014HospitalAdoptionDataBrief.pdf. Accessed March 9, 2016.

13. United States Department of Labor Bureau of Labor Statistics. Industries at a glance. http://www.bls.gov/iag/tgs/iag622.htm#iag622emp1.f.P. Accessed March 8, 2016.

14. Faulkner M, Aveyard B. Is the hospital sick role a barrier to patient participation? *Nurs Times.* 2002;98:35-36.

15. American Hospital Association. A patient's bill of rights. http://www.carroll.edu/msmillie/bioethics/patbillofrights.htm. Accessed March 8, 2016.

16. The American Hosptial Association. The patient care partnership. http://www.aha.org/advocacy-issues/communicatingpts/pt-care-partnership.shtml. Accessed March 8, 2016.

17. Dolgin JL. The legal development of the informed consent doctrine: Past and present. *Camb Q Healthc Ethics.* 2010;19:97-109.

18. Centers for Medicare & Medicaid Services. Clarification of evaluation and management payment policy. CMS manual system, pub 100–02, Medicare benefit policy, transmittal 147. https://www.cms.gov/Regulations-and-Guidance/Guidance/Transmittals/downloads/R147BP.pdf. Accessed March 8, 2016.

19. Patient Advocate Foundation. Second opinions. http://www.patientadvocate.org/help.php/index.php?p=691. Accessed March 8, 2016.

20. Shortell S, Reinhardt U. *Improving Health Policy and Management.* Ann Arbor, MI: Health Administration Press; 1992.

21. Centers for Medicare & Medicaid Services. Hospital discharge appeal notices. https://www.cms.gov/Medicare/Medicare-General-Information/BNI/Downloads/CMS-4105-F-.pdf. Accessed March 8, 2016.

22. Federal Trade Commission. United States Department of Justice. Reorganization of the hospital system. http://www.justice.gov/atr/chapter-3-industry-snapshot-hospitals#7. Accessed March 8, 2016.

23. Radach Spang H, Bazzoli GJ, Arnould RJ. Hospital mergers and savings for consumers: Exploring new evidence. *Health Aff.* 2001;20:156. http://content.healthaffairs.org/content/20/4/150. Accessed April 9, 2016.

24. Delbanco TL, Stokes DM, Cleary PD, et al. Medical patients' assessments of their care during hospitalization: Insights for internists. *J Gen Intern Med.* 1995;10:679-685.

25. Gerteis M, Leviton SE, Daily J, Delbanco T. *Through the Patient's Eyes: Understanding and Promoting Patient-Centered Care.* San Francisco, CA: Jossey-Bass; 1993.

26. Sunshine L, Wright JW. *The Best Hospitals in America.* New York, NY: Henry Holt and Company; 1987.

27. Rundle RL. We hope you enjoy your stay. *The Wall Street Journal.* November 22, 2004. http://www.wsj.com/articles/SB110082005042278666. Accessed April 18, 2016.

28. Kropf R. Planning for health services. In: Kovner AR, ed. *Health Care Delivery in the United States.* New York: Springer; 1995:353.

29. Zuckerman A. The next wave of mergers and acquisitions. What's your organization's position? *Healthc Financ Manage.* 2009;63:60-63.

30. Cognizant. Cognizant 20-20 insights: five key trends reshaping the future of healthcare. http://www.cognizant.com/InsightsWhitepapers/Five-Key-Trends-Reshaping-the-Future-of-Healthcare.pdf. Accessed March 8, 2016.

31. Kohn LT, Corrigan JM, Donaldson MS. *To Err Is Human: Building a Safer Health System.* National Academies Press; March 1, 2000.

32. The Commonwealth Fund. Five years after "to err is human": what have we learned? 2005. http://www.commonwealthfund.org/Publications/In-the-Literature/2005/May/Five-Years-After--To-Err-Is-Human---What-Have-We-Learned.aspx. Accessed March 21, 2016.

33. ProPublica. How many die from medical mistakes in U.S. Hospitals? https://www.propublica.org/

article/how-many-die-from-medical-mistakes-in-us -hospitals Accessed March 21, 2016.

34. Milbank Memorial Fund. A picture of progress on hospital errors. 2015. http://www.milbank.org /the-milbank-quarterly/search-archives/article/4022 /a-picture-of-progress-on-hospital-errors. Accessed March 21, 2016.

35. Donnabedian A. Evaluating the quality of medical care. 1966. *Milbank Q.* 2005;83:691-729.

36. The Institute for Healthcare Improvement. The IHI triple aim. http://www.ihi.org/engage/initiatives/tripleaim /Pages/default.aspx. Accessed March 8, 2016.

37. Wennberg JE, Gittlesohn A. Small area variation in health care delivery. *Science.* 1973;182:1102-1108.

38. The Commonwealth Fund. Leapfrog Group offers first web-based compendium of quality incentive and reward programs. http://www.commonwealthfund .org/publications/press-releases/2004/jun/leapfrog -group-offers-first-web-based-compendium-of -quality-incentive-and-reward-programs. Accessed August 27, 2016.

39. Dworkin RW. Where have all the nurses gone? *National Aff.* 2002;148:23-36.

40. Needleman J, Buerhaus PI, Stewart M, Zelevinsky K, Mattke S. Nurse staffing in hospitals: Is there a business case for quality? *Health Aff.* 2006;25:204-211.

41. Auerbach DI, Buerhaus PI, Staiger DO. Registered nurse supply grows faster than projected amid surge in new entrants ages 23-26. *Health Aff.* 2011;30:2286-2292.

42. Health Resources and Services Administration. The future of the nursing workforce: national- and state-level projections, 2012–2025. 2012. http://bhpr .hrsa.gov/healthworkforce/supplydemand/nursing /workforceprojections/nursingprojections.pdf. Accessed March 21, 2016.

43. American Association of Colleges of Nursing. Nursing shortage. April 24, 2014. http://www.aacn.nche .edu/media-relations/fact-sheets/nursing-shortage. Accessed March 21, 2016.

44. The RAND Corporation. RB4522: Assessing the appropriateness of care: How much is too much? 1998. http://www.rand.org/pubs/research_briefs/RB4522 /index1.html. Accessed March 8, 2016.

45. ABIM Foundation. Choosing wisely. http://www .choosingwisely.org/. Accessed March 8, 2016.

46. Glabman M. Hospitalists: The next big thing? *Trustee.* 2005;58:6-11.

47. American Board of Internal Medicine. MOC requirements. http://www.abim.org/maintenance-of -certification/moc-requirements/focused-practice -hospital-medicine.aspx. Accessed March 20, 2016.

48. The American Board of Family Medicine. Recognition of focused practice in hospital medicine (RFPHM). https://www.theabfm.org/moc/rfphm.aspx. Accessed March 8, 2016.

49. Society of Hospital Medicine. Hospital-focused practice. http://connect.hospitalmedicine.org/hfp/home. Accessed March 8, 2016.

50. Society of Hospital Medicine. Centers for Medicare & Medicaid services grants billing code for hospitalists. http://www.hospitalmedicine.org/Web /Media_Center/Press_Release/2016/medicaid-code- feb25.aspx?utm_source=Web_banner&utm_medium =web&utm_content=2.25_Bill%20Code&utm_ campaign=Advocacy_16. Accessed March 8, 2016.

51. Jablow M. The public health imperative: revising the medical school curriculum. https://www.aamc.org /newsroom/reporter/may2015/431962/public-health .html. Accessed March 8, 2016.

52. Becker's Hospital Review. The road to population health: key considerations. http://www.beckershospitalreview. com/hospital-physician-relationships/the-road -to-population-health-key-considerations.html. Accessed March 8, 2016.

53. Nahm S, Mack G. Goodbye, post-acute care. "Heavy-lifting" will shift to community-based care. *Mod Healthc.* 2013;43:26.

54. Blumenthal D, Abrams M, Nuzum R. The Affordable Care Act at 5 years. *N Engl J Med.* 2015;372:2451-2458.

55. Booz and Company. Healthcare reform and hospital systems preparing for the future means structural transformation. http://www.strategyand.pwc.com /media/uploads/Strategyand-Healthcare-Reform -Hospital-Systems-Structural-Transformation .pdf?frombooz=1. Accessed March 8, 2016.

56. Healthcare M. Taking a different path: annual M&A report shows year of strong growth, rise of nontraditional deals. http://www.modernhealthcare .com/article/20130126/MAGAZINE/301269951. Accessed March 8, 2016.

57. Business Wire. Newly published report: 2014 health care services M&A market sees growth in deal volume and value of transactions, according to Irving Levin Associates, Inc. March 31, 2015. http://www .businesswire.com/news/home/20150331006369 /en/Newly-Published-Report-2014-Health-Care -Services#.VRv4s-FKZsZ. Accessed March 21, 2016.

58. Healthcare Financial Management Association. Hospital deal uptick continues. October 21, 2015. http://www.hfma.org/Content.aspx?id=42986. Accessed August 27, 2016.

59. Gunderman R. Should doctors work for hospitals? *The Atlantic.* 2014. http://www.theatlantic.com /health/archive/2014/05/should-doctors-work-for -hospitals/371638/. Accessed April 8, 2016.

60. Hospital cost-containment strategies that earn the respect of rating agencies. *Healthcare Financial Management.* 2016;70:32-35.

61. Becker's Hospital Review. Hospital M&A outlook 2012: 5 key trends. http://www.beckershospitalreview. com/hospital-transactions-and-valuation/

hospital-maa-outlook-2012-5-key-trends.html. Accessed March 3, 2016.

62. Centers for Medicare & Medicaid Services. Accountable care organizations (ACO). https://www.cms.gov/Medicare/Medicare-Fee-for-Service-Payment/ACO/index.html?redirect=/Aco. Accessed March 8, 2016.

63. Centers for Medicare & Medicaid Services. Shared savings program. https://www.cms.gov/Medicare/Medicare-Fee-for-Service-Payment/sharedsavingsprogram/index.html?redirect=/sharedsavingsprogram/. Accessed March 8, 2016.

64. Centers for Medicare & Medicaid Services. Advance payment ACO model. https://innovation.cms.gov/initiatives/Advance-Payment-ACO-Model/. Accessed March 8, 2016.

65. Kaiser Health News. Accountable care organizations, explained. http://khn.org/news/aco-accountable-care-organization-faq/. Accessed March 8, 2016.

66. Centers for Medicare & Medicaid Services. Pioneer ACO model. https://innovation.cms.gov/initiatives/Pioneer-ACO-Model/. Accessed March 8, 2016.

67. Centers for Medicare & Medicaid Services. Summary of final rule provisions for accountable care organizations under the Medicare shared savings program. https://www.cms.gov/Medicare/Medicare-Fee-for-Service-Payment/sharedsavingsprogram/Downloads/ACO_Summary_Factsheet_ICN907404.pdf. Accessed March 8, 2016.

68. Centers for Medicare & Medicaid Services. Next generation accountable care organization model (NGACO model). January 11, 2016. https://www.cms.gov/Newsroom/MediaReleaseDatabase/Fact-sheets/2016-Fact-sheets-items/2016-01-11.html. Accessed March 21, 2016.

69. McWilliams JM, Landon BE, Chernew ME, Zaslavsky AM. Changes in patients' experiences in Medicare accountable care organizations. *N Engl J Med.* 2014; 371:1715-1724.

70. O'Callaghan E, Turner N, Renwick L, et al. First episode psychosis and the trail to secondary care: Help-seeking and health-system delays. *Soc Psychiatry Psychiatr Epidemiol.* 2010;45:381-391.

71. American College of Physicians. Detailed summary—Medicare shared savings/accountable care organization (ACO) program. https://www.acponline.org/system/files/documents/running_practice/delivery_and_payment_models/aco/aco_detailed_sum.pdf. Accessed March 8, 2016.

72. McGuireWoods. Health reform for hospitals and health systems. https://www.mcguirewoods.com/news-resources/publications/health_care/health%20reform%20for%20hospitals.pdf. Accessed March 8, 2016.

73. Deloitte Center for Health Solutions. Value-based purchasing: A strategic overview for health care industry stakeholders. http://www.orthodirectusa.com/wp-content/uploads/2013/07/US_CHS_ValueBasedPurchasing_031811.pdf. Accessed March 8, 2016.

74. Centers for Medicare & Medicaid Services. Hospital value-based purchasing. https://www.cms.gov/Medicare/Quality-Initiatives-Patient-Assessment-Instruments/hospital-value-based-purchasing/index.html?redirect=/Hospital-Value-Based-Purchasing/. Accessed March 8, 2016.

75. Centers for Medicare & Medicaid Services. Hospital value-based purchasing. https://www.cms.gov/Outreach-and-Education/Medicare-Learning-Network-MLN/MLNProducts/downloads/Hospital_VBPurchasing_Fact_Sheet_ICN907664.pdf. Accessed March 8, 2016.

76. Centers for Medicare & Medicaid Services. Fiscal year (FY) 2016 results for the CMS hospital value-based purchasing program. https://www.cms.gov/Newsroom/MediaReleaseDatabase/Fact-sheets/2015-Fact-sheets-items/2015-10-26.html. Accessed March 8, 2016.

77. The Commonwealth Fund. New study: 20 percent of hospitalized Medicare patients readmitted to hospital within 30 days; half rehospitalized without seeing a doctor after discharge. http://www.commonwealthfund.org/publications/press-releases/2009/apr/new-study-20-percent-of-hospitalized-medicare-patients-readmitted-to-hospital-within-30-days. Accessed March 8, 2016.

78. Centers for Medicare & Medicaid Services. Hospital readmissions reduction program (HRRP). https://www.cms.gov/Medicare/Medicare-Fee-for-Service-Payment/AcuteInpatientPPS/Readmissions-Reduction-Program.html. Accessed March 8, 2016.

79. Zuckerman RB, Sheingold SH, Orav EJ, Ruhter J, Epstein AM. Readmissions, observation, and the hospital readmissions reduction program. *N Engl J Med* 2016. http://www.ncbi.nlm.nih.gov/pubmed/26910198. Accessed April 8, 2016.

80. Centers for Medicare and Medicaid Services. New data shows Affordable Care Act reforms are leading to lower hospital readmission rates for Medicare beneficiaries. December 6, 2013. https://blog.cms.gov/2013/12/06/new-data-shows-affordable-care-act-reforms-are-leading-to-lower-hospital-readmission-rates-for-medicare-beneficiaries/. Accessed March 21, 2016.

81. Centers for Medicare & Medicaid Services. Bundled payments for care improvement (BPCI) initiative: general information. https://innovation.cms.gov/initiatives/bundled-payments/. Accessed March 8, 2016.

82. LewinGroup. CMS bundled payments for care improvement (BPCI) initiative models 2–4: year 1 evaluation & monitoring annual report. https://innovation.cms.gov/Files/reports/BPCI-EvalRpt1.pdf. Accessed March 8, 2016.

83. Centers for Medicare & Medicaid Services. Fact sheet: Two-midnight rule. https://www.cms.gov/Newsroom/MediaReleaseDatabase/Fact-sheets/2015-Fact-sheets-items/2015-10-30-4.html. Accessed March 8, 2016.

84. Health Policy Briefs. The two-midnight rule. *Health Aff*. January 22, 2015. http://www.healthaffairs.org/healthpolicybriefs/brief.php?brief_id=133. Accessed March 8, 2016.

85. Becker's Hospital CFO. CMS releases OPPS rule for 2016, finalizes two-midnight changes: 10 things to know. http://www.beckershospitalreview.com/finance/cms-releases-opps-rule-for-2016-finalizes-two-midnight-changes-10-things-to-know.html. Accessed March 8, 2016.

86. Schnecker, L. Another 50 hospitals join fight against two-midnight pay cut. *Mod Healthc*. January 11, 2016. http://www.modernhealthcare.com/article/20160111/NEWS/160119990. Accessed March 8, 2016.

87. Centers for Medicare & Medicaid Services. The merit-based incentive payment system (MIPS) & alternative payment models (APMs). https://www.cms.gov/Medicare/Quality-Initiatives-Patient-Assessment-Instruments/Value-Based-Programs/MACRA-MIPS-and-APMs/MACRA-MIPS-and-APMs.html. Accessed March 8, 2016.

88. Health Affairs Blog. MACRA: New opportunities for Medicare providers through innovative payment systems (updated). http://healthaffairs.org/blog/2015/09/28/macra-new-opportunities-for-medicare-providers-through-innovative-payment-systems-3/. Accessed March 8, 2016.

89. Centers for Medicare & Medicaid Services. CMS quality measure development plan: Supporting the transition to the merit-based incentive payment system (MIPS) and alternative payment models (APMs) (draft). December 18, 2015. https://www.cms.gov/Medicare/Quality-Initiatives-Patient-Assessment-Instruments/Value-Based-Programs/MACRA-MIPS-and-APMs/Draft-CMS-Quality-Measure-Development-Plan-MDP.pdf. Accessed March 21, 2016.

90. Richman BD, Schulman KA. A cautious path forward on accountable care organizations. *JAMA*. 2011;305:602-603.

91. Caldwell P. Epic fail: Digitizing America's medical records was supposed to help patients and save money. Why hasn't that happened? *Mother Jones*. 2015. http://www.motherjones.com/politics/2015/10/epic-systems-judith-faulkner-hitech-ehr-interoperability. Accessed April 8, 2016.

92. Saleem JJ, Flanagan ME, Wilck NR, Demetriades J, Doebbeling BN. The next-generation electronic health record: Perspectives of key leaders from the US department of veterans affairs. *J Am Med Inform Assoc*. 2013;20:e175-177.

93. Digital Health Nexus. How to design next-generation EHR data models. June 4, 2012. http://www.healthcareguy.com/2012/06/04/how-to-design-next-generation-ehr-data-models/. Accessed April 8, 2016.

CHAPTER 5

Ambulatory Care

CHAPTER OVERVIEW

This chapter reviews the major elements of ambulatory (outpatient) care and discusses developments associated with the American Reinvestment and Recovery Act (ARRA) and the Patient Protection and Affordable Care Act (ACA). Ambulatory care encompasses a diverse and growing sector of the healthcare delivery system. Physician services are the chief component; however, hospital outpatient and emergency departments, community health centers, departments of health, and voluntary agencies also contribute important services, particularly for underserved and vulnerable populations. Ambulatory surgery is a continuously expanding component of ambulatory care as new technology allows more procedures to be performed safely and efficiently. Finally, telehealth is discussed as an expanding field affecting the evolving delivery system.

▶ Overview and Trends

Ambulatory care comprises healthcare services that do not require overnight hospitalization. Once largely consisting of visits to private physicians' offices and hospital outpatient clinics and emergency departments, ambulatory care today encompasses a broad and expanding array of services.

New technological advancements allow medical and diagnostic procedures previously requiring hospitalization to be performed on an outpatient basis. Surgical procedures that previously required a hospital stay are now routinely performed on a same-day, ambulatory basis.

In addition to new diagnostic and treatment tools available in the outpatient setting and the advanced technology that made outpatient treatment safe and effective, financial mandates also drove services into the ambulatory arena. In the late 1980s, prospective hospital reimbursement replaced retrospective payment on a national scale through Medicare's initiation of the diagnosis-related group (DRG) payment system. The new payment system provided financial incentives to decrease the duration of inpatient stays and to increase service delivery efficiency. Hospitals responded to the new payment system by shifting services amenable to outpatient delivery from the more expensive inpatient environment to less expensive and more efficient ambulatory delivery settings.

Both DRGs and pressures from healthcare insurers and purchasers to control costs contributed to the rapid expansion of managed care. With the goal of providing services in the least expensive, most effective manner possible, managed care organizations exerted a powerful influence that compelled a shift toward the use of ambulatory services to replace more expensive inpatient care.

Ambulatory care capacity has undergone exponential increases in both the hospital-based and non-hospital-based, or "freestanding," settings. Historically, hospitals operated virtually all ambulatory or outpatient clinics within their main facilities or in contiguous facilities on the hospital campuses. Many hospitals still operate ambulatory clinics on-site, and many have retained ambulatory surgical services within their main facilities. For some hospitals, converting underused inpatient units to ambulatory surgical facilities within the hospital provided a cost-effective means to accommodate the shift in site of care.

Beginning in the 1980s, hospitals expanded their service networks to include geographically distributed freestanding ambulatory care facilities throughout their service areas, both for routine diagnosis and treatment and for surgical services. Two factors influenced this trend for hospitals. First, the 1980s and 1990s saw increased consumer demand for conveniently located, easily accessible facilities and services. Second, with the growing concerns of inner-city hospitals about competition with other institutions for market share of profitable outpatient services and referrals for inpatient care, hospitals recognized the need to expand their service distribution network by establishing conveniently located facilities. Hospitals also recognized that ambulatory surgical services could be operated more efficiently off-site, removed from complexities such as operating room scheduling that required accommodation to a vast array of physician and inpatient needs.

Independent of hospital organizations, for-profit corporations' freestanding facilities providing ambulatory, primary, specialty, and surgical services proliferated. In addition to profitability and cost-control features attractive to insurers, responsiveness to consumer preferences also was a primary driver in these developments.

The decade of the 1990s saw a rapid upward trend in the number of ambulatory care facilities owned and operated by hospitals, physicians, and independent chains. Services provided by these facilities are diverse and represent a response to population demographics in their respective service areas as well as reimbursement opportunities. A partial listing of the array of ambulatory care facilities includes cancer treatment, diagnostic imaging of many different types, renal dialysis, pain management, physical therapy, cardiac and other types of rehabilitation, outpatient surgery, occupational health, women's health, and wound care.

A significant corollary to developments in ambulatory care delivery for hospital-operated and independent organizations has been physicians' entry into the business of outpatient diagnostic, treatment, and surgical services previously available to their practices in only the hospital setting. The same factors operative in the larger industry—technological advances making the purchase, maintenance, and operation of required equipment feasible and cost effective in freestanding facilities; consumer demand for convenient, user-friendly environments; and profitability—continued driving this development.

Physician involvement in this arena paralleled that of hospitals in practice areas, such as ophthalmologic surgery for lens replacement and laser therapy, certain types of gynecologic surgery, fiber-optic gastrointestinal diagnosis, chemotherapy, renal dialysis, computed tomography, magnetic resonance imaging, and more. The implications of this trend for hospitals' business volume and revenue were significant as physicians and hospitals emerged as competitors engaged in the

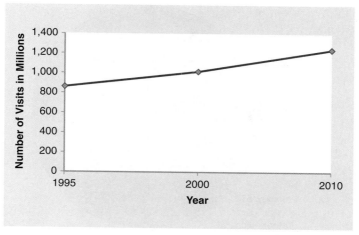

FIGURE 5-1 **Annual Number of Ambulatory Care Visits in Millions, United States, 1995–2010**
Data from CDC/NCHS, Health, United States, 2014.

same lines of business. These developments significantly altered the long-standing relationships between physicians and their affiliated hospitals.[1]

The ambulatory care delivery system is changing and growing as its various organization models evolve, including new efforts to measure quality relative to costs. The service constellation also is growing and becoming more diverse with many service delivery hybrids. With the implementation of the Patient Protection and Affordable Care Act (ACA) and accompanying proliferation of new care delivery models such as patient-centered medical homes (PCMHs) and accountable care organizations (ACOs) that emphasize population health, the roles of both primary and specialty ambulatory services are evolving along with their respective reimbursement systems. This chapter provides a framework for understanding the origins, development, and future direction of this important sector of the healthcare delivery system that continues on the growth trajectory shown by **FIGURE 5-1**.[2] The data presented is the most recent available from the National Center for Health Statistics (NCHS).

▶ Private Medical Office Practice

Private physician office practices constitute the predominant mode of ambulatory care in the United States. In 2012, the most recent year for which data are available, the NCHS estimated that patients made 929 million visits to physician offices. Approximately 56 percent of visits were made to physicians in the fields of general and family practice, pediatrics, internal medicine, and obstetrics and gynecology, and 17 percent were made to physicians in the fields of orthopedic surgery, ophthalmology, dermatology, and psychiatry. The remaining 27 percent encompassed visits to an array of other specialist physicians. **FIGURE 5-2** provides a snapshot of the distribution of physician office visits by specialty.[3]

The way physicians organize and operate their private practices has evolved from a variety of factors. Physician group practice can be traced to the Mayo Clinic in the late 1800s, and generated

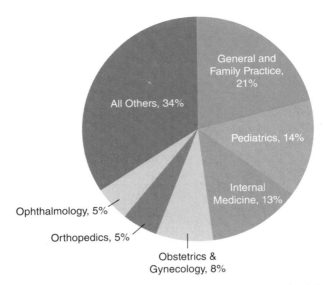

FIGURE 5-2 **Percent Distribution of Office Visits by Physician Specialty: United States, 2012**

Data from CDC/NCHS National Ambulatory Medical Care Survey 2012 State and National Summary Tables.

considerable controversy among physicians at the time. A 1932 report by a New York private foundation's Committee on the Costs of Medical Care endorsed organized group practices and the use of insurance payments. The American Medical Association (AMA) had long opposed the group practice model and condemned the report, declaring that salaried physicians practicing in groups were unethical. The controversy erupted into a legal battle when Group Health Insurance was organized in Washington, DC, in 1937. The AMA expelled all Group Health Insurance—salaried physicians. Hospitals received lists of so-called reputable physicians who were not part of group practices. The Washington, DC, Medical Society and the AMA were subsequently indicted, found guilty, and fined for having conspired to monopolize medical practice.[4] For the next few decades negative confrontations occurred as physicians sought participation in developing group health plans. Participating physicians were socially ostracized and denied hospital privileges. By the 1950s, due to effective legal challenges against organized medicine and a physician shortage, opposition to group practice subsided.

Before 1960, most physicians operated solo practices. Over ensuing years, specialization, changing economics, and the desire for more control over their lifestyles caused physicians to group together, either in single fields, such as primary care, or into multispecialty groups.

The old solo-practice model made the physician responsible for his or her entire patient caseload 24 hours a day, every day of the year. Before the proliferation of specialties, these physicians provided all medical care for their patients, with the exception of surgery or occasional consultation. The demands on their time and stamina were enormous. Aside from occasional coverage arrangements with a colleague to allow for brief time off, their schedules were relentless and unpredictable.

Beginning in the 1960s, many factors influenced a shift from the solo mode of private practice to group practice. Social movements in the United States yielded heightened awareness of lifestyle adaptations that allowed accommodation for personal growth and balance between professional and personal responsibilities. In the same period, medical specialization burgeoned as the growth in medical knowledge and technologic advances increased exponentially. Rapidly advancing knowledge in every field of medicine and the resulting specialization created new challenges for the solo generalist and the specialist. Most obvious were increasing demands on physicians to maintain a command of an exponentially growing body of diagnostic and therapeutic knowledge in their fields.

The introduction of Medicare reimbursement in 1966 dramatically altered the private medical office and its administrative processes. Before this development, physician reimbursement came from largely two sources—personal patient payments or third-party private insurance. Billing and collection were relatively simple. When Medicare began providing coverage for everyone at the age of 65 years, private physicians' offices found themselves dealing with a vast array of new government regulations and fee schedules. In addition, many Medicare recipients also carried supplemental private insurance contracts. Government regulation, complexity, and volume of billing requirements burgeoned. Solo-practice office administration, once the province of the physicians themselves, with possibly a receptionist and bookkeeper, now required an increased level of sophistication and a great deal more time and attention.

Other factors also influenced the shift to group practice. Inflation fueled office lease and rental expenses. The need for more sophisticated administrative support services increased with advancing technology and more complex billing and record-keeping. As technology advanced and diagnostic equipment became available for in-office use, groups could benefit from sharing equipment acquisition costs and ensuring the patient volume necessary to justify ongoing staffing and maintenance. Group practice could provide other economies of scale through shared administrative overhead.

Group practice evolved in two forms. One consisted of groups of physicians in the same discipline, usually primary care, surgery, obstetrics, or pediatrics. The other form was multidisciplinary specialty practices, usually including primary care physicians in collaboration with specialists or subspecialists. There were important features that both generalist and specialist physicians found more attractive in group practice than solo practice. Although typically each physician carried his or her own caseload of patients, physicians could arrange a routine, preplanned schedule of after-hours and weekend and vacation coverage.

With the continuing growth of medical knowledge required to maintain state-of-the-art competencies and an ever-expanding range of diagnostic and therapeutic alternatives, group practice enabled physicians to access each other's knowledge and experience in an informal consultative environment. This interchange of information provided professional support and introduced an informal system of peer review to each physician's practice, which, in theory, could contribute to the quality of care.

Multispecialty group practices evolved for many of the same reasons as single-specialty groups. For specialists, a major benefit was that group membership reduced reliance on patient referrals from other community physicians because economic incentives made keeping the business inside the group beneficial to all members. Patients also benefited by having diagnosis, treatment, and consultation services available at one location. Surgical group practices evolved similarly to those in the general and other specialty medical fields for similar reasons; however, surgeons tend to avoid multispecialty grouping. Instead, most are either general surgeons or specialists in such areas as colorectal, cardiothoracic, vascular, or orthopedic surgery.

In 2012, almost two-thirds of physicians were working in group practices, ranging in size from 2 to 11 physicians per group.[3] Today an increasing number of physicians are choosing employment by hospitals over private practice. The American Hospital Association reported in 2012 that the number of physicians employed by hospitals grew 32 percent since 2000.[5] A 2014 survey reported that 21 percent of all physicians in all specialties are employed by a hospital.[6]

From physicians' perspectives, hospital employment has become attractive due to factors such as flat reimbursement rates, complex insurance and health information technology requirements, high malpractice premiums, and the desire for greater work–life balance. For hospitals, employing physicians provides opportunities to gain market share for admissions, the use of diagnostic testing and other outpatient services, and referrals to high-revenue specialty services.[7]

In the 1990s, many hospitals acquired physician practices with the goals of capturing new market share, ensuring inpatient admissions, bringing new volume to ancillary departments such as laboratory and radiology, and improving service delivery efficiency to meet the demands of managed care. In succeeding years, hospitals divested from these arrangements due to financial losses resulting from low physician productivity and high overhead expense.[8] However, in the past decade, hospital acquisitions of physician practices accelerated rapidly as hospitals prepared for health reform by creating physician networks that are well-positioned to negotiate with health plans, manage coordination of care, monitor quality, and contain costs. There is strong indication that hospital leaders will continue active physician recruitment in the foreseeable future.[8] In the past, hospitals targeted primary care physicians for employment but now are also seeking employment from specialists in anticipation of creating "closed integrated healthcare delivery systems."[8] In addition to physicians, staff of hospital-owned physician practices may include nurses, nurse practitioners, physician assistants, medical office assistants, laboratory personnel, clerical staff, information technology personnel, and case management staff. Given the dynamics of health reform, acquiring physician practices is preparing hospitals to cope with a spectrum of scenarios that range from continuing fee-for-service payment to population health management and financial risk-based reimbursement.[8]

▶ Integrated Ambulatory Care Models

Traditional ambulatory care models reimbursed providers for services on a piecework basis, without requirements for coordinating services between or among providers. This piecework reimbursement promoted using a high volume of interventions, offered providers no compensation for effort to efficiently coordinate services on behalf of patient needs, and lacked methods to aggregate information on patient outcomes.[9] Historically, these models have been service focused rather than patient focused and, as a result, highly fragmented and inefficient. ACA system reforms include healthcare delivery and reimbursement principles that make patient health outcomes, rather than delivery of discrete services, the primary focus. In addition, reforms place new emphasis on providers' responsibilities for the overall health outcomes of their total population of patients, not just individuals. This emphasis requires integration and coordination of care across the spectrum of patient needs and among multiple providers in all sectors of the health and human services delivery system. The ACA provides resources to support the development and testing of two service delivery and reimbursement models, PCMHs and ACOs. The overarching goals of these models are to make medical care more effective and efficient and thereby to improve the health of populations and reduce costs, while increasing both patient and provider satisfaction. The timely, coordinated, and efficient delivery of ambulatory primary care and specialty services is central to both of these models.

To achieve the goals of these programs requires an information system to undergird multiple providers, institutions, payers, and regulators with sufficient sophistication to support all of their needs that go well beyond just supporting good patient care. Commenting on a study conducted with the Rand Corporation regarding physician discontent with EHRs, AMA President Dr. Steven

J. Stack noted, "Now is the time to recognize that requiring electronic health records to be all things to all people—regulators, payers, auditors and lawyers—diminishes the ability of the technology to perform the most critical function—helping physicians care for their patients."[10] Dr. Stack and others believe that the current siloed health IT infrastructure is not yet capable of providing the necessary IT functions to meet all these needs.

Patient-Centered Medical Homes

The Patient-Centered Medical Home (PCMH), described as the "main policy vehicle to reinvigorate U.S. primary care,"[11] is a "team-based model of care led by a personal physician who provides continuous and coordinated care throughout a patient's lifetime to maximize health outcomes."[12] The PCMH is responsible for providing all of a patient's healthcare needs or appropriately arranging a patient's care with other qualified professionals. This includes the provision of preventive services, treatment of acute and chronic illness, and assistance with end-of-life issues. The PCMH applies to all ages of patients with a distinctive orientation toward individual patients' partnership with the provider team, in all aspects of their care. The model recognizes that the current reimbursement system fails to meaningfully address multiple patient needs and provider demands for a comprehensive, coordinated, and integrated approach to managing all aspects of an individual's health. As such, the PCMH embodies recommendations for major reimbursement reforms that compensate physicians for the time required to provide and arrange for the holistic care necessary to meet the full spectrum of patient needs, not only for in-office, face-to-face encounters.[9] As described by the Agency for Healthcare Research and Quality (AHRQ), the PCMH model embodies a philosophy of advanced primary care (APC) based on the five core principles summarized below, which address the Institute for Healthcare Improvement "Triple Aim" of improved population health, improved patient experience of care, and reductions in per-capita costs:[13,14]

1. The PCMH supports patients learning to manage and organize their care based upon preferences and ensures that patients, families, and caregivers are included in the development of care plans. It encourages patients to participate in quality-improvement research, and health policy efforts.
2. Comprehensive: The PCMH offers holistic care from a team of providers that is accountable for the patient's physical and behavioral health needs, including prevention and wellness, acute, and chronic care.
3. Coordinated: The PCMH ensures that care is organized across all elements of the broader healthcare system, including specialty care, hospitals, home health care, community services, and long-term care supports. (Elements of the broader healthcare system are referred to as the "medical neighborhood.")
4. Accessible: The PCMH delivers accessible service with shorter waiting times, enhanced in-person hours, 24/7 electronic or telephone access, and alternative methods of communication through health information technology.
5. Committed to Quality and Safety: The PCMH demonstrates commitment to quality improvement and the use of data and health information technology and other tools to assist patients and families making informed decisions about their health.

The PCMH model is not new; it was described in 1967 by the American Academy of Pediatrics and in 2004 by the American College of Physicians and the American Academy of Family Physicians (AAFP).[15] With increasing recognition of the healthcare delivery systems' stark inadequacies of care continuity, safety, and quality, and increasing pressures to reduce costs and waste, the model gained widespread support. In 2006, the Patient-Centered Primary Care Collaborative (PCPCC) was created to advocate for improvement in the primary care delivery model. By 2012, the PCPCC consisted of more than 1,000 member organizations, including patient advocate groups, several large national employers, most of the nation's primary care physician associations, health benefits companies, trade associations, academic health centers, and healthcare quality improvement associations.[16] The 2016 PCPCC report, "The Patient-Centered Medical Home's Impact on Cost and Quality, Annual Review of Evidence 2014–2015," notes that 30 publications indicate "a clear trend showing that the medical home drives reductions in healthcare costs and/or unnecessary utilization such as ED visits, inpatient hospitalizations and hospital readmissions."[13] The 30 publications released between 2014 and 2015 included 17 peer-reviewed studies, 4 state government evaluations, 6 industry reports, and 3 independent evaluations of federal initiatives.[13] Twenty-one of 23 studies that reported on cost measures found reductions in one or more measures, and 23 of 25 studies reporting on utilization found reductions in one or more measures.[13] However, an AAFP report on these findings, while citing that the "medical home shows promise," noted the absence of research on "health outcomes, patient experience, and physician satisfaction," elements considered crucial to evaluating the new care delivery model.[17] Currently, more than 90 commercial and not-for-profit health plans are leading PCMH or patient-centered primary care initiatives. Many employers offer advanced primary care and PCMH benefits to thousands of employees and millions of patients are attributed to PCMHs in private practices, community health centers, hospital ambulatory care networks, and independent physician associations. In the public sector, millions are receiving patient-centered primary care through 44 state Medicaid programs, the federal employee health plan and the U.S. military and Veterans Administration.[18]

The ACA included many provisions to support primary care and development of the PCMH model. These provisions may be categorized under the broad headings of expanded Medicaid coverage eligibility, new Medicaid and Medicare payment enhancements, primary care payment reforms initiatives, and workforce development.[19] Five years following its implementation, there are notable developments in primary care funded by the ACA, examples of which are outlined below.

First, the 31 states and District of Columbia, which expanded Medicaid eligibility under the ACA, succeeded in enrolling more than 6 million previously uninsured individuals, thereby creating new access to services.[20]

Second, the ACA required, and provided full funding for, all state Medicaid programs to pay primary care physicians and certain other physicians providing primary care services at Medicare rates (an average 73 percent increase) for the years 2013 and 2014.[21] A study in 10 states reported that "available primary care appointments rose by nearly 8 percent among providers already accepting Medicaid patients, as compared with an increase of only approximately 1 percent among privately insured patients."[22] Fifteen states opted to continue the payment increase with state funds in 2015; 23 states and the District of Columbia opted to revert to pre-ACA rates; and 12 states did not decide.[22] Future study and comparisons of results from states' decisions about payment increases will be needed to inform federal and state policymaking.

Third, through the Primary Care Incentive Payment Program, the ACA provided a 10 percent Medicare payment bonus from 2011 to 2015 for physicians, nurse practitioners, clinical nurse specialists, and physician assistants for whom primary care services account for at least 60 percent of their Medicare charges.[23,24] The Medicare Payment Advisory Commission recommended continuation of additional payments to primary care physicians for 2016 in the form of a per-beneficiary payment to encourage continued movement away from the fee-for-service, volume-driven payment system.[25] The recommendation awaits Congressional action.

Fourth, other initiatives using alternative payment models (APMs) with incentives as the centerpiece increased from 26 in 2009 (prior to ACA passage) to 114 in 2013; patients covered by initiatives increased from almost 5 million to nearly 21 million in the same period.[26] The Center for Medicare and Medicaid Innovation (CMMI) is engaged in projects to test innovative payment and service delivery models to reduce expenditures and enhance quality of care.[27] One such CMMI project is the Multi-payer Advanced Primary Care Practice Demonstration (MAPCP) launched in 2011 as a state-led multi-payer collaboration to help primary care practices transform into medical homes. Through MAPCP, Medicare participates in eight existing state multi-payer health reform initiatives that include both Medicaid and private payers. The program pays a monthly care management fee for beneficiaries served by advanced primary care practices to cover costs of care coordination, improved access, patient education, and other services that support chronically ill patients. By the end of the demonstration program in 2015, approximately 1,200 PCMHs serving more than 900,000 Medicare beneficiaries were expected to be participating.[28] Another CMMI project is the Comprehensive Primary Care (CPC) Initiative, a multi-payer initiative begun in 2012 to foster collaboration between public and private healthcare payers to strengthen primary care.[29] Under the CPC's State Innovation Models (SIM) Initiative, the Centers for Medicare and Medicaid Services (CMS) awarded nearly $300 million to 25 states to design or test innovative healthcare payment and service delivery models.[30]

The CPC identified five comprehensive primary care functions aligned with ACA goals to reward value and care coordination rather than volume and to offer population-based care management fees and shared savings opportunities to participating primary care practices:

1. Risk-stratified case management to customize care plans according to level of patient needs
2. Access and continuity of care
3. Planned care for chronic conditions and preventive care
4. Patient and caregiver engagement
5. Coordination of care across the medical neighborhood[31]

To help participating practices achieve these functions, CPC offers three main supports: enhanced payment, data feedback, and learning activities and technical assistance.[31] By 2015, the CPC had engaged 38 public and private payers and almost 2,200 providers serving approximately 2.7 million patients, including an estimated 410,000 Medicare and Medicaid beneficiaries at 474 practice sites.[32] In its second, four-year round of funding commencing in 2014, the CMS awarded more than $660 million for 28 states, three territories, and the District of Columbia to continue designing and testing healthcare payment and service delivery models that improve healthcare system performance.[33] Though requiring time and effort to implement, preliminary evaluations of multi-payer arrangements including the MAPCP demonstration and the CPC initiative indicate the healthcare providers and payers are finding participation worthwhile.[13]

Fifth, in the realm of primary care workforce development, the ACA has succeeded in the early stages of implementing ACA budget-authorized primary care objectives. President Obama's 2016 fiscal year budget invests $14.6 billion through three initiatives.[34] The first allocates $4 billion for the National Health Service Corps in fiscal years 2015–2020 to support 15,000 providers with scholarships and loan repayments in exchange for commitment to work in medically underserved areas. The second targets the Graduate Medical Education (GME) program with $5.2 billion to support training for 13,000 medical residents over 10 years. The third initiative provides $5.4 billion for increased reimbursements for Medicaid primary care.[34]

Recognizing that 55 percent of all medical office visits are for primary care and that only 4–7 percent of healthcare dollars are spent on primary care, experts agree that to successfully promote adoption and sustainability of the PCMH model, the fee-for-service payment model must be changed and new payment models must provide support for required practice infrastructure enhancements as well as incentives for PCMH participation.[13] In addition to providing financial support, initiatives and demonstrations have major goals of reducing the administrative burdens of performance and quality monitoring and reporting for primary care practices which are widely viewed as significant barriers to PCMH implementation.[13] The need to consolidate reporting requirements is identified by many research studies and highlighted by a study of 23 health plans covering 121 million commercial enrollees which identified 546 distinct performance measures among plans and widespread variations in both public and private programs.[35]

Catalyzed by the ACA's directions toward implementing a value-driven system, and recognizing the vast, unaligned and burdensome array of quality measurement and reporting required by the fractured payment and delivery systems, the Core Quality Measures Collaborative was established in 2015. Comprised of the CMS, America's Health Plans, the National Quality Forum, and a select group of health professionals, its purpose is "to build the kind of quality measurement that includes manageable reporting requirements for providers, alignment by reporting entities, and a focus on health outcomes that are more meaningful to consumers, providers, and payers than many process-based measures."[36] In 2016, CMS released seven core measure sets for use across commercial and government payers to reduce the quality measures reporting burden for physician practices and offer consumers information that can be used in decision-making.[37] Also in 2015, the Medicare Access and CHIP (Children's Health Insurance Program) Reauthorization Act (MACRA) was signed into law. In addition to major additional reforms for Medicare and Medicaid payment that are outlined in other chapters of this text, the MACRA will have critical impacts on primary care. Beginning in 2015, the MACRA shifts Medicare clinical reimbursement to value-based payments over the period until 2019 and beyond, with two innovative payment pathways for PCMHs, the Merit-Based Incentive Payment System (MIPS) and APMs.[38] The new payment pathways streamline previously separate multiple and disparate quality-reporting requirements into a single program and provide new financial incentives to reward healthcare providers for achieving higher quality in patient outcomes.[39]

There is much still to be learned about the challenges of PCMHs achieving intended reductions in cost and improvements in quality. Continuing research abounds on various dimensions of PCMHs, with mixed results.[40,41] A growing body of scientific evidence is demonstrating that PCMHs are saving resources by reducing hospital and emergency department visits, attenuating health disparities and improving patient outcomes.[13,42] However, research findings also point out continuing challenges. For example, patient engagement in quality improvement is a critical component of the PCMH. A survey of 112 PCMH practices in 22 states reported that fewer than one-third of PCMH practices actually engage patients in quality improvement efforts.[40] Also, experts studying the transition of primary care practices to the PCMH model report many inherent challenges, in addition to implementing supportive payment reforms.[41] The National Committee for Quality Assurance (NCQA), which provides the most widely adopted educational programs for transforming primary care practices into PCMHs and grants formal recognition to almost 7,000 PCMHs and 35,000 clinicians, notes that providers attempting transformation to the PCMH model may experience steep learning curves or may not have the capabilities, commitment, and resources to sustain transformation.[43,44] The NCQA further notes that, "practices may face technological or legal challenges with electronic access privacy and liability" and challenges in building the required coordination with an array of other community-based resources.[43] A Commonwealth Fund report notes, "To become a PCMH, most practice organizations must undergo wrenching cultural and system changes."[45] Researchers reporting on a nation-wide survey of PCMH initiatives find, "it is likely that changing practice behavior and culture will take substantial effort and time."[26] Regarding the future of the PCMH, authors of a report on 14 AHRQ grants on primary care practice transformation observed, "Looking toward the future, transformation is not optional. The transformation of primary care is essential to achieving the triple aim of better outcomes, better value, and better experience of care."[41]

Accountable Care Organizations

The ACA adopted the ACO model, which is a group of providers and suppliers involved in patient care that work together to coordinate care for the patients they serve under the traditional Medicare fee-for-service program.[46] Primary care is considered the cornerstone of the ACO model and ideally, PCMHs will be the primary care component of ACOs for the Medicare population. Like PCMHs, ACOs are designed to ensure care coordination so that all patients receive timely and appropriate care and avoid unnecessary duplication of services, medical emergencies, and hospitalizations. An ACO may include the following types of provider groups and suppliers of Medicare-covered services:[46]

- ACO professionals, including physicians and hospitals in group practice arrangements
- Networks of individual practices of ACO professionals
- Partnerships or joint venture arrangements between hospitals and ACO professionals or hospitals employing ACO professionals
- Other Medicare providers and suppliers as approved by U.S. Department of Health and Human Services

Each ACO must be a legally constituted entity within its state with a governing board that includes service providers, suppliers, and Medicare beneficiaries. Each one must take responsibility for at least 5,000 Medicare beneficiaries for a period of three years.[46] To qualify for participation, ACOs must meet Medicare-established quality measures of care appropriateness, coordination, timeliness, and safety.[46] Provider participation in an ACO is voluntary, and Medicare recipients participating in ACOs are not restricted from using physicians outside their ACO.[46]

The ACA provides a payment structure for ACOs that combines fee-for-service payments with shared savings and bonus payments linked with specific quality performance standards for which all providers in an ACO are accountable.[47] Like the payment structure for PCMHs, the ACOs shift fee-for-service interventions toward financial rewards for maintaining patients' health. In 2016, CMS reported that 477 shared savings ACOs were serving 8.9 million Medicare fee-for-service beneficiaries.[48] In 2016 CMS also launched a new ACO model, the "Next Generation ACO" (NGACO), which includes 21 organizations experienced with care coordination through current and prior ACO initiatives and whose providers are prepared to assume greater financial risks in exchange for higher financial rewards.[48] In launching the NGACO, CMS noted that the new model is in accordance with the goal of tying 30 percent of fee-for-service Medicare payments to APMs such as ACOs by the end of 2016, and tying 50 percent of such payments to these models by the end of 2018.[48]

▶ Other Ambulatory Care Practitioners

In addition to physicians, a number of other licensed healthcare professionals conduct practices in ambulatory settings. Among the most common are dentists, podiatrists, social workers, psychologists, physical therapists, and optometrists. Like physicians, they may practice singly or in single-specialty or multi-specialty groups. For example, there are general solo-practice dentists and multi-specialty dental groups that provide general preventive and curative services, as well as services in specialties such as periodontics and orthodontics. Likewise, psychologists in a group may include both generalists and specialists in forensic, child, and other types of psychological interventions.

▶ Ambulatory Care Services of Hospitals: History and Trends

Acute-care not-for-profit hospitals have operated outpatient clinics since the 1800s. The early ones were located predominantly in urban centers whose indigent populations lacked access to private medical care. At that time, the provision of outpatient services was largely a function of government-sponsored public hospitals. With the proliferation of the not-for-profit hospitals beginning in the early 1900s, outpatient clinics provided a means for those hospitals to fulfill part of their charitable mission by serving low-income populations who had little, if any, access to private physicians. Hospital outpatient clinics also provided a teaching setting for university-affiliated hospitals, which trained physicians as part of their community mission. Because hospital outpatient clinics served needy populations, they were a low-status component of the hospital and were characterized as the "stepchild of the institution."[49] Often, medical students and hospital-affiliated physicians of lowest rank agreed to staff the clinics in return for earning hospital admitting privileges.

Today, hospital outpatient clinics still function as community safety nets for needy populations; however, the status of those clinics is vastly different from their historical predecessors. Far from the "stepchild" image, hospitals now view outpatient clinical services as providing a channel for inpatient admissions and major revenue sources from the use of hospital ancillary services.

Today's hospital outpatient clinics are organized along the lines of private physician group practices and are aesthetically pleasant, well equipped, and customer oriented. Trends in treatment in the hospital outpatient setting as contrasted with inpatient care are clear. With respect to the hospitals' financial picture, in 1990 outpatient services revenue constituted 23 percent of total U.S. voluntary hospital revenues.[50] This figure has continued to rise over succeeding decades, with the outpatient share of total hospital revenue reaching 45 percent in 2013.[51] Hospital admissions began declining in 2005 with a steady decline noted through 2013 and projected to continue in 2014.[52,53] In contrast, during the period 2005–2012, hospital outpatient visits, including visits to the emergency department, rose steadily, increasing by 15 percent.[52]

Because hospital outpatient services were designed to provide teaching and research opportunities, they have been organized along the lines of human organ systems and the diseases affecting them. For example, medical clinics, in addition to general medicine, might include clinics for dermatology (skin), cardiology (heart), gastroenterology (digestive tract), rheumatology (bone and connective tissue), and other specialties. In addition to general surgery, surgical clinics might include specialties such as orthopedics, obstetrics and gynecology, and others. This type of organizational structure allowed focus on particular patient complaints and illnesses. Beyond this benefit, however, the complex interactions among physicians and patients inherent in this anatomic organization of services have both positive and negative implications for both.

For patients, specialty clinics provide a focused approach to diagnosis and treatment by physicians with special training in their particular conditions. Also, medical teaching responsibilities in clinics often result in thorough patient examination, diagnostic work-ups and case review for the healthcare students' benefit, which might not otherwise occur in a nonteaching setting.

Hospital-based specialty clinics also have drawbacks for patients. Often, specialty clinics treat patients only on certain days each week or month. Patients with multiple conditions may have to visit several specialty clinics, necessitating return visits during which a number of different physicians examine them. Because communication among physicians in different specialty clinics can be problematic, patients may receive conflicting advice or instruction, may be medicated inappropriately with drugs prescribed by several different specialists, or may "fall through the cracks" when a complaint arises that does not fit the specialty area of one of their providers. Similarly for the physician, this type of categorical treatment environment requires a high degree of initiative to maintain accurate, current information on patients treated by multiple specialists. Such communication challenges among clinical settings are ripe for the implementation of PCMHs.

Beginning in the early 1980s, several influences began to have an impact on how hospital outpatient clinic services were organized and delivered. One major influence was the adoption of prospective hospital reimbursement, which emphasized decreased lengths of stay and reduced inpatient revenues. Another major factor was the influence of managed care and its emphasis on the role of primary medical care.

Facing declining inpatient revenue, increasing fiscal pressures, and emphasis on primary medicine, hospitals reorganized and expanded outpatient services that focused heavily on primary care. Teaching hospitals planned jointly with their affiliated medical schools, and nonteaching facilities followed suit to expand the array of outpatient services with primary care as the core. Teaching hospitals also created primary care centers under the direction of paid, full-time faculty department heads with administrative, clinical, and teaching responsibilities. Primary care physician employees were organized into group models along the lines of private group practices. This primary care model provided a rational structure for the general medical care of clinic patients and helped ensure appropriate referrals and coordination of patient care within and among outpatient clinic specialty units.

The group model of primary care also supported hospitals' teaching mission by alleviating reliance on voluntary physician staffing of clinic sessions and student supervision responsibilities. Medical students and medical residents were provided a more supportive and consistent learning environment by continuously interacting with members of the practice group instead of interacting with different mentors over the course of their rotations. Patients benefited from improved coordination of their care and the opportunity to develop relationships with attending physicians. Developments in the organization of primary care in hospital-based clinics have made a major contribution to the coordination and appropriate delivery of health care to consumers of hospital-based outpatient clinic services.

Trends in the volume of hospital outpatient clinic caseloads and payment sources will be subjects of great interest as hospital markets continue consolidating and the ACA continues implementation over the next years. Now, more than 20 percent of hospitals are participating in PCMH projects.[53] Outcomes of these PCMH projects and the experience gained likely will contribute to future policy decisions regarding costs and improvements in the quality of care.

▶ Hospital Emergency Services

In 2011, U.S. hospitals operated 4,461 hospital emergency departments (EDs), 189 fewer than in 2000.[54] However, during the same period, annual emergency department visits increased 26.2 percent, from 108 million to 136.3 million.[55] The increase in ED visits is attributed to overall population growth, increase in illness-related diagnoses, and lack of private health insurance. The uninsured and Medicaid patients demonstrated the greatest increase in rates of ED use as compared with privately insured patients.[56]

According to the 2011 National Ambulatory Medical Care Survey, 15.7 percent of patients arrived at the ED via ambulance and 16.2 million ED visits, or 11.9 percent, resulted in hospitalization.[57,58] In 2011, more than five times as many individuals who visited the ED were discharged as were admitted to the same hospital.[59] Infants under 1 year of age and adults aged 85 years and older had the highest rates of ED visits. The older adults were far more likely to be admitted to the same hospital in which they visited the ED.[59]

Of expected sources of payment for ED visits in 2011, private insurance accounted for 34.9 percent, Medicaid or Children's Health Insurance Program for 31.8 percent, and Medicare for 18.4 percent. Uninsured patients accounted for 16 percent. (This combined total exceeds 100 percent because more than one source of payment may be reported per visit.[60]) EDs are the primary portal of entry for hospital admission for uninsured and publicly insured patients.[59]

In the past, like other teaching hospital outpatient clinics, the ED was a place of indenture for medical students or medical residents who were required to provide coverage as a component of their training. Often, to earn extra income, medical residents would contract to "moonlight" extra hours for their assigned hospital or for other hospital EDs. Nonteaching hospitals also often hired medical residents on a contracted basis to cover the ED or required attending staff to provide rotating coverage. These staffing configurations were less than ideal. Physicians working in EDs often had little training or experience with the illnesses and injuries encountered there and this haphazard ED staffing was abandoned by the mid-1980s. Expanded knowledge, techniques, and equipment available for the care of critically ill and injured patients and concerns about liability resulted in dramatic changes in how EDs are staffed and organized. Since 1979, emergency medicine has been recognized as a medical specialty with accompanying requirements for extended specialty training and experience to attain board certification, as in the other medical specialty fields.[61] Now, EDs are staffed by physicians qualified by training and experience in emergency medicine. Many corporations employ groups of board-qualified or board-certified emergency medicine physicians and contract their services to hospitals. Medical schools with accredited training programs in emergency medicine may staff their affiliated hospitals' EDs as a faculty practice group, providing clinical training for emergency department medical residents.

ED staff includes nurses with advanced education and training in the triage and care of critically ill or injured patients. It also includes an array of other personnel who provide medical and nursing assistance and clerical support. Depending on the needs of the population served by the hospital, ED staff also may include mental health professionals and social workers. On-call arrangements with hospital medical staff of other departments or with contracted professionals assist ED staff to meet patient needs.

Although designed to care for life-threatening illness or injury, the public looks to EDs for medical care that ranges from critically urgent to routine and reasons for ED visits encompass a broad spectrum. Because state and federal regulations require that hospitals turn no one away from an ED without an appropriate medical assessment, patients have learned that EDs are a guaranteed source of care regardless of their ability to pay or the nature of their complaint. EDs use a standardized system for evaluating patient condition upon ED arrival to determine the time frame in which patients require intervention. This Emergency Severity Index (ESI) includes five levels: (1) immediate, (2) emergent (1–14 minutes), (3) urgent (15–60 minutes), (4) semi-urgent (1–2 hours), (5) non-urgent (2–24 hours).[62] In 2011, 8 percent of ED visits, equating to more than 10 million visits, were deemed to be non-urgent, and therefore not requiring emergency intervention[63] (see **FIGURE 5-3**).

One contributing factor to inappropriate ED use is patients' self-interpretation of symptoms. Also, when physicians receive calls regarding potentially serious complaints, and it is neither practical nor appropriate for the patient to be evaluated in the private office, physicians may direct patients to the ED for immediate care. Physicians also may use the EDs to perform certain tests or examinations requiring equipment not available in their offices.

EDs are organized to treat episodes of serious illness and injury and therefore are not a good choice for routine care. First, care is much more expensive than in an appropriate ambulatory setting because it consumes the time of specialist personnel for conditions in which that level of personnel is unnecessary. Second, waiting times are often long because life-threatening cases appropriately have priority. Third, the ED, by its nature, is not organized or staffed to provide follow-up care. To facilitate follow-up care, ED staff often refers patients to ambulatory care services.

Increased ED use coupled with ED closures has resulted in a phenomenon called "ED crowding." Decades-long reports have cited the ongoing need to divert ambulances to alternative EDs because of immediate lack of capacity.[64,65] A solution to crowding has gained traction

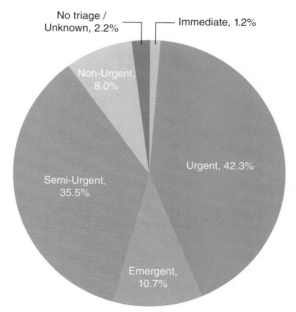

FIGURE 5-3 **Triage Status of Emergency Department Visits, United States, 2011**

Data from CDC/NCHS National Hospital Ambulatory Medical Care Survey: 2011.

among hospital EDs in the form of clinical observation units (COUs). Established as dedicated locations adjacent to hospital EDs or as beds located in other areas of the hospital, COUs use a period of 6–24 hours to triage, diagnose, treat, and monitor patient responses while common complaints such as chest pain, abdominal pain, cardiac arrhythmias, and congestive heart failure are assessed.[66] After the assessment period, a determination is made whether to discharge or admit the patient to the hospital.[67] COUs enable ED staff to move patients out of the immediate ED triage queue, thus decreasing ED stress.[66] The use of COUs is endorsed by the American College of Emergency Physicians, the Society of Hospital Medicine, and other professional organizations as a means to prevent unnecessary hospitalization, increase hospital revenue, and promote patient safety, among other benefits.[67]

Despite the well-documented recognition that inappropriate ED use drives up costs and lacks continuity of care, individuals without resources or who may be unaware of other sources of care find the ED their most accessible choice. Even for individuals with a usual source of primary care, lack of provider availability outside normal business hours contributes to ED use for non-urgent conditions.[68] In accordance with the ACA goal of improving access to primary care, recent research evidence suggests that extended-hours access such as that required in the PCMH model can help to reduce unnecessary ED use and hospitalizations.[68,69] Such findings are adding strength to the rationale for continued robust support for primary care practices' pivotal role in meeting the population's basic needs.

▶ Non-hospital-Based (Freestanding) Facilities

Non-hospital-based or freestanding ambulatory care facilities may be owned and operated by hospitals, hospital systems or physician groups, or independent for-profit or not-for-profit single entities or corporate chains. Many hospital systems, independent entities, and chains operate multiple ambulatory care facilities that provide a wide array of services, including ambulatory surgery, occupational health services, physical rehabilitation, substance abuse treatment, renal dialysis, cancer treatment, diagnostic imaging, cardiovascular diagnosis, sports medicine, and urgent/emergent care. Technology advances, entrepreneurial business opportunities, cost-reduction initiatives, and consumer preferences for convenient services continue to advance freestanding services as major components of the healthcare delivery system.

The following provides an overview of the major types of freestanding facilities that play roles in the rapid expansion of ambulatory care services.

Urgent Care Centers

The first urgent care centers opened in the 1970s. The Urgent Care Association of America (UCAOA) describes urgent care as "health care provided on a walk-in, no-appointment basis for acute illness or injury that is not life or limb threatening, and is either beyond the scope or availability of the typical primary care practice or retail clinic."[70] Some urgent care centers also provide other health services such as occupational medicine, travel medicine, and sports and school physicals.[70] In most states, urgent care centers do not require licensure separate from that of a typical physician office that operates under the physician's license.[71]

A UCAOA 2015 survey estimates that there are more than 7,100 U.S. urgent care centers, providing an average of nearly 14,000 annual visits per center.[72,73] As **FIGURE 5-4** depicts, ownership is diverse, including hospitals, physician groups, corporate entities, and others.[73]

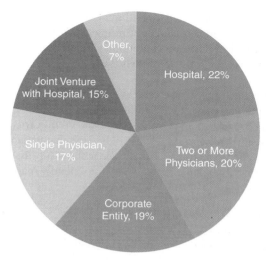

FIGURE 5-4 **Ownership of Urgent Care Centers**

Data from Urgent Care Association of America, "Benchmarking Survey Headlines Summary." Available from http://c.ymcdn.com/sites/www.ucaoa.org/resource/resmgr/Infographics/2015_BM_Survey_Headlines_Sum.pdf.

Operating with extended hours including evenings, weekends, and holidays, and accepting patients on a walk-in basis, urgent care centers are filling gaps in the delivery system created by the inflexibility of private physician appointment scheduling and unavailability during nonbusiness hours. This convenience factor is highlighted by the report that two-thirds of urgent care patients have a regular primary care physician.[73] Urgent care centers provide user-friendly alternatives to the chaotic environment and long waiting times of hospital EDs. In the UCAOA 2015 survey noted above, 90 percent of patients experienced a waiting time of 30 minutes or less, with their entire care episode completed in 60 minutes or less.[73] Typically located in highly visible facilities such as storefronts in commercial areas, urgent care centers offer convenience and ease of accessibility to their consumers, and their numbers are increasing.[73] Because they are a less-expensive alternative to the hospital ED, health plans usually fully reimburse members' use of urgent care facilities when their physicians are not available. Costs for patients and insurers are also a major factor in urgent care center popularity. The 2015 UCAOA survey places the average cost of an urgent care visit at $150 versus the average cost of an ED visit at $1,354.[74] The cost differential is significant as increasing numbers of Americans subscribe to high-deductible health plans in which they pay out-of-pocket charges until an annual spending threshold is met.

Most urgent care centers emphasize that they do not provide ongoing care for chronic conditions, although they may be the site where a chronic condition such as diabetes or hypertension is initially diagnosed. If patients lack a routine source of care, staff may encourage patients to establish a relationship with a primary doctor and may provide information about physicians or primary care centers that are accepting new patients to encourage continuity.

Urgent care physicians are typically specialists in internal, family, or emergency medicine. Established in 1997, the American Board of Urgent Care Medicine offers certification in the field of urgent care medicine to qualified candidates who have successfully completed an Accreditation Council for Graduate Medical Education residency in emergency medicine, family practice, general surgery, internal medicine, obstetrics and gynecology, or pediatrics; meet several other requirements for experience in the field and continuing medical education; and pass a certification examination.[75] Individual urgent care centers may be granted certification by the UCAOA upon meeting specific criteria for staffing models, facility equipment, hours of operation, and other requirements.[76]

In addition to physicians, urgent care centers may employ registered nurses, nurse practitioners, physician assistants, and may provide radiology and basic laboratory services. Acceptable payment typically includes all forms of insurance, cash, and credit cards.

The emergence of urgent care centers is a clear indication that patients perceive them as a positive alternative to the hospital ED, and for individuals without a primary physician's availability, meet nonemergency needs in a convenient and consumer-friendly manner.

Retail Clinics

Retail clinics, operated at retail sites such as pharmacies and supermarkets, are a growing form of ambulatory care. The first retail clinics opened in 2000 in the Minneapolis–St. Paul area in grocery stores.[77] Expanding from approximately 300 retail clinic sites in 2007, current projections estimate that the number of retail clinic sites will grow to 2,400 in 2016, with a 14 percent growth annually through 2017.[78] Total annual patient visits to retail clinics have reached 10.5 million.[79] Clinics operate in 41 states and the District of Columbia,[80] and typically are located in brand name retailers such as pharmacies, grocery and "big box" stores[79] such as CVS pharmacies, Walgreens, Wal-Mart, and Target stores. Most retail clinics are owned by pharmacies and big box retailers.[79] Known by consumer-friendly names, such as "MinuteClinic" and "TakeCare," the clinics represent an entrepreneurial response to patient demand for fast, affordable treatment of easy-to-diagnose conditions. Staffed by nurse practitioners or physician assistants, a physician is not required on-site, although many clinics have physician consultation available by phone. Most clinics accept Medicare, Medicaid, private insurance, and Worker's Compensation insurance.[79] In 2015, 80 percent of visits to clinics within CVS and Walgreens were covered by insurance.[81] There is no federal regulation of retail clinics, and pertinent state legislation has been very limited, affecting clinics in fewer than 10 states.[80,82]

In the reforming healthcare delivery system, proliferation of these clinics has captured the attention of both health systems and payers. First, the cost of care initiated at retail clinics is significantly lower than physician offices, urgent care centers, and EDs. Second, the wide geographic coverage of retail sites and convenient hours of operation have made retail clinics attractive to health systems. For health systems, retail clinic locations expand market reach into new areas, expand the primary care network to new populations, and reduce unnecessary ED visits.[79] More than 100 partnerships between retail clinics and health systems have been established.[79] Payers are integrating retail clinics into their networks to reduce costs. For example, Blue Cross Blue Shield of Minnesota has developed an "aligned incentive" ACO that now accounts for 40 percent of its network spending. This ACO-like product developed with Allina Health Network "wraps" the health network with other providers, including retail clinics.[79]

Reactions to retail clinics from the organized medical community vary from acceptance as a patient choice to opposition. Primary care physicians have many concerns about quality and continuity of care and competition. The AAFP has the retail clinic phenomenon under continuing study. In 2013 it issued a policy affirming its belief that the PCMH is best suited to improving the quality of care. In this policy, the AAFP opposed expansion of retail clinic services beyond minor acute illness and chronic medical conditions and agreed that retail clinics can be a component of patient-centered care while coordinating with primary care physicians to avoid fragmentation.[83] In a 2015 position paper, the American College of Physicians issued recommendations addressing retail clinic expansion noting that, "retail health clinics should serve as an episodic alternative to care from an established primary care practice for relatively healthy patients without complex medical histories."[84] Upon release of the recommendations, the ACP President acknowledged, "Health care delivery models are changing and our patients are embracing and exploring alternatives to the traditional office practice."[84]

As retail clinics continue proliferating, more research is required to learn about how these entities will fit into the reformed delivery system. This growing ambulatory care enterprise is under close observation by employers, insurers, retailers, investors, and the medical and consumer communities. It is clear that retail clinics are established in the mainstream of primary healthcare delivery and will likely continue to be an important component of future primary care delivery systems.

Ambulatory Surgery Centers

The NCHS defines ambulatory surgery as "surgical and nonsurgical procedures performed on an ambulatory (outpatient) basis in a hospital or freestanding center's general operating rooms, dedicated ambulatory surgery rooms, and other specialized rooms such as endoscopy units and cardiac catheterization labs."[85] Federal tracking and reporting on ambulatory surgery through the National Survey of Ambulatory Surgery was first conducted from 1994 to 1996, but discontinued due to lack of resources. After a 10-year hiatus, it was conducted again in 2006, with plans reported in 2015 to include this survey in the National Hospital Ambulatory Medical Care Survey in the future.[86] Therefore, where applicable, ambulatory surgery data is gleaned from other most-recent available sources.

Ambulatory or outpatient surgery accounted for more than 64.5 percent of all surgeries performed in hospitals in 2012.[87] Since the 1990s the total number of ambulatory surgery centers (ASCs) including hospital and non-hospital based, has more than doubled.[88] Now, there are more than 6,000 ASCs operating in the United States, of which 5,344 are Medicare-certified.[89] Between 2000 and 2007 the number of Medicare-certified ASCs increased at an average annual rate of 7.3 percent.[90] Since 2007 the growth rate has slowed to an annual average of 2.6 percent.[89] Ninety-seven percent of ASCs operate as for-profit entities and 91 percent are located in urban settings.[89] Approximately 22.3 percent of ASCs are owned or managed by an ASC management and development company.[89] Physicians have ownership interest in 90 percent of ASCs, hospitals have ownership interest in 21 percent, and 3 percent are owned entirely by hospitals.[91]

In the 1970s, physicians led the development of ASCs because they saw opportunities to establish high-quality and cost-effective alternatives to inpatient surgery. ASCs were physicians' solutions to frustration with hospital bureaucracy, operating room schedule difficulties, and patient inconvenience. ASCs provided physicians with a high degree of professional autonomy in procedure scheduling and in selecting staff, equipment, and facilities best suited to their specialties and patient needs and preferences.[91]

Advancements in medical technology and changes in reimbursement criteria were the two primary drivers for ambulatory surgical procedures as alternatives to inpatient surgery. One of the most significant factors was advancements in anesthesia that resolved safely and quickly.[91] Advancements in surgical equipment and techniques reduced or eliminated the invasiveness of many procedures and their complications and risks. With these and other technological advances making outpatient surgery safe, mounting financial pressures resulted in Medicare and private insurers requiring that certain procedures be performed in the less costly ambulatory setting unless physicians were able to document the necessity of hospitalization. The initial years of the shift from inpatient to ambulatory surgery provided opportunities for hospitals to convert underused inpatient space into efficient, cost-effective care delivery areas, encouraging the development of separate surgical management systems for ambulatory and complicated cases. At the same time well-managed ASCs quickly became profitable.

Hospitals responded to the demand for ambulatory surgery as they faced competition from newly formed physician-directed freestanding facilities and insurer demands for lower costs. In 1982, Medicare expanded coverage to include ambulatory surgical procedures and between 1982 and 1992, outpatient surgeries in community hospitals increased by more than 200 percent, while inpatient surgical procedures declined by more than 32 percent.[88,92]

ASCs are among the most highly regulated healthcare entities. Forty-three states and the District of Columbia require licensure of ASCs; the remaining seven states have some form of regulatory requirement.[91] All ASCs qualifying for Medicare reimbursement must undergo a process entailing compliance with federal standards on staff qualifications, safety, equipment, and management.[91] Many ASCs also voluntarily submit to accreditation reviews by The Joint Commission, the Accreditation Association for Ambulatory Health Care, the American Association for the Accreditation of Ambulatory Surgery Facilities, or the American Osteopathic Association.[91] Beginning in 2015, ASCs serving Medicare beneficiaries will participate in a new CMS ASC Quality Reporting Program. ASCs failing to submit required data or to meet established quality criteria may receive a 2 percent reduction in subsequent years' payment update.[93]

Quality and the patient care experience have benefited significantly from improved technology applied in the ambulatory setting. Patients experience fewer complications, much faster recovery, and less disruption to normal activity than from inpatient surgery. Continuing advances in surgical procedures and anesthetic agents, postoperative management, and other evolving technology provide future opportunities to move even more types of inpatient surgery into the ambulatory setting. Patients view ASC facilities as user friendly and responsive to their needs with 92 percent reporting a high degree of satisfaction.[91]

Federally Qualified Health Centers

Federally qualified health centers (FQHCs) originated during Lyndon Johnson's presidency in the mid-1960s and represented a facet of that administration's social reform movement labeled the "war on poverty." Originally authorized by the Office of Economic Opportunity, the Public Health Service assumed coordinating responsibility in the mid-1970s. Funded under Section 330 of the Public Health Service Act, these centers were established in urban and rural communities with common characteristics rooted in federal funding requirements, including focus on needs of the underserved, comprehensive primary care, professional staffing, community involvement, and partnerships between the public and private sectors.[94] Subsequent amendments to Section 330 established specialized primary care programs for migrant farm workers, the homeless, and residents of public housing.[94]

FQHCs may be organized under the aegis of local health departments (LHDs) as part of larger not-for-profit human service organizations or as stand-alone, not-for-profit corporations. All FQHCs must comply with federal requirements to:[94]

■   Serve a medically underserved population
■   Provide appropriate and necessary services with fees adjusted on patients' ability to pay

- Demonstrate sound clinical and financial management
- Be governed by a board, a majority of which includes health center patients

The FQHC model emphasizes coordinated and comprehensive care and reductions in health disparities for low income individuals, racial and ethnic minorities, rural communities, and other underserved populations.[95] Reflecting these emphases, FQHCs are staffed by multi-disciplinary teams that include physicians, nurse practitioners, physician assistants, nurses, dental providers, midwives, behavioral healthcare providers, social workers, health educators, and many others.[95] This team approach assists patients to overcome geographic, cultural, linguistic, and other barriers and assists patients in linking with other supportive programs and services.[95] FQHCs are required to provide a full range of primary care and preventive services in the fields of family medicine, internal medicine, pediatrics, obstetrics and gynecology, and dentistry including screenings, laboratory testing, and radiology, and where appropriate, pharmacy services.[96] As population needs dictate, centers also may provide transportation, language translation, and health education services. Currently, 98 percent of FQHCs use electronic health records, a 51 percent growth in the use of electronic health records since 2010.[97] Two-thirds of FQHCs have earned designation as PCMHs.[98]

FQHC grants are administered by the Health Resources and Services Administration (HRSA) of the U.S. Department of Health and Human Services. Fees for services are based on income, and services are offered without charge for the neediest patients; no patient may be denied services due to inability to pay.[98] The FQHC program has grown substantially over the years, and in 2014 nearly 1,300 centers operate 9,000 delivery sites providing care to nearly 22.8 million patients in every state, the District of Columbia, Puerto Rico, U.S. Virgin Islands, and the Pacific Basin.[95] Fifty percent of patients are members of ethnic and minority groups; 28 percent lack health insurance; 47 percent depend on Medicaid; and 31 percent are children.[95,99] **FIGURE 5-5** illustrates the insurance status of FQHC patients.[100]

Since 2009, FQHCs have increased the number of patients served by nearly 6 million and now 1 out of every 14 U.S. citizens relies on a HRSA-funded clinic for primary care.[95]

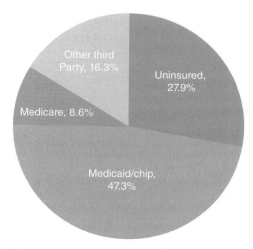

FIGURE 5-5 **Health Center Patients by Insurance Status, 2014**

Data from Health Resources & Services Administration. Retrieved from: bpch.hrsa.gov./uds/datacenter.aspx

The pivotal role of FQHCs in meeting healthcare needs of America's most vulnerable and underserved citizens received significant support during President Obama's administration. In 2009 the administration earmarked $600 million in the ARRA to support major construction and renovation projects at 85 FQHCs in 30 states and to support their adoption of electronic health records and other health information technology systems.[101]

In 2010, the ACA established the Community Health Center Fund providing $11 billion over a five-year period that included:[95]

- $9.5 billion to:
  - Support ongoing health center operations
  - Create new health center sites in medically underserved areas
  - Expand preventive and primary healthcare services, including oral health, behavioral health, pharmacy, and/or enabling services, at existing health center sites
- $1.5 billion to support major expansion, renovation, and construction of new FQHC sites

In 2015 through the ACA, the HRSA Health Center Program awarded the following:[95]

- $271 million to establish approximately 430 new FQHC sites
- $36.3 million to 1,113 FQHCs to recognize quality-improvement activities
- $51.3 million to support 210 FQHCs to establish or expand behavioral health services
- $6.4 million to hire outreach and eligibility assistance workers to assist people with enrollment for affordable health coverage
- $100 million commencing in 2016 to support 310 health centers to improve and expand delivery of substance abuse services

In 2011 under a provision of the ACA, CMS launched a three-year pilot program to test the development of the PCMH model for FQHC Medicare beneficiaries.[102,103] Conducted at 434 FQHCs, the demonstration project provided financial incentives to support the FQHCs in adopting care coordination practices recognized by the NCQA.[103] The demonstration project concluded in 2014. Issued in 2015, the second of three evaluation reports on this demonstration project noted, "In fact, despite substantial growth in the number of practices pursuing APC attributes and the support being offered to them, evidence supporting the effectiveness of PCMH transformation in improving both quality and cost/utilization outcomes has been mixed."[104] The evaluation report cited the need for more data analysis and application of additional methods to identify elements of the demonstration that are associated with process and outcomes improvements.[104]

Public Health Ambulatory Services

The delivery of ambulatory health services by state, county, or municipally supported governmental entities has its roots in the early American ethic of community responsibility for the care of needy residents. Since the colonial period, altruistic citizens sought the charity of the community to provide for the less fortunate by supporting the development of almshouses to care for the needy and for orphaned children. Many of these institutions became the precursors of community hospitals.

With the evolution of state and local governments' roles in providing welfare services, and the development of the public health discipline in the late 1800s and early 1900s, tax-supported state and LHDs began providing ambulatory personal health services. The public health community's successful campaigns in controlling childhood and other communicable diseases were rapidly followed by the recognition of the emergence of chronic disease by the medical-care community. This recognition resulted in major shifts of resources toward specialized medical care, to the detriment of public health's preventive agenda.[105] In addition to maintaining its basic mission to promote and protect the public's health and safety, the public health community was expected to mount new initiatives to promote healthy lifestyles, provide safety-net services to needy populations, and expand regulatory oversight to accommodate the rapidly expanding medical care industry.[105]

Ambulatory health services that became the domain of health departments included the administration of preventive public health measures such as cancer and chronic disease screening, immunization, high-risk maternal and infant care, family planning, tobacco control, and tuberculosis and sexually transmitted disease screening and treatment. Some LHDs also established FQHCs or other types of community health centers to provide a range of primary care services to needy individuals of all ages.

Today the scope of ambulatory care services delivered by public health departments ranges across a wide spectrum from prevention-oriented programs, such as immunizations, well-baby care, smoking cessation, and cancer and chronic disease screening and education, to a full range of personal health services offered through ambulatory care centers. Historically, support for ambulatory public health services has included combinations of city, county, and state funding, plus federal and state disease-specific or block grant funds.

Public health ambulatory services staff may include physicians, nurses, aides, social workers, public health educators, community health workers, and clerical and administrative staff, who function under the overall administrative direction of a local health officer. This health officer may or may not be a physician, depending on the population size of the jurisdiction and individual state or municipal requirements. Depending on the geographic area, the governmental aegis may be state, county, or city.

Findings of the National Association of County & City Health Officials (NACCHO) 2013 *National Profile of Local Health Departments* reveal the extent to which LHDs are providing ambulatory services.[106] The following data is gleaned from the profile. With responses from 2,000 LHDs of 2,532 surveyed, the report reveals that a significant proportion of local public health agencies continues to provide directly an array of ambulatory services. As examples of the services most frequently provided, adult and child immunizations top the list at 90 percent of respondents. Eighty-three percent of LHDs reported services to screen for tuberculosis and 76 percent provided tuberculosis treatment. Sexually transmitted disease screening and treatment were offered by 64 percent and 60 percent of LHDs, respectively. Fifty-five percent of respondents reported providing family planning services. Few LHDs provide direct clinical services to mothers and children, such as obstetrical care (8 percent), prenatal care (27 percent), and well-child clinics (32 percent).

In 2015, NACCHO released results from another report, *Findings from the 2015 Forces of Change Survey*, which highlights changes in LHD's service constellations resulting from economics and the reforming healthcare delivery system.[107] The survey findings note that some LHDs have decreased clinical services and that more than one-third of LHDs are serving fewer patients in clinics compared with the prior year. Examples of changes include 14 percent reductions in immunizations, maternal and child health services, and diabetes screenings. Possible reasons cited for service reductions and decreased clinic volume include newly insured patients' options due to the ACA, the growing availability of alternative providers such as urgent care clinics, and LHD staffing constraints. Noting concomitant increases in population-oriented services such as obesity prevention (24 percent) and tobacco, alcohol, and other drug prevention (23 percent), the report suggests that the ACA's population emphasis is influencing LHDs' decisions about use of resources in population-based, rather than individual service directions.

Ambulatory services of public health agencies are facing many challenges including constrained resources and the need to adapt to changes in the healthcare delivery system. LHDs recognize their roles in sustaining essential public health services in their communities and continue seeking additional revenue streams, including billing for some clinical services, in order to remain as important resources for their communities' most vulnerable citizens.

Not-for-Profit Agency Ambulatory Services

Not-for-profit agencies operate a variety of ambulatory healthcare services throughout the United States. Not-for-profit ambulatory services have evolved from many sources, often cause-related, to address needs of population groups afflicted by specific diseases or types of conditions. Asthma, diabetes, multiple sclerosis, and cerebral palsy are a few of the conditions addressed. As not-for-profit organizations, many are chartered by states as charitable organizations and maintain tax-exempt status with the Internal Revenue Service. These designations allow them to solicit charitable contributions for which their donors may receive tax deductions. Governed by boards of directors who receive no compensation for their services, these organizations may be operated by an all-volunteer staff or employ numerous paid professionals and have annual operating budgets of several million dollars.

Voluntary ambulatory healthcare agencies often were established through the advocacy of special interest groups that desired to address the healthcare or health-related needs of a population group whose needs were not being adequately met by existing community services. Some operate as single entities, and others as independent affiliated agencies of national organizations. Planned Parenthood Federation of America is an example of one such organization. Its clinics provide preventive care, education, gynecologic care, and contraception methods in numerous locations throughout the United States. Another example is the Alzheimer's Association, which provides or assists affected individuals and their caregivers with specialized education and social support and promotes research into causes of and treatment for the disease. Frequently, legislative advocacy related to the organization's interests at the federal, state, and local levels is a major component of not-for-profit organization activity.

Financial support for voluntary ambulatory healthcare agencies is diverse. Sources may include charitable contributions, private payment, third-party insurance reimbursement (including Medicare and Medicaid), and federal, state, or local government grants. In many agencies, a large proportion of clients is uninsured or underinsured and lacks personal resources, making financial subsidies crucial to continued viability. Agencies with missions to serve the neediest members of the community continue meeting challenges posed by the ebb and flow of government grant dollars and community economic conditions that affect philanthropic support through efficient business practices and a variety of private fundraising activities.[108] Although voluntary agencies provide only a small fraction of the ambulatory care services, as compared with hospitals and other ambulatory care organizations, they are important as repositories of community values, as symbols of community charity and volunteerism, and as advocates for populations with special needs.

▶ Telehealth

Though not exclusively in the province of ambulatory care, telehealth (sometimes referred to as telemedicine) is a rapidly expanding field that is increasingly recognized as having a significant impact on the evolving delivery system in general, and on ambulatory medicine in particular. There are definite benefits to telehealth from a population health perspective, such as providing care in locations where none exists, i.e. rural areas, or connecting home-bound patients to physician consultations. Telehealth bridges patient contact with physicians at their offices or institutions or even at a patient's residence. The Center for Connected Health Policy defines telehealth as, "A collection of means or methods for enhancing health care, public health, and health education delivery and support using telecommunications technologies." Telehealth uses four modalities:[109]

1. Live video (synchronous): Real-time interaction substituting for an in-person encounter using audiovisual telecommunications technology.
2. Store and forward (asynchronous): Transmission of recorded health history that may include digital image results of diagnostic procedures transmitted to a provider (usually a specialist) who uses the information to evaluate a case.
3. Remote patient monitoring (RPM): Personal health and medical data collection from a patient via electronic communication technologies, transmitted to a provider.
4. Mobile health: Mobile communications devices such as cell phones, tablets, and personal digital assistants that send messages ranging from promoting healthy behaviors to alerts about public health threats.

While the benefits of telehealth in terms of cost-containment and physician and patient convenience may seem obvious, insurers have been slow in adopting reimbursement for these services. Slow adoption has been attributed principally to the lack of an exact definition of services for billing purposes and accompanying fears that telehealth services will actually add charges rather than substitute for in-person patient encounters.[110] Medicare has remained highly reluctant to participate and restricts payment to only rural residents and specific clinical sites. Medicaid reimbursement is much more flexible.[110] Now, payers' attitudes are changing with the recognition that burgeoning numbers of older Americans who will require monitoring for chronic diseases face transportation challenges in both urban and rural areas, and that patients have increasing expectations for convenient services.[110] Today, 29 states and the District of Columbia require that private insurers cover telehealth the same as they cover in-person services, and in 2016, Congress initiated action on Medicare to relax some restrictions.[110] With opportunities for improving access, reducing costs, and responding to patient demands, the utilization of telehealth can be expected to grow.

▶ Continued Future Expansion and Experimentation

The focus of the healthcare delivery system in the United States has shifted from hospitals to expanded use of ambulatory care services. Continuing advances in medical technology, cost-reduction initiatives, and patient demands for convenient, accessible services will drive future ambulatory care growth in all settings. As healthcare marketplace reforms continue, the PCMH and ACO models will continue to be subjects of intense study. Analyses will provide fertile opportunities for health services research to inform practitioners and policymakers about these models' effectiveness in achieving the goals of higher quality care, reduced costs, and patient satisfaction.

KEY TERMS FOR REVIEW

Accountable Care
   Organization (ACO)
Ambulatory Care
Ambulatory Surgery Center
   (ASC)

Clinical Observation Unit (COU)
Federally Qualified Health
   Center (FQHC)
Not-for-profit Ambulatory
   Services

Patient-Centered Medical
   Home (PCMH)
Retail Clinic
Telehealth
Urgent Care Center

CHAPTER ACRONYMS

AAFP American Academy of Family Physicians
ACA Patient Protection and Affordable Care Act of 2010
ACO Accountable Care Organization
ACP American College of Physicians
AHRQ Agency for Health Research and Quality
AMA American Medical Association
APC Advanced primary care
ARRA American Recovery and Reinvestment Act
ASC Ambulatory surgery center
CHIP Children's Health Insurance Program
CMMI Center for Medicare and Medicaid Innovation
COU Clinical observation unit
CPC Comprehensive Primary Care Initiative
DRG Diagnosis-related group
ED Emergency department

ESI Emergency severity index
HRSA Health Resources and Services Administration
MACRA Medicare Access and CHIP Reauthorization Act of 2015
MAPCP Multi-payer Advanced Primary Care Practice
MIPS Merit-based Incentive Payment System
NACCHO National Association of County & City Health Officials
NCHS National Center for Health Statistics
NCQA National Committee for Quality Assurance
NGACO Next generation accountable care organization
PCMH Patient centered medical home
PCPCC Patient-centered Primary Care Collaborative
SIM State Innovation Model
UCAOA Urgent Care Association of America

References

1. Berenson RA, Ginsburg PB, May JH. Hospital–physician relations: Cooperation, competition, or separation? *Health Aff.* 2007;26(1):w31-w43. http://content.healthaffairs.org/content/26/1/w31/suppl/DC1. Accessed January 7, 2016.
2. CDC, NCHS. Health, United States, 2014. Table 82. http://www.cdc.gov/nchs/data/hus/2014/082.pdf. Accessed January 7, 2016.
3. CDC, NCHS. National Ambulatory Care Medical Care Survey: 2012 State and National Summary Tables. http://www.cdc.gov/nchs/data/ahcd/namcs_summary/2012_namcs_web_tables.pdf. Accessed January 7, 2016.
4. Raffel MW, Raffel NK. *The U.S. Health System: Origins and Functions.* 4th ed. Albany, NY: Delmar Publishers; 1994:36-44.
5. Hospitals and Health Networks Daily. Hospital statistics chart rise in physician employment. http://www.hhnmag.com/articles/5455-hospital-statistics-chart-rise-in-physician-employment. Accessed January 7, 2016.
6. Becker's Hospital Review. 8 statistics on physician employment. http://www.beckershospitalreview.com/hospital-physician-relationships/8-statistics-on-physician-employment.html. Accessed January 7, 2016.
7. Center for Studying Health System Change. Rising hospital employment of physicians: better quality, higher costs? http://www.hschange.com/CONTENT/1230/. Accessed January 9, 2016.
8. Kocher R, Sahni R. Hospitals' race to employ physicians—the logic behind a money-losing proposition.

N Engl J Med. 2011;364:1791. http://www.nejm.org/doi/full/10.1056/NEJMp1101959. Accessed January 9, 2016.

9. American College of Physicians. Enhance care coordination through the patient centered medical home (PCMH). https://www.acponline.org/system/files/documents/running_practice/delivery_and_payment_models/pcmh/understanding/pcmh_back.pdf. Accessed January 9, 2016.

10. American Medical Association. AMA calls for design overhaul of electronic health records to improve usability. http://www.ama-assn.org/ama/pub/news/news/2014/2014-09-16-solutions-to-ehr-systems.page. Accessed March 20, 2016.

11. Reid RJ, Coleman K, Johnson EA, et al. The group health medical home at year two: cost savings, higher patient satisfaction, and less burnout for providers. *Health Aff.* 2010;29:835. http://content.healthaffairs.org/content/29/5/835.full?sid=cfd8ecd0-e777-4e67-ad88-b32d17e2658c. Accessed January 9, 2016.

12. American College of Physicians. Patient-centered medical home. http://www.acponline.org/running_practice/delivery_and_payment_models/pcmh/. Accessed January 9, 2016.

13. Patient-centered Primary Care Collaborative. The patient-centered medical home's impact on cost and quality annual review of evidence, 2014–2015. http://www.milbank.org/uploads/documents/PCPCC_2016_Report.pdf. Accessed February 10, 2016.

14. Institute for Healthcare Improvement. IHI Triple Aim Initiative. http://www.ihi.org/engage/initiatives/TripleAim/Pages/default.aspx. Accessed January 10, 2016.

15. American College of Physicians. The advanced medical home: a patient-centered, physician-guided model of health care. Position paper. Philadelphia, PA: American College of Physicians; 2006. https://www.acponline.org/acp_policy/policies/adv_medicalhome_patient_centered_model_healthcare_2006.pdf. Accessed August 29, 2016.

16. Patient-Centered Primary Care Collaborative. Benefits of implementing the PCMH: A review of cost and quality results, 2012. https://www.pcpcc.org/sites/default/files/media/benefits_of_implementing_the_primary_care_pcmh.pdf. Accessed January 10, 2016.

17. American Academy of Family Physicians. Medical homes show steady progress nationally, report finds. http://www.aafp.org/news/practice-professional-issues/20160205medicalhomes.html. Accessed February 10, 2016.

18. Patient-Centered Primary Care Collaborative. PCPCC's Strategic Plan 2015–2018. https://www.pcpcc.org/resource/pcpccs-strategic-plan-2015-2018. Accessed February 10, 2016.

19. Safety Net Medical Home Initiative. Health reform and the patient-centered medical home: Policy provisions and expectations of the Patient Protection and Affordable Care Act. http://www.safetynetmedicalhome.org/sites/default/files/policy-brief-2.pdf. Accessed January 10, 2016.

20. Rand Corporation. Health coverage grows under Affordable Care Act. May 6, 2015. http://www.rand.org/news/press/2015/05/06.html. Accessed January 10, 2016.

21. The Henry J. Kaiser Family Foundation. Increasing Medicaid primary care fees for certain physicians in 2013 and 2014: a primer on the health reform provision and final rule. December 2012. Policy Brief. December 2012. https://kaiserfamilyfoundation.files.wordpress.com/2013/01/8397.pdf. Accessed January 10, 2016.

22. Blumenthal D, Abrams M, Nazum R. The Affordable Care Act at 5 Years. *N Engl J Med.* 2015;372:2451-2458. http://www.nejm.org/doi/full/10.1056/NEJMhpr1503614. Accessed January 11, 2016.

23. U.S. Department of Health and Human Services, Centers for Medicare and Medicaid Services. Primary Care Incentive Payment Program (PCIP). https://www.cms.gov/Medicare/Medicare-Fee-for-Service-Payment/PhysicianFeeSched/Downloads/PCIP-2012-Payments.pdf. Accessed January 11, 2016.

24. Medicare Payment Advisory Commission. Report to the Congress Chapter 5. Per Beneficiary Payment for Primary Care. June 2014. http://www.medpac.gov/documents/reports/chapter-5-per-beneficiary-payment-for-primary-care-(june-2014-report).pdf?sfvrsn=2. Accessed January 11, 2016.

25. Medicare Payment Advisory Commission. Medicare Payment Advisory Commission Releases Report on Medicare Payment Policy. March 2015. http://www.medpac.gov/documents/press-releases/medpac-releases-march-2015-report-on-medicare-payment-policy.pdf?sfvrsn=0. Accessed January 11, 2016.

26. Edwards ST, Bitton A, Hong J, Landon BE. Patient-centered medical home initiatives expanded in 2009–13: providers, patients, and payment incentives increased. *Health Aff.* 2014;33:1823-1831. http://content.healthaffairs.org/content/33/10/1823.full?sid=f4452d2e-764a-498b-93d3-dfc152c5a380. Accessed January 11, 2016.

27. Centers for Medicare and Medicaid Services. About the CMS Innovation Center. https://innovation.cms.gov/About/index.html. Accessed January 13, 2016.

28. Centers for Medicare and Medicaid Services. Multi-payer advanced primary care practice (MAPCP) demonstration fact sheet. https://www.cms.gov/Medicare/demonstration-projects/demoprojectsevalrpts/downloads/mapcpdemo_factsheet.pdf. Accessed January 11, 2016.

29. Centers for Medicare and Medicaid Services. Comprehensive primary care initiative. https://innovation.cms.gov/initiatives/comprehensive-primary-care-initiative/. Accessed January 11, 2016.

30. Centers for Medicare and Medicaid Services. State innovation models initiative: General information. https://innovation.cms.gov/initiatives/state-innovations/. Accessed January 11, 2016.

31. Taylor EF, Dale S, Peikes D, et al. Mathematica Policy Research. Evaluation of the Comprehensive Primary Care Initiative: First Annual Report, January 2015. https://innovation.cms.gov/files/reports/cpci-evalrpt1.pdf. Accessed January 11, 2016.

32. Centers for Medicare and Medicaid Services. Comprehensive Primary Care Mid-year 2015 Snapshot. https://innovation.cms.gov/Files/x/cpci-fastfacstmy2015.pdf. Accessed January 11, 2016.

33. Centers for Medicare and Medicaid Services. State Innovation Models Initiative: Round Two. https://innovation.cms.gov/initiatives/State-Innovations-Round-Two/. Accessed January 11, 2016.

34. U.S. Department of Health and Human Services. Health Care Fact Sheets. Creating health care jobs by addressing primary care workforce needs. March 2015. http://www.hhs.gov/healthcare/facts-and-features/fact-sheets/creating-health-care-jobs-by-addressing-primary-care-workforce-needs/index.html. Accessed January 11, 2016.

35. Higgins A, Veselovskiy G, McKown L. Provider performance measures in private and public programs: achieving meaningful alignment with flexibility to innovate. *Health Aff*. 2013;32:1453. http://content.healthaffairs.org/content/32/8/1453.full?sid=577bc305-0c70-4fd6-877e-6788c9195e50. Accessed January11, 2016.

36. Conway PH. The Core Quality Measures Collaborative: A Rationale and Framework for Public-Private Quality Measure Alignment. Health Affairs Blog. http://healthaffairs.org/blog/2015/06/23/the-core-quality-measures-collaborative-a-rationale-and-framework-for-public-private-quality-measure-alignment/. Accessed January 11, 2016.

37. Centers for Medicare and Medicaid Services. Core Quality Measures Collaborative Release. February 16, 2016. https://www.cms.gov/newsroom/mediarelease database/fact-sheets/2016-fact-sheets-items/2016-02-16.html. Accessed August 29, 2016.

38. Conway PH. MACRA: New Opportunities for Medicare Providers Through Innovative Payment Systems (Updated). Health Affairs Blog. http://healthaffairs.org/blog/2015/09/28/macra-new-opportunities-for-medicare-providers-through-innovative-payment-systems-3/. Accessed January 12, 2016.

39. Centers for Medicare and Medicaid Services. The merit-based payment system (MIPS) and alternative payment models (APMs): Delivery system reform, medicare payment reform, and the MACRA. https://www.cms.gov/Medicare/Quality-Initiatives-Patient-Assessment-Instruments/Value-Based-Programs/MACRA-MIPS-and-APMs/MACRA-MIPS-and-APMs.html. Accessed January 12, 2016.

40. Han E, Scholle SH, Morton S, Bechtel C, Kessler R. Survey shows that fewer than a third of patient-centered medical home practices engage patients in quality improvement. *Health Aff*. 2013;32:368-375. http://content.healthaffairs.org/content/32/2/368.short. Accessed January 12, 2016.

41. McNellis RJ, Genevro JL, Meyers DS. Lessons learned from the study of primary care transformation. *Ann Fam Med Suppl*. 2013;11:S1-S5. http://www.annfammed.org/content/11/Suppl_1/S1.full.pdf±html. Accessed January 12, 2016.

42. National Committee for Quality Assurance. Latest evidence: Benefits of the patient-centered medical home. https://www.ncqa.org/Portals/0/Programs/Recognition/NCQA%20PCMH%20Evidence%20Report,%20June%202015.pdf. Accessed January 12, 2016.

43. National Committee for Quality Assurance. The future of patient-centered medical homes. http://www.ncqa.org/Portals/0/Public%20Policy/2014%20Comment%20Letters/The_Future_of_PCMH.pdf. Accessed January 13, 2016.

44. National Committee for Quality Assurance. PCMH recognition. http://www.ncqa.org/Programs/Recognition/Practices/PatientCenteredMedicalHomePCMH.aspx. Accessed January 13, 2016.

45. The Commonwealth Fund. *Guiding Transformation: How Medical Practices Can Become Patient-Centered Medical Homes*. http://www.commonwealthfund.org/~/media/Files/Publications/Fund%20Report/2012/Feb/1582_Wagner_guiding_transformation_patientcentered_med_home_v2.pdf. Accessed January 9, 2016.

46. Centers for Medicare and Medicaid Services. Summary of final rule provisions for accountable care organizations under the Medicare shared savings program. https://kaiserhealthnews.files.wordpress.com/2014/04/aco_summary_factsheet_icn907404.pdf. Accessed January 13, 2016.

47. Baxley L, Borkan J, Campbell T, Davis A, Kuzel T, Wender R. In pursuit of a transformed health care system: From patient centered medical homes to accountable care organizations and beyond. *Ann Fam Med*. 2011;9:466-467. http://www.annfammed.org/content/9/5/466.full. Accessed January 14, 2016.

48. Centers for Medicare and Medicaid Services. Next generation accountable care organization model (NGACO Model). https://www.cms.gov/Newsroom/MediaReleaseDatabase/Fact-sheets/2016-Fact-sheets-items/2016-01-11.html. Accessed January 14, 2016.

49. Knowles JH. The role of the hospital: The ambulatory clinic. *Bulletin of the New York Academy of Medicine.* 1965;41:68–70.

50. Fraser I, Lane L, Linne E. Ambulatory care: A decade of change in health care delivery. *The J Ambul Care Manage.* 1993;16:1-8.

51. American Hospital Association. Trendwatch chartbook 2015. Table 4.2: Distribution of Inpatient vs. Outpatient Revenues, 1993–2013. http://www.aha.org/research/reports/tw/chartbook/2015/chapter4.pdf. Accessed January 14, 2016.

52. National Center for Health Statistics. Health, United States, 2014: With special feature on adults aged 55-64. Hyattsville, MD. 2015. Table 91. Hospital Admissions, average length of stay, outpatient visits, and outpatient surgery, by type of ownership and size of hospital: United States, selected years 1975–2012. http://www.cdc.gov/nchs/data/hus/hus14.pdf#listtables. Accessed January 14, 2016.

53. Robeznieks A. Hospitals saw fewer admissions, more outpatients in 2013. *Mod Healthc.* January 27, 2015. http://www.modernhealthcare.com/article/20150127/NEWS/301279903. Accessed January 14, 2016.

54. American Hospital Association. Trendwatch Chartbook 2015. Supplementary data tables, utilization and volume. Table 3.3: Emergency department visits, emergency department visits per 1,000 and number of emergency departments, 1993–2013. http://www.aha.org/research/reports/tw/chartbook/2015/table3-3.pdf. Accessed January 14, 2016.

55. National Center for Health Statistics. Health, United States, 2014: With Special Feature on Adults Aged 55-64. Hyattsville, MD. 2015. Table 82 (page 2 of 3). Visits to physician offices, hospital outpatient departments, and hospital emergency departments, by age, sex and race: United States, selected years 1995–2011. http://www.cdc.gov/nchs/data/hus/hus14.pdf#082. Accessed January 14, 2016.

56. Hernandez-Boussard T, Burns CS, Wang NE, Baker LC, Goldstein BA. The Affordable Care Act reduces emergency department use by young adults: Evidence from three states. *Health Aff.* 2014;33:1648–1654. http://content.healthaffairs.org/content/33/9/1648.full.pdf±html?sid=11df7e6a-0859-445f-9f1e-12b5ed7c368b. Accessed January 14, 2016.

57. Centers for Disease Control and Prevention. National Center for Health Statistics. National Ambulatory Medical Care Survey: 2011. Table 5. Mode of arrival at emergency department by patient age: United States, 2011. Emergency department visits resulting in hospital admission, by selected patient and visit characteristics: United States, 2011. http://www.cdc.gov/nchs/data/ahcd/nhamcs_emergency/2011_ed_web_tables.pdf. Accessed January 15, 2016.

58. Centers for Disease Control and Prevention. National Center for Health Statistics. National Ambulatory Medical Care Survey: 2011. Table 25. Emergency department visits resulting in hospital admission, by selected patient and visit characteristics: United States, 2011. http://www.cdc.gov/nchs/data/ahcd/nhamcs_emergency/2011_ed_web_tables.pdf. Accessed January 15, 2016.

59. Weiss AJ (Truven Health Analytics), Wier LM (Truven Health Analytics), Stocks C (AHRQ), Blanchard J (Rand). Overview of emergency department visits in the United States, 2011. HCUP Statistical Brief # 174. June 2014. Agency for Healthcare Research and Quality, Rockville, MD. https://www.hcup-us.ahrq.gov/reports/statbriefs/sb174-Emergency-Department-Visits-Overview.pdf. Accessed January 15, 2016.

60. Centers for Disease Control and Prevention. National Center for Health Statistics. National ambulatory medical care survey: 2011. Table 6. Expected sources of payment at emergency department visits: United States, 2011. http://www.cdc.gov/nchs/data/ahcd/nhamcs_emergency/2011_ed_web_tables.pdf. Accessed January 15, 2016.

61. American Board of Emergency Medicine. History: ABEM in the 1960s and 1970s. https://www.abem.org/public/general-information/history. Accessed January 25, 2016.

62. Gilboy N, Tanabe T, Travers D, Rosenau AM. Emergency severity index (ESI): A triage tool for emergency department care, version 4. Implementation Handbook 2012 edition. AHRQ publication no. 12-0014. Rockville, MD. Agency for Healthcare Research and Quality. November 2011. http://www.ahrq.gov/sites/default/files/wysiwyg/professionals/systems/hospital/esi/esihandbk.pdf. Accessed January 25, 2016.

63. Centers for Disease Control and Prevention. National Center for Health Statistics. National hospital ambulatory medical care survey: 2011. Table 7. Triage status of emergency department visits, by selected patient characteristics, United States, 2011. http://www.cdc.gov/nchs/data/ahcd/nhamcs_emergency/2011_ed_web_tables.pdf. Accessed January 25, 2016.

64. U.S. Government Accountability Office. Report to the Chairman, Committee on Finance, U.S. Senate. Hospital emergency departments: Crowding continues to occur and some patients wait longer than recommended time frames. April 2009. http://www.gao.gov/assets/290/289048.pdf. Accessed August 30, 2016.

65. CDC National Center for Health Statistics. Media brief. Almost half of hospitals experience crowded emergency departments. http://www.cdc.gov/nchs/pressroom/06facts/hospitals.htm. Accessed January 25, 2016.

66. Napoli A. Emergency department observation units offer efficiencies that cut cost, improve care.

Mod Healthc. http://www.modernhealthcare.com/article/20141101/MAGAZINE/311019978. Accessed January 25, 2016.

67. Asudani D, Tolia, V. Pros and cons of clinical observation units. *The Hospitalist.* November 1, 2013. http://www.the-hospitalist.org/article/pros-and-cons-of-clinical-observation-units/. Accessed January 25, 2016.

68. O'Malley AS. After-hours access to primary care practices linked with lower emergency department use and less unmet medical need. *Health Aff.* 2013;32:175-181. http://content.healthaffairs.org/content/32/1/175.full.pdf±html. Accessed January 27, 2016.

69. Pourat N, Davis A, Chen X, Vrungos S, Kominski G. In California, primary care continuity was associated with reduced emergency department use and fewer hospitalizations. *Health Aff.* 2015;34:1113-1120. http://content.healthaffairs.org/content/34/7/1113. Accessed January 27, 2016.

70. Urgent Care Association of America. The case for urgent care. http://c.ymcdn.com/sites/www.ucaoa.org/resource/resmgr/Files/WhitePaperTheCaseforUrgentCa.pdf. Accessed February 2, 2016.

71. Urgent Care Association of America. Industry FAQs. http://www.ucaoa.org/?page=IndustryFAQs. Accessed February 2, 2016.

72. Becker's Hospital Review. 20 things to know about urgent care. http://www.ucaoa.org/blogpost/1190415/239114/20-Things-to-Know-About-Urgent-Care--2016. Accessed February 16, 2016.

73. Urgent Care Association of America. Benchmarking survey headlines summary, 2015. http://c.ymcdn.com/sites/www.ucaoa.org/resource/resmgr/Infographics/2015_BM_Survey_Headlines_Sum.pdf. Accessed February 9, 2016.

74. Urgent Care Association of America. Urgency or emergency? http://c.ymcdn.com/sites/www.ucaoa.org/resource/resmgr/Media/UCAOA-Infographic-UCvsER_FIN.pdf. Accessed February 9, 2016.

75. American Board of Urgent Care Medicine. Board certification. http://www.abucm.org/general-info.html. Accessed August 31, 2016.

76. Urgent Care Association of America. UCAOA accreditation. http://www.ucaoa.org/?UCAOA Accreditation. Accessed February 10, 2016.

77. Scott MK. Health care in the express lane: Retail clinics go mainstream. Oakland, CA: HealthCare Foundation. September 2007. http://www.chcf.org/publications/2007/09/health-care-in-the-express-lane-retail-clinics-go-mainstream. Accessed February 12, 2016.

78. Accenture. Number of U.S. retail health clinics will surpass 2,800 by 2017, Accenture forecasts. https://newsroom.accenture.com/news/number-of-us-retail-health-clinics-will-surpass-2800-by-2017-accenture-forecasts.htm. Accessed February 14, 2016.

79. Bachrach D, Frohlic J, Garcimonde A, Nevitt K. Building a culture of health: the value proposition of retail clinics. The Robert Wood Johnson Foundation. http://www.rwjf.org/content/dam/farm/reports/issue_briefs/2015/rwjf419415. Accessed February 14, 2016.

80. National Conference of State Legislatures. Retail health clinics: state legislation and laws. http://www.ncsl.org/research/health/retail-health-clinics-state-legislation-and-laws.aspx. Accessed February 14, 2016.

81. Japsen B. Insurance covers four in five visits to CVS and Walgreen clinics. *Forbes.* http://www.forbes.com/sites/brucejapsen/2015/05/02/as-cvs-and-walgreen-play-doctor-insurance-picks-up-the-tab/#685666f1471d. Accessed February 16, 2016.

82. Ollove M. States forgo special rules for commercial walk-in health clinics. The Pew Charitable Trusts: stateline. http://www.pewtrusts.org/en/research-and-analysis/blogs/stateline/2016/01/05/states-let-commercial-walk-in-health-clinics-grow-unregulated. Accessed February 18, 2016.

83. American Academy of Family Physicians. Retail clinics. http://www.aafp.org/online/en/home/policy/policies/r/retailhealth.html. Accessed February 18, 2016.

84. American College of Physicians. Retail clinics best used as backup to a patient's primary care physician. https://www.acponline.org/acp-newsroom/retail-clinics-best-used-as-backup-to-a-patients-primary-care-physician. Accessed February 18, 2016.

85. Cullen KA, Hall MJ, Golosinskiy A. Ambulatory surgery in the United States, 2006. *National Health Statistics Reports.* 2009;(11). Revised. Hyattsville, MD: National Center for Health Statistics. http://www.cdc.gov/nchs/data/nhsr/nhsr011.pdf. Accessed February 20, 2016.

86. Centers for Disease Control and Prevention. National Survey of Ambulatory Surgery. http://www.cdc.gov/nchs/nsas.htm. Accessed February 20, 2016.

87. National Center for Health Statistics. Health, United States, 2014: With Special Feature on Adults Aged 55-64. Hyattsville, MD. 2015. Table 91. Hospital admissions, average length of stay, outpatient visits, and outpatient surgery, by type of ownership and size of hospital: United States, selected years 1975–2012. http://www.cdc.gov/nchs/data/hus/hus14.pdf#091. Accessed January 14, 2016.

88. Casalino LP, Devers KJ, Brewster LR. Focused factories? Physician-owned specialty facilities. *Health Aff.* 2003;22:56-67. http://content.healthaffairs.org/content/22/6/56.full.html. Accessed February 23, 2016

89. Becker's ASC Review. 50 things to know about the ambulatory surgery center industry. http://www.beckersasc.com/lists/50-things-to-know-about-the-ambulatory-surgery-center-industry.html. Accessed February 23, 2016.

90. KNG Health Consulting LLC. An analysis of recent growth of ambulatory surgical centers. Final report. June 2009. http://cascacolorado.com/wp-content/uploads/2009/06/KNG-Health-ASC-Growth-Factors-Final-Report-6-012-09.pdf. Accessed February 23, 2016.

91. Ambulatory Surgery Center Association. Ambulatory surgery centers: A positive trend in health care. Update 2011. http://www.ascassociation.org/ASCA/Resources/ViewDocument/?DocumentKey=7d8441a1-82dd-47b9-b626-8563dc31930c. Accessed February 23, 2016.

92. Ambulatory Surgery Center Association. History. 1980s. http://www.ascassociation.org/aboutus/whatisanasc/history. Accessed February 23, 2016.

93. Centers for Medicare and Medicaid Services. ASC quality reporting program. http://www.qualityreportingcenter.com/asc/program_information/. Accessed February 25, 2016.

94. U.S. Department of Health and Human Services. Health Resources and Services Administration. Bureau of Primary Health Care. The health center program: Program requirements. http://bphc.hrsa.gov/about/requirements/index.html. Accessed February 25, 2016.

95. Health Resources and Services Administration. Bureau of Primary Health Care Health Center Program. http://bphc.hrsa.gov/about/healthcentersaca/healthcenterfactsheet.pdf. Accessed February 25, 2016.

96. U.S. Code. Health Center Program Statute: Section 330 of the Public Health Service Act (42 U.S.C. §254b). http://uscode.house.gov/view.xhtml?edition=prelim&req=42±usc±254b&f=treesort&fq=true&num=20&hl=true. Accessed February 25, 2016.

97. U.S. Department of Health and Human Services. Health Resources and Services Administration. The health center program: Serving America's communities for 50 years. Infographic 2015. http://bphc.hrsa.gov/about/pdf/nhcw2015infographicfull.png. Accessed February 27, 2016.

98. U.S. Department of Health and Human Services. Health Resources and Services Administration. What is a health center? http://bphc.hrsa.gov/about/what-is-a-health-center/index.html. Accessed February 27, 2016.

99. National Association of Community Health Centers. Fact sheet: America's health centers. http://nachc.org/wp-content/uploads/2015/06/Americas-Health-Centers-March-2016.pdf. Accessed August 31, 2016.

100. U.S. Department of Health and Human Services. Health Resources and Services Administration. Health Center Program. 2014 health center data. http://bphc.hrsa.gov/uds/datacenter.aspx. Accessed February 27, 2016.

101. The White House Office of the Press Secretary. President Obama announces Recovery Act awards to build, renovate community health centers in more than 30 states. https://www.whitehouse.gov/the-press-office/president-obama-announces-recovery-act-awards-build-renovate-community-health-cente. Accessed February 27, 2016.

102. Centers for Medicare and Medicaid Services. New Affordable Care Act support to improve care coordination for nearly 200,000 people with Medicare. https://www.cms.gov/Newsroom/MediaReleaseDatabase/Fact-sheets/2011-Fact-sheets-items/2011-06-06.html. Accessed February 27, 2016.

103. Centers for Medicare and Medicaid Services. FQHC advanced primary care practice demonstration. https://innovation.cms.gov/initiatives/fqhcs/. Accessed February 27, 2016.

104. Kahn K, Timbie JW, Friedberg MW, et al. Evaluation of CMS FQHC APCP demonstration: Second annual report. https://innovation.cms.gov/Files/reports/fqhc-scndevalrpt.pdf. Accessed March 1, 2016.

105. McGinnis M. Can public health and medicine partner in the public interest? *Health Aff.* 2006;25:1048-1049. http://content.healthaffairs.org/content/25/4/1044.full.pdf±html. Accessed March 3, 2016.

106. National Association of County & City Health Officials. 2013 national profile of local health departments. http://archived.naccho.org/topics/infrastructure/profile/upload/2013-National-Profile-of-Local-Health-Departments-report.pdf. Accessed March 6, 2016.

107. National Association of County & City Health Officials. The changing public health landscape. Findings from the 2015 forces of change survey. http://nacchoprofilestudy.org/wp-content/uploads/2015/04/2015-Forces-of-Change-Slidedoc-Final.pdf. Accessed March 6, 2016.

108. Alliance for Advancing Nonprofit Health Care. The value of nonprofit health care. http://www.nonprofithealthcare.org/reports/5_value.pdf. Accessed March 6, 2016.

109. Center for Connected Health Policy. What is telehealth? http://cchpca.org/what-is-telehealth. Accessed March 7, 2016.

110. Herman B. Virtual reality: More insurers are embracing telehealth. *Mod Healthc.* February 22, 2016. http://www.modernhealthcare.com/article/20160220/MAGAZINE/302209980. Accessed March 7, 2016.

CHAPTER 6

Medical Education and the Changing Practice of Medicine

CHAPTER OVERVIEW

This chapter provides an overview of the evolution in medical education from the colonial apprentice system to today's high-technology, specialty-oriented instruction in the basic sciences and clinical fields. It includes discussions of the Health Information Technology for Economic and Clinical Health (HITECH) Act, the Affordable Care Act (ACA), and resulting impacts on medical education and practice. Updates are provided on evidence-based clinical practice guidelines, specialty physicians called hospitalists, physician report cards, and health information technology (HIT). New information is presented on open access to the biomedical literature and new ethical issues are reviewed. The chapter concludes with a discussion of the future direction of medical education and healthcare reform.

▶ Medical Education: Colonial America to the 1800s

There were no medical schools in colonial America. Women treated the sick at home with the help of medicinal herbs, the advice of friends, and self-help publications of questionable credibility. Only a few of the university-trained physicians in Europe came to the colonies. Those European physicians trained other physicians in an apprentice relationship. Because there was no formal method of testing or licensing new physicians after they concluded their apprenticeship, they were free to practice with no regulation.

Flag: © Lightix/Shutterstock

The first medical school in America was established in 1756 at the College of Philadelphia (later the University of Pennsylvania). In 1768, a second was founded at King's College (later Columbia University). Both schools graduated only a small number of students each year.

Training under a single physician remained the most common method of physician education until the founding of hospitals in the mid-1700s. Physicians brought their own apprentices to the hospital, and they encouraged other students to observe patient treatment. This practice became so popular that the Philadelphia Hospital began charging a fee to students who were not apprenticed to physicians on the staff. By 1773, the hospital felt it had become necessary to regulate this training system and initiated a program whereby an aspiring physician would pay a fee to the hospital and be formally apprenticed to the institution for five years.[1] Physicians were granted a certificate on the completion of their apprenticeship.

By 1800, only four new U.S. medical schools had been added. Harvard University established a medical school in 1783 and Dartmouth College, in 1797. The schools were small, with three or four faculty members teaching all courses, and there were still very few restrictions on who could practice medicine. The first law concerning medicine in the colonies was enacted in Virginia in 1639 to control physician fees.[2] Various states attempted to enact medical licensing legislation during the 1700s and early 1800s, but "by the time of the Civil War, not a single state had a medical licensure act in effect."[2] As the number of medical schools grew, their diplomas came to be viewed as licenses to practice.

In 1821, Georgia became the first state to restrict medical licenses to graduates of medical schools. Opposition was strong, especially from the apprentice-trained physicians. However, as physicians from medical schools began to outnumber those from the apprentice system, the Doctor of Medicine (MD) degree became the standard of competence.

The endorsement of formal medical education over apprenticeship training encouraged an increase in the number of medical schools. Many of the new medical schools had weak programs and no hospital affiliations. In 1892, Harvard became the first medical school to require four years of training. In 1893, Johns Hopkins initiated a four-year curriculum as part of a pioneering effort to improve medical education. The Johns Hopkins model became the standard for the subsequent reform of all medical education.

Many medical schools during this period operated without strict admission requirements, a well-trained faculty, or a place for clinical observation and practice. Consequently, the quality of a medical degree varied greatly from school to school. Medical societies were organized to improve the quality of education and practice. The first such society was the Medical Society of Boston, organized in 1736.[2]

By the mid-1800s, most states had medical societies. In 1847, most of the state societies were affiliated with the newly formed American Medical Association (AMA). The goal of the AMA at the time was to improve medical education. The AMA's early attempts to reform or close some of the weaker medical schools often were ineffective; many AMA members were professionally associated with weaker schools and had a vested interest in keeping them open.[1] As a result, attempts to establish a national standard for medical teaching floundered for a few decades.

The Association of American Medical Colleges (AAMC), founded in 1876 by 22 medical schools, supported a four-year curriculum such as the one introduced by the medical schools of Harvard and Johns Hopkins. However, it lacked the influence at that time to accomplish the desired medical education reforms.

▶ Flexner Report and Medical School Reforms

In 1904, the AMA created a new Council on Medical Education and began the *Journal of the American Medical Association*. The AMA used the journal to publish medical school failure statistics on state board licensing examinations and to group schools in categories by their failure rates.

The most important educational reform accomplishment of the AMA began in 1905 when it enlisted the Carnegie Foundation to investigate and rate medical schools. Abraham Flexner of the Foundation led a study of the medical schools in the United States and Canada. He proposed to examine the entrance requirements at each institution, the size and training of the faculty, endowment fees, the quality of laboratories, and the relationship between the medical schools and hospitals.

Flexner started his educational survey of all 155 medical schools in the United States and Canada in 1909. He visited each school, interviewing the dean and faculty members and inspecting laboratories and equipment. He summarized the observations he made during each visit and mailed his summary to the dean for verification. The deans and faculty of each school cooperated happily with Flexner in the mistaken belief that Carnegie was contemplating a contribution to their school.

Flexner's full report, "Medical Education in the United States and Canada," was published by the Carnegie Foundation in 1910. The report was an accurate description of the assets and liabilities of each medical program and its teaching facilities. Overall, the report was a searing indictment of most medical schools of the time. Some were referred to as a "disgrace" and a "plague spot." The report recommended corrective measures. In the aftermath of this criticism, some schools closed while others consolidated. Soon after, some attempted to make improvements based on the report's recommendations. Flexner had proposed that the number of schools be reduced from 155 to 31, but a decade later the number had only been reduced to 85.[1]

Not all observations in Flexner's report were negative. Dartmouth, Yale, and Columbia were able to make alterations that improved the quality of their programs. Schools that received praise for excellent performance in the United States and Canada included Harvard, Western Reserve, McGill, the University of Toronto, and especially Johns Hopkins, which was described as a "model for medical education."

Formulated by an independent body, the Flexner Report gave increased leverage to medical reformers. Licensing legislation was pursued more vigorously, and new requirements for the length of medical training and for the quality of laboratories and other facilities were established. The AMA and the AAMC accelerated their efforts at reform and, in 1942, established the Liaison Committee on Medical Education to serve as the official accrediting body of medical schools.

One of the most important outcomes of Flexner's report was its stimulation of financial support for medical education from foundations and wealthy individuals. Schools that received the most favorable ratings from Flexner shared most of the money. Because most were associated with universities, the university-affiliated medical schools gained significant influence over the direction of medical education.[1]

▶ Transition from Academic Medical Centers to Academic Health Centers

Federal research grants of the 1950s and 1960s encouraged research-oriented medical schools and their teaching hospitals to become the country's centers of scientific and technologic advances in health care. Most of the large tertiary-care hospitals affiliated with the approximately 80 medical schools operating at that time attracted patients with complicated medical conditions and were getting better results than their smaller unaffiliated counterparts were.

Because university medical complexes were increasingly recognized as leading the way toward a more sophisticated and effective healthcare system, the federal government assisted in extending that expertise through the regional medical program legislation of 1965 and associated funding.

One of many federal grant programs of the 1960s, the regional medical program legislation supported the development of programs across the United States to upgrade medical knowledge about the leading causes of death: heart disease, cancer, and stroke. The regional medical programs supported research, continuing professional education, service innovation, and regional networking among hospitals and other healthcare facilities. By 1974, however, the university-based regional medical programs had lost their political support and disbanded.

However, by 1974 university-based academic medical centers were well established as the proponents of cutting-edge advances in research and clinical medicine. By the early 1980s, federal support had increased the number of medical schools to 127. Academic medical centers broadened into academic health centers by adding to their complexes professional healthcare programs such as nursing, pharmacy, dentistry, and allied health. Together with their large teaching hospitals and other clinical facilities, these academic health centers became a powerful force in the healthcare arena.

Academic health centers became the principal places of education and training for physicians and other healthcare personnel, the sites for most basic research in medicine, and the clinical settings in which many of the advances in diagnosis and treatment were tested and perfected. Today, the teaching hospitals of academic health centers are also major providers of the most sophisticated patient care required by trauma centers, burn centers, and neonatal intensive care centers, and the technologically advanced treatment of cancer, heart disease, and neurologic and other acute and chronic conditions. In addition to their complex tertiary-care services, teaching hospitals also provide much of the primary care for the economically disadvantaged populations in their geographical regions.

While the teaching hospitals of the 145 academic health centers represent only 7 percent of the nation's 5,627 hospitals (about 400 hospitals), they provide 37 percent of all hospital charity care, 24 percent of all Medicaid hospitalizations, and 59 percent of all pediatric Intensive Care Unit beds.[3-5] The highly specialized, high-technology nature of academic health centers makes them the most expensive type of facility in America's healthcare system. Care provided at the teaching hospitals often is more expensive because student physicians order more diagnostic tests and procedures and often must consult with senior doctors regarding diagnoses and treatment procedures. As health care has shifted from an era of abundant resources to one of more stringent economic constraints, academic health centers have been under increasing pressure to reduce high-cost activities or face ballooning deficits that could threaten their survival.[6]

Medical schools' diverse research, teaching, and patient care responsibilities require them to generate revenues from multiple sources. A major source of revenue is the clinical practice of faculty who provide care to patients in addition to their responsibilities for teaching medical students. In fiscal year 2014, the largest proportion, 40 percent, of the total revenue of the U.S. fully accredited medical schools came from their faculty practice plans in which medical school faculty provided medical care to patients. This is a 7.6 percent increase from the previous fiscal year. In the same year, federally supported research grants and contracts contributed about 15 percent, a 5 percent decrease from the previous year. Medical schools receive relatively smaller proportions of their total revenue from state and local government appropriations, hospital programs, tuition and fees, federal and other grants and contracts, and endowments.[7] The increasing proportion of practice revenue in medical school budgets has put more pressure on faculty to provide more revenue-generating patient care while still maintaining their teaching and academic standards.

The cost of medical care is generally higher in academic health centers relative to non-teaching hospitals because of the added time and expenses for educational activities that are inextricably linked with patient care. Recognizing this, Centers for Medicare & Medicaid Services (CMS) pays academic medical centers an Indirect Medical Education (IME) adjustment on its Medicare claims to offset this added cost.[8]

▶ Graduate Medical Education

There are two types of physicians: the Medical Doctor (MD) and the Doctor of Osteopathic Medicine (DO). MDs are also known as allopathic physicians. Although both MDs and DOs may use all accepted methods of treatment, including drugs and surgery, DOs place special emphasis on the body's musculoskeletal system. As of March 2016, there were 145 accredited schools of allopathic medicine[5] and 31 accredited colleges for degrees in osteopathy.[9]

No one national agency grants licenses to practice medicine. Instead, a physician must obtain a license from the medical board of the state in which they plan to practice. Each state has independent requirements about who may practice within the state and may have special requirements or restrictions for licensure. To provide direct patient care, after successful completion of medical school, physicians are required to complete a 3- to 7-year graduate medical education. This consists of a residency, and possibly a fellowship, accredited by the Accreditation Council for Graduate Medical Education (ACGME) in one of the recognized medical specialties or subspecialties. Formerly the Liaison Committee for Graduate Medical Education established in 1972, the ACGME was established in 1981. In 2000, it became an independent, not-for-profit organization with the following mission: "We improve health care and population health by assessing and advancing the quality of resident physicians' education through accreditation."[10]

"In academic year 2013–2014, there were approximately 9,600 ACGME-accredited residency and fellowship programs in 130 specialties and subspecialties at approximately 700 sponsoring institutions. Active full-time and part-time residents and fellows numbered more than 120,000."[11] Given the large number of programs, over many years, questions have arisen about program quality and responsiveness to personnel supply and specialty distribution issues. Reflecting these concerns, U.S. residency programs were described at the 1992 Macy Foundation conference, "Taking Charge of Graduate Medical Education: To Meet the Nation's Needs in the 21st Century," as "responsive principally to the service needs of hospitals, the interests of the medical specialty societies, the objectives of the residency program directors, and the career preferences of the medical students."[12]

Initiated in 1998 and then fully implemented in all residency training programs in 2012, ACGME made major changes in how the nation's medical residency programs are accredited through the establishment of an outcomes-based evaluation system called the "Outcome Project." The new system measures medical residents' competencies in performing essential tasks necessary for clinical practice today.[13] Reports thus far on the results of the Outcome Project are scant. One qualitative study that interviewed four experts states:[14]

> "Despite repeated entreaties by educational leaders, very few articles have been published to describe the reliability, validity, and reproducibility of educational methods for teaching or evaluating the competencies. As a result, objective metrics are lacking more than a decade after launching…[the] Outcome Project. Even measurement of medical knowledge—the most time-honored competency—remains problematic."

The same report concludes:

> The Outcome Project "…remains a work in progress, the results of which will not be known for 10 to 20 years or maybe never, since the changes afoot in medicine and society may dwarf any positive or negative impacts of the Outcome Project."

There has been a projected shortage of physicians in the United States for a variety of reasons including an aging population and the increased numbers of individuals with complex, chronic diseases. "In a comparison of 11 industrialized nations' experience, the U.S. number of practicing physicians per 1,000 population was second lowest at 2.5, compared with 2.3 for Japan, which was the lowest rate, 4.2 for Norway (per 2012 data), which was the highest rate, and the median of 3.1."[15] In response to the projected shortages, in 2006 the AAMC and others called for a 30 percent increase in the number of U.S. medical school graduates. Since then, the number of graduates has increased by 23 percent and will likely hit the 30 percent goal by 2020.[16]

As noted earlier, CMS supports hospitals' residency training programs in recognition of the added expenses entailed by training requirements. However, CMS limited the number of residents per hospital in 1997, to 1996 levels. There were a few small exceptions including allowing rural hospitals to climb to 130 percent of the number of their slots at 1996 levels. Since then, despite a steady increase in the number of allopathic and osteopathic medical school graduates, the number of CMS-funded residency slots has remained essentially unchanged since 1996.[16]

Congress has not passed legislation to increase the number of residency slots for more than 20 years. In an attempt to help address the issue, a provision of the Patient Protection and Affordable Care Act (ACA) of 2010 authorized CMS to redistribute available residency training slots from hospitals that have closed or underutilized their slots to hospitals in need of additional residents.[15] In this redistribution, priority is given to primary care and general surgery in states with the lowest physician-to-population ratios.[17] The ACA also promotes residency training in outpatient settings and in rural and underserved areas by increasing flexibility in the laws and regulations that govern Medicare's residency program funding.[17] Although this ACA provision will help optimize the use of available CMS funded residency slots, the gap between U.S. medical school graduates and available U.S. residency slots will increase at a time when projected physician shortages in the United States will become more pronounced.[16]

Whether the provisions of the ACA will succeed in ameliorating the imbalances in both the medical specialty and primary care workforces to meet American society's medical care needs and whether the ACGME outcome-based evaluation system will be implemented successfully to assist in that endeavor remain open questions. As in so many other aspects of health care, it is likely that market forces combined with policy decisions will determine the outcomes.

▶ Delineation and Growth of Medical Specialties

In its early history, the AMA resisted the development of medical specialties due to concerns about fragmenting care. The AMA's slow response to specialty interests prompted specialists to form their own societies and associations. In the last half of the 1800s, physicians interested in ophthalmology, otology, gynecology, obstetrics, and pediatrics formed their own specialty groups. In the early 1900s, with specialization increasing among physicians, specialty hospitals were founded in some cities, and general practitioners found themselves eased out of hospitals by specialists.

In response, the American Academy of General Practice was formed in 1947 to advocate general practice departments in hospitals. It was not until 1969, however, that general practice, now called family medicine, became a recognized specialty.

Deficient Training of Medical Specialists

Despite the growth in the number of specialists, at the time of the Flexner Report there was no standard for adequate specialty training. The length of specialty training required by various medical schools and hospitals ranged from just a few weeks to three years, and the quality of graduating specialists could vary from excellent to incompetent. A physician with almost any level of training could practice as a specialist.

In 1917, the U.S. Army, in need of physicians, examined the qualifications of physicians who wished to be classified as specialists, and the results were shocking. Though many had practiced as specialists for years, very high percentages of self-declared physician specialists were rejected by the service as unfit to practice as specialists, and some were deemed unfit to practice in any branch of medicine at all.

As improved technology and the development of safer and more effective anesthesia and antiseptic techniques made surgery a more acceptable medical option, the demand for surgery grew and the numbers of surgeons and hospitals increased in response. The American College of Surgeons, established in 1912, set up an oversight board and established practice standards in 1917 for certifying specialist surgeons. At the same time, the AMA started inspecting internship sites and produced a list of approved sites.

Although both the AMA and the American College of Surgeons began to rate the quality of postgraduate training, they quickly realized they could not make their findings public, and the results were suppressed. In 1924, the AMA Council on Medical Education began to approve hospitals for residency specialty training programs. For the next 40 years, residency programs were initiated in hospitals with little regard for the quality of the training experience. Often poorly planned and supervised, residents' educational experiences were deemed secondary to their obligations as medical house staff to serve whatever patient load they were assigned. Assigned to single departments, the opportunities for developing expert clinical knowledge and skills varied with the interest and teaching skills of a few attending physicians in the department. Educational standards and reform were needed, and half a century after the Flexner Report was published, the AMA again requested an outside examination of the medical education process. The AMA commissioned a Citizens Committee on Graduate Medical Education, chaired by John S. Mills, who issued his report in 1966. Key recommendations of the report included the elimination of independent internships and the awarding of accreditation of residency training programs to institutions rather than to individual medical departments. In 1970, the AMA endorsed the inclusion of the first year of graduate medical education in a program approved by an appropriate residency review committee (RRC). The term *internship* was dropped, and by 1980 the AMA had issued recommendations for broad training in the first postdoctoral year.

The current curriculum requirements for becoming a specialist are well defined and standardized. The physician must graduate from a medical school, serve in a residency program in an approved setting, and pass a qualifying specialty examination. The appropriate specialty board then certifies the physician. The boards are sponsored by the major specialty society in the specific area of study and the appropriate specialty section of the AMA.

▶ Certification of Physicians with Board Examinations

Any discussion of medical training requires the clarification between accreditation and certification. Training programs such as medical residencies are accredited to ensure they have the necessary resources, personnel, and curriculum to produce well-qualified trainees. Certifying organizations such as medical boards support a certification process that usually includes a board examination, which if completed successfully, indicates that the individual physician who is certified has demonstrated the necessary knowledge and skills to practice medicine safely and effectively. The terms, "certification" referring to professionals and "accreditation" referring to training programs will be used consistently throughout this chapter.

With regard to physicians, boards were formed for each specialty to provide a process to ensure physicians who "pass" are properly trained and capable to practice medicine safely and effectively. The American Board of Ophthalmology, established in 1933, was the first specialty board. In the same year, an advisory board for medical specialties, the American Board of Medical Specialties (ABMS), was established as an independent, not-for-profit organization. The mission of ABMS "is to serve the public and the medical profession by improving the quality of health care through setting professional standards for lifelong certification in partnership with Member Boards."[18] The last specialty board, the American Board of Medical Genetics and Genomics, was created in 1991.

Each member board can sponsor the creation of numerous subspecialty certifications. Some specialty boards such as Allergy and Immunology sponsor no subspecialty certifications. Some of the subspecializations are specific to just one sponsoring specialty board such as the subspecialization of Cardiovascular Disease (Cardiology), which is only a subspecialization of internal medicine. Other subspecialties traverse multiple specialty boards such as Sleep Medicine, which is sponsored as a subspecialty certification of Anesthesiology, Family Medicine, Internal Medicine, Otolaryngology, Pediatrics, and Psychiatry and Neurology. (Psychiatry and Neurology is one board.) Each of these specialty boards sponsors its own Sleep Medicine Certification, writes its own certification requirements, and creates and administers its own board examination. This can be very confusing to patients as they may see a subspecialist "sleep doctor" who is a specialist, first, in any of the aforementioned specialties.

In addition, some subspecialty certifications are offered to those who do not have certification of the sponsoring specialty board. For example, the four-year-old subspecialty of Clinical Informatics is sponsored by the two ABMS member boards of Pathology and Preventive Medicine. Pathology only offers its subspecialty certification to those holding a Pathology specialty certification while Preventive Medicine offers its subspecialty certification to those who hold a specialty certification in any of the ABMS member boards.[19] The establishment of the Clinical Informatics subspecialization is very timely as the adoption of electronic health records and other health information technology becomes the standard in medical practice. The creation of this subspecialization recognizes the importance of the clinical informatics field to the practice of medicine. It is one where its physicians have the training and experience to solve some of the significant challenges and unintended consequences of the use of health information technology in the practice of medicine. This includes the population tools needed to meet the new value-based care reporting requirements soon to be implemented by CMS. See Chapters 3 and 4 for discussion of the value-based reporting requirements.

As of 2016, ABMS member boards offer specialty certification in 37 specialties and 85 subspecialties. The number of subspecialties has continued to increase as the science of medicine has advanced. The current and complete list of medical specialties and subspecialties is available from the ABMS.[20] The ABMS also publishes a helpful guide that provides a detailed and in-depth look at how specialty and subspecialty certification is structured.[21]

A typical path for training physicians in the United States is completion of education, training, and certification in the following sequence:

1. Undergraduate degree with a core in biology, chemistry, math, and many other disciplines (4 years)
2. Medical school accredited by the AAMC (4 years)
3. Residency specialty training accredited by the ACGME (3–7 years)
4. Certification by one of the ABMS boards in the medical specialty of the physician's residency by passing a board examination
5. Optional fellowship(s) accredited by the ACGME (1–4 years each)
6. Optional certification(s) by the ABMS boards in the medical subspecialties based on the fellowship(s) completed.

To keep their certification(s) active, most physicians participate in the ABMS Program for Maintenance of Certification (MOC). The MOC program requires periodic professional knowledge self-assessments and/or practice improvement activities in the specialty or subspecialties in which one or more certification is held.[22] For example, after initial specialty certification in internal medicine, a 10-year clock begins during which a physician must complete a prescribed number of ABMS-sponsored educational and quality improvement activities on a time line designed for their specialty. Only after the physician fulfills the MOC requirements does the physician become eligible to take the internal medicine recertification exam. This process then repeats every 10 years for the duration of the physician's medical practice.[22] The MOC program is designed to help ensure that physicians keep their medical knowledge up-to-date and adopt quality-improvement processes in their practices as they progress through their medical careers.

The MOC program has not been without detractors, as some physicians complain that the requirements are too time consuming for busy practicing physicians and that the quality of the MOC training programs are substandard. In 2015, one of the ABMS member boards, the American Board of Internal Medicine (ABIM), acknowledged these criticisms in its MOC program and has developed a plan to address these weaknesses.[23,24]

▶ Accreditation of Graduate Physician Training

All of the specialty boards require that to be eligible to sit for a board examination (i.e., to be "board eligible"), the candidate physician must have successfully completed an accredited residency. In 1928, the AMA published the guidelines for approved residencies that set educational accreditation standards for residencies. The ACGME, formed in 1981 by the ABMS, the American Hospital Association, the AMA, the AAMC, and the Council of Medical Specialty Societies, extends authority to RRCs to determine the standards for its residencies. The ACGME specifies the curriculum, teaching methods, trainee assessment, program evaluation, faculty requirements for each residency and fellowship in detail. For a residency or fellowship to become ACGME accredited, a hospital or university that is sponsoring the training must submit a detailed application and plan for operation and evaluation of the residency or fellowship according to exacting ACGME specifications. In addition, all accredited programs go through periodic reaccreditation cycles that include site visits to ensure each accredited training program is maintaining ACGME standards. Should a program fall short during a reaccreditation cycle, the ACGME has several options from minor sanctions up to and including immediate suspension of accreditation status.

In addition to the controls of ACGME and its five parent organizations, numerous influences affect different aspects of residency content and training. These include the 24 specialty boards, RRCs, hospital directors, medical school deans, program directors, training directors, faculty, house staff, and specialty societies. The problems inherent in this complex system of control will intensify as legislated healthcare reforms require:

- Changes to accommodate specialty imbalance
- Physician supply
- Reductions in funding
- Shifts from inpatient to ambulatory care
- Increased emphasis on primary care
- Reconfigurations of practice and reimbursement taking shape in the healthcare industry

Hospitalists are rapidly assuming the care of inpatients in U.S. hospitals and replacing the role of patients' primary care physicians in hospital care, as described more extensively in Chapter 4. They are not following the usual paradigm of an ACGME-accredited training program and an ABMS-sponsored board examination. While there is not yet a specific and distinct board certification available for hospitalists, in the early 1990s the ABIM created the Focused Practice in Hospital Medicine (FPHM) as part of its MOC program for its Internal Medicine Board Certification. To become board certified as a hospitalist in internal medicine, physicians must first obtain board certification in internal medicine and then select a track in internal medicine's MOC program—either general internal medicine MOC or the FPHM. The FPHM is the path that certifies physicians as hospitalists. Physicians cannot participate in both the MOC for internal medicine and the FPHM. As physicians with certification in other medical specialties increase their presence as hospitalists, it is likely that a method of certification more similar to the traditional path will emerge in the future.

▶ Physician Workforce Supply and Distribution

By the mid-1960s, the federal government predicted there would be a national shortage of physicians in the United States. New policies and programs were established to increase the number of physicians by increasing medical school funding. In the 20 years between 1980 and 2000, the total number of physicians in the United States increased from 467,679 to 813,770—an increase of 74 percent. The overall physician-to-population ratio during the same period increased from 207 to 296 per 100,000 people. However by 2014, the physician-to-population ratio decreased to 265.4 physicians per 100,000 people.[25]

Calculating present and future physician supply needs is a challenging and complex exercise. There is an absence of a national, comprehensive methodology as well as difficulty in assessing physician productivity, or how many patients physicians see or reasonably can see in specified time frames. In addition, wide variations in the number of physicians practicing in various geographic regions remains a pressing problem in the current healthcare delivery system. The number of active physicians providing patient care per 100,000 people in each state varies from a high of more than 432.4 per 100,000 population in Massachusetts to a low of 184.7 per 100,000 population in Mississippi. States having the highest ratio of physicians per population are concentrated regionally in the northeastern states.[25] The low supply of physicians in rural and inner-city communities continues to create a medical care delivery crisis for populations living in these underserved areas.

Most U.S. hospitals depend on International Medical Graduates (IMGs) to help fill their residency positions, as more residency program slots are available than the number of available U.S. medical school graduates each year. In the 2014–2015 class, approximately 25 percent of hospital residencies were filled by IMGs.[26,27] This has been the case for several years. Now, approximately 25 percent of the active physician workforce in the United States is composed of IMGs.[27] Most foreign medical graduates gained entry to the U.S. healthcare system by completing an accredited medical residency in the United States. Due to concerns about a lack of basic clinical and communication skills among some IMGs, since 1998 IMGs have been required to pass a clinical skill assessment prior to entering a U.S. residency. Although there was a surge of IMG entrants immediately before the requirement went into effect, there was a significant drop in IMG entrants after the requirement was initiated. However, the quality of the applicants has improved while still providing enough IMGs to fill the residency positions not taken by U.S. medical graduates.[28]

Although most residencies are funded through CMS, additional funding sources are available. For example, some states fund residencies in an attempt to address areas of critical shortages such as in primary care and nephrology.

▶ Ratios of Generalist to Specialist Physicians and the Changing Demand

Primary care or generalist physicians are broadly defined as physicians practicing family medicine, general internal medicine, or general pediatrics. Physicians practicing obstetrics and gynecology also are sometimes included as primary care practitioners. For years, the numbers of generalist physicians have been considered too low to meet the basic healthcare needs of large segments of the general population. Additionally, the emphasis on medical diagnosis and treatment by combinations of specialist and subspecialist physicians rather than preventive medicine and lifestyle management has been criticized as contributing significantly to the complexity and rising costs of medical care.

In the early 1990s, the growth of managed care raised concerns that the longstanding 60:40 ratio of medical specialists to primary care physicians would leave the United States with an inadequate number of primary care physicians and an oversupply of specialists. Those forecasts led to a number of federal and state policies that encouraged the training of more primary care practitioners. A significant increase in the number of physicians practicing in the primary care fields of family medicine and pediatrics followed. The adequacy of the supply of primary care physicians and the number of training programs for medical students, which had appeared to meet population needs for primary care in years past, have recently been reexamined during the current era of healthcare delivery reform.[29]

In contrast to earlier predictions, the marketplace demand for medical specialists has not decreased, due to factors such as general population growth and the aging of the baby-boom population, who as they age require additional and more complex medical care provided by specialists.[30] "The ratio of generalist physicians to specialists in this country reversed from about 80:20 in 1930 to 20:80 in 1970. Since then we have seen family physicians, general internists, general pediatricians, and osteopathic physicians carry on the generalist tradition, but their aggregate numbers today are no more than 30 percent."[31]

The ratio favoring specialty practice results from individual career choices made by medical students before graduation. One of the most important influences of academic health centers is the socialization process that shapes the skills, values, and attitudes of future physicians and other healthcare professionals. Other factors that influence the choice of specialty include significant income differentials between primary care and specialty practice, work–life balance preferences, and the types of outpatient clinical practice sites in which residents receive training. These outpatient sites often are overcrowded hospital outpatient clinics that serve large numbers of poor and medically difficult patients with overburdened teaching faculty.

Considering the origins of the specialist–generalist imbalance, it is significant that until very recently almost every aspect of most medical school and teaching hospital experiences favored the practice of specialty medicine. Many medical students who intended to become generalist physicians at the onset of their medical education were induced by exposure to the medical education environment to change their minds in favor of becoming specialists.

With the passage of the ACA in 2010, by 2015, there were approximately 16.4 million fewer uninsured people in the United States who are increasing the demand on the current system for services they likely postponed in the past such as primary care and preventive medicine.[32] In 2012, despite the highest per-capita spending on health care in the world and an aging population, and despite the increased demand for health care resulting from the ACA, the ratio of U.S. physicians to 1,000 people was second lowest at 2.5 as compared to Japan at 2.3 (the lowest) and to Norway at 4.2 (the highest).[16] Because of the previously noted 1997 CMS cap on the number of residency slots it funds each year and the push to increase the number of medical school graduates, the total number of first-year ACGME accredited residency positions has grown at an annual rate of 1 percent from 2002 to 2014.[16] At the same time, the number of MD and DO graduates has been growing at an annual rate of 2.8 percent.[16] Approximately 29,000 residents completed training in 2015 and approximately 29 percent of these have become primary care physicians.[16] The AAMC estimates that with the slow 1 percent projected annual increase in the number of physicians, by 2025, there will be short fall of between 12,500 and 31,100 primary care physicians and between 28,200 and

63,700 specialists.[30] In addition, approximately 28 percent of practicing physicians are aged 60 and older and therefore likely to retire in the next decade.[16] Despite the proposed shortages, beginning in 2015, U.S. medical schools have begun to graduate more MDs and DOs than there are U.S. residency program slots to accommodate.[16] Congress will need to act to fund additional residency program slots or there will be a large and growing pool of successful medical school graduates whose medical careers will not begin due to lack of residency slots, despite a critical shortage of physicians.

Many ACA provisions were aimed at improving access to primary health care and addressing the urgent need for an expanded primary care workforce.[33] These provisions included allowing hospitals to better utilize unused CMS-funded residency slots and loan repayment programs for physicians who agreed to work in primary care in underserved areas. The ACA also funded the National Health Service Corps to recruit primary care providers to work in underserved areas and provided more than $200 million in grants for community-based "teaching health centers" to establish more primary care residency programs.[33]

▶ Preventive Medicine

In 1991, the Pew Charitable Trusts published a report that outlined factors expected to drive future health care. They concluded that an approach that stresses disease prevention would characterize future healthcare systems. The report emphasized that health concerns should be addressed at a community level and that medical schools should require physician training learning in community environments. The need to focus on preventive care and treatment techniques that use technology to the patient's advantage was a challenge facing new physicians, which was also recognized many years ago.[34]

The practice of medicine and medical education, however, has a history of poor results in establishing health promotion and disease prevention as a high priority in the U.S. healthcare system. This is largely because the delivery system and its reimbursement incentives have evolved as an acute illness complaint–response system. Provider payment incentives always have favored intervention after the fact rather than prevention, in spite of strong evidence of the cost-effectiveness of primary prevention. As a result, the United States currently spends most of its healthcare dollars treating diseases that could have been prevented. Parameters for prevention are established in many areas, but past studies have shown that only a small percentage of physicians adhere to the guidelines.[35]

More recently, however, rising public awareness, media pressure, and enlightened leadership have produced some innovative and productive collaborations between clinical and preventive medicine. Practicing physicians have participated in public health measures to prevent vaccine-preventable childhood diseases, sexually transmitted diseases, and HIV infection that depend on physician case reporting, immunization, and education. They also have continued to collaborate in community prevention campaigns for problems such as childhood obesity, diabetes, smoking cessation, cholesterol education, and early cancer detection.

For collaborations between clinical medicine and public health to expand and grow, there is strong recognition of the need for significant changes in all areas of medical education, accountability measures, and healthcare financing.[36] A 2012 report of the Institute of Medicine, "Primary

Care and Public Health: Exploring Integration to Improve Population Health," offers new perspectives on how the primary care and public health sectors can leverage healthcare workforce and provisions in the ACA to advance a population-based, prevention-oriented mind-set in the healthcare delivery system. The report offers several suggestions for community-level linkages of academic health centers' strengths with provider and community resources to research, develop, and implement sustainable delivery system changes that will result in improved health status of populations.[37]

▶ Changing Physician–Hospital Relationships

Historically, physicians and hospitals maintained a unique relationship that brought both of them profits from a single source—patient admission. The independence and autonomy of physicians were respected, and their financial relationship with the hospital in the care of patients was overlooked by paying physicians separately on a fee-for-service basis and the hospital on the basis of costs incurred. Because hospitals were dependent on physicians to admit patients and make use of the hospitals' resources, hospitals courted physicians by providing them with equipment, staff, and other perquisites with little regard for the effects on hospital costs.

Physicians had responsibilities to the hospital as an institution and to the patients they admitted to the hospital. As a component of a hospital's governance structure, the medical staff organization was responsible to the board of trustees and the hospital administration for many organizational activities that required medical expertise. Through the medical staff organization and its committees, physicians have been obligated to provide the knowledge and authority to establish clinical policies and procedures, perform utilization review, ensure quality, and determine the credentialing standards for admission to the hospital's medical staff.[38]

The roles and responsibilities of physicians have changed from the time when physicians were the sole determinants of hospital admission criteria, the ordering of diagnostic tests and therapeutic procedures, the establishment of the length of hospital stays, decisions on the use of hospital-owned services and other resources, and referrals. In the current environment of constrained and reconfigured reimbursement systems, heightened accountability, and physician entrepreneurship, the relationships between physicians and hospitals are different and often strained.

Under the prospective payment system, hospitals are at financial risk if physicians allow lengths of inpatient stays to exceed insurer criteria. New payment criteria penalize hospitals financially if treatment results in costly complications or the need for readmission.[39,40] As a result, hospitals must monitor and question physician decisions. Another reason why physicians can no longer ignore the financial consequences of their clinical decisions includes health plans selecting hospitals to serve their members based on operating efficiency and cost-effectiveness. Physicians who are not sensitive to the impact of their practice patterns on the financial burden of the hospitals where they have privileges and who do not cooperate in keeping the hospital financially competitive likely will not be viewed favorably by hospital administration.

In addition to these stresses on the internal relationships of hospitals and physicians, there are external conflicts. Advanced technology and the economic environment cause hospitals and physicians to become competitors for patient business. The growth of group practice along with advanced technologies that permit many procedures that formerly required hospitalization to be performed in ambulatory settings have given physicians the financial resources and patient volume to acquire the necessary equipment and trained staff to allow them to independently own and operate ambulatory centers. These entrepreneurial activities have placed physicians in direct competition with hospitals.

In addition to the employment of hospitalists, increasing employment of primary care and specialist physicians by hospitals has been one response to the changing healthcare system environment. The number of physicians directly employed by hospitals grew by 34 percent between 2000 and 2010. In one year alone, between 2013 and 2014, physicians directly employed by hospitals increased from 10 percent to 21 percent.[41] This trend is the result of changing interests on the part of both physicians and hospitals. From physicians' perspectives, employment has become desirable due to factors such as flat reimbursement rates, complex insurance and health information technology (HIT) requirements, high malpractice premiums, and a desire for greater work–life balance. For hospitals, employing physicians provides opportunities to gain market share for admissions, the use of diagnostic testing and other outpatient services, and referrals to high-revenue specialty services.[42] In addition, hospital executives cite physician–hospital integration as an important strategy to prepare for payment reforms such as accountable care organizations and penalties for hospital readmissions.[43] The AMA has raised concerns about the potential effects of employment requirements on the physician–patient relationship. In a policy issued in late 2012, the AMA reminds physicians that "in any situation where the economic or other interests of the employer are in conflict with patient welfare, patient welfare must take priority." The AMA statement also notes that physicians should inform patients about any financial incentives that may impact treatment options.[44] Clearly, the competition for patients in the reformed environment has vastly changed traditional hospital–physician relationships.[45]

Evidence-Based Clinical Practice Guidelines

Clinical practice guidelines are systematically developed protocols used to assist practitioner and patient decisions about appropriate health care by defining the roles of specific diagnostic and treatment modalities in patient diagnosis and management. The protocols contain recommendations that are based on scientific evidence gathered from a rigorous systematic review and synthesis of the published medical literature and are, therefore, described as evidence-based.[46]

Clinical practice guidelines evolved in the late 1970s and early 1980s after the publication of data showing wide variations in the applications of medical procedures in different regions of the United States and increased use of questionable, inappropriate, and unnecessary services that added significantly to the increasing costs of health care. It is important to note that the variations in the level of healthcare interventions were so great as to suggest that physicians were unaware of the relative effectiveness of various procedures and that patients were not benefiting from much of the care they received.

Health services researchers conjectured that assessments of the outcomes or relative effectiveness of various medical procedures would lead to practice guidelines and eliminate ineffective, unnecessary, or inappropriate procedures and their related costs. To this end, Congress created the Agency for Health Care Policy and Research in 1989, now renamed the Agency for Healthcare Research and Quality (AHRQ). The agency was directed to fund outcomes and health services research to start developing practice guidelines. After a slow start, the agency began releasing practice guidelines for specific conditions. Although fewer than two dozen guidelines had been released by 1995, the agency's efforts sparked a great deal of guideline development by other institutions and agencies. The RAND Corporation, medical specialty societies, health maintenance organizations, insurers, and many other professional healthcare organizations have produced clinical practice guidelines that have subsequently been reviewed and evaluated. For a clinical practice guideline to be considered for AHRQ approval it must meet these criteria[47]:

- The guideline must contain systematically developed recommendations, strategies, or other information to assist healthcare decision-making in specific clinical circumstances.
- The guideline must have been produced under the auspices of a relevant professional organization (e.g., medical specialty society, government agency, healthcare organization, or health plan).
- The guideline development process must have included a verifiable, systematic literature search and review of existing evidence published in peer-reviewed journals.
- The guideline must be current and the most recent version (i.e., developed, reviewed, or revised within the last five years).

More than 2,000 active, evidence-based clinical practice guidelines that have met these AHRQ evaluation criteria have been collected in a database, organized by searchable topics, and made available online at the AHRQ's National Guideline Clearinghouse.[48] The AHRQ also maintains a searchable database of nearly 5,000 archived guidelines that have been updated or withdrawn.

Evidence-based clinical practice guidelines are considered to be the most objective and least biased clinical practice guidelines that serve as a means to assist in preventing the use of unnecessary treatment modalities and in avoiding negligent events, with patient safety and the delivery of consistent high-quality care as foremost priorities.[49] With government agencies, health systems, third-party payers, and specialty societies promoting the use of evidence-based clinical practice guidelines, they have become an integral part of current medical practice. The widespread application of evidence-based clinical practice guidelines is expected to continue to have a significant effect on medical practice.

▶ Physician Report Cards and "Physician Compare"

In the 1970s, the AMA code of ethics explicitly prohibited "information that would point out differences between doctors." Thirty-two states passed laws supporting the AMA's position. The laws were intended to prevent misleading or competitive advertising of office hours, charges, or services. The position of organized medicine, however, reflected a long history of protecting physician performance from public scrutiny.[50]

Subsequently, state laws supporting the AMA's position were determined to be violations of the First Amendment. Passage of freedom of information acts that prohibited governments from hiding information from the public removed the barriers that prevented the public from comparing the performance of physicians. In 1986, when the Health Care Financing Administration (now renamed CMS) released hospital-specific mortality rates for Medicare patients, the information dam was broken. In December 1991, the publication *Newsday* reported the first information regarding physician performance ever made public.[51] Never again would the public be denied access to government data about the quality of medical care. The publication was based on New York State's pioneering effort to compare and publish hospital-specific, severity-adjusted heart surgery mortality rates. Although New York State had intended to publish only the names of the hospitals involved, a *Newsday* freedom of information request, supported by the Supreme Court of the State of New York, forced the release of the rankings of the heart surgeons involved.[51]

Within less than a decade, the contentious matter of exposing the comparative performance of physicians on a wide spectrum of variables has been resolved in favor of the consumers of medical care. Many states have passed legislation that gives the public access to physician information, including disciplinary records, malpractice actions, and whether a physician has lost privileges at a hospital.

Medical societies in general support physician-profiling programs that report a physician's education, training, licensure, and membership in professional societies, state disciplinary actions, and serious misdemeanor convictions. They have, however, objected strongly to the inclusion of medical malpractice and hospital disciplinary information out of concern that such information would be taken out of context, possibly misinterpreted by the consumer, and possibly not adequately reflective of the quality of care provided by the physician. Now, as a component of the ACA, in 2010 CMS launched a "Physician Compare" website that is a companion to its previously established "Hospital Compare" site. Originally established as a directory of Medicare participating physicians, CMS has taken a slow, step-wise approach to adding additional information to the site. In 2011 and 2012 CMS added information on physicians participating in the Physician Quality Reporting System (PQRS) and the Electronic Prescribing Incentive Program. The PQRS is a quality-improvement program that establishes a number of key quality metrics on physician practice. The Electronic Prescribing Incentive Program was a financial incentive to promote the use of electronic prescribing. The Physician Compare program uses some of the data generated by these programs to help report on group practice and eventually individual physician quality. In 2014 Physician Compare added diabetes and heart disease performance data for 66 group practices and five measures of heart disease and diabetes care for 146 accountable care organizations serving patients enrolled in Medicare.[52] As of April 2016, quality data is only reported at the group practice level. CMS plans to continue to add more quality data for group practices and add quality data for individual physicians later in 2016. Concerns will continue about data collection methods and the fairness, accuracy, and objectivity of the comparative data used in all types of reports about physician performance. Although increased transparency is expected to contribute to the quality of care, physician performance reports likely will have significant limitations. These limitations will be true for both the medical provider and the consumer due to the complexity of collecting data from a wide variety of data sources and putting them in one standardized form that patients can understand.[52]

▶ Health Information Technology and Physician Practice

The introduction of HIT into the practice of medicine has signaled a new era in clinical practice to both new and established physicians. Incentives for the adoption of electronic health records (EHR) by the HITECH Act, the ACA, and most recently, the Medicare Access & CHIP Reauthorization Act of 2015 (MACRA) have pushed physicians and other healthcare workers to integrate this new technology into their practice of medicine. Health information technologies have transformed the practice of medicine in many ways. While there is a great deal of evidence that HIT holds the promise to dramatically improve the quality of care and reduce its cost, there also have been a number of unfortunately unintended consequences.[53-55] For a much more detailed discussion on this important and timely topic, see Chapter 3.

Medical schools and teaching hospitals have responded to this epic change in the practice of medicine by introducing HIT training into their coursework and biomedical informatics into their curricula. Unfortunately, medical school curricula are already packed full, and adding yet another new curricular area is extremely challenging given it must compete with a plethora of other new proposed areas such as quality improvement, systems-based practice, evidence-based practice, and a number of initiatives in public health. Medical schools have been unable to keep pace with the rapid changes. Wald et al provide an excellent summary of the current state of this important issue[56]:

> The actual teaching of HCIT [Health Care Information Technologies] competencies, however, is likewise not keeping pace with the burgeoning use of HCIT.[57] For example, few medical schools have explicit processes for assessing medical informatics competencies within the Association of American Medical Colleges' Medical School Objectives Project.[58] Currently, no EHR-related competencies are indexed in the ACGME requirements framework, nor are EHR-related questions included in the United States Medical Licensing Examination. Given the scarcity of existing formal pedagogy, medical education curriculum and professional development initiatives for preparing both future providers and seasoned clinicians to effectively use EHRs are warranted. In particular, medical students need to be "informed consumers who understand both the power and vulnerabilities of the tools they will be using in their practices."[59]

A study of third-year medical students reported generally positive attitudes toward the use of EHR in an ambulatory setting. Students noted that they received more feedback on their electronic charts than on paper charts. However, students were concerned about the use of the EHR interfering with doctor–patient encounters.[60]

As mentioned previously, the ABMS has also recently approved a new physician subspecialty certification in Clinical Informatics, a recognition of the importance of HIT and the science of biomedical informatics to the medical community and the practice of medicine.

▶ Escalating Costs of Malpractice Insurance

The steeply rising costs of medical liability insurance are a continuing concern for practicing physicians, medical schools, and teaching hospitals. In the last decade, schools of medicine and hospitals have seen their liability premium costs increase from 6 to 10 times—from thousands to millions. In some states, physicians, especially specialists, have seen their premiums triple or quadruple in just a few years. Rising liability insurance costs reflect steep increases in the amount of malpractice jury awards. Also, during economic downturns such as the recent recession, insurance companies that depended on investment income are forced to raise premiums to keep their businesses viable. In addition, there is fairly good evidence that physicians who fear malpractice lawsuits practice "defensive medicine" causing unproductive or unnecessary care, which has been estimated to cost about $6 billion per year. This figure does not include litigation costs, damages, or settlement costs.[61] The effect has been demoralizing to many physicians, some to the point where they move their practice to locations with less-expensive malpractice insurance costs.[50]

▶ Ethical Issues

Two developments have focused attention on a number of issues in medical ethics. Rather than concerns about unethical or unprofessional conduct, these ethical issues reflect the practice-based dilemmas faced by physicians working in the rapidly changing healthcare environment.

The first set of ethical concerns relates to the policies promoted by health insurers. Efforts of such organizations to manage the financing, costs, accessibility, or quality of care delivered cause them to subject physicians to a range of guidelines, treatment parameters, peer reviews, and financial incentives and penalties. Cost-avoidance policies that require preauthorization for the more expensive procedures, substitution of less expensive tests and medications, and restraint of hospitalization in favor of alternative ambulatory services raise questions about increased risks to patients.

An opposite set of ethical concerns could be raised about the risk to patients subjected to the practices of fee-for-service traditional medicine, which the health insurers try to avoid—unnecessary hospitalizations, needless or inappropriate tests and procedures, ineffective treatments, and uncoordinated care provided by multiple providers. There is no question, however, that particular control strategies of health insurers present related ethical issues. Increasingly, physicians admit they may have to exaggerate the severity of an illness in order to help patients get necessary care. Systems that encourage deceitful practices detract from the professional standards of medicine.

The second development creating vexing ethical issues is the remarkable advance in technologic capability. Medicine's ability to prolong the lives of severely brain-injured patients, increasingly premature infants, terminally ill or brain-dead patients, and others with no promise of functional survival has increased the need for ethical guidelines. At present, individual physicians decide how they will advise the families of such patients. If the family and the physician cannot agree about treatment, there is no set procedure for deciding what to do. These and other ethical dilemmas brought about by the technologic advances in medicine present formidable challenges to the ethics committees of hospitals and professional organizations.

Among the most critical of future ethical issues are those related to advances in the field of molecular biology and gene manipulation and therapy. The $1,000 genome—technology that allows scientists to sequence an individual's entire DNA in less than 72 hours for approximately $1,000—will likely decrease to $100 in 10 years. Such sequencing is now becoming a standard of care for forms of childhood cancer where the tumor can be sequenced and the effectiveness of various chemotherapeutics can be predicted based on the genome of the tumor. As genome sequencing becomes more common, a host of unintended consequences and ethical issues will arise. How genomics data can and should be used and who can use it is just beginning to be discussed. One example dilemma is what future obligations are for the holders of a person's genome data. Traditional lab tests are analyzed, reported, acted upon, and then archived. Genomic data is much different given that as more discoveries are made, reanalysis of patients' genomic data could provide extremely valuable information for predicting future disease states and healthcare decision making. By whom, how, and whether such periodic reanalysis is performed is one of many ethical questions yet to be vetted in our society. How individual medical practitioners are supposed to cope with the deluge of information that is a human genome is another as of yet unanswered question. Amid all the potential benefits of these remarkable scientific advances are fears of the unethical applications of such technology. Now more than ever, the application of sound ethical principles to the practice of medicine is becoming increasingly important.

▶ Physicians and the Internet

The vast majority of the world's biomedical literature (approximately 5,500 journals) are actively indexed by the National Library of Medicine, one of the National Institutes of Health, in Washington, DC. *PubMed*, a web-based search engine of this enormous body of biomedical knowledge, is just one of millions of potential sources of medical information available to physicians and their patients through the Internet.

The major tenet of evidence-based practice is that physicians consult and use the latest scientific evidence to inform medical decision-making for their patients.[62] To do this proactively is a practical impossibility due to the sheer volume of new medical information generated on an ongoing basis. A recent study estimated that a primary care physician would need to devote 627.5 hours per month in order to review the estimated 7,287 articles published in 341 primary care-related journals and indexed in *PubMed*.[63] This expectation is obviously absurd. Therefore, physicians often rely on what is termed "point of care knowledge resources" or expert summaries of the latest medical evidence, indexed by topical area and targeted for clinicians caring for patients. These summaries often come with a subscription cost, but they allow physicians to quickly locate the latest evidence, which is summarized concisely, on an as-needed basis. Such "point of care knowledge resources" are usually highly vetted and maintained by experts in the field so that all the information is periodically reviewed to incorporate the latest evidence as it is published. The Internet, however, has no "police" to ensure that all of the millions of sites with medically related information are correct, accurate, or up to date. This often creates confusion among patients and some physicians who are not savvy consumers of the biomedical literature. A recent Google search on "pneumonia" yielded more than 34 million results. It is becoming increasingly difficult for patients and physicians to cope with the sheer volume and utility of medical information available through the Internet.

Ironically, the vast majority of peer-reviewed biomedical journals are not freely available on the Internet and require subscription fees for access. In past years, this was the situation, even for articles published about research findings funded by the National Institutes of Health or other federal agencies. However, in 2009 the NIH Public Access Policy was mandated by Congress. The policy requires authors of all scientific papers on NIH-funded research that are published in the peer-reviewed biomedical journals to deposit their accepted manuscripts in a repository maintained by the National Library of Medicine that is freely searchable on the Internet.[64] The repository, *PubMed Central*, is distinct from *PubMed* that only indexes the articles and does not contain the full articles. Since the NIH policy was implemented, several additional federal agencies adopted the policy including the CDC, Department of Defense, Department of Agriculture, and the AHRQ. This entire body of biomedical literature freely available to the public via the Internet still represents only about 20 percent of all the biomedical literature published in peer-reviewed journals.[65] Despite the potential of current Internet technology, a large portion of the biomedical literature is not freely available to those outside of typical university settings that can afford the subscriptions costs for its physicians and researchers.

▶ **Future Perspectives**

Medicine has made astounding progress in the last 50 years. An increasing number of highly specialized physicians and support personnel have achieved marvels of technical accomplishment. The U.S. medical education establishment has had a central role in these laudable achievements.

However, in the World Health Organization report in 2000, the United States was ranked 15th in overall performance and number one in expenditures, yielding the now famous overall ranking of 36th—between the countries of Costa Rica and Slovenia.[66] In a 2014 report produced by the Commonwealth Fund, a private United States foundation whose mission is to promote a high-performing equitable healthcare system, indicates that the United States is dead last among the 11 national healthcare systems it evaluated. From the report[67]:

> The United States health care system is the most expensive in the world, but this report and prior editions consistently show the U.S. underperforms relative to other countries on most dimensions of performance. Among the 11 nations studied in this report— Australia, Canada, France, Germany, the Netherlands, New Zealand, Norway, Sweden, Switzerland, the United Kingdom, and the United States—the U.S. ranks last, as it did in the 2010, 2007, 2006, and 2004 editions of [the report].

Although the report includes some promise for an improved performance of the U.S. healthcare system as a result of the implementation of the ACA, the report concludes " ... from the perspectives of both physicians and patients, the U.S. healthcare system could do much better in achieving value for the nation's substantial investment in health."[67] Initiatives of the HITECH Act to advance the effective use of HIT, the ACA to promote robust development of the primary care workforce, and MACRA to improve the quality of care delivered are all causes for optimism.

The U.S. medical education infrastructure will require transformative change to instill the competencies necessary in future generations of physicians and allied health personnel to improve the quality and reduce the costs of the future U.S. healthcare system. This will include new curricula including population health, clinical informatics, systems-based practice, quality improvement, and other domains of knowledge perhaps not yet discovered or identified as being important.

The challenges of including substantial additions to the already overloaded medical school curricula clearly are a tall order for the current medical education infrastructure. The problem will likely lie more in what to eliminate so the new competencies can be included rather than just identifying what should be added for the future. In 2012, U.S. medical licensing examination began testing students on public health principles with more emphasis on public health planned for future examinations. In 2014, the ABMS gave the first board examination in clinical informatics, the new subspecialty for physicians wanting to apply the science of clinical informatics to improve the quality of care while reducing its costs. So positive change in the medical education establishment is possible and is occurring. "Efforts to develop health professionals who can improve health, and not just deliver care, should be a continuing priority for the academic medicine and public health communities."[68]

In his landmark report of 1910, Abraham Flexner presaged the situation of today:

> His (the physician's) relationship was formerly to his patient—at most to his patient's family, and it was almost altogether remedial. If the patient had something wrong with him the doctor was called in to cure it. Payment of a fee ended the transaction. But the physician's function is fast becoming social, preventive, and systems' based rather than individual and curative. Upon him society relies to ascertain, and through measures essentially educational, to enforce the conditions that prevent disease and make positively for physical and moral well-being.[69]

Historically, medicine responded to the American public's desire to have the best and the most of medical services. But medicine now has a new responsibility—to help the American public understand that the challenges of improving health status and its costs are beyond the sole grasp of traditional system "insiders." Collaborative partnerships between the medical education establishment and other health- and community-serving professionals and organizations, citizens, policy makers, and elected officials will be required and in new ways. Without this, the creation of a new form of healthcare organization that ensures a coherent, efficient, and effective healthcare delivery system for all Americans will not be possible.

KEY TERMS FOR REVIEW

Academic Health Center
Accreditation Council on
  Graduate Medical Education
  (ACGME)
Active Evidence-based Clinical
  Practice Guidelines
Agency for Healthcare Research
  and Quality (AHRQ)

American Board of Medical
  Specialties (ABMS)
Flexner Report
Focused Practice in Hospital
  Medicine (FPHM)
Hospitalist
Indirect Medical Education
  (IME) Adjustment

Maintenance of Certification
  (MOC) Program
NIH Public Access
  Policy
Physician Compare
PubMed Central

CHAPTER ACRONYMS

ACGME Accreditation Council on Graduate
  Medical Education
AAMC Association of American Medical
  Colleges
AHRQ Agency for Healthcare Research
  and Quality
ABMS American Board of Medical Specialties
AMA American Medical Association
EHR Electronic Health Record
FPHM Focused Practice in Hospital Medicine

HIT Health Information Technology
HITECH Health Information Technology
  for Electronic and Clinical Health
IMG International Medical Graduate
MACRA Medicare Access & CHIP
  Reauthorization Act of 2015
MOC Maintenance of Certification
NIH National Institutes of Health
RRC Residency Review Committee

References

1. Barsukiewicz CK, Raffel MW, Raffel NK. *The US Health System: Origins and Functions*. 6th ed. Clifton Park, NY: Delmar/Cengage Learning; 2010.

2. Jones RS. Organized medicine in the United States. *Ann Surg*. 1993;217:423-429.

3. American Hospital Association. Fast facts on US hospitals. http://www.aha.org/research/rc/stat-studies/101207fastfacts.pdf. Accessed February 18, 2016.

4. American Association of Medical Colleges. Why teaching hospitals are important to all Americans. https://www.aamc.org/newsroom/keyissues/teaching_hospitals/253374/teaching-hospitals.html. Accessed February 18, 2016.

5. American Association of Medical Colleges. Medical schools. https://www.aamc.org/about/membership/378788/medicalschools.html. Accessed March 25, 2016.

6. Kohn L. The consequences of current financing methods for the future roles of AHCs. In: *Academic Health Centers: Leading Change in the 21st Century*. National Academies Press; 2004:chap 6. http://www.nap.edu/openbook.php?record_id=10734&page=92. Accessed March 25, 2016.

7. American Association of Medical Colleges. Table 1: Revenues supporting programs and activities at fully-accredited U.S. medical schools FY2014. https://www.aamc.org/download/434264/data/fy2014_medical_school_financial_tables.pdf. Accessed March 25, 2016.

8. Centers for Medicare & Medicaid Services. Indirect medical education (IME). https://www.cms.gov/medicare/medicare-fee-for-service-payment/acuteinpatientpps/indirect-medical-education-ime.html. Accessed March 25, 2016.

9. American Association of Colleges of Osteopathic Medicine. U.S. colleges of osteopathic medicine. http://www.aacom.org/become-a-doctor/us-coms. Accessed March 25, 2015.

10. Accreditation Council for Graduate Medical Education. Mission, vision, and values. http://www.acgme.org/About-Us/Overview/Mission-Vision-and-Values. Accessed March 25, 2016.

11. Accreditation Council for Graduate Medical Education. About us. http://www.acgme.org/About-Us/Overview. Accessed March 25, 2016.

12. Morris T, Sirica C. Taking charge of graduate medical education to meet the nation's needs in the 21st century. Paper presented at conference sponsored by the Josiah Macy, Jr., Foundation. June, 1992. New York, NY.

13. Accreditation Council for Graduate Medical Education. ACGME announces plan to transform how medical residency programs will educate future physicians for a changing health care system. February 22, 2012. http://www.prnewswire.com/news-releases/acgme-announces-plan-to-transform-how-medical-residency-programs-will-educate-future-physicians-for-a-changing-health-care-system-140051823.html. Accessed March 25, 2016.

14. Manthous CA. On the outcome project. *Yale J Biol Med.* 2014;87:213-220.

15. American Association of Medical Colleges. AAMC summaries of DGME and IME sections of the health reform bill and CMS proposed rules implementing these provisions. https://www.aamc.org/download/163590/data/summaries_of_gme_sections_of_health_reform_bill_.pdf. Accessed March 25, 2016.

16. Grover A, Orlowski JM, Erikson CE. The nations physician workforce and future challenges. *Am J Med Sci.* 2016;351:11-19.

17. Henry J. Kaiser Family Foundation. Summary of the Affordable Care Act. April 25, 2013. http://kff.org/health-reform/fact-sheet/summary-of-the-affordable-care-act/. Accessed March 25, 2016.

18. American Board of Medical Specialties. ABMS mission statement. http://www.abms.org/about-abms/governance/abms-mission-statement/. Accessed March 28, 2016.

19. American Board of Preventive Medicine. Clinical informatics board certification. http://www.theabpm.org/abpm_clinical_informatics.pdf. Accessed March 28, 2016.

20. American Board of Medical Specialties. Specialty and subspecialty certificates. http://www.abms.org/member-boards/specialty-subspecialty-certificates/. Accessed March 28, 2016.

21. American Board of Medical Specialties. ABMS guide to medical specialties. http://www.abms.org/media/84812/guide-to-medicalspecialties_05_2015-2.pdf. Accessed March 28, 2016.

22. American Board of Medical Specialties. Steps toward initial certification and MOC. http://www.abms.org/board-certification/steps-toward-initial-certification-and-moc/. Accessed March 28, 2016.

23. Bendix J. We got it wrong: ABIM does about-face on recent MOC changes. *Med Econ.* 2015;92:61.

24. American Board of Internal Medicine. ABIM announces immediate changes to MOC program. February 5, 2015. http://www.abim.org/news/abim-announces-immediate-changes-to-moc-program.aspx. Accessed March 28, 2016.

25. American Association of Medical Colleges. 2015 state physician workforce data book. November 2015. http://members.aamc.org/eweb/upload/2015StateDataBook%20(revised).pdf. Accessed March 30, 2016.

26. American Association of Medical Colleges. Table B3. Number of active residents, by type of medical school, GME specialty, and gender 2014–2015. https://www.aamc.org/data/448482/b3table.html. Accessed March 30, 2016.

27. Whelan GP, Gary NE, Kostis J, Boulet JR, Hallock JA. The changing pool of international medical graduates seeking certification training in US graduate medical education programs. *JAMA.* 2002;288:1079-1084.

28. United States Government Accountability Office. Foreign medical schools: Education should improve monitoring of schools that participate in the federal student loan program. June 2010. http://www.gao.gov/assets/310/306021.pdf. Accessed April 4, 2016.

29. Peccoralo LA, Callahan K, Stark R, DeCherrie LV. Primary care training and the evolving healthcare system. *Mt Sinai J Med.* 2012;79:451-463.

30. American Association of Medical Colleges. Physician supply and demand through 2025: key findings. March 2015. https://www.aamc.org/download/426260/data/physiciansupplyanddemandthrough2025keyfindings.pdf. Accessed April 3, 2016.

31. The Huffington Post. Upside down health care: why it matters. October 28, 2011. http://www.huffingtonpost

.com/john-geyman/generalist-vs-specialist-care
_b_927759.html. Accessed April 3, 2016.

32. United States Department of Health and Human Services. The Affordable Care Act is working. http://www.hhs.gov/healthcare/facts-and-features/fact-sheets/aca-is-working/index.html. Accessed April 3, 2016.

33. United States Department of Health and Human Services. Title V. Health care workforce. August 28, 2015. http://www.hhs.gov/healthcare/about-the-law/read-the-law/index.html#collapseFive. Accessed April 3, 2016.

34. O'Neil EH. Education as part of the health care solution. Strategies from the Pew Health Professions Commission. *JAMA*. 1992;268:1146-1148.

35. Inwald SA, Winters FD. Emphasizing a preventive medicine orientation during primary care/family practice residency training. *J Am Osteopath Assoc*. 1995;95:267-268, 271-265.

36. Association of Academic Health Centers. Out of order, out of time: the state of the nation's health workforce. http://www.aahcdc.org/policy/AAHC_OutofTime_4WEB.pdf. Accessed April 3, 2016.

37. The National Academies of Sciences Engineering and Medicine. Primary care and public health: exploring integration to improve population health. March 28, 2012. http://www.nationalacademies.org/hmd/Reports/2012/Primary-Care-and-Public-Health.aspx. Accessed April 3, 2016.

38. Kovner A. *Health Care Delivery in the United States*. 5th ed. New York, NY: Springer; 1995.

39. Zuckerman RB, Sheingold SH, Orav EJ, Ruhter J, Epstein AM. Readmissions, observation, and the hospital readmissions reduction program. *N Engl J Med*. 2016. http://www.ncbi.nlm.nih.gov/pubmed/26910198. Accessed April 8, 2016.

40. Centers for Medicare & Medicaid Services. Readmissions reduction program (HRRP). https://www.cms.gov/Medicare/Medicare-Fee-for-Service-Payment/AcuteInpatientPPS/Readmissions-Reduction-Program.html. Accessed March 8, 2016.

41. Becker's Hospital Review. 8 statistics on physician employment. July 14, 2014. http://www.beckershospitalreview.com/hospital-physician-relationships/8-statistics-on-physician-employment.html. Accessed April 9, 2016.

42. Singleton T, Miller P. The physician employment trend: what you need to know. *Fam Pract Manag*. 2015;22:11-15.

43. Gunderman R. Should doctors work for hospitals? *The Atlantic*. 2014. http://www.theatlantic.com/health/archive/2014/05/should-doctors-work-for-hospitals/371638/. Accessed April 8, 2016.

44. Pear R. Doctors warned on "divided loyalty". *The New York Times*. December 26, 2012. http://www.nytimes.com/2012/12/27/health/27doctors.html?ref=health&_r=1. Accessed April 3, 2016.

45. Casalino LP, November EA, Berenson RA, Pham HH. Hospital-physician relations: two tracks and the decline of the voluntary medical staff model. *Health Aff*. 2008;27:1305-1314.

46. National Heart Lung and Blood Institute. About systematic evidence reviews and clinical practice guidelines. http://www.nhlbi.nih.gov/health-pro/guidelines/about#what. Accessed April 3, 2016.

47. Agency for Healthcare Research and Quality. National Guideline Clearinghouse fact sheet. http://www.ahrq.gov/research/findings/factsheets/errors-safety/ngc/national-guideline-clearinghouse.html. Accessed April 3, 2016.

48. Agency for Healthcare Research and Quality. National guideline clearinghouse guidelines by topic. http://www.guideline.gov/browse/by-topic.aspx. Accessed April 3, 2016.

49. Shea KG, Sink EL, Jacobs JC, Jr. Clinical practice guidelines and guideline development. *J. Pediatr Orthop*. 2012;32 Suppl 2:S95-100.

50. Special report, docs fight to hide lawsuits. *New York Daily News, Sports Final*. April 17, 2000: 12.

51. Zinman D. Heart surgeons rated: State reveals patient-mortality records. *New York Newsday*. 1991;A.

52. Health Affairs website. Health policy briefs: Physician Compare. December 11, 2014. http://www.healthaffairs.org/healthpolicybriefs/brief.php?brief_id=131. Accessed April 3, 2016.

53. Gephart S, Carrington JM, Finley B. A systematic review of nurses' experiences with unintended consequences when using the electronic health record. *Nurs Adm Q*. 2015;39:345-356.

54. Sittig DF, Ash JS, Singh H. The safer guides: empowering organizations to improve the safety and effectiveness of electronic health records. *Am J Manag Care*. 2014;20:418-423.

55. Ryan AM, McCullough CM, Shih SC, Wang JJ, Ryan MS, Casalino LP. The intended and unintended consequences of quality improvement interventions for small practices in a community-based electronic health record implementation project. *Med Care*. 2014;52:826-832.

56. Wald HS, George P, Reis SP, Taylor JS. Electronic health record training in undergraduate medical education: bridging theory to practice with curricula for empowering patient- and relationship-centered care in the computerized setting. *Acad Med*. 2014;89:380-386.

57. Triola MM, Friedman E, Cimino C, Geyer EM, Wiederhorn J, Mainiero C. Health information technology and the medical school curriculum. *Am J Manag Care*. 2010;16:SP54-56.

58. McGowan JJ, Passiment M, Hoffman HM. Educating medical students as competent users of health information technologies: the MSOP data. *Stud Health Technol Inform*. 2007;129:1414-1418.

59. Shortliffe EH. Biomedical informatics in the education of physicians. *JAMA*. 2010;304:1227-1228.

60. Rouf E, Chumley HS, Dobbie AE. Electronic health records in outpatient clinics: perspectives of third year medical students. *BMC Med. Educ*. 2008;8:13.

61. Kass JS, Rose RV. Medical malpractice reform-historical approaches, alternative models, and communication and resolution programs. *AMA J Ethics*. 2016;18:299-310.

62. Sackett DL, Straus SE, Richardson WS, Rosenberg W, Haynes RB. *Evidence-Based Medicine. How to Practice and Teach EBM*. 2nd ed. London, UK: Harcourt Publishers. 2000.

63. Alper BS, Hand JA, Elliott SG, et al. How much effort is needed to keep up with the literature relevant for primary care? *J Med Libr Assoc*. 2004;92:429-437.

64. United States Department of Health and Human Services. NIH public access policy. https://publicaccess.nih.gov/index.htm. Accessed April 4, 2016.

65. Lindberg DAB, Humphreys BL. Rising expectations: access to biomedical information. *IMIA Yearbook*. 2008:165-172.

66. World Health Organization. The world health report 2000. Health systems: improving performance. http://www.who.int/whr/2000/en/whr00_en.pdf. Accessed April 4, 2016.

67. The Commonwealth Fund. Mirror, mirror on the wall, 2014 update: how the U.S. health care system compares internationally. 2014. http://www.commonwealthfund.org/publications/fund-reports/2014/jun/mirror-mirror. Accessed April 4, 2016.

68. Maeshiro R, Koo D, Keck CW. Integration of public health into medical education. 2011. http://www.ajpmonline.org/article/S0749-3797(11)00511-3/pdf. Accessed April 4, 2016.

69. Flexner A. Medical education in the United States and Canada. 1910. http://archive.carnegiefoundation.org/pdfs/elibrary/Carnegie_Flexner_Report.pdf. Accessed April 4, 2016.

CHAPTER 7

The Healthcare Workforce

CHAPTER OVERVIEW

This chapter defines the major healthcare professions, with particular emphasis on their educational preparation, credentials, numbers, and roles in the healthcare delivery system. Factors that influence demand for the various healthcare providers also are reviewed. The chapter concludes with a discussion of health workforce policy developments in light of the Patient Protection and Affordable Care Act of 2010 and some expectations for the future.

Health care is one of the nation's largest and most important industries as well as one of its largest employers. The Department of Labor estimates that in May of 2015, 12 million people have healthcare-related occupations, representing 9 percent of the total workforce.[1] In addition, "Healthcare occupations and industries are expected to have the fastest employment growth and to add the most jobs between 2014 and 2024."[2]

Although hospitals are still a major employer, recent employment growth has been primarily among health maintenance organizations, ambulatory clinics and services, home health providers, and offices of health practitioners.

▶ Health Professions

There are more than 200 occupations and professions in the healthcare field. As the healthcare system continues to change, making use of new technology, expanding in some sectors and contracting in others, new occupations and professions will continue to appear. The personnel of those new occupations and professions will be required to possess more specialized knowledge and more sophisticated skills.

Specialization to attain higher levels of technical competence also reduces the flexibility of providers to develop more efficient staffing patterns. Specialization among the workforce increases personnel costs, as additional employees are required to perform specific tasks. Smaller service facilities, especially in rural areas, are burdened most by the need for infrequently used specialists.

As a result, there is growing acceptance of multi-skilled health practitioners. Hospitals, in particular, are employing individuals trained in more than one skill. A large number of combinations are feasible: for example, occupational therapy assistants are also serving as physical therapy assistants, radiologic technologists are performing ultrasound imaging, and a variety of nonclinical personnel are performing phlebotomy.

Credentialing and Regulating Health Professionals

Government regulation of the health professions is considered the safeguard to protect the public from incompetent and unethical practitioners. Because each state assumes and exercises most of that responsibility, how healthcare occupations are regulated and the manner in which regulation is carried out vary from state to state. About 50 health occupations are regulated throughout the United States.

Regulatory restrictions limit healthcare service organizations and agencies in how they may use personnel and limit their ability to implement innovative ways to provide patient care. Similarly, regulatory restrictions influence educational programs to focus curricula on what has been prescribed by regulatory boards and their related accrediting bodies. Many states have taken steps to revise their credentialing systems to provide greater flexibility and responsiveness to fast-changing healthcare technology.[3]

The healthcare occupations are regulated through four mechanisms:

1. State licensure
2. Professional certification
3. Maintenance of certification (the newest procedure)
4. Registration

Currently licensure is provided at the state level where state law defines the scope of practice to be regulated and the educational and testing requirements that must be met to engage in a particular profession's practice. Licensure, the most restrictive of the four mechanisms of regulation, is intended to restrict entry or practice in certain occupations and to prevent the use of professional titles by those without predetermined qualifications. For example, it is illegal for individuals to perform procedures defined in state statutes as medicine or dentistry or to call themselves physicians or dentists without the appropriate license. Because practicing a medical profession without a state-required license is illegal, licensure is the most powerful mechanism to regulate a profession because of the potential legal penalties, up to and including incarceration.

Most states empanel medical licensing boards that are primarily composed of practitioners, but these panels now may include other experts as well as community members. Licensing boards provide two essential functions. First, they determine who may begin practicing in their state by insuring that applicants hold the appropriate credentials, are not under sanction by any other state medical licensing board, and do not have a criminal record. The second function is to investigate allegations of malpractice and physician impairment and then impose appropriate sanctions and/or required treatment and/or supervision. Medical licensing boards have broad authority to mandate treatment for addiction, require supervision to practice, impose practice limitation (e.g., not treat women unless a chaperone is present during all patient encounters) up to and including partial or total suspension of licensure. Medical boards also can make recommendations to the state's attorney general for prosecution if a practitioner's behavior is believed to be criminal. The current state-level licensing system has come under criticism for not being sufficiently responsive to patient complaints, for emphasizing practitioners' right to practice, for not providing harsher sanctions, and for not sufficiently involving the community of patients in the processes.[3]

The second mechanism of professional regulation is certification. Certification is the regulating process under which a professional organization, such as a national board, attests to the educational achievements and performance abilities of persons in a healthcare field of practice. Certification is usually not state-based and it is a much less restrictive regulation than licensing. Certification means that the individual has obtained advanced or specialized training in a particular area of practice consistent with an established body of metrics. For example, this applies to physicians who have completed a residency program and have successfully passed a board certification examination for a particular medical specialty. Certification allows the public, employers, and third-party payers to determine which practitioners are appropriately qualified in their specialty or occupation.

Certification generally has no provision for regulating impaired or misbehaving practitioners other than dropping them from certification. Unlike the licensed professions, the certified occupations have no legal basis for preventing an impaired or professionally delinquent individual who is uncertified from practicing. It is left to third-party payers or employers to ensure a practitioner in a profession that does not require licensure is validly certified.

The third mechanism that regulates healthcare occupations is maintenance of certification (MOC). Because most occupations in the healthcare field are based on a constantly changing body of knowledge, it is important for all healthcare practitioners to keep up with the latest science, treatments, and standards of care. Traditionally, MOC entailed simple requirements from a state licensing board or professional certifying organization on the number of hours of continuing education (CE) credits a practitioner should obtain per year. CE venues produced educational conferences to meet quality standards and awarded attendees with CE credits based on the number of hours of conference time attendees could apply to meet licensing or certification requirements.

In the past decade, many certifying organizations believed that CE credits alone were not sufficient to ensure practitioners were remaining current in all the latest trends of medicine, including systems-based practice and implementing quality improvement processes. As an example, the American Board of Internal Medicine (ABIM) created a continuous MOC program that is synchronized with an every-10-year recertification board exam. In order to be eligible to sit for the next recertification exam, the MOC program required a physician to complete a certain number of medical knowledge self-assessment modules produced by the ABIM and perform practice-improvement activities as outlined by an ABIM program on a specified time line. The ABIM also created a new credential, "Participating in MOC." Physicians who met all the recertification and MOC deadlines would have this phrase appear on the ABIM website's physician directory of board-certified physicians. Physicians who did not comply with MOC requirements, even if they met the 10-year board exam recertification period and are "board certified," would have the words "Not participating in MOC" next to their name in the ABIM physician directory.[4]

The growing financial costs and time to meet the expanding MOC requirements in internal medicine and other professions has risen substantially to the point of generating a significant backlash from various physician communities.[5] In fact, the ABIM issued an open letter apologizing for an overly aggressive and poorly designed MOC program, suspending its requirement for a MOC practice improvement module in 2015 ".. for at least two years."[6] Given the current backlash on MOC in the physician community, there will likely be many changes to come in this rapidly changing area.

The fourth mechanism of regulation is registration. Registration began as a mechanism to facilitate contacts and relationships among members of a profession and potential employers or the public. It is the least rigorous of the regulatory processes, ranging from simple listings or registries of persons offering a service, such as private duty nurses, to national registration programs of professional or occupational groups that require educational and testing qualifications. Because most registration programs are voluntary, they do not include parameters for competence or disciplinary actions.[7]

▶ Healthcare Occupations

Space does not nearly allow for the description of all healthcare occupations but the following are major occupational categories:

Physicians

There are 145 American Association of Medical Colleges (AAMC)-accredited medical schools in the United States and 17 in Canada that award the Doctor of Medicine (MD) degree. In 2006, the AAMC set a target for a 30 percent increase in the number of first-year medical students based on 2002 enrollment data (16,448 first year students in 2002). Although not attained by 2015 as originally planned, the projected first year enrollment for 2019 is 21,304 (a 29.2 percent increase from 2002).[8] In the AAMC's *2014 Medical School Enrollment Survey*, the majority of AAMC-accredited medical schools expressed a concern that the number of CMS-funded residency slots has not kept up with the increasing number of American medical school graduates[8] See Chapter 6 for a more detailed discussion on this topic. In the last three decades, the proportion of female physicians in both active practice and in training has been increasing steadily. In 2013, 46 percent of trainees in ACGME accredited residency and fellowship training programs were women.[9] In 2014, 33 percent of practicing physicians in the United States were women.[10] In 2015, 50 percent of students in AAMC accredited U.S. medical schools were women.[11] Given these trends, the percentage of women practicing physicians will likely approach that of men in the next two decades.

The number of minority students enrolled in medical schools now constitutes more than one-third of medical school enrollees. In 2015, 62 percent of the medical school graduates were white, 7.4 percent black, 9.4 percent Hispanic, 22.9 percent Asian, and the remainder either foreign, Native American, or of mixed or unknown race.[11]

There are 31 accredited colleges of osteopathy that offer the Doctor of Osteopathy (DO) degree. In the last two decades their enrollment has nearly doubled, and they now graduate more than 4,800 students per year; this is more than 20 percent of all U.S. medical students.[12] From the American Association of Colleges of Osteopathic Medicine:[13]

> Osteopathic medicine provides all of the benefits of modern medicine including prescription drugs, surgery, and the use of technology to diagnose disease and evaluate injury. It also offers the added benefit of hands-on diagnosis and treatment through a system of therapy known as osteopathic manipulative medicine. Osteopathic medicine emphasizes helping each person achieve a high level of wellness by focusing on health promotion and disease prevention.

Doctors of medicine and doctors of osteopathy share the same privileges in most all U.S. hospitals. Doctors of osteopathy practicing in the United States make up 7 percent of all the physicians in the country.[13]

Although medical education in the United States begins in medical school, it continues intensively for up to eight or more years of graduate medical training (training after medical school). Most states require a minimum of one year of graduate medical education before a physician can be licensed. However, increasing numbers of payers and healthcare employers are requiring board certification as the new minimum.

Residency training prepares a physician to practice in a medical specialty or subspecialty. Successfully completing a residency makes a physician "board eligible," in other words, eligible to sit for one of the 24 medical specialty boards. Post-residency training, called a fellowship, can lead to certification in a subspecialty. Likewise, successful completion of a fellowship makes a physician "board eligible" to sit for a subspecialty board exam. See Chapter 6 for a more detailed explanation of the various stages of physician training.

In the past, U.S. medical schools have consistently graduated fewer new physicians per year than there were available slots in U.S. residency and fellowship programs. Traditionally, empty slots not filled by American medical school graduates are filled by physicians trained in medical schools outside of the United States. The responsibility for evaluating the credentials of international medical graduates (IMGs) entering the United States to enter residency programs lies with the Educational Commission for Foreign Medical Graduates, a private not-for-profit organization sponsored by major U.S. medical organizations, including the American Association of Medical Colleges. In 2015, a total of 3,641 IMGs matched for U.S. residency training program slots[14] and 1,503 IMGs matched for fellowship training programs.[15]

The impetus for this influx is the demand for resident house officers in both teaching and nonteaching hospitals. Many hospitals, particularly those in rural or inner-city areas, depend heavily on foreign medical graduates to staff their clinical services.

After finishing residency training, most IMGs remain in the United States to practice. As a result, IMGs now constitute about one-fourth of the active U.S. physician workforce. Also, a relatively stable group of about 1,350 U.S. citizens attend medical schools outside the country and return to the United States to practice each year. With the increase in American medical school graduates, the availability of U.S. residency slots for foreign medical school graduates is likely to change significantly over the next few years.

About 35 percent of more than 700,000 practicing physicians in the United States are in primary care, general pediatrics, family medicine, or general internal medicine practice. Almost two-thirds of this country's physicians limit their practice to one of the many medical subspecialties. Employment of physicians and surgeons is projected to grow by 14 percent from 2014 to 2024, as the expanding population of baby boomers will increase demand for physician services.[16]

Nevertheless, there are serious shortages in rural and low-income areas that affect the efficiency and quality of medical care. Depending on the region of the country, several of a wide range of medical specialists are in short supply.[16]

Nursing

Nursing was a common employment position for women during the 1800s through association with religious or benevolent groups. A physician, Ann Preston, organized the first training program for nurses in the United States in 1861 at Women's Hospital of Philadelphia. Training was open to all women "who wished greater proficiency in their domestic responsibilities."[17]

In the early 1900s, hundreds of new hospitals were built under the aegis of religious orders, ethnic groups, industrialists, and elite groups of civic-minded individuals. Because student nurses were a constantly renewable source of low-cost hospital workers, even some of the smallest hospitals maintained nursing schools.[17] Hospital nursing school programs, therefore, were primarily sources of on-the-job training rather than academic programs. As educational programs evolved, stronger academic components were introduced, eventually leading to baccalaureate degrees instead of hospital diplomas.

Before World War I, nursing was divided into three domains—public health, private duty, and hospital. Public health nursing was considered the elite pursuit and recognized as instrumental in the campaign against tuberculosis and promoting infant welfare. Few nurses worked for hospitals. In 1920, more than 70 percent of nurses worked in private duty, about half in patients' homes and half for private patients in hospitals.

The war emphasized the effectiveness of hospitals, and they soon became the center of nursing education in the increasingly specialized acute-care medical environment. The social medicine and public health aspects of nursing were subjugated to the image of nursing as a symbol of patriotism, national sacrifice, and efficiency. The war experience established nurses as dedicated associates in hospital science. Nursing leaders promoted the idea of upgrading the nursing profession through high-quality hospital nursing schools, preferably associated with universities. The choice to idealize the role of the nurse as dedicated and deferential to the physician specialist in the hospital marginalized the independent role of the nurse in social medicine and public health.[18]

Registered Nurses

Different levels of nursing education were developed at a variety of educational institutions. A registered nurse (RN) can be trained in a two-year associate degree program at a community college or a junior college, a two- to three-year diploma program offered through a hospital, or a four- to five-year bachelor's of science degree program at a university or college.

The increasing complexity in health care forced specialization in nursing as it did in medicine. Nurses with a bachelor's degree could undertake advanced studies in several clinical areas to develop the needed competence for teaching, supervision, or advanced practice. Advanced practice RNs took on various advanced practice roles such as nurse practitioners, clinical nurse specialists, nurse anesthetists, or nurse midwives. By the 1960s, master's degree and doctoral programs were developed for nurses who wished to specialize.

The latest available survey of the RN population published in 2014 from the U.S. Bureau of Labor Statistics indicated that in 2012, 2.9 million RNs were in active practice in the United States. Assuming RNs continue to train at current levels and accounting for new entrants and attrition, the RN supply is expected to reach 3.8 million in 2025, a 33 percent increase. However, the nationwide demand for RNs is projected to grow more slowly than the supply such that by 2025, the projected demand will be 3.5 million, a 21 percent increase over 2012 numbers.[19] However, the national-level projection of a surplus of RNs does not reflect the projected imbalance of RNs at the state level. Sixteen states are projected to have RN shortages where state supply of RNs is not expected to keep up with state-specific demand. "States projected to experience the greatest shortfalls in the number of RNs by 2025 are Arizona (with 28,100 fewer RNs than needed) followed by Colorado and North Carolina (each with 12,900 fewer RNs than needed)."[19] One reason for the projected national level surplus is that RNs are working longer before retirement than in the past. Auerbach et al in a recent study found that nurses retiring in the period 1991–2012 did so an average of 2.5 years later than their counterparts did during 1969–1990.[20]

Another reason for the projected national level surplus is the increasing number of nursing school graduates. There has been a 108 percent increase in the number of nurses passing the

National Council Licensure Examination for RNs (NCLEX-RN) during the 2001–2011 period.[21] The NCLEX-RN is the examination that RNs must pass to receive their nursing license in the United States and Canada.

Accurately projecting the actual national need for RNs and the estimated national supply is a complex and inexact task. In fact, several nursing organizations promote different estimates that project a significant national nursing shortage in the next decade.[22] All sources of projections agree on one point: There will very likely be significant growth in the number of RNs in the next decade. Whether there will be a sufficient number of RNs to meet the actual future need is open for debate.

Another source of RNs in the United States has been RNs recruited from other countries. The number of internationally educated nurses increased from 6,600 in 2001, peaked at 22,879 in 2007, declined steadily down to 6,108 in 2011, and has remained at this level since then. "Steady increases in the earlier part of the decade were followed by a substantial decrease after 2007, immediately following the economic recession. U.S.-educated NCLEX-RN candidates, on the other hand, experienced steady and sustained growth from 2001 to 2010, more than doubling their numbers by the end of the decade. These data suggest that the in-migration of internationally educated nurses may be sensitive to the effects of the macroeconomic climate as well as the domestic production of nurses."[21]

As stated at the beginning of this chapter, the educational training pathway to becoming an RN can traverse through a diploma, or associate's, bachelor's, or master's degrees program. Almost 90 percent of nurses now receive their basic education in an institution of higher education compared with 20 percent in 1960. Today approximately 55 percent of the RN workforce holds a bachelor's degree or higher and this number has slowly increased over the last decade by approximately 5 percent.[21] In October of 2010, the Institute of Medicine report recommended an increase in the proportion of nurses with bachelor's degrees to 80 percent by 2020.[21] According to the American Association of Colleges of Nursing (AACN) 2014 Annual Report, 44 percent of employers now require a baccalaureate degree for new hires while 79 percent require or strongly prefer baccalaureate-prepared nurses.[24]

Nurses began to specialize during the 1950s. After World War II, nurses were in short supply, and hospitals began to group the least physiologically stable patients in one nursing unit for intensive care. The more competent nurses cared for the sickest patients. This initiated the critical care nurse specialty and the need for staff nurses continued to grow.

According to the 2013 AACN annual survey, nursing PhD enrollments increased by 49 percent between 2004 and 2012 while Doctor of Nursing Practice (DNP) increased 22 percent in the one year between 2012 and 2013.[25] There are now more than 323 U.S. schools that have at least one of the three types of doctoral programs in nursing: DNP, PhD, DNSc.[26,27] The DNP builds on the liberal arts or scientific education that prepared students to take the state licensing exam to practice as an RN. The DNP degrees are professional doctorates that prepare nurses for advanced clinical practice. The nursing PhD is an academic degree with requirements similar to the PhD in other fields—extensive preparation in a narrow field and a dissertation. A nursing PhD typically prepares students for academic positions in nursing schools and for nursing-related research. The DNSc (Doctor of Nursing Science) degree is grounded in research and theory and considered equivalent to the PhD in nursing by the National Science Foundation and the U.S. Department of Education. The current trend of colleges of nursing is to discontinue the DNSc in favor of the PhD.

TABLE 7-1 shows the distribution of employed RN nurses by setting.[21]

TABLE 7-1 Estimated Number of RNs, by Setting of Employment

	Census 2000 Estimate	ACS 08–10 Estimate	Estimated Growth/Decline	% Change in Growth
Hospitals	1,427,497	1,785,304	357,807	25.1%
Nursing Care Facilities	189,594	208,051	18,457	9.7%
Offices of Physicians	156,559	134,231	−22,328	−14.3%
Home Healthcare Services	101,895	105,922	4,027	4.0%
Outpatient Care Centers	70,224	131,022	60,798	86.6%
Other Healthcare Services	66,723	153,449	86,726	130.0%
Elementary and Secondary Schools	51,495	61,323	9,828	19.1%
Employment Services	45,835	58,362	12,527	27.3%
Insurance Carriers and Related Activities	22,919	25,155	2,236	9.8%
Administration of Human Resource Programs[1]	20,509	38,136	17,627	85.9%
Justice, Public Order and Safety Activities[2]	14,793	18,137	3,344	22.6%
Offices of Other Health Practitioners	13,346	7,596	−5,750	−43.1%
Colleges and Universities including Junior Colleges	12,637	16,320	3,683	29.1%
Residential Care Facilities without Nursing	10,853	9,928	−925	−8.5%
All Other Settings[3]	70,397	71,705	1,308	1.9%
Totals	2,275,276	2,824,641	549,365	24.1%

[1]Category includes RNs whose jobs focus primarily on administration.

[2]Category includes the majority of nurses working in public health settings.

[3]For this analysis, all settings holding less than 1 percent of the RN population have been recoded to "Other."

HRSA analysis of the American Community Survey (ACS) 2008–2010 three-year file and Census 2000 Long Form 5 percent sample.

According to the U.S. Census Bureau, nursing remains a predominantly female profession, but the proportion of male RNs has increased from 8 percent in Census 2000 to 9 percent in 2010.[21]

Increases also are occurring in the number of RNs identifying themselves as members of a racial/ethnic minority. The U.S. Census Bureau reports that Caucasian RNs have declined in proportion, from more than 80 percent in 2000 to approximately 75 percent in 2010.[19] The trend for increased minority racial/ethnic group RNs in the workforce is expected to advance even more rapidly in the future as minority racial/ethnic groups are increasingly represented in the recently graduated nurse population currently entering the healthcare workforce. "According to AACN's report on 2012–2013 Enrollment and Graduations in Baccalaureate and Graduate Programs in Nursing, nursing students from minority backgrounds represented 28.3 percent of students in entry-level baccalaureate programs, 29.3 percent of master's students, and 27.7 percent of students in research-focused doctoral programs."[28]

Hospital consolidations in response to market forces have affected nursing employment in several ways. Hospital workforces have been reorganized to adjust to fiscal restraints, reductions in the number of admissions, and shortened lengths of stay. At the same time, increases in the intensity of nursing care required by more complicated illnesses of inpatients require higher nurse-to-patient ratios. Thus, although many hospitals employ fewer nurses for inpatient care, those retained are expected to maintain clinically sophisticated nursing skills, monitor staff with a lower level of training to provide direct patient care, and manage units with high proportions of seriously ill patients.

Fewer nurses taking care of more severely ill patients, combined with the requirements to supervise nonprofessional and unlicensed personnel performing nursing tasks, have increased nursing workloads and affected morale. According to the American Nurses Association, 96 percent of nurses report fatigue at the beginning of their shift, 54 percent report excessive workloads, and 50 percent indicate they have insufficient time with patients.[29]

Although important concerns remain about the continued aging of the currently employed RN population and the difficulty of schools of nursing in expanding nursing enrollment due to lack of faculty, there are promising developments. There has been a recent increase in the number of nursing graduates taking the licensure exam, and hospitals are developing innovative ways to increase enrollment in schools of nursing. Some facilities offer attractive sign-on bonuses to recruit new graduates. In addition, many schools of nursing are adding accelerated programs as a way to bring nurses to the workforce more quickly.[30] The Robert Wood Johnson Foundation, with a long history of supporting nurses, is addressing one of the roots of the problem with projects to change the frustrating nursing work environment through alterations of both physical facilities and hospital cultures. The changes are intended to decrease the amount of time nurses spend on non-nursing tasks to permit them to focus on the more satisfying responsibilities of maintaining the quality of patient care.[31]

Licensed Practical Nurses

A licensed practical nurse (LPN) or licensed vocational nurse (LVN) works under the direct supervision of an RN or physician. One-year LPN/LVN training is offered at about 1,100 state-approved technical or vocational schools or community or junior colleges. Programs include both classroom study and supervised clinical practice. Like RNs, LPN/LVNs must pass a state licensing examination.

According to the U.S. Bureau of Labor Statistics, there were a total of 719,900 LPN/LVNs active in the U.S. workforce in 2014.[32] The demand for LPN/LVNs in other work settings, however, is increasing, and employment overall in this occupation is expected to increase by 16 percent from 2014 to 2024. The U.S. Bureau of Labor Statistics reports the breakdown of the industries LPN/LVNs work in is as follows:

- 38 percent nursing homes and residential care facilities that provide assisted living
- 17 percent state, local, and private hospitals
- 13 percent physician offices
- 11 percent home health care
- 7 percent government jobs

Nurse Practitioners

Nurse practitioners (NPs) are RNs with advanced education and clinical experience. Nurse practitioners provide primary and specialty care, and they are allowed to prescribe medicine in most states. Each state specifically defines practice requirements and allowed parameters for this type of advanced practice nursing role. Most nurse practitioners specialize. Neonatal nurse practitioners work with newborns. Pediatric nurse practitioners treat children from infancy through adolescence. School nurse practitioners serve students in elementary and secondary schools, colleges, and universities. Adult and family nurse practitioners are generalists who serve adults and families. Occupational health nurse practitioners work in industry providing on-the-job care. Psychiatric nurse practitioners serve people with psychiatric or emotional problems. Geriatric nurse practitioners care for older adults. Nurse practitioners also work in hospitals and assist surgeons or other interventionists (e.g., cardiologists who perform intra-arterial catheterization and orthopedic surgeons who perform joint replacements) manage patients in the hospital with pre- and post-surgical regimens. Nurse practitioner services allow physicians to perform a larger number of procedures by freeing them from much of the routine pre- and post-procedure patient management activities.

The earliest nurse practitioners were nurse midwives and nurse anesthetists. A nurse midwife is usually an RN who completes a one- or two-year master's degree program in nurse midwifery after completing RN training. They are licensed by the state and also may be required to be certified by the American College of Nurse Midwives. Currently, almost all midwife-assisted births take place in a hospital or birthing clinic. Although nurse midwives can perform vaginal deliveries on their own, they all work with obstetricians who they can call in for complications and unanticipated emergencies or when a patient requires a caesarian section.

The roots for the nurse anesthetist specialty go back more than a century when nurses administered anesthesia in Catholic hospitals. Early training was provided in hospitals, but in 1945 the American Association of Nurse Anesthetists established a certification program. Nurse anesthetists are now required to have a master's degree from an accredited school and must pass the national certification examination. Most nurse anesthetists work with physician anesthesiologists in hospitals, ambulatory surgery centers, and urgent care centers providing comprehensive care to patients requiring anesthesia.[33]

The current nurse practitioner movement began in the 1960s because of the shortage of physicians. The goal was to have specially prepared nurses augment the supply of physicians by working as primary care providers in pediatrics, adult health, geriatrics, and obstetrics. Nurse practitioners had to overcome resistance from organized medicine and legal difficulties caused by restrictions in most state nurse practice acts (the statutes defining nursing scope of practice), which prohibited nurses from diagnosing and treating patients. Nurse practitioners sought state-by-state changes in nurse practice acts, and by 1975 most states had started certifying or accepting the national certification of nurse practitioners, nurse midwives, and nurse anesthetists.[34]

Two-thirds of the first nurse practitioner programs were brief certificate-granting programs, and one-third were master's programs. The programs primarily trained for practice in pediatrics, midwifery, maternity, family medicine, adult health, or psychiatry. As in most ventures into uncharted territory, several approaches to nurse practitioner preparation were tested. Eventually, an RN with a master's degree became the requirement for national certification and recertification.

Efforts at healthcare cost containment have increased the demand for cost-effective nurse practitioners. Rural hospitals, with limited reserves of physicians, make substantial use of nurse practitioners and physician assistants. These "mid-level" practitioners are considered to be a cost-effective means to expand the scope of service in primary care.[35]

According to the National Center for Health Statistics, "In 2009, 49.1 percent of office-based physicians were in practices that used nurse practitioners (NP), certified nurse midwives (CNM), or physician assistants (PA)."[36] The high regard for nurse practitioners among both other medical personnel and the public is evidenced by the fact that there are now more than 400 accredited master's programs in the United States for the preparation of nurse practitioners[27] that graduate approximately 17,000 nurse practitioners each year.[37]

Physician Assistants

The emergence of physician assistants (PAs) closely parallels that of nurse practitioners. In the 1960s, there was a shortage of healthcare providers. Duke University initiated the first PA program in 1965.[38] It was a new provider model designed to benefit from the experience and expertise of the many hospital corpsmen and medics that were discharged from the armed forces during the Vietnam War. As the flow of returning corpsmen and medics tapered off, individuals without prior healthcare training were accepted into PA programs. Unlike nurse practitioners, who have additional training after completion of an RN, PAs need an undergraduate degree in science as a requirement for PA school admission.

PA training programs are accredited by the Accreditation Review Commission on Education for the Physician Assistant. Today, there are 210 accredited PA education programs. Most offer a master's degree, some offer a bachelor's degree, and a few offer associate's degrees. Beginning with the class that matriculates in 2020, all PA programs must transition to offering a graduate degree in order to maintain accreditation.[39]

Unlike medical assistants who perform routine clinical and clerical tasks, PAs are formally trained to provide diagnostic, preventive, and therapeutic healthcare services as delegated by the physician. PAs take medical histories, order and interpret laboratory tests and x-rays, make diagnoses, and prescribe medications as allowed by law in the 50 states and the District of Columbia. Many PAs are employed in specialties such as internal medicine, pediatrics, family medicine, orthopedics, and emergency medicine. Others specialize in surgery and may provide preoperative and postoperative care and act as first or second assistants during surgery. PAs usually provide healthcare services under the supervision of a physician, although the degree of supervision required varies among states.

PAs are certified through an examination from the National Commission on Certification of Physician Assistants. Those who pass this exam have the credential Physician Assistant-Certified (PA-C). All physician assistants must be licensed by the state in which they practice. In 2014, there were 94,400 PAs in the United States. The U.S. Department of Labor projects a significant increase in the employment of PAs over the next decade due to the aging population, the increased emphasis on cost reduction in health care, and a growing patient population due to the implementation of the ACA.[40]

Clinical Nurse Specialists

A different, but related, type of advanced nursing practice role is the clinical nurse specialist. This specialty role was developed in response to the specific nursing care needs of increasingly complex patients. Like specialist physicians, clinical nurse specialists are advanced-practice specialists with in-depth knowledge and skills that make them valuable adjunct practitioners in specialized clinical settings. The training requirements vary by state but generally include an RN plus either a master's or doctorate degree (PhD or DNP) in nursing.[41]

Dentistry

Dentistry in early America was primitive. Tooth extraction was performed by itinerant tooth drawers, the neighborhood doctor or barber, or sometimes the local blacksmith. Because there were no regulations, anyone could practice dentistry, and skilled craftsmen and artisans turned their talents to dental practice.

Dentistry began its emergence from a trade to a profession in the 1800s. Until about 1850 almost all prominent dentists were medical doctors who had chosen dentistry rather than general medicine as their vocation.[42] Dental schools were established to replace preceptorships, and dental practitioners participated in developing laws to regulate the profession.[42]

In 1840, the State of Maryland chartered the first dental school, the Baltimore College of Dental Surgery. The course of study lasted two years, the same number of years required for a medical degree. By 1884, 28 dental colleges existed. Although a few were affiliated with universities, most were privately owned. New York took the lead in regulating the profession by licensure. In 1868, New York established a board of censors to examine candidates, which later became the State Board of Dental Examiners. By the end of the century, most other states also had passed licensure laws.

The mix of university-affiliated and independent dental schools resulted in significant variations in the quality of dental education. In 1922, 12 years after the Carnegie Foundation for the Advancement of Teaching had issued the Flexner Report evaluating U.S. medical education, the foundation created a commission to examine dental education. The commission's report appeared in 1926 and resulted in a complete reorganization of dental education in the United States.[43]

World War II brought about profound changes in Americans' attitudes toward dentistry. Citizens were shocked to learn that the dental health of the nation's young men was deplorable. Among the first 2 million draftees summoned by the Selective Service System, one of five lacked even the minimum standard of 12 functioning teeth. The Selective Service had to eliminate all dental standards to avoid mass disqualification of selectees. As a consequence, after the war, the United States made a vigorous effort to improve the dental health of the country's population.

Before World War II, dentists were not involved in public health, and few dental schools taught anything on the subject. A decade after the first graduate course of study in dental public health was established in the 1940s by the University of Michigan, the new field of public health dentistry emerged in the United States. Today, a number of schools have established courses leading to advanced degrees in the field, and there is an American Board of Dental Public Health to certify public health dental specialists.

The U.S. Public Health Service established the National Institute of Dental Research in 1948. Ultimately incorporated into the National Institutes of Health, the National Institute of Dental Research played a major role in advancing basic and applied dental research.

Also beneficial to dentistry during the postwar years was the increase in insurance group plans that provide payment for routine dental care and, in certain instances, more extensive dentistry at an additional premium. By 1980, almost 100 million Americans were covered, to some degree, by a dental insurance plan; today, it is a common employee benefit.

In 2014, the U.S. Census reported there were a total of 151,500 dentists with an 18 percent projected annual growth rate. The rapid growth rate is due to the popularity of cosmetic dental procedures, the increasing access to dental insurance, and the fact that aging patients are keeping their teeth much longer than in the past.[44]

To practice in a dental specialty, a dentist must complete a dental residency after dental school in the specialty of choice and then usually must qualify for a special state-based dental license.[44] Dentistry currently includes nine practice specialties:

1. Dental public health
2. Endodontics
3. Oral and maxillofacial pathology
4. Oral and maxillofacial radiology
5. Oral and maxillofacial surgery
6. Orthodontics and dentofacial orthopedics
7. Pediatric dentistry
8. Periodontics
9. Prosthodontics

Specialty recognition of dental anesthesiology as an additional dental specialty was considered and rejected by the American Dental Association (ADA) 2012 House of Delegates.[45] However, there is a certification for dental anesthesiologists offered by the American Dental Board of Anesthesiology which requires both an oral and written examination.[46]

In contrast to the predominance of specialization in the practice of medicine, more than 85 percent of the more than 151,500 practicing dentists in the United States are general practitioners.[47] According to the Commission on Dental Accreditation (CoDA), the organization that accredits all dental schools in the United States, there were 65 accredited dental schools that graduated 5,491 dentists in 2014, 47.4 percent of whom were female.[48] Graduates receive a Doctor of Dental Surgery (DDS), Doctor of Dental Medicine (DDM), or Doctor of Medical Dentistry (DMD) degree.

Increased outreach efforts to recruit racial/ethnic minority dental school applicants have been made over the last three decades. However, the proportion of some racial and ethnic minorities graduating from U.S. dental schools is still low. The 2014 CoDA survey demonstrates the following proportion of racial and ethnic minorities among graduating dentists in 2014:[48] Fifty-five percent are White non-Hispanic, 22 percent are Asian, and the rest are African-American and other minorities.

Overall, dentists are working fewer hours for increased earnings. Dentistry has successfully resisted managed care and capitated payments and remains a "cottage industry." With most dentists in solo practice choosing to serve only those with dental insurance or the fiscal means to pay prevailing fees out-of-pocket, many of the population groups with the greatest need for dental services continue to be underserved. While neither dental education nor the dental practice model have traditionally placed a high priority on the creation of a dental safety net for underserved populations, the implementation of the Affordable Care Act (ACA) may be having an impact. According to a recent survey, young adults aged 18–24 are less likely to report that cost is a barrier to their dental care than in the past.[49] This may be due to the impact of the ACA's requirement that dental plans for children up to 18 years of age be included in all health insurance exchanges, either bundled with a health insurance plan or as a standalone policy. All adults taken as a whole report cost as the most significant barrier to dental care across all insurance types (i.e., private, Medicare, Medicaid, and uninsured.)[49]

Pharmacy

Pharmaceutical practice dates back to ancient Egypt, Rome, and Greece. The first apothecaries appeared in Europe during the 1100s. By 1546, the Senate of the city of Nuremberg, Germany, recognized the value of standardizing drugs to ensure uniformity in filling prescriptions.[50]

Hospital pharmacists were apprentice physicians in early America. In the early 1800s, medicine and pharmacy separated, and by 1811 the New York Hospital had a full-time pharmaceutical practitioner. The American Pharmaceutical Association was organized in 1852. Professional training programs were developed for pharmacists, and by 1864 there were eight colleges of pharmacy in the United States.[50]

In 2014, 134 colleges of pharmacy were accredited to confer degrees by the American Council on Pharmaceutical Education.[51] Pharmacy programs grant a Doctor of Pharmacy (PharmD) degree after at least six years of postsecondary study. The PharmD degree has replaced the Bachelor of Pharmacy degree, which is no longer awarded. Many colleges of pharmacy also offer a master's or PhD degree after completion of a PharmD program for pharmacists who want more laboratory or research experience to prepare them for research positions with pharmaceutical companies or to teach at a university. After graduation, each pharmacist is licensed by passing a state examination and completing an internship with a licensed pharmacist. Schools of pharmacy graduate about 15,000 students annually.[52] The 2014 U.S. Census reported the number of active pharmacists in the United States was 297,100.

The Census Bureau projects the number of pharmacists will grow by 3 percent per year. This projected growth rate is considerably less than most other healthcare occupations.[53] This is likely due to a recent increase in the number of pharmacy schools and, therefore, the level of competition for available jobs.[52,54]

In 1976, the American Pharmaceutical Association created the Board of Pharmaceutical Specialties. It has since approved nuclear pharmacy, nutrition support pharmacy, oncology pharmacy, pharmacotherapy, psychiatric pharmacy, ambulatory care pharmacy (added in 2011), critical care pharmacy (added in 2013), and pediatric pharmacy (added in 2013) as the eight specialties in which pharmacists may be certified.[55]

Forty-two percent of pharmacists work in retail pharmacies, many of which are owned by large commercial chains. There, they may supervise other employees, manage overall business needs, computerize patients' records, and advise physicians and patients about drug dosage, side-effects, and interaction with other medications. Nineteen percent of pharmacists work in hospitals, and the balance are employed by clinics, nursing homes, health maintenance organizations, and the federal government.[56] Many pharmacists work after hours in all-night retail pharmacies or in hospitals. Because of the increased use of mail-order pharmacies, the number of jobs in the pharmacy retail segment is expected to decline slightly.[54]

Podiatric Medicine

Podiatric medicine is concerned with the diagnosis and treatment of diseases and injuries of the lower leg and foot. Podiatrists can prescribe drugs; order radiographs, laboratory tests, and physical therapy; set fractures; and perform surgery. They also fit corrective inserts called orthotics, design plaster casts and strappings to correct deformities, and design custom-made shoes.

As of 2014, the U.S. Census reports a total of 9,600 practicing podiatrists[57] and nine accredited schools in the United States where students can apply after graduating from college.[58] Graduates obtain a Doctor of Podiatric Medicine (DPM) degree. The four years of professional training is similar to that for physicians. Most podiatrists spend three or more years completing a residency in a hospital after they graduate.[58] Podiatrists also may take postgraduate training and become board certified in the specialties of primary care in podiatric medicine, diabetic foot wound care and footwear, limb preservation and salvage, or podiatric surgery. All doctors of podiatric medicine are licensed by the state in which they practice. Podiatric care is more dependent on disposable income than other medical services. While Medicare and most private health insurance programs cover acute medical and surgical foot services, as well as diagnostic radiographs and leg braces, routine foot care ordinarily is not covered. One notable exception is that Medicare covers diabetic foot care with a podiatrist for those over the age of 65.

Chiropractors

Chiropractors treat the whole body without the use of drugs or surgery. Special care is given to the spine, because chiropractors believe that misalignment or irritations of spinal nerves interfere with normal body functions. Today, there are 15 accredited chiropractic programs and 22 accredited chiropractic institutions in the United States.[59] Students need at least 90 credit hours of previous undergraduate education before applying to one of the accredited programs or institutions. After completion of the Doctor of Chiropractic Degree, all states require licensure. In 2014, the U.S. Department of Labor estimated there are 45,200 chiropractic practitioners. Projections to 2024 indicate this number will increase to more than 53,100, an expected growth rate of 17 percent for chiropractic employment over the 2014–2024 decade.[60] This will help meet the increasing demand for chiropractic care as the aging population in the United States becomes more likely to experience musculoskeletal and joint problems and seek chiropractic care.[61] Patients are generally satisfied or more satisfied with chiropractic care than standard medical care.[62] For specific conditions resulting in back pain, chiropractors achieve outcomes that are comparable with those of physicians.[63]

Chiropractic practice has strong public support, and chiropractors have used that patronage to make significant gains in legal and legislative areas. Regardless of medicine's questions about chiropractic's lack of scientifically proven effectiveness, chiropractors achieved Medicare coverage and participate in most managed care plans, and many other insurance policies contain some form of chiropractic coverage.

Optometry

A Doctor of Optometry examines patients' eyes to diagnose vision problems and eye disease, prescribes drugs for treatment, and prescribes and fits eyeglasses and contact lenses. An optometrist should not be confused with an ophthalmologist or an optician. An ophthalmologist is a physician who specializes in the treatment of eye diseases and injuries and uses drugs, surgery, or the prescription of corrective lenses to correct vision deficiencies. An optician is a licensed health professional who fits eyeglasses or contact lenses to individual patients as prescribed by ophthalmologists or optometrists.

Optometrists must graduate from 1 of the 23 accredited four-year colleges of optometry and pass both written and clinical examinations of the state board to obtain a license to practice.[64] The U.S. Census Bureau estimated there were 40,600 practicing optometrists in 2014 and project that this number will increase by 27 percent over the decade from 2014 to 2024.[65] This will likely be due to the aging population and the increased insurance coverage as a result of the ACA.[66] Persons above 45 years of age visit optometrists and ophthalmologists more frequently because of the onset of vision problems in middle age and the increased likelihood of cataracts, glaucoma, diabetes, and hypertension in old age.

One-year residency programs are available for optometrists who wish to specialize in family practice optometry, pediatric optometry, geriatric optometry, low-vision rehabilitation, cornea and contact lenses, refractive and ovular surgery, vision therapy and rehabilitation, ocular disease, and community health optometry.[64]

Optometrists usually work in private practice, but many are now forming small group practices. Optometrists may hire opticians and optometric assistants to help them increase their productivity and thus care for more patients.

Healthcare Administrators

Like any other business, health care needs good management to keep it running smoothly. Healthcare administrators are managers who plan, organize, direct, control, or coordinate medical and health services in hospitals, clinics, nursing care facilities, and physicians' offices. Many healthcare administrators are employed in hospital settings, and others work for insurers, clinics, or medical group practices. Employment opportunities are numerous with 333,000 jobs for healthcare administrators as of 2014.[67]

Bachelors, masters, and doctoral degree programs in healthcare administration are offered by a variety of colleges and universities. At least 70 schools have accredited programs leading to a master's degree in health services administration. There are also short certificate or diploma programs, usually lasting less than one year, in health services administration or in medical office management. However, a bachelor's degree in medical administration currently is considered the minimum entry-level educational degree required for higher-level management positions.[66]

Allied Health Personnel

Unlike professionals in medicine, dentistry, nursing, and pharmacy, allied health personnel represent a varied and complex array of healthcare disciplines. Allied health personnel support, complement, or supplement the professional functions of physicians, dentists, or other health professionals in delivering health care to patients, and they assist in environmental health control, health promotion, and disease prevention. A number of more recent categories of healthcare specialists were created to implement the new procedures and equipment, and the diagnostic, surgical, and therapeutic techniques that proliferated during the last three decades. Allied health occupations encompass 80 different allied health professions and represent approximately 60 percent of all healthcare providers.[69]

The range of allied health professions may be understood best by classifying them according to the functions they serve, grouped into the following four categories:

1. Laboratory technologists and technicians
2. Therapeutic science practitioners
3. Behavioral scientists
4. Support services

Some allied health disciplines may be included in more than one of these functional classifications.

▶ Technicians and Technologists

There is a rapidly growing number of technicians and technologists, including such major categories as cardiovascular technicians and technologists, clinical laboratory technicians, emergency medical technicians, health information technicians, nuclear medicine technologists, cytotechnologists, histologic technicians and technologists, surgical technologists, occupational safety and health technicians, pharmacy technicians, and many more. Because space does not allow for a discussion of all of these important health vocations, the following descriptions include only some representative disciplines in this allied health category.

Laboratory Technologists and Technicians

Clinical laboratory technologists and technicians have a critically important role in diagnosing disease, monitoring physiologic functions and the effectiveness of interventions, and performing highly technical procedures. Technologists, also known as clinical laboratory scientists or medical technologists, usually have a bachelor's degree in one of the life sciences. Clinical laboratory technicians, also known as medical technicians or medical laboratory technicians, generally require an associate's degree or a certificate.

Among their roles, clinical laboratory personnel analyze body fluids, tissues, and cells checking for bacteria and other microorganisms; analyze chemical content; test drug levels in blood to monitor the effectiveness of treatment; and match blood for transfusion.

The National Accrediting Agency for Clinical Laboratory Sciences currently approves/accredits 618 programs for clinical laboratory technologists and technicians.[70] Employed graduates of those programs number more than 328,200, and more than 50 percent of those employed work in hospitals. Most of the others work in physician offices or diagnostic laboratories. Employment growth in the next decade is projected to remain steady as the aging of the general population is expected to lead to an increased need for diagnosis through testing of medical conditions such as type 2 diabetes and cancer, and the development of new laboratory tests.[71]

Radiologic and Magnetic Resonance Imaging Technologists

A radiologic technologist works under the supervision of a radiologist, a physician who specializes in the use and interpretation of radiographs and other medical imaging technologies. The radiologic technologist uses radiographs (x-rays), fluoroscopic equipment, and high-tech imaging machines such as ultrasonography, computed tomography, magnetic resonance imaging (MRI), and positron emission tomography (PET). These technologies produce images that allow physicians to study the internal organs, bones, and the metabolic activity of these structures. Formal training programs in radiologic technology range in length from one to four years and lead to a certificate, associate's degree, or bachelor's degree. Two-year associate's degrees are the most prevalent. The Joint Review Committee on Education in Radiology accredited more than 710 formal programs in 2014.[72]

In 2014, there were 230,600 radiologic and MRI technologists in the United States with a projected increase of 9 percent over the 2014–2024 decade. The increase is due to the increase in the aging population and because there will be an increase in medical conditions that will require medical imaging to assist with diagnosis.[73]

Nuclear Medicine Technology

Nuclear medicine technologists use diagnostic imaging techniques to detect and map radioactive drugs in the human body. They administer radioactive pharmaceuticals to patients and then monitor the characteristics and functions of tissues or organs in which the radiopharmaceuticals localize. Abnormal areas show higher or lower concentrations of radioactivity than do normal ones.

Nuclear medicine technologists are prepared in one-year certificate programs offered by hospitals to those who are already radiologic technologists, medical technologists, or RNs; or, they may be trained in two- to four-year programs offered in university schools of allied health. Nuclear medicine technologists must meet the minimum federal standards on the administration of radioactive drugs and the operation of radiation detection equipment. In addition, about half of all states require technologists to be licensed. Technologists also may obtain voluntary professional certification or registration.[74]

▶ Therapeutic Science Practitioners

Therapeutic science practitioners are essential to the treatment and rehabilitation of patients with diseases and injuries of all kinds. Physical therapists, occupational therapists, speech pathology and audiology therapists, radiation therapists, and respiratory therapists are only some of the allied health disciplines in this category.

Physical Therapy

Physical therapists provide services that help restore function, improve mobility, relieve pain, and prevent or limit physical disabilities of patients suffering from injuries or disease. They restore, maintain, and promote overall fitness and health. They review patients' medical histories and measure patients' strength, range of motion, balance, coordination, muscle performance, and motor function. They then develop and implement treatment plans that include exercises to develop flexibility, strength, and endurance. They also may prescribe exercises for patients to do at home.

Physical therapists also may use electrical stimulation, hot or cold compresses, and ultrasound to relieve pain and reduce swelling. They teach patients to use assistive and adaptive devices, such as crutches, prostheses, and wheelchairs. Physical therapists supervise physical therapy assistants to aid them in meeting the needs of an increasing number of patients. Physical therapy assistants earn associate's degrees and take a national certifying examination. Physical therapists may practice as generalists or specialize in areas such as pediatrics, geriatrics, orthopedics, sports medicine, neurology, or cardiopulmonary physical therapy. Physical therapists most often work in the offices of other health practitioners or in hospitals. They also may be employed in clinics, nursing homes, and home healthcare settings. In 2014, there are 210,900 physical therapists in the United States and the Census Bureau projects a 34 percent increase by 2024 due to the aging population and greater access to care because of the ACA. Employment opportunities have grown rapidly in the physical therapy field, and the demand now exceeds the supply.[75]

According to the Commission on Accreditation in Physical Therapy Education (CAPTE), there were 233 accredited physical therapy programs in 2015.[76] All programs offer a Doctor of Physical Therapy (DPT) degree.[77] DPT programs are usually three years in duration and require a bachelor's degree with requirements in the basic sciences including anatomy, physiology, biology, and physics. All states require physical therapists to be licensed. Some physical therapists choose to become board-certified in one of eight physical therapy specialty areas such as orthopedics, sports, and geriatric physical therapy. Board certification in a specialty area requires 2,000 hours of clinical work or completion of a residency program accredited by the American Physical Therapy Association in the specialty area.[77]

Occupational Therapy

Occupational therapists assist patients in recovering from accidents, injuries, or diseases to improve their ability to perform tasks in their daily living and work environments. Occupational therapists work with a wide range of patients, from those with irreversible physical disabilities to those with mental disabilities or disorders. Occupational therapists assist patients in caring for their daily needs such as dressing, cooking, and eating. They also use physical exercises and other activities to increase strength and dexterity, visual acuity, and hand–eye coordination. Occupational therapists instruct in the use of adaptive equipment such as wheelchairs, splints, and aids to improve mobility. They also may design or make special equipment needed by patients at home or at work to perform activities of daily living or work responsibilities. Therapists may collaborate with clients and employers to modify work environments so that clients can maintain employment.

Occupational therapists require at least a master's degree and some are now entering the profession with doctoral degrees. State licensure is required for practice. They work in medical offices, nursing homes, community mental health centers, adult day care programs, rehabilitation centers, and residential care facilities. There were a total of 114,600 occupational therapists in the United States in 2014, with growth projected at 27 percent over the following decade.[78]

Speech-Language Pathology

Speech-language pathologists, sometimes called speech therapists, treat patients with speech problems, swallowing, and other disorders in hospitals, schools, clinics, and private practice. Approximately half of all speech pathologists are employed in the education system—from preschools to universities. Speech-language pathologists use written and oral tests and special instruments to diagnose the nature of an impairment and develop an individualized plan of care. They may teach the use of alternative communication methods, including automated devices and sign language.

More than 250 colleges and universities offer graduate programs in speech-language pathology. A master's degree and a state license are required to practice. The number of speech-language pathologists in 2014 was 135,400 and is expected to grow in the next decade by 21 percent as the general population ages with increased instances of health conditions such as strokes, brain injuries, and hearing loss, all requiring speech-language therapy intervention.[79]

▶ Behavioral Scientists

Behavioral scientists are crucial in the social, psychological, and community and patient educational activities related to health maintenance, prevention of disease, and accommodation of patients to disability. They include professionals in social work, health education, community mental health, alcoholism and substance abuse services, and other health and human service areas.

Social Work

Social workers counsel patients and families to assist them in addressing the personal, economic, and social problems associated with illness and disability. They arrange for community-based services to meet patient needs after discharge from a health facility. A bachelor's degree in social work is required for entry-level positions as caseworkers or mental health assistants. Clinical social workers require a master's degree plus two years of supervised experience in a clinical setting. Doctoral-level programs prepare social workers for advanced clinical practice, research, and academic careers.

Social workers provide social services in hospitals and other health-related settings. Medical and public health social workers provide patients and families with psychosocial support in cases of acute, chronic, or terminal illnesses. Mental health and substance abuse social workers assess and treat persons with mental illness or those who abuse alcohol, tobacco, or other drugs.[80]

As of June 2015, the Council on Social Work Education listed 506 accredited bachelor's programs and 238 accredited master's in social work degree programs.[81]

In 2014 there were 649,300 social workers active in the United States. This number is projected to grow by 12 percent over the subsequent decade. Specifically in the healthcare field, the projected growth rate is 19 percent as needs increase for social workers with backgrounds in gerontology, substance abuse treatment, and mental health.[82]

Rehabilitation Counselor

A rehabilitation counselor gives personalized counseling, emotional support, and rehabilitation therapy to patients limited by physical or emotional disabilities. Patients may be recovering from illness or injury, have psychiatric problems, or have intellectual deficits. After an injury or illness is stabilized, the rehabilitation counselor tests the patient's motor ability, skill level, interests, and psychological makeup and develops an appropriate training or retraining plan. The goal is to maximize the patient's ability to function in society.

A master's degree often is required to be licensed or certified as a rehabilitation counselor. Licensing requirements differ from state to state. Usually counseling services require state licensure, but other services such as vocational training or job placement assistance may not. Licensure usually requires a master's degree and 2,000–4,000 hours of supervised clinical experience. The Commission on Rehabilitation Counselor Certification offers certification, but this is not required for all jobs and in all states. There are 120,100 rehabilitation counselors as of 2014 and the projected growth rate is 9 percent over the next 10 years as the population ages and advanced medical care saves more lives. In addition, legislation requiring equal employment rights for persons with disabilities will increase the demand for counselors to prepare disabled people for employment.[83]

▶ Support Services

Support services are necessary for the highly complex and sophisticated system of health care to function. Service specialists perform administrative, operational, and management duties and often work closely with direct providers of healthcare services. Health information administrators, dental laboratory technologists, electroencephalographic technologists, food service administrators, surgical technologists, and environmental health technologists are just some of the allied health professionals in this category.

Health Information Administrators

Health information administrators are responsible for the activities of the medical records departments of hospitals, skilled nursing facilities, managed care organizations, rehabilitation centers, ambulatory care facilities, and a number of other healthcare operations. They plan, implement, and maintain information systems and associated policies that permit patient data to be received, recorded, stored, and retrieved easily to assist in diagnosis and treatment. A significant function they provide is supporting the billing and coding operations for healthcare organizations. Health information administrators supervise the staff in the medical records department and are responsible for maintaining the confidentiality of all the information within their departments.

The Commission on Certification for Health Informatics and Information Management (CAHIIM) provides a national certification examination for Registered Health Information Administrators. A bachelor's degree from a training program accredited by the CAHIIM is the entry level for certification.[84] Currently, there are more than 59 bachelor's level and 5 master's degree level training programs accredited by CAHIIM.[85]

Complementary and Integrative Medicine Practitioners

Rather than diminishing the public's interest in alternative forms of health care, the increasing sophistication of scientific medicine, and perhaps its limitations, have fostered a receptive climate for alternative forms of therapy. Across the country, there is widespread interest in complementary, integrative, and alternative modalities.

Each of these modalities has a specific definition. Complementary medicine is used together with mainstream medicine. An example of complementary medicine would be seeking treatment with an acupuncturist to treat allergies in addition to obtaining conventional allergy medication prescribed by an allergist. When the same healthcare provider offers both complementary and mainstream medicine in a coordinated manner, this is called integrative medicine. Alternative medicine is the use of non-mainstream treatments in place of conventional medicine.[84] In the past, complementary and alternative medicine was also known as CAM before the new term, *integrative medicine* was introduced by the National Institutes of Health. Integrative medicine involves bringing together conventional medicine with complementary medicine in a coordinated way.[86]

In 1992, with one-third of Americans resorting to so-called *alternative therapies*, the National Institutes of Health created an Office of Alternative Medicine to examine the efficacy of these therapies. In 1998, when more than 40 percent of Americans reported the use of alternative or complementary therapies, the Office of Alternative Medicine was elevated to the National Center for Complementary and Alternative Medicine, and its mandate was expanded. On December 17, 2014, the relatively new center was renamed to reflect the updated terminology of integrative medicine and is now called the National Center for Complementary and Integrative Health (NCCIH).

In 2012, data from the National Health Interview Survey (NHIS) reported that 33 percent of U.S. adults and 12 percent of children used at least one complementary health approach. The most commonly used complementary health approach was dietary supplements (i.e., supplements other than vitamins or minerals). The majority of adults who use dietary supplements do so to maintain wellness rather than to treat a specific ailment. The most commonly used dietary supplement by adults and children was fish oil (12 percent of adults and 1.1 percent in children). Other frequently used supplements were probiotics, melatonin, glucosamine/chondroitin, Echinacea, and garlic. The mind–body approaches most commonly used were yoga, chiropractic manipulation, meditation, and massage therapy. The proportion of adults who used yoga in 2012 (9.5 percent) increased substantially from the past NHIS (5.1 percent in the 2002 survey). Yoga use by children increased from 2.3 percent in 2007 to 3.1 percent in 2012.[87]

Along with alternative modalities came new classes of alternative practitioners. To name a few, there are certified Trager practitioners, who rock and cradle the patient's body for relaxation and mental clarity; doctors of naturopathy, who use natural healing methods that include diet, herbal medicine, and homeopathy; advanced certified Rolfers, who use deep massage to restore the body's natural alignment; and registered polarity practitioners, who use touch and advice on diet, self-awareness, and exercise to balance energy flow. Although professional medical societies strongly oppose naturopathy, considering the practice "unscientific" and "irrational," naturopathic doctors have made great strides in the last few years. Although they do not have medical degrees and are trained in loosely monitored schools, they are able to generate strong public support within state legislatures.[88]

The gains of alternative practitioners reflect the public's frustrations with conventional medicine, high drug prices, media reports of disproved treatments, and the lack of effectiveness for the treatment of chronic pain. The interest of insurance companies in alternative forms of medicine is also important. Many insurers have taken the position that when traditional medicine is ineffective and an alternative form of therapy, such as acupuncture for chronic pain, costs less and satisfies the patient, they will pay for it. As a result, several states now require insurance companies to cover naturopathic procedures and other techniques, such as acupuncture.[89]

The relatively new field of integrative medicine is rapidly taking hold where physicians take a whole-person approach and strive to treat the person and not just a disease. Physicians now perform post-residency fellowships in integrative medicine,[90] and some medicine residencies offer optional tracks or emphasis in integrative medicine.[91,92]

Medical Assistant

Almost all patients who have visited a physician's office have encountered a medical assistant. In fact, many patients often incorrectly identify them as nurses as they are ubiquitous in virtually all ambulatory healthcare facilities. Typical duties of medical assistants are checking patients in for appointments, recording of vital signs, verifying insurance, scheduling, performing some patient testing, and providing post-visit instructions and general support. "Many patients in primary care now have more face and phone time with a medical assistant than they do with their primary-care doctor, who increasingly is hidden from our view, funneled toward the most complex patient visits coming through their doors each day."[93]

The educational requirements for medical assistants are usually a high-school diploma followed by a one-year training program at a community college, vocational school, technical school, or university. These programs typically lead to a certificate while some two-year programs offer associate's degrees. Medical assistants are not required to be licensed or certified. However, some employers prefer medical assistants who have been certified by one of several certifying bodies.

In 2014, there were 591,300 medical assistants in the United States with a projected 23 percent increase over the next 10 years due to the aging population, the increasing number of group practices, implementation of the ACA, and the increasing volume of quality data that will need to be collected for accountable care organizations.[94]

▶ Factors That Influence Demand for Health Personnel

Without attempting to include all interrelated factors that influence demand for various types of health personnel, it is important to recognize some major determinants of the size and nature of the healthcare employment sector. Regardless of the potential for legislatively mandated reforms of the healthcare system, the number and skill requirements of each discipline within the healthcare workforce depend on the interdependence of the following factors.

Changing Nature of Disease, Disability, and Treatment

The aging of the population and advances in the treatment of acute and life-threatening conditions result in increased survival of people with chronic illness or disabilities. The growing number of patients with deteriorating mental capacities, cardiac conditions, cancer, stroke, head and spinal cord injuries, neonatal deficits, and congenital disorders significantly increases the demand for workers who provide and support prolonged medical treatment, rehabilitation, and nursing home or custodial care.

Physician Supply

Although many categories of health personnel perform independently of physicians, most of the decisions regarding the use of healthcare resources, the acceptance of other therapeutic modalities, and the treatment provided by nonphysicians, are made by physicians. It is therefore important to recognize that the anticipated changes in the numbers and types of physicians will have a direct impact on the demand for many other types of healthcare personnel.

Technology

Medical and nonmedical technology used in the provision of health care has important implications for the number and skill requirements of the healthcare workforce. Advances in medical imaging, new pharmaceuticals, and health information and communications technologies have the potential to both increase and decrease the demand for various kinds of personnel. Some technologies, such as transluminal coronary angioplasty and positron emission tomography, have led to the elimination of more laborious medical interventions. Others, such as sophisticated remote patient monitoring systems, telehealth, and more robust home care services have facilitated shifts to new service settings, such as ambulatory surgical centers. Also, automation of clinical laboratory testing has reduced the need for laboratory personnel. Thus, the mix of skills and the numbers of personnel ebb and flow with the discovery, application, and sun-setting of technologies, treatments, and drugs.

Expansion of Home Care

Healthcare reforms will continue the shift in health service delivery sites from acute care hospitals toward ambulatory, home care, and long-term care settings. With the emphasis on cost containment and value, the home care component of the healthcare industry is expected to expand significantly in the next decade. In addition, there is a growing body of evidence that therapy provided in the home can help patients recover faster, is safer, and reduces hospital readmissions.

Corporatization of Health Care

Solo practice among health professionals is becoming a practice pattern of the past for many reasons. The increase in group practices and hospital employment of physicians, the development of several forms of provider organizations, and new models for physician payment are likely to reduce solo private practice dramatically to only highly specialized and small niches. The assembly of vertically integrated health systems that link hospitals, nursing homes, home care, and other services along with the diversification of health providers into various health-related corporate ventures all reflect the corporatization of health care.

Since the beginning of the most recent U.S. recession (2007–2009), employment in health care continued to rise in ambulatory care, nursing, and residential care. While overall nationwide employment dropped steadily during the recession, the healthcare industry showed continued growth by adding almost 500,000 jobs. This was also the case during previous economic recessions in 1990 and 2001.[95] Strong growth in the healthcare workforce is likely to continue for the foreseeable future. Between 2014 and 2024, the U.S. Bureau of Labor Statistics predicts a 21.8 percent increase in healthcare sector jobs compared to an increase of 4.8 percent projected for all other non-healthcare related jobs.[96]

▶ Healthcare Workforce Issues and the Patient Protection and Affordable Care Act

Policy makers at every level of government, insurers, educators, providers, and consumers have a vested interest in the issues that pertain to the healthcare workforce. The Association of Academic Health Centers clearly defined those issues in a 1994 publication. Remarkably, the issues remain active almost 25 years later:[97]

- The adequacy of supply of health professionals, such as nurses, allied health professionals, primary care physicians, and geriatricians
- The geographic distribution of health professionals, especially shortages in rural and underserved urban areas
- The underrepresentation of minorities in all health professions
- The potential supply and poor distribution of specialty physicians
- The questions about the appropriate scope of practice for various health professionals and concern about legal restrictions on scope of practice for nonphysician practitioners
- The concern about the quality and relevance of the health professions' educational programs; whether educational institutions are producing the health professionals needed for an effective and productive workforce
- The costs associated with educating health professionals. The competency testing of healthcare professionals
- The redefinition of health professions as technology and the delivery system change and as various professions reconsider the credentials needed to practice within the profession
- The concern about the supply of faculty to train health professionals

These issues remain central to the ACA's workforce initiatives and were key to its establishment of a new National Health Care Workforce Commission (NHCWC). The NHCWC's composition included 15 representatives from the areas of healthcare workforce and health professionals, educational institutions, employers, third-party payers, healthcare services and health economics research, consumers, labor unions, and state or local workforce investment boards. The NHCWC was given an overall mandate to evaluate and make recommendations for numerous dimensions of the nation's healthcare workforce. This included education and training support for existing and potential new workers at all levels, efficient workforce deployment, professional compensation, and coordination among different types of providers. The Commission also was charged with monitoring grants awarded under ACA workforce development initiatives and submitting two reports to Congress each year. As proposed in the ACA, the NHCWC was recognized as potentially having the most significant influence on shaping the nation's future healthcare workforce policies.[98] Members of the Commission were appointed in 2010. However, despite the protests of 26 U.S. academic health science centers,[99] Congress has not funded the Commission and it has never met.[100]

Nevertheless, the ACA includes provisions to address workforce issues in addition to establishment of the NHCWC.[101] These include:

■ Increasing workforce supply by enhancing federal student loans for several health professions including primary care and geriatric physician, nurses, allied health personnel, public health workers, and those working in underserved areas
■ Enhancing workforce education and training, including cultural competency, through grants for primary care, dental health, mental health, nursing, public health personnel, community health personnel, those working with disabled individuals, and those working in rural settings
■ Supporting the existing healthcare workforce through increased funding for minority applicants to the health professions and a primary care extension program to educate providers about evidence-based therapies, health promotion, chronic disease management and mental health
■ Strengthening primary care through redistributions of unfilled residency positions to address shortages, increased funding for primary care residency-training programs at teaching health centers and establishing a demonstration program to increase graduate nurse training
■ Improving access to healthcare services through increased funding for federally qualified health centers, state and medical school support to improve and expand emergency services for children, and new support for coordinating and integrating primary and specialty care in community-based mental health settings

▶ The Future: Complexities of National Healthcare Workforce Planning

The United States has never planned comprehensively or strategically for the development and deployment of its healthcare workforce and, as a result, "the preparation of each generation of health workers is just as fragmented and confusing as the healthcare system they will one day join."[101] Federal and state governments, educational institutions, professional organizations, insurers, and provider institutions have had separate and often conflicting interests in health workforce education and training, regulation, financing, entry-level preparation, and scope of practice. The various levels at which policy decisions have been made and the disparate interests that influence those decisions have presented major obstacles to ensuring a coherent, efficient, and rational health workforce in the United States. Complex supply and demand factors influence workforce requirements, and the prediction of future requirements is severely confounded by the lack of uniform data at national and state levels across the professions.[102] Supply factors include variables such as income variations among professions, licensure requirements, and transferability of skills. Demand is affected by factors such as population demographics, consumer expectations, and payment systems. In the upcoming years, the current workforce shortages in professions such as generalist physicians, nurses, and mental health workers; the disproportionate geographic distribution of many types of providers in urban and rural areas; and underrepresentation by minorities in the health professions are major focal points of the ACA and were intended to be central to the NHCWC. The aging population, the shifting nature of diseases, healthcare delivery and reimbursement reforms, new technology, and economic factors will continue to change consumer demands and provider expectations, all lending more complexity to the challenges of planning for future workforce requirements.

The continued influx of previously uninsured individuals as a result of the ACA alone will put unprecedented stresses on delivery system personnel. In fact, there is mounting evidence that since implementation of the ACA, there has been an increase in the stress and burnout levels of primary care physicians. A survey conducted in 2014 indicates that more than 54.4 percent of U.S. primary care physicians exhibited at least one clinical sign of burnout, and this level had increased from 45.5 percent in 2011.[103] It will be necessary to modify the roles and scope of practice of many of the healthcare professions to adapt to changing service patterns.

The ACA and its workforce-related provisions include opportunities to take actions that have the potential to result in meaningful improvements in national workforce planning, development, and deployment. Already one of the nation's largest industries, healthcare employment will continue to experience significant growth.[96] Unfortunately, to date, Congressional gridlock has prevented funding of the NHCWC and other key portions of the ACA that could potentially address some of the stressors and deficiencies in the current healthcare workforce and the healthcare system as a whole. The centrality of the healthcare workforce to the quality, costs, and accessibility of the healthcare delivery system makes these improvements essential to the future of healthcare delivery in the United States.

KEY TERMS FOR REVIEW

Accreditation
Alternative Medicine
Behavioral Scientist
Certification
Complementary Medicine
Health Information Administrator
International Medical Graduates (IMGs)
Integrative Medicine
Laboratory Technologists and Technicians
Licensure
Maintenance of Certification (MOC)
National Center for Complementary and Integrative Health (NCCIH)
National Health Care Workforce Commission (NHCWC)
Nurse Practitioner
Osteopathic Medicine
Physician Assistant (PA)
Registration
Therapeutic Science Practitioner

CHAPTER ACRONYMS

ACA Affordable Care Act
AACN American Association of Colleges of Nursing
AAMC American Association of Medical Colleges
ABIM American Board of Internal Medicine
CNM Certified Nurse Midwife
CAHIIM Commission on Accreditation for Health Informatics and Information Management
CAPTE Commission on Accreditation in Physical Therapy Education

CoDA Commission on Dental Accreditation
CE Continuing Education
DDS Doctor of Dental Surgery
DDM Doctor of Dental Medicine
DMD Doctor of Medical Dentistry
MD Doctor of Medicine
DNP Doctor of Nursing Practice
DO Doctor of Osteopathy
PharmD Doctor of Pharmacy
DPT Doctor of Physical Therapy
IMG International medical graduate
LPN Licensed Practical Nurse
LVN Licensed Vocational Nurse

MRI Magnetic Resonance Imaging
MOC Maintenance of Certification
NCCIH National Center for Complementary and Integrative Health
NCLEX-RN National Council Licensure Examination for RNs
NHCWC National Health Care Workforce Commission
NHIS National Health Interview Survey
NP Nurse Practitioner
PA-C Physician Assistant-Certified
PA Physician Assistant
RN Registered Nurse

References

state-level projections, 2012–2025. December 2014. http://bhpr.hrsa.gov/healthworkforce/supplydemand /nursing/workforceprojections/nursingprojections .pdf. Accessed April 28, 2016.

20. Auerbach DI, Buerhaus PI, Staiger DO. Registered nurses are delaying retirement, a shift that has contributed to recent growth in the nurse workforce. *Health Aff.* July 16, 2014;33:1-7.

21. United States Department of Health and Human Services. Health Resources and Services Administration. The U.S. Nursing workforce: trends in supply and education. April 2013. http://bhpr.hrsa.gov/health workforce/reports/nursingworkforce/nursing workforcefullreport.pdf. Accessed April 28, 2016.

22. American Association of Colleges of Nursing. Nursing shortage fact sheet. April 24, 2014. http://www.aacn .nche.edu/media-relations/NrsgShortageFS.pdf. Accessed April 28, 2016.

23. The Institute of Medicine of the National Academies. The future of nursing: leading change, advancing health. October 5, 2010. http://www.nationalacademies.org /hmd/Reports/2010/The-Future-of-Nursing-Leading -Change-Advancing-Health.aspx. Accessed May 31, 2016.

24. American Association of Colleges of Nursing. Annual report 2014: building a framework for the future. http://www.aacn.nche.edu/aacn-publications/annual -reports/AnnualReport14.pdf. Accessed April 29, 2016.

25. Kirschling JM. Reflections on the future of doctoral programs in nursing. January 30, 2014. http://www .aacn.nche.edu/dnp/JK-2014-DNP.pdf. Accessed April 29, 2016.

26. College Atlas. Doctor of nursing science (DNSC, DNS or DSN) degree. May 22, 2015. http://www .collegeatlas.org/doctor-of-nursing-science-degrees .html. Accessed May 19, 2016.

27. American Association of Colleges of Nursing. Institutions offering doctoral programs in nursing and degrees conferred 2015. http://www.aacn.nche.edu /research-data/DOC.pdf. Accessed April 29, 2016.

28. American Association of Colleges of Nursing. Enhancing diversity in the workforce. March 16, 2015. http://www.aacn.nche.edu/media-relations/fact -sheets/enhancing-diversity. Accessed April 29, 2016.

29. American Nurses Association. Nurse staffing. http:// www.nursingworld.org/MainMenuCategories /ThePracticeofProfessionalNursing/NurseStaffing. Accessed April 29, 2016.

30. American Association of Colleges of Nursing. Accelerated nursing programs. January 14, 2014. http:// www.aacn.nche.edu/students/accelerated-nursing -programs. Accessed April 29, 2016.

31. Robert Wood Johnson Foundation. A new era in nursing: transforming care at the bedside. April 10, 2007. http://www.rwjf.org/en/library/research/2007/04 /a-new-era-in-nursing.html. Accessed April 29, 2016.

32. United States Bureau of Labor Statistics. Occupational Outlook Handbook. Licensed practical and licensed vocational nurses. May 2014. http://www.bls.gov /ooh/healthcare/licensed-practical-and-licensed -vocational-nurses.htm. Accessed May 8, 2016.

33. United States Bureau of Labor Statistics. Occupational Outlook Handbook. Nurse anesthetists, nurse midwives, and nurse practitioners. 2014. http://www.bls.gov/ooh /healthcare/nurse-anesthetists-nurse-midwives-and -nurse-practitioners.htm. Accessed May 8, 2016.

34. Bullough B, Bullough VI. *Nursing Issues for the Nineties and Beyond.* New York: Springer; 1994.

35. Poghosyan L, Lucero R, Rauch L, Berkowitz B. Nurse practitioner workforce: a substantial supply of primary care providers. *Nurs Econ.* 2012;30:268-274.

36. United States Centers for Disease Control and Prevention. National Center for Health Statistics. NCHS data brief no. 69 nurse practitioners certified nurse midwives and physician assistants in physician offices. August 2011. http://www.cdc.gov/nchs/data /databriefs/db69.pdf. Accessed May 10, 2016.

37. American Association of Nurse Practioners. NP facts. November 23, 2015. https://www.aanp.org/images /documents/about-nps/npfacts.pdf. Accessed May 10, 2016.

38. Yale School of Medicine. Physician associate program: history of the profession. http://paprogram.yale.edu /profession/history_profession.aspx. Accessed May 19, 2016.

39. Accreditation Review Commission on Education for the Physician Assistant. Accredited PA programs. http://www.arc-pa.org/accreditation/accredited -programs/. Accessed August 30, 2016.

40. United States Bureau of Labor Statistics. Occupational Outlook Handbook. Physicians assistants. 2014. http:// www.bls.gov/ooh/healthcare/physician-assistants .htm. Accessed May 12, 2016.

41. National Association of Clinical Nurse Specialists. CNS facts. 2016. http://www.nacns.org/html/cns-faqs .php. Accessed May 10, 2016.

42. Ring M. *Dentistry: An Illustrated History.* New York: Harry N. Abrams; 1985.

43. Loevy HT, Kowitz AA. Dental development in the midwest of America. *Int Dent J.* 1992;42:157-164.

44. United States Bureau of Labor Statistics. Occupational Outlook Handbook. How to become a dentist. December 17, 2015. http://www.bls.gov/ooh/healthcare/dentists .htm#tab-4. Accessed May 11, 2016.

45. American Dental Association. Specialty recognition for dental anesthesiology rejected. October 30, 2012. http://www.ada.org/en/publications/ada-news/2012 -archive/october/specialty-recognition-for-dental -anesthesiology-rejected. Accessed May 11, 2016.

46. American Dental Board of Anesthesiology. About the ADBA. 2006. http://www.adba.org/about.html. Accessed May 11, 2016.

47. United States Bureau of Labor Statistics. Occupational Outlook Handbook. Dentists: Job prospects. 2014. http://www.bls.gov/ooh/healthcare/dentists.htm#tab-6. Accessed May 11, 2016.

48. Commission on Dental Accreditation. Program surveys. 2014. http://www.ada.org/en/coda/find-a-program/program-surveys. Accessed May 11, 2016.

49. Health Policy Institute and the American Dental Association. Why adults forgo dental care: evidence from a new national survey. November 2014. http://www.ada.org/~/media/ADA/Science%20and%20Research/HPI/Files/HPIBrief_1114_1.ashx. Accessed May 11, 2016.

50. Higby GJ. American hospital pharmacy from the colonial period to the 1930s. *Am J Hosp Pharm*. 1994; 51:2817-2823.

51. Accreditation Council for Pharmacy Education. Accreditation Council for Pharmacy Education annual report. 2014. https://www.acpe-accredit.org/pdf/2014AnnualReport.pdf. Accessed May 11, 2016.

52. Pharmacy Times. The pharmacy job crisis: blame the pharmacy school bubble. May 26, 2015. http://www.pharmacytimes.com/contributor/alex-barker-pharmd/2015/05/the-pharmacy-job-crisis-blame-the-pharmacy-school-bubble. Accessed May 11, 2016.

53. United States Bureau of Labor Statistics. Occupational Outlook Handbook. Pharmacists. 2014. http://www.bls.gov/ooh/healthcare/pharmacists.htm. Accessed May 11, 2016.

54. United States Bureau of Labor Statistics. Occupational Outlook Handbook. Pharmacists: job outlook. 2014. http://www.bls.gov/ooh/healthcare/pharmacists.htm#tab-6. Accessed May 11, 2016.

55. Board of Pharmacy Specialties. About BPS. http://www.bpsweb.org/about-bps/. Accessed May 11, 2016.

56. United States Bureau of Labor Statistics. Occupational Outlook Handbook. Pharmacists: work environment. 2014. http://www.bls.gov/ooh/healthcare/pharmacists.htm#tab-3. Accessed May 11, 2016.

57. United States Bureau of Labor Statistics. Occupational Outlook Handbook. Podiatrists. 2014. http://www.bls.gov/ooh/healthcare/podiatrists.htm. Accessed May 11, 2016.

58. United States Bureau of Labor Statistics. Occupational Outlook Handbook. Podiatrists: how to become a podiatrist. 2014. http://www.bls.gov/ooh/healthcare/podiatrists.htm#tab-4. Accessed May 11, 2016.

59. Association of Chiropractic Colleges. http://www.chirocolleges.org/members.html. Accessed May 19, 2016.

60. United States Bureau of Labor Statistics. Occupational Outlook Handbook. Chiropractors. 2014. http://www.bls.gov/ooh/healthcare/chiropractors.htm. Accessed May 11, 2016.

61. United States Bureau of Labor Statistics. Occupational Outlook Handbook. Chiropractors: job outlook. 2014. http://www.bls.gov/ooh/healthcare/chiropractors.htm#tab-6. Accessed May 11, 2016.

62. Hertzman-Miller RP, Morgenstern H, Hurwitz EL, et al. Comparing the satisfaction of low back pain patients randomized to receive medical or chiropractic care: Results from the UCLA low-back pain study. *Am J Public Health*. 2002;92:1628-1633.

63. Rubinstein SM, Middelkoop Mv, Assendelft WJ, Boer MRd, Tulder MWv. Spinal manipulative therapy for chronic low-back pain. *Cochrane Database of Systematic Review*. 16 February 2011:188.

64. United States Bureau of Labor Statistics. Occupational Outlook Handbook. Optometrists: how to become an optometrist. 2014. http://www.bls.gov/ooh/healthcare/optometrists.htm#tab-4. Accessed May 11, 2016.

65. United States Bureau of Labor Statistics. Occupational Outlook Handbook Optometrists. 2014. http://www.bls.gov/ooh/healthcare/optometrists.htm. Accessed May 11, 2016.

66. United States Bureau of Labor Statistics. Occupational Outlook Handbook Optometrists: job outlook. 2014. http://www.bls.gov/ooh/healthcare/optometrists.htm#tab-6. Accessed May 11, 2016.

67. United States Bureau of Labor Statistics. Occupational Outlook Handbook. Medical and health services managers. 2014. http://www.bls.gov/ooh/management/medical-and-health-services-managers.htm. Accessed May 11, 2016.

68. United States Bureau of Labor Statistics. Occupational Outlook Handbook. Medical and health services managers: how to become a medical or health services manager. 2014. http://www.bls.gov/ooh/management/medical-and-health-services-managers.htm#tab-4. Accessed May 11, 2016.

69. Explorehealthcareers.org. Allied health professions overview. May 9, 2016. http://explorehealthcareers.org/en/Field/1/Allied_Health_Professions.aspx. Accessed May 11, 2016.

70. National Accrediting Agency for Clinical Laboratory Sciences 2015 Annual Report; http://www.naacls.org/getattachment/12e2c198-ac20-4a93-9336-27360b20a112/2015-Annual-Report.aspx. Accessed August 30, 2016.

71. United States Bureau of Labor Statistics. Occupational Outlook Handbook. Medical and clinical laboratory technologists and technicians. 2014. http://www.bls.gov/ooh/healthcare/medical-and-clinical-laboratory-technologists-and-technicians.htm. Accessed May 11, 2016.

72. Joint Review Committee on Education in Radiology. Organizational report of the Joint Review Committee on Education in Radiologic Technology. 2015. https://www.jrcert.org/sites/jrcert/uploads/documents/2015_Organizational_Report.pdf. Accessed May 11, 2016.

73. United States Bureau of Labor Statistics. Occupational Outlook Handbook. Radiologic and MRI technologists. 2014. http://www.bls.gov/ooh/healthcare/radiologic-technologists.htm. Accessed May 11, 2016.

74. United States Bureau of Labor Statistics. Occupational Outlook Handbook. How to become a nuclear medicine technologist. 2014. http://www.bls.gov/ooh/healthcare/nuclear-medicine-technologists.htm#tab-4. Accessed May 11, 2016.

75. United States Bureau of Labor Statistics. Occupational Outlook Handbook. Physical therapists. 2014. http://www.bls.gov/ooh/healthcare/physical-therapists.htm. Accessed May 12, 2016.

76. Commission on Accreditation in Physical Therapy Education. Welcome to CAPTE. 2016. http://www.capteonline.org/home.aspx. Accessed May 12, 2016.

77. United States Bureau of Labor Statistics. Occupational Outlook Handbook. How to become a physical therapist. 2015. http://www.bls.gov/ooh/healthcare/physical-therapists.htm#tab-4. Accessed May 12, 2016.

78. United States Bureau of Labor Statistics. Occupational Outlook Handbook. How to become an occupational therapist. 2014. http://www.bls.gov/ooh/healthcare/occupational-therapists.htm#tab-4. Accessed May 12, 2016.

79. United States Bureau of Labor Statistics. Occupational Outlook Handbook. Speech-language pathologists. 2014. http://www.bls.gov/ooh/healthcare/speech-language-pathologists.htm#tab-1. Accessed May 12, 2016.

80. United States Bureau of Labor Statistics. Occupational Outlook Handbook. How to become a social worker. 2014. http://www.bls.gov/ooh/community-and-social-service/social-workers.htm#tab-4. Accessed May 12, 2016.

81. Council on Social Work Education. Annual report 2014–2015. http://www.cswe.org/File.aspx?id=83135. Accessed May 12, 2016.

82. United States Bureau of Labor Statistics. Occupational Outlook Handbook. Social workers: job outlook. 2014. http://www.bls.gov/ooh/community-and-social-service/social-workers.htm#tab-6. Accessed May 12, 2016.

83. United States Bureau of Labor Statistics. Occupational Outlook Handbook. Rehabilitation counselors. 2014. http://www.bls.gov/ooh/community-and-social-service/rehabilitation-counselors.htm#tab-1. Accessed May 12, 2016.

84. Commission on Certification for Health Informatics and Information Management. RHIA overview. http://www.ahima.org/certification/RHIA. Accessed May 12, 2016.

85. Commission on Certification for Health Informatics and Information Management. Program directory. 2016. http://www.cahiim.org/directoryofaccredpgms/programdirectory.aspx. Accessed May 14, 2016.

86. National Center for Complementary and Integrative Health. Complementary, alternative, or integrative health: what's in a name? March 29, 2016. https://nccih.nih.gov/health/integrative-health. Accessed May 13, 2016.

87. National Center for Complementary and Integrative Health. What complementary and integrative approaches do Americans use? Key findings from the 2012 National Health Interview Survey. November 4, 2015. https://nccih.nih.gov/research/statistics/NHIS/2012/key-findings. Accessed May 13, 2016.

88. National Center for Complementary and Integrative Health. Draft minutes of the tenth meeting. January 28, 2002. https://nccih.nih.gov/about/naccam/minutes/2002jan.htm. Accessed May 13, 2016.

89. Rubenstein S. *Wall Street Journal.* September 22, 2002; D7.

90. American Board of Physician Specialties. Integrative medicine fellowships. http://www.abpsus.org/integrative-medicine-fellowships. Accessed May 13, 2016.

91. University of New Mexico Department of Internal Medicine. Integrative medicine in residency (IMR track). http://medicine.unm.edu/education/integrative/residency.html. Accessed May 13, 2016.

92. University of California Irvine School of Medicine. Department of Family Medicine. UC Irvine integrative medicine program. http://www.familymed.uci.edu/residency/Integrative_Medicine.asp. Accessed May 31, 2016.

93. Modern Healthcare. Commentary: the underappreciated role of medical assistants. May 5, 2018. http://www.modernhealthcare.com/article/20160506/NEWS/160509937?utm_source=modernhealthcare&utm_medium=email&utm_content=20160506-NEWS-160509937&utm_campaign=financedaily. Accessed May 12, 2016.

94. United States Bureau of Labor Statistics. Occupational Outlook Handbook. Medical assistants. 2014. http://www.bls.gov/ooh/healthcare/medical-assistants.htm#tab-1. Accessed May 12, 2016.

95. United States Bureau of Labor Statistics monthly labor review. Employment in health care: a crutch for the ailing economy during the 2007–09 recession. April 2011. http://www.bls.gov/opub/mlr/2011/04/art2full.pdf. Accessed May 13, 2016.

96. University of Albany Center for Health Workforce Studies. Health care employment projections, 2014–2024: an analysis of Bureau of Labor Statistics projections by setting and by occupation 2016, http://chws.albany.edu/archive/uploads/2016/04/BLS-Health-Care-Employment-Projections_2016.pdf. Accessed May 13, 2016.

97. McLaughlin C. Health work force issues and policy-making roles. In Larson P, Osterweis M, Rubin E, eds. *Health Work Force Issues for the 21st century.* Washington, DC: Association of Academic Health Centers; 1994:1-3.

98. Congressional Research Service. Public health, workforce, quality, and related provisions in the patient protection and Affordable Care Act (PPACA). June 7, 2010. NHCWC Accessed May 14, 2016.

99. Association of Academic Health Centers. Letter to the Committee on Appropriations, U.S. House of Representatives. June 11, 2013. http://www.aahcdc.org /Policy/Correspondence/View/tabid/78/ArticleId /121/To-Chairs-and-Ranking-Members-of-the -Appropriations-Committees-AAHC-Members-Sign -on-Letter-in-Support-of-the-National-Health-Care -Workforce-Commission.aspx. Accessed May 14, 2016.

100. Association of Academic Health Centers. Crucial health workforce commission languishes with no funding June 2013. http://www.aahcdc.org/Policy /PressReleases/PRView/tabid/85/ArticleId/122 /Crucial-Health-Workforce-Commission-Languishes -With-No-Funding.aspx. Accessed May 14, 2016.

101. Hahn A, Sussman J. Foundations and health care reform 2010: Policy brief: improving workforce efficiency. Brandeis University: The Heller School for Social and Policy Management. July 14, 2010; http:// sillermancenter.brandeis.edu/PDFs/Workforce%20 Policy%20Brief%20in%20conf%20template%20v2 .pdf. Accessed May 14, 2016.

102. Bipartisan Policy Center. The complexities of national health care workforce planning: executive summary. October 18, 2011. http://bipartisanpolicy.org/sites /default/files/Workforce%20study_Public%20 Release%20040912.pdf. Accessed May 14, 2016.

103. Shanafelt TD, Hasan O, Dyrbye LN, et al. Changes in burnout and satisfaction with work-life balance in physicians and the general US working population between 2011 and 2014. *Mayo Clin Proc.* 2015; 90:1600-1613.

CHAPTER 8

Financing Health Care

CHAPTER OVERVIEW

This chapter reviews the most currently data available on national healthcare expenditures and sources of payment. It also provides an historical overview of the developments that played major roles in creating the current national healthcare financing infrastructure. Major factors that affect healthcare costs are discussed as well. Because healthcare costs are inextricably bound to quality issues, the chapter discusses quality initiatives linked with healthcare spending. Significant trends in healthcare cost and quality are reviewed, along with underlying reasons for changes. The roles of the private sector and government as payers are presented. Throughout the chapter, features of the Patient Protection and Affordable Care Act (ACA) are integrated with updated information on the ACA's implementation. Lastly, the progress with federal rulemaking for implementation of the Medicare Access and CHIP Reauthorization Act of 2015 (MACRA) is discussed.

Implementation of the ACA of 2010 continues through 2019 with effects through many succeeding years. The ACA already has had a significant impact on health insurance regulation, has made access to health insurance for millions of Americans affordable, and has implemented ongoing efforts to transform the healthcare delivery payment system from a volume-based to a value-based system. However, it is important to recognize that the ACA does not change the fundamental structure of the U.S. healthcare financing system. As in the past, healthcare expenditures in the United States continue to be financed through a mosaic combination of private and public sources.

In 2015, a majority of working Americans under the age of 65 had private health insurance coverage provided by their employers.[1] In the entire population, due to the ACA's offerings through insurance exchanges, the percentage of individuals with coverage purchased directly from an insurance company increased by 3.8 percent between 2013 and 2014, representing an increase of approximately 10 million.[2] Fifty-seven percent of employers offer health benefits to their workers, a proportion unchanged since 2005.[3] However, during the past two decades, and

Flag: © Lightix/Shutterstock

especially during the economic recession of 2007–2009, employment-based health insurance coverage declined.[4] The number of Americans without health insurance coverage increased steadily over the years prior to implementation of the ACA, topping 40 million in the first years of the millennium.[4]

In 2011, for the first time in several years, the number of uninsured Americans dropped by more than one million, primarily due to an influx of newly insured young adults who benefited from a provision in the ACA legislation that required healthcare insurers to allow parents to keep adult children on their health insurance plans up to age 26.[5]

The primary federal health insurance programs are Medicare and Medicaid. Medicare covers healthcare services for most individuals over 65 years of age and disabled individuals. Medicaid covers services for low income populations. The federal government now also provides subsidies for individuals purchasing health insurance through ACA-authorized state and federal health exchanges (now known as "health insurance marketplaces").[1]

Financing of the U.S. healthcare system continues to evolve from a variety of influences, including provider, employer, purchaser, consumer, and political factors. As pointedly reflected in national healthcare reform debates, these influences produced major tensions. Issues included the role and responsibility of the government as payer, financial responsibilities of employers as purchasers of health insurance, and the impacts of payment systems on quality. Despite passage and implementation of the ACA, controlling the rising healthcare costs and the large numbers of Americans still uninsured under the ACA continue as two major challenges.[4]

▶ Healthcare Expenditures in Perspective

National health expenditures (NHEs) and trends are reported annually by the National Center for Health Statistics of the Centers for Disease Control and Prevention, the Office of the Actuary, National Health Statistics Group, and the U.S. Department of Health and Human Services (DHHS), Centers for Medicare & Medicaid Services (CMS). Expenditures are reported and tracked over time using a standard format that identifies both the private and public sources of funds as well as the objects of expense. Reports are issued annually, two years following closure of the reporting period. **TABLE 8-1** provides one example of this type of report for 2014.[6]

In 2014, NHEs totaled more than $3.0 trillion, 17.5 percent of the gross domestic product (GDP), or $9,523 per person (**FIGURE 8-1**).[7]

The GDP is the broadest quantitative measure of a nation's total economic activity, representing the monetary value of all goods and services produced within a nation's geographic borders over a specified time period.

In 2014, NHEs increased 5.3 percent from an increase of 2.9 percent the prior year.[8] The increase in expenditures followed five years of slow expenditure growth.[9] The 2014 growth is attributed to two primary factors: ACA-related health insurance coverage expansions, especially for Medicaid and private health insurance, and significant increases in retail prescription drug expenditures that represented the largest annual increase since 2002. A new hepatitis C treatment drug costing $11.3 billion was the major factor in 2014 drug cost increases.[9] Prescription drug expenditures for 2014 totaled $ 297.7 billion.[7]

Expenditures for personal healthcare services in 2014 represented more than 84 percent, or $2.6 trillion of the total NHEs.[7] Hospital care at $971.8 billion and physician plus clinical services at $603.7 billion in total comprised 52 percent of 2014 NHEs.[7] (See **FIGURE 8-2**.)[10]

TABLE 8-1 National Health Expenditures, 2014, by Source of Funds and Type of Expenditures: Calendar Year 2014

Year and Type of Expenditure	Total	Out of Pocket	Health Insurance	Private Health Insurance	Medicare	Medicaid	Other Health Insurance Programs[1]	Other Third Party Payers[2]	Government Public Health Activities	Investment
					Amount in Billions					
Year 2014										
National Health Expenditures	$3,031.3	$329.8	$2,216.9	$991.0	$618.7	$495.8	$111.4	$251.7	$79.0	$153.9
Health Consumption Expenditures	2,877.4	329.8	2,216.9	991.0	618.7	495.8	111.4	251.7	79.0	–
Personal Health Care	2,563.6	329.8	2,000.3	868.8	580.7	444.9	105.9	233.5	–	–
Hospital Care	971.8	31.4	840.8	362.1	250.3	168.0	60.4	99.7	–	–
Professional Services	801.6	121.1	605.4	338.4	158.4	80.3	28.3	75.1	–	–
Physician and Clinical Services	603.7	54.0	482.2	254.7	138.4	64.0	25.2	67.4	–	–
Other Professional Services	84.4	21.3	55.8	29.7	19.6	6.3	0.2	7.3	–	–
Dental Services	113.5	45.7	67.3	54.1	0.4	10.1	2.8	0.5	–	–
Other Health, Residential, and Personal Care[3]	150.4	5.9	102.5	11.4	5.2	83.9	2.0	42.1	–	–
Home Health Care[4]	83.2	7.4	73.1	8.3	34.7	29.6	0.5	2.7	–	–
Nursing Care Facilities and Continuing Care Retirement Communities[4,5]	155.6	41.2	103.1	13.1	35.7	49.6	4.7	11.3	–	–
Retail Outlet Sales of Medical Products	401.0	123.0	275.3	135.5	96.4	33.5	10.0	2.6	–	–
Prescription Drugs	297.7	44.7	250.9	127.3	86.4	27.3	9.9	2.0	–	–
Durable Medical Equipment	46.4	23.6	22.2	8.2	7.7	6.1	0.1	0.6	–	–

(continues)

TABLE 8-1 National Health Expenditures, 2014, by Source of Funds and Type of Expenditures: Calendar Year 2014 (*continued*)

Year and Type of Expenditure	Total	Out of Pocket	Health Insurance						Government Public Health Activities	Investment
			Health Insurance	Private Health Insurance	Medicare	Medicaid	Other Health Insurance Programs[1]	Other Third Party Payers[2]		
Other Non-durable Medical Products	56.9	54.7	2.3	–	2.3	–	–	0.0	–	–
Government Administration[6]	40.2	–	36.5	–	9.5	22.6	4.4	3.7	–	–
Net Cost of Health Insurance[7]	194.6	–	180.1	122.2	28.5	28.3	1.1	14.5	–	–
Government Public Health Activities	79.0	–	–	–	–	–	–	–	79.0	–
Investment	153.9	–	–	–	–	–	–	–	–	153.9
Research[8]	45.5	–	–	–	–	–	–	–	–	45.5
Structures and Equipment	108.3	–	–	–	–	–	–	–	–	108.3

[1] Includes Children's Health Insurance Program (Titles XIX and XXI), Department of Defense, and Department of Veterans Affairs.

[2] Includes worksite health care, other private revenues, Indian Health Service, workers' compensation, general assistance, maternal and child health, vocational rehabilitation, other federal programs, Substance Abuse and Mental Health Services Administration, other state and local programs, and school health.

[3] Includes expenditures for residential care facilities (NAICS 623210 and 623220), ambulance providers (NAICS 621910), medical care delivered in non-traditional settings (such as community centers, senior citizens centers, schools, and military field stations), and expenditures for Home and Community Waiver programs under Medicaid.

[4] Includes freestanding facilities only. Additional services of this type provided in hospital-based facilities are counted as hospital care.

[5] Includes care provided in nursing care facilities (NAICS 6231), continuing care retirement communities (623311), state and local government nursing facilities, and nursing facilities operated by the Department of Veterans Affairs (DVA).

[6] Includes all administrative costs (federal and state and local employees' salaries, contracted employees including fiscal intermediaries, rent and building costs, computer systems and programs, other materials and supplies, and other miscellaneous expenses) associated with insuring individuals enrolled in the following health insurance programs: Medicare, Medicaid, Children's Health Insurance Program, Department of Defense, Department of Veterans Affairs, Indian Health Service, workers' compensation, maternal and child health, vocational rehabilitation, Substance Abuse and Mental Health Services Administration, and other federal programs.

[7] Net cost of health insurance is calculated as the difference between CY incurred premiums earned and benefits paid for private health insurance. This includes administrative costs, and in some cases, additions to reserves, rate credits and dividends, premium taxes, and plan profits or losses. Also included in this category is the difference between premiums earned and benefits paid for the private health insurance companies that insure the enrollees of the following programs: Medicare, Medicaid, Children's Health Insurance Program, and workers' compensation (health portion only).

[8] Research and development expenditures of drug companies and other manufacturers and providers of medical equipment and supplies are excluded from "research expenditures" but are included in the expenditure class in which the product falls.

NOTE: Numbers may not add to totals because of rounding. The figure 0.0 denotes amounts less than $50 million. Dashes (–) indicate "not applicable." Dollar amounts shown are in current dollars. Percent changes are calculated from unrounded data.

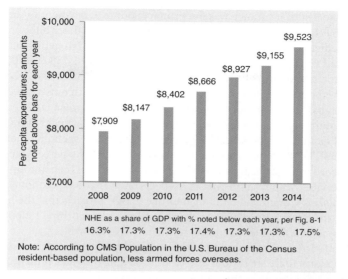

FIGURE 8-1 **National Healthcare Expenditures Per Capita and Their Share of the Gross Domestic Product, 2008–2014**

Data from National Health Expenditures per Capita and Their Share of the Gross Domestic Product, 2008-2014. Source: Centers for Medicare and Medicaid Services, Office of the Actuary, National Health Statistics Group. Retrieved from: https://www.cms.gov/research-statistics-data-and-systems/statistics-trends-and-reports/nationalhealthexpenddata/nationalhealthaccountshistorical.html.

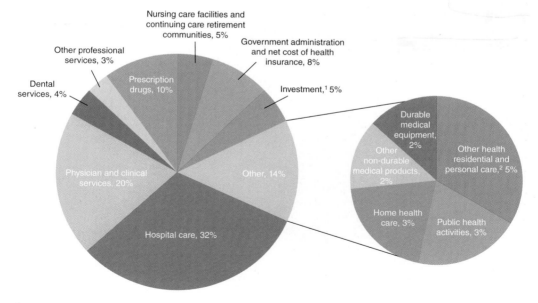

[1] Includes Noncommercial Research (2 percent) and Structures and equipment (4 percent).
[2] Includes expenditures for residential care facilities, ambulance providers, medical care delivered in non-traditional settings (such as community centers, senior citizens centers, schools, and military field stations), and expenditures for Home and community Waiver programs under Medicaid.
Note: Sum of pieces may not equal 100 percent due to rounding.

FIGURE 8-2 **The Nation's Health Dollar ($3.0 Trillion), Calendar Year 2014, Where It Went**

Centers for Medicare & Medicaid Services, Office of the Actuary, National Health Statistics Group.

In 2014, private health insurance was the primary source of payment for healthcare services, with an outlay of $991.0 billion.[10] Medicare, with expenditures of $618.7 billion, was the next largest source, and Medicaid ranked as third largest at $495.8 billion.[10] Together, all public sources of funding represented 43 percent of total health expenditures in 2014.[10] (See **FIGURE 8-3**.)

Historically, the rate of growth in healthcare expenditures (HCEs) has been an overarching concern of both the private and government sectors as HCE growth outstripped general inflation by significant margins.[11] U.S. healthcare spending per person has grown faster on average than the nation's economic output per capita for the past few decades.[1] As a percent of the GDP, HCEs were 9.5 percent in 1985 and now represent 17.5 percent.[1,7] Healthcare spending increases that exceed growth in the overall GDP are not sustainable.[1] This is because the percentage of the GDP used for health care absorbs an increasing share of individuals' incomes, constraining consumption of other goods and services, with resulting negative effects on the national economy. Without changes in current laws, the U.S. Congressional Budget Office (CBO) projects that the healthcare share of GDP will increase to 25 percent by 2040. Such projections provide strong rationale for the private and government sectors' initiatives to control healthcare cost growth.[1]

Although insured Americans view the U.S. healthcare delivery system as superior to that of other developed nations, there are serious questions regarding the value returned for vastly greater U.S. expenditures, while citizens of those other nations experience better health outcomes.

The Organization for Economic Cooperation and Development (the OECD) is composed of 34 nations committed to democratic principles and economic progress.[12] One of its functions is the compilation of comprehensive comparable statistics on health and health systems across its members.[13] The most recent OECD report based on 2013 data notes that U.S. health spending, with a 17.5 percent share of the GDP, is an "outlier among other OECD countries," who devote an average of 8.9 percent to health spending.[13] Also based on 2013 data from the OECD and other sources, a 2015 Commonwealth fund report compared the United States with 12 other high-income OECD members on healthcare spending, use of services, and prices.[14] The

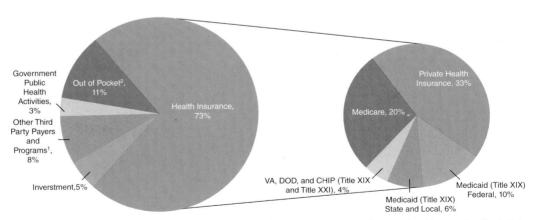

[1] Includes worksite health care, other private revenues, Indian Health Service, workers, compensation, general assistance, maternal and child health, vocational rehabilitation, Substance Abuse and Mental Health Service Administration, school health, and other federal and state local programs.
[2] Includes co-payments, deductibles, and any amounts not covered by health insurance.
Note: Sum of pieces may not equal 100 percent due to rounding.

FIGURE 8-3 **The Nation's Health Dollar ($3.0 Trillion), Calendar Year 2014: Where It Came From**

Centers for Medicare & Medicaid Services, Office of the Actuary, National Health Statistics Group.

United States was the only country in the study group that did not have a universal healthcare system. Some key findings included:

- As the highest spender, the percent of GDP the United States devoted to health care was 50 percent higher than the next highest spender (France at 11.6 percent) and almost double the 8.8 percent of the United Kingdom.
- U.S. per-resident private spending for health insurance and other related costs was more than five times the amount spent in Canada, the second-highest-spending country.
- Differentials in cost between the United States and other countries are due to more use of expensive technologies and significantly higher prices rather than to higher hospitalization rates or use of physician services.
- The United States was the only country whose share of GDP for healthcare spending exceeded the share of GDP expended for social services.
- Compared with its peer nations, U.S. population health outcomes are poor with the lowest life expectancy and the highest rates of infant mortality. The report suggests that the relatively low spending on social services in the United States may be a contributor to poor health outcomes because health disparities are inadequately addressed.[14]

Noting that the report reflects the pre-ACA implementation period, the authors suggest that ACA initiatives to better link social services with health care may hold promise to improve the health status of the U.S. population.[14]

Waste, Fraud, and Abuse

Studies by the Institute of Medicine (IOM) and U.S. Congressional Budget Office (CBO) indicate that 30–40 percent of total U.S. health spending is "wasted," providing services of no discernible value and inefficiently providing valuable services; this is another significant dimension of U.S. healthcare spending.[15] A 2012 study highlighted five categories of health spending waste that estimated unnecessary costs totaling between $476 and $992 billion per year.[16] Primary causes of waste identified included failures of care delivery and care coordination, overtreatment, administrative complexity, and overpricing.[16] Successfully mitigating these causes is very complex, involving issues such as general system disorganization, provider behaviors, patient behaviors, perverse economic incentives, and market forces. One example of professional efforts is the Choosing Wisely Campaign discussed in Chapter 4. Launched in 2012 by the American Board of Internal Medicine Foundation in concert with Consumer Reports and more than 70 professional medical societies, its intent is to avoid, "wasteful or unnecessary medical tests, treatments and procedures."[17] Because the Campaign involves judgments about the clinical value of interventions that have the potential to affect physician and healthcare organization revenue, robust discussions continue about its appropriate applications.[18]

It is no surprise that a $3+ trillion enterprise invites fraud and abuse. The Federal Bureau of Investigation estimated that fraudulent billings to public and private healthcare programs were 3–10 percent of total health spending, or $75–$250 billion."[19] With fraud and abuse draining substantial resources from the healthcare system, there has been a decades-long history of collaboration among the U.S. Department of Justice, the Office of the Inspector General of the DHHS, and other government agencies to combat these issues.[20] The following are some examples of antifraud and abuse initiatives.

Begun in 1997, the Health Care Fraud Abuse and Control Program had returned more than $27.8 billion to the Medicare Trust Fund by 2015.[20] In 2007, the U.S. Attorney General and DHHS

Secretary created a multifaceted approach with a Health Care Fraud Prevention and Enforcement Action Team (HEAT) to use "cutting-edge technology to identify and analyze suspected fraud and to build complex healthcare fraud cases quickly and efficiently."[19] A key component of HEAT is an interagency Medicare Fraud Strike Force.[20] In 2015, CMS reported that the Strike Force had charged more than 2,800 individuals involved in more than $8.7 billion in fraud, with a 95 percent conviction rate.[20] Another initiative is the interagency Health Care Fraud Prevention Partnership that includes federal agencies, states, private health plans, and associations. This initiative deploys fraud-detection technology similar to that used by credit card companies.[20] However, sophisticated criminal schemes involving providers, patients, drug dealers, and others continue to evolve.[19,21]

A perspective on healthcare financing in the United States requires a grasp of much more than the numbers; it requires an appreciation for many other factors. Some of these include the human dimensions of healthcare providers; a propensity to maintain the status quo; and many social, political, and economic factors that interplay in this enormous industry.

▶ Drivers of Healthcare Expenditures

Numerous interrelated factors contribute to healthcare expenditures. As discussed briefly below, key factors include:

- Aging population
- New drugs and medical and diagnostic technology
- Emphasis on specialty medicine
- Large numbers of uninsured and underinsured
- Volume-based reimbursement incentives
- Labor intensity

Estimates in 2014 place the population 65 years of age and older at 44.7 million, 14.1 percent of the population, or about one in every seven Americans.[22] Persons over the age of 65 are the major consumers of inpatient hospital care. According to the most recent federal data, these individuals account for more than one-third of all hospital stays and nearly one-half of all days of hospital care.[23] In addition, Medicare beneficiaries with four or more chronic conditions generate 80 percent of all Medicare spending, and half of Americans age 65 years or older visit an emergency department in the last month of life.[24,25] Aging has a large effect on federal health spending due to virtually all Americans' eligibility for Medicare at age 65.[1]

New pharmacologic agents and medical and diagnostic technology and services come at a high price.[26] Increased access to drug coverage through Medicare and managed care and "direct-to-consumer" marketing of prescription drugs via all types of media contributed to increases in prescription drug usage and costs.[27]

Technologically advanced diagnostic and treatment innovations require expensive equipment, computerization, and highly trained personnel. The large capital investments to finance technological innovations drove economic and professional incentives for their use, unbounded by requirements to justify their cost or the validity of their clinical benefits. The tendency to favor broad, rather than discretionary, use of technology grew with rapidly increasing availability of new technology and its profitability.

Growth in specialized medicine occurred as medical science and technology advanced. Americans' preference for specialty care resulted in high utilization and rapidly rising costs. Unlike other developed nations, where physician specialists represent half or fewer of physicians, 70 percent of practicing physicians in the United States are specialists.[28] Since the 1940s, when employers offset post-World War II wage controls with fully paid health insurance benefits, working Americans were insulated from healthcare costs. Americans demanded what they perceived as the "best" care, placing a high value on the use of expensive specialty care. For most, the costs of treatment were irrelevant, and physicians' recommendations were uninhibited by economic considerations for their well-insured patients. Historically, U.S. health insurance models carried no prohibitions against patient self-referrals to specialty care until the 1980s when managed care placed strong restrictions on patient self-referrals to specialists.

According to U.S. Census Bureau, among all developed countries of the world, the United States had the highest proportion of population without health insurance coverage.[29] Without health insurance, individuals often do not receive timely preventive, acute, and chronic care. Frequently, this results in their using high-cost emergency care. Un- and underinsured individuals tend to delay seeking care and are more likely than insured individuals to enter care in later stages of disease and require hospitalization.[30,31] Both private and government healthcare-financing mechanisms continue to be major influences in volume-driven healthcare expenditures. Fee-for-service reimbursement that financially rewards the volume of services delivered continues to provide profit-driven incentives that drive healthcare expenditures. In spite of earlier reforms, such as the prospective hospital payment reimbursement system of the 1980s and managed care (discussed later in this chapter), the fee-for-service system is still largely in use today. ACA provisions are attempting to move financial incentives toward value-based rather than volume-based approaches.

Health care is a labor-intensive industry that employs some of the most highly educated, trained, and compensated individuals in the U.S. workforce. As such, it is inherently expensive. Employment growth due to technology, the aging population, and other factors are anticipated to continue as significant drivers of healthcare expenditures.[32]

▶ Evolution of Private Health Insurance

As early as the mid-1800s, a movement by benevolent societies and unions began to insure workers against lost wages resulting from work-related accidents.[33] Later, insurance to cover lost wages resulting from catastrophic illness was added to accident policies.[33] It was not until the 1930s that health insurance began paying part or all costs of medical treatment. The basic concept of health insurance is antithetical to the central premise by which "insurance" was historically defined. Whereas insurance originally guarded against the low risk of rare occurrences such as premature death and accidents, the health insurance model that evolved provided coverage for predictable and discretionary uses of the healthcare system as well as unforeseen and unpredictable health events. Known as indemnity insurance because it protected individuals from a portion of financial risk associated with the costs of care, health insurance companies set allowable charges for services, and providers could bill the patient for any excess.[34] Coverage for routine healthcare services added a new dimension to the concept of insurance. Indemnity coverage prevailed until the advent of managed care in the 1970s.

The Rise of Blue Cross and Blue Shield and Commercial Health Insurance

In 1930, a group of Baylor University teachers contracted with Baylor Hospital in Dallas, Texas, to provide coverage for hospital expenses.[35] This arrangement created a model for the development of what was to become Blue Cross, a private, not-for-profit insurance empire that grew over the succeeding four decades into the dominant form of health insurance in the United States. The Blue Shield plans providing physician payments began shortly after Blue Cross, and by the early 1940s, numerous Blue Shield plans were operating across the country.[35]

The establishment and subsequent growth of the "Blues" signaled a new era in U.S. healthcare delivery and financing. They played a significant role in establishing hospitals as the centers of medical care proliferation and technology and, by reimbursing for expensive services, they put hospital care easily within the reach of middle-class working Americans for the first time. The insulation from costs of care provided by the Blues had a major impact on utilization. By the late 1930s, annual hospital admission rates for Blue Cross enrollees were 50 percent higher on average than for the nation as a whole.[36] In addition to contributing to increased utilization of hospital services by removing financial barriers, the Blue Cross movement had other lasting impacts on national policy making. Rosemary Stevens noted, "In the United States, the brave new world of medicine was specialized, interventionist, mechanistic and expensive—at least as interpreted, through prepayment, for workers in major organizations."[36] By 1940, the Blue Cross movement was a major financing alternative that squelched forces that had long lobbied for a form of national health insurance, a concept opposed vehemently by private medicine.[36]

Uniform features of all Blue Cross plans included not-for-profit status, supervision by state insurance departments, direct payments through contracts with providers, and the use of community rating. Community-rated insurance allowed all individuals in a defined group to pay single premiums without regard to age, gender, occupation, or health status.[37] Community rating helped ensure nondiscrimination against groups with varying risk characteristics to provide coverage at reasonable rates for the community as a whole.

For-profit commercial health insurers entered the market in significant numbers in the decade following start-up of Blue Cross and Blue Shield. However, as the commercial insurers entered the marketplace, they used experience-rated insurance and based premiums on groups' historically documented patterns of claims.[37] Unbounded by the requirement for community rating by the not-for-profit Blues, they used experience rating to charge higher premiums to less-healthy individuals and successfully competed for the market of healthier individuals by offering lower premiums. By the early 1950s, commercial insurers had enrolled more subscribers than the Blues.[38] To remain competitive, the Blues were forced to switch to experience-rated insurance to avoid attracting a disproportionate share of high-risk individuals for whom commercial insurance was prohibitively expensive.[36]

▶ Transformation of Health Insurance: Managed Care

The transformation occurred for many reasons. In summary, it resulted from concerns over rising costs and quality issues. Today, health insurance in the United States is synonymous with managed care and managed care organizations (MCOs), also known by the term "health plans," are the vehicles through which almost all Americans receive health insurance coverage.

Throughout the 1960s and early 1970s, rapidly increasing expenditures accompanied by quality concerns captured the attention of government and private policy makers. Medicare costs were spiraling upward with concerns about quality, and in the private sector, large employers, as the primary private health insurance purchasers, advocated for changes to control costs.[39] These concerns and other factors ultimately resulted in the Nixon administration's proposal for the Health Maintenance Organization (HMO) Act that was enacted in 1973.[36] Although many employer groups had used principles of managed care for prior decades through contracts with healthcare providers to serve employees on a prepaid basis, provisions of the HMO Act opened participation to the employer-based market, allowing the rapid proliferation of managed care plans.[36]

The HMO Act of 1973 provided loans and grants for the planning, development, and implementation of combined insurance and healthcare delivery organizations and required that comprehensive preventive and primary care services be included in the HMO arrangements.[34]

The legislation mandated employers with 25 or more employees to offer an HMO option if one was available in their area.[34]

HMOs combined providers and insurers into one organizational entity. Managed care is population based rather than individually based. The population basis enables the insurer to actuarially determine projected use of services related to age, gender, occupation, and other factors. Population groups' claims histories are used to set premium levels. All forms of managed care entail interdependence between the provision of and payment for healthcare services. It is a system through which care-providing groups or networks and beneficiaries share financial risk with an insurer for medical care and health maintenance.

By linking insurance with service delivery and financial risk, managed care intended to reverse the financial incentives in the fee-for-service model, which historically had rewarded providers financially for service volume and focused on illness treatment rather than prevention.

Financial risk-sharing between insurers and providers in managed care took two primary forms. The first form is prepayment or capitation, through which providers are paid a preset amount in advance for services their insured population is projected to need in a given period. Capitation pays providers for services on a per-member-per-month basis. Under capitation, providers receive payment whether or not services are used. If providers exceed the predetermined payment level, they may suffer financial penalties. If providers use fewer resources than projected, they may retain the excess as profit. The second form of financial risk-sharing is withholds, in which a percentage of the monthly capitated fee is withheld from provider payments to cover potential cost overruns for services such as specialty referrals or hospitalizations. All, part, or none of the withholds may be returned to providers at the end of specified period, depending on financial performance.[34] The key element of all provider prepayment arrangements is cost-conscious, efficient, and effective care.

For beneficiaries, managed care transfers financial risk in two forms: co-payments and deductibles. Co-payments require beneficiaries to pay a set fee each time they receive a covered service, such as a co-payment for each physician office visit. Deductibles require beneficiaries to meet predetermined, out-of-pocket expenditures before a managed care plan assumes payment responsibility for the balance of charges.

Initially, there were two major types of HMOs. The first was a staff model. It employed groups of physicians to provide most healthcare needs of its members. HMOs often provided some specialty services within the organization and many contracted for services with community specialists. In the staff model, the HMO operated facilities in which its physicians practiced, providing on-site support services such as radiology, laboratory, and pharmacy. The HMO purchased hospital care and other services for its members through fee-for-service or prepaid contracted arrangements. Staff model HMOs were referred to as "closed panel" because they employed the physicians who provided the majority of their members' care, and those physicians did not provide services outside the HMO membership. Similarly, community-based physicians could not participate in HMO member care without authorization by the HMO.[34]

The second type of HMO stimulated by the 1973 legislation was the individual practice association (IPA). IPAs are physician organizations composed of community-based independent physicians in solo or group practices that provide services to HMO members. An IPA HMO did not operate facilities in which members received care but rather provided its members services through private physician office practices. Like the staff model HMO, the IPA HMO purchased hospital care and specialty services not available through IPA-participating physicians from other providers on a prepaid or fee-for-service basis. Some IPA HMOs allowed physicians to have a nonexclusive relationship that permitted treatment of nonmembers as well as members; however, HMO relationships with an IPA also could be established on an exclusive basis. In this scenario, an HMO took the initiative in recruiting and organizing community physicians into an IPA to serve its members. Because the HMO was the organizing entity in such an arrangement, it was common for the HMO to require exclusivity by the IPA, limiting its services only to that HMO's membership.[34] The staff model and IPA-type organizations illustrate two major types of HMOs, but many hybrid forms of managed care organizations (MCOs) emerged throughout the 1980s and 1990s in response to cost and quality concerns as well as to purchaser and consumer preferences. The following sections summarize two examples.

Preferred provider organizations (PPOs) are managed care plans that may be owned by various types of organizations such as HMOs, hospitals, physician groups, and physician/hospital joint venture groups.[34] PPOs contract for services from physicians, hospitals, and other healthcare providers to form a network of participating preferred providers who agree to a PPO's cost and utilization control parameters.[34] Employer health benefit plans and health insurance companies may contract with PPOs to purchase healthcare services for their beneficiaries. PPOs exercise purchasing power by negotiating payment rates for services with providers. PPOs derive this power by covering large groups of beneficiaries.[34] Participating providers benefit from a guaranteed flow of business, and physicians are not required to share in financial risk as a condition of participation. By providing predictable admission volume, PPOs help hospitals to project occupancy rates and revenue. Beneficiaries benefit because PPOs do not restrict the use of out-of-network providers. However, using out-of-network providers does incur additional costs, typically in the form of higher co-payments. In 2015, PPOs were the most popular managed care plans, encompassing 56 percent of covered workers among large employers and 41 percent of covered workers among small employers.[40]

A point-of-service (POS) plan is a hybrid of HMO and PPO plans. It is called "point-of-service" because beneficiaries can select whether to use a provider in a POS-approved network or seek care outside the POS plan network when a particular medical need arises. Although POS plans require beneficiaries to select an in-network primary care provider, POS plans offer the flexibility to choose providers outside of a MCO's approved provider network without requirement of a referral. However, like in PPOs, selecting an out-of-network provider without a primary care referral can incur significant out-of-pocket costs.[41] In 2015, POS plans represented 6 percent of firms with more than 200 workers and 19 percent of covered employee enrollment in firms with fewer than 200 workers.[40]

The organizational forms of managed care continued to evolve because of changing marketplace conditions, including purchaser preferences, beneficiary demands, and other factors. With the numbers and types of managed care organizations, clear distinctions among them are no longer possible.[34] The emergence of PPOs as the most popular beneficiary choice represented a means to involve insurers and providers in negotiating fees and monitoring utilization while giving beneficiaries more choice. Today, the staff model HMO is almost non-existent due to many factors including beneficiary demands for more choice of providers, large capital outlays associated with facility maintenance, and increased competition from IPA models.[42]

Throughout the 1990s, market factors that enabled large health insurance purchasers to aggressively negotiate provider arrangements contributed to the impact of expenditure-cutting managed care initiatives. The surge in managed care enrollment in the 1990s with decreases in premiums contributed to a decline in the average annual growth of national healthcare expenditures.[43] However, after four years of decline, health insurance premiums increased 8.2 percent in 1998, more than double the increase of the previous three years.[44] The insurance "underwriting cycle," in which insurers underprice during periods of market development and then increase premiums later to restore profitability, was viewed as a major reason for premium increases. A 1997–2001 literature analysis of MCO performance indicated that, overall, MCOs did not accomplish their early promises to change clinical practice and improve quality while lowering costs.[45] Findings suggested that a systematic revamping of information systems, coupled with appropriate incentives and revised clinical processes, were required to produce the desired changes in cost and quality performance.[45]

Managed Care Backlash

In what was termed the managed care "backlash" beginning in the late 1990s, organized medicine, other healthcare providers, and consumers protested MCO policies on choice of providers, referrals, and other practices that were viewed as unduly restrictive.[34] A federal commission was established to review the need for guidelines in the managed care industry. In 1998, President Clinton signed legislation that imposed patient protection requirements on private insurance companies providing health coverage to federal workers.[46] Public dissatisfaction with constraints over the right to receive necessary care and the freedom of physicians to refer patients to specialists received wide publicity. Ultimately, the states took the lead in the patients' rights arena and, beginning in 1998, state legislatures enacted more than 900 laws and regulations addressing both consumer and provider protections.[47] Over the years, expanded beneficiary choices, patient rights' legislation, rescindments of physician restrictions on referrals, and other factors have served to reverse many of the issues that spawned the backlash.[34]

High-Deductible Health Plans

Beginning in 2001, an effect of the managed care backlash was seen in the form of employers offering health insurance plans that allowed employees to make personal decisions about their coverage.[48] First dubbed "Consumer-Driven Health Plans," the plans are now commonly known as High-Deductible Health Plans (HDHPs). The goals of HDHPs are to entice employees with lower premium costs in exchange for agreeing to make out-of-pocket up-front payments for health services. The HDHP intends to encourage cost-consciousness about the use of healthcare services.[48] Today, HDHPs are the second most common type of plan offered by employers, with 24 percent of U.S. workers selecting this option.[49] Since 2009, the percent of employees covered by HDHPs has tripled.[49]

The Internal Revenue Service (IRS) sets criteria for HDHPs' minimum deductible and maximum out-of-pocket cost limits.[48] HDHPs may have a health savings account option (HSA) or health reimbursement arrangement (HRA); both are governed by IRS criteria. HSAs are tax-free, employers and employees may make contributions, and their availability is not limited to only employer-sponsored health plans. The HSA is used for reimbursing employees for out-of-pocket expenses required to meet an HDHP's deductible.[48,50] HSAs are owned by employees and are therefore portable as an employee may change employers. An HRA is a reimbursement arrangement between employers and employees that reimburses employees for out-of-pocket medical expenses and health insurance premiums to which employers contribute tax-free dollars. Unlike HSAs, HRAs are owned by employers and are therefore not portable.[48,51] Research has yielded mixed results on whether HDHPs actually reduce costs, and there is concern that HDHPs may actually cause individuals to refrain from accessing appropriate medical care.[48,50] Researchers note that HDHPs are now a staple of U.S. health insurance but caution that much more research is needed to identify what may be "unintended consequences"[50] of using them.

▶ Managed Care Today

The organizational forms of managed care have continued evolving over past decades because of changing marketplace conditions, purchaser preferences, beneficiary demands, and other factors. Today, with the large numbers and types of managed care plans, clear distinctions among them are no longer possible.[34] The significance of managed care in both the private and public sectors is clear from the most recent numbers. In 2015, in the private sector, employer-sponsored health insurance covered 147 million people—57 percent of the U.S. population under 65 years of age.[49] Of those, 111 million or more than 75 percent were covered by managed care plans, divided among PPO (52 percent), HMO (14 percent) and POS (10 percent) plans.[49] The remaining 24 percent enrolled in HDHPs also may participate in managed care because PPO and POS plans may be HDHPs.[48]

In the government sector in 2016, 57 million Americans were covered by Medicare, with 17.6 million or 31 percent of all Medicare beneficiaries enrolled in Medicare Advantage, Medicare's managed health insurance program.[52] Since the 1970s, Medicare participants may receive their benefits through private insurers, primarily HMOs, instead of the traditional Medicare program.[52] In this arrangement, Medicare pays the private insurers using capitation on a per-member-per-month basis, plus an additional amount for prescription drug coverage.[52] Between 2004 and 2015, the number of Medicare participants selecting Medicare Advantage plans tripled.[52] In 2016, responding to rising Medicare Advantage costs as compared with traditional Medicare, the CMS instituted a two-year phased in reduction of payment increases to private health plans administering the Advantage program.[53] In 2014, the Medicaid program had 55.2 million beneficiaries or almost 77 percent enrolled in a type of managed care.[54] The origins and operation of Medicare and Medicaid, the federal government's primary health insurance programs, are discussed later in this chapter.

MCOs and Quality

The most influential managed care quality organization is the National Committee for Quality Assurance (NCQA). The NCQA was formed in 1979 at the request of the federal Office for Health Maintenance Organizations (HMOs), sponsored by the Group Health Association of America and the American Association of Foundations for Medical Care.[55] The NCQA is an independent, not-for-profit organization deriving its revenue primarily from fees for accreditation services.[56] The NCQA is the nation's largest accreditor of MCOs, which provide health insurance coverage to more than 136 million people.[57]

The NCQA evaluates participating organizations on a voluntary basis. NCQA accreditation and recognition programs cover a broad spectrum. In addition to MCOs, examples include accreditation for PPOs and managed behavioral healthcare organizations, and recognition for providers in certain specialty practices and disease-management programs.[58] MCO accreditation entails rigorous reviews of all aspects of the respective organizations, including quality management and improvement, service utilizations management, provider credentialing, members' rights and responsibilities, and communications with subscribers about wellness and prevention.[59] In 1989, a partnership among the NCQA, MCOs, and employers developed the Health Plan Employer Data and Information Set (HEDIS).[55] The HEDIS (now called the Healthcare Effectiveness Data and Information Set) provides a standardized method for MCOs to collect, calculate, and report information about their performance to allow employers, other purchasers, and consumers to compare plans on costs and quality. The HEDIS has evolved through several stages of development and continuously refines its measurements through rigorous reviews and independent audits. The data set contains measures of MCO performance, divided among the following seven domains:[60]

- Effectiveness of care
- Access/availability of care
- Experience of care
- Utilization and risk adjusted utilization
- Relative resource use
- Health plan descriptive information
- Measures collected using electronic clinical data systems

The CMS requires that all Medicare managed care plans publicly report HEDIS data, and the NCQA requires all accredited plans to allow public reporting of their clinical quality data. A number of states also require plans providing Medicaid managed care to publicly report HEDIS data.[57,61]

The NCQA/HEDIS data provide important standardized measures of cost and quality for employers who purchase health coverage for employees. The data also supply critical feedback to providers in efforts to achieve quality improvement. The 2015 NCQA report, "The State of Health Care Quality" includes quality and consumer satisfaction data on more than 1,000 health plans covering 171 million people or 54 percent of the U.S. population.[62] The report assists healthcare system stakeholders in identifying quality gaps and opportunities for improvement and promotes the advancement of evidence-based care.[63]

MCOs also use internal methods to manage quality and costs. Data systems monitor claims information and track service utilization. MCOs use evidence-based clinical practice guidelines for patients with potentially high-cost conditions and disease-management programs (DMPs). Disease management is a system of coordinated healthcare interventions and communications for populations in which patient self-care efforts are significant.[64,65] DMPs identify high-risk individuals and incorporate methods, such as patient self-management education, proactive patient outreach, and performance feedback to providers. Candidates for disease-management programs are identified from claims data and enrolled in DMP services to reduce the potential for expensive services, such as emergency department visits and hospitalization. DMPs also may use clinical specialists who provide monitoring and support to patients with disease-management issues.[64] High-risk individuals may be requested to use telemetric monitoring devices, may be periodically contacted by an insurer's professional staff to monitor health status, or may be requested to use some combination of these tactics. Employer purchasers, a number of states, and the federal government endorsed disease-management programs for their employees and Medicaid and Medicare recipients.[66] However, ongoing research has continued to question the effectiveness of DMPs in achieving their goals.[67,68]

▶ Private Health Insurance Cost Trends

In the decade 2005–2015, annual premiums for employer sponsored single and family healthcare coverage increased by an average of 5 percent. In 2015, single coverage premiums were $6,251, and family coverage premiums were $17,545.[49] In spite of onerous predictions that new ACA employer requirements would cause employers to decrease hiring of full-time workers, to change full-time workers to part-time status, or to increase new employee waiting periods to obtain health insurance coverage, only small percentages of employers made such changes.[49]

However in 2015, employee cost burdens for health insurance remained substantial, with the proportion of covered workers whose health plans required a deductible increasing from 55 percent in 2006 to 81 percent in 2015.[49] In 2015, on average, covered workers contributed approximately 18 percent of premiums for single coverage and approximately 29 percent for family coverage. **FIGURE 8-4** illustrates the extent to which employees' cost burden for family health insurance coverage has grown. Between 2005 and 2015, total premium costs grew by 61 percent and employees' contribution to health insurance premiums grew by 83 percent (Figure 8-4).[49]

While the rate of health insurance premium growth has been low over the past decade (averaging approximately 5 percent), health insurance deductibles, or the amounts employees must pay before insurance coverage begins, have risen significantly in the past five years. Since 2010, deductible amounts have increased by 67 percent.[49,69] The overall effect is that employees have an increasing financial responsibility for the costs of their health care.

Both employers and employees have obvious interests in trying to stem the rising tide of health insurance costs. That more employers are offering—and increasing numbers of employees are opting for—HDHPs is one example of how these interests are manifested. Employers also seek to control health insurance premium increases through design changes in the health plans offered. Known as "benefit buy-downs," changes may include increasing co-payments and/or coinsurance.[70] On the premise that encouraging improvements in employees' health will help curb costs, employers are using tactics such as health risk assessments and biometric screenings under the

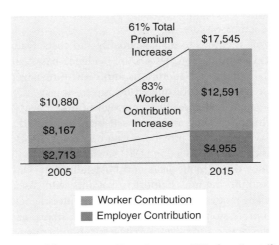

FIGURE 8-4 Average Annual Health Insurance Premiums and Worker Contributions for Family Coverage, 2005 and 2015

Reproduced from Kaiser/HRET Survey of Employer-sponsored Health Benefits, 2005–2015 broad rubric of "wellness programs." In 2015, 50 percent of employers with more than 200 employees who provided health benefits either offered or required assessments to identify health risks.[49] Sixty-two percent of those employers offered incentives for completing an assessment.[49] Biometric screening that measures risk factors such as body weight and blood pressure is another tactic, and some companies use financial penalties and rewards for employees' meeting specific outcomes.[49] In 2015, *Healthcare Finance News* reported findings of a survey noting that "80 percent of employers are offering wellness and health improvement programs, spending on average a record $693 per worker."[71] However, pervasive controversies remain in the economic and academic research communities about the effectiveness of these programs in both financial and personal terms and the ethics and legality of employers' requirements for participation.[71,72] In 2014, the Equal Employment Opportunity Commission sued three companies on the basis that their wellness programs violated federal anti-discrimination laws.[71]

▶ Self-Funded Insurance Programs

Since the late 1970s, self-funded health insurance (full or partial) and self-insurance of employee health benefits became increasingly common among large employers.[73] Today, more than 82 percent of employers with 500 or more employees self-insure and about 26 percent of employers with between 100 and 499 employees do so.[74] Through the self-funded mechanism, the employer collects premiums and pools these into an account it uses to pay for medical benefit claims instead of using a commercial carrier. Self-funded plans often use the services of an actuarial firm to set premium rates and a third-party administrator (TPA) to administer benefits, pay claims, and collect data on utilization.[75] Many TPAs also provide case-management services for potentially extraordinarily expensive cases to help coordinate care and control employer risk of catastrophic expenses.[75]

Self-funded plans offer significant advantages to employers, such as avoiding additional administrative and other charges made by commercial carriers which may be as high as 12 percent of premiums collected.[74] By self-funding benefits, employers also can avoid taxes on health insurance premiums paid and accrue earnings on the cash reserves held in the health insurance benefit account.[76] A major stimulus to the development of self-insurance programs was their exemption from the Employee Retirement and Income Security Act of 1974 (ERISA), which mandates minimum benefits under state law. This exemption allows employers much greater flexibility in designing benefit packages and provides another mechanism to control benefit costs. In addition, under the ACA, self-insured plans are exempt from a new excise tax on health insurance premiums, community ratings on premiums, and mandates to provide what the ACA terms "essential health benefits."[74]

▶ Government as a Source of Payment: A System in Name Only

Federal and state governments and, to a lesser extent, local government, finance healthcare services. Federal funding originally focused on specific population groups, providing health care for those in government service, their dependents, and particular population groups, such as Native Americans. Today, a combination of public programs, chief among them the federal Medicare program and the joint federal–state Medicaid program, constitutes nearly 40 percent of total national care expenditures.[8] In addition to Medicare and Medicaid, which operate under the DHHS in the Centers for Medicare & Medicaid Services, the DHHS has nine other operating divisions with a very broad spectrum of activities covering the entire lifespan of individuals, health professional development, military and veterans' health services, and research. These and other government supported services are discussed in Chapter 11 of this text.

In the absence of a comprehensive national health and social services policy, government's role in financing healthcare services can be described as a system only in the loosest interpretation of that term. It may be more accurate to describe government's various roles in healthcare financing as a mosaic of individual programs of reimbursement, direct payments to vendors, grants, matching funds, and subsidies.

As a source of healthcare service payments, the financing system operates primarily in a vendor–purchaser relationship, with government contracting with healthcare providers rather than providing services directly.[77] A prime example is the Medicare program, in which the federal government purchases hospital, home health, nursing home, physician, and other medical services under contract with suppliers. The Medicaid system operates similarly.

America's history of fierce resistance from the private sector, principally from organized medicine and other stakeholders with vested interests, has not allowed development of a comprehensive national healthcare system. Although the ACA creates federally supported programs to enable coverage of the majority of the nation's uninsured, it does not result in anything that could be characterized as a national system of health care.

Medicare and Medicaid comprise the majority of public spending on health and are reviewed in the following sections.

Medicare

Were it not for the vigorous opposition of the private sector led by the AMA, the Social Security Act of 1935, the most significant social legislation ever enacted by the U.S. government, would have included a form of national health insurance. It took 30 more years, during which time many presidential and congressional acts for national health insurance had been proposed and defeated, until Congress enacted Medicare, "Health Insurance for the Aged," as Title XVIII of the Social Security Act, in 1965. When Medicare was enacted, approximately only one-half of the elderly had any type of health insurance. This insurance usually covered only inpatient hospital costs, and much of healthcare spending was paid for out-of-pocket.[77] Today, Medicare covers 57 million Americans, including most 65 years and older, younger individuals who receive Social Security Disability Insurance benefits, and individuals with end-stage kidney disease and amyotrophic lateral sclerosis (Lou Gehrig's Disease) following their eligibility for Social Security Disability Insurance benefits. As noted earlier in this chapter, in 2014 Medicare expenditures totaled $618.7 billion, and they are projected to grow to $1.1 trillion by 2024.[78]

The enactment of Medicare legislation was an historical benchmark, signaling government's entry into the personal healthcare financing arena. The Medicare program was established under the aegis of the Social Security Administration, and hospital payment was contracted to local intermediaries chosen by hospitals. More than 90 percent of hospitals chose their local Blue Cross association as the intermediary. In response to organized medicine's opposition to government certification, the Social Security Administration agreed to accreditation by the private Joint Commission on Accreditation of Hospitals (now the Joint Commission) as meeting the certification requirement for Medicare participation. Describing the enactment of Medicare as a "watershed," Rosemary Stevens wrote the following (pp. 281–282):[36]

Thus with the stroke of a pen, the elderly acquired hospital benefits, the hospitals acquired cost reimbursement for these benefits, the Blue Cross Association was precipitated into prominence as a major national organization (since the national contract was to be with the association, with subcontracting to local plans), and the Joint Commission was given formal government recognition.

The Medicare amendment stated that there should be "prohibition against any federal interference with the practice of medicine or the way medical services were provided" (pp. 286–287).[36] Ultimately, however, the government's acceptance of responsibility for payment for the care of older adults generated a flood of regulations to address cost and quality control of the services and products for which it was now a major payer.[36]

As originally implemented, the Medicare program consisted of two parts, Part A and Part B, which remain fundamentally the same today. In subsequent years, legislative amendments added Parts C and D. Each is discussed below. It is important to note that from inception, Medicare coverage was not comprehensive, and that remains true today. Beneficiaries are required to share costs through deductibles and coinsurance, and many beneficiaries purchase supplemental health insurance policies to assist with costs that Medicare does not cover.

Part A pays for inpatient hospital care, limited-skilled nursing facility care, home health care related to a hospital stay, and hospice care. Part A is mandatory and is financed principally from a 2.9 percent payroll tax with equal amounts contributed by employees and employers.[79,80] Individuals and couples with incomes over certain thresholds contribute at a higher rate.[80] In general, individuals who have contributed for at least 40 quarter years of employment (approximately 10 years) are entitled to Part A without paying a premium.[79] However, in 2016, deductibles were $1,288 for a hospital stay of 1 to 60 days, and coinsurance of $161 per day was required for between 21 and 100 days in a skilled nursing facility.[79] Medicare does not pay for long-term care in skilled nursing facilities.

Part B, supplementary medical insurance, is a voluntary program covering physician services, outpatient hospital services, end-stage renal disease services, outpatient diagnostic tests, medical equipment and supplies, and certain home health services.[79] About 75 percent of Part B is financed by general federal revenues and 25 percent by premiums paid by beneficiaries, typically through automatic deductions from monthly Social Security payments.[79] Individuals and couples with incomes over certain thresholds pay higher premiums.[80]

Medicare Part C, "Medicare + Choice," was added by the Balanced Budget Act of 1997.[81] As discussed earlier in this chapter, Medicare Part C allowed private health plans to administer Medicare contracts, with beneficiary enrollment on a voluntary basis.[52] The Medicare Prescription Drug, Improvement, and Modernization Act of 2003 (MMA) changed Part C to "Medicare Advantage," revising the administration of Medicare managed care programs to entice additional participation.[81] Part C pays private health plans a capitated monthly payment to provide all Part A and Part B services and Part D services (discussed below) if offered by the plan.[79] Plans can offer additional benefits or alternative cost-sharing arrangements that are at least as generous as the standard Parts A and B benefits under traditional Medicare.[79] In addition to the normal Part B premium, beneficiaries who choose to participate in Part C may pay monthly premiums based on services offered.[79] Beneficiary enrollment in these private health plans has increased substantially over the past decade.[52] (See **FIGURE 8-5**.)

Medicare Part D for prescription drug coverage was added by the Medicare Prescription Drug, Improvement, and Modernization Act of 2003.[82] Participation is voluntary, and in 2016, participants were required to meet a deductible of $360 and incurred an average estimated monthly

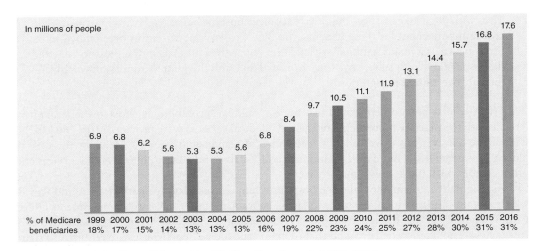

FIGURE 8-5 **Total Medicare Private Health Plan Enrollment, 1999–2016**

Reproduced from The Henry J. Kaiser Family Foundation. Medicare advantage. May 2016. Available from http://files.kff.org/attachment/Fact-Sheet-Medicare-Advantage. Accessed June 1, 2016.

premium of $41 and a 25 percent coinsurance charge up to an annual coverage limit of $3,310. In 2017, CMS predicts that enrollment will reach 44.5 million individuals.[79] As originally implemented, Part D had a coverage gap that became known as the "donut hole." The gap meant that when costs reached the annual limit of $3,310, beneficiaries would have no coverage until reaching total out-of-pocket spending of $4,850.[79,82] The ACA gradually closes the gap by phasing in a combination of drug manufacturer discounts and increased federal subsidies by 2020.[79]

Medicare Cost Containment and Quality: A Brief History

Within a few years after implementation, Medicare spending was significantly exceeding projections. Although hospital costs for the growing population of older adults increased more rapidly than expected, the galloping increases over projected Medicare expenses could not be explained by that phenomenon alone. In the decade after Medicare enactment, several amendments to the Social Security Act made significant changes. In general, amendments during the first five years increased the types of covered services and expanded the population of eligible participants. During later periods, amendments addressed concerns about rising costs and quality.

A 1976 study by the U.S. Human Resources Administration reviewed the first 10 years of Medicare hospital expenses and attributed less than 10 percent of increases to utilization by the older adult population. Almost two-thirds of the increase over projected hospital costs was attributed to huge growth in hospital payroll and non-payroll expenses, including profits.[36]

Medicare's hospital reimbursement mechanism was cost-based and retrospective on a per-day-of-stay basis. This cost-based reimbursement fueled utilization of services and hospital capital expansion, which was augmented by new and expensive medical technology. Paid on a retrospective basis for costs incurred, hospitals had no incentives for efficiency. When Medicare and Medicaid were enacted in 1965, the annual rate of increase in healthcare expenditures was close to the annual increase in gross domestic product. By 1967, healthcare expenditures began rising at double the prior rate. Five years later, federal healthcare expenditures had undergone a sixfold increase over the 1965 level.[83]

Medicare Cost Containment and Quality: 1965–1985

In Medicare's first two decades, many initiatives attempted to slow spiraling costs and address quality concerns. They were largely unsuccessful. The 1966 Comprehensive Health Planning Act provided federal support to states for conducting local health planning to ensure adequate health facilities and avoid duplication.[84] In 1974, the Health Planning Resources and Development Act replaced the Comprehensive Health Planning Act with local health systems agencies to coordinate and justify health facility and service plans based on quantified population needs.[83] The Act also mandated organizations to obtain approval from a state planning agency before starting any major capital project, and several states adopted what became known as "certificate-of-need" regulations for this purpose. Congress repealed the federal mandate in 1987, but 36 states still maintain some form of certificate-of-need program.[85] Health systems agencies were unsuccessful in materially influencing decisions about service or technology expansion because their processes were dominated by institutional and stakeholder vested interests. Concurrent with attempts to slow cost increases through planning, a number of other initiatives took shape that related to concerns over Medicare costs and service quality.

Professional standards review organizations (PSROs) established in 1972 were the first federal attempt to review the costs and quality of care provided under Medicare. PSROs were composed of local physicians who performed record reviews and made recommendations to local Blue Cross agencies, the Medicare payment intermediary. Plagued by questionable effectiveness and high administrative costs, PSROs were replaced by professional review organizations (PROs) in 1984 and are now known as quality improvement organizations (QIOs).[86,87] QIOs are groups of physicians and other health professionals in each state who are paid by the CMS to review the quality of care provided to Medicare beneficiaries.[87]

In another effort to reduce spending, the Federal Budget Reconciliation Act of 1980 amended the Medicare legislation with a strong focus on reducing the number and length of Medicare hospitalizations through increased use of home healthcare services.[88] Amendments eliminated many prior restrictions on Medicare recipients' eligibility for home care and lifted the exclusion of for-profit home healthcare agencies from Medicare participation in states that did not require agency licensure.[88] Ironically, not only did the amendments not succeed in their intended purpose, they ultimately resulted in more amendments in the late 1990s to curb explosive home care service expenditures and widespread provider financial abuses.[88]

The rate of Medicare cost growth continued rising in spite of cost-control efforts of the 1970s and early 1980s for two primary reasons: (1) existing payment methods incentivized the provision of more services, and (2) increases in expensive technology.[89] In addition, Medicare's fee-for-service payment structure was becoming outmoded as employer-sponsored plans, Medicaid, and private insurance companies embraced the managed care principles of pre-payment and shared financial risk.

In 1983 Medicare enacted a new case payment system that radically changed hospital reimbursement. The new system shifted hospital reimbursement from a fee-for-service retrospective mode to a pre-paid prospective mode, or prospective payment system (PPS). Using diagnosis-related groups (DRGs), the new system provided a patient classification method to relate the type of patients a hospital treated (i.e., age, sex, gender, diagnoses) to costs.[89] The PPS based hospital payments on established fees-for-services required to treat specific diagnoses rather than on discreet units of services. The DRGs grouped more than 10,000 International Classification of Disease codes into more than 500 patient categories. Patients within each category are grouped for similar clinical conditions and expected resource use.[90] DRGs are a clinically coherent set of patient classes that relate a hospital's case mix to its resource demands and associated costs. The payment an individual hospital receives under this system is calculated using input from a variety of other data known to impact costs, such as hospital teaching status and wage data for its geographic location.[89]

The PPS was intended to provide incentives for the hospital to spend only what was needed to achieve optimal patient outcomes. If outcomes could be achieved at a cost lower than the preset payment, the hospital could retain the balance of unexpended payment. If a hospital spent more to treat a case than allowed, it absorbed the excess costs. The PPS also financially provided for cases classified as "outliers" because of complications.[90] The PPS did not build in allowances to the payment rate for direct medical education expenses for teaching hospitals, hospital outpatient expenses, or capital expenditures. These continued to be reimbursed on a cost basis. By 10 years following implementation by Medicare, forms of the PPS were adopted by 21 state Medicaid programs and about two-thirds of Blue Cross/Shield Plans.[91]

The PPS raised many concerns among healthcare system stakeholders, including fears about premature hospital discharges, hospitals' questionable ability to streamline services to conform to prospective payments, and the home healthcare industry's capacity to accommodate an increased caseload due to earlier discharges. In 1986 Congress established the Prospective Payment Assessment Commission (ProPAC) to monitor the effects of the PPS and evaluate its performance on financial and quality.[89,92]

"Quicker and sicker" was the slogan popularized by the media during the first years of the PPS to characterize the drive for shorter hospital stays. The media also popularized the term "patient dumping," referring to hospitals transferring patients to other hospitals because they were deemed to be at high risk for expensive and potentially unprofitable services.

Subsequent research on the PPS impact indicated that most concerns were unfounded and that DRGs had a measurable impact on slowing the overall Medicare spending growth rate.[93] Research compared quality indicators before and after PPS implementation, revealing little effect on Medicare patient readmission rates and mortality rates.[92] In a study of almost 17,000 Medicare patients admitted to hospitals for five common serious diagnoses, post-PPS findings saw both a 24 percent decrease in the average length of stay for these conditions and an overall improvement in mortality rates among the five diagnoses studied.[92]

Concerns about patient dumping were addressed in the 1985 federal budget by the Emergency Medical Treatment and Labor Act (EMTALA), passed into law in 1986. The EMTALA required hospitals to screen everyone who presented in their emergency departments and to treat and stabilize the condition prior to transfer to another hospital.[94] Stiff financial penalties, as well as risk of Medicare de-certification by the Joint Commission for inappropriately transferring patients, accompanied the EMTALA provisions.[94]

Concerns about the capacity of the home healthcare industry to meet anticipated increases in demand dissipated quickly. The industry responded by creating new or expanding existing home healthcare services.[95] Hospitals did not experience the predicted negative financial impact, and they actually posted substantial profits.[92] In fact, the federal government partially justified subsequent reductions in prospective payment on the basis that early payments were too high relative to costs.[92] It was even suggested that the large financial surpluses generated by not-for-profit hospitals in the early years of prospective payment fueled hospital costs by making new resources available for investment.[92]

Medicare Cost Containment and Quality: 1986–2006

Historically, physicians set fee-for-service charges, insurers paid their claims, and patients paid any difference between the insured payment and actual bill.[87] Medicare Part B physician reimbursement was established as fee-for-service, based on prevailing fees within geographic areas. Burgeoning Medicare physician annual payment-rate increases averaging 18 percent between 1975 and 1987 provoked legislative action.[96] In 1984, Congress enacted a temporary price freeze for physician services.[96] Assessments of the price freeze suggested that physicians offset lower fees by increasing the volume of services.[96] Continuing concerns over Medicare's growth in physician payments and overuse of costly specialty care prompted further action.

The 1989 federal budget established a new method of Medicare physician reimbursement effective in 1992, using a resource-based relative value scale (RBRVS) to replace the fee-for-service reimbursement system.[91] The prior payment system, which was based on charges alone, favored the use of more costly diagnostic and surgical procedures over cognitive and primary care services.[91] The RBRVS intended to make physician payments equitable across various types of services, specialties, and geographic locations. To accomplish this, the "resource" components of the scale took into account total physician work, practice expenses, and malpractice expenses.[91] The "value" of physicians' work incorporates elements such as the time required to perform a procedure, physical and mental effort, skill, judgment, and stress.[91] Fee determinations also incorporate geographic differences in price and overall national physician expenditures.[91] Use of the RBRVS scale continues with a committee of the AMA and national medical specialty societies providing input to the CMS on annual updates.[97]

Medicare reforms enacted by the PPS, managed care influences, market competition, technology advances, and consumerism continued producing changes in the delivery system. The PPS had demonstrated that "more is not necessarily better," as lengths of stay declined with no apparent negative impact on the quality of patient care. Then, in the early 1990s, the nation witnessed vigorous debates regarding the Clinton administration's proposal for a national health system, the National Health Security Act. Although the Act never reached a Congressional vote, months of debate thrust national concerns about escalating Medicare spending, barriers to services, beneficiary costs, and provider choice into the public spotlight. Popular and political sensitivities rose against the backdrop of escalating national predictions about potential insolvency of the Hospital Insurance Trust Fund.[98]

Several trends supported major changes in the Medicare system. First, the CBO projected that Medicare cost growth could not be sustained without cuts in other government programs, major tax increases, or larger budget deficits.[99] Second, as noted earlier in this chapter, Medicare's fee-for-service structure was outmoded, as employer-sponsored plans, Medicaid, and private insurance embraced managed care principles of pre-payment. Third, Medicare coverage left significant gaps requiring co-pays and coinsurance that many beneficiaries were unable to meet. Acknowledging the President's and Congress's discord on a national health reform program, in 1995 Congress focused on slowing Medicare cost growth and achieving broader choices for Medicare beneficiaries through managed care plans as models of cost containment and consumer satisfaction.[99]

The federal budget negotiations for 1997 reflected pressures to produce a balanced budget and to respond meaningfully to national health issues from consumer and cost-containment perspectives. The resulting Balanced Budget Act (BBA) created major new policy directions for Medicare. The BBA's impact on Medicaid is discussed later in this chapter.

The BBA proposed to reduce growth in Medicare spending through savings of $115 billion over five years, most of which was derived from reductions in payments to providers.[100] As the largest Medicare spender, the BBA targeted hospitals as the source of more than one-third of total anticipated savings. Among several other cost-cutting provisions, it also increased cost-sharing among Medicare beneficiaries.[100] Another major BBA provision extended the PPS to hospital outpatient services, home health agencies, skilled nursing facilities and inpatient rehabilitation facilities.[87]

Decreased Medicare spending growth between 1998 and 2002 demonstrated the immediate impact of the BBA. After growing at an average annual rate of 11.1 percent for 15 years, the average annual rate of Medicare spending growth between 1998 and 2000 dropped to 1.7 percent, resulting in approximately $68 billion in savings.[101]

As discussed earlier in this chapter, the BBA also opened the Medicare program to private insurers through the Medicare+Choice Program.

The BBA established federal commissions to carry out monitoring and recommendation functions. These included the Medicare Payment Advisory Commission (MedPAC) and an independent National Bipartisan Commission on the Future of Medicare, whose functions include analyzing numerous dimensions of Medicare's financial condition and benefits design over time and providing advisory reports to Congress.[102,103]

BBA Medicare implementation drew widespread challenges and delays with opposition from industry stakeholder groups. As a result, just prior to many of the BBA's provisions taking effect, President Clinton signed the Balanced Budget Refinement Act of 1999, providing $17.5 billion to restore cuts to sectors negatively impacted by the BBA and outlining delayed implementation schedules for many of the BBA's original mandates.[104]

Due to large MCO withdrawals from the Medicare+Choice program because of reduced Medicare reimbursement and market shifts reducing profitability, in 2000 Congress enacted the Benefits Protection and Improvement Act that increased participating MCO and provider payments.[105]

In 2001, the CMS inaugurated the "Quality Initiative," encompassing every dimension of the healthcare delivery system supported by Medicare payments. The Quality Initiative includes hospitals, nursing homes, home healthcare agencies, physicians, and other facilities.[106] The program collects and analyzes data to monitor conformance with standards of care and performance. In addition to the Quality Initiative, the Medicare Quality Monitoring System "processes, analyzes, interprets and disseminates health-related data to monitor the quality of care delivered to Medicare fee-for-service beneficiaries."[107] Since 2003, the Medicare administration also has continued experimenting with hospital pay-for-performance plans that emphasize the quality of patient outcomes and avoidance of unnecessary costs.[108] Pay-for-performance experiments are reflected in several ACA initiatives to address Medicare costs and quality discussed in subsequent sections of this chapter.

With the goal of providing public, valid, and user-friendly information about hospital quality, in 2005 Medicare launched the website Hospital Compare, in a collaboration with the Hospital Quality Alliance, a public–private partnership organization. Hospital Compare includes common conditions and criteria that assess the consistency of individual hospital performance with evidence-based practice; reporting is required for hospitals to qualify for Medicare payment rate updates.[109] Inaugurated in 2006, data from the Hospital Consumer Assessment of Healthcare Providers and Systems (HCAHPS) surveys was added to the Hospital Compare information, providing patient perspectives on their hospital experience.[110]

Medicare Cost Containment and Quality: 2007–Present

In 2007, CMS announced that beginning in 2008 Medicare would no longer pay hospitals for extra costs associated with treatment for what are considered preventable medical errors. This policy change was made through a federal budget mandate that required the CMS to identify conditions that: (1) are high-cost and/or high volume, (2) result in assignment of a case to a higher payment DRG when the condition is a secondary diagnosis, and (3) could reasonably have been prevented through use of evidence-based treatment guidelines.[111] CMS refers to the conditions covered under this mandate as "hospital-acquired conditions" (HACs) and publishes a list containing 14 categories of such conditions.[111] Examples include catheter-acquired urinary tract infections, foreign objects retained after surgery, surgical-site infections, and falls or trauma during hospitalization.[111] Also in 2007, the CMS announced that Medicare would no longer pay additional costs for preventable errors known as "never-events."[112] The term *never-event* was introduced in 2001 by the National Quality Forum (NQF), an independent organization of healthcare experts that advises the federal government on the best evidence-based practices.[112,113] Never-events are egregious, usually preventable errors that result in death or significant disability, such as surgery performed on the wrong body part or use of contaminated drugs or devices in a healthcare setting.[112]

The ACA contained numerous provisions affecting Medicare that reflect the law's overarching population-based approach and the drive to transition from a volume-driven to a value-driven system of care. These provisions are discussed in the following paragraphs. Several of these provisions are discussed in detail in Chapter 4 in the context of hospital care. While some of the summaries listed below appear in Chapter 4, their importance to the history of Medicare cost containment and quality merit reiteration here. As available, results from implementation of provisions also are discussed. In reviewing results, remember that for the most part, the provisions have been in effect for only a few years. Given the enormity of the proposed system transformation and the technical and behavioral changes required, it will take many more years of experimentation and research to identify, enact, and embed policies and practices that result in positive balances between costs and quality. Discussed later in this chapter, the Medicare Access and CHIP Reauthorization Act of 2015 (MACRA) will create many more opportunities for experimentation with the links between cost and quality.

Partnership for Patients. Beginning in 2011, CMS dedicated up to $1 billion over three years to test care models to reduce hospital-acquired conditions and improve transitions in care. This public–private partnership supported efforts of physicians, nurses, and other clinicians to make care safer and to better coordinate patients' transitions from hospitals to other settings. More than 6,000 organizations, including more than 3,000 hospitals, joined Partnership for Patients. The CMS estimates that the program has potential to save 60,000 lives and reduce millions of preventable injuries and complications in patient care with savings up to $50 billion over 10 years.[114] Following the 2014 release of a positive CMS report on results, leading quality experts raised concerns about the validity of CMS findings.[115,116]

Bundled Payments for Care Improvement. Inaugurated in January 2013, the Bundled Payments for Care Improvement (BPCI) recognized that separate Medicare fee-for-service payments for individual services provided during a Medicare beneficiary's single illness often result in fragmented care with minimal coordination across providers and settings and resulted in rewarding service quantity rather than quality. The BPCI links payment for services to an episode of patient care that results in hospitalization. It tests whether, as prior research has shown, bundled payments can align incentives for hospitals, post-acute care providers, physicians, and other healthcare personnel to work closely together across many settings to achieve improved patient outcomes at lower cost.[117] In 2016, there were 1,522 BPCI participants including, among others, acute care hospitals, physician group practices, home healthcare agencies, and skilled nursing facilities.[118] In April 2016, CMS implemented a mandated "Comprehensive Care for Joint Replacement Model" BPCI for hip and knee replacements requiring participation by 800 hospitals in 67 geographic areas. In issuing this mandate, the CMS noted that more than 400,000 of these procedures are performed annually at a Medicare hospitalization cost of $7 billion with wide variations in cost and quality.[119]

Comprehensive Primary Care Initiative. Launched in 2012 in select markets, this initiative tested a model to support primary care practices to provide higher-quality, more coordinated, and patient-centered care.[114] It concluded in 2016. In addition to regular fee-for-service payments, CMS paid 497 primary care practices in seven regions throughout the United States a monthly fee to help patients with serious or chronic diseases follow personalized care plans; give patients 24-hour access to care and health information; deliver preventive care; engage patients and their families in care plans; and work together with other doctors, including specialists, to improve care coordination.[114,120] In an evaluation of the Comprehensive Primary Care (CPC) at its midway point in 2014, participating practices reported progress with changes in service delivery but had not yet shown savings in Medicare expenditures or material improvements in quality of care or patients' experience of care.[120] In April 2016, the CMS announced a new program, "Comprehensive Primary Care Plus," commencing in January 2017 that will operate for five years. The model incorporates principles of the advanced primary care medical home and uses a combination of Medicare fee-for-service payments and performance-based financial incentives. Participation is voluntary and medical practices must apply to the CMS for inclusion. In 2016 CMS was recruiting physician practices and state and commercial health plans to test the model that it expects will include up to 20,000 physicians and 25 million patients.[121,122]

Federally Qualified Health Center Advanced Primary Care Practice Demonstration. Begun in 2011, this demonstration evaluates the impact of advanced primary care practice on improving care, focusing on prevention, and reducing healthcare costs among Medicare beneficiaries served by Federally Qualified Health Centers (FQHCs). With additional support from CMS in collaboration with HRSA, the demonstration tests FQHCs' ability to become formally recognized as patient-centered medical homes using teams of physicians and other health professionals to coordinate care for up to 195,000 Medicare patients. Concluded in 2014, the demonstration was undergoing final evaluation in 2016.[114,123]

Accountable Care Organizations. The subject of experimentation in the private sector since 1998, in 2016 there were 838 accountable care organizations (ACOs) of all types operating, with a total of 23.8 million participants across 50 states and the District of Columbia.[124] Commercial insurers covered 17 million ACO members; Medicare covered 8.2 million; and Medicaid covered 2.9 million.[124] The ACA adopted the ACO model, consisting of groups of providers and suppliers of health care, health-related services, and others involved in caring for Medicare patients to voluntarily work together to coordinate care for the patients they serve under the original Medicare (not the Medicare Advantage) program.[125] ACOs intend to address the costly results of healthcare system fragmentation by ensuring care coordination across multiple providers for the entire spectrum of a patient's needs. The intent under the ACA was to create a variety of ACO organizations with different financial incentive models to track and then identify the models that worked best. ACOs are administered by Medicare and can be structured in several different ways that are outlined in Chapter 4.[126] However, each ACO must be a legally constituted entity within its state and include healthcare providers, suppliers, and Medicare beneficiaries on its governing board. It also must take responsibility for at least 5,000 Medicare beneficiaries for a period of three years.[127] To qualify for support under the ACA, ACOs must meet Medicare-established quality measures of care appropriateness, coordination, timeliness, and safety.[127] Medicare recipients participating in ACOs are not restricted from using physicians outside of their ACO.[127]

Reports on ACOs' quality improvement and financial performance during the early years of this ACA initiative are mixed.[128,129,130]

Hospital Value-Based Purchasing Program. CMS began implementing value-based purchasing (VBP) pilot projects in 2003; this model has been replicated by private insurers as well, structured to provide incentives to discourage inappropriate, unnecessary, and costly care.[73] Now mandated by the ACA, the VBP program applies to more than 3,500 U.S. hospitals, enabling them to earn incentive payments based on clinical outcomes and patient satisfaction.[131] Quality is measured based on a hospital's Total Performance Score (TPS) determined by how well it met a number of specific patient care and outcome objectives. In 2016, the CMS reported that more than half of participating hospitals will earn financial incentives for exceeding quality goals, a material increase over the prior period.[132]

Readmissions Reduction Program. The intent of the program is to encourage hospitals to improve the quality and continuity of care beyond the acute episode that resulted in the initial hospitalization. In 2009 prior to ACA enactment, 20 percent of all Medicare fee-for-service payments ($17 billion annually) were for unplanned readmissions.[77] Beginning with discharges on October 1, 2012, the ACA requires CMS to reduce payments to hospitals for the readmission of patients with specified diagnoses within 30 days of discharge from a prior hospitalization.[133] A 2016 analysis compared readmissions rates for targeted conditions before and after implementation of the reduction program. The analysis found reductions in readmissions for targeted and non targeted conditions alike, suggesting an overall positive impact.[134]

Medicare Access and CHIP Reauthorization Act of 2015. The most significant health policy development of the past decade in terms of cost containment and quality improvement after the ACA is the Medicare Access and CHIP Reauthorization Act of 2015 (MACRA).[135] In addition to repealing a severely flawed Medicare physician reimbursement formula, the "Sustainable Growth Rate," the law has very broad effects on the continued advancement of the population and value-based approaches for the Medicare program.[136] The Children's Health Insurance Program (CHIP) aspect is discussed in the later Medicaid section of this Chapter.

The MACRA focuses upon quality improvement coupled with value-based payments as the centerpieces of clinical practices. The law establishes a new Quality Payment Program (QPP) that allows physicians to select participation in one of two CMS system options that define the way in which they will be reimbursed for services under Medicare.[136] Payment details are discussed in Chapter 4 and summarized here.

The first option is participation in the Merit-Based Incentive Payment System (MIPS).[136] MIPS eliminates three prior programs that affected physician Medicare payment adjustments and combines them into one program, assigning four weighted-performance categories of quality, resource use, clinical practice improvement activities and meaningful use of certified electronic health-record technology.[136] A combined score on performance categories will determine whether physicians receive a Medicare payment increase, no increase, or reduction.[135] The second option is participation in an alternative payment model (APM), such as an ACO, patient-centered medical home (PCMH), or BPCI, in which providers accept some measure of financial risk in return for potentially enhanced reimbursements.[136] Participation in an APM exempts physicians from MIPS payment adjustments and provides an annual lump-sum payment based on 5 percent of the prior year's estimated aggregate expenditures under the Medicare fee schedule.[135] If physicians do not select a system or are not approved for APM participation, CMS will assign them to a MIPS.[137] Consistent with the ACA's drive toward value-driven performance and departure from volume-driven fee-for-service reimbursement, APM participation is favored by the CMS.[137] This direction was clearly signaled by the 2015 CMS announcement that 30 percent of traditional Medicare payments would be tied to APMs by the end of 2016 and that 50 percent of payments would be tied to these models by the end of 2018.[135] The CMS is offering more lucrative potential bonus opportunities and fee increases in APMs as compared with MIPS.[137] Also in this regard, in 2016 the CMS announced the availability of $10 million in competitive grants over three years to support clinical practices with technical assistance for transition to APMs.[138]

Finally, it is important to recognize that as a new law, the MACRA must undergo a rulemaking process that transitions the law's intent into the implementation details that bring it to life. Rulemaking occurs in dynamic political, economic, and professional environments and can take years.[137] Approximately one year after MACRA's passage, on April 27, 2016, the DHHS issued the required "Notice of Proposed Rulemaking" to solicit input from stakeholders on implementation of its key provisions.[139] The CMS intends to begin measuring clinician performance through the MACRA in January 2017 with payments based on those measures beginning in 2019.[139] Understandably, the MACRA has evoked strong positions from numerous stakeholders that will surely continue throughout the rulemaking process with potentially material effects on the law's final impact and the timing of its implementation.[137]

▶ Medicaid and the Children's Health Insurance Program

Medicaid became law as Title XIX of the Social Security Act amendment of 1965. Medicaid is administered by the CMS and is a joint federal–state program in which federal and state support is shared. The federal government matches state expenditures based on the federal medical assistance percentage (FMAP), which is adjusted annually based on a state's average personal income compared with the national average.[140] The FMAP can be no lower than 50 percent for states with the highest average incomes or greater than 83 percent for states with lower incomes.[79] Therefore, states are guaranteed a federal match of at least $1 for each $1 they spend, and lower-income states receive considerably higher match amounts for each $1 spent.

Before Medicaid's implementation, healthcare services for the economically needy were provided through a patchwork of programs sponsored by state and local governments, charitable organizations, and community hospitals. Medicaid is the primary source of medical assistance for millions of low-income and disabled Americans, providing health coverage to many who otherwise would be unable to obtain health insurance. In 2016, Medicaid enrollment stood at 72.4 million individuals, including disabled adults and children, the elderly, and 34.9 million children in the Children's Health Insurance Program (CHIP).[141,142] Medicaid represents a major source of national healthcare expenditures, accounting for approximately 19 percent of $2.6 trillion in personal health services spending and almost 32 percent of spending for nursing home care in 2014.[6] Medicaid bears significant responsibility for funding long-term care services because Medicare and private health insurance often furnish only limited coverage for these needs. Medicaid is the third-largest source of healthcare coverage in the United States after private employer-based coverage and Medicare.[143]

The federal government establishes broad program guidelines, but states design, implement, and administer their own Medicaid programs. Because rate-setting formulas, procedures, and policies vary widely among states and the District of Columbia, it is essentially comprised of 51 different programs. Medicaid requires states to cover individuals who meet certain minimum categorical and financial eligibility standards. Medicaid beneficiaries include children, pregnant women, adults in families with dependent children, the aged, blind and/or disabled, and individuals who meet certain minimum income eligibility criteria. Many adults who qualify for Medicaid are working, but earn wages too low to afford private coverage.[144] Approximately 65 percent of children on Medicaid live in households with at least one full-time worker.[144] The CBO estimates that almost one-half of Medicaid beneficiaries are children who consume 21 percent of Medicare spending. The 14 percent of beneficiaries who are blind and disabled have the highest consumption of Medicaid spending, at 44 percent.[145]

In general, the program provides three types of coverage:

1. Health insurance for low-income families with children
2. Long-term care for older Americans and individuals with disabilities
3. Supplemental coverage for low-income Medicare beneficiaries for services not covered by Medicare, including Medicare part B premiums, deductibles, and coinsurance. These individuals are known as "dual eligibles."[143,146]

Medicaid federal guidelines establish a mandated core of basic medical services for state programs including:[147]

■ Inpatient hospital services	■ Laboratory and x-ray services
■ Outpatient hospital	■ Family planning services
■ Preventive, diagnostic and treatment, including immunizations	■ Nurse-midwife
■ Nursing facility	■ Certified pediatric and family nurse practitioner
■ Home health	■ Freestanding birth center
■ Physician	■ Transportation to medical care
■ Rural health clinic	■ Tobacco cessation
■ Federally qualified health center	

Examples of optional benefits states may cover are optometry, physical therapy, occupational therapy, chiropractic, dental services, and hospice.[147] States also have the flexibility to extend coverage to higher income groups under specific circumstances.[79]

Medicaid is funded principally from federal matching dollars to states and state general funds.[140] Medicaid is considered a "countercyclical" program in that difficult economic times result in increases in Medicaid eligibility, thereby increasing states' financial burdens as they experience budget stresses.[140] In such instances, Congress may act to increase matching support as it did during the 2008 recession.[140] Unlike Medicare, which reimburses providers through intermediaries such as Blue Cross, Medicaid directly reimburses service providers.

Children's Health Insurance Program

The Balanced Budget Act of 1997 included an initiative, the State Children's Health Insurance Program (SCHIP), which complemented the Medicaid program by targeting uninsured children whose family income was too high to qualify for Medicaid and too low to afford private health insurance.[148] Subsequently renamed the Children's Health Insurance Program (CHIP), with the goal of enrolling 10 million children, it was the largest expansion of health insurance coverage for children in the United States since Medicaid began.[87] Called the "Connecting Kids to Coverage" campaign, the CHIP has been continuously funded since inception and was reauthorized by the ACA in 2010 for five years.[87] Provisions of the MACRA of 2015 will make $32 million available to assist 38 community organizations in 27 states to enroll eligible children in Medicaid and CHIP. Funding is targeted to areas where access to health care has been lagging, including among Native Americans, children with learning disabilities, children residing in rural communities, and teens.[149] In 2014, 8.1 million children were enrolled in CHIP.[150] In 2016, a combined total of 34.9 million children participated in CHIP and Medicaid.[141]

▶ Medicaid Managed Care

Until the early 1990s, most Medicaid beneficiaries received Medicaid coverage through fee-for-service arrangements. Over time that practice shifted with states using managed care arrangements to provide coverage to beneficiaries. Under managed care, beneficiaries receive part or all of their Medicaid services from healthcare providers that are paid by organizations under contract with the state. Managed care organizations receive a monthly capitated payment for a specified benefit package and are responsible for the provision and coverage of services.

In 2016, almost two-thirds of 72 million Medicaid beneficiaries were enrolled in private managed care plans in 39 states and the District of Columbia.[151] In April 2016, CMS announced a final rule on a major overhaul of the Medicaid and CHIP managed care program regulations to be effective in phases over three years starting in mid-2017.[151] The rule was heralded as "a regulatory milestone in the life of Medicaid" and a change "that will determine Medicaid's transformation from a welfare program into a pillar of national health reform and a major player in the health plan market."[152] The CMS characterizes the rule as "modernizing" Medicaid managed care by aligning its policies and practices with other managed health insurance programs. To accomplish this, the rule supports states in reforming delivery systems and improving quality through participation in APMs, improving beneficiaries' experience, and increasing program accountability and transparency.[151] In essence, the new rule intends to bring the practices and performance of Medicaid managed care health plans up to the standards now expected in the general managed care marketplace.

▶ Medicaid Quality Initiatives

The CMS Center for Medicaid and CHIP services has principal responsibility for developing and carrying out Medicaid and CHIP quality initiatives through working partnerships with state programs.[153] The Center carries out a broad range of activities in collaboration with states to support formulation, coordination, integration, implementation, and evaluation of national programs and policies related to Medicaid and CHIP.[153]

Medicaid also carries out voluntary quality monitoring and reporting programs with states. The 2009 CHIP reauthorization required establishment of quality standards for children's care, resulting in development of a core set of seven measurement areas: access to care, preventive care, maternal and perinatal health, behavioral health, care of acute and chronic conditions, oral health, and experience of care.[154,155] The ACA required a similar set of quality standards for adults.[156,157] As guidance to providers, each of the children and adult measures includes recommended activities.

The "Partnership for Medicaid," a non-partisan, nationwide coalition of physicians, other healthcare providers, and stakeholders is advocating for development of a Medicaid standardized quality measurement framework across all states.[158] Noting that because Medicaid programs are designed on a state-by-state basis, the absence of such a framework hampers sharing of best practices, undermines innovation, and limits policy makers' understanding of the Medicaid program.[158] Among recommendations is a phased-in approach to establishing mandatory, meaningful reporting by all states.[158]

▶ Medicaid Expansion Under the Affordable Care Act

As initially legislated by the ACA, states' participation in the expansion was mandatory. However, a 2012 U.S. Supreme Court decision made states' participation optional.[159] Beginning in 2014, the ACA allowed states to expand Medicaid eligibility to individuals under age 65 with family incomes up to 133 percent of the federal poverty level.[79] By mid-2016, 31 states and the District of Columbia had expanded Medicaid coverage.[160] The ACA provides for federal payment of 100 percent of state expenditures related to coverage for newly eligible individuals through calendar year 2016; the federal matching rate drops gradually to 90 percent in 2020, where it will remain.[79]

According to the CBO, Medicaid enrollment of newly eligible individuals grew by 55 percent between 2014 and 2015, resulting in more than 9 million newly insured individuals.[161] In the 29 states which had expanded Medicaid coverage in 2015, average Medicaid enrollment increased by 18 percent accompanied by an average of 17.7 percent increase in spending.[162] This compares with all 50 states and the District of Columbia in 2015, where Medicaid enrollment on average increased by 13.8 percent with an average spending increase of 13.9 percent.[162] Because Medicaid expansion states received 100 percent federal matching funds for new enrollments in 2015, growth in state spending from states' general funds was much slower than total Medicaid spending.[162] (See **FIGURE 8-6**.)

With only two full years since the start of the expansion, research on many dimensions of its effects continues and much more research will be needed to evaluate its effects over time. However, prior extensive, scientifically rigorous research has strongly substantiated the value of having health insurance. Such research was the foundation for a U.S. Council of Economic Advisors 2014 report on the importance of expanding Medicaid to cover the uninsured.[163] The report highlighted benefits such as:

- Having a usual source of care and being better able to obtain care when needed
- Receiving recommended preventive care including disease screenings
- Relief from the financial burdens of medical costs and fewer catastrophic out-of-pocket expenses
- Experiencing improved mental health

Also, 2015 findings reported by the Kaiser Commission on Medicaid and the Uninsured from a 50-state survey of Medicaid directors included positive administrative effects of the ACA requirements on state Medicaid agencies. Among these were extensive streamlining of the Medicaid enrollment and renewal processes including the use of information technology, and improved reporting systems that may contribute to future resource efficiencies.[164]

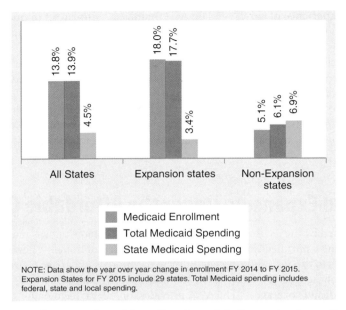

FIGURE 8-6 **FY 2015 Enrollment and Total Spending Growth in Expansion States Far Exceeded Non-expansion States; State Spending Growth Was Lower**

Reproduced from The Henry J. Kaiser Family Foundation. Medicaid enrollment & spending growth: 2015–2016. Available from http://kff.org/medicaid/issue-brief/medicaid-enrollment-spending
-growth-fy-2015-2016/. Accessed April 29, 2016.

▶ Disproportionate Share Hospital Payments

Since 1986, federal law requires Medicaid payments to states called disproportionate share hospital (DSH) payments for hospitals serving large numbers of Medicaid and low-income, uninsured individuals.[165] The law establishes an annual DSH allotment for each state that limits the federal contribution of total statewide payments and limits hospital-specific payments to 100 percent of costs that are not compensated by Medicaid.[140,165] DSH payments provide critical financial supplements to hospitals serving the neediest populations. In 2015, the federal allotment to states was $11.9 billion.[166] Under the assumption that the ACA would significantly decrease the number of uninsured individuals, the law originally called for reductions in the DSH state allotments between 2014 and 2020. However, recent legislation delayed start of the reductions until 2018, which will then continue to 2025.[140]

▶ Healthcare-Financing Mandates of the Affordable Care Act for Individuals and Employers

Beginning in 2014, the ACA required most Americans to carry health insurance coverage or pay a penalty. This requirement is known as the individual mandate or "shared responsibility" requirement of the law.[167] Coverage that fulfills this requirement includes employer-provided insurance, Medicaid, or personally purchased policies. The penalty for not having coverage is either a flat dollar amount or a percentage of income above the tax-filing threshold and increases annually. In

2016, the penalty was $695 for adults and $347.50 per child (up to $2,085 per family).[167] Groups exempt from the penalty include individuals for whom the cost of insurance would exceed 8 percent of their income, people with incomes below the federal requirement for tax filing, religiously exempt individuals, undocumented immigrants, incarcerated individuals, and members of tribal nations.[168] Making health insurance affordable for as many Americans as possible is the centerpiece of the ACA. Uninsured individuals incur enormous costs to society. Prior to adoption of the ACA, costs were estimated at $50 billion per year in unpaid medical bills.[169] These costs are passed on to the insured through increased insurance premiums. The individual mandate is critical to achieve affordability by spreading insurance risk, and therefore costs, over the highest proportion of the population as possible.

The Individual Mandate and Health Insurance Marketplaces

To facilitate insurance enrollment, the ACA required states to establish health benefit exchanges, now known as health insurance marketplaces (HIMs), and create separate HIMs for employers with fewer than 100 full-time equivalent employees through the Small Business Health Options Program (SHOP).The SHOPs may qualify small employers for tax credits of up to 50 percent of premium costs.[170] Through participation of several insurance companies in each state, the HIMs created a competitive health insurance market by providing consumers with web-based, easily understandable, comparative information on plan choices and standardized rules regarding health plan offers and pricing.[171]

The ACA gave states the option to create their own HIMs. If a state opted not to do so or was unable to do so, the DHHS established and administered the HIM. In 2016, 13 states and the District of Columbia operated their own HIM, 34 states had federally facilitated HIMs, and 4 states operated HIMs with federal assistance.[172] The ACA provided an indefinite fiscal appropriation for DHHS grants to states for planning and establishing HIMs through 2015, after which HIMS were expected to be self-sustaining.[173]

To participate in HIMs, health insurance plans must meet federal requirements for minimum coverage known as "essential health benefits." Essential benefits include services in the following 10 categories:[173]

1. Ambulatory patient services
2. Emergency services
3. Hospitalization
4. Maternity and newborn care
5. Mental health and substance use disorder services, including behavioral health treatment
6. Prescription drugs
7. Rehabilitative and habilitative services and devices
8. Laboratory services
9. Preventive and wellness services and chronic disease management
10. Pediatric services, including oral and vision care

Eligibility to purchase insurance through an exchange is open to American citizens and legal immigrants whose employers do not provide health insurance and those for whom the cost of employer-sponsored coverage is prohibitive.[173] Acceptance into plans is guaranteed.[173] To help make coverage affordable, the federal government provides varying levels of advance and refundable premium tax credits and cost-sharing subsidies based on personal income.[173]

The Employer Mandate

The ACA employer mandate began in 2015 and requires all businesses with 50 or more full-time equivalent (FTE) employees to provide health insurance to at least 95 percent of their full-time employees and dependents up to age 26, or pay a fee by 2016. There are several nuances to employer penalties for failing to provide health insurance coverage, but in general, they are subject to a $2,000 fee per full-time employee (in excess of 30 employees). The mandate does not apply to businesses with 49 or fewer employees.[174]

▶ The Affordable Care Act: Insurance Coverage Progress and Costs

It is important to note that reports on Americans' gaining insurance coverage due to the ACA is a dynamic challenge. Although data from enrollments through the HIMs, Medicaid, and CHIP are quite specific, much other reported data represents projections and extrapolations. Thus, it is challenging to achieve exact counts of those enrolled under ACA provisions versus those who would have enrolled without the ACA.[175,176,177] Therefore enrollment data represent averages over specific time periods rather than exact numbers at points in time. For example, people shift (or drop) coverage as circumstances change, and many included in enrollment statistics may never actually participate due to non-payment of premiums or other reasons.[176,177] Nonetheless, data do allow reasonable representations of the ACA in enabling previously uninsured Americans to obtain health insurance coverage.

One year prior to the ACA's enactment in 2010, the U.S. Census Bureau estimated that 48.6 million Americans or about 15.7 percent were uninsured.[178] HIM plan enrollments began in 2013. By the end of 2015, 11.2 million individuals had selected or were automatically re-enrolled in HIM plans.[179] By 2015, new Medicaid and CHIP enrollments in the states choosing to expand coverage totaled approximately 10 million.[177] By 2016, individuals enrolled through the HIMs, Medicaid expansion, and CHIP reduced the number of uninsured Americans by an estimated 21.2 million to about 27 million, or 10 percent of the population, an unprecedented level.[177,180] Numerous factors will affect future trends, but assuming existing laws remain unchanged, the CBO projects that about 10 percent of the population under 65 years of age will remain uninsured in the next decade.[177]

ACA implementation and operation costs are reported by the CBO and the Joint Committee on Taxation (JCT), which also compiles projections for future periods. Net costs of the ACA insurance provisions in 2016 are estimated at $110 billion, with net total costs over the decade 2017–2026 projected at $1.4 trillion.[177] On an annual basis, costs translate to estimates of $5,000 per HIM enrollee and $3,500 per Medicaid and CHIP enrollee.[175] Included in the net costs are the income-based subsidies for HIM enrollees (approximately 80 percent of HIM enrollees qualify for premium subsidies), and the costs of Medicaid and CHIP and tax credits provided to small employers.[177] The net costs also take into account federal revenue derived from individual penalties for not obtaining health insurance, employer penalties for declining to offer health insurance that meets federal standards, and other penalties and taxes.[177] Compared with the CBO and JCT projection made just prior to the ACA's 2010 enactment, the current estimate for the next decade's costs are $157 billion less or 25 percent lower.[177] (See **FIGURE 8-7**.) As an indication that ACA insurance provisions are now woven in the federal

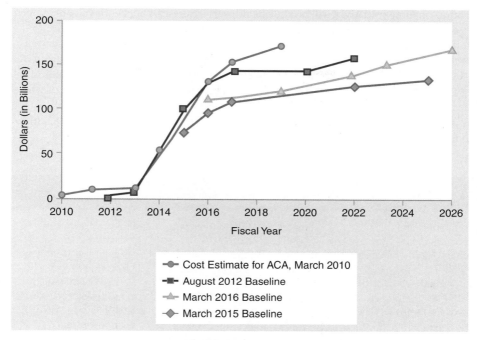

FIGURE 8-7 **Congressional Budget Office (CBO) and Joint Committee on Taxation Estimates (JCT) of the Net Budgetary Effects of the Insurance Coverage Provisions of the Affordable Care Act**

Reproduced from Congressional Budget Office. Federal subsidies for health insurance coverage for people under age 65: 2016–2026. Available from https://www.cbo.gov/sites/default/files/114th -congress-2015-2016/reports/51385-HealthInsuranceBaseline.pdf. Accessed May 25, 2016.

insurance funding fabric, in 2015 the CBO and JCT noted that subsequent reports will no longer separately identify the ACA's insurance coverage provisions on the federal budget. Instead, these effects will be included as part of overall reporting.[176]

▶ Continuing Challenges and Innovations

Transformation of the U.S. healthcare financing system through payment reform coupled with a population health focus will continue posing a daunting array of issues. Paying for changes is only one issue. Breaking loose from old philosophies, value systems, and the politics that have brought the U.S. healthcare enterprise to its paradoxical state of superior technology while it remains plagued by profit-driven waste will pose overarching challenges. As noted in this chapter, U.S. healthcare costs compared with other developed nations are unjustifiable when comparing this country's health status with other developed nations that spend far less.

However, innovation is occurring. ACA provisions are reaching millions with affordable health insurance and initiatives such as bundled payments and accountable care organizations linking costs with quality. The new MACRA legislation, if implemented as intended, will take historic steps with more equitable provider reimbursement linked with quality of care. Other ongoing initiatives such as the hospital readmissions reduction program are showing promising results.

Many other ongoing initiatives will provide health services researchers with valuable information for developing and refining future efforts to control costs and improve quality.

Today, U.S. health care remains entrenched in a much-too-costly and profit-driven reward system that surely will not passively acquiesce to change. As journalist Steven Brill stated in a searing 2013 review of U.S. healthcare delivery system costs entitled "Bitter Pill: Why Medical Bills Are Killing Us," "When we debate healthcare policy, we seem to jump right to the issue of who should pay the bills, blowing past what should be the first question: Why exactly are the bills so high?"[181] In this next phase of reform, Mr. Brill's query may be a quintessential issue for U.S. citizens and their policy makers.

KEY TERMS FOR REVIEW

Accountable Care Organization (ACO)
Alternative Payment Model (APM)
Balanced Budget Act of 1997 (BBA)
Bundled Payments for Care Initiatives (BPCI)
Capitation
Children's Health Insurance Program (CHIP)
Community-Rated Insurance
Diagnosis-Related Groups (DRGs)
Disease-Management Program (DMP)
Disproportionate Share Hospital (DSH)

Emergency Medical Treatment and Labor Act (EMTALA)
Employer Mandate
Experience-Rated Insurance
Financial Risk Sharing
Health Insurance Marketplace (HIM)
Healthcare Effectiveness Data and Information Set (HEDIS)
High-Deductible Health Plan (HDHP)
HMO Act of 1973
Indemnity Insurance
Individual Mandate
Medicaid
Medicare
Medicare Access and CHIP Reauthorization Act of 2015 (MACRA)

Medicare Advantage
Medicare Modernization and Prescription Drug Act of 2003 (MMA)
National Committee for Quality Assurance (NCQA)
Point of Service Plan (POS)
Preferred Provider Organization (PPO)
Prospective Payment System (PPS)
Quality Payment Program (QPP)
Self-Funded Health Insurance
Third-Party Administrator (TPA)
Value-Based Purchasing (VBP)

CHAPTER ACRONYMS

ACA Patient Protection and Affordable Care Act of 2010
AHRQ Agency for Healthcare Research and Quality
CMS Centers for Medicare and Medicaid Services
DHHS Department of Health and Human Services
FMAP Federal Medical Assistance Percentage
GDP Gross Domestic Product
HAC Hospital-Acquired Condition

IOM Institute of Medicine
MCO Managed Care Organization
MIPS Merit-Based Incentive Payment System
NHE National Health Expenditures
NQF National Quality Forum
OEDC Organization of Economically Developed Countries
PCMH Patient-Centered Medical Home
PSNET Patient Safety Network
RBRVS Resource-Based Relative Value Scale

References

1. Congressional Budget Office. The long-term outlook for major federal health care programs. In: *The 2015 Long-Term Budget Outlook*. June 2015. http://www.cbo.gov/sites/default/files/114th-congress-2015-2016/reports/50250/50250-breakout-Chapter2-2.pdf. Accessed April 9, 2016.

2. Fronstin P. Issue brief #419: sources of health insurance coverage: a look at changes between 2013 and 2014 from the March 2014 and 2015 current population survey. Employee Benefit Research Institute. http://files.kff.org/attachment/summary-of-findings-2015-employer-health-benefits-survey. Accessed April 9, 2016.

3. The Kaiser Family Foundation and Health Research and Educational Trust. Employer health benefits 2015 summary of findings. http://files.kff.org/attachment/summary-of-findings-2015-employer-health-benefits-survey. Accessed April 9, 2016.

4. The Kaiser Commission on Medicaid and the Uninsured. The uninsured: a primer: key facts about health insurance and the uninsured in the era of health reform. http://files.kff.org/attachment/primer-the-uninsured-a-primer-key-facts-about-health-insurance-and-the-uninsured-in-the-era-of-health-reform. Accessed April 11, 2016.

5. Aizenman NC. Number of uninsured Americans drops by 1.3 million, Census report shows. *The Washington Post*. September 12, 2012. http://articles.washingtonpost.com/2012-09-12/national/35494577_1_young-adults-number-of-uninsured-americans-employer-sponsored-coverage. Accessed April 11, 2016.

6. Centers for Medicare & Medicaid Services. Historical. Downloads: NHE Tables. Table 1. https://www.cms.gov/research-statistics-data-and-systems/statistics-trends-and-reports/nationalhealthexpenddata/nationalhealthaccountshistorical.html. Accessed April 12, 2016.

7. Centers for Medicare & Medicaid Services. Historical. Downloads. NHE summary including share of GDP CY 1980–2014. https://www.cms.gov/research-statistics-data-and-systems/statistics-trends-and-reports/nationalhealthexpenddata/nationalhealthaccountshistorical.html. Accessed April 12, 2016.

8. Centers for Medicare & Medicaid Services. National health expenditures 2014 highlights. https://www.cms.gov/Research-Statistics-Data-and-Systems/Statistics-Trends-and-Reports/NationalHealthExpendData/Downloads/highlights.pdf. Accessed April 12, 2016.

9. Martin AB, Hartman H, Benson J, Catlin A, National Health Expenditure Accounts Team. National health spending in 2014: faster growth driven by coverage expansion and prescription drug spending. *Health Aff*. 2016;35:150-160. http://content.healthaffairs.org/content/35/1/150. Accessed April 10, 2016.

10. Centers for Medicare & Medicaid Services, Office of the Actuary, National Health Statistics Group. The health care dollar: where it went and where it came from. 2014. https://www.cms.gov/Research-Statistics-Data-and-Systems/Statistics-Trends-and-Reports/NationalHealthExpendData/Downloads/PieChartSourcesExpenditures2014.pdf. Accessed April 10, 2016.

11. Altman SH, Tompkins CP, Eilat E, Glavin MPV. Escalating health care spending: is it desirable or inevitable? *Health Aff*. 2003;(w3):1-14. http://content.healthaffairs.org/content/early/2003/01/08/hlthaff.w3.1.full.pdf. Accessed April 11, 2016.

12. Organization for Economic Cooperation and Development. About the OECD. http://www.oecd.org/about/. Accessed April 16, 2016.

13. Organization for Economic Development. Focus on health spending, OECD health statistics 2015. https://www.oecd.org/unitedstates/Country-Note-UNITED%20STATES-OECD-Health-Statistics-2015.pdf. Accessed April 16, 2016.

14. Squires D, Anderson C. U.S. health care from a global perspective: spending, use of services, prices, and health in 13 countries. *The Commonwealth Fund*. http://www.commonwealthfund.org/publications/issue-briefs/2015/oct/us-health-care-from-a-global-perspective. Accessed April 16, 2016.

15. Milstein A, Gilbertson E. American medical home runs. *Health Aff*. 2009;28:1317-1326. http://content.healthaffairs.org/content/28/5/1317.full.pdf. Accessed April 16, 2016.

16. Lallemand NC. Health Policy Brief: reducing waste in health care. *Health Aff*. December 13, 2012. http://healthaffairs.org/healthpolicybriefs/brief_pdfs/healthpolicybrief_82.pdf. Accessed April 16, 2016.

17. ABIM Foundation. Choosing wisely. http://www.choosingwisely.org. Accessed March 8, 2016.

18. Morden N, Colla CH, Sequist TD, Rosenthal MB. Choosing wisely—the politics and economics of labeling low-value services. *N Engl J Med*. 2014;0370:589-592. http://www.nejm.org/doi/full/10.1056/NEJMp1314965. Accessed April 18, 2016.

19. Morris L. Combating fraud in health care: an essential component of any cost containment strategy. *Health Aff*. 2009;28:1351-1356. http://content.healthaffairs.org/content/28/5/1351.full.pdf. Accessed April 18, 2016.

20. Centers for Medicare & Medicaid Services. The health care fraud and abuse control program protects consumers and taxpayers by combating health care fraud. March 19, 2015. https://www.cms.gov/Newsroom/MediaReleaseDatabase/Fact-sheets/2015-Fact-sheets-items/2015-03-19.html. Accessed April 18, 2016.

21. Schnecker L. What's the matter with Florida? Healthcare fraud flourishes despite enforcement

efforts. *Modern Health Care*. May 9, 2016. http://www.modernhealthcare.com/article/20160507/MAGAZINE/305079988. Accessed May 21, 2016.

22. U.S. Department of Health and Human Services. Administration on Aging. *A Profile of Older Americans: 2014*. http://www.aoa.acl.gov/aging_statistics/Profile/2014/docs/2014-Profile.pdf. Accessed March 6, 2016.

23. Centers for Disease Control and Prevention. 2010 National hospital discharge survey, number and rate of hospital discharges, average length of stay and days of care, number and rate of discharges by sex and age, 2010. July 2010. http://www.cdc.gov/nchs/data/nhds/2average/2010ave2_ratesexage.pdf. Accessed April 12, 2016.

24. Boult C, Counsell SR, Leipzig RM, Berenson RA. The urgency of preparing primary care physicians to care for older people with chronic illnesses. *Health Aff.* 2010;29:811-818. http://content.healthaffairs.org/content/29/5/811.full.pdf±html. Accessed April 12, 2016.

25. Grudzen C, Richardson LD, Baumlin KM, et al. Redesigned geriatric emergency care may have helped reduce admissions of older adults to intensive care units. *Health Aff.* 2015;34:788-795. http://content.healthaffairs.org/content/34/5/788.full.pdf±html. Accessed April 12, 2016.

26. Chernew ME, Jacobson PD, Hofer TP, Aaronson KD, Fendrick AM. Barriers to constraining health care cost growth. *Health Aff.* 2004;23:122-128. http://content.healthaffairs.org/content/23/6/122.full.pdf±html. Accessed April 12, 2016.

27. Levit K, Smith C, Cowan C, Lazenby H, Martin A. Inflation spurs health spending in 2000. *Health Aff.* 2002;21:172-181. http://content.healthaffairs.org/content/21/1/172.full.pdf±html. Accessed April 12, 2016.

28. The Huffington Post. Upside down health care: why it matters. October 28, 2011. http://www.huffingtonpost.com/john-geyman/generalist-vs-specialist-care_b_927759.html. Accessed May 8, 2016.

29. DeNavas-Walt C, Proctor BD, Smith JC. *U.S. Census Current Population Reports, P60-236, Income, Poverty, and Health Insurance Coverage in the United States: 2008*. Washington, DC: U.S. Government Printing Office. 2009. http://www.census.gov/prod/2009pubs/p60-236.pdf. Accessed May 8, 2016.

30. The Henry J. Kaiser Family Foundation. Health care costs: a primer: key information on health care costs and their impact. May 2012. http://kff.org/report-section/health-care-costs-a-primer-2012-report/. Accessed May 8, 2016.

31. American College of Physicians and American Society of Internal Medicine. The cost of the lack of health insurance. 2004. https://www.acponline.org/acp_policy/policies/cost_of_lack_of_health_insurance_1999.pdf. Accessed May 8, 2016.

32. United States Bureau of Labor Statistics. Employment projections: 2014–24 summary. December 8, 2015. http://www.bls.gov/news.release/ecopro.nr0.htm. Accessed April 5, 2016.

33. Institute of Medicine (U.S.) Committee on Employment-Based Health Benefits. Field MJ, Shapiro HT, eds. *Employment and Health Benefits: A Connection at Risk*. Washington DC: National Academies Press (US); 1993; Shumpeter, J. Origins and Evolution of Employment-Based Health Benefits. Available from: http://www.ncbi.nlm.nih.gov/books/NBK235989/. Accessed May 8, 2016.

34. Kongstvedt PR. *Essentials of Managed Health Care*. 6th ed. Sudbury, MA: Jones & Bartlett Learning; 2012.

35. Lichtenstein, M. Health insurance from invention to innovation: a history of the Blue Cross and Blue Shield companies. Blue Cross/Blue Shield. http://www.bcbs.com/blog/health-insurance.html?referrer=https://www.google.com/#.V1cDXb0uF50. Accessed May 8, 2016.

36. Stevens R. *In Sickness and in Wealth: American Hospitals in the Twentieth Century*. New York, NY: Basic Books; 1989.

37. Leduc JLK. Community versus experience rating health insurance. Connecticut General Assembly Office of Legislative Research. https://www.cga.ct.gov/2008/rpt/2008-R-0377.htm. Accessed May 10, 2016.

38. Thomasson M. Economic History Association. Health insurance in the United States. http://eh.net/?s=Health±insurance±in±the±United±States. Accessed April 16, 2016.

39. Kovner AR, Knickman JR, eds. *Health Care Delivery in the United States*. 10th ed. New York, New York: Springer Publishing Company; 2011.

40. Long M, Rae M, Claxton G. PPO enrollment: comparison of the availability and cost of coverage for workers in small firms and large firms: update from the 2015 employer health benefits survey. The Henry J. Kaiser Family Foundation. http://kff.org/private-insurance/issue-brief/a-comparison-of-the-availability-and-cost-of-coverage-for-workers-in-small-firms-and-large-firms-update-from-the-2015-employer-health-benefits-survey/. Accessed May 11, 2016.

41. Small Business Majority. Plan characteristics and types: Affordable Care Act health coverage guide. http://healthcoverageguide.org/reference-guide/coverage-types/plan-characteristics-and-types/#Point-of-Service±Plans±%28POS%29. Accessed May 11, 2016.

42. Trespacz KL. Staff-model HMOs: don't blink or you'll miss them. *Managed Care Magazine*. July 1999. http://www.managedcaremag.com/archives/1999/7/staff-model-hmos-dont-blink-or-youll-miss-them. Accessed May 12, 2016.

43. Smith S, Heffler S, Freeland M. The next decade of health spending: a new outlook. *Health Aff*. 1999;18(4):86-95. http://content.healthaffairs.org/content/18/4/86.citation. Accessed May 12, 2016.

44. Levit K, Cowan C, Lazenby H, et al. Health spending in 1998: signals of change. *Health Aff*. 2000;19:124-132. http://content.healthaffairs.org/content/19/1/124.full.pdf±html. Accessed May 12, 2016.

45. Miller RH, Luft HS. HMO plan performance update: an analysis of the literature, 1997–2001. *Health Aff*. 2002;21:63-86. http://content.healthaffairs.org/content/21/4/63.full.pdf±html. Accessed May 12, 2016.

46. U.S. Department of Health and Human Services. White House Backgrounder. President Clinton releases report documenting actions federal government is taking to implement a patients' bill of rights and urges voters to send back a Congress that shares his commitment to pass legislation to assure protections for all health plans. November 2, 1998. http://archive.hhs.gov/news/press/1998pres/981102.html. Accessed May 14, 2016.

47. National Conference of State Legislatures. Managed care state laws and regulations including consumer and provider protections. September, 2011. http://www.ncsl.org/issues-research/health/managed-care-state-laws.aspx. Accessed May 14, 2016.

48. Health Policy Brief. High-deductible health plans. *Health Aff*. February 4, 2016. http://healthaffairs.org/healthpolicybriefs/brief_pdfs/healthpolicybrief_152.pdf. Accessed May 17, 2016.

49. The Henry J. Kaiser Family Foundation and Health Research & Educational Trust. 2015 employer health benefits survey: summary of findings. http://kff.org/report-section/ehbs-2015-summary-of-findings/. Accessed May 17, 2016.

50. Islam I. Trouble ahead for high deductible health plans? *Health Affairs Blog*. October 7, 2015. http://healthaffairs.org/blog/2015/10/07/trouble-ahead-for-high-deductible-health-plans/. Accessed May 17, 2016.

51. Lindquist R. Health reimbursement arrangement (HRA) - what is it? Zane Benefits. Small Business Employee Benefits and HR Blog. May 26, 2016. https://www.zanebenefits.com/blog/bid/97288/Health-Reimbursement-Arrangement-HRA-What-is-it. Accessed May 30, 2016.

52. The Henry J. Kaiser Family Foundation. Medicare advantage. May 2016. http://files.kff.org/attachment/Fact-Sheet-Medicare-Advantage. Accessed June 1, 2016.

53. Herman B. Final Medicare advantage rates largely shun health plan lobbying. *Modern Healthcare*. April 4, 2016. http://www.modernhealthcare.com/article/20160404/NEWS/160409961. Accessed May 26, 2016.

54. Centers for Medicare & Medicaid Services. Medicaid managed care enrollment and program characteristics 2014. https://www.medicaid.gov/medicaid-chip-program-information/by-topics/data-and-systems/medicaid-managed-care/downloads/2014-medicaid-managed-care-enrollment-report.pdf. Accessed May 17, 2016.

55. McPartland G. Birth of the national committee for quality assurance. Kaiser Permanente. http://kaiserpermanentehistory.org/tag/hedis/. Accessed May 3, 2016.

56. Iglehart JK. The National Committee for Quality Assurance. *N Engl J Med*. 1996;335:995

57. National Committee for Quality Assurance. The National Committee for Quality Assurance "gold standard" for health plan accreditation. 2013. https://www.ncqa.org/Portals/0/Newsroom/2014/NCQA_Gold_Standard_%20Accreditation.pdf. Accessed May 3, 2016.

58. National Committee for Quality Assurance. What is recognition? http://www.ncqa.org/Programs/Recognition.aspx. Accessed May 3, 2016.

59. National Committee for Quality Assurance. NCQA health plan accreditation. http://www.ncqa.org/Portals/0/Programs/Accreditation/HPA_Web_July2014.pdf. Accessed May 3, 2016.

60. National Committee for Quality Assurance. HEDIS compliance audit program. http://www.ncqa.org/tabid/205/Default.aspx. Accessed May 3, 2016.

61. National Committee for Quality Assurance. HEDIS data submission. http://www.ncqa.org/hedis-quality-measurement/hedis-measures/hedis-data-submission. Accessed May 3, 2016.

62. National Committee for Quality Assurance. State of health care quality: introduction. http://www.ncqa.org/report-cards/health-plans/state-of-health-care-quality/2015-table-of-contents/introduction. Accessed May 3, 2016.

63. National Committee for Quality Assurance. The state of health care quality report 2015. http://www.ncqa.org/report-cards/health-plans/state-of-health-care-quality. Accessed May 3, 2016.

64. Academy of Managed Care Pharmacy. Concept series paper on disease management. http://www.amcp.org/WorkArea/DownloadAsset.aspx?id=9295. Accessed May 19, 2016.

65. Innovations Exchange Team with Meyer, J. Chronic disease management can reduce readmissions. Agency for Health Care Research and Quality. https://innovations.ahrq.gov/perspectives/chronic-disease-management-can-reduce-readmissions. Accessed May 12, 2016.

66. Fireman B, Bartlett, J, Selby J. Can disease management reduce health care costs by improving quality? *Health Aff*. 2004;23:63-75. http://content.healthaffairs.org/content/23/6/63.full.pdf±html. Accessed May 11, 2016.

67. Mays GP, Au M, Claxton G. Convergence and dissonance: evolution in private sector approaches to disease management and care coordination. *Health Aff.* 2007;20:1683-1691. http://content.healthaffairs.org/content/26/6/1683.full.pdf±html. Accessed May 11, 2016.

68. Geyman JP. Disease management: panacea, another false hope, or something in between? *Ann Fam Med.* 2007;5:257-260. http://www.ncbi.nlm.nih.gov/pmc/articles/PMC1886482/. Accessed May 11, 2016.

69. Tracer Z. Employer health insurance costs slow as workers pay bigger share. *Bloomberg News.* September 22, 2015. http://www.bloomberg.com/news/articles/2015-09-22/employer-health-insurance-costs-slow-as-workers-pay-bigger-share. Accessed May 11, 2016.

70. AON Hewitt. 2011 health insurance trend driver survey. http://www.aon.com/attachments/thought-leadership/2011_Health_Insurance_Trend_Driver_Survey.pdf. Accessed May 26, 2016.

71. Healthcare Finance News Staff. Employer wellness programs spend record $693 per worker. March 26, 2015. http://www.healthcarefinancenews.com/news/employer-wellness-programs-spend-record-693-worker#.Vpe66ZMrL1J. Accessed May 26, 2016.

72. Mattke S. When it comes to the value of wellness, ask about fairness, not just about effectiveness. *Health Affairs Blog.* March 18, 2015. http://healthaffairs.org/blog/2015/03/18/when-it-comes-to-the-value-of-wellness-ask-about-fairness-not-just-about-effectiveness/. Accessed May 26, 2016.

73. Moran DW. Whence and whither health insurance? A revisionist history. *Health Aff.* 2005;24:1415-1425. http://content.healthaffairs.org/content/24/6/1415.full.pdf±html. Accessed May 28, 2016.

74. Goforth A. The rise of self-funding. BenefitsPro.com. March 9, 2015. http://www.benefitspro.com/2015/03/09/the-rise-of-self-funding?page=3. Accessed May 16, 2016.

75. Rinck A. What is a third party administrator (TPA)? Zane Benefits: Small Business Employee Benefits and HR Blog. December 9, 2012. https://www.zanebenefits.com/blog/bid/244838/What-is-a-Third-Party-Administrator-TPA. Accessed May 27, 2016.

76. Parker DC. Responding to trends in group health plans. *HR Crossing.* http://www.hrcrossing.com/article/270112/Human-Resources-Responding-to-Trends-in-Group-Health-Plans/. Accessed August 31, 2016.

77. U.S. Congressional Budget Office. The long-term outlook for health care spending: sources of growth in projected federal spending on Medicare and Medicaid: an overview. 2007. http://www.cbo.gov/publication/41646. Accessed May 20, 2016.

78. U.S. Congressional Budget Office. March 2016 Medicare baseline by fiscal year. https://www.cbo.gov/sites/default/files/51302-2016-03-Medicare.pdf. Accessed May 20, 2016.

79. Department of Health and Human Services. Fiscal year 2017 budget in brief. Advancing the health, safety and well-being of the nation. http://www.hhs.gov/sites/default/files/fy2017-budget-in-brief.pdf. Accessed April 9, 2016.

80. The Henry J. Kaiser Family Foundation. The facts on Medicare spending and financing. http://kff.org/medicare/fact-sheet/medicare-spending-and-financing-fact-sheet/. Accessed May 14, 2016.

81. Department of Health and Human Services. Assistant Secretary for Legislation (ASL). Hash M. Testimony on Medicare+Choice implementation. http://www.hhs.gov/asl/testify/t980730a.html. Accessed May 11, 2016.

82. The Henry J. Kaiser Family Foundation. The Medicare part D prescription drug benefit. http://kff.org/medicare/fact-sheet/the-medicare-prescription-drug-benefit-fact-sheet/. Accessed May 3, 2016.

83. Scandlen G. Myth busters #4: the death of health planning. National Center for Health Policy Analysis. *Health Policy Blog.* July 27, 2011. http://healthblog.ncpa.org/myth-busters-4-the-death-of-health-planning/. Accessed May 3, 2016.

84. Melhado E. Health planning in the United States and the decline of public-interest policymaking. *Millbank Q.* 2006;84:359-440. http://www.ncbi.nlm.nih.gov/pmc/articles/PMC2690168/. Accessed May 4, 2016.

85. National Conference of State Legislatures. Certificate of need state health laws and programs. January 2016. http://www.ncsl.org/research/health/con-certificate-of-need-state-laws.aspx. Accessed April 29, 2016.

86. Government Accountability Office. Implementation of the PSRO program. http://www.gao.gov/assets/100/98419.pdf. Accessed April 28, 2016.

87. Shi L, Singh D. *Delivering Health Care in America: A Systems Approach.* Burlington, MA: Jones & Bartlett Learning; 2012.

88. Department of Health and Human Services. Assistant Secretary for Legislation (ASL). Vladeck B. Testimony on reforming the Medicare home health benefit. March 5, 1997. http://www.hhs.gov/asl/testify/t970305a.html. Accessed April 28, 2016.

89. Department of Health and Human Services Office of the Inspector General. Medicare hospital prospective payment system: how DRG rates are calculated and updated. August, 2001. http://oig.hhs.gov/oei/reports/oei-09-00-00200.pdf. Accessed April 28, 2016.

90. Mistichelli J. National Reference Center for Bioethics Literature. Diagnosis-related groups and the prospective payment system: forecasting social implications. http://bioethics.georgetown.edu/publications/scopenotes/sn4.pdf. Accessed May 12, 2016.

91. McCormack LA, Burge RT. Diffusion of Medicare's RBRVS and related physician payment policies. *Health Care Finance Rev.* 1994;16:159-173. http://www.ncbi.nlm.nih.gov/pmc/articles/PMC4193488/. Accessed May 14, 2016.

92. Thorpe KE. Health care cost containment: results and lessons from the past 20 years. In: Shortell SM, Reinhardt UE, eds. *Improving Health Policy and Management*. Ann Arbor, MI: Health Administration Press; 1992:244-246.

93. Russell LB, Manning CL. The effect of prospective payment on Medicare expenditures. *N Engl J Med*. 1989; 320:439-444. http://www.nejm.org/doi/pdf/10.1056 /NEJM198902163200706. Accessed May 12, 2016.

94. American Academy of Emergency Physicians. EMTALA. March 26, 2012. http://www.aaem.org /em-resources/regulatory-issues/emtala. Accessed May 4, 2016.

95. Fishman EZ, Penrod JD, Vladeck B. Medicare home health utilization in context. *Health Serv Res*. 2003;38:107-112. http://www.ncbi.nlm.nih.gov/pmc /articles/PMC1360876/. Accessed May 12, 2016.

96. Kovner A. *Jonas' Health Care Delivery in the United States*. 5th ed. New York, NY: Springer; 1995.

97. American Medical Association. Overview of the RBVS. http://www.ama-assn.org/ama/pub/physician -resources/solutions-managing-your-practice /coding-billing-insurance/medicare/the-resource -based-relative-value-scale/overview-of-rbrvs.page?. Accessed May 12, 2016.

98. Davis PA. Medicare: Insolvency projections. Congressional Research Service. July 3, 2013. https://www.fas.org/sgp/crs/misc/RS20946.pdf. Accessed April 12, 2016.

99. Reischauer RD. Medicare beyond 2002; preparing for the baby boomers. *Brookings Review*. 1997;15:24. http:// www.brookings.edu/research/articles/1997/06/summer -useconomics-reischauer. Accessed April 12, 2016.

100. National Association of Social Workers. Balanced Budget Act of 1997, Public Law 105-33: significant changes made in children's health, welfare, Medicaid and Medicare. http://www.socialworkers.org/archives /advocacy/updates/1997/grbudget.htm. Accessed May 14, 2016.

101. Medicare Payment Advisory Commission. Report to the Congress: Medicare payment policy (March 2003), chapter 1, context for Medicare spending. http://www.medpac.gov/documents/reports/Mar03 _Entire_report.pdf?sfvrsn=0. Accessed May 15, 2016.

102. MedPac. About MedPAC. http://medpac.gov/-about -medpac-. Accessed May 15, 2016.

103. The Commonwealth Fund. After the bipartisan commission: what next for Medicare? http:// www.commonwealthfund.org/usr_doc/altman _bipartisan_353.pdf. Accessed August 31, 2016.

104. U.S. Department of Health and Human Services. Balanced Budget Refinement Act of 1999: highlights. November 18, 1999. http://archive .hhs.gov/news/press/1999pres/19991118b.html. Accessed May 16, 2016.

105. Ross MN. Paying Medicare + Choice plans: the view from MedPAC. *Health Aff*. http://content .healthaffairs.org/content/early/2001/11/28/hlthaff .w1.90.full.pdf. Accessed May 9, 2016.

106. Centers for Medicare & Medicaid Services. Quality initiatives - general information. April 3, 2013. https:// www.cms.gov/Medicare/Quality-Initiatives-Patient -Assessment-Instruments/QualityInitiativesGenInfo /index.html?redirect=/qualityinitiativesgeninfo/. Accessed May 16, 2016.

107. Leavitt MO. Report to congress: improving the Medicare quality improvement organization program - response to the Institute of Medicine study. http://www.cms.gov/Medicare/Quality-Initiatives -Patient-Assessment-Instruments/Quality ImprovementOrgs/downloads/QIO_improvement _RTC_fnl.pdf. Accessed May 18, 2016.

108. Werner R, Kolstad JT, Stuart EA, Polsky D. The effect of pay-for-performance in hospitals: lessons for quality improvement. *Health Aff*. 2011;30:690-698. http://content.healthaffairs.org/content/30/4/690. Accessed May 18, 2016.

109. Centers for Medicare & Medicaid Services. Hospital compare. https://www.cms.gov/medicare/quality -initiatives-patient-assessment-instruments/hospital qualityinits/hospitalcompare.html. Accessed May 18, 2016.

110. Hospital Consumer Assessment of Healthcare Providers and Systems. HCAHPS fact sheet. July, 2010. http://www.hcahpsonline.org/files/HCAHPS%20 Fact%20Sheet%202010.pdf. Accessed May 18, 2016.

111. Centers for Medicare & Medicaid Services. Hospital-acquired conditions. https://www.cms .gov/Medicare/Medicare-Fee-for-Service-Payment /HospitalAcqCond/Hospital-Acquired_Conditions .html. Accessed May 21, 2016.

112. Patient Safety Network. Patient safety primer: never events. https://psnet.ahrq.gov/primers/primer/3 /never-events. Accessed May 21, 2016.

113. National Quality Forum. NQF's history. http://www .qualityforum.org/about_nqf/history/. Accessed May 21, 2016.

114. Centers for Medicare & Medicaid Services. The Affordable Care Act: helping providers help patients. https://www.cms.gov/Medicare/Medicare -Fee-for-Service-Payment/ACO/Downloads /ACO-Menu-Of-Options.pdf. Accessed May 16, 2016.

115. Department of Health and Human Services. New HHS data shows major strides made in patient safety, leading to improved care and savings. https:// innovation.cms.gov/Files/reports/patient-safety -results.pdf. Accessed May 9, 2016.

116. Pronovost P, Jha AK. Did hospital engagement networks actually improve care? *N Eng J Med*. 2014. 371:691-693. http://www.nejm.org/doi/full/10.1056 /NEJMp1405800. Accessed May 9, 2016.

117. Centers for Medicare & Medicaid Services. Bundled payments for care improvement (BPCI) initiative: general information. https://innovation.cms.gov /initiatives/bundled-payments/. Accessed May 9, 2016.

118. Centers for Medicare & Medicaid Services. Bundled payments for care improvement initiative (BPCI). https://www.cms.gov/Newsroom /MediaReleaseDatabase/Fact-sheets/2016-Fact -sheets-items/2016-04-18.html. Accessed May 9, 2016.

119. Centers for Medicare & Medicaid Services. Comprehensive care for joint replacement model. https://innovation.cms.gov/initiatives/cjr. Accessed May 9, 2016.

120. Dale SB, Ghosh A, Peikes DN, et al. Two-year costs and quality in the comprehensive primary care initiative. N Engl J Med. 2016;374:2345-2356. http:// www.nejm.org/doi/full/10.1056/NEJMsa1414953. Accessed May 12, 2016.

121. Centers for Medicare & Medicaid Services. Comprehensive primary care plus. https:// innovation.cms.gov/initiatives/comprehensive -primary-care-plus. Accessed May 12, 2016.

122. Dickson V. CMS unveils primary care plus. Modern Healthcare. April 16, 2016. http:// www.modernhealthcare.com/article/20160416 /MAGAZINE/304169908. Accessed May 12, 2016.

123. Kahn K, Timble JW, Friedberg MW, et al. Evaluation of CMS's federally qualified health center (FQHC) advanced primary care practice (APCP) demonstration: final second annual report. The Rand Corporation. http://www.rand .org/content/dam/rand/pubs/research_reports /RR800/RR886z1/RAND_RR886z1.pdf. Accessed May 12, 2016.

124. Muhlstein D, McClellen M. Accountable care organizations in 2016: private and public-sector growth and dispersion. April 21, 2016. Health Affairs Blog. http://healthaffairs.org/blog/2016/04/21/accountable -care-organizations-in-2016-private-and-public -sector-growth-and-dispersion/. Accessed May 23, 2016.

125. American Hospital Association. Committee on Research. AHA research synthesis report: accountable care organizations. Chicago: American Hospital Association; 2010. http://www.aha.org/research/cor /content/ACO-Synthesis-Report.pdf. Accessed May 19, 2016.

126. Centers for Medicare & Medicaid Services. Accountable care organizations (ACO). https:// www.cms.gov/Medicare/Medicare-Fee-for-Service -Payment/ACO/index.html?redirect=/Aco. Accessed March 8, 2016.

127. Centers for Medicare & Medicaid Services. Summary of final rule provisions for accountable care organizations

(ACOs) under the Medicare shared savings program. https://www.cms.gov/Medicare/Medicare-Fee-for -Service-Payment/sharedsavingsprogram/Downloads /ACO_Summary_Factsheet_ICN907404.pdf. Accessed March 8, 2016.

128. Kaiser Health News. Accountable care organizations, explained. http://khn.org/news/aco-accountable-care -organization-faq/. Accessed March 8, 2016.

129. McWilliams JM, Landon BE, Chernew ME, Zaslavsky AM. Changes in patients' experiences in Medicare accountable care organizations. N Engl J Med. 2014;371:1715-1724.

130. O'Callaghan E, Turner N, Renwick L, et al. First episode psychosis and the trail to secondary care: help-seeking and health-system delays. Soc Psychiatry Psychiatr Epidemiol. 2010;45:381-391.

131. Centers for Medicare & Medicaid Services. Hospital value-based purchasing. https://www.cms.gov /Medicare/Quality-Initiatives-Patient-Assessment -Instruments/hospital-value-based-purchasing /index.html?redirect=/Hospital-Value-Based -Purchasing/. Accessed March 8, 2016.

132. Centers for Medicare & Medicaid Services. Fiscal year (FY) 2016 results for the CMS hospital value -based purchasing program. https://www.cms.gov /Newsroom/MediaReleaseDatabase/Fact-sheets/2015 -Fact-sheets-items/2015-10-26.html. Accessed March 8, 2016.

133. Centers for Medicare & Medicaid Services. Readmissions reduction program (HRRP). https:// www.cms.gov/Medicare/Medicare-Fee-for-Service -Payment/AcuteInpatientPPS/Readmissions -Reduction-Program.html. Accessed March 8, 2016.

134. Zuckerman RB, Sheingold SH, Orav EJ, Ruhter J, Epstein AM. Readmissions, observation, and the hospital readmissions reduction program. N Engl J Med. 2016;374:1543-1551. http://www.ncbi.nlm.nih .gov/pubmed/26910198. Accessed April 8, 2016.

135. Conway PH, Gronniger T, Pham H, et al. MACRA: new opportunities for Medicare providers through innovative payment systems (updated). Health Affairs Blog. September 28, 2015. http://healthaffairs .org/blog/2015/09/28/macra-new-opportunities-for -medicare-providers-through-innovative-payment -systems-3/. Accessed May 26, 2016.

136. Centers for Medicare & Medicaid Services. The merit-based incentive payment system (MIPS) & alternative payment models (APMS): MACRA: delivery system reform, Medicare payment reform. https://www.cms.gov/Medicare/Quality -Initiatives-Patient-Assessment-Instruments/Value -Based-Programs/MACRA-MIPS-and-APMs /MACRA-MIPS-and-APMs.html. Accessed March 10, 2016.

137. Findlay, S. Health policy brief: Medicare's new physician payment system. Health Aff. http://

healthaffairs.org/healthpolicybriefs/brief_pdfs/healthpolicybrief_156.pdf. Accessed May 26, 2016.

138. Morse S. CMS makes $10 million in grants available to help with MACRA transition. *Medical Practice Insider.* June 10, 2016. http://www.medicalpracticeinsider.com/news/cms-makes-10-million-grants-available-help-macra-transition. Accessed June 13, 2016.

139. Department of Health and Human Services. Medicare Access and CHIP Reauthorization Act of 2015 quality improvement program: notice of proposed rulemaking. https://www.cms.gov/Medicare/Quality-Initiatives-Patient-Assessment-Instruments/Value-Based-Programs/MACRA-MIPS-and-APMs/NPRM-QPP-Fact-Sheet.pdf. Accessed June 13, 2016.

140. Snyder L, Rudowitz R. Medicaid financing: how does it work and what are the implications? The Henry J. Kaiser Family Foundation. Issue Brief. May 20, 2015. http://kff.org/medicaid/issue-brief/medicaid-financing-how-does-it-work-and-what-are-the-implications/. Accessed May 8, 2016.

141. Centers for Medicare & Medicaid Services. Medicaid & CHIP: March 2016 monthly applications, eligibility determinations and enrollment report. May 25, 2016. https://www.medicaid.gov/medicaid-chip-program-information/program-information/downloads/march-2016-enrollment-report.pdf. Accessed May 9, 2016.

142. Department of Health and Human Services. 2014 annual report on the quality of health care for adults enrolled in Medicaid. November 2014. https://www.medicaid.gov/medicaid-chip-program-information/by-topics/quality-of-care/downloads/2014-adult-sec-rept.pdf. Accessed May 9, 2016.

143. Almanac of Policy Issues. Medicaid: an overview. September 2000. http://www.policyalmanac.org/health/archive/hhs_medicaid.shtml. Accessed May 7, 2016.

144. Medicaid.gov. Medicaid overview: it's July 4th - Independence day! https://www.medicaid.gov/medicaid-50th-anniversary/overall-medicaid/overview-medicaid-anniversary.html. Accessed May 31, 2016.

145. Center on Budget and Policy Priorities. Policy basics: introduction to Medicaid. http://www.cbpp.org/research/health/policy-basics-introduction-to-medicaid. Accessed May 21, 2016.

146. The Henry J. Kaiser Family Foundation. Medicaid's role for dual eligible beneficiaries. August 2013. https://kaiserfamilyfoundation.files.wordpress.com/2013/08/7846-04-medicaids-role-for-dual-eligible-beneficiaries.pdf. Accessed September 1, 2016.

147. Medicaid.gov. Benefits. https://www.medicaid.gov/medicaid-chip-program-information/by-topics/benefits/medicaid-benefits.html. Accessed May 6, 2016.

148. Lambrew JM. The state children's health insurance program: past, present, and future. The Commonwealth Fund, February 2007. http://www.commonwealthfund.org/publications/fund-reports/2007/feb/the-state-childrens-health-insurance-program--past--present--and-future. Accessed May 9, 2016.

149. HHS.gov. CMS announces $32 million to increase number of children with quality, affordable health coverage. http://www.hhs.gov/about/news/2016/06/13/cms-announces-32-million-increase-number-children-with-quality-affordable-health-coverage.html#. Accessed June 15, 2016.

150. The Henry J. Kaiser Family Foundation. Total number of children ever enrolled in CHIP annually. http://kff.org/other/state-indicator/annual-chip-enrollment/. Accessed May 14, 2016.

151. HHS.gov. HHS issues major rule modernizing Medicaid managed care. http://www.hhs.gov/about/news/2016/04/25/hhs-issues-major-rule-modernizing-medicaid-managed-care.html. Accessed May 15, 2016.

152. Rosenbaum S. Ushering in a new era in Medicaid managed care. *The Commonwealth Fund.* http://www.commonwealthfund.org/publications/blog/2015/jul/ushering-in-a-new-era-in-medicaid. Accessed May 15, 2016.

153. Centers for Medicare & Medicaid Services. Center for Medicaid and CHIP services. https://www.cms.gov/About-CMS/Agency-Information/CMSLeadership/Office_CMCSC.html. Accessed May 12, 2016.

154. Medicaid.gov. CHIPRA. https://www.medicaid.gov/chip/chipra/chipra.html. Accessed May 13, 2016.

155. Medicaid.gov. Core set of children's health care quality measures for Medicaid and CHIP (child core set). https://www.medicaid.gov/medicaid-chip-program-information/by-topics/quality-of-care/downloads/2016-child-core-set.pdf. Accessed May 13, 2016.

156. Medicaid.gov. Adult health care quality measures: initial core set of adult health care quality measures for Medicaid-eligible adults. https://www.medicaid.gov/medicaid-chip-program-information/by-topics/quality-of-care/adult-health-care-quality-measures.html. Accessed May 13, 2016.

157. Medicaid.gov. Core set of adult health care quality measures for Medicaid (adult score set). https://www.medicaid.gov/medicaid-chip-program-information/by-topics/quality-of-care/downloads/2016-adult-core-set.pdf. May 13, 2016.

158. Siegel B, Murray M, Hawkins D. Time to take Medicaid quality seriously. April 14, 2015. *Health Affairs Blog.* http://healthaffairs.org/blog/2015/04/14/time-to-take-medicaid-quality-seriously/. Accessed May 13, 2016.

159. Russell K. Court holds that states have choice whether to join Medicaid expansion. SCOTUSblog. http://www.scotusblog.com/2012/06/court-holds

-that-states-have-choice-whether-to-join-medicaid
-expansion/. Accessed May 13, 2016.

160. The Henry J. Kaiser Family Foundation. Status of
state action on the Medicaid expansion. March
2014.   http://kff.org/health-reform/state-indicator
/state-activity-around-expanding-medicaid-under
-the-affordable-care-act/. Accessed May 13, 2016.

161. Jost T. CBO lowers marketplace enrollment projections,
increases Medicaid growth projections (updated).
Health Affairs Blog. January 2016. http://healthaffairs
.org/blog/2016/01/26/cbo-lowers-marketplace
-enrollment-projections-increases-medicaid-growth
-projections/. Accessed May 16, 2016.

162. The Henry J. Kaiser Family Foundation. Medicaid
enrollment & spending growth: FY 2015 & 2016.
http://kff.org/medicaid/issue-brief/medicaid
-enrollment-spending-growth-fy-2015-2016/.
Accessed April 29, 2016.

163. Executive Office of the President of the United
States. The Council of Economic Advisors. Missed
opportunities: the consequences of state decisions
not to expand Medicaid. July 2014. https://www
.whitehouse.gov/sites/default/files/docs/missed
_opportunities_medicaid.pdf. Accessed June 3, 2016.

164. The Henry J. Kaiser Family Foundation. Medicaid
and CHIP eligibility, enrollment, renewal and cost-
sharing policies as of January 2016: findings from
a 50-state survey. http://kff.org/report-section
/medicaid-and-chip-eligibility-enrollment-renewal
-and-cost-sharing-policies-as-of-january-2016
-executive-summary/. Accessed May 16, 2016.

165. Medicaid.gov. Medicaid disproportionate share
hospital (DSH) payments. https://www.medicaid
.gov/medicaid-chip-program-information/by
-topics/financing-and-reimbursement/medicaid
-disproportionate-share-hospital-dsh-payments
.html. Accessed May 19, 2016.

166. The Henry J. Kaiser Family Foundation. Federal
Medicaid disproportionate share hospital (DSH)
allotment. FY 2015. http://kff.org/medicaid/state
-indicator/federal-dsh-allotments/. Accessed May
19, 2016.

167. Obamacare Facts. Obamacare individual mandate.
http://obamacarefacts.com/obamacare-individual
-mandate/. Accessed May 4, 2016.

168. Chow A. Who is exempt from Obamacare's mandate?
FindLaw. Law & Daily Life blog. September 28, 2013.
http://blogs.findlaw.com/law_and_life/2013/09
/who-is-exempt-from-obamacares-mandate.html.
Accessed May 19, 2016.

169. Gruber J. Why we need the individual mandate. Center
for American Progress. April 8, 2010. https://www
.americanprogress.org/issues/healthcare/report

/2010/04/08/7720/why-we-need-the-individual
-mandate/. Accessed May 19, 2916.

170. Obamacare Facts. SHOP exchange: small business
health options program. http://obamacarefacts.com
/insurance-exchange/shop-exchange/. April 10,2016.

171. Obamacare Facts. What is the health insurance
marketplace? http://obamacarefacts.com/insurance
-exchange/health-insurance-marketplace. Accessed
May 16, 2016.

172. The Henry J. Kaiser Family Foundation. State health
insurance marketplace types, 2016. http://kff.org
/health-reform/state-indicator/state-health-insurance
-marketplace-types/. Accessed May 20, 2016.

173. Uberoi NK, Mach AL, Fernandez B. Overview of
health insurance exchanges. Congressional Research
Service. June 10, 2015. https://www.fas.org/sgp/crs
/misc/R44065.pdf. Accessed May 24, 2016.

174. Obamacare Facts. Obamacare employer mandate.
http://obamacarefacts.com/obamacare-employer
-mandate/. Accessed May 24, 2016.

175. Obamacare Facts. Obamacare enrollment numbers.
http://obamacarefacts.com/sign-ups/obamacare
-enrollment-numbers/. Accessed May 25, 2016.

176. Congressional Budget Office. Updated estimates of the
insurance coverage provisions of the Affordable Care
Act. https://www.cbo.gov/sites/default/files/114th
-congress-2015-2016/reports/49892/49892
-breakout-AppendixB.pdf. Accessed May 25, 2016.

177. Congressional Budget Office. Federal subsidies for
health insurance coverage for people under age
65: 2016–2026. https://www.cbo.gov/sites/default
/files/114th-congress-2015-2016/reports/51385
-HealthInsuranceBaseline.pdf. Accessed May 25, 2016.

178. U.S. Census Bureau. Health insurance coverage
in the United States: 2014. http://www.census.gov
/library/publications/2015/demo/p60-253.html.
Accessed May 25, 2016.

179. Department of Health and Human Services. Assistant
Secretary for Planning and Evaluation. Health
insurance marketplaces 2016 open enrollment
period. January 7, 2016. https://aspe.hhs.gov/sites
/default/files/pdf/167981/MarketPlaceEnrollJan2016
.pdf. Accessed May 25, 2016.

180. Diamond D. Thanks, Obamacare: American's
uninsured rate is below 10% for first time ever.
Forbes. August 12, 2015. http://www.forbes.com/sites
/dandiamond/2015/08/12/for-first-time-americas
-uninsured-rate-is-below-10/#5ffdeff7741c.
Accessed April 12, 2016.

181. Dubrava P. A summary of "bitter-pill: why medical
bills are killing us," by Steven Brill. *Holding the Light.*
http://patriciadubrava.com/?p=187. Accessed June
9, 2016.

CHAPTER 9

Long-Term Care

CHAPTER OVERVIEW

Long-term care needs are not confined only to older Americans, but older Americans are the fastest-growing proportion of the population and are the major consumers of long-term care services. Advances in medical care have made a longer life span possible, with accompanying challenges presented by chronic disease and physical limitations. This chapter provides an overview of the major components of the diverse array of long-term care services available in institutional, community-based, and home-based settings for individuals in all age groups who require long-term care. This chapter also reviews components of the Patient Protection and Affordable Care Act that affect long-term care services and recent developments in this area of health care.

Each individual life span, from birth to death, can be seen as a connected flow of events—a continuum. The unrelenting progression of time is the one constant that expresses the diverse range of life's possibilities. An infant may be born with a birth defect, a young adult may suffer a head injury from an automobile accident, or an older adult may have a stroke. Unanticipated events such as these have a profound long-term impact on an individual's capacity to develop or to maintain abilities for self-care and independence. These individuals may require very different kinds and intensities of personal care assistance, healthcare services, and/or psychosocial and housing services over an extended segment of their life span.

The age, diagnosis, and ability to perform personal self-care and the sites of care delivery vary widely for recipients of long-term care. Thus, long-term care requires diversified, yet coordinated, services and flexibility within the service system to respond to recipients' changing needs over time.

The ideal healthcare delivery system provides participants with comprehensive personal, social, and medical care services. This ideal system requires mechanisms that continually guide and track individual clients over time through the array of services at all levels and intensities of care that they require.[1] Because it generates a continuous flow of high costs over an extended period, long-term care has a particular need to use what the American Hospital Association calls a seamless continuum of care[2] that promotes the highest quality of life but still responds to growing public concerns about cost-effectiveness.[3] The particular package of services provided to each person should be tailored to meet his or her needs. Service needs vary from assistance with personal care and basic needs for food and safe shelter, to rehabilitation when possible, to socialization opportunities. Additionally, the type and extent of physical disability and the intensity of services required determine the location of long-term care. For example, an older individual with paralysis after a stroke may be able to remain at home with services that dovetail with family caregivers in the home. Another person with a similar disability may require nursing home placement because that environment best meets the particular requirements of the situation.

Configuring a package of services that promotes independence and maintains lifestyle quality as far as possible within personal, community, and national resources makes the variety of long-term care services complex and sometimes confusing. Concern about cost-effectiveness and the desire to accommodate personal and family desires, finances, and reimbursement eligibility result in the need for both the availability of an array of services and coordination of those services to meet individual needs in the most effective way.

Population demographics and the types and availability of healthcare services in the United States have evolved over the past 50 years. The economic ramifications of a rapidly increasing population of older Americans, advances in medicine making life-sustaining measures available, and an emphasis on preventive care and healthy lifestyles all have impacted the continued growth of the population who require or potentially will require long-term care services. Older adults represent the largest population group requiring long-term care services. Current estimates place the population 65 years of age and older at 44.7 million, 14.1 percent of the population, or about one in every seven Americans.[4] The number of persons aged 65 years or older is expected to grow to 21.7 percent of the population by 2040, totaling 82.3 million. A current U.S. Census projection estimates that the population 65 years or older will more than double in number between 2013 and 2060, reaching 98.2 million by year 2060.[4] The "oldest old" population, 85 years of age and older, is expected to grow from 5.8 million in 2010 to 8.7 million by 2030, with projections that this group will reach 19 million by 2050 (**FIGURES 9-1** and **9-2**).[4,5]

Many people will grow old alone because of smaller family size, single parenting, and divorce. The increasing economic need for family members to delay retirement and work outside the home also reduces the availability of family caregivers to participate in the informal family caregiving system. Family members are now more geographically dispersed, decreasing their availability to care for dependent, older family members.

▶ Development of Long-Term Care Services

The colonists who emigrated from Europe to the New World brought with them many of the social values and institutional models of their native countries. One of these, the almshouse, was a place where people who were sick or disabled or older adults who lacked adequate family or financial support could be cared for in a communal setting. Charitable community members purchased private homes and converted them to almshouses that operated as communal residences. Municipal and county governments also created homes and "infirmaries" to care for impoverished older adults. These early models were the basis for "homes for the elderly," which existed until the economic upheavals of the Great Depression and the restructuring of the social welfare system after World War II.

The economic devastation experienced during the Great Depression of the 1930s affected the availability of long-term care services, especially homes for older adults, in several ways. Operating

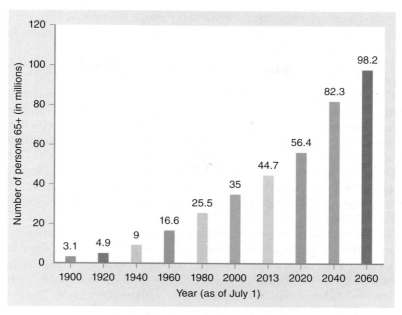

FIGURE 9-1 Projected Number (in Millions) of Persons 65 Years of Age or Older by 2060
U.S. Bureau of the Census.

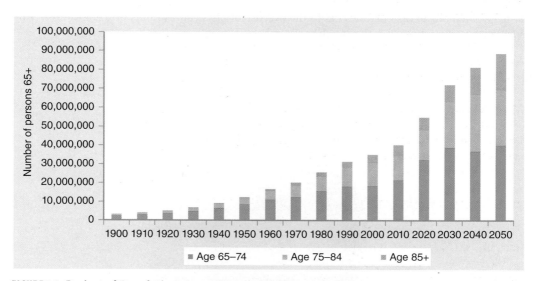

FIGURE 9-2 Projected Population, Age 65 Years and Older, 2000–2050
U.S. Bureau of the Census.

small private nursing homes became attractive to people in financial danger of losing their homes to mortgage foreclosure because taking in outsiders and providing care generated a new source of income. After the Great Depression, many local charitable agencies could no longer afford to provide care based on the almshouse tradition, and the federal government became more involved in developing, overseeing, and paying for long-term care services as part of the social welfare reforms, such as the 1935 Social Security Act.[6] The Social Security Act provided financial assistance for particular categories of older Americans and people with disabilities. Additionally, the Social Security Act established a form of old age and survivor's insurance that allowed workers and their employers to contribute to a fund that supplemented retirement income. This form of income security reduced the extent of indigence frequently found in the older population and increased the amount of secure income available to older Americans for services and care in later years. Government lending programs available to not-for-profit organizations beginning in the 1950s spurred the development of nursing homes in this sector; major growth in the proprietary (for-profit) sector did not occur until after the passage of Medicare and Medicaid legislation in 1965. The Centers for Medicare & Medicaid Services (CMS) reported the ownership basis of nursing homes in the *Nursing Home Data Compendium, 2013*. Now, more than two-thirds operate on a for-profit basis (**FIGURE 9-3**).[7]

Public and private homes for older adults often varied in the adequacy of care and the kinds of services provided. Nursing homes often were viewed as places where minimal custodial care required to meet the basic needs of food, clothing, and shelter was provided, sometimes in unhygienic and inhumane environments. Frequently, nursing homes were places where older and frail adults, some of society's most vulnerable members, were taken to die. They were not seen as options where residents could receive needed care to prolong or enhance the quality of their lives. Physical care often was substandard, and emotional, spiritual, and social needs were ignored. Because many frail, older people suffer from perceptual and cognitive disabilities in addition to physical disabilities, their behavior in a group setting was often considered by nursing home staff to be problematic and sometimes led to the overuse of physical restraints or chemical restraints such as sedatives and mood-altering drugs.

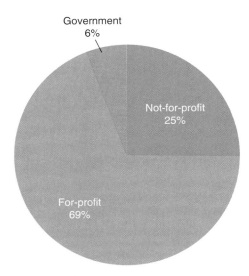

FIGURE 9-3 **Percent Distribution of Nursing Homes by Type of Ownership.**
Data from Centers for Medicare & Medicaid Services Nursing Home Data Compendium, 2013.

The provision of home nursing care also has a long tradition in the United States as an alternative to institutional care provided in hospitals and nursing homes. Family members traditionally have provided home care to their own relatives. An interest in providing formal professional home care services began in the late 1800s as a social response to the unhealthy living conditions of immigrants residing in urban tenements. Such crowded and unsanitary conditions became a public health concern because they were frequently implicated in the spread of contagious diseases, such as tuberculosis, typhoid, and smallpox. Agencies such as the Visiting Nurses Association were established to provide trained nurses to tend to the sick in their homes. Their role quickly expanded to include preventive education regarding hygiene, nutrition, and coordination of social welfare interventions, especially in caring for society's most vulnerable ill, low-income or disabled populations.[8]

The passage of Medicare and Medicaid legislation in 1965 provided more stable sources of reimbursement than were previously available only through private pay and charitable funding and promoted the expansion of the long-term care industry. Medicare and Medicaid affected the long-term care industry in several ways. These programs established minimum requirements for standards of care and services for providers to qualify for reimbursement. They also provided funding sources for older Americans, people with disabilities, and those lacking the means to pay for care. This funding simultaneously attracted both the scrupulous and the unscrupulous into the long-term care industry, as it quickly became apparent that being a provider of long-term care could be very profitable.

The long-term care industry came under increasing scrutiny in the early 1970s during congressional hearings on the nursing home industry, after the publication of several hundred exposés in newspapers and additional publications such as the Nader Report and Mary Adelaide Mendelson's book, *Tender Loving Greed*. The litany of nursing home corruption and abuses that were exposed during that period included the following:[9,10]

- Care that did not recognize the right to human dignity
- A lack of activities for residents
- Untrained and inadequate staff, including untrained administrators
- Unsanitary conditions
- Theft of residents' belongings
- Inadequate safety precautions (especially fire protection)
- Unauthorized and unnecessary use of restraints
- Both overmedication and undermedication of patients
- Failure to act in a timely manner on complaints and reprisals against those who complained
- Discrimination against patients who were members of minority groups
- A lack of dental and psychiatric care
- Negligence leading to injury and death
- Ineffective inspections and nonenforcement of laws that were meant to regulate the nursing home industry
- Reimbursement fraud

These congressional hearings and simultaneous public outcry resulted in stricter enforcement of Medicare and Medicaid guidelines and credentialing, increased establishment and enforcement of nursing home and home care licensure, more active accreditation procedures by The Joint Commission, laws related to the reporting of elder abuse, federal guidelines regulating the use of physical restraints, and establishment of ombudsman programs. All these measures led to a much more regulated and responsive long-term care industry. Vocal and astute consumers also have provided economic and social mandates for high-quality standards of care including meaningful, organized quality-assurance processes to be maintained in the long-term care industry overall. The Omnibus Budget Reconciliation Act of 1987 legislated new guidelines and restrictions on the use of physical and chemical restraints, established a nursing home resident bill of rights, mandated quality assurance standards, established a standard survey process, and mandated training and educational requirements for nursing home staff.[11]

▶ Modes of Long-Term Care Service Delivery

Long-term care facilities (LTCFs) are institutions such as nursing homes, skilled nursing facilities (SNFs), and assisted-living facilities that provide health care to people who are unable to manage independently in the community. This care may represent custodial or chronic care management or short-term rehabilitative services.[12] The site of care delivery categorizes long-term care programs. Institution-based services are those long-term care services provided within an institution such as a nursing home, hospital with inpatient extended care or rehabilitation facility, or inpatient hospice. Community-based services coordinate, manage, and deliver long-term care services such as adult day-care programs, residential group homes, or care in the recipient's home.

Skilled Nursing Care

A skilled nursing facility (SNF) that is Medicare and Medicaid certified is defined as "a facility, or distinct part of one, primarily engaged in providing skilled nursing care and related services for people requiring medical or nursing care, or rehabilitation services."[13] Skilled nursing care is provided by or under the direct supervision of licensed nursing personnel, such as registered nurses and licensed practical nurses, and emphasis is on the provision of 24-hour nursing care and the availability of other types of services. Nursing home residents can be of any age, although most are adults in their later years. The typical nursing home resident is an older woman with cognitive impairment who was living alone on a limited income before nursing home placement. The decreased ability to function independently and a lack of family caregivers are additional factors associated with an increased risk of nursing home admission.

In 2013, the CMS reported that 1.4 million Americans resided in 15,643 SNFs.[7] One of seven or approximately 14 percent of SNF residents are under the age of 65 years, and six of seven or approximately 86 percent are 65 years of age and older.[14] Because SNFs are only one portion of the array of types of long-term care facilities, and an LTCF may provide more than one level of service in the same facility, an exact number of residents in skilled nursing care has been much more difficult to ascertain. The biennial National Study of Long-Term Care Providers (NSLTCP) sponsored by the Centers for Disease Control and Prevention/National Center for Health Statistics (NCHS) is a groundbreaking initiative first implemented in 2012. These recurring studies monitor and detail ongoing trends in the major sectors of the paid, regulated provision of long-term care. The NSLTCP reports include data and overview summaries about nursing homes, home healthcare agencies, hospices, residential care communities, and adult day-services centers. The NSLTCP reports provide reliable and timely statistical information about residents and participants receiving long-term care, agencies that provide those services, and descriptions of services provided.[15]

Annual national expenditures for care in nursing care facilities and continuing care communities in 2014 alone totaled $155.6 billion. Medicare and Medicaid paid the largest portion (55 percent), and 45 percent was funded by out-of-pocket, private insurance, other third party or other health

TABLE 9-1 Sources of Payment for Nursing Home Care*, 2014		
Source of Payment	**Amount in Billions***	**Percentage**
Total	155.6	100.0
Medicare	35.7	22.9
Medicaid	49.6	31.9
Other third-party/other health insurance	16.0	10.3
Private (out of pocket, other private funds)	41.2	26.5
Private insurance	13.1	8.4

*Care in nursing home facilities and in continuing care retirement communities. Numbers may not add to totals due to rounding.
Modified from Centers for Medicare and Medicaid Services.

insurance. (See **TABLE 9-1**.)[16] At an average of $250 per day for a private room and $220 per day for a semiprivate room, the 2015 national average cost per resident had reached $91,250 per year for a private room and $80,300 per year for a semiprivate room.[17] The nursing home industry remains a dominant sector of the long-term care industry, with expenditures for care in a nursing home reported as almost double those for home care.[16]

Despite the burgeoning numbers of older Americans, national nursing home occupancy rates have declined from 84.5 percent occupancy in 1995 to 80.8 percent occupancy in 2013.[18] Many factors are cited as contributing to the decline in SNF occupancy rates. Today's older adults are healthier, delaying the need for skilled nursing services. The vastly increased availability of assisted-living facilities, defined later in this chapter, and the availability of other community-based assistance through day care and home care also are playing roles in delaying the need for SNF care.

Typical staffing in SNFs includes a physician medical director, a nursing home administrator, a director of nursing, at least one registered nurse on the day and evening shifts, and either a registered nurse or a licensed practical nurse on the night shift. Certified nursing assistants provide direct custodial care under the supervision of licensed nursing personnel and represent the majority of all nursing staff employed by SNFs.[19] SNFs use the services of an array of ancillary professionals who may be employed by the SNFs or contracted. These services include physical therapy, occupational therapy, pharmacy, nutrition, recreational therapy, podiatry, dentistry, laboratory, and hospice.[19] Support staff, including dietary, laundry, housekeeping, and maintenance workers, complete the employee complement. The licensed nursing home administrator, along with the owner/operator, is responsible for carrying out the regulatory mandates regarding the mix and ratio of licensed and unlicensed personnel and the availability of licensed nursing personnel on an around-the-clock basis to provide skilled care and supervision.

Nursing homes are highly regulated by both state licensure and federal certification. The 1987 Omnibus Budget Reconciliation Act increased government involvement in nursing home industry regulation by[11]:

- Mandating regularly scheduled comprehensive assessments of the functional capacity of residents in nursing homes
- Establishing training standards for nursing home aides
- Placing restrictions on the use of physical restraints and psychoactive drugs
- Establishing a nursing home resident bill of rights
- Setting guidelines for the role of the medical director, including continuing education, involvement, and responsibility

States license nursing home administrators. Individual states set criteria for licensure in relationship to minimum age, educational requirements, passing examination scores, and continuing education requirements. The National Association of Boards of Examiners of Long-Term Care Administrators "develops and administers the licensing examinations that administrators take to get licensed by their respective states."[20] The examination is required by all states and the District of Columbia.[20] A lack of nursing home compliance with state and federal mandates can lead to penalties such as direct fines, exclusion from Medicare and Medicaid certification, and withdrawal of nursing home licensure. Accreditation through The Joint Commission provides an additional quality check. Although highly desirable, The Joint Commission accreditation remains voluntary.

A 1986 report by the Institute of Medicine, "For Profit Enterprise in Health Care," synthesized research on the quality of nursing home care based on for-profit and not-for-profit ownership noting that for-profit and investor-owned nursing homes tend to provide care of lower quality than their not-for-profit counterparts.[21] These findings have been replicated by other studies over the years.[22] In 2011, the Government Accountability Office reported findings of a first-ever analysis of the 10 largest for-profit nursing home chains, which noted among other findings that these facilities had "the lowest staffing levels; the highest number of deficiencies identified by public regulatory agencies and the highest number of deficiencies causing harm or jeopardy to residents."[22] It is important to note that research findings do not necessarily apply to an individual nursing home as "some for-profit nursing facilities give excellent care and some not-for-profit nursing facilities give poor care, but the general rule is documented in study after study: not-for-profit nursing facilities generally provide better care to their residents."[22] In response to concerns such as these, the Patient Protection and Affordable Care Act (ACA) requires Medicare- and Medicaid-certified SNFs to publicly disclose detailed ownership information, accountability requirements, expenditures, and other information related to quality indicators. It also requires these facilities to publish standardized information reported on the publicly accessible *Nursing Home Compare* website that enables Medicare enrollees to compare facilities.[23]

Assisted-Living Facilities

Assisted-living facilities (ALFs) are appropriate for long-term care for individuals who do not require skilled nursing services and whose needs lie more in the custodial and supportive realm. While a universal interagency definition of assisted living has not yet been achieved, key components include 24-hour oversight, housekeeping services, provision of at least two meals a day, and personal assistance with at least two of the following: bathing, dressing, medications. An underlying philosophy includes accommodation of individual resident's personal needs to promote independence in a home-like residential setting, coupled with activities and opportunities that

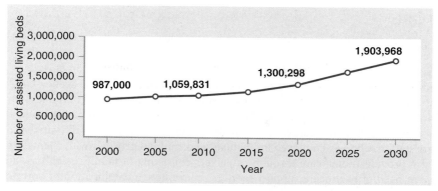

FIGURE 9-4 Projected Growth of Assisted Living Beds Based on Population Growth for Those 75 Years and Older

National Center for Assisted Living, reprinted with permission.

promote community and family involvement and maximize resident's dignity, autonomy, choice, and safety.[24] Assisted-living facilities vary significantly in size, ranging from just a few residents to several hundred. They may take the form of small to large homes with just a few residents or large multi-unit apartment complexes with several hundred residents. Many assisted-living facilities contract with home health agencies to provide skilled nursing care and with hospice service providers when such services are needed by individual residents.

The assisted-living population is expected to grow to almost 2 million individuals by 2030 (**FIGURE 9-4**).[24] The typical assisted-living resident is described as an 87-year-old female who requires assistance with two or more activities of daily living and who will reside in assisted living for an average of 22 months.[25]

States carry out oversight and regulation of assisted-living facilities at varying levels. These variations in laws and regulations create a diverse operating environment as well as a wide range of terminology and available services for consumers. The quality of facilities, care, and services therefore may be an exclusive function of the policies of the owner organization or a combination of owner and organization policies coupled with state regulatory oversight.

Costs of assisted living are borne largely from private resources, although in certain circumstances supplemental Social Security income, private health insurance, long-term care insurance (LTCI), or special government rent subsidies for low-income older adults may apply. Estimates place the average monthly cost at more than $3,600, but costs can range across a broad continuum depending on the level of amenities desired in a facility and the types of services required. Residents most often fund accommodations from personal resources or from LTCI policies.[16–17]

Residential institutions such as adult homes, board and care homes, and group homes for people with mental or developmental disabilities also represent assisted-living arrangements. Care provided in adult homes has been available only to people who are for the most part healthy but limited in their ability to do their own housekeeping, household maintenance, and cooking. Residents must be able, for the most part, to meet their own personal care needs for dressing, eating, bathing, toileting, and ambulation unassisted. Oversight of residents may include services such as supervision of medications to the extent of reminding residents to take their medication or providing some assistance with bathing, grooming, transportation, laundry, and simple housekeeping.

Home Care

Home care is community-based care provided to individuals in their own residences. Home care may be either a long-term provision of supportive care and services to chronically ill clients to avoid institutionalization or short-term intermittent care of clients after an episode of illness or hospitalization. Home care may be provided through the formal system of agency-employed professional home care providers, such as registered nurses, licensed practical nurses, home health aides, physical therapists, occupational therapists, speech-language pathologists, social workers, personal care aides, and homemakers, who make home visits. A considerably smaller number of home care staff may be self-employed individuals who contract privately with clients. An informal system also provides home care through caregivers consisting of family, neighbors, and friends of people in need of healthcare support services. Very often, a combination of both formal and informal systems delivers home care.

Professional home care services originated in social welfare initiatives in the early 1900s in public response to the horrific living conditions of immigrants in U.S. industrialized cities. Public health concerns also gained impetus at that time as the "germ theory" of disease became accepted, and local, state, and national health departments and agencies mandated the control of contagious disease using preventive hygiene and sanitation measures as public health standards.

After Medicare's enactment of reimbursement for home care services in 1965, the number of Medicare-certified home health agencies (HHAs) grew more than threefold to 5,983 between the years 1967 and 1985, with public health agencies dominating the home care industry.[26] In the late 1980s, significant additional growth in the number of agencies ceased due to Medicare reimbursement issues.[26] However, with Medicare reimbursement changes since the 1990s, the number of Medicare-certified, hospital-based, and freestanding for-profit home health agencies grew rapidly.[26] The home care industry expanded its scope of services in response to demographic, economic, and legislative changes that include:

- An increase in the number of older persons and their expressed desire to remain in their own homes for care whenever possible
- Decreased numbers of informal caregivers that are available to provide in-home care to their relatives
- Increased innovations in high-technology home care that have redefined and expanded the categories of diseases and chronic conditions that can be cared for effectively in the home
- Medicare and Medicaid reimbursement that supported expanded coverage
- The 1999 Olmstead decision of the Supreme Court that upheld the right of citizens to receive care in the community

In 2013, about 3.5 million Medicare beneficiaries received home health services from 12,613 home health agencies at a Medicare cost of $17.9 billion.[27] Approximately 70 percent of the freestanding home healthcare agencies were classified as proprietary or for-profit.[28] Medicare remains the largest payer for home healthcare services, accounting for almost 42 percent of total annual home care expenditures in 2014 (**TABLE 9-2**).[16]

Eligibility for Medicare reimbursement of home care services originally included four criteria:

1.   Home care must include the provision of skilled nursing care or physical, occupational, or speech therapy; or medical social services; or a combination of any of these services as warranted by the patient's condition.
2.   The person must be confined to the home.

TABLE 9-2 Sources of Payment for Home Health Care		
Source of Payment	**Amount in Billions***	**Percentage**
Total	83.2	100.0
Medicare	34.7	41.9
Medicaid	29.6	35.6
Other third-party/other health insurance	3.2	3.9
Private (out of pocket, other private funds)	7.4	8.9
Private insurance	8.3	9.9

*Numbers may not add to totals due to rounding.

Modified from Centers for Medicare & Medicaid Services.

3. A physician must order that home care services are required.
4. The home care agency must meet the minimum quality standards as outlined by Medicare and must be Medicare certified.

In 2011 under the Affordable Care Act, Congress added more eligibility criteria for Medicare reimbursement for home care to those listed above. Additional criteria included a requirement for Medicare beneficiaries receiving home care to have a face-to-face office visit encounter or a telehealth visit with a physician or nurse practitioner when home health care is ordered. This change was intended to ensure that beneficiaries receive a complete evaluation when home health care is ordered. Tighter supervision of therapy services provided under the home health benefit also was included. Under the new requirement, patients must be assessed by a qualified therapist at specific therapy intervals. The additional review was intended to serve as a safeguard against manipulation of therapy visits to garner increased payments.[28]

In 2006 the Centers for Medicare & Medicaid Services had recommended a "postacute care" (PAC) reform plan that emphasized a patient-centered approach giving more choice and control of post-hospitalization services to patients and caregivers, providing a seamless continuum of care through better service coordination, and ensuring quality services in the most appropriate setting.[29] The reform plan, called "Medicaid Money Follows the Person" (MFP), set demonstration projects in motion through 2011 by providing grants to states for additional federal matching funds for Medicaid beneficiaries making the transition from an institution back to their homes or to other community settings. The ACA extended the MFP demonstrations through 2016. By mid-2015, 44 states and the District of Columbia had received federal grants under the program and more than 52,140 Medicaid beneficiaries had transitioned through the MFP demonstration and another 10,265 transitions were in process. MFP is due to expire at the end of 2016, leaving questions about whether states will be able to continue to offer all MFP services if the program is not re-authorized.[30]

Other long-term care provisions under the ACA include a "Community First Choice Option in Medicaid," which provides states with an increased federal Medicaid matching rate to support community-based attendant services for individuals who require an institutional level of care[31,32]; The "State Balancing Incentive Program" enhances federal matching funds to states to increase the proportion of Medicaid long-term services and support dollars allocated toward home and community-based services.[32] This program established the Federal Coordinated Health Care Office, charged "to improve the integration of benefits and increase coordination between federal and state governments for individuals receiving both Medicare and Medicaid benefits." This office has launched state demonstration projects to identify and evaluate delivery systems and payment models for individuals eligible for both Medicare and Medicaid that can be rapidly tested and, if successful, replicated in other states.[33]

Research published between 2000 and 2013 in the *New England Journal of Medicine*, the *American Journal of Managed Care*, *Journal of the American Geriatrics Society*, *Health Care Financing Review*, *Cochrane Database of Systematic Reviews*, and other sources notes the significant cost-effectiveness of home care when compared with the higher costs of providing institutional care for a variety of conditions such as the need for intravenous antibiotic therapy, diabetes, chronic obstructive pulmonary disease, congestive heart failure, and in the provision of palliative care for advanced illnesses.[34]

Medicare certification of home care agencies requires state licensing.[35] Most states issue a license for one year and require resubmission of an application and an annual state reinspection performed by a survey team. The state licensing agency has the right to investigate complaints and to conduct periodic reviews of all licensure requirements. The few agencies that treat only private pay or private insurance patients may not require a license; however, most home healthcare agencies want to participate in Medicare and Medicaid, so they maintain certification standards. Participation in voluntary accreditation indicates that home care agencies have a commitment to continuous quality improvement. Organizations that are actively engaged in the accreditation process for home healthcare agencies include the Community Health Accreditation Program, the Joint Commission, and the Accreditation Commission for Health Care, Inc.

Until the proliferation of social programs in the 1960s and 1970s, individuals requiring long-term health care usually were a cared for by family members and/or friends in the family home. This informal care system provided a valuable social service at little or no public cost. This arrangement is still the most used system of long-term care as family members care for more than 80 percent of the older adults needing some level of assistance. The informal care system offers significant savings to the public; however, the potential for caregivers to suffer physical and emotional burnout and the growing inability of family caregivers to fully manage care without outside assistance have begun to diminish these savings.

Recent estimates place the number of unpaid family caregivers who provide hands-on care for persons age 50 or older at more than 34.2 million. Most adult caregivers assist family members, most commonly a parent or parent-in-law. The majority of caregivers are female, 60 percent of whom, in addition to providing caregiving to a family member, also are employed outside the home.[36] Family caregivers frequently are required to make major compromises in their finances, lifestyles, and personal freedom to care for family members. The costs can be high. Stresses experienced by the caregiver can lead to exhaustion, illness, and depression.[37] In addition, with increased longevity, middle-aged individuals often find themselves caring for their children and their aged parents simultaneously. Dubbed the "sandwich generation,"[38] these caregivers suffer even more stress from this dual role, which in many cases becomes a triple role for those who also provide care for their grandchildren. Respite care, discussed later in this chapter, is one mechanism to provide solutions to this dilemma. Employers also experience losses because of the demands of caregiving on their employees. One study estimated the annual costs of lost productivity for U.S. businesses due to caregiving at nearly $34 billion.[39] Employer costs are associated with worker replacement, absenteeism, workday interruptions, elder care crises, and supervisory time.[36,39] Some larger employers are responding with flexible scheduling and other considerations to help accommodate their employees' caregiving responsibilities for family members.[39]

Estimates place the market value of long-term care delivered by unpaid family members and friends at more than $470 billion per year[40], almost double the annual national healthcare expenditures for nursing home and home care combined. The economic and personal contributions of the informal caregiving system form the foundation of the nation's chronic care system and deserve more policy-level attention and support. The federal government took an important first step to assist family caregivers through the Family Medical Leave Act (FMLA) of 1993, providing up to 12 workweeks of unpaid leave per year for the birth of a child or adoption of a child, or for employees to care for themselves or a sick family member, while ensuring continuation of health benefits and job security.[41] However, the FMLA has serious shortcomings. It provides only for unpaid leave, a criterion that makes its use financially unfeasible for many individuals. Also, the FMLA does not cover workers in companies of 50 or fewer employees, or those employed for less than a year, effectively excluding approximately 40 percent of U.S. workers.[41,42]

Some states have implemented programs to assist caregivers by expanding paid leave provisions. California was a leader when it enacted the Paid Family Leave Law in 2002, allowing workers up to six weeks of partially paid leave to bond with a new biological, adopted, or foster child or to care for a seriously ill family member.[42] While only New Jersey and Rhode Island have followed suit with California and enacted paid leave legislation or regulations for private sector employees, several additional states currently are considering such legislation.[42] To encourage consideration of paid leave legislation, since 2014, the Obama administration has awarded $1.75 million to states to study the issue.[42] As discussed earlier, provisions of the ACA have potential to lessen the burden on informal caregivers by enabling increased Medicaid payment flexibility to support home and community-based services. Particularly relevant to family caregivers, the ACA also created an "Independence at Home Medical Practice Pilot Program" to provide Medicare beneficiaries with multiple chronic conditions with home-based primary care services and a "Community Care Transitions Program" for high-risk Medicare beneficiaries following hospital discharge. The ACA also requires federally funded geriatric education centers to provide free or low-cost training for family caregivers.

Historically, home healthcare services have been vulnerable to breaches in operational integrity. In the 1990s, the Clinton administration and Congress responded to large Medicare and Medicaid spending increases and concerns about service quality and fiscal integrity with an antifraud and abuse pilot project, Operation Restore Trust.[43] The project investigated selected home health agencies and other organizations in five states with the highest rates of use. Operation Restore Trust was expanded in future years to selected home healthcare agencies in 12 states and included training for agency surveyors in identifying care improperly billed to Medicare.[43]

Clinton's Balanced Budget Act of 1997 included provisions to enable the Health Care Financing Administration (now called the Center for Medicare & Medicaid Services) to control costs and address service quality issues more effectively in Medicare-certified home healthcare agencies and contained several measures to thwart fraudulent practices by home health clients and agencies.[44] Also in 1997, the Department of Health and Human Services promulgated new regulations requiring home health agencies to implement a standardized reporting system, the Outcomes and Assessment Information Set, to monitor patients' conditions and satisfaction with services.[45]

Vigorous antifraud and abuse initiatives continue in the Medicare program through its partnerships with the Department of Justice, the Federal Bureau of Investigation, the Office of the Inspector General, and several other federal and state law enforcement agencies.[46] Home healthcare services are an integral component of the healthcare delivery system's continuum, which can provide an effective, safe, and humane alternative to institutional care for the medical treatment and personal care of individuals of all ages. Ideally, lessons learned from continuing initiatives to thwart abuses and improve quality and the ACA provisions that support expanded home- and community-based services will help to ensure that home health care fulfills its purposes in ensuring the highest-possible quality of life for all recipients of these services.

Hospice Care

Hospice is a philosophy supporting a coordinated program of care for the terminally ill. The most common criterion for admission into a hospice is that the applicant has a diagnosis of a terminal illness with a limited life expectancy of six months or less. Aggressive medical treatment of the patient's disease may no longer be medically feasible or personally desirable. The disease may have progressed despite available medical treatments, making continuance of curative treatment futile or intolerable, or the patient may elect to discontinue such treatment for a variety of personal reasons, such as continued deterioration of quality of life related to treatment side-effects.

The term palliative care often is used synonymously with hospice care. Palliative care is care or treatment given to relieve the symptoms of a disease rather than attempting to cure the disease. Pain, nausea, malaise, and emotional distress caused by feelings of fear and isolation are only some of the difficulties that patients encounter during the terminal stages of an illness. Hospice treatment is directed toward maintaining the comfort of the patient and enhancing the patient's quality of life and sense of independence for as long as possible.

Hospice has its historical roots in medieval Europe. Hospices were originally way stations where travelers on religious pilgrimages received food and rest. Over time, the concept evolved into sanctuaries where impoverished people or those who were sick or dying received care.

English physician Dame Cicely Saunders established St. Christopher's, a hospice located in a London suburb, in 1967, and it became a model for the modern hospice. Here, terminally ill patients received intensive symptom management, modern techniques of pain control, and psychological and emotional support. She brought the founding concepts of the modern hospice to the United States in a lecture tour in the late 1960s, during which she emphasized that dying patients were also on a kind of pilgrimage and needed a more responsive environment than could be provided in high-technology, impersonal, cure-oriented hospitals.

The U.S. hospice movement began as a consumer-based grassroots movement supported by volunteer and professional members of the community. Today, 28 percent of hospice organizations are operating as not-for-profit entities, whereas for-profit hospice organizations have multiplied over the years and now represent about 68 percent of hospice organizations (**FIGURE 9-5**).[47]

U.S. founders shared the belief that the hospice concept was a more humane alternative to the technology-driven, curative emphasis in hospitals. Because the medical system can view choosing to discontinue aggressive medical treatment as a failure, terminally ill patients can feel depersonalized and isolated inside a traditional hospital setting. Ideally, the physician, the patient, and the patient's family jointly recognize the need to refer the patient to a hospice when deciding to stop curative treatment.

The first U.S. hospice was established in New Haven, Connecticut, in 1974. The number of hospices has increased steadily every year, with more than 6,100 hospices now serving between 1.6 and 1.7 million individuals annually (**FIGURES 9-6** and **9-7**).[47] Growth in the availability of hospice

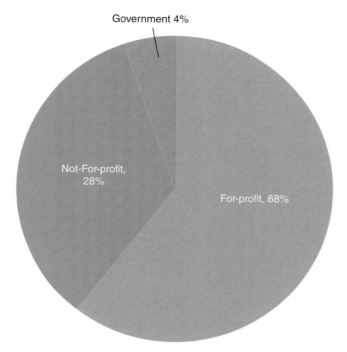

FIGURE 9-5 Tax Status of Medicare-Certified Hospice Agencies

Modified from NHPCO Facts and Figures: Hospice Care in America. Alexandria, VA: National Hospice and Palliative Care Organization, September 2015.

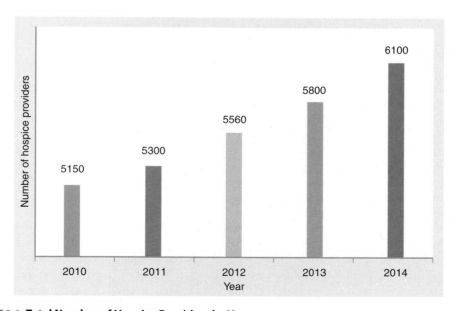

FIGURE 9-6 Total Number of Hospice Providers by Year

Reproduced with permission from NHPCO Facts and Figures: Hospice Care in America. Alexandria, VA: National Hospice and Palliative Care Organization, September 2015.

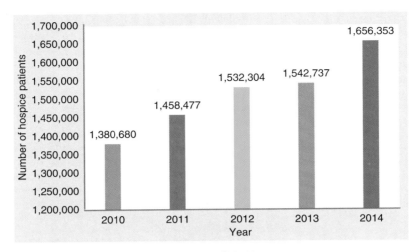

FIGURE 9-7 **Total Hospice Patients Served (estimated) By Year**

Reproduced with permission from NHPCO Facts and Figures: Hospice Care in America. Alexandria, VA: National Hospice and Palliative Care Organization, September 2015.

care followed the enactment of 1982 legislation that extended Medicare coverage to hospice services, allowing the movement to escape its prior dependency on grant support and philanthropy. A 73-fold increase in the number of hospice agencies occurred between 1984 and 1998. In 2011, approximately 44.6 percent of all U.S. deaths occurred in hospice care. Updated data on the number of deaths occurring in hospice care is available from the Centers for Disease Control and Prevention.[47]

Consistent with the hospice philosophy, a multidisciplinary team of nurses, social workers, counselors, physicians, and therapists provides services. Hospices also provide drug therapies and medical appliances and supplies. Bereavement services for surviving family members continue for a year or longer after the patient's death. Most hospice organizations also provide bereavement services for the larger community.[47]

A variety of different settings accommodates hospice care, including patient homes, hospitals, SNFs, assisted-living facilities, or hospice inpatient facilities. The most important unifying concept about hospice is that no matter where the care is delivered, a specialized multidisciplinary team of healthcare professionals works together to manage the patient's care. Physicians direct multi-disciplinary team members with each team member contributing particular skills and expertise to assist in managing pain, alleviating emotional distress, promoting comfort, and maintaining the independence of the hospice patient. Hospice care encompasses the patient's family and routinely includes counseling (including bereavement counseling), spiritual support, and respite care for family members.

The hospice philosophy emphasizes volunteerism, and it is the only healthcare provider category whose Medicare certification requires that at least 5 percent of total patient care hours are contributed by volunteers. In 2014, the National Hospice and Palliative Care Organization estimated that more than 430,000 volunteers assisted hospice organizations with 19 million contributed hours of service such as provision of respite care for families, child care assistance, and other supportive non-medical assistance.[47,48] Volunteers from the community are actively encouraged to participate in a wide range of hospice activities, including direct services to patients and families, clerical services, and other support services and assistance with fundraising.

Hospice care has demonstrated its cost savings in care for the terminally ill. The unique blend of care provided by specialized teams, use of volunteers, and frequent use of family members as primary caregivers in the home decrease expenses. The focus on palliative care rather than on cure-oriented care also decreases the cost. A number of research studies have examined the savings from the use of hospice care. Similar to Medicare, annual Medicaid expenditures for hospice care represent only a small fraction of total expenditures.[47]

Managed care organizations and traditional health insurers recognize both the human and economic benefits of hospice care and typically include hospice in their benefit packages. Insurers may have their own team of hospice-type providers within their respective networks or may contract with community hospice organizations to provide hospice care. Medicare-eligible subscribers of Medicare-participating health plans are automatically eligible for hospice care, and services must be provided through a Medicare-certified hospice organization. Patients are not required to obtain a referral from their health plan or to discontinue their managed care contract in order to receive hospice care.

A basic tenet of the hospice philosophy is that hospice care should be available regardless of the ability to pay. When a patient does not have health insurance and does not qualify for Medicare or Medicaid, hospice services still may be available. A hospice may offer a sliding payment scale to patients, with the hospice drawing on internal funds garnered through its fundraising activities to supplement available patient payments.

Ongoing quality assurance to monitor care quality is an inherent concept in hospice care. Three standards used most frequently are licensure, certification, and accreditation. Licensure is based on state-imposed statutes as part of the consumer protection code of a state. Not all states have such licensing statutes. States that have licensing statutes require that hospices within their jurisdiction meet the standards set forth in the law. Certification means that hospices have been examined on the federal level and have been found to at least minimally meet the mandated requirements for Medicare and Medicaid reimbursement. A hospice program that is not certified may still operate legally, but it is ineligible to bill Medicare or Medicaid for its services. As identified above, the same three organizations which accredit home healthcare agencies also accredit hospice agencies.

Respite Care

Family caregivers continue to be a key factor in providing care for many long-term care recipients in their communities, rather than placing them in institutions. Providing care up to 24 hours a day can place enormous physical and emotional stress on family caregivers.

Respite care is temporary surrogate care given to a patient when that patient's primary caregiver(s) must be absent. In the 1970s, formal respite-care programs originated to meet the increasing need for assistance after the rapid deinstitutionalization of individuals who had developmental disabilities or mental illness. Since then, the respite-care model has expanded to include any family-managed care program that helps to avoid or forestall the placement of a patient in a full-time institutionalized environment by providing planned, intermittent caregiver relief. Respite care offers an organized, reliable system in which both patient and primary caregiver are the beneficiaries.

Respite care may be offered in a variety of settings: the home; a day care situation; or institutions with overnight care, such as hospitals, nursing homes, or group homes. Respite-care auspices may include private, public, and voluntary not-for-profit agencies. The length of respite care varies, but it is intended to be short term and intermittent.

Respite-care services are highly differentiated. Some are very structured and self-contained; others are highly flexible and exist in a more casual support capacity. A number of services are oriented to treating only patients with a particular ailment, but, for many, the only criterion the patient must meet for admission is that he or she requires supervised medical treatment and nursing care, which usually has been provided by family or friends as primary caregivers. Respite models include:

- Alzheimer's disease care on an inpatient basis with admissions lasting for several weeks
- Community-based, adult day-care centers that offer nursing, therapeutic, and social services
- In-home assistance, where visiting homecare or personal care aides supply services
- Temporary patient furloughs to a hospital or nursing home at regular intervals

Respite-care program staffing varies widely, deploying both professionals and nonprofessionals. For example, respite care could be as informal as having a member from the caregiver's church come into the home for a few hours while the caregiver goes out or as professional as a specialized dementia day-care program where nurses, aides, and recreational and physical therapists are specifically educated to care for dementia patients in a structured, caregiving environment. When respite care entails overnight care in an institutional setting, such as a nursing home, hospital, or group home, the staff providing care is the same staff employed by the institution to provide care to their regular patients in the institution.

Formal respite programs in the United States that are financially accessible to all in need have remained sparse. One of the greatest barriers limiting the expanded use of respite care is cost. Family caregivers operating on a limited budget may have difficulty finding funds to compensate a respite provider. Although some respite providers offer care on a sliding scale, almost any fee may exceed the financial means of the family. In these situations, not-for-profit organizations may assist by providing respite assistance at a tolerable cost for patients who meet certain financial or medical parameters.

Historically, there have been few provisions in the Medicare and Medicaid programs to support formal respite care. Medicare contains no allowances for respite, unless services are provided by a Medicare-certified hospice, Medicare-certified hospital, or Medicare-certified nursing home, and co-pay fees are required. The person receiving respite care may be responsible for 5 percent of the Medicare-approved amount for respite care. For example, if Medicare pays $100 per day for inpatient respite care, the co-pay would be $5 per day.[49] Each time a patient receives respite care, Medicare covers up to five days. There is no limit to the number of times that a patient can receive respite care. The amount paid for respite care can change each year.[49] Medicaid has stringent requirements regarding the specific type and length of care provided as well as financial eligibility for services and does not pay for respite care directly. Often states use waivers to apply federal funds to offset respite costs for eligible Medicaid recipients. Some states allow family members to receive a wage subsidy for respite services for persons over the age of 60 with very low incomes, but eligibility, types of care, and funding vary on a state-by-state basis.[50] Available respite programs offered by voluntary agencies as the result of federal grants often provide service for only specific medical conditions, such as Alzheimer's disease. Both proprietary and not-for-profit organizations are developing specialized dementia and related respite-care programs in response to recent federal legislation. Many specialized dementia respite-care programs currently are developed and marketed to private pay customers, but such programs often are beyond the financial capacity of many families.

One of the major barriers to responsive changes in reimbursement for respite care has been that funding mechanisms have viewed respite care as meeting a social, rather than an acute medical care, need. In addition, community systems of respite care can be difficult to organize because the level of need is intermittent and unpredictable. Family caregivers, rather than the patients who actually receive the care, often are viewed as the most direct beneficiaries of respite care. With the indisputable conclusion that respite-care programs offer society value and cost savings through postponement or avoidance of costly institutionalization, bipartisan federal legislation was developed in 2003 to address respite-care issues. Entitled the Lifespan Respite Care Act, more than 200 national, state, and local organizations advocated its passage, culminating in its signing into law in 2006.[51] The law authorized $289 million over five years for state grants to develop respite programs. According to the National Family Caregivers Association (now renamed Caregiver Action Network or CAN), the 2006 Act defined respite programs as "coordinated systems of accessible, community-based respite-care services for family caregivers of children and adults with special needs."[51] Passage of this legislation was a landmark because it provided a nationwide acknowledgment of the inherent economic value of the informal family-provided care system. To date, 33 states and the District of Columbia have received Lifespan Respite Care Program grants.[52] The Lifespan Respite Care Reauthorization Act of 2015 requests $75 million, $15 million each year for fiscal years 2016–2020.[52] In addition, as a major thrust of federal initiatives, the U.S. Administration on Aging (AoA) has continued to pilot several demonstration programs targeted at determining the cost-effectiveness and consumer acceptability of various combinations of community-based services that support older persons' ability to continue living independently. For the fiscal year 2016, the AoA Administration for Community Living requested Congress to fund $386.2 million for home- and community-based support services, an increase of over $38 million above the fiscal year 2015 enacted level.[53]

Adult Day Care

An adult day care center may provide a supervised program of social activities and custodial care (social model), medical and rehabilitative care through skilled nursing (medical model), or specialized services for patients with Alzheimer's disease or other forms of dementia. An adult day care center operates during daytime hours in a protective group setting located outside the recipient's home. The primary intent of adult day care is to prevent the premature and inappropriate institutionalization of older adults by providing socialization, health care, or both. Older adults maintain their mental and physical well-being longer and at a higher level when they continue to reside in their homes and their communities. Furthermore, for those who depend on the services of a regular family caregiver, an adult day care center can provide respite for the caregiver and therapeutic social contacts for the care recipient.[54]

The concept of adult day care grew out of social concern for the quality of life and care of older adults based on the work of Lionel Cousins, who in the 1960s established the first adult day care center in the United States to "prepare patients for discharge by teaching and promoting independent living skills."[55] Originally, development and growth in such programs were slow because there was no national policy to support the program concept and no permanent funding base, because the prototype Medicare and Medicaid programs supported and encouraged institutionalization. However, as the cost of institutionalization, the inhumanity of many nursing homes, and the burden placed on family caregivers were recognized, the focus of long-term care was redirected toward support of community-based care as a preferred alternative to institutionalization. In 1978, only 300 adult day care centers existed nationwide; but, according to the National Adult Day Services Association, by 2010, 4,000 were in operation, 80 percent of which were operated by not-for-profit organizations.[56] By 2014, the number of adult day care centers in operation had increased to more than 5,685.[57]

The services that adult day care centers offer are similar, but the emphasis varies with the model they follow. Most adult day care centers offer a variety of medical, psychiatric, and nursing assessments; counseling; physical exercises; social services; crafts; and rehabilitation in activities of daily living skills. Special-purpose adult day care centers serve particular populations of clients, such as veterans, older persons with mental illnesses, the blind, people with Alzheimer's disease, or people with cerebral palsy, for example.

Staffing patterns of adult day care programs vary from program to program and are directly related to the type of program and specific services offered; the mix of unskilled to skilled employees depends on the kinds of services being offered. Programs based on the medical model are more likely to employ more registered nurses, occupational therapists, and physical therapists to provide skilled assessment, direct care, and rehabilitative therapies than in a social model, where aides may perform most of the custodial care and a recreational therapist may be employed to plan and deliver recreational and socialization activities. The number of clients enrolled in an adult day care program varies according to the staffing pattern and facility size. The cost of care may vary widely depending on the range and scope of services provided. Medicare generally does not provide reimbursement for day care services. Medicaid may provide reimbursement for services in a medical model day care program, but this practice varies from state to state. Often, services are paid for through private fees or through programs supported by grant funds or by charitable or religious organizations.

Most centers are licensed by the states in which they operate.[56] Most also are certified by the particular community agency that is funding the day care center. Licensure and credentialing ensure that the day care center meets at least the minimum standards and guidelines set by the overseeing agency that provides grant funding to the community agency and ensure that the overseeing agency has met all criteria for obtaining underlying federal government grants. Adult day care standards, which include organizational measurement and quality and information systems and outcomes quality, were first published in 1999 by the Commission on Accreditation of Rehabilitation Facilities along with the National Adult Day Services Association. The standards provide quality guidance to adult day care management, as well as recognition of the value of adult day care services in the overall continuum of long-term care.[58]

▶ Innovations in Long-Term Care

Innovative long-term care services that meet the diverse medical needs, personal desires, and lifestyle choices of older Americans have made important strides over the years. The continuum of care model recognizes the complex configuration of individual needs and encourages the implementation of programs and services of adequate variety, intensity, and scope to provide the best configuration of care to any individual. Concepts such as aging in place, life care communities, naturally occurring retirement communities, and high-technology home care are some of the changes that offer enriched alternatives to long-term care recipients.

Aging in Place

Moving to a nursing home or dependent care facility is seen by many as a change in lifestyle to be steadfastly avoided for as long as possible. Most people prefer to remain actively engaged in their own support and care, in their own residence, and within the context of their own family. Research indicates enhanced quality of life and longevity when older adults are able to remain in their own residences. The term aging in place in the context of older and frail persons refers to at least partial fulfillment of this desire. An aging-in-place healthcare system allows older adults to maintain their health while living as independently as possible in their own homes, without a costly, and in many cases traumatic, move to an institutional setting. At the federal, state, and local governmental levels, as evidenced by legislation, and at the grassroots level, an increasingly favorable light is shining on the well-documented cost-effectiveness of healthcare programs that encourage the aging-in-place concept and the concurrent maintenance of independent living.

Aging-in-place programs bring together a variety of health and other supportive services to enable participants to live independently in their own residences for as long as safely possible. Services that participants receive most frequently include:

- Nursing services provided by registered and licensed nurses
- Home care aide assistance
- Homemaker services to assist with meals and housekeeping
- A 24-hour emergency response system
- Home-delivered groceries
- Transportation to healthcare appointments

In 1972, a model of aging-in-place service delivery, called On Lok Senior Health Services, was established as a demonstration project to provide health services to a selected population of frail older people in San Francisco. The term *On Lok* derives from the Chinese language, meaning "peaceful and happy abode."[59] Participants in the On Lok program live in their own residences, and an interdisciplinary team of healthcare professionals manages their health care. When institutional care is required (either in a nursing home or hospital) or ancillary diagnostic or specialty physician services are needed, they are provided through contractual arrangements with outside providers. The prototype program was so successful that Congress mandated replication of this model by the establishment of demonstration programs, called the Program for All-Inclusive Care for the Elderly (PACE), in other parts of the country.[59] The early success of PACE was evidenced by the fact that although clients were certified as eligible for nursing home placement, only 6 percent were placed in nursing homes; the rest were able to remain in their homes.[60] Also impressive was the low hospitalization rate of participants when compared with typical Medicare beneficiaries with similar health status. Through provisions of the Balanced Budget Act of 1997, PACE earned a permanent status as a Medicare-approved benefit.[60]

Continuing Care Retirement and Life Care Communities

Continuing care retirement communities (CCRCs) are available for those Americans who do not wish to stay in their own homes as they get older yet are essentially well enough to avoid institutionalization. Recent estimates have placed the number of licensed CCRCs at nearly 1,900,[61] accommodating more than 600,000 older Americans,[62] with the numbers of both the licensed facilities and their residents increasing every year. More than 80 percent of CCRCs have been operated by not-for-profit organizations.[61] CCRCs provide residences on a retirement campus, typically in apartment complexes designed for functional older adults. Unlike ordinary retirement communities that offer only specialized housing, CCRCs offer a comprehensive program of social services, meals, and access to contractual medical services in addition to housing. There are three types of CCRCs[63]:

- Life care or extended contract/continuing life care community (CLCC): This is the most expensive option. It offers unlimited assisted living, medical treatment, and skilled nursing care without any additional charges as the resident's needs change over time.
- Modified contract: This contract offers a set of services provided for a specified length of time. When that time is expired, other services can be obtained but will have higher monthly fees.
- Fee-for-service contract: The initial enrollment fee may be lower, but assisted living and skilled nursing are paid for at their market rates.

According to the American Association of Retired Persons (AARP), CCRCs provide the most expensive of all long-term care options and require an entrance fee as well as monthly charges.[63] Fees depend on a variety of factors including the resident's health status, the type of housing chosen, the size of the facility, and the type of service contract.[63] Cost varies widely, and such programs require upfront entrance fees that can range from $100,000 to $1 million. Monthly charges can range from $3,000 to $5,000, but they may increase as needs change.[63] However, as advocates for this lifestyle point out, many Americans approaching their retirement years have sufficient equity in their homes and investment income to pay the required entrance and monthly maintenance fees.

CLCCs achieve financial viability by using an insurance-based model and, as such, are regulated by state insurance departments as well as other regulatory agencies to which their services may be subject in their respective states. The program administrators establish eligibility criteria for participants using actuarial data from the insurance industry. The future lifetime medical costs of participants are anticipated, and rates and charges are set accordingly. Prospective CLCC residents are provided a contract outlining what the CLCC provides in terms of home accommodations, social activities, services and amenities, and access to on-site levels of health care. Most CLCCs require a one-time entrance fee and a monthly fee as previously mentioned. There are many variations to the types of contracts offered.[64] In general, services may include the following:

- Meals
- Scheduled transportation
- Housekeeping services
- Housing unit maintenance
- Linen and personal laundry
- Health monitoring
- Wellness programs
- Some utilities
- Social activities
- Home health care
- Skilled nursing care

A life care community offers more comprehensive benefits and support systems for older persons than any other option available today in the United States. Fewer than 1 percent of older citizens have taken advantage of this option in the past, in great part because of the expense and the requirement of an extended contractual commitment.

Naturally Occurring Retirement Communities

A naturally occurring retirement community (NORC) is a term coined by Professor Michael Hunt of the University of Wisconsin–Madison in the 1980s to describe apartment buildings where most residents were 60 years of age or older. Now, the NORC acronym is widely used to describe apartment complexes, neighborhoods, or sections of communities where residents have opted to remain in their homes as they age.[65] Today, numerous communities throughout the United States formally recognize NORCs.

The U.S. AoA recognized NORCs through the development of a competitive grant awards program for demonstration projects designed to test and evaluate methods to assist older Americans in their desire to age in place. Community centers and other not-for-profit organizations competed for grant funding, and demonstration projects were enacted in several states. NORC programs use a combination of services such as case management, nursing, social and recreational activities, health education, transportation, nutrition, and referral linkages to enhance quality of life and safety for older adults who wish to remain in their homes during their aging process.[65] NORCs have appeared to hold much potential as a positive alternative to institutionalization and offer possible cost savings for individuals and government.[66]

High-Technology Home Care: Hospitals Without Walls

Traditionally, home health care focused on providing supportive care to persons with long-term disability and chronic disease. Changes in reimbursement mechanisms to a prospective payment system based on diagnosis-related groups (DRGs) led to the more rapid discharge of all patients from hospitals after episodes of hospitalization for acute illness, exacerbation of chronic disease, progression of disability, or surgery. Patients frequently are discharged to their homes while still requiring advanced intensive therapeutic treatments and relying on complex, high-technology services such as ventilators, kidney dialysis, intravenous antibiotic therapy, parenteral nutrition, or cancer chemotherapy.

The delivery of high-technology home care not only is more cost-effective than hospitalization or institutionalization in a nursing home, but it also allows the client to move from the dependent patient role to the more autonomous role as a client in their own residence. Home healthcare agencies have accommodated this trend toward provision of advanced high-technology therapy in the home setting through innovations in the type and organization of the specialty services they provide. Improvements and innovations have taken place in the portability, mobility, reliability, and cost of medical devices such as intravenous therapy pumps, long-term venous access devices, continuous ambulatory peritoneal dialysis equipment, and ventilators. Innovative teams of skilled practitioners in specialized areas such as intravenous therapy and kidney dialysis and the concurrent development of innovative support teams of pharmacists and specialty technicians who prepare and deliver necessary intravenous, parenteral nutrition, and dialysis fluids and medications have made the home setting an appropriate environment for the delivery of high-technology therapies.

▶ Long-Term Care Insurance

Long-term care insurance (LTCI) is one financing option for the various components of long-term care. The earliest long-term care policies were first offered in the 1960s and covered only care in nursing homes.[67] In 2016, the National Association of Insurance Commissioners reported that the long-term care insurance market covers more than 7 million Americans and that LTCI policies provide coverage for long-term care in a variety of setting options such as nursing homes, assisted living, or in the home.[67] Individuals purchase the majority of policies, but an increasing number of employers are now offering coverage through group purchase plans. The federal government has encouraged the purchase of long-term care policies by offering tax deductions to employers who offer long-term care insurance as a benefit. Almost all long-term care insurance policies sold today meet federal standards, specified by the Health Insurance Portability and Accountability Act of 1996, for favorable tax treatment. Many states also offer incentives to individuals in the form of income tax deductions for the purchase of tax-qualified long-term care policies.[68] However, in ominous developments of the past few years, many long-term care insurers have left the market, and those remaining are facing financial difficulties for a variety of reasons.[69] Major net effects include soaring premiums for subscribers, increasing numbers of policy abandonments, and consumer reluctance to purchase the insurance in the first place.[69]

The ACA included a provision, the Community Living Assistance Services and Supports Act (CLASS Act), to establish a national voluntary long-term care insurance program funded through payroll deductions by persons at least 18 years of age. However, by late 2011, amid much controversy, the Department of Health and Human Services eliminated the program with analysts noting that the CLASS Act suffered from "serious design flaws." Advocates lamented the withdrawal of the Act as losing an opportunity to shift costs from the Medicaid program to private insurance.[70]

The benefits of LTCI policies vary across a broad spectrum. The most desirable policies cover services across the continuum of potential long-term care needs, with maximum subscriber flexibility. Specialists counsel buyers to be wary of limitations relative to inflationary factors in the costs of coverage, renewal clauses, limits on payments for various modes of long-term care, requirements for prior hospitalization for eligibility for home care, cancellation features of policies, and lifetime benefit limits. As with life insurance, the premium cost reflects age and health status at purchase of the policy. LTCI companies also use underwriting criteria and may reject applicants or increase premiums for individuals with pre-existing conditions that render them at high risk for future long-term care services.

Insurance industry advocates and other analysts contend that individuals and society will benefit in the future from the proliferation of LTCI. In this view, public dependency, especially on Medicaid, to fund long-term care needs would decrease, and individuals would have the ability to access the highest quality long-term care services without risk of impoverishment.[71]

The decision to invest in an LTCI product is very personal and depends on many factors, primarily on the level of assets the individual has or expects to have at risk if long-term care is required. Other alternatives to LTCI, such as transferring assets to children to become financially eligible for Medicaid, using the equity in a home in a reverse mortgage, selecting special living arrangements, and using personal savings, are not universally applicable. All these options must be carefully assessed against the cost of LTCI to make viable and appropriate future plans.

▶ **Future of Long-Term Care**

The United States will need more and diverse long-term care programs in the future to serve increasing needs, especially of older adults. Some of the causes underlying the intensifying need for diverse long-term care service options include:

- Changes in U.S. population demographics
- Social and economic changes in families

- Increasingly sophisticated medical technology
- Greater consumer sophistication and demands

Services such as the provision of transitional health care after hospitalization for medically complex patients through integrated organizations such as patient-centered medical homes and accountable care organizations are components of system reforms to prevent hospital readmissions and improve community-based coordination of care. Demonstrated cost-effectiveness and expressed patient preferences for community-based care are reflected in the ACA provisions. As discussed earlier, the ACA promotes increased consumer choice, flexibility, care coordination, and community-based rather than institutional care, holding promise for a more rational, less costly, and more coordinated long-term care system.

The ACA's CLASS Act drew national attention to the need for universal financial coverage for long-term care and a potentially positive development occurred in 2013 in response to its elimination. A provision of the American Taxpayer Relief Act of 2012 required establishment of a Federal Long-term Care Commission effective in January, 2013.[72] Constituted with a bi-partisan panel of 15 political appointees with expertise in the long-term care industry, the Commission was charged to develop "a plan for the establishment, implementation, and financing of a comprehensive, coordinated, and high quality system that ensures the availability of long-term services and supports for individuals in need of such supports… " by September, 2013.[72,73] Based upon its recommendations, the commission was granted authority to introduce legislation to Congress but never did so with one member noting, "We didn't have the resources or time to get that done."[73] Kaiser Health News reported that the Commission had "meager financing for its operations, few staff members and little time" and because of delays in member appointments, had only 100 days to meet the deadline for its report.[73] Ultimately, the Commission issued its report with nine members in agreement with recommendations and six opposed. Five of the dissenting members issued alternative recommendations and concluded that the Commission's recommendations "do not fulfill its comprehensive charge."[72] With a disappointing end product to the Commission's work, a dissenting member, a Georgetown University Public Policy Institute scholar, reported, "The fundamental issue in getting people the long-term services and supports they need is an issue of financing and this commission did not address that issue."[73]

In the face of failed federal efforts to address long-term care costs and growing financial challenges among long-term care insurers, it remains clear that political will and continuing advocacy on many fronts will be required to meet the long-term care needs of the burgeoning population of older Americans and others requiring long-term care.

Long-term care employees have traditionally been paid less and given less status than workers in acute-care health services. The long-term care industry is enduring an employment crisis with an inadequate number and quality of applicants to fill vacancies in direct caregiver positions across all industry sectors. Factors contributing to the long-term care employment crisis include the following[74]:

- The growing need for services
- Competition among employers for qualified employees
- Workload and working conditions
- Employee turnover
- Wages and benefits constrained by reimbursement policies
- A lack of social supports for workers, including child care and transportation
- A lack of opportunities for education and career mobility

Staffing shortages seriously affect the quality of long-term care services. The industry's ability to develop innovative approaches to attracting and retaining staff will have important implications as service demands swell with the aging of the baby-boom generation. Supported by government, not-for-profit organizations, and major philanthropies, identifying solutions to the staffing crises in long-term care has been the subject of ongoing research at academic and policy development institutions throughout the country.[71,75] In a recent positive development, the U.S. Department of Labor extended federal wage protections to the nation's 2 million home care workers through an amendment to the Federal Fair Labor Standards Act. Effective January 1, 2016, for the first time, home care workers will be entitled to the federal minimum wage, time-and-a-half pay for overtime, and pay for time spent traveling between client homes.[76] Advocates believe these new federal protections may make home care employment more attractive and help ease the ongoing recruitment and retention challenges in the industry.[76] Until recently, the needs of the informal caregiver system were virtually ignored. Significant legislative action at the federal and state levels only recently began to recognize these needs in terms of employer allowances and other programmatic and economic considerations at the federal and state levels. In hopeful signs, several state legislatures now have paid family medical leave under consideration.

An undercurrent of concern continues to run beneath all aspects of long-term healthcare delivery, especially with regard to the development of responsive, patient-centered, quality-driven, accessible, affordable, and cost-effective healthcare services for all citizens—including the society's most vulnerable: people with chronic disabilities and frail older adults. As exemplified by the demise of the CLASS Act and the failure of the Commission on Long-term Care to produce legislation, it is not possible to predict if or how Congress and the long-term care industry will develop solutions to the crises in meeting present and future long-term care needs for older Americans and others in need of these services. Insurance industry experts suggest the need for a national long-term care strategy that incorporates four primary components: education and awareness, caregiving, healthy aging, and long-term care financing (**FIGURE 9-8**). It is certain however, that research and advocacy for long-term care reforms will be ongoing. As an example, in 2012 under the auspices of the Convergence Center for Policy Resolution, a not-for-profit, non-partisan organization, the Long-Term Care Financing Collaborative (LTCFC) convened to develop "widely supportable and actionable recommendations for a public and private insurance-based financing system that empowers all people to receive high quality services and supports."[77] The LTCFC membership includes a diverse group of policy experts and stakeholders representing a broad political spectrum. In its latest report issued in February 2016, the LTCFC outlined five reform proposals[77]:

- Clear private and public roles for long-term care financing
- A new universal catastrophic long-term care insurance program to shift the current welfare based system to an insurance model.
- Redefining Medicaid long-term services and supports to allow greater autonomy and choice in service settings
- Encouraging private long-term care insurance initiatives to lower cost and increase enrollment
- Increasing retirement savings and improving public education on long-term care costs and needs

Given the industry's current unmet needs and rising demands, experimentation, innovation, and advocacy in the long-term healthcare system are sure to continue.

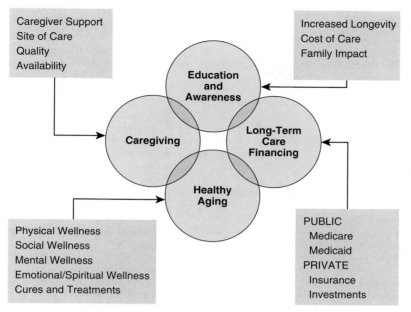

FIGURE 9-8 Components of a National Long-Term Care Strategy
Reproduced from Genworth Financial, reprinted with permission.

KEY TERMS FOR REVIEW

Aging in Place
Assisted Living
Continuing Care
   Retirement Community
   (CCRC)

Continuing Life Care
   Community (CLCC)
Hospice
Long-Term Care Facility
   (LTCF)

Naturally Occurring Retirement
   Community (NORC)
Palliative Care
Respite Care
Skilled Nursing Facility (SNF)

CHAPTER ACRONYMS

ACA Affordable Care Act
ALF Assisted Living Facility
AoA Administration on Aging
CAN Caregiver Action Network
CCRC Continuing Care Retirement Community
CLASS Act Community Living Assistance
   Services and Supports Act
CLCC Continuing Life Care Community
CMS Centers for Medicare and Medicaid Services
DRGs Diagnosis-Related Groups
FMLA Family Medical Leave Act
HHAs Home Health Agencies

LTCF Long-Term Care Facility
LTCFC Long-Term Care Financing Collaborative
LTCI Long-Term Care Insurance
NHPCO National Hospice and Palliative Care
   Organization
NCHS National Center for Health Statistics
NORC Naturally Occurring Retirement
   Community
NSLTCP National Study of Long Term Care
   Providers
PACE Program for All-Inclusive Care for the Elderly
SNF Skilled Nursing Facility

References

1. Evashwick CJ. Strategic management of a continuum of care. *J Long-Term Care Admin*. 1993;21:13-24.
2. Shortell SM. *Transforming Health Care Delivery: Seamless Continuum of Care*. Chicago, IL: American Hospital Publishing; 1994:1-7.
3. Jack CM, Paone DL. *Toward Creating a Seamless Continuum of Care: Addressing Chronic Care Needs*. Chicago, IL: Section for Aging and Long-Term Care Services of the American Hospital Association; 1994:3-5.
4. U.S. Department of Health and Human Services, Administration on Aging. A profile of older Americans: 2014. http://www.aoa.acl.gov/aging_statistics/Profile/2014/docs/2014-Profile.pdf. Accessed February 1, 2016.
5. U.S. Department of Health and Human Services. Administration for Community Living. Administration on Aging (AoA). Projected future growth of the older population by age: 1900–2050: persons 65 and older. http://www.aoa.acl.gov/aging_statistics/future_growth/future_growth.aspx#. Accessed February 4, 2016.
6. Shore HH. History of long-term care. In: Goldsmith SB, ed. *Essentials of Long-Term Care Administration*. Gaithersburg, MD: Aspen; 1994:5-6.
7. Centers for Medicare & Medicaid Services. CMS Nursing Home Data Compendium, 2013. https://www.cms.gov/Medicare/Provider-Enrollment-and-Certification/CertificationandComplianc/downloads/nursinghomedatacompendium_508.pdf. Accessed February 4, 2016.
8. Pavri JM. Overview: one hundred years of public health nursing: visions of a better world. *Imprint*. 1994;4:43-48.
9. Glasscote RM, Beigel A, Butterfield A, et al. *Old Folks at Homes: A Field Study of Nursing and Board and Care Homes*. Washington, DC: American Psychiatric Association; 1976.
10. Moss FE, Halamandaris VJ. *Too Old, Too Sick, Too Bad*. Gaithersburg, MD: Aspen; 1977:15-37.
11. Evans JM, Fleming KC. Medical care of nursing home residents. *Mayo Clin Proc*. 1995;70:694.
12. Centers for Disease Control and Prevention. Nursing homes and assisted living (long-term care facilities [LTCFs]) http://www.cdc.gov/longtermcare/. Accessed September 5, 2016.
13. Long-Term Care Education.com. Skilled care facilities. http://www.ltce.com/learn/skilledcare.php. Accessed September 5, 2016.
14. National Center on Elder Abuse. Fact Sheet: Abuse of residents of long term care facilities. February 2012. https://ncea.acl.gov/resources/docs/Abuse-LongTermCare-Facilities-2012.pdf. Accessed September 5, 2016.
15. Centers for Disease Control and Prevention. National study of long-term care providers: An introduction. http://www.cdc.gov/nchs/data/nsltcp/NSLTCP_FS.pdf. Accessed February 4, 2016.
16. Centers for Medicare & Medicaid Services. National health expenditure data: Table 2: Aggregate, annual percent change, percent distribution and per capita amounts, by type of expenditure: selected calendar years 1960–2014. Table 14: Home health care services expenditures; levels, percent change, and percent distribution, by source of funds: selected calendar years 1970–2014. Table 15: Nursing care facilities and continuing care retirement communities expenditures; levels, percent change, and percent distribution, by source of funds: selected calendar years 1970–2014. https://www.cms.gov/Research-Statistics-Data-and-Systems/Statistics-Trends-and-Reports/NationalHealthExpendData/NationalHealthAccountsHistorical.html. Accessed February 4, 2016.
17. Genworth 2015 Cost of Care Survey. Genworth Financial Inc. https://www.genworth.com/dam/Americas/US/PDFs/Consumer/corporate/130568_040115_gnw.pdf. Accessed February 5, 2016.
18. National Center for Health Statistics. *Health, United States, 2014: With Special Feature on Adults Aged 55-64*. Hyattsville, MD: 2015. Table 101. Nursing homes, beds, residents and occupancy rates, by state: United States, selected years 1995–2013. http://www.cdc.gov/nchs/data/hus/hus14.pdf. Accessed February 5, 2016.
19. Jones AL, Dwyer LL, Bercovitz AR, Strahan GW. The National Nursing Home Survey: 2004 overview. National Center for Health Statistics. *Vital Health Stat*. 2009;13(167):3. http://www.cdc.gov/nchs/data/series/sr_13/sr13_167.pdf. Accessed February 5, 2016.
20. Association of Boards of Examiners of Long Term Care Administrators. Programs. http://www.nabweb.org/programs. Accessed September 5, 2016.
21. The National Academy of Sciences. *For-profit Enterprise in Health Care*. Washington, DC: National Academy Press; 1986:510-515.
22. Center for Medicare Advocacy. Non-profit vs. for-profit nursing homes: is there a difference in care? 2012. http://www.medicareadvocacy.org/non-profit-vs-for-profit-nursing-homes-is-there-a-difference-in-care/. Accessed February 5, 2016.
23. Center for Medicare Advocacy. Health reform: the nursing home provisions. 2010. http://www.medicareadvocacy.org/health-reform-the-nursing-home-provisions/. Accessed February 5, 2016.
24. National Center for Assisted Living. *Facts and Trends: The Assisted Living Sourcebook 2001*. http://www.ahcancal.org/research_data/trends_statistics/Documents/Assisted_Living_Sourcebook_2001.pdf. Accessed February 6, 2016.

25. National Center for Assisted Living. Resident profile. https://www.ahcancal.org/ncal/resources/pages/residentprofile.aspx. Accessed September 5, 2016.

26. National Association for Home Care and Hospice. Basic statistics about home care: Updated 2010. http://www.nahc.org/assets/1/7/10hc_stats.pdf. Accessed February 6, 2016.

27. Medicare Payment Advisory Commission. MEDPAC report to Congress: Medicare payment policy. Chapter 9: Home health care services. March 2015. http://www.medpac.gov/docs/default-source/reports/chapter-9-home-health-care-services-march-2015-report-.pdf?sfvrsn=0. Accessed September 5, 2016.

28. L&M Policy Research. Home health study report. January 11, 2011. https://www.cms.gov/Medicare/Medicare-Fee-for-Service-Payment/HomeHealthPPS/downloads/HHPPS_LiteratureReview.pdf. Accessed September 5, 2016.

29. Centers for Medicare & Medicaid Services. Policy council document: post acute care reform plan. September 28, 2006. http://www.cms.gov/Medicare/Medicare-Fee-for-Service-Payment/SNFPPS/Downloads/pac_reform_plan_2006.pdf. Accessed February 6, 2016.

30. Watts MO, Reaves EL, Musumeci M. Money follows the person: A 2015 state survey of transitions, services and costs. Executive summary. The Henry J. Kaiser Family Foundation. Kaiser Commission on Medicaid and the Uninsured. October 16, 2015. http://files.kff.org/attachment/report-money-follows-the-person-a-2015-state-survey-of-transitions-services-and-costs/. Accessed September 5, 2016.

31. Walker L. Health care reform improves access to Medicaid home and community-based services. American Association of Retired Persons, Public Policy Institute. June 2010. www.aarp.org/health/health-care-reform/info-06-2010/FS-192.html. Accessed February 7, 2016.

32. Reaves EL, Musumeci M. Medicaid and long-term services and supports: a primer. The Henry J. Kaiser Family Foundation. December 15, 2015. http://kff.org/medicaid/report/medicaid-and-long-term-services-and-supports-a-primer/. Accessed February 14, 2016.

33. Reinhard SC, Kassner E, Houser A. How the Affordable Care Act can help move states toward a high-performing system of long-term services and supports. *Health Aff.* March 2011;30:447-453. http://content.healthaffairs.org/content/30/3/447.full.html. Accessed February 14, 2016.

34. American Association for Homecare. Cost effectiveness of homecare. https://www.aahomecare.org/issues/cost-effectiveness-of-homecare. Accessed February 14, 2016.

35. Centers for Medicare & Medicaid Services. Home health providers. April 9, 2013. http://www.cms.gov/Medicare/Provider-Enrollment-and-Certification/CertificationandComplianc/HHAs.html. Accessed February 14, 2016.

36. AARP Public Policy Institute and National Alliance for Caregiving and. Caregivers of older adults: a focused look at those caring for someone age 50+. June 2015. http://www.aarp.org/content/dam/aarp/ppi/2015/caregivers-of-older-adults-focused-look.pdf. Accessed September 5, 2016.

37. Family Caregiver Alliance. Caregiving and ambiguous loss. December 11, 2013. National Center on Caregiving. http://www.caregiver.org/caregiving-and-ambiguous-loss. Accessed February 20, 2016.

38. Pierret CR. The "sandwich generation": women caring for parents and children. *Mon Labor Rev.* September 2006:1-9. http://www.bls.gov/opub/mlr/2006/09/art1full.pdf. Accessed February 20, 2016.

39. MetLife Mature Market Institute and National Alliance for Caregiving. The MetLife caregiving cost study: productivity losses to U.S. businesses. July 2006. http://www.caregiving.org/data/Caregiver%20Cost%20Study.pdf. Accessed February 20, 2016.

40. Reinhard SC, Feinberg LF, Choula R, Houser A. *Valuing the Invaluable: 2015 update.* AARP Public Policy Institute, July 2015. http://www.aarp.org/content/dam/aarp/ppi/2015/valuing-the-invaluable-2015-update-new.pdf. Accessed February 20, 2016.

41. Mayer G. The Family and Medical Leave Act (FMLA): an overview. September 28, 2012. Congressional Research Service. https://www.fas.org/sgp/crs/misc/R42758.pdf. Accessed February 20, 2016.

42. Farmer L. Paid family leave gets new momentum in states. Governing the States and Localities. September 2015. http://www.governing.com/topics/mgmt/gov-paid-family-leave-states.html. Accessed March 18, 2016.

43. U.S. Department of Health and Human Services. Secretary Shalala launches new "Operation Restore Trust:" expanded initiative builds on 23-1 recovery success. May 20, 1997. http://archive.hhs.gov/news/press/1997pres/970520.html. Accessed February 20, 2016.

44. U.S. Department of Health and Human Services, Assistant Secretary for Legislation. Testimony on the Balanced Budget Act Home Health Provisions by Nancy-Ann Min DeParle, Administrator, Health Care Financing Administration. March 31, 1998. http://www.hhs.gov/asl/testify/t980331a.html. Accessed February 20, 2016.

45. Shaughnessy PW, Crisler KS, Hittle DF, Schlenker RE. Summary of the report on OASIS and outcome-based quality improvement in home health care: research and demonstration findings, policy implications, and considerations for future change. March 2002. Centers for Medicare & Medicaid. http://www.cms.gov/Medicare/Quality-Initiatives-Patient-Assessment-Instruments/HomeHealthQualityInits/downloads

/hhqioasisreportsummary.pdf. Accessed February 20, 2016.

46. Centers for Medicare & Medicaid Services. Medicare fraud and abuse: prevention, detection and reporting. November 2012. http://www.cms.gov/Outreach -and-Education/Medicare-Learning-Network-MLN /MLNProducts/downloads/Fraud_and_Abuse.pdf. Accessed February 20, 2016.

47. National Hospice and Palliative Care Organization. NHPCOfactsandfigures:hospicecareinAmerica,2015ed. http://www.nhpco.org/sites/default/files/public /Statistics_Research/2015_Facts_Figures.pdf. Accessed February 28, 2016.

48. Hospice Foundation of America. Become a Volunteer. 2016. http://hospicefoundation.org/Volunteer. Accessed February 28, 2016.

49. Centers for Medicare & Medicaid Services. Your Medicare coverage: hospice & respite care. https:// www.medicare.gov/coverage/hospice-and-respite -care.html. Accessed February 28, 2016.

50. Helpguide.org. Respite care. February 2016. helpguide. org/articles/caregiving/respite-care.htm. Accessed February 28, 2016.

51. U.S. Administration on Aging. The lifespan respite care program. http://www.caregiving.org/pdf/coalitions /The_Year_of_the_Caregiver_Greg_Link.pdf. Accessed February 28, 2016.

52. National Respite Coalition.Seeking congressional cosponsors for Lifespan Respite Care Reauthorization Act of 2015 (HR3913). http://archrespite.org/images /Lifespan_Reauthorization/2015_Reauthorization /Legislative_Alert_2016.pdf. Accessed March 19, 2016.

53. U.S. Department of Health and Human Services. Administration for Community Living. Fiscal Year 2016: *Justification of Estimates for Appropriations Committees.* p. 33. http://www.acl.gov/About_ACL /Budget/docs/FY_2016_ACL_CJ.pdf. Accessed March 6, 2016.

54. Cefalu CA, Heuser M. Adult day care for the demented elderly. *Am Fam Phys.* 1993;47:723-724.

55. Lamden RS, Tynan CM, Warnke J, et al. Adult day care. In: Goldsmith SB, ed. *Long-Term Care Administration Handbook.* Sudbury, MA: Jones and Bartlett; 1993:395-396.

56. National Respite Network and Resource Center. Adult day care: one form of respite for older adults. August 18, 2010. http://www.care-givers.com/DBArticles/pages /viewarticle.php?id=49. Accessed March 8, 2016.

57. National Adult Day Services Association. About adult day services. http://www.nadsa.org/learn-more /about-adult-day-services/. Accessed March 8, 2016.

58. MacDonnell C. CARF accredits adult day care. *Nurs Homes.* 1999;48:53.

59. Miller JA. *Community-Based Long-Term Care.* New York, NY: Sage; 1991.

60. Deloitte & Touche, LLP, and Deloitte & Touche Consulting Group, LLC. *The Balanced Budget Act of 1997, Public Law 105-33 Medicare and Medicaid Changes.* Washington, DC: Deloitte & Touche, LLP; 1997.

61. Maag S. CCRCs today: the real deal about retirement communities. LeadingAge. January 17, 2012. http:// www.leadingage.org/How_to_Respond_to_Media _Inquiries.aspx. Accessed March 8, 2016.

62. Powell R. Pros, cons: Continuing care retirement community. *USA Today.* October 18, 2014. http:// www.usatoday.com/story/money/columnist/powell /2014/10/18/continuing-care-independent-living -assisted-living-powell/17447609/. Accessed March 8, 2016.

63. American Association of Retired Persons. About continuing care retirement communities: learn what they are and how they work. http://www.aarp.org /relationships/caregiving-resource-center/info-09 -2010/ho_continuing_care_retirement_communities. html. Accessed March 8, 2016.

64. Senior Resource for Continuing Care Retirement Communities. Continuing care retirement communities (CCRCs) and lifecare. http://www .seniorresource.com/hccrc.htm. Accessed March 8, 2016.

65. NORCs: An Aging in place initiative. What is NORC SSP? Available at http://norcs.org/norc-paradigm. Accessed March 8, 2016.

66. Ormond BA. Black KJ. Tilly J, Thomas S. Supportive services programs in naturally occurring retirement communities. U.S. Department of Health and Human Services, Office of the Assistant Secretary for Planning and Evaluation (ASPE). November 2004. https://aspe .hhs.gov/basic-report/supportive-services-programs -naturally-occurring-retirement-communities. Accessed March 8, 2016.

67. National Association of Insurance Commissioners & The Center for Insurance Policy and Research. Long-term care. http://www.naic.org/cipr_topics /topic_long_term_care.htm. Accessed March 20, 2016.

68. Ujvari K, AARP Public Policy Institute. Long-term care insurance: 2012 Update. http://www.aarp.org /health/medicare-insurance/info-06-2012/long-term -care-insurance-2012-update,html. Accessed March 20, 2016.

69. Ostrov BF. Long-term care insurance: less bang, more buck. Kaiser Health News. March 17, 2016. http:// khn.org/news/long-term-care-insurance-less-bang -more-buck/. Accessed March 20, 2016.

70. Gleckman H. Requiem for the CLASS Act. *Health Aff.* December 2011;30(12):2231-2234. http://content .healthaffairs.org/content/30/12/2231.full. Accessed March 8, 2016.

71. Merlis M. *Financing Long-Term Care in the Twenty-first Century: The Public and Private Roles.* Institute for Health Policy Solutions. New York, NY: The Commonwealth Fund. 1999:20. http://www.commonwealthfund.org/~/media/files/publications/fund-report/1999/sep/long-term-care-financing-in-the-twenty-first-century--the-public-and-private-roles/merlis343-pdf.pdf. Accessed March 20, 2016.

72. Center for Medicare Advocacy. Federal commission on long-term care concludes its work. September 19, 2013. http://www.medicareadvocacy.org/federal-commission-on-long-term-care-concludes-its-work/. Accessed March 20, 2016.

73. Jaffe S. Long-term panel releases recommendations but fails to offer plan to help pay for services. Kaiser Health News. September 13, 2013. http://khn.org/news/long-term-care-commission-recommendations/. Accessed March 20, 2016.

74. Institute for the Future of Aging Services. The long-term care workforce: can the crisis be fixed? January 2007. http://www.leadingage.org/uploadedFiles/Content/About/Center_for_Applied_Research/Center_for_Applied_Research_Initiatives/LTC_Workforce_Commission_Report.pdf. Accessed March 8, 2016.

75. Stone R, Harahan MF. Improving the long-term care workforce serving older adults. *Health Aff.* 2010;29:109-115. http://content.healthaffairs.org/content/29/1/109.full.pdf±html. Accessed March 20, 2016.

76. Paraprofessional Healthcare Institute. Home care workers deserve minimum wage & overtime. http://phinational.org/campaigns/home-care-workers-deserve-minimum-wage-protection. Accessed March 20, 2016.

77. Convergence Center for Policy Resolution. Long-Term Care Financing Collaborative. Diverse group of policy experts and stakeholders proposes major long-term care reforms. http://www.convergencepolicy.org/wp-content/uploads/2016/02/LTCFC-Press-Release-for-2.22.16-FINAL-FINAL.pdf. Accessed March 20, 2016.

CHAPTER 10

Behavioral Health Services

Susan V. McLeer, MD, MS

CHAPTER OVERVIEW

This chapter provides an overview of behavioral health services in the United States. It examines historical trends and the forces affecting the distribution and types of behavioral health services. Epidemiologic data on the prevalence of psychiatric and substance disorders compared with the nation's behavioral healthcare needs highlights gaps in service adequacy. Continuing changes in organization and fiscal structures resulting from the implementation of the Patient Protection and Affordable Care Act (ACA) are examined. The response of individual states to the ACA, specifically regarding Medicaid expansion and its impact on behavioral health services, is highlighted. Special challenges of the homeless and incarcerated mentally ill populations are noted. Behavioral health workforce shortages are discussed as are opportunities for improvement in the financing and delivery of behavioral health services throughout the nation.

The United States Congress, in response to the imperative of addressing issues of cost, quality, and access to healthcare services, passed the Patient Protection and Affordable Care Act of 2010 (ACA). The nation is still in the implementation phases for the ACA, which will continue through 2018. When ACA insurance enrollment began in 2013, approximately 44.8 million persons of all ages were uninsured. By the third quarter of 2015, the law's impact had decreased the number of uninsured to 28.8 million, 9.1 percent of the total population, with 16 million fewer uninsured than in 2013.[1] Historically, this is the lowest rate of uninsured Americans. Yet, there is ongoing political polarization regarding whether or not the ACA is necessary, effective, or even harmful, with opinions divided along political party lines. Currently, both houses of the Congress have a Republican majority and President Obama is in his final year of office. The 2016 presidential and congressional elections will occur prior to this edition's publication, making it impossible to predict the political climate of 2017 and beyond. However, over the past five years, there has been considerable contention about the ACA from the Republican majority, with more than

50 attempts to repeal the law finally resulting in a repeal bill sent to the President in January 2016 that he promptly vetoed.[2] Congressional gridlock and record-low legislative productivity has been an ongoing problem for six years. Nonetheless, change is happening. The paradigms used for providing care and the mechanisms for funding programs and individual care are undergoing rapid change.

In the midst of this change process, a new lexicon has emerged, requiring definitions. "Mental health care" now is often referred to as "behavioral health care," with psychiatric care, a medical subspecialty, being but one aspect of an integrated approach to needed services. Usage of terms throughout the country is not uniform. Some jurisdictions, such as states or counties, have departments of mental health, whereas others have departments of behavioral health. The concept of "patient" has been replaced with "consumer" or "person/people." All of these terms will be used in the chapter, depending on the time period and discussion context.

The paradigm for service provision to individuals has shifted from a treatment plan model, which formerly used a diagnosis-anchored, "problem-based" list, to a model that is "strength-based." The "Recovery Movement" has been well underway since 2004 and advocates for the provision of holistic care within the obvious context that a psychiatric illness or behavioral health issue is but one aspect of a person's life. The task of recovery is self-directed, individualized, and person-centered. It is founded on the principles that consumers must have opportunities for choice, self-direction, and empowerment. The model is similar to that used in working with individuals with other disabilities.

The implementation of the ACA, with a significant drop in the number of uninsured throughout the country, has enabled many more people to seek care. This is turn, has resulted in a workforce shortage in the behavioral health field. The workforce shortage is resulting in yet another paradigm shift in service delivery wherein psychiatrists are starting to think more about providing population-based services integrated with primary care providers than restricting services to only those provided directly in psychiatrists' individual, office-based practices. These issues will be discussed more fully later in this chapter.

▶ Historical Overview

In the early years of our nation, the mentally ill were confined at home, in jails, or in almshouses, where they received no care and suffered severely. By 1817, a philosophical change occurred in Philadelphia when the Quakers established the first freestanding "asylum" where people with mental illness could receive kind, but firm, treatment while engaged in work, education, and recreation.[3] Effective biological treatments were nonexistent, but psychosocial care was heavily influenced by the European movement for the moral treatment of the mentally ill. Unfortunately, few people nationally could access such care, and most continued to be confined under the most adverse circumstances in overcrowded asylums and hospitals that housed not only the mentally ill, but also criminals and homeless people.

Little changed until the end of World War I, when thousands of soldiers returned, suffering from "war neurosis." This condition, also called "shell shock," was synonymous with current criteria for posttraumatic stress disorder. Finally, in the 1930s and more than a decade after World War I ended, the first effective biological treatments for various types of mental illness emerged in the forms of insulin coma, drug-induced convulsions, electroconvulsive therapy, and psychosurgery. With the end of World War II, the federal government became active in the mental health field, passing the National Mental Health Act in 1946, which resulted in the establishment of the National Institute of Mental Health (NIMH). Federal, state, and county public funds were allocated for mental health training, research, and service. The Department of Veterans Affairs recognized the need for increased services and established psychiatric hospitals and clinics.

During the 1940s and 1950s, psychiatric care was mainly provided in state-operated psychiatric hospitals.[4] By the mid-1950s, the public psychiatric hospital population peaked at more than half a million people.[5] Fortuitously, this peak corresponded with the development of the first psychoactive medications specifically targeting psychiatric disorders. These agents, chlorpromazine (Thorazine) and reserpine, were used for the treatment of schizophrenia and other psychotic disorders. These pharmaceutical advances profoundly changed patterns of care, reducing the need for convulsive therapies and psychosurgery, and provided patients with effective interventions that allowed them to live outside of a psychiatric hospital. New outpatient services were developed as were transitional residential facilities, or halfway houses, for the mentally ill. As discussed later in this chapter, in addition to pharmaceutical advances, the implementation of new social programs and the development of community mental health centers for outpatient treatment facilitated a dramatic flow of discharges from psychiatric hospitals over succeeding years. From its peak in the mid-1950s at more than half a million people, by 1994 the number of inpatients in public psychiatric hospitals stood at approximately 72,000.[5]

In 1955, Congress established the Joint Commission on Mental Illness and Health. The Commission attacked the quality of care and inadequate patient access to care in large state and county psychiatric hospitals. The Commission's report stimulated a substantial shift in sites for the provision of mental health services from inpatient state and county psychiatric hospitals to outpatient facilities. This was the first time a federal body had intervened to manage the allocation of resources for the mentally ill. In 1956, Social Security and Disability Insurance became accessible to the mentally ill.

By the early 1960s, the winds of change had been whipped up not only by the Commission, but also by the development of new psychotropic medications and psychosocial treatments that could provide effective intervention outside the hospital. Congress passed the Mental Retardation Facilities and Community Mental Health Centers Construction Act of 1963, resulting in new federal support for community-based services. Subsequently, entitlement programs became accessible to the mentally ill, Medicaid and Medicare in 1965, Supplemental Security Income (SSI) in 1974, and housing subsidies, among others.

Throughout the 1960s and 1970s, the federal government became even more involved in financing mental health care. Community mental health centers developed and expanded, and more health professionals entered the mental health field. By 1980, the number of patient care episodes delivered in organized mental health settings increased nearly fourfold, from 1.7 million to 7 million.[6] Most patients were seen in outpatient settings, and few were severely mentally ill.[7] Insurers became concerned that psychiatric care was an uncontrolled healthcare cost and started limiting coverage for the treatment of mental illness. This was done by placing limits on the amount of service that would be reimbursed, such as lifetime limits, irrespective of the nature of the illness, and by developing discounted fee-for-service contracts with the costs of psychiatric care being reimbursed as a percentage of cost, a system that used different metrics than those used for reimbursement of the cost for non-psychiatric illnesses. Furthermore, insurers, concerned that psychiatric care would drain their coffers, started issuing contracts that outsourced care and coverage for mental health care, a process referred to as carve-outs. Another method insurers used for cost control was capitation, as discussed in Chapter 8. With capitation, a set amount is paid for care of a defined patient population, irrespective of the amount of service provided. Through these financing initiatives, non-parity of mental illness insurance coverage with insurance coverage for other categories of illness was established. When non-parity occurred, the behavioral health system was defined as "different" from other parts of the healthcare system. The issue of non-parity in coverage has plagued the financing mechanisms for behavioral health care for decades.

Simultaneously, with the development of new insurance structures and with a shift in focus toward ambulatory care within community mental health centers, many severely mentally ill patients, who formerly had been warehoused in large state or county psychiatric hospitals, were discharged from institutions to community boarding and nursing homes. This deinstitutionalization movement was presented as important to the rehabilitation of those with severe mental illness. Emphasis was placed on the necessity of providing service in community settings. States, through Medicaid, received financial incentives to move patients from inpatient settings to boarding houses. However, community resources remained limited for a variety of reasons, and many severely ill psychiatric patients were not able to access necessary services.

By the late-1970s, healthcare costs had soared, and the federal government became concerned with identifying mechanisms for restraining health-related spending. Limited access to care, including financial barriers, continued to plague those with psychiatric disorders, limiting individual recovery. Consequently psychosocial rehabilitation programs were expanded under Medicaid. Medicaid payment for outpatient behavioral health care was expanded and co-payment requirements for case management services were reduced. Patients with severe and persistent mental illness became eligible for SSI funding. These changes resulted in a substantial shift in quality of life for this population; however, by the mid-1980s, programs were sharply curtailed again, with cutbacks in housing subsidies, social services, and increased exclusion of people with psychiatric and substance abuse disorders from SSI benefits.

By 1990, the locus of mental health care in the United States had shifted from inpatient to outpatient settings. Of the 1.7 million episodes of mental health services delivered in 1955, 77 percent were in inpatient settings and 23 percent in outpatient programs. By 1990, 67 percent of the 8.6 million episodes of mental health services delivered were provided in outpatient programs, 7 percent in partial hospitalization settings (not 24-hour facilities), and 21 percent in inpatient services.[8]

Since the 1990s, because of constant and rigorous pressure placed on Congress and legislative bodies by advocacy groups, the focus on severe psychiatric illness returned. The Medicare Prescription Drug Improvement and Modernization Act of 2003 expanded drug coverage for older Americans. The Child Health Insurance Program (CHIP), originally enacted in 1987 and financed jointly by federal and state governments, increased the number of insured children in low-income families. The issue of insurance parity for psychiatric and behavioral health care was finally addressed through the Wellstone–Domenici Parity Act of 2008.[9]

Through insurance coverage for people previously uninsured for financial reasons, or barriers due to pre-existing conditions, the ACA improves access to behavioral health services. In these ways, the ACA supports and reinforces the concept of insurance parity.[10]

However, in spite of advancements in therapies, financial assistance, and social supports for the severely mentally ill, negative effects of deinstitutionalization remain pervasive and persistent in the forms of homelessness and criminal incarceration among these individuals. The Substance Abuse and Mental Health Services Administration (SAMHSA) estimates that 26.2 percent of sheltered homeless persons have a severe mental illness and that 34.7 percent of the same population have chronic substance abuse issues.[11] Another estimate is that, at minimum, 26 percent of America's homeless, 165,000 individuals, were seriously mentally ill at any given point in time.[12] In 2014, health policy experts noted that "69 percent of them (jail inmates) have problems related to drugs, alcohol, or both and 64 percent meet the criteria for mental illness at the time of their booking or during the 12 months prior to their arrest."[13] Citing reductions in availability of inpatient mental health services and under-funding of community mental health services, the same authors note that "jails and prisons have become the de facto mental health "system" for millions of under- or uninsured people with mental health problems and co-occurring mental health and substance abuse conditions."[13] Further, the American Psychiatric Association reports that incarcerated individuals now appear to have more severe types of mental illness than in the past, including psychotic and major mood disorders.[14] For the mentally ill, homelessness and risks of incarceration are highly interrelated. Because homeless persons are at a severe disadvantage in accessing, obtaining, and maintaining needed treatment, their untreated conditions can lead to behaviors that subject them to incarceration. This phenomenon is not only profoundly deleterious to mentally ill persons, but also to their communities where they overburden already-overcrowded hospital emergency departments and strain law enforcement agency resources.[15] With the Medicaid expansion and emphases on care coordination, the ACA offers hope for improving care for both homeless and incarcerated mentally ill persons. However, it is clear that given changes needed in the still very disjointed care delivery system, reaping the benefits of the reforming system for these highly vulnerable populations with complex needs will be extremely challenging for providers and policy makers.[13]

▶ Recipients of Psychiatric and Behavioral Health Services

Psychiatric illness is widespread in the U.S. population. The most recent statistics from the NIMH report that approximately 44 million, or 18 percent of American adults, experience a mental illness in a given year.[16] **FIGURE 10-1** depicts overall prevalence by gender, age groups, and race.[16]

However, many mental health disorders are temporary and have minimal effects on personal functioning. A subgroup of the population with diagnosed mental illnesses is classified as having a serious mental illness (SMI), resulting in "serious functional impairment which substantially interferes with or limits one or more major life activities."[17] This subgroup, estimated at 10 million adults aged 18 years or older, represents approximately 4 percent of all U.S. adults.[17] This subgroup represents those at greatest risk and having the greatest need for service. **FIGURE 10-2** depicts the overall prevalence of SMI and prevalence by gender, age groups, and race.[17]

Neuropsychiatric disorders are the leading cause of disability in the United States surpassing cardiovascular disease, cancer, and unintentional injuries as measured in units encompassing the total burden of disease and defined as disability-adjusted life years (DALYs). DALYs represent the total number of years lost to illness, disability, or premature death within a given population. They are calculated by adding the number of years of life lost to the number of years lived with disability for a certain disease or disorder. **FIGURE 10-3** depicts World Health Organization estimates of categories of diseases and disorders and the percentage each category contributes to the total DALYs for the United States. As shown, neuropsychiatric disorders are the leading cause of disability in the United States, followed by cardiovascular and circulatory diseases.[18] (See Figure 10-3.)

As depicted by **FIGURE 10-4**, of all DALYs caused by disorders in the mental and behavioral category, mood disorders and drug use account for more than 63 percent of the total.[19] Figure 10-4 provides a percentage breakdown of total U.S. DALYs in the mental and behavioral disorders category.

People and their families suffer immeasurably from mental illness. Studies of the measurable costs for mental illness have examined both direct costs for behavioral health services and treatment as well as expenditures and losses secondary to disability. Estimates based on a 2002 database indicated that

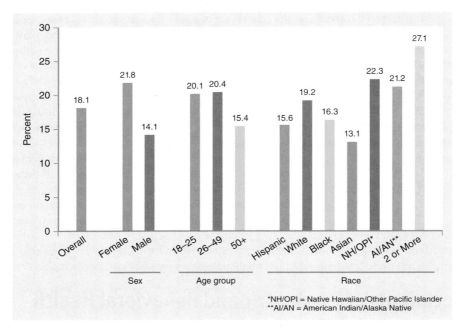

FIGURE 10-1 **Prevalence of Any Mental Illness Among U.S. Adults (2014)**

Reproduced from National Institute of Mental Health: Substance Abuse and Mental Health Services Administration.

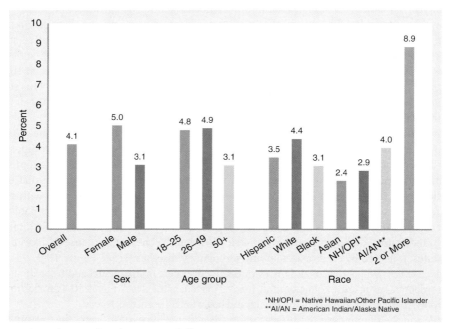

FIGURE 10-2 **Prevalence of Serious Mental Illness Among U.S. Adults (2014)**

Reproduced from National Institute of Mental Health: Substance Abuse and Mental Health Services Administration.

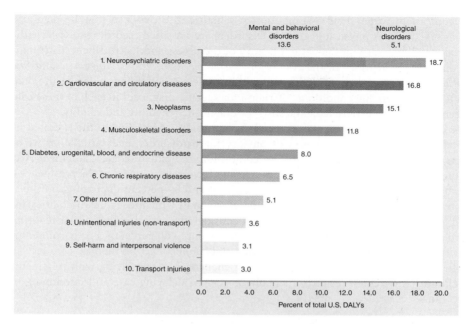

FIGURE 10-3 **Top 10 Leading Disease/Disorder Categories Contributing to U.S. DALYs (2010)**
Reproduced from National Institute of Mental Health: Substance Abuse and Mental Health Services Administration.

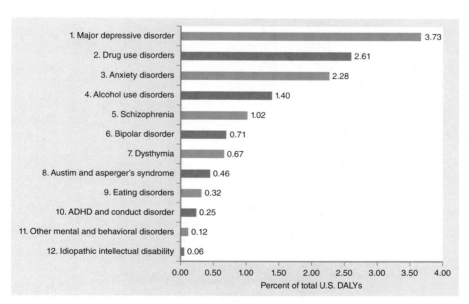

FIGURE 10-4 **U.S. DALYS for Mental and Behavioral Disorders as a Percent of Total U.S. DALYs**
Reproduced from National Institute of Mental Health: Substance Abuse and Mental Health Services Administration.

costs are comprised of disability benefits payments, healthcare expenditures, and lost earnings.[20] (See **FIGURE 10-5**.) Federal estimates project 2014 expenditures on mental health and substance abuse treatment alone at $239 billion, an increase of $121 billion or 49 percent since 2003.[21]

In contrast to widely held assumptions, psychiatric disorders can now be diagnosed and treated as effectively as physical disorders. Disorders are classified according to criteria that provide predictability regarding the natural history of the illness and its treatment. Currently, there are 22 diagnostic categories in the *American Psychiatric Association's Diagnostic and Statistical Manual of Mental Disorders (DSM-V)*, and within these categories there are specific diagnostic criteria for more than 300 conditions.[22] Criteria for specific diagnoses in each of these categories have been subjected to extensive field testing for diagnostic reliability and validity.

The co-existence of two diagnoses is called comorbidity. According to the National Institute of Mental Health, nearly half of those with any psychiatric disorder meet criteria for two or more disorders, with severity strongly related to comorbidity.[23] Epidemiologic Catchment Area Program studies in both clinical and nonclinical settings have determined that the prevalence of substance abuse comorbidity ranges between 23 percent and 80 percent depending on the specific psychiatric diagnosis.[24] In addition, clinical studies of people with intellectual disabilities, formerly referred to as mental retardation, have revealed considerable variation in prevalence estimates of co-morbid psychiatric disorders, ranging from 30 percent to 60 percent.[25] Furthermore, mentally ill individuals have great difficulty in identifying and connecting with medical care services, and even when they do so, may have overwhelming challenges in complying with treatment plans. These circumstances often result in mentally ill persons delaying care and developing medical complications.

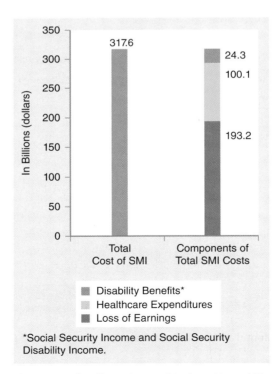

FIGURE 10-5 **Annual Total Direct and Indirect Costs of Serious Mental Illness in 2002**

▶ Treatment Services

As noted above, in 2014, approximately 44 million adults ages 18 or older—18 percent of the adult population—met criteria for at least one psychiatric disorder in the previous 12-month period. Among the 20 million adults with a substance abuse disorder, more than 50 percent had a co-morbid psychiatric disorder. Among the 44 million known to have a mental illness, only 40 percent were able to access mental health treatment services.[26] In the subgroup with greatest need for treatment, those diagnosed with a SMI, only 42 percent received some form of treatment.[27] These data do not take into consideration whether or not treatment was of adequate duration or quality. Those with SMI are most often treated within the mental health sector; however, others, less-severely afflicted, receive services and treatment in other settings. For example, within a 12-month period, of those who were diagnosed with a mental health problem, 41.1 percent received some treatment, including 12.3 percent treated by a psychiatrist, 16.0 percent treated by a non-psychiatrist mental health specialist, 22.8 percent treated by a primary care provider, 8.1 percent treated by a human services provider, and 6.8 percent treated by a complementary and alternative medical provider.[28] The lack of care was greatest in traditionally underserved groups, such as the elderly and racial and ethnic minorities, as well as people with low incomes or no health insurance. Another notably underserved group was those living in rural areas where behavioral health services were not available.

▶ Barriers to Care

There are multiple factors associated with lack of access to care. These include:

- Provider geographic distribution
- Financial limitations
- Lack of or inadequate health insurance
- Stigma
- Misunderstandings about the treatability of conditions
- Personal and provider attitudes
- Cultural issues
- A poorly organized care delivery system

Patients with a mental illness and a substance use disorder experience additional barriers secondary to the stigma associated with substance abuse.

Substance abuse, including alcoholism, is a chronic brain disease, like many other psychiatric disorders. However, the general community and, more disturbingly, providers tend not to view substance abuse and addiction as a chronic illness but often instead attribute causality to a lack of will or a moral failure. Furthermore, if there is a relapse, rather than seeing the relapse as a characteristic of the disease, the person who has relapsed is apt to be removed from the treatment program. This is due to providers failing to recognize that by its nature, substance abuse is a chronic illness and is subject to fluctuations that include improvements in function, periods of stabilization, and relapses.[29]

Children and Adolescents

Data on the use of mental health services by children and adolescents diagnosed with mental disorders first became available in 1999 following a NIMH survey of children and adolescents between ages 9 and 17. Only 9 percent of children and adolescents had been able to access and receive some mental health services in the general medical and specialty mental health delivery sectors. This accounted for fewer than half of those with a diagnosed mental illness. The study found that the largest provider of services to children and youth was the school system.[30] In 2009, results from a larger study indicated that the prevalence of mental health disorders in children aged 4–17 had increased more than 40 percent between the mid-1990s and 2006, with 7 percent of this population being diagnosed with at least one psychiatric illness. Increased sensitivity and use of screening tools by primary care physicians appeared to have had a major effect on findings. The rate of mental illness diagnosis among children aged 4–17 seen in primary care offices doubled between 1996 and 2006.[31] However, access to care remains problematic, particularly for children with severe disorders. The American Association for Child and Adolescent Psychiatry reported in 2016 that there is an ongoing critical shortage of U.S. child and adolescent psychiatrists compounded by severe geographic maldistribution particularly in low-socioeconomic and rural areas.[32]

Clinical research involving children and adolescents suffering from mental illness has lagged considerably behind that for adults. Inadequate research has been particularly notable regarding pharmaceuticals to treat all types of children's illnesses. In response, Congress passed two laws to increase the study of drugs in children. In 2002, the Best Pharmaceuticals for Children Act (BPCA) was enacted and reauthorized in 2007 to establish and conduct a program for pediatric drug development through the National Institutes of Health (NIH). The BPCA's intent is threefold:[33]

- Identify and prioritize drugs needing study
- Develop study requests in collaboration with NIH, Food and Drug Administration, and other organization experts
- Conduct studies on priority drugs after manufacturers decline to do so.

The Pediatric Research Equity Act (PREA) of 2003 recognized that some drugs that work for adults may not work for children. The Act also recognizes that a drug's use in children may entail safety concerns or dosage parameters that differ from those in adults. For these reasons, PREA requires drug companies to study products in children for the same use for which they were approved in adults.[34] These laws have resulted in some gains. Prior to their enactment, more than 80 percent of the drugs approved for adult use were being used in children, even though their safety and effectiveness had not been established in children. Today, the number has been reduced to about 50 percent. Clearly, there remains much need for improvement.[34]

Although diagnostic techniques have been highly refined through standardized diagnostic interviews and symptom rating scales that facilitate accurate identification of those in need of service, research funding for treatment of mental illness in childhood and adolescence has not kept pace. The effects of a mental disorder on the developmental process of children are only beginning to be appreciated, but they clearly impact development in emotional, social, and cognitive domains. Moreover, few practitioners access research findings regarding treatment efficacy, and there are inadequate numbers of well-trained child and adolescent psychiatrists available for the population at risk. The need for expanding the workforce, developing early interventions, providing treatment and rehabilitation services, and seeking enhanced funding for research is critical.

Older Adults

Although many advances have been made in the treatment of mental disorders, a crisis looms in providing behavioral health services to the older population. The number of persons ages 65 years or older is expected to grow to 21.7 percent of the population by 2040, totaling 82.3 million.

A current U.S. Census projection estimates that the population 65 years or older will more than double in number between the years 2013 and 2060, reaching 98.2 million by year 2060. People 65 years old and older represented 12.9 percent of the population in 2009, but this group is expected to increase in number and represent 19 percent of the population, more than 72.1 million people, by 2030.[35] In addition to this increase in sheer volume, epidemiologic studies have indicated that baby-boomer cohorts have high prevalence rates for depression, suicide, anxiety, and alcohol and drug abuse.[36]

Studies have indicated that one in four older Americans has a significant psychiatric disorder, with depression and anxiety disorders being the most common. The prevalence of psychiatric disorders in the aging population is expected to more than double over the next 25 years with numbers increasing from 7 to 15 million people. In addition, there looms yet another problem regarding the abuse of alcohol and substances, particularly the abuse and misuse of prescription medication. Estimates note that 1.7 million older adults abused substances and alcohol and that the prevalence is expected to increase to 4.4 million by 2020.[37]

The implications of these findings on future resource allocation decisions are enormous. Although older adults suffer from many of the same mental disorders as their younger counterparts, diagnosis and treatment are complicated by medical conditions that mimic or mask psychiatric disorders. Older adults also are more likely to be reluctant to report symptoms and tend to emphasize physical complaints, minimizing complaints about their mental status. Stereotypes about aging predispose older adults to believe that adverse mental changes are to be expected, contributing to a tendency to minimize the symptoms associated with a psychiatric disorder. Fears of developing dementia are omnipresent and add to reluctance in symptom disclosure. Such concerns make assessment and accurate diagnosis challenging. [38]

▶ The Organization of Psychiatric and Behavioral Health Services

Psychiatric disorders and behavioral health problems are treated by an array of providers representing multiple disciplines working in both public and private settings. The loose coordination of facilities and services has resulted in the mental health delivery system being referred to as a de-facto mental health service system,[39] structured with four highly compartmentalized sectors characterized by poor inter-sector communication and isolated funding streams.[40]

The psychiatric and behavioral health sector consists of behavioral health professionals, such as psychiatrists, psychologists, psychiatric nurses, psychiatric social workers, and behavioral health clinicians working in outpatient settings. More recently, providers are hiring peer specialists, people with a psychiatric or substance abuse disorder, who are trained to help others in accessing care and developing a recovery plan. Early reports suggest that peer specialists are particularly helpful in enhancing treatment compliance and community integration.

Most acute care is provided in psychiatric units of general hospitals or beds located throughout hospitals. Intensive treatment for adults and children is provided in private psychiatric hospitals, with residential treatment centers being available for children and adolescents. Public-sector facilities include state and county mental hospitals and multiservice facilities that provide or coordinate a wide range of outpatient, intensive case management, partial hospitalization, or inpatient services. Very few long-term care inpatient facilities remain, with most care being provided within the community. Currently, there is a movement away from large community residential facilities for the mentally ill toward an increased focus on independent living accommodations such as apartments for mentally ill people in need of housing. Case managers work with people to enhance their daily living skills, their use of the public transportation systems, and their ability to access care as well as other resources within the community.

The primary care sector consists of healthcare professionals, such as internists, family practitioners, pediatricians, and nurse practitioners in private office-based practices, clinics, hospitals, and nursing homes. This sector often is the initial point of contact and may be the only source of mental health services for a large proportion of people with psychiatric or behavioral health disorders. The rates of mental health diagnosis in the primary care setting have increased materially in the past decade, doubling for children and increasing by almost 30 percent for adults.[7]

The human services sector consists of social service agencies, school-based counseling services, residential rehabilitation services, vocational rehabilitation services, criminal justice/prison-based services, and religious professional counselors. With the recession of 2008, the role of this sector shifted as many states faced significant challenges in balancing their budgets. With increased unemployment and business closures, state revenues were deficient. Consequently, many states decreased services within the human service and mental health sectors, with few of these services being restored as of the first quarter of 2016. This has resulted in people with mental illness facing even greater financial and resource barriers to accessing care. In addition, many have experienced significant losses in welfare benefits that have resulted in an inability to pay insurance co-pays for service visits and, more importantly, an inability to pay co-pays for medication. Decreased personal revenues, including reductions in state-supported general assistance, have resulted in an increase in the homeless population and an increased feeling of desperation among those mentally ill people who have limited financial resources. These economic circumstances and resulting barriers to care have caused exacerbations of symptoms among mentally ill persons who previously had been stable and productive. Co-morbid substance use and abuse has increased as well as petty crimes. As a consequence, many people with SMI have transitioned from the psychiatric and behavioral health sector into the human service sector, specifically into the criminal justice and prison system. Compounding the tragedy of imprisonment is the limited and variable quality of treatment programs for substance abuse and mental illness within the prison health system. Costs for treating people with a psychiatric disability in prisons far exceed the costs of treating and supporting them within the community. The old adage of "a penny wise, a pound foolish" appears to apply to those states where budget cuts have shifted care from programs specifically designed to care for people with mental illness and substance abuse disorders into the criminal justice and prison systems. It remains an abysmal reality that, in fact, U.S. prisons of today have earned a remarkable resemblance to the early asylums that warehoused individuals prior to scientific understanding of mental illness and treatment. Mentally ill prisoners, like their counterparts from the 1700s and 1800s, without political voice, are among the most vulnerable people in U.S. society.

The volunteer support network sector consists of self-help groups and family advocacy groups. This sector has been invaluable in shifting public attention to people with persistent and severe mental illness. Advocacy groups also have had a major impact on Congress in its appropriations for funding research focused on mental illness and substance abuse disorders through the National Institutes of Health. Numerous national and state public and private advocacy organizations participate in efforts to illuminate the needs of mentally ill and disabled persons at the federal state and local levels. Organizations encompass a broad range of activities from lobbying federal and state legislatures on legal and funding issues to promoting behavioral health awareness and reducing mental illness stigma.[41] For organization details, readers are encouraged to consult the reference noted and its numerous links.

▶ Paradigm Shifts

Within the last five years, there have been two paradigm shifts directed toward turning the de-facto mental health system into a more integrated and effective system of care.

Recovery Oriented Systems of Care

The recovery transformation of the mental health system was first introduced in 2002 by the Freedom Commission on Mental Health, established by executive order of President George W. Bush.[42] In 2004, there was a National Consensus Conference on Mental Health Recovery and Mental Health Systems Transformation.[43] This invitational conference was sponsored by the U.S. Department of Health and Human Services and the Interagency Committee on Disability Research in partnership with six other federal agencies. At this conference, recovery was cited as the single most important goal for transforming mental health care in America. The focus on choice, strength-based empowerment of the consumer, and the establishment of hope for a better life culminated in a true paradigm shift for both assessment and treatment planning.

Recovery is the process of pursuing a fulfilling and contributing life, regardless of the difficulties one has faced. The Recovery Oriented Systems of Care (ROSC) provides a holistic and integrated approach to care, seeking to enhance a person's positive self-image and identity. The overarching goals in ROSC are to empower mentally ill people through the provision of choices and a vision of a hopeful future. Evaluations, formerly focused on establishing a diagnosis and a list of problems, are now, through the ROSC, person-centered and strength-based. Diagnoses and specific problems remain important but are now viewed as issues that must be managed within the context of life goals that have the potential to enhance the person's quality of life and self-identity. Actively linking a person's strengths with family and community resources are critical steps. Peer specialists facilitate initial contacts between a person and the providers of care, and facilitate a person's connections with resources in the community. Resources may be illness related, but they also may be related to the planning of leisure activities, shopping, and other normalizing activities. The ROSC shifts care from the old episodic care model to one that emphasizes continuity. Choice is provided through the treatment planning process. Both providers and individuals are encouraged to focus beyond symptoms of mental illness and articulate needs and desires for housing, utilization of public transportation systems, employment, leisure activities, or even a weight-reduction strategy. In ROSC, the traditional treatment plan targeting symptom reduction shifts to that of a "hope plan" for the individual's future.[44]

Integration of Primary Care and Behavioral Health Services

More than 60 percent of people with psychiatric illness are unable to access any kind of psychiatric care, and more than half of those who do, access and receive care in primary care settings.[21] In addition, people with psychiatric illness, particularly those with SMI, die 15–20 years earlier than people without psychiatric illness.[45] Moreover, many of the medications used to treat SMI pose an increased risk for the development of metabolic syndrome (high cholesterol, diabetes, and heart disease) whereas others have complex interactions with other medications that the person may be taking for non-psychiatric conditions. As a result, it is crucial that behavioral health services become increasingly integrated with primary care services. From the perspective of the primary care providers, there is great need for consultation from psychiatrists and behavioral health specialists, particularly given that primary care providers carry much of the burden for early diagnosis of mental illness and substance abuse disorders.

Yet, psychiatrists and other behavioral health professionals have traditionally not been involved with the primary care treatment team. Finances have been a major barrier to involvement, particularly the problems posed by insurance non-parity, which has made it difficult, if not impossible, for the behavioral health clinicians to cover costs within a primary care setting.

The ACA provides the mechanisms and funding for massive expansion of insurance coverage through private health insurance exchanges and Medicaid expansion. Under the ACA, the individual mandate for health insurance coverage requires that if the insurance plan provides coverage for psychiatric and behavioral health care, then that coverage must be equivalent to that provided for non-psychiatric medical disorders. However, an insurer is not required to offer coverage for all behavioral health conditions. This means that insurers, not infrequently, use this loophole as a methodology for trimming costs. Hence insurers are able to continue decreasing access to services for behavioral health care. Nonetheless, new models of care are emerging that emphasize the integration of behavioral health services with primary care. Multiple models for facilitating such integration are being studied, with the Collaborative Care Model as the most prominent and evidence-based.[46-48] Within the Collaborative Care Model, the behavioral health provider is not a psychiatrist, but an individual with behavioral health training, such as a psychologist with a master's or doctoral degree, a social worker, or a case worker. Behavioral health providers are usually embedded in a primary care office or clinic and use a variety of screening tools and standardized rating scales to identify patients in need of care. The psychiatrist, as a medical specialist, provides much indirect patient care by reviewing screening interview and standardized rating scales results, conducting caseload-focused registry reviews, and providing follow-up consultation with the behavioral health specialists and the primary care provider. Direct patient care by the psychiatrist is infrequent, but it may be required for complicated cases which are not responding adequately to care provided through the primary care physician and/or the behavioral health specialist.

To date, widespread implementation of integrated care models has been hindered by two major issues: (1) the availability of sustainable funding, and (2) the availability of a sufficient behavioral healthcare workforce. Sustainable financing mechanisms have not been developed adequately or established for any of the integrated care models. Siloed funding streams and the lack of mechanisms for reimbursing providers for indirect patient care through the currently predominant fee-for-service billing systems are a substantial part of the problem. Effective models of integrated care, for the most part, have had grant funding from either the federal or state governments, with some having private foundation funding. As discussed in several other topics of this text, the issue remains as to what mechanisms will be developed that are sufficient for sustainable funding. Bundled payments, case-based rates, and global capitation are under consideration as possible mechanisms for sustaining funding of integrated care programs.

Integrated care also requires access to a considerable behavioral healthcare workforce. Many of the current behavioral health specialists and psychiatrists will require retraining to acquire skills and techniques necessary for working with a population-based care model. Many specialty organizations are working on the development and implementation of new training for practitioners. Many of the retraining programs are being supported by grant funding at this time. What is clear is that the new skills and techniques for service delivery must be subsumed by established training programs if future needs are to be met. Finally, the use of telemedicine for providing care to remote communities and underserved areas will be a critical part of the answer to workforce shortages.[47,49] Nonetheless, even with the challenges of funding programs and workforce development, there is much optimism among both providers and insurers regarding the integration of psychiatric and primary care services. Early reports suggest that the integrative methodology improves health outcomes and, in the long run, will decrease healthcare costs.[50, 51]

▶ Financing Psychiatric and Behavioral Health Services

Mental health services are funded in many ways, including private health insurance, Medicaid, Medicare, state and county funding, as well as contracts and grants. As noted in the historic review of mental health services, the history of insurance coverage for behavioral health services has been one of unequal coverage for psychiatric and behavioral health disorders when compared to coverage for non-psychiatric medical illnesses. As explained previously, "non-parity" has been used to describe insurance inequalities. Insurance inequalities have taken many forms and imposed severe limitations on the amount and kind of care people with chronic and severe mental illness, such as schizophrenia, have been able to access. Recognizing that schizophrenia is a chronic illness not unlike some of the non-psychiatric chronic illnesses, such as multiple sclerosis, diabetes, stroke, and heart disease, it becomes apparent that the insurers have produced huge inequities biased against people with mental illness.

The Mental Health Parity Act of 1996 was approved by the U.S. Congress with overwhelming bipartisan support. Enacted in 1998, this legislation equated aggregated lifetime limits and annual limits for mental health services with aggregate lifetime and annual limits for medical care; however, the law allowed many cost-shifting loopholes, such as setting limits on psychiatric inpatient days, prescription drugs, outpatient visits, raising coinsurance and deductibles, and modifying the definition of medical necessity.[52] The Act did not require employers to offer mental health coverage, nor did it impose any limits on insurance co-payments, deductibles, days, or visits. Furthermore, coverage was not required for people suffering from substance use and abuse disorders, which are psychiatric disorders with substantial public health significance.

In 2008, contained within the Emergency Economic Stabilization Act, Senators Paul Wellstone (D-Minnesota) and Pete Domenici (R-New Mexico) proposed the Mental Health Parity and Addiction Equity Act (MHPAEA) to build upon the Mental Health Parity Act of 1996. Enacted in 2008 with bipartisan support, the law took effect in October 2009. It was intended to end health insurance benefit inequity between mental health and substance abuse benefits and medical/surgical benefits for group health plans with more than 50 employees. Significant features of the legislation include the following:

- Equity coverage applicable to all deductibles, co-payments, coinsurance, and out-of-pocket expenses and to all treatment limitations including frequency of treatment, numbers of visits, days of coverage, or other similar limits
- Parity coverage for annual and lifetime dollar limits with medical coverage
- Broad definition of mental health and substance abuse benefits
- If a plan offers two or more benefit packages, the parity requirements apply to each package
- Mental health/substance abuse benefit coverage is not mandated, but if a plan offers such coverage, it must be provided at parity with other medical/health benefits coverage

- A group health plan or coverage that provides out-of-network coverage for medical/surgical benefits also must provide out-of-network coverage, at parity, for mental health/substance use disorder benefits
- Preserves existing state parity laws and would only preempt a state law that "prevents the application" of the federal act. Therefore, state parity laws applicable to health insurance coverage continue in effect unless the state laws conflicts with Act's ban on inequitable financial requirements and treatment limitations.[53]

However, as of the end of 2015, it was clear that the intent of the MHPAEA can still be avoided by applying non-quantitative treatment limitations (NQTLs) for almost all of the psychiatric and substance abuse disorders and applying few NQTLs to non-psychiatric illnesses. NQTLs are defined as treatment limits "which otherwise limit the scope or duration of benefits for treatment and are not expressed numerically."[54] An example of an NQTL is applying a requirement for pre-authorization of services.[54] Clearly, regulators need to develop:

- Standards for disclosure of criteria for medical/surgical benefits
- Standards that health plans should use in establishing that the plans have applied NQTLs in a "comparable and no more stringent manner" than for medical/surgical benefits
- Standards for determining what constitutes "recognized clinically appropriate standards of care"
- Standards for delineating parity in scope of service.[55]

Public Funding of Behavioral Health Care

Because historically, many U.S. citizens lacked adequate or even basic health insurance coverage for the treatment of psychiatric or substance abuse disorders, most people with severe mental illness had coverage through publicly funded insurance, such as Medicaid or managed Medicaid programs funded by the states, with federal matching funds based on preset formulas discussed in detail in Chapter 8. With regard to financing mental health services, the ACA is clearly a "game changer," through its appropriation of an estimated $100 billion over a 10-year period (2010–2019) in mandatory funding and authorization of another $100 billion over the same time period in discretionary funding, subject to the Congress' annual appropriation process. Assuming the ACA stays largely intact through political changes of the next years, the insurance reforms it mandates can be expected to have a major impact on the financing of psychiatric and behavioral health care.

In July 2012, the Congressional Budget Office estimated that 55 million Americans under the age of 65 and 20 percent of those over the age of 65 were uninsured.[56] Most uninsured people, because of limited finances, have been less likely to seek care for symptoms of mental illness. Under the ACA, the pool of insured people has been expanded considerably by two mechanisms: (1) the establishment of state-based affordable health insurance exchanges, and (2) the expansion of Medicaid. As noted previously in this chapter, because of the ACA, the percentage of uninsured Americans dropped to 9.2 percent, an historic low.[1]

As discussed extensively in this text, the ACA requires most Americans to obtain basic health insurance coverage. Significant for behavioral health, the ACA mandates behavioral health coverage for most health insurers, and parity is required both under the ACA and the MHPAEA. However, as has been discussed in this chapter, there still remain additional mechanisms for restricting benefits for mental health services through NQTLs.[55]

The ACA targeted Medicaid for expansion by January 1, 2014, providing eligibility for nearly all people under the age of 65 with income below 138 percent of the federal poverty level (FPL). This expansion would have affected millions of low-income adults, with and without children, and in some instances children currently covered through the CHIP. It was anticipated that if all states participated in the Medicaid expansion, by 2020, an additional 20 million people would be covered by Medicaid.[57] Theoretically, this expansion of Medicaid would have improved access to psychiatric and behavioral health services. However, the decision of the U.S. Supreme Court in June 2012 enabled states to opt out from Medicaid expansion. This decision decreased the number of people covered under Medicaid, but those individuals, still being mandated to carry insurance, were eligible to purchase basic insurance through the state health insurance exchanges; they were eligible for a subsidy to make the purchasing of insurance relatively affordable. However, states also can decrease the number of people on Medicaid by seeking Medicaid federal waivers to alter Medicaid benefits. Waivers have had a particularly adverse impact on people with SMI. The ACA Medicaid expansion is discussed in detail in Chapter 8 of this text.

Prior to the ACA, the federal government's matching funds to states covered the majority of costs for providing care to Medicaid beneficiaries, with each state's federal matching funds dependent on its per-capita income. CHIP was financed by both the state and the federal government, with federal matching funds at a capped amount determined by block grants, significantly higher than that for Medicaid. The ACA made states' Medicaid expansion "budget neutral" by covering 100 percent of expansion costs with federal funding for 2014–2016 and 90 percent of expansion costs in 2020 and beyond.[58]

The significance of the ACA for U.S. behavioral health services is enormous. Millions of previously disenfranchised, low-income people and their children now have access to Medicaid coverage, removing major financial barriers to accessing psychiatric and behavioral healthcare services. However, in accord with the U.S. Supreme Court's decision of June 2012, at March 2016, 31 states and the District of Columbia had adopted the expansion, 16 states had not, and 3 states had Medicaid expansion under consideration.[58]

Because of state Medicaid expansion decisions, Medicaid eligibility remains limited for those in states which have not participated. Low-income individuals in these states fall into a coverage gap, with too much income to qualify for Medicaid eligibility and too little income to qualify for federal subsidies in purchasing health insurance through Marketplace exchanges.[59]

An estimated 2.9 million adults fall into this coverage gap, most living in the southern regions of the United States. More than half of the people in the coverage gap are people of color. Nearly two-thirds of the adults affected live in a family with a working family member, but the worker does not have a job which offers health insurance. As **FIGURE 10-6** illustrates, adoption of Medicaid expansion by all states would eliminate this coverage gap by making many more people eligible for financial assistance.[59] **FIGURE 10-7** depicts the reach of ACA's intended Medicaid coverage expansion to low-income adults.[59]

Cost Containment Mechanisms

As in other healthcare sectors, managed care programs were designed to control costs through financial incentives which reward outcomes of care, not service utilization. Today, of the approximately 90 percent of Americans who have health insurance, or 154.3 million people, 49 percent of the non-elderly U.S. adult population receive health insurance through their employers. The remainder is insured through other means, with non-group private insurance

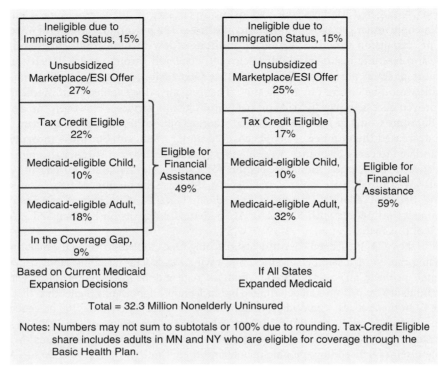

FIGURE 10-6 Adoption of Medicaid Expansion

If all states adopted the Medicaid expansion, the coverage gap would be eliminated and 59 percent of the nonelderly uninsured would be eligible for financial assistance

Modified from: The Henry J. Kaiser Family Foundation. The Kaiser Commission on Medicaid and the Uninsured. Who is impacted by the coverage gap in states that have not adopted the Medicaid expansion?

accounting for 6 percent, Medicaid 19 percent, Medicare 13 percent, and other public insurers 2 percent.[60] Employer surveys indicate that 99 percent of all workers covered by employer benefits are enrolled in some type of managed care plan.[61] Managed care systems for people with mental illness tightly control utilization and closely monitor heavy users of mental health services. Before the passage of the MHPAEA of 2008, managed care firms often did not incorporate coverage for mental illness in their basic contracts because of concerns about the costs of chronic care. If coverage was provided, it was "carved out," and outsourced to a subcontractor, known as a Managed Behavioral Healthcare Organization (MBHO), which would assume the financial risk as well as the benefits of managing budgets and authorization for access to mental health services. The past practice of limiting mental health benefits to a greater extent than general healthcare benefits is no longer permitted under the federal parity laws, and the U.S. Department of Labor has been charged with monitoring and insuring compliance with parity laws and regulations.

Public sector initiatives have paralleled private sector efforts in using MBHOs to control costs. Recent research indicates that MBHOs, both within the public and private sector, have facilitated access and coordinated care for those in greatest need as more people with SMI are now more likely to receive mental health specialty services than in the past.[62, 63]

As enacted, the ACA Medicaid expansion would cover adults up to 138% FPL in all states, filling long-standing gaps in coverage.

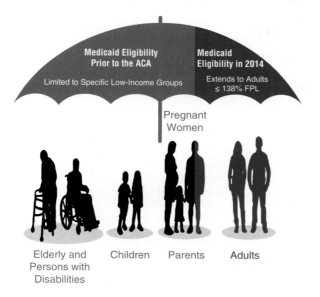

Notes: 138% FPL = $16,242 for an individual and $27,724 for a family of three in 2015.

FIGURE 10-7 **The Reach of ACA's Intended Medicaid Coverage Expansion to Low-Income Adults**

Reproduced from: The Henry J. Kaiser Family Foundation. The Kaiser Commission on Medicaid and the Uninsured. Who is impacted by the coverage gap in states that have not adopted the Medicaid expansion?

▶ The Future of Psychiatric and Behavioral Health Services

As previously noted, there have been significant paradigm changes in psychiatric and behavioral healthcare and service organization. Qualitatively, the shift to a recovery model of care provides for a strength-based system, individualized in accord with client-directed life goals and objectives, with the psychiatrist being but one component of an array of providers. First, the hope is that the new paradigm will produce a substantial, sustained shift from the practitioner or provider-driven system focused on diagnosis-anchored problems. Second, it is cautiously anticipated that continued experimentation will produce findings that support the move toward fully integrating psychiatry and behavioral health services with primary care and away from a separate and more isolated model of care. Both of these shifts will be transforming events, which will qualitatively change the face of psychiatric and behavioral health care, if not all health care nationally. However, the real "game changer" is the ACA, which, for vast numbers of Americans, will assure access to affordable health insurance and mandate parity of behavioral health benefits. As these new initiatives and healthcare laws are implemented, it is expected that overall health services will be improved by assuring increased access to needed psychiatric and behavioral health services, and by increasing the likelihood that those with SMI will be able to access primary care services. Integration of behavioral health with primary care services will go a long way in reducing untoward effects from drug interactions as well as early interventions for illnesses that are more likely to occur in those with psychiatric illness and on psychotropic medications, such as Type II Diabetes Mellitus and high cholesterol. It is a time of great change and promise in the healthcare delivery system as a whole and for the behavioral health services sector in particular. It is also a time that will require practitioners to be extraordinarily flexible in embracing change with a heightened recognition of the vulnerability of the mentally ill population.

KEY TERMS FOR REVIEW

Carve-out
Comorbidity
Deinstitutionalization
Disability-Adjusted Life Years (DALYS)

Managed behavioral healthcare organization (MBHO)
Non-parity
Non-quantitative Treatment Limitations (NQTLs)

Recovery-Oriented Systems of Care (ROSC)
Serious Mental Illness (SMI)

CHAPTER ACRONYMS

NIMH National Institute of Mental Health
MHPAEA Mental Health Parity and Addition Equity Act of 2008

SAMHSA Substance Abuse and Mental Health Services Administration
SSI Supplemental Security Income

References

1. Martinez ME, Cohen RA, Zammitti EP. Health insurance coverage: early release of estimates from the national health interview survey, January–September 2015. http://www.cdc.gov/nchs/data/nhis/earlyrelease/insur201602.pdf. Accessed April 11, 2016.

2. White D. President Obama vetoes Affordable Care Act repeal. *Time.* January 8, 2016. http://time.com/4173152/president-obama-vetoes-affordable-care-act-repeal/. Accessed March 21, 2016.

3. Bockoven JS. *Moral Treatment in Community Mental Health.* New York: Springer; 1972.

4. Fisher WH, Geller JL, Pandani JA. The changing role of the state psychiatric hospital. *Health Aff.* 2009; 28;676-677. http://content.healthaffairs.org/content/28/3/676. Accessed April 12, 2016.

5. PBS Frontline. Deinstitutionalization. Special reports. The new asylums. http://www.pbs.org/wgbh/pages/frontline/shows/asylums/special/excerpt.html. Accessed April 12, 2016.

6. Klerman GL. The psychiatric revolution of the past 25 years. In: Gove WR, ed. *Deviance and Mental Illness. Newbury Park, CA:* Sage Publishing; 1982:180.

7. Mechanic D. Establishing mental health priorities. *Milbank Q.* 1994;72:501-514.

8. Redick RW, Witkin MJ, Atay JE, Manderscheid RW. The evolution and expansion of mental health care in the United States between 1955 and 1990. In: Mental Health Statistical Note 210. Washington, DC: U.S. Department of Health and Human Services; 1994.

9. Glied SA, Frank RG. Better but not best: recent trends in the well-being of the mentally ill. *Health Aff.* 2009; 28:637-638. http://content.healthaffairs.org/content/28/3/637.full.pdf±html. Accessed March 22, 2016.

10. 111th U.S. Congress. Public Law 111-148. *The Patient Protection and Affordable Care Act.* Washington, DC: U.S. Government Printing Office; March 23, 2010.

11. Substance Abuse and Mental Health Services Administration. Current statistics on the prevalence and characteristics of people experiencing homelessness in the United States. http://homeless.samhsa.gov/ResourceFiles/hrc_factsheet.pdf. Accessed April 12, 2016.

12. Mental Illness Policy ORG. 250,000 mentally ill are homeless. The number is increasing. http://mentalillnesspolicy.org/consequences/homeless-mentally-ill.html. Accessed April 12, 2016.

13. Regenstein M, Rosenbaum S. What the Affordable Care Act means for people with jail stays. *Health*

Aff. 2014.33:449. http://content.healthaffairs.org/content/33/3/448. Accessed April 12, 2016.

14. Aufderheide D. Mental illness in America's jails and prisons: toward a public safety/public health model. Health Affairs Blog. April, 2014. http://healthaffairs.org/blog/2014/04/01/mental-illness-in-americas-jails-and-prisons-toward-a-public-safetypublic-health-model/. Accessed April 12, 2016.

15. Treatment Advocacy Center. No room at the inn. Trends and consequences of closing public psychiatric hospitals. http://www.tacreports.org/bedstudy. Accessed April 12, 2016.

16. The National Institute of Mental Health. Any mental illness (AMI) among U.S. adults. http://www.nimh.nih.gov/health/statistics/prevalence/any-mental-illness-ami-among-us-adults.shtml. Accessed March 21, 2016.

17. The National Institute of Mental Health. Serious mental illness (SMI) among U.S. adults. http://www.nimh.nih.gov/health/statistics/prevalence/serious-mental-illness-smi-among-us-adults.shtml. Accessed March 21, 2016.

18. The National Institute of Mental Health. U.S. leading categories of diseases/disorders. http://www.nimh.nih.gov/health/statistics/disability/us-leading-categories-of-diseases-disorders.shtml. Accessed March 21, 2016.

19. The National Institute of Mental Health. U.S. DALYS contributed by mental and behavioral disorders. http://www.nimh.nih.gov/health/statistics/disability/us-dalys-contributed-by-mental-and-behavioral-disorders.shtml. Accessed March 21, 2016.

20. The National Institute of Mental Health. Annual total direct and indirect costs of serious mental illness. http://www.nimh.nih.gov/health/statistics/cost/index.shtml. Accessed March 21, 2016.

21. Levit KR, Kassed CA, Coffey RM, McKusick DR, et al. *Projections of National Expenditures for Mental Health and Substance Abuse Treatment: 2004–2014.* SAMHSA Publication No. SMA 08-4326. Rockville, MD: Substance Abuse and Mental Health Services Administration, 2008. https://store.samhsa.gov/shin/content/SMA08-4326/SMA08-4326.pdf. Accessed March 22, 2016.

22. American Psychiatric Association. *Diagnostic and Statistical Manual of Mental Disorders.* 5th ed. Washington, DC: American Psychiatric Press; 2013.

23. National Institute of Mental Health. Questions and answers about the National Comorbidity Survey Replication (NCSR) Study. http://www.nimh.nih.gov/health/topics/ncsr-study/questions-and-answers-about-the-national-comorbidity-survey-replication-ncsr-study.shtml. Accessed March 22, 2016.

24. Regier DA, Farmer ME, Rae DS, et al. Comorbidity of mental disorders with alcohol and other drug abuse: results from the Epidemiological Catchment Area (ECA) Study. *JAMA.* 1991;264:2511-2518.

25. Kerker BD, Owens PL, Zigler E, Horwitz SM. Mental health disorders among individuals with mental retardation: challenges to accurate prevalence estimates. *Public Health Rep.* 2004;119(4):409-417.

26. National Alliance on Mental Illness. Mental health by the numbers. https://www.nami.org/Learn-More/Mental-Health-By-the-Numbers. Accessed March 24, 2016.

27. Treatment Advocacy Center. What percentage of individuals with serious mental illness are receiving no treatment? http://www.treatmentadvocacycenter.org/resources/assisted-outpatient-treatment/about-aot/159. Accessed March 24, 2016.

28. Wang PS, Lane M, Olfson M, Pincus HA, Wells KB, Kessler RC. Twelve-month use of mental health services in the United States: results from the National Comorbidity Survey Replication. *Arch Gen Psychiatry.* 2005; 62(6):629-640. http://www.ncbi.nlm.nih.gov/pubmed/15939840. Accessed March 20, 2016.

29. National Institute on Drug Abuse, National Institutes of Health, U.S. Department of Health and Human Services. Addiction is a chronic disease. http://archives.drugabuse.gov/about/welcome/aboutdrugabuse/chronicdisease/. Accessed March 24, 2016.

30. U.S. Department of Health and Human Services. *Mental Health: A Report of the Surgeon General—Chapter 6.* Rockville, MD: U.S. Department of Health and Human Services, Substance and Mental Health Services Administration, Center for Mental Health Services, National Institutes of Health, National Institute of Mental Health; 1999:409. https://profiles.nlm.nih.gov/ps/access/NNBBHS.pdf. Accessed March 24, 2016.

31. Glied SA, Frank RG. Better but not best: recent trends in the well-being of the mentally ill. *Health Aff.* 2009; 28:639-640. http://content.healthaffairs.org/content/28/3/637.full.pdf±html. Accessed March 22, 2016.

32. American Academy of Child and Adolescent Psychiatrists. AACAP workforce factsheet. http://www.aacap.org/aacap/resources_for_primary_care/Workforce_Issues.aspx. Accessed April 13, 2016.

33. National Institutes of Health. About the BPCA: background of the Best Pharmaceuticals for Children Act. https://bpca.nichd.nih.gov/about/Pages/Index.aspx. Accessed April 13, 2016.

34. Food and Drug Administration. FDA takes steps to encourage pediatric drug studies. http://blogs.fda.gov/fdavoice/index.php/tag/best-pharmaceuticals-for-children-act-bpca/. Accessed April 13, 2016.

35. U.S. Department of Health and Human Services, Administration on Aging. A Profile of Older Americans: 2014. http://www.aoa.acl.gov/aging_statistics/Profile/2014/docs/2014-Profile.pdf. Accessed March 24, 2016.

36. Regier DA, Boyd JH, Burke JD Jr, et al. One month prevalence of mental disorders in the United States: based on five epidemiological catchment area sites. *Arch Gen Psychiatry.* 1988;45:977-986.

37. Bartels SJ, Blow FC, Brockmann LM, Van Citters AD. Substance abuse & mental health among older Americans: the state of the knowledge and future directions. Older American Substance Abuse and Mental Health Technical Assistance Center, Substance Abuse and Mental Health Services Administration. 2005. http://gsa-alcohol.fmhi.usf.edu/Substance%20Abuse %20and%20Mental%20Health%20Among%20 Older%20Adults-%20The%20State%20of%20 Knowledge%20and%20Future%20Directions.pdf. Accessed March 24, 2016.

38. U.S. Department of Health and Human Services. *Mental Health: A Report of the Surgeon General— Chapter 6.* Rockville, MD: U.S. Department of Health and Human Services, Substance and Mental Health Services Administration, Center for Mental Health Services, National Institutes of Health, National Institute of Mental Health; 1999:340-341. https:// profiles.nlm.nih.gov/ps/access/NNBBHS.pdf. Accessed March 24, 2016.

39. Regier DA, Narrow WE, Rae DS, Manderscheid RW, Locke BZ, Goodwin FK. The de facto US mental and addictive disorders service system: epidemiological catchment area prospective 1-year prevalence rate of disorders and services. *Arch Gen Psychiatry.* 1995;50:85-94.

40. U.S. Department of Health and Human Services. *Mental Health: A Report of the Surgeon General— Chapter 6.* Rockville, MD: U.S. Department of Health and Human Services, Substance and Mental Health Services Administration, Center for Mental Health Services, National Institutes of Health, National Institute of Mental Health; 1999:406-407. https:// profiles.nlm.nih.gov/ps/access/NNBBHS.pdf. Accessed March 24, 2016.

41. American Hospital Association. Connecting with national behavioral health organizations. http:// www.aha.org/advocacy-issues/mentalhealth/natlorgs .shtml. Accessed April 14, 2016.

42. President's New Freedom Commission on Mental Health. *Achieving the Promise: Transforming Mental Health Care in America, Executive Summary, 3-4.* July 2003. http://govinfo.library.unt.edu/mentalhealthcommission /reports/FinalReport/downloads/downloads.html. Accessed March 24, 2016.

43. U.S. Department of Health and Human Services. Substance Abuse and Mental Health Services Administration. Interim Report of the President's New Freedom Commission on Mental Health. October 29, 2002. http://govinfo.library.unt.edu/mentalhealth commission/reports/Interim_Report.htm. Accessed March 24, 2016.

44. U.S. Department of Health and Human Services. Substance Abuse and Mental Health Services Administration. *Transforming Mental Health Care in America: The Federal Action Agenda.* 2005. http://cretscmhd.psych .ucla.edu/nola/Video/MHR/Governmentreports /TRANSFORMING%20MENTAL%20HEALTH %20CARE%20IN%20AMERICA.pdf. Accessed March 24, 2016.

45. Newcomer JW, Hennekens CH. Early death rate for severe mental illness and risk of cardiovascular disease. *JAMA.* 2007;298(15):1794-1796.

46. Katon WJ, Von Korff M, Lin E, et al. Collaborative management to achieve treatment guidelines: impact on depression in primary care. *JAMA.* 1995;273:1026-1031.

47. Katon, WJ, Lin EH, Von Korff M, et al. Collaborative care for patients with depression and chronic illnesses. *N Engl J Med.* 2010;363:2611-2620.

48. Raney LE. Integrating primary care and behavioral health: the role of the psychiatrist in the collaborative care model. *Am J Psychiatry.* 2015;172:721-728.

49. Fortney JC, Pyne JM, Mouden SB, et al. Practice-based versus telemedicine-based collaborative care for depression in rural federally qualified health centers: a pragmatic randomized comparative effectiveness trial. *Am J Psychiatry.* 2013;170:414-425. http:// www.ncbi.nlm.nih.gov/pmc/articles/PMC3816374/. Accessed March 22, 2016.

50. Collins C, Hewson DL, Munger R, Wade T. Evolving Models of Behavioral Health Integration in Primary Care. New York: Millbank Memorial Fund, 2010. http://www.milbank.org/uploads/documents/10430 EvolvingCare/10430EvolvingCare.html. Accessed March 25, 2016.

51. Butler M, Kane RL, McAlpine D, et al. *Integration of Mental Health/Substance Abuse and Primary Care.* Washington, DC: Agency for Healthcare Research and Quality, U.S. Department of Health and Human Services; 2008. http://www.ahrq.gov/sites/default/files /wysiwyg/research/findings/evidence-based-reports /mhsapc-evidence-report.pdf. Accessed March 21, 2016.

52. Health Policy Brief. Mental health parity. *Health Aff.* April 3, 2014. http://www.healthaffairs.org/health policybriefs/brief.php?brief_id=112. Accessed March 24, 2016.

53. Mental Health America. Fact Sheet: Paul Wellstone and Pete Domenici Mental Health Parity and Addiction Equity Act of 2008. http://takeaction.mentalhealthamerica .net/site/PageServer?pagename=Equity_Campaign _detailed_summary. Accessed March 24, 2016.

54. Mental Health America.net. Parity implementation coalition. http://www.mentalhealthamerica.net/sites /default/files/final%20detailed%20summary.pdf. Accessed March 24, 2016.

55. U.S. Department of Labor. Mental Health Parity and Addiction Equity Act: Sub-regulatory guidance in the form of frequently asked questions (FAQs). http://www.dol .gov/ebsa/faqs/faq-aca7.html. Accessed March 24, 2016.

56. Congressional Budget Office. Estimates for the insurance coverage provisions of the Affordable Care Act updated for the recent Supreme Court decisions.

July 2012. http://www.cbo.gov/sites/default/files/cbofiles /attachments/43472-07-24-2012-CoverageEstimates .pdf. Accessed March 24, 2016.

57. Kaiser Commission on Medicaid and the Uninsured. The cost and coverage implications of the ACA Medicaid expansion: national and state-by-state analysis. November 2012. http://kff.org/health-reform /report/the-cost-and-coverage-implications-of-the/. Accessed March 24, 2016.

58. Families USA. A 50-state look at Medicaid expansion. February, 2016. http://familiesusa.org/product/50-state -look-medicaid-expansion. Accessed March 25, 2016.

59. The Henry J. Kaiser Family Foundation. The Kaiser Commission on Medicaid and the Uninsured. Who is impacted by the coverage gap in states that have not adopted the Medicaid expansion? January 2016. Slides #14 and #6. http://kff.org/slideshow /who-is-impacted-by-the-coverage-gap-in-states-that -have-not-adopted-the-medicaid-expansion/. Accessed March 25, 2016.

60. The Henry J. Kaiser Family Foundation. Health insurance coverage of the total population. http:// kff.org/other/state-indicator/total-population/#table. Accessed March 25, 2016.

61. The Henry J. Kaiser Family Foundation. Employer health benefits survey 2015. Exhibit 4.3. http://kff .org/report-section/ehbs-2015-section-four-types-of -plans-offered/. Accessed March 25, 2016.

62. Mechanic D, Bilder S. Treatment of people with mental illness: a decade-long perspective. *Health Aff.* 2004;23:93. http://content.healthaffairs.org/content /23/4/84.full.html. Accessed March 25, 2016.

63. Dixon K. Implementing mental health parity: the challenge for health plans. *Health Aff.* 2009;28:663-665. http://content.healthaffairs.org/content/28/3/663.full .html. Accessed March 25, 2016.

CHAPTER 11

Public Health and the Role of Government in Health Care

CHAPTER OVERVIEW

This chapter presents the history of governmental efforts to promote population health through disease prevention and intervention. It traces efforts to protect the public's health, begun in early European history and transferred to Colonial America, with emphasis on their purpose, motivation, and results. Trends in the rise and historical challenges of America's federal, state, and local partnerships in the delivery of public health services are described, as well as the activities of private and voluntary agencies. Barriers to effective preventive services that result from an inadequate population perspective in the U.S. healthcare system are discussed. Updates on the public health impacts of the Patient Protection and Affordable Care Act (ACA) are provided. Selected enduring and emerging domestic and global public health issues are discussed in a current and future context.

▶ Public Health Defined

The term *public health* most broadly defined, refers to efforts communities make to cope with the health problems that arise when people live in groups. Community life creates the need to control the transmission of communicable diseases, maintain a sanitary environment, provide safe water and food, and sustain disabled and low-income populations.[1] More specifically, the World Health Organization defines public health as, "all organized measures (whether public or private) to prevent disease, promote health, and prolong life among the population as a whole."[2] The Centers for Disease Control and Prevention (CDC) defines public health as "the science of protecting and improving the health of families and communities through promotion of healthy lifestyles, research for disease and injury prevention, and detection and control of infectious diseases."[3]

Grounded in the tenets of social justice, public health applies the principles of medicine, epidemiology, statistics, social and behavioral sciences, environmental sciences, and other disciplines

Flag: © Lightix/Shutterstock

in order to achieve the best possible health status for populations. Unlike clinical medicine which focuses on individuals, public health is concerned with achieving and maintaining healthy living circumstances for entire populations in areas as small as neighborhoods or as large as regions of the world.

Public health is unique in its interdisciplinary approach and methods, its emphasis on preventive strategies, its linkage with government and political decision making, and its dynamic adaptation to new problems placed on the agenda. Above all else, it is a collective effort to identify and address the unacceptable realities that result in preventable and avoidable health and quality of life outcomes. It is the composite of efforts and activities that are carried out by people and organizations committed to these ends.[4]

In its population perspective, public health has continued to adapt and apply various ecological models to its pursuits. These models take into account the vast number of factors or determinants that impact the health status of groups. Health determinants include factors such as:

- Physical environments
- Political conditions
- Human biology and genetics
- Social factors such as economic circumstances; discrimination by race, ethnicity, gender, or sexual orientation; and the availability of familial or other social supports
- Behavioral choices
- Cultural norms

The interdependence and interaction of these factors coalesce to produce effects on population health.[5,6] Ecological models help to identify the most expeditious path to developing effective population-based interventions.

▶ Early History

The world history of public health is a fascinating study of civilized society's attempts to deal with the biologic, social, and environmental forces that have contributed to the pervasive problems of morbidity and mortality. It also chronicles the efforts of governments and societies to aid unfortunate citizens handicapped by illness, disability, and poverty. The following observations set the stage for understanding the development of the U.S. governments' role in the evolution of public health in the United States.

Throughout history, public health activities have reflected the current state of knowledge regarding the nature and cause of the diseases that afflict humankind, the practices used for their control or treatment, and the dominant social ideologies of political jurisdictions. The ancient Hebrews codified concepts of spiritual cleanliness and community responsibility. The ancient Greeks practiced systems of personal hygiene to promote mind/body balance. The ancient Romans were the first to develop public health as a governmental matter beyond individual practice. Their engineering and administrative accomplishments provided citizens with clean water, effective sewage disposal, and swamp drainage that were the forerunners of politically sanctioned environmental public health protections. In addition, the Roman Empire is credited for establishing a network of infirmaries to treat illness among its soldiers. These infirmaries are considered to be the first public hospitals.[7]

The medieval period after Rome fell was characterized by the disintegration of the cities and anarchy. The overpopulated walled towns built to withstand enemy attacks crowded community members together in the unhealthiest circumstances. The pest-ridden, unsanitary, and over-crowded living conditions provided fertile environments for disease epidemics that decimated large segments of those populations. Superstitious, demonic, and theological theories of epidemic disease displaced ancient concerns for personal hygiene and environmental quality.[8]

The Renaissance that followed was characterized by a great revival of learning. Along with advances in art, literature, and philosophy, there was a renewed interest in science and medicine. From the 1500s to the 1700s, public health was shaped by two countervailing trends.[9] Although the administration of rudimentary medical and nursing services continued to be the responsibility of towns and other local units, the concept of the modern state was beginning to emerge.

Because only a political jurisdiction that protected and cared for its citizens could reap the continuing economic benefits of production and world trade, healthy laborers and soldiers became valuable commodities. Thus in the centralized national governments of Europe between the 1500s and the 1700s, maintaining the health of laborers and soldiers became important economic, polit-ical, and public health concerns.

Public Health in England

In England, the Elizabethan Poor Laws of 1601 addressed the issue of the "lame, impotent, old, blind, and such other among them being poor and not able to work" without dealing directly with health matters.[9] The law was expanded subsequently to include the provision of nursing and medical care.

It was also in England that the collection and analysis of national statistics regarding industrial production and demographics began in the 1600s. The work of the father of political arithmetic, William Petty (1623–1687), and the statistical analyses of his friend John Graunt (1620–1674) established the importance of vital statistics. This led to such epidemiologic tools as population-specific and disease-specific morbidity and mortality rates, life tables, and the calculus of probability. Vital statistics contained in the *Bills of Mortality*, publicly posted weekly in London, cited numbers of recorded deaths and causes. These led to a better understanding of the social phenomena that were factors in the occurrence of disease and death.[10]

By the 1800s, the industrialization of England had made poverty and social distress increas-ingly prevalent. In that climate, the drastic Poor Law Amendment Act of 1834 was passed. The dual intent was to reduce the rates of populations' dependency and free the labor market to spur industrialization. The law required that able-bodied people and their families be given aid only in exchange for their labor in regulated workhouses whose conditions were to be harsher than those of the lowest-paid workers.[11]

The circumstances of the new industrial society, factories, and the congested dwellings of urban environments produced new health problems, and diseases flourished and spread. In his *Report on the Sanitary Condition of the Labouring Population of Great Britain* (1842), Edwin Chad-wick described decrepit housing, unclean water, and filthy streets, all of which he asserted contrib-uted to crime, disease, and immorality. The Public Health Act of 1848, passed by Parliament in the wake of a cholera epidemic threat, fell far short of addressing the conditions Chadwick brought to light, but a General Board of Health was created which Chadwick headed from 1848 to 1854.[12]

Although the subsequent history of public health in England is a chronicle of social change, epidemics, and political machinations, the growth of its sanitary reform movement and the cre-ation of the General Board of Health in 1848 established the British as world leaders in public health philosophy and practice. Public health in early America was heavily influenced by the med-ical and administrative experience of the British.[9]

Development of U.S. Public Health and Government-Supported Services

The history of public health in the United States from the early colonial period to the end of the 1800s followed a development pattern similar to that in England. Widespread epidemics such as yellow fever and cholera stimulated sanitary reforms, and the early cities and towns began to assume responsibility for the collective health of their citizens. Public medical care in the United States, however, bore the stigma of its "Poor Law" legacy. The New York Poor Law of 1788 provided that any town or city could establish an almshouse, and within a few years, most towns and cities had done so. Although there was a series of shocking exposés of terrible conditions in many of these facilities, the concept of the almshouse and town-employed physicians remained the mainstay of sick people among the low-income population until the Great Depression of the 1930s.

Lemuel Shattuck, a Massachusetts statistician, conducted U.S. sanitary surveys similar to those of Chadwick in England. In his 1850 Report of the Sanitary Commission, he documented differences in morbidity and mortality rates in different locations and related them to various environmental conditions. He argued that the city or state was responsible for the environment. Although largely ignored at the time of its release, the report has come to be considered one of the most influential documents in the evolution of public health in the United States.[13]

In 1865, emulating the Shattuck survey in Massachusetts, the New York City Council of Hygiene and Public Health published a shocking exposé of unsanitary conditions in the city. Within a year, New York City passed a law that created a city board of health. Creating an appropriate administrative structure for local public health efforts became a turning point for public health in the United States.

As in England and other countries, early federal public health initiatives were motivated more by economic and commercial concerns than humanitarian values. For instance, the U.S. Public Health Service was established in 1798 as the Marine Hospital Service when President John Adams signed into law an act providing for the care and relief of seamen who were sick or disabled.[14] Because healthy sailors were a valuable commercial commodity, and because the seaport towns only took responsibility for their own citizens, it was left to the federal government to provide health services to the seamen and passengers of the important shipping industry. The citizens of seaports also were concerned that the personnel of foreign ships did not transmit diseases contracted elsewhere.

In 1801 the first marine hospital was established at Washington Point in Virginia, and other hospitals were established in port cities along the East Coast. In 1870, the Marine Hospital Service was reorganized as a national hospital system with central headquarters in Washington, DC. The medical officer in charge in the position of "supervising surgeon" was later given the title of "surgeon general." The title of surgeon general for the chief medical officer of the United States is still in use today.[14] In light of the commercial motivation for its creation, the Marine Hospital Service was established as a component of the Treasury Department.

In 1889, Congress established the Public Health Service Commissioned Corps. Envisioned as a mobile force of physicians to assist the nation in fighting disease and protecting health, the Corps was set up along military lines, with titles and pay corresponding to Army and Navy grades and physicians subject to duty wherever assigned.[14] The discovery of the microbes causing infectious diseases such as tuberculosis, cholera, diphtheria, and typhoid fever during the 1880s and 1890s created a revolution in medical thought and practice. The Hygienic Laboratory was established at the Marine Hospital on Staten Island, New York, in 1887 to apply the methods of this new science of bacteriology to the diagnosis and study of epidemic diseases.[15] In 1891, the bacteriologic laboratory in the Staten Island Marine Hospital was moved to Washington, DC, where it was expanded to include pathology, chemistry, and pharmacology. The establishment of this single-room bacteriological laboratory by the U.S. Marine Hospital Service marked the beginning of the National Institutes of Health and laid the groundwork for government-supported scientific research in the United States.[15]

Eleven years later, in 1902, a new law changed the Marine Hospital Service's name to Public Health and Marine Hospital Service. In 1912, the Public Health Service Commissioned Corps' name was changed to the U.S. Public Health Service (PHS), its present designation. In the same year, Congress broadened the powers of the PHS by authorizing investigations into human diseases (such as tuberculosis, hookworm, malaria, and leprosy), sanitation, water supplies, and sewage disposal.[14] From this modest start, the Public Health Service underwent a series of reorganizations and expansions until it became a major agency of the U.S. Department of Health and Human Services (DHHS), responsible for the largest public health program in the world.[14]

In 1933, it became apparent that state and local governments with limited tax revenues required help from the federal government to provide welfare assistance, and the Federal Emergency Relief Act was passed. It provided federal aid to the states and authorized general medical care for acute and chronic illness, obstetric services, emergency dental extractions, bedside nursing, drugs, and medical supplies. Because participation by the states was optional, the act was not implemented in many parts of the country.[16]

The passage of the Social Security Act of 1935 ended the era of makeshift federal and state programs to meet the health needs of sick people among the low-income population. Title VI of the Act was instrumental in the expansion of the Public Health Service. It gave the Public Health Service the authority to assist states, counties, health districts, and other political subdivisions to establish and maintain public health services. Title VI provided the impetus for all political jurisdictions to create public health agencies and services. After 141 years, the Public Health Service was removed from the Treasury Department to become a component of the new Federal Security Agency, created in 1939 to bring together most of the health, welfare, and educational services scattered throughout the federal government.[15] In 1946, the Federal Security Agency also was expanded to include the Children's Bureau and the Food and Drug Administration. During World War II, the Public Health Service carried out emergency health and sanitation efforts that contributed substantially to the country's defense efforts. Since 1946, the Public Health Service has provided national leadership in hospital planning, research, and operation.

The Federal Security Agency was a non-cabinet-level agency. In 1953, the Public Health Service, along with the other components of the Federal Security Agency, was transferred to the newly created Department of Health, Education and Welfare (HEW) to ensure that the areas of health, education, and social security were represented in the President's cabinet.[15] During the next decades, the healthcare industry faced multiple challenges of coping with a rapidly expanding U.S. population, rising public expectations for health services, a host of technologic advances in medicine, and healthcare workforce issues. In 1979, in response to HEW's burgeoning challenges and under pressure from the National Education Association to create a cabinet-level department of education, Congress approved renaming HEW to Department of Health and Human Services (DHHS), with the education component transferred to a new Department of Education.[17]

▶ Government Responsibilities for Health and Public Health

In a 2003 report, *The Future of the Public's Health in the 21st Century,* the National Academy of Sciences noted:

> An effective public health system that can assure the nation's health requires the collaborative efforts of a complex network of people and organizations in the public and private sectors, as well as an alignment of policy and practice of governmental public health agencies at the national, state, and local levels. In the United States, governments at all levels (federal, state, and local) have a specific responsibility to strive to create the conditions in which people can be as healthy as possible. For governments to play their role within the public health system, policy makers must provide the political and financial support needed for strong and effective governmental public health agencies.[18]

The 2003 report underscores the importance of remembering the pivotal roles of numerous non governmental organizations and individuals in maintaining effective public health systems. Governmental partnerships and cooperation with such organizations and individuals are often the primary channels through which government organizations are able to accomplish their objectives. These include hospitals and healthcare providers, businesses, churches, schools, transportation systems, community coalitions, the justice system, philanthropic organizations, and the media.[19] The public health services of voluntary agencies are discussed later in this chapter.

All three levels of government in the United States—federal, state, and local—play significant roles in financing and regulating public health services. All three levels also maintain agencies and systems that directly or indirectly deliver health care and promote improved population health status.[7]

The following sections highlight selected characteristics and key activities implemented by federal, state, and local government agencies in promoting, protecting, and assuring the public's health. The section on local roles also includes the important contributions of government and non governmental "essential" hospitals that provide a safety net for vulnerable populations.

Federal Responsibilities

The principal entities through which the federal government enacts its responsibilities in promoting and maintaining health include the DHHS, the Veterans Health System (a component of the Department of Veterans Affairs), and the Department of Defense Military Health System.

The federal government maintains broad policy-making and operational responsibilities to promote and protect the health of U.S. citizens while ensuring the implementation of both preventive and protective public health practices. At the policy level, the federal government plays crucial roles in leading, exercising regulatory powers, and setting health goals, policies, and standards that are models for the nation. It contributes operational and financial resources. It supports research, higher education, and advancements in science and technology that contribute to the effectiveness of public health at all levels.[19] Federal public health responsibilities include:

- Ensuring that all levels of government have the capabilities to provide essential public health services (described later in this chapter)
- Taking action when health threats span more than one state, a region, or the entire nation

■ Taking action where solutions to public health problems may be beyond the jurisdiction of individual states

■ Assisting states when their expertise or resources are not adequate to effectively respond to a public health emergency such as a natural disaster, bio-terrorism, or an emerging disease threat

■ Facilitating development of public health goals in collaboration with state and local governments and other relevant stakeholders[19]

The DHHS is the federal government's principal agency concerned with health protection, health promotion, and the provision of health and other human services to vulnerable populations.[20] The 2017 proposed DHHS budget is $1.1 trillion. **FIGURE 11-1** provides a summary of the 2017 budget outlays.[20]

With more than 79,000 full-time equivalent employees, DHHS programs carry out activities through the following 11 operating divisions:

1. *Administration for Children and Families (ACF):* The ACF promotes the economic and social well-being of children, youth, families, and communities, focusing special attention on vulnerable populations such as children in low-income families, refugees, and Native Americans. Particular focal areas include providing child-care support for working families, improving outcomes for children and families in the child welfare system, increasing child support, and strengthening Head Start programs. With more than 1,400 full-time equivalent employees, the agency's 2017 proposed budget is $63 billion.

2. *Administration for Community Living (ACL):* The ACL works to maximize the independence, well-being, and health of older adults, people with disabilities across their lifespan, and their families and caregivers. With more than 200 full-time equivalent employees, the agency's proposed 2017 budget is $2.1 billion.

$1,145 billion in outlays

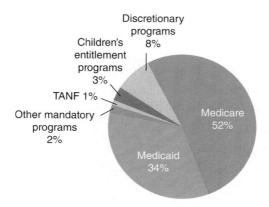

FIGURE 11-1 President's Proposed Budget for the Department of Health and Human Services by Distribution of Funds, Fiscal Year 2017

3. *Agency for Healthcare Research and Quality (AHRQ):* The AHRQ's mission is to produce evidence to make health care safer, higher quality, more accessible, equitable, and affordable. It is also charged to work within the DHHS and with other partners to ensure that evidence produced is understood and used. The agency employs more than 300 full-time equivalent staff and has a proposed 2017 budget of $470 million.

4. *Agency for Toxic Substances and Disease Registry (ATSDR):* The ATSDR operates under the aegis and budget of the CDC. Its purposes are to apply the best science and research to safeguard the public from exposures to hazardous substances. It conducts surveillance, education, and training and supports public health assessments through applied research. The CDC's proposed 2017 budget allocates $75 million for the ATSDR.

5. *Centers for Disease Control and Prevention (CDC):* The mission of the CDC is to protect America from health, safety, and security threats, both foreign and domestic. Its mission also promotes quality of life and prevention of leading causes of disease, injury, disability, and death. With more than 11,000 full-time equivalent employees, the proposed 2017 budget is $6.98 billion.

6. *Centers for Medicare & Medicaid Services (CMS):* CMS finances the Medicare and Medicaid programs, the Children's Health Insurance Program (CHIP), private health insurance programs, program integrity initiatives (anti-fraud and abuse), and operating costs. CMS accounts for more than 86 percent of total DHHS spending. (See Figure 11-1.) In addition, CMS finances the ACA's Center for Medicare Innovation, state grants, and demonstration projects. Medicare currently insures 58 million Americans, 49 million of whom are 65 years and older, and 9 million of whom are disabled. Medicaid, the joint federal–state program, provides coverage for low-income individuals, families, and children, and nursing home stays for low-income older adults. The DHHS estimates that in 2017, more than 70 million people on average will receive healthcare coverage through Medicaid. The CMS proposed 2017 budget is $1 trillion.

7. *Food and Drug Administration (FDA):* The FDA protects public health by assuring the safety, efficacy, and security of human and veterinary drugs, biological products, medical devices, the nation's food supply, cosmetics, and products that emit radiation. The FDA advances public health by helping to speed innovations that make medicines more effective, safer, and affordable, and by helping the public get accurate, science-based information about using medicines and foods to maintain and improve their health, including regulation of tobacco use. With more than 16,700 full-time equivalent employees, the 2017 FDA budget proposal is $5.1 billion.

8. *Health Resources and Services Administration (HRSA):* HRSA is the primary federal agency dedicated to improving health and achieving health equity through access to quality services, a skilled health workforce, and innovative programs. HRSA's programs provide health care to people who are geographically isolated or economically or medically vulnerable. Among many other programs, it funds federally qualified health centers; the National Health Services Corps that provides primary medical, dental, and mental health care to underserved populations; workforce training; and loan programs. HRSA's full-time equivalent employment is approximately 2,100. Its proposed 2017 budget is $10.7 billion.

9. *Indian Health Service (IHS):* The IHS mission is to raise the physical, mental, social, and spiritual health of American Indians and Alaska Natives to the highest level. The IHS operates more than 650 facilities including hospitals, health centers, and clinics.

With more than 15,000 full-time equivalent employees, the IHS proposed budget for 2017 is $6.6 billion.

10. *National Institutes of Health (NIH):* The NIH is the U.S. medical research agency and leads the world in supporting innovative, multi-disciplinary, biomedical and behavioral research. NIH investments across its 27 institutes and centers in basic research support the translation of scientific discovery into tangible improvements in healthcare interventions. With approximately 18,000 full-time equivalent employees, the proposed 2017 NIH budget is $33.1 billion.

11. *Substance Abuse and Mental Health Services Administration (SAMHSA):* SAMHSA's mission is to reduce the impact of substance abuse and mental illness on America's communities. SAMHSA programs help provide treatment and services for people with mental and substance use disorders, support families of people with mental and substance use disorders, and strive to prevent costly behavioral health conditions. Staffed with more than 600 employees, the 2017 proposed SAMHSA budget is $4.3 billion.[20]

The DHHS also includes six offices under the direction of the DHHS secretary that encompass program matters ranging across general management, hearings and appeals, health information technology, civil rights, fraud and abuse, and responses to public health emergencies.[20]

Veterans Health Administration

First established to provide care for Civil War veterans who were disabled or indigent, the Veterans Health Administration (VHA) system grew to become one of the world's largest healthcare delivery systems. The VHA is a component of the U.S. Department of Veteran's Affairs (VA) and is the country's largest healthcare system and a significant component of America's medical education system. The VA owns and operates 150 hospitals, most of which are affiliated with medical schools, and 819 community-based outpatient clinics throughout the United States. The VA serves approximately 22 million veterans with a 2017 proposed budget of more than $182.3 billion.[21] Thirty-eight percent of the total proposed VA budget, or $69.3 billion, is dedicated to veterans' health services.[21] With more than 1,700 sites of care including hospitals, outpatient clinics, rehabilitation centers, and nursing homes, the VHA projects serving almost 9 million individuals in 2016.[22]

Because the VHA system has a long-term relationship with its patients, it has access to each patient's complete medical record, an advantage over private medicine that, in theory, reduces both costs and medical errors. Likewise, this long-term relationship should be expected to foster more preventive care, higher-quality services, and greater patient satisfaction and cost savings. However, as noted in Chapter 4, major deficiencies in the VHA health system have come to light regarding egregious delays in veterans' access to services. These have called the system's credibility into question. Administrative and other reforms are underway with the intent to remedy this situation.

Department of Defense Military Health System

The Department of Defense Military Health System operates one of the largest healthcare organizations in the nation and provides both direct healthcare services and support for U.S. active duty personnel, military retirees, survivors, and their dependents.[23] The system is composed of 15 integrated networks of military hospitals and clinics. Eleven of these facilities are in the United States and four are overseas, including 56 hospitals and 365 clinics that employ more than 58,000 civilians and more than 86,000 military personnel.[24,25] Components of the system include Army, Air Force, and Navy military treatment facilities and the TRICARE healthcare program. TRICARE is a health insurance program available to those covered under the military health system and offers both managed-care and fee-for-service options. TRICARE managed-care providers include those at military treatment facilities and a network of civilian providers administered through regional contracts with civilian managed care organizations. The fee-for-service option also covers care provided by civilian providers who have not joined the TRICARE network. TRICARE brings together the healthcare resources of the uniformed services and supplements them with networks of civilian healthcare professionals, institutions, pharmacies, and other suppliers to provide access to high-quality healthcare services.[23]

State and Local Government Responsibilities

The following sections focus on the central state and local roles in public health. In reviewing these sections, it is important to note the many relationships, shared resources, and responsibilities between and among the federal, state, and local government sectors. For example, states have significant roles in administering federal grant initiatives, and local health departments carry out important surveillance, data collection, and program implementation activities on behalf of state health agencies.

State Roles

State governments have significant influences on healthcare delivery and public health through their departments and agencies such as health, insurance, education, and social services. States function as regulators of health insurance companies, licensors and regulators of health professionals, regulators of quality of care in state-licensed facilities, and analysts of healthcare costs and quality.[26] Many states also operate mental health institutions, support medical and other health professional schools, and may act as lead organizations to channel federal or other support to local or regional health jurisdictions. Chief among states' obligations is their matching funds requirements for the joint federal/state Medicaid program.[26] Also, since the implementation of the ACA, 20 states have opted to develop and operate health insurance marketplaces either solely or in federal partnerships, creating yet another pivotal role for states in the healthcare system.[27] The primary sources of state health agency funding include federal support (53 percent) and state general funds (24 percent).[28]

In its 2014 report, the Association of State and Territorial Health Officials (ASTHO) described characteristics and activities of state health agencies in *ASTHO State Public Health, Volume Three*, using extensive surveys of 48 states and the District of Columbia.[28]

The aggregate state health agency workforce is estimated at 101,000 full-time equivalent employees whose roles encompass a wide range of occupational classifications.[28] **TABLE 11-1** lists the top ten occupational classifications by average number of full-time equivalent employees in the reporting state health agencies.[28]

Leadership of state health agencies is carried out by a top state health official, typically in the title of "commissioner." In 76 percent of states, this position is appointed by the state governor.[28] Almost three-fourths of all top state health officials have medical degrees and almost 50 percent hold the Master of Public Health degree. In 53 percent of states, official statutes require the top state official to hold a medical degree.[28]

TABLE 11-1 Top Ten Occupational Classifications by Average Number of State Health Agency Full-Time Equivalent (FTE) Employees, 2012

Occupational Classification	Average Number of FTEs	Number of States Reporting
Administrative/Clerical	395.3	39
Public Health Nurse	223.3	37
Environmental Health Worker	116.4	34
Public Health Manager	97.1	37
Lab Worker	78.3	34
Social Worker	75.9	26
Epidemiologist/Statistician	52.0	37
Health Educator	51.6	34
Nurse Practitioner	42.1	13
Nutritionist	35.6	38

Modified from Association of State and Territorial Health Officials, *ASTHO Profile of State Public Health, Volume Three*, Washington, DC: Association of State and Territorial Health Officials, 2014.

Based upon the ASTHO survey findings, the following are brief descriptions of six primary categories of state health agency activity and selected tables highlighting the percentage of state health agencies participating in activities. Most tables include activities in which at least 50 percent of responding states participate, and therefore, are not inclusive of all state agency activities. To access more detail on each of the six state categories and other information, readers are encouraged to consult the ASTHO website referenced above from which the following information is derived.

1. *Administering federal initiatives:* State health agencies have primary responsibilities for the administration and fiscal performance of several federal programs. **TABLE 11-2** lists the 10 initiatives for which state health agencies most often report responsibility.

2. *Population-based primary prevention and screening for diseases and medical conditions:* State health agencies engage in a wide array of primary preventive services. As **TABLE 11-3** lists, the most prominent of these relate to tobacco, HIV, and sexually transmitted diseases.

3. *Technical assistance and training:* State health agencies maintain partnerships across local health departments, emergency medical services, healthcare providers, hospitals, laboratories, and other state and community-based organizations. In this role, they provide technical assistance and support on a variety of topics. **TABLE 11-4** lists partners with percentages obtaining technical assistance by topics. As Table 11-4 indicates, local health departments are the most frequent users of technical assistance.

4. *Laboratory services:* The most common testing performed by state health agency laboratories is bioterrorism agent testing (96 percent), foodborne illness testing (96 percent), and influenza typing (94 percent). The next most common tests are for newborn screening (73 percent) and blood lead testing (50 percent).

TABLE 11-2 Percent of State Health Agencies with Responsibility for Federal Initiatives, 2012

Federal Initiative	Percent of State Health Agencies with Responsibility
Public Health Emergency Preparedness cooperative agreement (CDC)	100
Maternal and Child Health—Title V	98
Vital Statistics (National Center for Health Statistics)	98
Preventive Health and Health Services Block Grant (CDC)	96
ASPR Hospital Preparedness Program Cooperative Agreement[1]	96
National Cancer Prevention and Control Program Grant (CDC)	94
Immunization Funding	92
Women, Infants, and Children Program (U.S. Department of Agriculture)	92
Healthy People	90
Injury Prevention	81

Modified from Association of State and Territorial Health Officials, *ASTHO Profile of State Public Health, Volume Three*, Washington, DC: Association of State and Territorial Health Officials, 2014.

TABLE 11-3 Selected Population-Based Primary Prevention Services Performed Directly by State Health Agencies, 2012

Service	Percentage of State Health Agencies Directly Performing Service
Tobacco	87
HIV	85
Sexually Transmitted Disease Counseling and Partner Notification	85
Nutrition	79
Physical Activity	77
Injury	66
Hypertension	53
Unintended Pregnancy	53
Violence	51

Modified from Association of State and Territorial Health Officials, *ASTHO Profile of State Public Health, Volume Three*, Washington, DC: Association of State and Territorial Health Officials, 2014.

TABLE 11-4 Technical Assistance Provided by State Health Agencies by Percentage of Partners Participating in Topics, 2012

State Health Agency Partner	Topics					
	Quality Improvement/ Accreditation	Data Management	Public Health Law	Policy Development	Workforce Issues	None of These Topics
Emergency Medical Services	83%	75%	63%	63%	63%	0%
Providers	87%	68%	55%	60%	62%	4%
Hospitals	90%	69%	58%	60%	46%	2%
Laboratories	88%	54%	44%	38%	40%	2%
Local Public Health Agencies	84%	74%	76%	84%	74%	10%
Nonprofits/ Community-Based Organizations	56%	44%	53%	71%	42%	16%

Modified from Association of State and Territorial Health Officials, *ASTHO Profile of State Public Health, Volume Three*, Washington, DC: Association of State and Territorial Health Officials, 2014.

5. *Regulation, inspection and licensing activities:* State health agencies play central roles in enforcing laws and regulations intended to protect the public's health and safety. As **TABLE 11-5** depicts, these activities cover a wide spectrum of activities that affect large segments of the population.

6. *Data collection, epidemiology, and surveillance activities:* State health agencies serve as primary organizations for the activities noted. These activities support a broad range of functions in enabling state and local health departments and others concerned with population health to monitor trends and to plan appropriate interventions. **TABLE 11-6** lists activities performed directly by at least 50 percent of state health agencies. Syndromic surveillance systems utilized by 94 percent of state health agencies are of particular importance in anticipating potential public health issues. These systems monitor data such as school and employment absenteeism, emergency call systems, volumes of emergency room visits, and other data sources to detect unusual patterns which may signal an evolving public health issue.

In addition to the activity highlights noted above, state health agencies carry out many more functions addressing public health issues. Examples include safeguarding and improving environmental quality, attenuating health disparities, improving health services access, supporting maternal and child health, and advocating for minority and rural health challenges.[28]

TABLE 11-5 Top 15 Regulation, Inspection, and Licensing Activities Performed Directly by State Health Agencies, 2012

Activity	Percentage of State Health Agencies Directly Performing Activity
Laboratories	89
Food Service Establishments	81
Hospitals	81
Trauma System	81
Emergency Medical Services	79
Lead Inspection	77
Public Swimming Pools	72
Long-Term Care Facilities	70
Nursing Homes	71
Body Piercing and Tattooing	64
Hospice	62
Campgrounds/RVs	60
Food Processing	60
Assisted Living	57
Smoke-Free Ordinances	55

Modified from Association of State and Territorial Health Officials, *ASTHO Profile of State Public Health, Volume Three*, Washington, DC: Association of State and Territorial Health Officials, 2014.

TABLE 11-6 Selected Data Collection, Epidemiology, and Surveillance Activities Performed Directly by State Health Agencies, 2012

Activities	Percentage of State Health Agencies Participating
Reportable Diseases	100
Communicable Infectious Diseases	98
Foodborne Illnesses	98
Vital Statistics Reporting	98
Morbidity Reporting	94
Perinatal Events or Risk Factors	94
Behavioral Risk Factors	94
Chronic Diseases	94
Syndromic Surveillance*	94
Environmental Health	92
Injury	92

Activities	Percentage of State Health Agencies Participating
Cancer Incidence	90
Adolescent Behavior	77

Modified from Association of State and Territorial Health Officials, *ASTHO Profile of State Public Health, Volume Three*, Washington, DC: Association of State and Territorial Health Officials, 2014.

Local Roles

The National Association of County and City Health Officials (NACCHO) report, *2013 National Profile of Local Health Departments*, provides detailed descriptions of local health department (LHD) characteristics and activities based upon survey responses received from 2,532 of 2,800 LHDs.[29] LHDs support and deliver a variety of health and health-related services and, as discussed in Chapter 5, provide direct patient care services in clinics or health centers, referrals for care, and other services particularly focused on underserved populations. Most LHDs (68 percent) are county-based while 20 percent serve cities or towns.[29] LHDs are supported by a variety of revenue sources. Approximately 80 percent of revenue is contributed from government sources: local funds (26 percent), state funds (21 percent), federal direct and pass-through funds (20 percent), and Medicaid (13 percent).[19]

The LHD workforce employs approximately 146,000 full-time equivalent personnel in a wide array of titles. **TABLE 11-7** lists the 10 employee occupations that include almost 80 percent of the LHD workforce.[29] Titles of LHD leadership executives vary widely throughout the United States and include, among others, director, health officer, nurse manager, and health commissioner. The

TABLE 11-7 Estimated Size of Workforce in Full-time Equivalents (FTEs) and Percent of Total Workforce of Top Ten Occupations in Local Health Departments, 2013

	Estimated Workforce Size	Percent of Total Workforce
Total FTEs	146,000	100.0
Selected Occupations		
Administrative or Clerical	35,000	23.9
Registered Nurse	27,700	19.0
Environmental Health Worker	13,300	9.1
Public Health Manager	10,100	6.9
Community Health Worker	6,700	4.6
Nursing Aide and Home Health Aide	5,400	3.7
Health Educator	5,100	3.5
Nutritionist	5,000	3.4
Behavioral Health Professional	4,000	2.7
Licensed Practical or Vocational Nurse	3,200	2.1
All Others	30,500	21.4

Data from: NACCHO *2013 National Profile of Local Health Departments*.

educational credentials of executives vary from associate's degrees to the doctoral level. Sixty percent of all leaders have earned a master's or doctoral degree.[29]

NACCHO describes LHD activities in four main categories by level of LHD participation
and other variables: (1) Programs and Services, (2) Emergency Preparedness and Response,
(3) Assessment, Planning and Improvement, and (4) Public Health Policy.[29] The following sections
summarize information from the NACCHO Profile:[29]

1.   *Programs and services:* LHDs engage in a wide variety of activities to promote the
     positive health status of their communities. Services provided in individual localities
     depend upon many variables including state laws and other requirements, community
     needs and priorities, available funding, and relationships with other health and human
     services providers and organizations. **TABLES 11-8** through **11-12** provide selected snap-
     shots of programs and services in which at least 50 percent of LHDs participate. Table
     contents are selected for illustrative purposes. LHDs provide many additional pro-
     grams and services which are detailed in the cited NACCHO report.

2.   *Emergency preparedness and response:* LHDs play important roles in responding to
     natural and other disasters as well as public health emergencies of many types. Their
     capacity, coupled with collaborations with an array of other community organizations
     and healthcare providers, is central in efforts to prevent and control disease outbreaks
     and environmental hazards. Their advance planning to deal with community public
     health emergencies is essential for safeguarding the public's health during times of
     threatening events. **TABLE 11-13** provides an overview of LHDs' participation in pre-
     paredness and response activities.

3.   *Assessment, planning, and improvement:* Periodic community health assessments, com-
     munity health improvement planning, and development of LHD strategic plans are
     mechanisms to help ensure that LHDs stay in touch with evolving community needs

TABLE 11-8 Ten Programs and Services Provided Directly and Most Frequently by Local Health Departments

Program or Service	Percentage of Local Health Departments Participating
Communicable/Infectious Disease Surveillance	91
Adult Immunization Provision	90
Child Immunization Provision	90
Tuberculosis Screening	83
Environmental Health Surveillance	78
Food Service Establishment Inspection	78
Tuberculosis Treatment	76
Food Safety Education	72
Population-Based Nutrition Services	69
Schools/Daycare Center Inspection	69

Modified from National Association of County and City Health Officials *2013 National Profile of Local Health Departments*.

TABLE 11-9 Screening for Diseases and Conditions in Which at Least 50 Percent of Local Health Departments Participate

Communicable Disease	Percent of Local Health Departments Participating
Tuberculosis Screening	83
Tuberculosis Treatment	76
Sexually Transmitted Disease Screening	64
Sexually Transmitted Disease Treatment	60
HIV/AIDS Screening	61
Non-Communicable Disease or Condition	
Blood Lead Screening	61
High Blood Pressure Screening	57

Modified from National Association of County and City Health Officials *2013 National Profile of Local Health Departments*.

TABLE 11-10 Epidemiology and Surveillance Services in Which at Least 50 Percent of Local Health Departments Participate

Epidemiology and Surveillance Services	Percentage of Local Health Departments Participating
Communicable/Infectious Disease	91
Environmental Health	78
Maternal and Child Health	61

Modified from National Association of County and City Health Officials *2013 National Profile of Local Health Departments*.

TABLE 11-11 Population-Based Primary Prevention Services Provided by at Least 50 percent of Local Health Departments

Primary Prevention Services	Percentage of Local Health Departments Participating
Nutrition	69
Tobacco	68
Physical Activity	52
Chronic Disease Programs	50

Modified from National Association of County and City Health Officials *2013 National Profile of Local Health Departments*.

TABLE 11-12 Regulation, Inspection and Licensing Services in Which at Least 50 percent of Local Health Departments Participate

Regulation, Inspection, or Licensing Services	Percentage of Local Health Departments Participating
Food Service Establishments	78
Schools/Day Cares	69
Public Swimming Pools	68
Septic Systems	66
Smoke-Free Ordinances	59
Private Drinking Water	56
Body Art	55
Hotels/Motels	50

Modified from National Association of County and City Health Officials *2013 National Profile of Local Health Departments.*

TABLE 11-13 Emergency Preparedness Activities in Which at Least 50 percent of Local Health Departments Participate

Emergency Preparedness Activity	Percentage of Local Health Departments Participating
Developed or Updated Written Emergency Plan	87
Provided Emergency Preparedness Training to Staff	84
Participated in Tabletop Exercises or Drills	76
Assessed Emergency Preparedness Competencies of Staff	66

Modified from National Association of County and City Health Officials *2013 National Profile of Local Health Departments.*

and plan effective interventions. Successful fulfillment of these activities is central to voluntary national public health accreditation discussed later in this chapter. As of 2013, 70 percent of LHDs had completed a community health assessment or a community health improvement plan during the past five years. However, only 43 percent of LHDs had completed an agency-wide strategic plan in the prior five years.

4. *Public health policy:* As discussed later in this chapter, policy development is one of the three core functions of public health. Given their intimate knowledge of the population health issues of their communities, LHDs are uniquely poised to provide input to government officials, elected policymakers, and advocacy groups about community needs and priorities. In 2012, NACCHO reported that 79 percent of LHDs communicated with legislators, regulatory officials, or other policymakers, 55 percent prepared issue briefs for policymakers, and 50 percent provided technical assistance regarding

proposed legislation, regulations, or ordinances. Local health departments use infor- mation technology systems to assist in implementing their responsibilities. The most predominant use of information technology is in maintaining immunization registries (85 percent of LHDs) and disease reporting systems (75 percent of LHDs). More than 60 percent of LHDs also use electronic systems to conduct surveillance of potentially significant public health events in real-time, such as disease outbreaks or bioterrorism attacks.[29] Most LHDs rely on e-mail alert systems, broadcast fax, and auto-dialing for their communications.

Seventy percent of all LHDs have a local board of health.[29] Boards of health are legally consti- tuted entities charged with protecting and promoting the health of the community.[19] Membership may be drawn from the local medical community, community stakeholders representing constitu- ent interests, elected and/or appointed public officials, and others deemed appropriate to provide input on public health matters. The most common board activities are advisement to the LHD or elected officials on policies and programs, adopting public health regulations, approving the LHD budget, and setting public health fees.[19]

In addition to the services of LHDs, more than 200 governmental and not-for-profit hospi- tals with emphasis on serving patients with limited or no access to health care due to financial circumstances or health conditions are classified as "essential hospitals."[30] Many essential hos- pitals are owned by city or county jurisdictions and are core safety-net providers of high-cost specialized services. These include trauma, community crisis response, pediatric and neonatal intensive care, psychiatric care, and burn care, which other hospitals may be unable or unwilling to provide.[30] In 2013, almost half of essential hospitals' discharges were minorities and about half of discharges and outpatient visits were for uninsured or Medicaid patients. In the same year, this small subset of U.S. hospitals operated nearly one-third of all U.S. Level I trauma centers and psychiatric-care beds and more than two-thirds of all burn-care beds available in nation's 10 largest cities.[31]

State and Local Health Department Relationships

Relationships among state and locally operated health departments are diverse, owing to the history of their development, nuances of state and local politics, and other factors. Because the relationships impact decisions about how best to implement effective public health strategies at state and local levels, the nature of the relationships has been the subject of significant research. This research has resulted in the classification of state and local public health departments in the following four categories as reported by a joint project of the ASTHO and the National Opinion Research Center of the University of Chicago:[19,32]

- *Centralized/largely centralized:* Seventy-five percent or more of the state's population is served by local health units that are led by employees of the state, and the state retains authority over many decisions relating to the budget, public health orders, and the selection of local health officials.
- *Decentralized/largely decentralized:* Seventy-five percent or more of the state's population is served by local health units that are led by employees of local governments, and the local governments retain authority over many decisions relating to the budget, public health orders, and the selection of local health officials.
- *Shared/largely shared:* Seventy-five percent or more of the state's population is served by local health units that meet one of these criteria: (1) local health units are led by state or local

employees, (2) local government has authority over many decisions relating to the budget, public health orders, and the selection of public health officials or where local health units are led by local employees, and the state retains many of those authorities.

■ *Mixed*: Within the state there is a combination of centralized, shared, and/or decentralized arrangements. No one arrangement predominates in the state.

Delineation of the categories provides a foundation for practical understanding among the entities and for subsequent research efforts on public health systems and services.

▶ Voluntary National Public Health Department Accreditation

The 2003 Institute of Medicine report, *The Future of the Public's Health in the 21st Century*, recommended establishment of a national steering committee to review the benefits of accrediting governmental public health agencies.[18] (Note that the Institute of Medicine was renamed *National Academy of Medicine* in 2015. References to its work prior to 2015 are attributed to its former title.) Up to this point, several states had managed statewide accreditation or related initiatives for local health departments.[33] In 2004, the CDC included accreditation as a key strategy in its plans.[33] In the same year, in collaboration with the CDC, the Robert Wood Johnson Foundation (RWJF) convened public health stakeholders to determine whether a voluntary national accreditation program for state and local health departments should proceed and achieved consensus to do so.[33] The RWJF initiative recognized that although many public service and health-related entities such as hospitals, schools, and universities had accreditation programs, no national accreditation program existed for public health departments.[34] Following three years of study and broad-based national input, the Public Health Accreditation Board (PHAB) was established in 2007 as a not-for-profit corporation to facilitate development of the accreditation process and manage its implementation.[33] Involving numerous public health professionals, other accreditation program and technical experts, feedback elicited through broad-based channels, and extensive pilot testing, accreditation standards and measures were formally adopted in 2011 by the PHAB, and the new accreditation program was launched.[33]

The goal of the voluntary national accreditation program "is to improve and protect the health of the public by advancing the quality and performance of Tribal, state and local territorial public health departments."[35] Organizations eligible for accreditation include governmental entities with primary statutory or legal responsibility for public health in a Tribe, state, territory, or local jurisdiction.[36] Accreditation requires a seven-step process that entails submission of extensive documentation to the PHAB, a site visit, and reports on conformance with PHAB-approved standards and measures.[37,38] In March 2016, the PHAB announced that since the launch of the national accreditation program in 2011, 117 public health departments and 1 integrated local public health department system had achieved accreditation.[39] In April 2016, the PHAB announced the establishment of the Public Health National Center for Innovations (PHNCI) with a three-year funding initiative from the Robert Wood Johnson Foundation. The goal of the PHNCI is to "identify, implement, and spread innovations in public health practice to help meet the health challenges of the 21st century in communities nationwide."[40]

▶ Public Health Organization Challenges and Responses

In 1985, the Institute of Medicine (IOM) Committee for the Study of the Future of Public Health convened regarding concerns about protecting the nation's health through an effective, organized public health sector and commenced a study of the status of public health in the United States The committee reported its findings and recommendations in 1988. The report included findings from research on the history of U.S. public health, research on the relationship of public health to clinical medicine and field reviews, and observations of federal, state, and local health agencies.[41] The report's chapters described "The Disarray of Public Health: A Threat to the Health of the Public," "An Assessment of the Current Public Health System: A Shattered Vision," and "Public Health as a Problem-solving Activity: Barriers to Effective Action."[41] The report also highlighted poor public health system organization across federal, state, and local levels; deficiencies in consistent and competent leadership; outdated public health legal parameters; inadequate financial support; inadequate data and surveillance infrastructures; and lack of effective linkages between the public and private sectors.[41]

The report made organizational, educational, financial, and political recommendations for addressing these complex and interrelated problems. Its strategies depended on sustained and strong financial support for existing public health agencies and stronger, more sharply focused leadership that could build increasingly productive links with the private and voluntary healthcare sectors. Unfortunately, as discussions in later sections of this chapter highlight, gaining and sustaining support for the recommended strategies continues to be a monumental challenge.

The 1988 IOM report was preceded by a 1980 federal initiative that advanced a 10-year national health improvement process described in, "Promoting Health/Preventing Disease: Objectives for the Nation," based upon a 1979 report of the Surgeon General. In response to the IOM report, in 1990, the DHHS published *Public Health Service: Healthy People 2000: National Health Promotion and Disease Prevention Objectives.*[42,43] *Healthy People 2000* provided 319 unduplicated objectives grouped in 22 priority areas with 21 focused on health promotion, protection, and preventive services and one priority area focused on surveillance and data systems development.[42] *Healthy People 2000* also emphasized the importance of local health departments in effectively carrying out the three core functions of public health assessment, policy development, and assurance as described by the IOM's report:[44]

1. *Assessment:* Collecting and analyzing data to define population health status and quantify existing or emerging health problems
2. *Policy development:* Generating recommendations from available data to address public health problems, analyzing options for solutions, and mobilizing public and community organizations through implementation plans
3. *Assurance:* Governmental public health agency responsibility to ensure that basic components of the healthcare delivery system are in place

These core health department functions are intended to put into operation, within resource and other constraints extant in their respective jurisdictions, the following generally accepted 10 essential health department performance responsibilities:

1. Monitor health status to identify and solve community health problems
2. Diagnose and investigate health problems and health hazards in the community

3. Inform, educate, and empower people about health issues
4. Mobilize community partnerships and action to identify and solve health problems
5. Develop policies and plans that support individual and community health efforts
6. Enforce laws and regulations that protect health and ensure safety
7. Link people as needed with personal health services and ensure the provision of health care when otherwise unavailable
8. Ensure the provision of a competent public and personal healthcare workforce
9. Evaluate the effectiveness, accessibility, and quality of person- and population-based health services
10. Research for new insights and innovative solutions to environmental health problems

FIGURE 11-2 depicts how the three core functions relate to the 10 essential services.

It is important to note that "research" is at the center of the figure, as its role is to inform the other functions. It is through the fulfillment of the three core public health functions and 10 essential services that public health departments protect the public against preventable communicable diseases, exposure to toxic environmental pollutants and harmful products, and poor-quality health care. These public health practices are the foundations of modern population-focused health care.

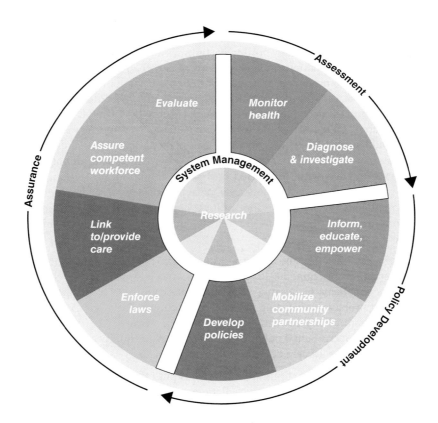

FIGURE 11-2 Three Core Functions and Ten Essential Public Health Services

As reported in 2001, the nation struggled to meet the goals of *Healthy People 2000*. The *Healthy People 2000 Final Review* noted that of the 319 objectives set in 1990, by 2000, the nation met 21 percent of targets; 41 percent showed improvement toward targets; 11 percent of targets showed mixed results; 2 percent showed no change; 15 percent moved negatively from targets; and 10 percent of target results could not be assessed due to data discrepancies.[45]

Healthy People 2010 built upon preceding targets to continue a framework for planning and action on achieving improvements in longevity and quality of life and provided additional emphases on decreasing health disparities. The final report on *Healthy People 2010* noted that progress was made in meeting or moving toward 71 percent of the program's targets.[43] However, there was little progress in reducing or eliminating health disparities. Disparities had not changed for 80 percent of the health objectives and had increased for an additional 13 percent.[43] Another disappointing finding from this report was that obesity rates increased across all age groups; for children aged 6 to 11 years, obesity rates rose 54.5 percent, and the proportion of obese adults rose 47.8 percent. On a positive note, the report cited substantial progress on heart disease and stroke reduction by meeting targets to reduce cholesterol levels and the levels of cigarette smoking.[43]

Healthy People 2020, like its predecessors, was crafted with extensive expert and public input and contains 1,200 objectives that span 42 distinct public health topic areas. In addition to encompassing the ongoing 2010 objectives, *Healthy People 2020* selected a set of 26 objectives, named "Leading Health Indicators" (LHIs), to communicate high-priority health issues and actions that can be taken to address them.[46] Selected examples of LHIs include:

- Persons with medical insurance
- Children receiving recommended doses of childhood vaccines
- Injury deaths
- Infant deaths
- Suicide
- Obesity among adults and children
- Persons visiting a dentist in the past year
- Sexually active females receiving reproductive health services in the past year
- Adolescents using alcohol or illicit drugs in past 30 days
- Adolescent cigarette smoking[47]

A 2014 interim report on LHI's accomplishments of *Healthy People 2020* notes modest gains toward achieving the *Healthy People 2020* targets for the 26 LHI objectives with 14 LHIs (53.9 percent) having either met their target or shown improvement.[47]

The goals and objectives of the *Healthy People* initiatives of the past three decades are commendable, and their delineation gives the government, private agencies, and organizations involved a sense of accomplishment. However, the absence of a cohesive, well-supported public health sector continues making achievement of the goals of these initiatives extremely challenging.

Public Health Accomplishments and Resource Challenges of the 20th and 21st Centuries

Accomplishments

The Centers for Disease Control and Prevention tracks historically significant public health accomplishments and trends. The CDC report, *Achievements in Public Health, 1990–1999: Changes in the Public Health System*, notes numerous public health accomplishments that contributed to significant improvements in both the health status and life expectancy of Americans throughout the 1900s and in the first decade of the 2000s.[48]

Using population-based strategies for disease and injury prevention coupled with unprecedented medical, biomedical, and scientific advances of the 1900s, public health contributed to remarkable declines in morbidity and mortality and dramatically changed the profiles of disease, injury, and death in the United States. For example, in the early 1900s, major health threats were infectious diseases associated with poor hygiene, sanitation, and nutrition; poor maternal and infant health; and diseases resulting from unsafe work conditions. Public health systems of the early 1900s that incorporated vaccinations, new antibiotics, and health education interventions resulted in major decreases in the impacts of infectious diseases and other conditions. In concert with community activism, many infectious diseases were conquered, diseases associated with nutritional deficiencies were vastly attenuated, maternal and infant health outcomes were improved, and diseases and injuries resulting from unsafe work conditions and motor vehicle-related injuries were reduced.[48,49] As many previously devastating infectious diseases (such as diphtheria, polio, and tuberculosis) were effectively controlled, in the last half of the 1900s, chronic conditions such as cardiovascular disease and cancer emerged as prominent causes of mortality, and the public health system engaged to identify related risk factors and introduce new interventions. The 1900s also saw development of enhanced morbidity and mortality surveillance, which helped maintain earlier successes and contributed to the development of new interventions.[48] Life expectancy at birth among U.S. citizens increased by 62 percent from 47.3 years in 1900 to 76.8 years in 2000.[49]

In the same period, epidemiological science acquired greater quantitative capacity that facilitated improvements in study design and periodic health surveys. Methods of data collection evolved from simple measures of disease prevalence to complex studies of precise analyses, such as cohort studies, case-control studies, and randomized controlled clinical trials.[48] Development of high-powered, computerized statistical testing allowed measurement of multiple variables collected in large-scale studies to be applied to development of tools for mathematical modeling. These advances allowed elucidation of disease risk factors and identification of effective interventions.[48]

The decade from 2000 to 2010 was marked by several public health accomplishments. Many new vaccines were introduced including rotavirus, meningococcal, herpes zoster, pneumococcal, and papillomavirus. A 2011 economic analysis on the use of vaccines reported that vaccination of each U.S. birth cohort using the current childhood immunization schedule prevents approximately 42,000 deaths and 20 million cases of disease, with net cost savings of nearly $14 billion in direct costs and $69 billion in total societal costs.[49]

Only a partial list of other significant public health accomplishments of this period include early identification of HIV/AIDS infection through expanded screening, elimination of canine rabies, reductions in tobacco use, reductions in childhood lead poisoning, enactment of motor vehicle safety policies, and, in concert with advances in clinical medicine, reductions in cardiovascular disease risk factors.

Many accomplishments from the 1900s to the present involve public health's use of the legal system to achieve desired population behavioral changes. Examples include state and local ordinances banning smoking in public locations; taxation of tobacco products; mandatory seat belt use; and federal, state, and local lead poisoning prevention and lead abatement regulations. Also, mandatory fortification of cereal grain products labeled as enriched contributed to a 36 percent reduction in the number of infants born with neural tube defects between 1996 and 2006, preventing these defects in an estimated 10,000 affected pregnancies, and resulting in a savings of $4.7 billion in direct costs.[49]

Resource Challenges

Despite the centrality of public health in providing critical systems and supports for the health of all Americans, historically, government funding for public health has competed with other more highly valued demands.[50] Such competition continues.

In 2006, the health policy journal, *Health Affairs* devoted its monthly issue to the "State of Public Health," in which the editors noted:[51]

> Public health has always been the neglected stepchild of U.S. healthcare system. It subsisted on whatever funding was left over after flashier parts of the system took their cut, and it took on tasks, such as being the provider of last resort for the uninsured and indigent, that no one else was willing to perform.

The editors cite the short-lived stimulus of funding infusion for public health infrastructure improvements created by the terrorist attacks and anthrax threats of 2001. The stimulus provided states with $5 billion, but no continuing funding was forthcoming to sustain efforts as states faced severe revenue shortfalls during the ensuing years of the U.S. economic downturn.[51] The subsequent decade did see progress in health departments' ability to respond to public health emergencies in areas such as preparedness planning, pharmaceutical and medical equipment distribution systems, and surveillance and communications. However, in the period from 2005 to 2012, federal funds for the CDC's support of state and local health departments' responses to a range of public health emergencies, including bioterrorism, were cut by more than 38 percent.[52]

A 2012 IOM report, *For the Public's Health: Investing in a Healthier Future* notes, "The poor performance of the United States in life expectancy and other major health outcomes as compared with its global peers reflects what the nation prioritizes. It spends extravagantly on clinical care but meagerly on other types of population-based actions that influence health more profoundly than medical services."[53] The report further notes that, " … to its detriment, society's fixation on clinical care, its delivery, and its financing overshadows population-based activities that more efficiently and effectively improve the nation's health," and cites insufficient funding for prevention of the health problems responsible for most morbidity and mortality.[53] The IOM report cited the health system's deficiencies in developing and implementing preventive strategies and the effects of these deficiencies on the U.S. economy and society. When the report was issued in 2012, IOM recommendations included doubling Congressional appropriations for public health from approximately $12 billion to $24 billion, noting that the recommended increase represented only a small fraction of the $2.5 trillion the nation spent on health in 2010, most of which was devoted to medical care.[53]

In 2015, the American Journal of Public Health published a policy brief with findings by City University of New York (CUNY) School of Public Health researchers, *Public Health's Falling Share of U.S. Health Spending.*[54] Researchers analyzed actual public health expenditure data spanning over five decades, 1960–2013, and projected 2014 expenditure data.[54] Findings reported inflation-adjusted per-capita public health spending rising from $39 in 1960 to a peak of $281 in 2008 and a decrease of 9.3 percent to $255 per capita in 2014. The public health share of total national health expenditures increased from 1.36 percent in 1960 to 3.18 percent in 2002, and decreased to 2.65 percent in 2014. The 2014 level represents a 17 percent decline since 2002 when funding surged due to the 2001 terrorist attacks.[54] Projections estimate that public health's share of national health expenditures will fall to 2.4 percent by 2023, or 25 percent below the 2002 level.[54] The report also noted that growth in public health spending between 1960 and 2001 resulted primarily from state and local governments, which contributed 80–90 percent of total public health spending in recent decades.[54] CUNY researchers calculated that if inflation-adjusted public health expenditures had remained at the 2008 level, an additional $40.2 billion would have been allocated to public health in the period 2009–2014.[54] Referring to the IOM report cited above, the CUNY report concluded that, "The current trajectory of health spending seems unlikely to close the funding gap identified by the Institute of Medicine panel."[54]

The ACA created the Prevention and Public Health Fund (the Fund), the nation's first mandatory funding stream dedicated to improving public health.[55] The Fund was intended to eliminate the previously unpredictable federal budget appropriations for public health and prevention programs. The ACA mandates the Fund's use to "improve health and help restrain the rate of growth in private and public sector healthcare costs."[55] The Fund's purposes emphasize the development of "a national prevention, health promotion, and public health strategy."[56] The ACA authorized $18.75 billion for the Fund for fiscal years 2010–2022, and $2 billion in each succeeding year.[55] The federal budget allocation for each year was set in the ACA law. However, specific uses of the Fund are determined annually by the Congressional budget appropriations process in consultation with the President and Congress.[55] The ACA allowed Congress to retain authority to set the Fund aside or to re-direct its resources to proposals outside of public health.[55]

Congressional prerogatives regarding the Fund played out to the detriment of the Fund purposes.[55] In 2012, Congress and the President approved legislation that cut the Fund by $6.25 billion over nine fiscal years (2013–2021) to offset Medicare payment adjustments to physicians.[55] In 2016, the Fund was reduced by $68 million through 2023 by automatic spending reductions to most federal programs resulting from Congressional deficit reduction initiatives.[55] The 2012 legislation and 2016 reductions left $932 million of the originally planned $2 billion for 2016 authorized by the ACA in 2010 (slightly less than 50 percent of intended Fund amount) for public health prevention, wellness, and preparedness activities.[55] These outcomes are prime examples of the ways in which public health resource priorities are pre-empted by political priorities. State and local health departments and community organizations such as hospitals that assist public health agencies continue bearing the impacts of underfunding.

The Federal Public Health Emergency Preparedness program funding for states and localities to prepare for and respond to all types of disasters decreased from a high of $940 million in 2002 to $661 million in 2016.[57] Federal funding for the Hospital Preparedness Program supporting these institutions' training and preparation of an array of community disasters has been reduced by more than 50 percent, from a high of $515 million in 2004 to $355 million in 2016. In 2012, on average, 12 percent of state health agency positions were vacant, with fewer than 25 percent of these in active recruitment for replacement.[28] Between 2010 and 2012, the number of state health agency full-time equivalent staff members declined by 5,000 and the agencies reduced disease and condition screening, maternal and child health services, and other services.[28] Spanning two fiscal periods from 2013 to 2015, 16 states reduced their public health budgets.[57] State health agency budget reductions have a ripple effect on non governmental state health agency public health partners as the ASTHO reported in 2012. Forty-four percent and 32 percent of state health agency contracts, grants, and awards were made to local health departments and not-for-profit organizations, respectively.[28]

Since 2008, LHDs eliminated an estimated 51,700 jobs resulting from layoffs due to hiring freezes or budget cuts; 61 percent of large LHDs (serving populations of 500,000 or more), reported job losses in 2014.[58]

Currently, with less than 3 cents of every U.S. healthcare dollar allocated to public health, the United States continues to shortchange American's healthcare needs. Public health's significant contributions make it clear that public health principles have far greater potential to improve the health status of all Americans than exponentially more expensive after-the-fact medical interventions. Public awareness must energize "political will" to bring material improvements to U.S. population health.[59]

▶ Public Health Services of Voluntary Organizations

The role of not-for-profit voluntary organizations as adjunct resources to government public health agencies is a major theme in the evolution of health care in the United States. Historically, private, not-for-profit organizations have shared responsibilities with government for meeting the needs of vulnerable populations.[60] Working partnerships between government public health agencies and not-for-profit healthcare organizations remain essential strongholds of the public health system.[18] In 2011 not-for-profit organizations received 32 percent of $6 billion distributed by state health agencies through contracts, grants, and awards.[28]

There is a host of voluntary agencies providing nursing home care, hospice care, home care, medical and vocational rehabilitation, and other personal healthcare services. A variety of voluntary agencies serves the special needs of persons with medical conditions such as AIDS, asthma, diabetes, cerebral palsy, hemophilia, and muscular dystrophy. Similar organizations support research on conditions such as cancer, heart disease, and respiratory disorders. Others, such as the American Red Cross, Planned Parenthood, and Meals on Wheels, focus on providing specific services to populations in need. Many voluntary agencies provide numerous valued and effective services that are not available in the private medical care sector.

The influence of large not-for-profit foundations, such as the RWJF, the Commonwealth Fund, and the Pew Charitable Trusts, on the advancement of health care from a population perspective has been considerable. By providing funds on a competitive basis to stimulate research and innovative program demonstrations, these and other philanthropic organizations have enabled organizations to engage in progressive health service delivery improvements that may otherwise have been years in development. In 2014, charitable contributions from all sources to not-for-profit health organizations exceeded $30 billion.[61]

The interdependence of government, private, and voluntary sector efforts has been both a bane and a blessing in the provision of health care in the United States. The U.S. healthcare system's disorderly evolution from a combination of charitable efforts, government responses to needs, and U.S. free enterprise resulted in a complex network that is technologically successful but plagued by costly inefficiencies, duplications, and inequities. Nevertheless, this pluralistic approach has endured and continues making material contributions to health system improvement through research to inform policymaking, demonstration programs to test system innovations, and support to reform system infrastructures.

▶ Relationships of Public Health and Clinical Medicine

Public health and clinical medicine have complementary roles in caring for the health of the American people. Although they often address the same health problems, their attention is directed at different stages of disease or injury. Clinical medicine devotes its most intensive resources to diagnosis, treatment, and health restoration for individuals. Clinicians define a successful outcome of a medical intervention as an individual's wellness.[62] Public health devotes its resources to identifying and implementing preventive strategies with a broad population focus through interventions such as environmental improvements, education promoting healthy behaviors and lifestyles, and reductions in barriers to healthcare access. Public health professionals characterize success "… as the reduction, delay, or prevention of a disease or disability for a group of individuals or community as a whole."[62]

The relationship between the disciplines of public health and clinical medicine has a lengthy history in America that formally began with the establishment of the Public Health Service Commissioned Corps in 1889. Among many other activities, Corps physicians assisted in combating large-scale disease outbreaks, conducted biomedical research, and rendered care to populations affected by disasters.[14,15] However, as the public health and medical professions evolved over succeeding years, the sectors diverged.

Conflicts between clinical medicine and public health were rooted in the medical profession's philosophical and economic concerns.[63] Private practice medicine considered extending the boundaries of public health as an opening wedge for usurping the physicians' role and the path to socialized medicine.[63] Physicians opposed public health's disease screening and primary care services such as mass vaccinations, even though these services targeted populations with the lowest incomes and populations groups which physicians chose not to serve.[63] Physicians asserted that public health agencies were intruding upon the physician–patient relationship and impinging upon their practices' income generating services.[63] Public health professionals came to view physicians as elitist and focused on financial gain, while physicians viewed public health as a politically motivated endeavor comprised of individuals of lesser scientific intellectual stature than themselves.[64]

An *American Journal of Public Health* report chronicling the history of this relationship throughout the 1900s notes, "The division of responsibility, authority, and power between public health and medicine has been a continuing source of concern and conflict. Although representatives of both fields have traditionally voiced strong commitments to health and social betterment, the relationship between public health and medicine has been characterized by critical tensions, covert hostilities, and at times, open warfare."[64] The report authors cite four primary reasons why the public health and clinical medicine sectors took divergent paths beginning in the early 1900s and continued in those paths during succeeding years:[64]

1. An increasingly powerful medical profession viewed public health initiatives such as requirements to report communicable diseases as infringing on the doctor–patient relationship. Physicians contended that these reports would deter patients from seeking treatment, while public health officials asserted that such reporting was justified to safeguard community health.

2. Public health services such as well baby care, disease screening, and school-based nursing were viewed by the medical profession as intrusions into its domains and income. Public health officials countered these protests as indicative of medicine's self-interest. The divide deepened as organized medicine succeeded in defeating legislative and administrative proposals to link clinical medicine and public health interventions with services such as maternal and infant health and neighborhood health centers.

3. Hospitals emerged as the centers of health care, shifting the focus from community-based preventive services to acute care. This shift was later fueled by the introduction of health insurance plans that lucratively supported the costs of hospital care.

4. Schools of public health were established as institutions separate from medical schools, and public health was increasingly recognized as a profession distinct from medicine. Further, as medicine became more highly specialized and scientifically oriented, public health increasingly viewed clinical medicine as disconnected from the social determinants of health.

Despite historical clashes in perspectives, there are many examples of the synergistic effects of public health and clinical medicine. The immunization of children and adults against a variety of preventable diseases is one example of how public health and medicine have worked together effectively. Many screening programs, such as for tuberculosis, colorectal and breast cancer, and hypertension, have linked the services of private medicine and the population-oriented services of public health through educational campaigns and cooperative agreements to treat patients with positive screening results. Further, public health and medicine remain deeply interdependent as medicine's link with individual community members provides a foundation for important public health functions.[62] Such functions include disease surveillance and infectious disease contact follow-up, maintenance of disease registries, vital statistics reporting, and participation in community health education campaigns.[62,66] In addition, examples abound about how physicians' knowledge and skills are invaluable to the public health enterprise by alerting authorities to unusual medical conditions that may pose threats to population health. Examples include the link of workplace exposure to carcinogenic vinyl chloride, discovery of a West Nile virus outbreak, re-emergence of drug-resistant tuberculosis, anthrax exposure following the 2001 terrorist attacks, and the recognition of toxic shock syndrome.[65] A recent striking example of medicine's pivotal role in public health was the initiative of a Flint, Michigan, pediatrician and her research team in publicly reporting alarming increases in blood lead levels among children in certain Flint neighborhoods. Her report was instrumental in exposing a public health disaster resulting from the diversion of the city's water supply from Lake Huron to the toxic Flint River.[66]

In the healthcare reform environment, public health and clinical medicine have stronger mandates than ever to collaborate, recognizing that neither sector alone can effectively achieve improved U.S. health status. Social determinants of health such as poverty, educational attainment, and economic self-sufficiency loom large and are beyond the scope of the biomedical model of medical care.[64,65] Concurrently, public health professionals recognize that enhanced collaborations with clinical medicine will form the pathway required to combine the best of clinical scientific expertise with the tenets of population health. A growing professional consensus that new models of care delivery and financing and melding population health and clinical medicine will provide the only viable solutions to improving U.S. population health status.[64] The ACA emphasis on population health and reimbursement incentives, aligned with population rather than individual outcomes, is proving key to begin closing the gap between public health and medicine. Changes have begun in accreditation standards for medical school curricula regarding the inclusion of population health and public health sciences and prevention along with revisions in national licensing examinations on these topics.[67] Accordingly, there are ongoing initiatives to integrate public health and medical education such as the American Association of Medical Colleges (AAMC)–CDC cooperative agreement.[68] Through the agreement, the CDC awards funds to the AAMC and other national academic associations to support improved teaching on public health concepts and provide practical experience for public health medical and nursing students.[68]

Political challenges in advancing public health principles are certain to continue both for the public health sector and clinical medicine. Public health and clinical advances that successfully controlled highly visible public health problems, such as outbreaks of poliomyelitis and other vaccine-preventable diseases in the mid-1900s, are mostly invisible to the American public, and therefore not politically attractive.

▶ **Public Health Ethics**

Following the issuance of the 1988 IOM report, "The Future of Public Health," the National Public Health Leadership Institute (PHLI) was established by the CDC in 1990 to address the infrastructure and system deficiencies cited by the report. The PHLI convened a network of senior public health leaders to collaborate on meeting public health infrastructure challenges.[69] The Public Health Leadership Society was created in 1993 by graduates of the PHLI. In 2000, the PHLI adopted the task of writing a public health code of ethics with the ultimate intent that it be adopted by public health organizations and institutions.[70] The need for a code of ethics recognized that public health's mandate to ensure and protect the health of the public is inherently moral. As such, the code draws from several ethical concepts relevant to human rights, distributive justice for the disenfranchised, and the duty to take action as an ethical motivation.[70] Different from the code of medical ethics, which is concerned with an individual and clinical focus, public health ethics are concerned with institutions' interactions with communities. Principles of public health ethical practice are as follows:[70]

1. Public health should address principally the fundamental causes of disease and requirements for health, aiming to prevent adverse health outcomes.
2. Public health should achieve community health in a way that respects the rights of individuals in the community.
3. Public health policies, programs, and priorities should be developed and evaluated through processes that ensure an opportunity for input from community members.
4. Public health should advocate and work for the empowerment of disenfranchised community members, aiming to ensure that the basic resources and conditions necessary for health are accessible to all.
5. Public health should seek the information needed to implement effective policies and programs that protect and promote health.
6. Public health institutions should provide communities with the information they have that is needed for decisions on policies or programs and should obtain the community's consent for their implementation.
7. Public health institutions should act in a timely manner on the information they have within the resources and mandate given to them by the public.
8. Public health programs and policies should incorporate a variety of approaches that anticipate and respect diverse values, beliefs, and cultures in the community.
9. Public health programs and policies should be implemented in a manner that most enhances the physical and social environment.
10. Public health institutions should protect the confidentiality of information that can bring harm to an individual or community if made public. Exceptions must be justified on the basis of the high likelihood of significant harm to the individual or others.
11. Public health institutions should ensure the professional competence of their employees.
12. Public health institutions and their employees should engage in collaborations and affiliations in ways that build the public's trust and the institution's effectiveness.

In 2002, the American Public Health Association became the first national organization to adopt the code. It was subsequently disseminated and adopted by numerous other national organizations.[70]

▶ The ACA and Public Health

This section reviews some of the many ACA public health provisions included in the ACA and, as available, provides updates. The summaries are not exhaustive and readers are encouraged to access the references cited for additional details.

National Prevention, Health Promotion and Public Health Council

ACA Title IV, "Prevention of Chronic Disease and Improving Public Health," established the National Prevention, Health Promotion and Public Health Council (the Council) in 2010 to develop and lead a national prevention strategy. Chaired by the U.S. Surgeon General, the Council's mandate is to build on existing federal programs such as *Healthy People 2020* and to make recommendations to the President and Congress for federal policy changes that support public health goals.[71–73] The Council currently provides leadership to and coordination of public health activities of 20 federal departments and agencies, and consults with outside experts and stakeholders.[72,73] The Council continues four strategic directions established in 2010: (1) building healthy and safe community environments, (2) expanding quality preventive services in both clinical and community settings, (3) empowering people to make healthy choices, and (4) eliminating health disparities. The Council's action plans are guided by commitments to identify opportunities to promote prevention, increase tobacco-free environments, and increase access to healthy, affordable foods.[74] Consistent with these commitments, in its most recent Report in 2014, the Council outlined several accomplishments made with community partners across the United States.[75] Examples include an almost 70 percent increase in the number of smoke-free college campuses between 2012 and 2013; more than 6,500 schools receiving certification for promoting nutrition and physical activity by the end of 2013; and a 672 percent increase in low-income individuals and families accessing the federal supplemental nutrition assistance program (SNAP) to access healthy foods at affordable costs by 2013.[75]

Health Care Workforce Development

The purpose of Title V of the ACA, "Health Care Workforce," is to improve access to and the delivery of healthcare services for all individuals, particularly low-income, underserved, uninsured, minority, health disparity, and rural populations.[76] To these ends, Title V mandated the establishment of a National Health Workforce Commission to review current and projected workforce needs and provide analyses and recommendations to Congress and the federal administration to align federal policies with national needs.[77] The Commission's expert 15-member panel was appointed in 2010, but because it has not received Congressional funding appropriation, has not convened.[77]

Title V has, however, awarded competitive grants to support state-level comprehensive workforce planning and implementation strategies.[78] To address needs of the underserved and health disparities, Title V also authorized incentive programs to attract professionals to work in medically underserved areas. For example, in 2013 with ACA funds, the HRSA awarded $9.3 million for student loan repayments to fourth-year medical students in exchange for agreement to work three years in an underserved area following completion of a primary care residency.[79] Title V also created a mandatory fund for the National Health Service Corps (NHSC) scholarship and loan repayment program and a "Ready Reserve Corp" within the U.S. Public Health Service to respond to national public health emergencies to be available for assignments in underserved communities.[80] In 2013, 94 percent of NHSC nurses were supported with ACA funding, and, in total, the NHSC loan-repayment program awarded approximately $170 million to various providers serving in high-need areas.[79,81] The ACA also established a new program to increase workforce supply by supporting nurse-managed health centers operated by advanced practice nurses who provide comprehensive primary care and wellness services to underserved populations.[81]

Title V took steps to decrease significant racial and ethnic disparities in the public health workforce. One example was the reauthorization and expansion of the Nursing Workforce Diversity Grants program to increase educational opportunities for individuals from disadvantaged backgrounds and from underrepresented racial and ethnic minorities in the registered nurse workforce. In 2014, $15.3 million was appropriated for this program.[81]

In summary, through both emphases on preventive services and important health workforce needs, ACA Titles IV and V address many public health issues that have a lengthy documented history. The impetus from those paying for health care (employers, organized consumers, and governments) for improved measures of health status and system performance created pressures that drove public health provisions of the ACA. As early accomplishments of the Council and workforce initiatives suggest, these provisions offer opportunities to both public health leaders and other stakeholders to increase collaborative emphases on preventive services in innovative ways.

▶ Current and Future: Enduring and Emerging Public Health Challenges

The United States faces major ongoing, emergent, and globally oriented public health challenges. The sections below discuss just a few examples. These discussions also highlight how in many situations, political, rather than population health interests determine the courses of action.

Enduring Public Health Issues

The focus on remedial medicine for Americans suffering from health disparities has denied the reality of system inequities. The major causes of disease and disability among many Americans are conditions that result from multiple causes that are not amenable to medicine's technologic remedies. While the vast majority of health spending is devoted to medical care, "There is strong evidence that personal behaviors and the environment are responsible for more than 70 percent of avoidable mortality and that health care is just one of several determinants of health."[18] While public health and clinical medicine have succeeded in conquering many diseases that plagued the United States in prior decades, there remain daunting challenges with the issues of health disparities associated with income, education, occupation, and chronic disease prevention and management.[82] According to the World Health Organization (WHO), non-communicable diseases (NCDs) account for 88 percent of total U.S. deaths.[83] The CDC reports that five causes account for 66 percent of U.S. NCD deaths among persons <80 years of age. The five causes and the CDC estimates of the percentage deemed potentially preventable are:[84]

Although early intervention through disease screening and timely medical treatment play important roles, reductions in the numbers of potentially preventable deaths requires remediation

U.S. Top Five Causes of Preventable Deaths	Percent Preventable
Diseases of the Heart	34
Cancer	21
Chronic Lower Respiratory Diseases	39
Cerebrovascular Diseases (Stroke)	33
Unintentional Injuries	39

Data from Centers for Disease Control and Prevention. Potentially preventable deaths from the five leading causes of death-United States, 2008-2010. Morbidity and Mortality Weekly Report. 2014;63:369-373. Available from http://www.cdc.gov/mmwr/pdf/wk/mm6317.pdf. Accessed May 12, 2016.

of risk factors associated with socioeconomic conditions, lifestyles, behaviors, cultural norms, and other determinants of health. Because historic presumptions prevail that such risks are not amenable to clinical interventions, personal behaviors have been largely considered as either outside the scope of the medical care system or immutable to change. Health insurance companies rarely have reimbursed providers for preventive services, thus reinforcing these presumptions and de-valuing non-medical interventions.

Against the backdrop of the meager percentage of U.S. health spending allocated to public health, to assess the impact of public health spending on reducing preventable deaths, researchers analyzed 13 years of funding and mortality from preventable causes of death from almost 3,000 local public health departments.[85] The goal was to determine whether changes in mortality rates from preventable causes of death were related to local public health department funding. Research findings indicated that public health spending is "one of the most consistent determinants of community-level preventable mortality."[85] The researchers also noted that, "the findings imply that the mortality reductions attributable to increases in public health spending are sizeable, and may exceed the reductions achievable through similar expansions in local medical care resources."[85] Another study by the American Public Health Association on returns for investment in public health notes that, "by investing in the prevention and treatment of the most common chronic diseases, the United States could save $218 billion per year in treatment costs and reduce the economic impact of disease by $1.1 trillion annually."[86]

Preventive public health initiatives of the ACA and longer-standing efforts such as *Healthy People 2020* and the CDC's Behavioral Risk Factor Surveillance System (BRFSS) are only two examples of government public health efforts to sustain presence on the frontlines in addressing enduring population health issues. BRFSS is a system that uses 450,000 interviews of U.S. adults annually and provides most states with their only sources of state-level data on health and health risk behavior related to chronic disease.[87] BRFSS findings are posted on its website and used by public health practitioners and researchers for purposes such as identifying and modifying health risk behaviors, evaluating public health programs, and developing prevention strategies at state and local levels.[87]

Limited health insurance and barriers to service access are only part of the reason why major health disparities exist across the United States.[88] The multi-dimensional determinants that influence the occurrence of preventable disease call for a similarly multi-dimensional approach, which cannot alone be the province of government public health programs or of clinical medicine. Today more than ever, all leaders and stakeholders in the quality of U.S. population health are called to align collaborations to create community environments that encourage healthier behaviors and invite engagement across the wide array of resources of public health, healthcare, and broader community sectors.[89]

Emergent Domestic Public Health Issues
Firearm Violence

The history of firearm violence in the United States is a pointed example of the influence of interest groups on U.S. policymakers. It serves as a strong reminder of the importance of the public health core functions of assessment and policy development that entail both development of evidence-based data and mobilizing advocacy to address serious public health issues. Because a discussion of the vast complexities of this issue, including the Second Amendment to the U.S. Constitution, is beyond the scope of this text, interested readers are encouraged to consult the cited references for more in-depth information.

In 2014, firearms deaths totaled 32,279, with 66 percent resulting from suicides and 34 percent from homicides.[90] Total deaths from firearms are now the third-leading cause of U.S. injury deaths ranking behind unintentional poisoning (42,032) and motor vehicle/traffic accidents (33,736). The age-adjusted annual death rate for firearm homicides, suicides, and accidental deaths is now the same as the rate for motor vehicle/traffic accidents, at 10.3 deaths per 100,000 population.[91]

Firearm-associated deaths and injuries were not considered a public health concern until 1989 when the American Medical Association (AMA) labeled them as "a critical public health issue."[92] Throughout the preceding two decades, these incidents were considered as residing in the criminal justice, mental health, and personal safety domains.[92]

In 1993 the *New England Journal of Medicine* reported study findings funded by the CDC's National Center for Injury Prevention that concluded, "... rather than confer protection, guns kept in the home are associated with an increase in the risk of homicide by a family member or intimate acquaintance."[93] Following media attention on the study, the National Rifle Association (NRA) mounted a campaign to eliminate the CDC National Center on Injury Prevention that had funded the study and enlisted U.S. House member, Jay Dickey, to author a budget amendment to do so.[93] While the Center survived, the results were a 1997 federal budget that stated, "none of the funds made available for injury prevention and control at the Centers for Disease Control and Prevention may be used to advocate or promote gun control." The budget also called for reallocation of $2.6 million previously available for firearm injury prevention research to a different purpose.[93] Under pressure and fear of retaliation from the NRA, both government and private organizations previously involved in firearm-related injury research curtailed their activities.[94]

In 2012, in response to the Newtown, Connecticut, school massacre, President Obama issued an executive order regarding many aspects of gun violence prevention, including reversal of the CDC research ban.[94] However up to the present, attempts to implement the President's executive order and reinstate funding have failed.[94]

As the 2017 federal budget was in Congressional review in 2016, more than 100 health care, public health, scientific organizations, and research universities issued a written appeal to the Senate and House appropriations committees through the American Public Health Association (APHA) to "... end the dramatic and chilling effect of the current rider language restricting gun violence research and to fund this critical work at the Centers for Disease Control and Prevention

(CDC)."[95] The appeal cited the effectiveness of prior federal public health research in developing policies that reduced injuries and deaths from other causes such as motor vehicle and traffic accidents, and noted the pivotal importance of evidence-based scientific research to development of effective gun violence prevention strategies.[95] The appeal contained a quote from former House Member Dickey, in which he stated that, "Doing nothing is no longer acceptable."[95] As the 2017 federal budget currently awaits approval, the fate of the funding restoration remains in the balance.

Even though mass shootings account for a very small percentage of firearm violence deaths, they have enlivened the debate about treating firearm violence as a public health issue. However, the real public health issue is not grounded in mass shootings; rather it is reflected by facts such as: (1) an average of 91 deaths occur every day from firearm-related violence,[95] and (2) more than $2.4 billion in hospitalization costs to treat firearm injuries are incurred each year, with approximately one-third of these costs uninsured.[96] The collective societal costs of firearm violence are estimated at $174 billion per year, not including other immeasurable costs such as human suffering, and individual and community fear and trauma.[97]

The debate about whether firearm deaths conform to the definition of a public health problem is particularly spurious when considering the history of the public health approach toward motor vehicle and traffic injuries and deaths. According to the CDC, six times as many people drove in 2000 than in 1925. The number of cars increased elevenfold and the number of miles driven increased tenfold.[98] In the same period, the annual death rate for motor vehicle and traffic accidents decreased by 90 percent.[98] A multi-pronged public health approach using research data, technologies, behavior change, expert scientific collaborations, public advocacy, and policy changes resulted in dramatically improved population health outcomes. Commenting on the effectiveness of the public health approach, the executive director of the APHA notes, "Time and time again, a public health approach to solving health threats is a proven, evidence-based approach to improving health and preventing injury."[98] As in the example of motor vehicle accidents, evidence-based research cannot be expected to eliminate gun violence, but research is necessary to contribute to its reduction.

Lead Poisoning

The recent water-borne lead poisoning crisis in Flint, Michigan, is one example of the complex emergent public health issues of this century which, like firearm violence, has its roots in a long history. A May 2016 *Health Affairs* article by David Rosner of Columbia University's Mailman School of Public School, "A Lead Poisoning Crisis Enters Its Second Century," summarizes a history of lead exposures in the United States and highlights many facets of how public health is inextricably enmeshed with and dependent upon politics, economics, and ethics.[99]

In 2011, the state of Michigan took over the finances of the impoverished city of Flint."[100] Cost-cutting measures included changing the source of Flint's water supply from Lake Huron to the Flint River.[100] Testing determined that Flint River water would be drinkable if treated with very inexpensive anti-corrosives that would prevent rust, iron, and poisonous lead from leaching into the supply, but this treatment was not done.[100,101] The city's water supply was sourced from the Flint River in May 2014, and resident complaints began almost immediately amid government officials' assurance of the safety of the water's quality.[100] In January 2015, Detroit offered to reconnect Flint's water to Lake Huron, but Flint management refused due to cost and other factors.[100] U.S. Environmental Protection Agency (EPA) tests showed toxic lead levels in residential water, but no EPA intervention followed.[100] A Flint resident concerned about health changes in her family contacted an expert on water quality, Virginia Tech professor Marc Edwards, and he launched an investigation.[100,102] Extensive testing results reported by Edwards to the EPA indicated Flint water lead content was at levels "that were two times the amount found in hazardous waste," and multiple times above federal regulations requiring corrective action." Still, no EPA action ensued, and the Michigan Department of Environmental Quality disputed the findings.[102] As Edwards was conducting his research, a Flint pediatrician and her research team analyzed state data and found blood-lead levels among children in certain neighborhoods to have doubled or tripled following the water supply diversion.[102,103] The pediatrician's report was first disputed by Michigan officials, but after one week, they agreed with her report.[100]

In October 2015, Flint's water was reconnected with Lake Huron after months of residents' dependence on bottled water, but not before 18 months of toxic lead exposure had occurred.[104]

In April 2016, the Michigan State Attorney General charged the director of the Flint water treatment plant and two Michigan environmental officials with a mix of misdemeanors and felonies.[105] Michigan's EPA regional leader and water quality director resigned.[101] Calls came for the resignation of Michigan's governor and Congressional hearings excoriated the EPA.[99] The extent of culpability by all those responsible for the disaster is yet to be determined while investigations continue.

The Flint disaster focused renewed attention on the devastating effects of lead poisoning. There is no safe blood lead level and no effective cure.[106,107] The effects of lead on children's neurological development are manifest in decreased intellectual capacity, attention disorders, and behavior problems.[106] Evidence also links lead exposure in adults to kidney disease and hypertension, and some research suggests links to Alzheimer's Disease, Parkinson's Disease, and schizophrenia.[106,107] Research also suggests that lead exposure has genetic-altering effects that may manifest in the offspring of those affected.[103,107] The Flint disaster also highlights the particular vulnerability of individuals living in poverty for whom serious additional lead exposures occur due to lead piping and residues of lead-based paint in older homes.[99,103,107]

An investigation by USA Today Network, reported in March 2016, "identified almost 2,000 additional water systems spanning all 50 states where testing has shown excessive levels of lead contamination over the past four years."[106] The systems which supply 6 million people reported lead levels exceeding EPA standards.[106] Citing the USA Today Network investigation in his *Health Affairs* article, Rosner notes, "Flint is only the tip of an enormous iceberg—which may be just one of a great many icebergs."[99]

In 1978 the United States banned the use of lead in paint, and in 1996, did likewise for gasoline.[107] Over the past 30 years, these and other public health measures produced dramatic declines in lead exposure, and today, *Healthy People 2020* includes as a goal the elimination of all elevated blood-lead levels and associated disparities.[103]

As the federal and state governments pour millions into remediation of the Flint disaster, it remains frustratingly clear that (1) the damaging effects of the human exposures cannot be cured and will be long-term at enormous human and economic costs, and (2) proactive measures by policymakers and the public health community are required to prevent future disasters of the same or even greater scope.

The Opioid Epidemic

The United States is experiencing an epidemic of drug overdose (poisoning) deaths. More persons died from drug overdoses in the United States in 2014 than during any previous year on record.[108] (Unless otherwise noted, the following information refers to 2014 U.S. reports, the most recently available.) A total of 47,055 drug overdose deaths occurred, representing a one-year increase of

6.5 percent.[108] There were approximately one and a half times more drug overdose deaths than deaths from motor vehicle crashes. Drug overdose deaths are the top cause of injury death in the United States.[108]

Opioids, primarily prescription pain relievers and heroin, are the main drugs associated with overdose deaths.[108] Since 1999, deaths from prescription opioids—drugs such as oxycodone, hydrocodone, and methadone—have quadrupled. In the same period, the number of prescription opioids sold in the United States also has quadrupled.[109] Between 2000 and 2014, nearly half a million people died from drug overdoses. Seventy-eight Americans die every day from an opioid overdose.[109] Non-fatal opioid overdoses requiring emergency department or hospital care have increased by a factor of six.[110] In 2011, prescription opioid abuse costs are estimated at more than $50 billion per year, including healthcare costs, workplace costs such as lost productivity, and criminal justice costs.[20]

The non-medical use of prescription drugs is highest among young adults, ages 18–25, who are the most prominent abusers of prescription opioid pain relievers, attention deficit hyperactivity disorder stimulants, and anti-anxiety drugs.[111] In 2014, 1,700 young adults died mainly from opioid prescription drug overdoses—more than died from overdoses of any other drug including heroin and cocaine combined.[111] Many more required emergency treatment.[111] In this group, there were 22 hospitalizations and 119 emergency room visits for every death.[111] In addition, there have been dramatic increases in neonatal abstinence syndrome (NAS) among infants whose mothers used opioids during pregnancy.[112] Affecting almost 22,000 infants in 2012, NAS saw a fivefold increase since 2000.[112] NAS is a syndrome in which newborns suffer drug withdrawal symptoms and often have low birth weight and respiratory complications. These newborns, whose length of hospital stay averages 16.1 days as compared with 2.1 days for other newborns, cost hospitals an estimated $66,700, compared with $3,500 for non-NAS newborns.[112] State Medicaid programs paid for 81 percent of the 2012 NAS newborn costs.[112]

The CDC notes that 2014 data demonstrate that the U.S. opioid overdose epidemic includes two distinct but interrelated trends: a 15-year increase in overdose deaths involving prescription opioid pain relievers and a recent surge in illicit opioid overdose deaths, driven primarily by heroin.[108] Drug overdose deaths from heroin have continued to increase sharply, and past misuse of prescription opioids is the strongest risk factor for heroin initiation and use.[108]

The origins of the epidemic lie in the healthcare industry itself, with a cultural shift that occurred in the mid-1990s as the medical specialty area of pain management emerged.[113] In 1995, the American Pain Society recommended adding pain as a vital sign for overall health assessments.[113] In 1996 the pharmaceutical company Purdue Pharma launched a promotion for its new drug, slow-release oxycodone (trade name OxyContin) for chronic back pain, touting that it would be unlikely to become addictive.[113] Physicians viewed the drug favorably for patients with chronic back pain, and in four years annual sales grew from $45 million to $1 billion.[113] (In 2007 Purdue Pharma pled guilty to federal criminal charges for misinforming physicians about OxyContin's addictive potential.)[113] In 2001 the Joint Commission issued pain standards, required for provider reimbursement.[113] The director of the Pain Medicine Division of Medical Education at Johns Hopkins University commented, "There was a time when doctors faced civil penalties and professional penalties for not prescribing opioids."[113] The pain-management culture and professional pressure to conform to pain treatment standards resulted in unwitting physicians unleashing a tsunami of addictive drug prescriptions and subsequent misuse. The number of opioid prescriptions written annually in the United States now almost equals the number of U.S. adults.[114]

An array of responses to the epidemic continues from state, federal, and local government enti-ties, the medical and mental health professions, community advocates, and others. Forty-nine states have enacted prescription drug monitoring programs (PDMPs).[115] PDMPs are electronic databases which track the prescription and dispensing of controlled drugs so pharmacists and prescribers can track individual patients' use history. This allows them to identify individuals at high risk who could benefit from intervention.[116] PDMPs in a number of states are showing positive results.[117]

In December 2015, the CDC issued a draft opioid-prescribing guideline.[118] In March 2016, the CDC issued a final guideline tailored to primary care clinicians who account for about half of opioid prescriptions.[119] The guideline addresses prescribing opioids for chronic pain and intends to improve communications between providers and patients about opioid risks and benefits, improve the safety and effectiveness of treatment, and reduce risks associated with long-term opi-oid therapy.[119]

In February 2016, the FDA announced several initiatives that included engaging the National Academies of Sciences, Engineering and Medicine, to assist with regulatory framework develop-ment and other near-term initiatives with the pharmaceutical industry to improve drug label-ing and to develop non-opioid pain relief alternatives.[114,120] In May 2016, the FDA approved an implantable form of the opioid addiction treatment drug, buprenorphine.[121] Previously available only in an oral form that required daily dosing, the new implants are active for six months and are expected to significantly enhance the effectiveness of medication-assisted treatment of opioid dependence.[121]

In March 2016, the U.S. Senate passed a bill proposing $600 million to fund many opioid-related interventions, such as grant programs for state and local governments for education and treatment and making the overdose-reversal drug naloxone more widely available.[122] In May 2016, the U.S. House of Representatives passed 18 bills related to the opioid epidemic.[123] House and Sen-ate action to reconcile the two versions of the bill and to develop a final legislative proposal with funding decisions are pending.[123] Also pending is a decision on President Obama's $1.1 billion 2017 federal budget request to address the epidemic.[20]

In March 2016, the U.S. Senate passed the Comprehensive Addiction and Recovery Act (CARA) with measures to reduce prescription opioid and heroin misuse that include evidence-based inter-ventions and prevention of overdose deaths.[124] Action pends a House of Representatives' review, where a companion bill was first introduced in 2014.[125]

In May 2016, the Coalition to Stop Opioid Overdose convened its first meeting, with mem-bers representing professional medical organizations, the pharmaceutical industry, and an array of other stakeholders.[126] Its legislative advocacy agenda includes expanded access to naloxone, pro-vider education, expanding medication-assisted treatment for opioid addiction, enhancing state PDMPs, and enacting the Comprehensive Addiction and Recovery Act.

Emergent Global Public Health Issues

The United States can be affected by public health threats or events throughout the world. Recent examples include the Ebola virus outbreak that began in 2013, the 2009 pandemic caused by the novel H1N1 influenza virus, and the 2003 outbreak of Severe Acute Respiratory Syndrome (SARS).[127] As the H1NI pandemic and SARS outbreak demonstrate, rapid international travel has effectively removed geographic borders from person-to-person infectious disease transmission. Diseases which once would have remained locally self-contained may now be carried across the world in hours.[128] For example, in 1900 the shipboard route from London to Hong Kong took 10 weeks.[129] Today the flight time between these destinations is approximately 12 hours.[130]

The following sections briefly describe the recent global health occurrences noted above and provide an overview of the 2016 Zika virus threat to the United States.

The Ebola Virus Outbreak

Ebola virus disease (EVD) first appeared in 1976 in Africa's South Sudan and the Democratic Republic of Congo.[131] EVD is an acute illness with an average mortality rate of 50 percent, whose symptoms include fever, fatigue, muscle pain, vomiting, diarrhea, and internal and external hemorrhage.[131] The EVD outbreak in West Africa began in December 2013 in Guinea and spread via land travel to Sierra Leone and Liberia, then by air travel to Nigeria and the United States, and subsequently by land travel to Senegal and Mali.[131,132] Total cases through February 2016 stood at 28,639 with 11,316 deaths.[133] A total of four EVD cases were diagnosed in the United States in 2014: One case originated in a traveler from Liberia, one in a traveler from Guinea, and two in healthcare personnel who had treated the traveler from Liberia during his U.S. hospitalization.[134] The traveler from Liberia succumbed to EVD while the others recovered.[134] In addition to its toll in morbidity and mortality, the EVD outbreak had enormous impacts in the three countries most affected (Guinea, Liberia, and Sierra Leone) and entailed billions in costs:[133]

■   In 2015 the economies of three countries suffered an estimated total loss of $2.2 billion..

■   With 881 EVD cases and 513 deaths among the three countries' healthcare workers, Liberia lost 8 percent of its physicians, nurses, and midwives; Sierra Leone and Guinea lost 7 percent and 1 percent of their healthcare workers respectively.

■   Costs of the international Ebola response totaled $3.6 billion in 2015. The United States allocated $2.4 billion, which included personnel, technical assistance, and other resources; Germany donated $165 million; the United Kingdom donated $364 million; and the World Bank donated $140 million.

In March 2016, the WHO declared that the EVD outbreak had ended.[132] In April 2016, the CDC announced commencement of EVD vaccine trials in Sierra Leone in partnership with the Sierra Leone College of Medicine and Allied Health Sciences and the Sierra Leone Ministry of Health and Sanitation.[135] In May 2016, promising results were reported on the initial phase of vaccine trials.[136]

H1N1 Pandemic

The novel H1N1 influenza pandemic of 2009 began in Mexico and within months had affected more than 214 countries, territories, and communities worldwide.[137,138] The virus was characterized as "novel" because there was little or no pre-existing population immunity.[139] In contrast with normal seasonal influenza effects, the CDC characterizes pandemic influenza as occurring infrequently (three times in the 1900s) and having rapid worldwide spread.[139] With high contagion quickly resulting in large numbers of cases, pandemic influenza typically overloads healthcare systems, depletes stocks of medical supplies and equipment, and disrupts the economy and society due to travel bans, event cancellations, and school and business closures.[139] The CDC estimated the final global death toll of the H1N1 pandemic at 284,000.[140] The CDC's final estimate of U.S. cases alone was 60.8 million with more than 12,000 deaths.[141] The WHO reports that the economic impact of the H1N1 pandemic remains unknown.[142] President Obama's 2017 federal budget proposal includes $125 million for pandemic influenza response including measures such as increased vaccine manufacture and stockpiling and provision of antiviral drugs.[20]

Severe Acute Respiratory Syndrome (SARS)

The 2003–2004 Severe Acute Respiratory Syndrome (SARS) epidemic began in a southern Chinese province, and within seven months, it resulted in 8,422 cases across 29 countries with a mortality rate of 11 percent.[143] In North America, there were 284 SARS cases, with 251 cases in the Canadian city of Toronto (41 deaths) and 33 in the United States (no deaths).[143] Ninety-eight percent of Canadian cases resulted from subsequent transmission from five imported cases. Ninety-four percent of U.S. cases (31) were imported from other countries.[143] The Toronto outbreak originated with a traveler from Hong Kong. Toronto's experience highlights the devastating human and economic costs of disease outbreaks. In economic terms alone, Toronto's estimated combined tourism and retail sales losses from the epidemic totaled $700 million.[144] The World Bank estimated that the SARS epidemic cost the world economy $54 billion.[145]

ZIKA Virus Threat

Zika is a disease caused by the Zika virus, which is spread to people primarily through the bite of an infected *Aedes* species of mosquito.[146] Evidence also indicates sexual transmission and other modes of transmission such as via blood transfusion and perinatal transmission are possible.[147] Symptoms are mild and usually do not prompt the need for medical attention.[146] The disease was first discovered in 1947 in rhesus monkeys in Uganda, with the first human case reported in 1952.[148] Since then, outbreaks of Zika have been reported in tropical Africa, southeast Asia, the Americas and the Pacific Islands.[146,147] In May 2015, the Pan American Health Organization (PAHO) issued an alert regarding the first Zika case in Brazil.[146] Characterized as an emerging virus by the WHO, Zika is spreading rapidly in the Americas due to the large susceptible population.[147] It is important to note that susceptible mosquito species may become infected by biting individuals circulating Zika virus in their bloodstreams, and, in turn, may infect other individuals.[149]

The Zika public health threat arises from its association with microcephaly (abnormal brain development) and other severe neurological disorders in babies born to infected mothers.[147] Zika infection also is associated with the occurrence of Guillain-Barré Syndrome (GBS), a rare, serious autoimmune neurological disorder that may occur at any age.[147] Unusual increases in GBS cases were noted by national health authorities following Zika outbreaks in French Polynesia and Brazil in 2013 and 2015.[147] By February 2016, Brazil had recorded 4,908 cases of microcephaly since the Zika outbreak began in 2015 (1,198 confirmed, 3,710 suspected) while the annual average number of cases previously recorded was 163.[150,151] Citing rapid spread, broad geographic distribution, and microcephaly cases, on February 1, 2016, the WHO declared the Zika outbreak a "Public Health Emergency of International Concern," and it launched a global strategy to guide an international response.[152] By the end of May 2016, 60 countries and territories reported continuing mosquito-borne transmission, and 13 countries and territories had reported an increased incidence of GBS associated with Zika.[147] At the same time, the CDC reported no locally acquired cases in United States, but it did report 591 cases associated with foreign travel including 11 sexually transmitted cases and one case of GBS.[153] The U.S. territories of American Samoa, Puerto Rico, and U.S. Virgin Islands together reported four travel-associated cases and 935 locally acquired cases, 96 percent of these in Puerto Rico.[153] At the same time, the CDC reported that with laboratory evidence of possible Zika infection, 168 pregnant women in the continental United States and 142 pregnant women in the U.S. territories were being monitored.[154]

The U.S. government response to the Zika outbreak principally involves the CDC, the NIH, the FDA, the U.S. Agency for International Development, and the Department of State.[148] These organizations carry out activities such as technical assistance and support in the United States and abroad. They also provide basic and vaccine research, coordination of diplomatic response, and financial assistance for partners such as the WHO and the PAHO.[148]

By mid-2016, the CDC had not estimated the risk for Zika spread in the continental United States. However, it did research the existence of two species of mosquitos which can carry Zika and have carried other viruses such as Dengue that have caused limited U.S. outbreaks in the past.[155] Another research study also focused on the U.S. mosquito population in the context of weather conditions, noting that several cities in the southern United States and along the East Coast offer favorable conditions for Zika's primary mosquito-carrying species.[156] Both studies cited pre-existing conditions required for an outbreak, including the introduction of the virus from international travelers.[155,156]

In February 2016, the Obama administration requested Congressional approval for $1.9 billion for the international and U.S. Zika response.[157] Months later on May 17, 2016, the Senate passed a $1.1 billion funding bill. A day later the House passed a $622 million funding bill, cutting funds previously allocated for the Ebola outbreak to offset Zika costs.[158] Reconciliation of the two proposals is expected to take months,[158] delaying international assistance and U.S. mosquito-control activities during the peak summer season of potential transmission. Failure to approve the administration's request will result in a $44-million cut in emergency preparedness funds for 60 U.S. health districts in all 50 states, affecting disease surveillance, laboratory services, mosquito control, and other emergency public health services.[159]

▶ **The Future**

Public health and the role of government in promoting improved U.S. population health status encompasses daunting challenges. In a culturally and increasingly ethnically diverse U.S. population of more than 320 million, and with beliefs and values spanning a vast spectrum, the highly personal and public issues of health and healthcare delivery are continuous subjects of controversy. This arises from several factors, including the understandably disparate views of the numerous health and public health system stakeholders, entrenched expectations among healthcare providers and the public, and priorities that shift with the winds of partisan politics. Almost all system changes are inherently difficult and are viewed as extracting costs from some stakeholder groups while benefitting others. Nonetheless, it is clear that the U.S. healthcare system remains desperately in need of continued reforms. It must continue on the trajectory of preventive health-oriented change emboldened by the ACA if it is to improve its population's health status commensurate with value-based versus volume-based expenditures.

Investments in the U.S. public health system are critical. Savings from implementation of public health measures in both human and economic terms over past decades are remarkable.[160] However, millions of Americans continue suffering from preventable diseases, and for the first time in American history, today's children are at risk of living shorter lives than their parents.[160]

Today, framing public health in a global context is an imperative of government's role in protecting public health.[127] A WHO report notes that since the 1970s, "newly emerging diseases have been identified at the unprecedented rate of one or more per year."[127] Commenting on the Toronto SARS epidemic, a WHO official noted, "Outbreaks and pandemics are unpredictable, but predictably recurrent," underscoring the U.S. involvement in international disease surveillance and control efforts.[161] In 2015, the United States announced the intent to commit $1 billion to the Global Health Security Agenda, a partnership with 30 countries to build capacity to respond to global infectious disease threats.[162] The proposed 2017 U.S. global health budget totals $10.3 billion and, if enacted, will be the highest level of global health funding in U.S. history.[163]

The future of public health and the role of government hold promise despite many challenges. Clinical medicine and public health are melding goals in education and practice. Healthcare delivery systems are slowly evolving to focus on prevention and cost-effectiveness. International public health concerns are receiving more appropriate attention as they may affect the U.S. population. As a world leader, the United States is called upon to continue improving the capacity for responding to global infectious disease threats that protect Americans and prevent the international spread of disease.[127]

KEY TERMS FOR REVIEW

Assessment
Assurance
Department of Health and
  Human Services (DHHS)
Ecological Model

National Prevention, Health
  Promotion and Public
  Health Council
Policy Development

Prescription Drug Monitoring
  Program
Prevention and Public Health
  Fund

CHAPTER ACRONYMS

ACF Administration for Children and Families
ACL Administration for Community Living
AHRQ Agency for Healthcare Research and Quality
APHA American Public Health Association
ASTHO Association of State and Territorial Health Officials
ATSDR Agency for Toxic Substances and Disease Registry
BRFSS Behavioral Risk Factor Surveillance System
CARA Comprehensive Addiction and Recovery Act
CDC Centers for Disease Control and Prevention
CMS Centers for Medicare and Medicaid Services
DHHS Department of Health and Human Services
EPA Environmental Protection Agency
EVD Ebola virus disease
FDA Food and Drug Administration

GBS Guillain-Barré Syndrome
HRSA Health Resources and Services Administration
IHS Indian Health Services
IOM Institute of Medicine
NACCHO National Association of County and City Health Officials
NCD Non-communicable disease
NHSC National Health Service Corps
NIH National Institutes of Health
PAHO Pan American Health Organization
PDMP Prescription Drug Monitoring Program
PHAB Public Health Accreditation Board
PHNCI Public Health National Center for Innovations
RWJF Robert Wood Johnson Foundation
SAMHSA Substance Abuse and Mental Health Services Administration
SARS Severe Acute Respiratory Syndrome
WHO World Health Organization

References

1. Salloway JL, Oberembt CM, et al. *A Coursebook in Health Care Delivery*. New York: Appleton & Lange; 1976:304-308.

2. Capital Area Public Health Network. What is public health? http://www.capitalareaphn.org/about/what-is-public-health. Accessed September 14, 2016.

3. Centers for Disease Control and Prevention Foundation. What is public health? http://www.cdcfoundation.org/content/what-public-health. Accessed April 7, 2016.

4. Turnock BJ. *Public Health, What It Is and How It Works*, 5th ed. Burlington, MA: Jones & Bartlett Learning; 2012:11.

5. Longest BB. *Health Policymaking in the United States*, 5th ed. Chicago, IL: Health Administration Press; 2010:16.

6. Goldsteen RL, Goldsteen K, Graham DG. *Introduction to Public Health*. New York: Springer Publisher Company; 2011:18-23.

7. British Broadcasting Corporation. Roman public health. http://www.bbc.co.uk/schools/gcsebitesize/history/shp/ancient/romanpublichealthrev2.shtml. Accessed April 7, 2016.

8. Medieval Life and Times. Medieval health. http://www.medieval-life-and-times.info/medieval-life/medieval-health.htm. Accessed April 7, 2016.

9. Rosen G. *A History of Public Health*. New York: MD Publications; 1957.

10. Children and Youth in History. London's bill of mortality (December 1664–December 1665). https://chnm.gmu.edu/cyh/primary-sources/159. Accessed April 7, 2016.

11. British Broadcasting Corporation. People and poverty. The poor law. http://www.bbc.co.uk/schools/gcsebitesize/history/shp/britishsociety/thepoorrev1.shtml. Accessed April 7, 2016.

12. Encyclopedia of World Biography 2004. Sir Edwin Chadwick. http://www.encyclopedia.com/topic/Sir_Edwin_Chadwick.aspx. Accessed April 7, 2016.

13. Winklestein W. Lemuel Shattuck: architect of American public health. *Epidemiology*. 2008;19:634. http://journals.lww.com/epidem/Fulltext/2008/07000/Lemuel_Shattuck__Architect_of_American_Public.21.aspx. Accessed April 7, 2016.

14. U.S. Public Health Service. Commissioned corps of the U.S. public health service: America's health responders. http://www.usphs.gov/aboutus/history.aspx. Accessed April 7, 2016.

15. National Library of Medicine. National Institutes of Health. Images from the history of the public health service. https://www.nlm.nih.gov/exhibition/phs_history/intro.html. Accessed April 7, 2016.

16. Yerby AS. Public medical care for the needy in the United States. In: DeGroot LJ, Ed. *Medical Care, Social and Organizational Aspects*. Springfield, IL: Charles C. Thomas; 1966:382-401.

17. Dictionary of American History. 2003. United States Department of Health and Human Services. http://www.encyclopedia.com/topic/United_States_Department_of_Health_and_Human_Services.aspx. Accessed April 8, 2016.

18. Committee on Assuring the Health of the Public in the 21st Century, Board on Health Promotion and Disease Prevention. *The Future of the Public's Health in the 21st Century*. Washington, DC: The National Academies Press; 2003:96. http://www.nap.edu/read/10548/chapter/3. Accessed April 15, 2016.

19. Centers for Disease Control and Prevention. United States public health 101. http://www.cdc.gov/stltpublichealth/docs/usph101.pdf. Accessed April 10, 2016.

20. Department of Health and Human Services. Fiscal year 2017 budget in brief. Advancing the health, safety and well-being of the nation. http://www.hhs.gov/sites/default/files/fy2017-budget-in-brief.pdf. Accessed April 9, 2016.

21. United States Department of Veterans Affairs. Budget in brief 2017. http://www.va.gov/budget/docs/summary/Fy2017-BudgetInBrief.pdf. Accessed March 21, 2016.

22. U.S. Department of Veterans Affairs. Veterans Health Administration. http://www.va.gov/health/. Accessed April 15, 2016.

23. Department of Defense. Final report to the secretary of defense: military health system review. Executive summary. http://archive.defense.gov/pubs/140930_MHS_Review_Final_Report_Main_Body.pdf. Accessed September 14, 2016.

24. Tricare. Military hospitals and clinics. http://www.tricare.mil/FindDoctor/AllProviderDirectories/Military.aspx?p=1. Accessed April 15, 2016.

25. Jansen DJ. Military medical care: questions and answers. Congressional Research Service. https://www.fas.org/sgp/crs/misc/RL33537.pdf. Accessed April 15, 2016.

26. Hess C, Schwartz S, Rosenthal J, Snyder A et al. State health policies aimed at promoting excellent systems: a report on states' roles in health systems performance. *National Academy for State Health Policy*. http://www.nashp.org/wp-content/uploads/sites/default/files/shapes_report.pdf. Accessed April 15, 2016.

27. Henry J. Kaiser Family Foundation. State health insurance marketplace types. 2016. http://kff.org/health-reform/state-indicator/state-health-insurance-marketplace-types/. Accessed April 15, 2016.

28. Association of State and Territorial Health Officials. ASTHO profile of state public health, volume three. Washington, DC: Association of State and Territorial

Health Officials; 2014. http://www.astho.org/Profile/Volume-Three/. Accessed April 16, 2016.

29. National Association of County & City Health Officials. 2013 national profile of local health departments. http://archived.naccho.org/topics/infrastructure/profile/upload/2013-National-Profile-of-Local-Health-Departments-report.pdf. Accessed March 6, 2016.

30. America's Essential Hospitals. About America's essential hospitals. http://essentialhospitals.org/about-americas-essential-hospitals/. Accessed April 16, 2016.

31. America's Essential Hospitals. Essential hospitals vital data: results of America's essential hospitals annual hospital characteristics report, FY 2013. http://essentialhospitals.org/wp-content/uploads/2015/03/Essential-Hospitals-Vital-Data-2015.pdf. Accessed April 16, 2016.

32. ASTHO/NORC. State public health agency classification: understanding the relationship between state and local public health. http://www.astho.org/Research/Major-Publications/ASTHO-NORC-Governance-Classification-Report/. Accessed April 16, 2016.

33. Public Health Accreditation Board. Public health department accreditation background. http://www.phaboard.org/about-phab/public-health-accreditation-background/. Accessed April 16, 2016.

34. Centers for Disease Control and Prevention. National voluntary accreditation for public health departments. February 2016. http://www.cdc.gov/stltpublichealth/hop/pdfs/nvaph_factsheet.pdf. Accessed April 16, 2016.

35. Public Health Accreditation Board. What is public health department accreditation? http://www.phaboard.org/accreditation-overview/what-is-accreditation/ Accessed April 16, 2016.

36. Public Health Accreditation Board. Who is eligible? http://www.phaboard.org/accreditation-overview/who-is-eligible/. Accessed April 16, 2016.

37. Public Health Accreditation Board. The seven steps of public health department accreditation. http://www.phaboard.org/accreditation-process/seven-steps-of-public-healthaccreditation/. Accessed April 16, 2016.

38. Public Health Accreditation Board. Standards and measures. http://www.phaboard.org/wp-content/uploads/PHAB-Standards-and-Measures-Version-1.0.pdf. Accessed April 16, 2016.

39. Public Health Accreditation Board. 154 million U.S. residents now protected by PHAB-accredited public health departments. http://www.phaboard.org/wp-content/uploads/PressReleaseFinalMarch2016.pdf. Accessed April 16, 2016.

40. Public Health Accreditation Board. Public health accreditation board launches national center for innovations. http://www.prweb.com/releases/2016/03/prweb13247536.htm. Accessed April 16, 2016.

41. National Academies of Sciences, Engineering, Medicine. *The Future of Public Health.* Washington, DC: National Academies Press; 1988:32. http://www.nationalacademies.org/hmd/Reports/1988/The-Future-of-Public-Health.aspx. Accessed April 26, 2016.

42. Centers for Disease Control and Prevention. National Center for Health Statistics. *Healthy People 2000.* http://www.cdc.gov/nchs/healthy_people/hp2000.htm. Accessed April 26, 2016.

43. National Center for Health Statistics. *Healthy People 2010 final review.* Hyattsville, MD: 2012. http://www.cdc.gov/nchs/data/hpdata2010/hp2010_final_review.pdf. Accessed April 27, 2016.

44. Centers for Disease Control and Prevention. Core functions of public health and how they relate to the 10 essential services. http://www.cdc.gov/nphpsp/documents/essential-phs.pdf. Accessed April 26, 2016.

45. National Center for Health Statistics. *Healthy People 2000* final review. Hyattsville, MD: Public Health Service. 2001. http://www.cdc.gov/nchs/data/hp2000/hp2k01.pdf. Accessed April 27, 2016.

46. National Center for Health Statistics. Leading health indicators. *Healthy People 2020.* https://www.healthypeople.gov/2020/Leading-Health-Indicators. Accessed April 27, 2016.

47. Department of Health and Human Services. *Healthy People 2020* leading health indicators: progress update. https://www.healthypeople.gov/sites/default/files/LHI-ProgressReport-ExecSum_0.pdf. Accessed April 28, 2016.

48. Centers for Disease Control and Prevention. Achievements in public health, 1990–1999: changes in the public health system. *Morbidity and Mortality Weekly Report.* http://www.cdc.gov/mmwr/preview/mmwrhtml/mm4850a1.htm. Accessed April 16, 2016.

49. Centers for Disease Control and Prevention. Ten great public health achievements—United States, 2001–2010. http://www.cdc.gov/mmwr/preview/mmwrhtml/mm6019a5.htm?s_cid=mm6019a5_w. Accessed April 18, 2016.

50. Shonick W. *Government and Health Services: Government's Role in the Development of U.S. Health Services, 1930–1980.* New York: Oxford University Press; 1995:460-464.

51. Public health partnerships and reform. Editorial. *Health Aff.* 2006;25:1016. http://content.healthaffairs.org/content/25/4/1016. Accessed April 18, 2016.

52. Trust for America's Health. Ready or not? Protecting the public's health from diseases, disasters, and bioterrorism. 2012. Robert Wood Johnson Foundation. http://www.hstoday.us/fileadmin/PDFs/TFAH2012ReadyorNot06.pdf. Accessed April 20, 2016.

53. Committee on Public Health Strategies to Improve Health. Institute of Medicine. *For the public's health: investing in a healthier future.* https://www.nationalacademies.org/hmd/~/media/Files/Report%20Files/2012/For-the-Publics-Health/phfunding_rb.pdf. Accessed April 20, 2016.

54. Himmelstein DU, Woolhandler S. Public health's falling share of US health spending. *American Journal of Public Health. Public Health Policy Brief.* November 12, 2015. http://org.salsalabs.com/o/307/images/AJPH.2015.302908.pdf. Accessed April 23, 2016.

55. American Public Health Association. Prevention and public health fund fact sheet. 2016. https://www.apha.org/~/media/files/pdf/factsheets/160127_pphf.ashx. Accessed April 26, 2016.

56. Staff of the Washington Post. *Landmark: The Inside Story of America's New Health-Care Law and What It Means for All of Us.* New York: Perseus Books Group; 2002:224.

57. Trust for America's Health. Investing in America's health: a state-by-state look at public health funding and key health facts. April 2016. http://www.healthyamericans.org/report/126/. Accessed May 3, 2016.

58. National Association of County & City Health Officials. The changing public health landscape: findings from the 2015 forces of change survey. June 2015. http://nacchoprofilestudy.org/wp-content/uploads/2015/04/2015-Forces-of-Change-Slidedoc-Final.pdf. Accessed May 3, 2016

59. O'Donnell J, Ungar L. Public health gets least money, but does most. *USA Today.* December 12, 2015. http://www.usatoday.com/story/news/nation/2015/12/07/public-health-gets-least-money-but-does-most/76888180/. Accessed May 3, 2016.

60. Seay JD, Vladeck BC. *Mission Matters: A Report on the Future of Voluntary Health Care Institutions.* New York: United Hospital Fund of New York; 1988.

61. Wilhelm A. Charitable giving in the U.S.: contributions to the health sector. Campbell & Company. http://www.campbellcompany.com/news/giving-usa-research-health-continues-rise. Accessed May 8, 2016.

62. Institute of Medicine. *Training Physicians for Public Health Careers.* Washington, DC: The National Academies Press; 2007:22. http://www.nap.edu/catalog/11915.html. Accessed May 8, 2016.

63. Ruis AR, Golden RN. The schism between medical and public health education: a historical perspective. http://www.academia.edu/6294811/The_Schism_between_Medical_and_Public_Health_Education_A_Historical_Perspective. Accessed May 8, 2016.

64. Brandt AM, Gardner M. Antagonism and accommodation: interpreting the relationship between public health and medicine in the United States during the 20th century. http://ajph.aphapublications.org/doi/pdf/10.2105/AJPH.90.5.707. Accessed May 8, 2016.

65. Lasker RD. Committee on Medicine and Public Health. *Medicine & Public Health: The Power of Collaboration.* New York: New York Academy of Medicine; 1997:90-106.

66. Gupta S, Tinker B, Hume T. Our mouths were ajar: doctor's fight to expose Flint's water crisis. Cable News Network. http://www.cnn.com/2016/01/21/health/flint-water-mona-hanna-attish/. Accessed May 10, 2016.

67. Maeshiro R, Koo D, Keck CW. Integration of public health into medical education. 2011. *Am J Prev Med.* http://www.ajpmonline.org/article/S0749-3797(11)00511-3/pdf. Accessed May 11, 2016.

68. Jablow M. The public health imperative: revising the medical school curriculum. Association of American Medical Colleges Reporter. May 2015. https://www.aamc.org/newsroom/reporter/may2015/431962/public-health.html. Accessed May 11, 2016.

69. Umble KE, Diehl SJ, Gunn A, Haws S. Developing leaders, building networks: an evaluation of the National Public Health Leadership Institute, 1991–2006. Chapel Hill, NC: North Carolina Institute for Public Health; 2007. https://sph.unc.edu/files/2015/03/nciph-phli-evaluation.pdf. Accessed May 11, 2016.

70. Thomas JC, Sage M, Dillenburg J, Guillory JV. A code of ethics for public health. Editorial. *Am J Public Health.* 2002;92:1057-1059. http://www.ncbi.nlm.nih.gov/pmc/articles/PMC1447186/pdf/0921057.pdf. Accessed May 11, 2016.

71. Staff of the Washington Post. *Landmark.* New York: Perseus Books Group; 2002:224.

72. The Institute for Healthcare Consumerism. Obama administration releases national prevention strategy. http://www.theihcc.com/en/communities/policy_legislation/obama-administration-releases-national-prevention-_gozwz678.html. Accessed May 18, 2016.

73. Majette GR. PPACA and public health: creating a framework to focus on prevention and wellness and improve the public's health. *J Law Med Ethics.* 2011;39:373-374. http://www2.law.csuohio.edu/newsevents/images/39JLME366.pdf. Accessed May 18, 2016.

74. National Prevention Council. National Prevention Council action plan. http://www.surgeongeneral.gov/priorities/prevention/strategy/npc-action-plan-fact-sheet.pdf. Accessed May 18, 2016.

75. National Prevention Council. Annual status report. Washington, DC: U.S. Department of Health and Human Services, Office of the Surgeon General. 2014. http://www.surgeongeneral.gov/priorities/prevention/2014-npc-status-report.pdf. Accessed May 19, 2016.

76. Staff of the Washington Post. *Landmark.* New York: Perseus Books Group; 2002:228-233.

77. Buerhaus PI, Retchin SM. The dormant National Health Care Workforce Commission needs congressional funding to fulfill its promise. *Health Aff.* 2013;32;2021-2024. http://content.healthaffairs.org/content/32/11/2021. Accessed May 18, 2016.

78. American Public Health Association Center for Public Health Policy. The Affordable Care Act's public health workforce provisions: opportunities and challenges. https://www.apha.org/~/media/files/pdf/topics/aca/apha_workforce.ashx. Accessed May 18, 2016.

79. Health Resources and Services Administration. Implementing our strategic plan: activities and accomplishments in fiscal year 2013. http://www.hrsa.gov/about/strategicplanimplementation2013.pdf. Accessed May 18, 2016.

80. Democratic Policy and Communications Center. The Patient Protection and Affordable Care Act. http://dpc.senate.gov/healthreformbill/healthbill52.pdf. Accessed May 18, 2016.

81. American Nurses Association. Health care transformation: the Affordable Care Act and more. June 18, 2014. http://nursingworld.org/MainMenuCategories/Policy-Advocacy/HealthSystemReform/AffordableCareAct.pdf. Accessed May 18, 2016.

82. Adler NE, Newman K. Socioeconomic disparities in health: pathways and policies. *Health Aff.* 2002;21;60-76. http://content.healthaffairs.org/content/21/2/60.full.pdf. Accessed May 11, 2016.

83. World Health Organization. United States of America: non-communicable diseases (NCD) country profiles. 2014. http://www.who.int/nmh/countries/usa_en.pdf. Accessed May 12, 2016.

84. Centers for Disease Control and Prevention. Potentially preventable deaths from the five leading causes of death—United States, 2008–2010. *Morbidity and Mortality Weekly Report.* 2014;63:369-373. http://www.cdc.gov/mmwr/pdf/wk/mm6317.pdf. Accessed May 12, 2016.

85. Mays GP, Smith SA. Evidence links increases in public health spending to declines in preventable deaths. *Health Aff.* 2011;30:1585-1593. http://content.healthaffairs.org/content/30/8/1585. Accessed May 14, 2016.

86. American Public Health Association. Public health and chronic disease: cost savings and return on investment. https://www.apha.org/~/media/files/pdf/factsheets/chronicdiseasefact_final.ashx. Accessed May 14, 2016.

87. Centers for Disease Control and Prevention. At a glance 2016: behavioral risk factor surveillance system. http://www.cdc.gov/chronicdisease/resources/publications/aag/pdf/2016/brfss-aag.pdf. Accessed May 14, 2016.

88. Centers for Disease Control and Prevention. CDC health disparities and inequalities report—United States, 2013. *Morbidity and Mortality Weekly Report.* 2013;62(Suppl 3):1,3,184. http://www.cdc.gov/mmwr/pdf/other/su6203.pdf. Accessed May 11, 2016.

89. Bauer UE, Briss PA, Goodman RA, Bowman BA. Prevention of chronic disease in the 21st century: elimination of the leading preventable causes of premature death and disability in the USA. *Lancet.* 2014;384;45-52. http://www.thelancet.com/pdfs/journals/lancet/PIIS0140-6736(14)60648-6.pdf. Accessed May 14, 2016.

90. Centers for Disease Control and Prevention. 10 leading causes of injury deaths by age group highlighting violence-related injury deaths, United States—2014. http://www.cdc.gov/injury/images/lc-charts/leading_causes_of_injury_deaths_violence_2014_1040w760h.gif. Accessed May 15, 2016.

91. Ingraham C. Guns are now killing as many people as cars in the U.S. *Washington Post.* December 17, 2015. https://www.washingtonpost.com/news/wonk/wp/2015/12/17/guns-are-now-killing-as-many-people-as-cars-in-the-u-s/. Accessed May 15, 2016.

92. Wintemute GJ. The epidemiology of firearm violence in the twenty-first century United States. http://www.annualreviews.org/doi/pdf/10.1146/annurev-publhealth-031914-122535. Accessed May 15, 2016.

93. Jamieson C. Gun violence research: history of the federal funding freeze. American Psychological Association. Psychological Science Agenda. February 2013. http://www.apa.org/science/about/psa/2013/02/gun-violence.aspx. Accessed May 15, 2016.

94. Frankel TC. Why the CDC still isn't researching gun violence, despite the ban being lifted two years ago. *The Washington Post.* January 14, 2015. http://www.washingtonpost.com/news/storyline/wp/2015/01/14/why-the-cdc-still-isnt-researching-gun-violence-despite-the-ban-being-lifted-two-years-ago/. Accessed May 16, 2016.

95. American Public Health Association. Letter to members of Senate and House Appropriations Committee leaders. April 6, 2016. http://www.apha.org/~/media/files/pdf/advocacy/letters/2016/160406_gunresearch.ashx. Accessed May 17, 2016.

96. Lee MK, Allareddy V, Rampa N, Nalliah R. Longitudinal trends in firearm related hospitalizations in the United States: profile and outcomes in 2000 to 2008. http://thecrimereport.s3.amazonaws.com/2/2d/4/2205/allareddy1_-_gun_victims_costs_more_than__16_billion_in_hospital_treatment_over_9_years.pdf. Accessed May 18, 2016.

97. Goozner M. Tackle gun violence like other public health problems. *Mod Healthc.* December 7, 2015. http://www.modernhealthcare.com/article/20151205/MAGAZINE/312059985. Accessed March 10, 2016.

98. Troisi C, Williams S. Troisi, Williams: public health approach can stem gun violence. *Houston Chronicle.* February 2, 2016. http://www.apha.org/~/media/files/pdf/advocacy/phact/troisigunviolenceoped2216v2.ashx. Accessed May 10, 2016.

99. Rosner D. A lead poisoning crisis enters its second century. *Health Aff.* 2016;35:756-759. http://content .healthaffairs.org/content/35/5/756. Accessed May 20, 2016.

100. Yan H. Flint water crisis timeline: how years of problems led to lead poisoning. CNN. March 3, 2016. http://www.cnn.com/2016/01/20/health/flint-water -crisis-timeline/index.html. Accessed April 16, 2016.

101. Bernstein L, Dennis B. Flint's water crisis reveals government failures at all levels. *Washington Post.* January 24, 2016. https://www .washingtonpost.com/national/health-science /flints-water-crisis-reveals-government-failures-at -every-level/2016/01/23/03705f0c-c11e-11e5-bcda -62a36b394160_story.html?tid=a_inl. Accessed April 16, 2016.

102. Kowlowski K. Virginia Tech expert helped expose Flint water crisis. *The Detroit News.* January 24, 2016. http://www.detroitnews.com/story/news/politics /2016/01/23/virginia-tech-expert-helped-expose -flint-water-crisis/79251004/. Accessed April 16, 2016.

103. Hanna-Attisha M, LaChance J, Sadler RC, Schnepp AC. Elevated blood lead levels in children associated with the Flint drinking water crisis: a spatial analysis of risk and public health response. *AJPH.* 2016;106:283-288. http://ajph.aphapublications.org /doi/pdf/10.2105/AJPH.2015.303003. Accessed April 16, 2016.

104. Lynch J, Ramirez CE. Flint reconnects to Detroit water system. October 16, 2015. http://www.detroitnews .com/story/news/local/michigan/2015/10/16/epa -flint-water/74053912/. Accessed April 16, 2016.

105. Gosk S, Rappleye H, Dokoupil T, Connor T. "Failed us all": 3 officials hit with charges in Flint water crisis. NBC News. April 20, 2016. http://www.nbcnews .com/storyline/flint-water-crisis/3-officials-charged -over-flint-water-crisis-n559186. Accessed April 22, 2016.

106. Young A, Nichols M. Beyond Flint: excessive lead levels found in almost 2,000 water systems across 50 states. *USA Today.* March 11, 2016. http://www .usatoday.com/story/news/2016/03/11/nearly-2000 -water-systems-fail-lead-tests/81220466/. Accessed April 16, 2016.

107. Rosen M. Lead's damage can last a lifetime, or longer. *Science News.* February 15, 2016. https://www .sciencenews.org/article/leads-damage-can-last -lifetime-or-longer?mode=magazine&context =3558. Accessed April 16, 2016.

108. Rudd R, Aleshire N, Zibbell JE, Gladden RM. Increases in drug and opioid overdose deaths— United States, 2000–2014. January 1, 2016. *Morbidity and Mortality Weekly Report.* 2016;64:1378-1382. http://www.cdc.gov/mmwr/preview/mmwrhtml /mm6450a3.htm. Accessed April 19, 2016.

109. Centers for Disease Control and Prevention. Understanding the epidemic: drug overdose deaths in the United States hit record numbers in 2014. http://www.cdc.gov/drugoverdose/epidemic/index .html. Accessed April 19, 2016.

110. Substance Abuse and Mental Health Services Administration. Prescription drug misuse and abuse. http://www.samhsa.gov/prescription-drug-misuse -abuse. Accessed April 19, 2016.

111. National Institute on Drug Abuse. Abuse of prescription (Rx) drugs affects young adults most. https://www.drugabuse.gov/related-topics/trends -statistics/infographics/abuse-prescription-rx -drugs-affects-young-adults-most. Accessed April 19, 2016.

112. National Institute on Drug Abuse. Dramatic increases in maternal opioid use and neonatal abstinence syndrome. https://www.drugabuse.gov /related-topics/trends-statistics/infographics /dramatic-increases-in-maternal-opioid-use-neonatal -abstinence-syndrome. Accessed April 19, 2016.

113. Johnson SR. The opioid abuse epidemic: how health care helped create a crisis. *Mod Healthc.* February 13, 2016. http://www.modernhealthcare.com/article /20160213/MAGAZINE/302139966. Accessed April 19, 2016.

114. Califf RM, Woodcock J, Ostroff S. A proactive response to prescription opioid abuse. *N Eng J Med.* 2016;10:1056. http://www.nejm.org/doi/full /10.1056/NEJMsr1601307. Accessed April 19, 2016.

115. National Alliance for Model State Drug Laws. 2015 annual review of prescription monitoring programs. http://www.namsdl.org/library/1810E284-A0D7 -D440-C3A9A0560A1115D7/. *Accessed April 20,* 2016.

116. Centers for Disease Control and Prevention. Prescription drug monitoring programs (PDMPs). http://www.cdc.gov/drugoverdose/pdmp/. Accessed April 20, 2016.

117. Centers for Disease Control. CDC Vital Signs. July 2014. Opioid painkiller prescribing. http://www.cdc .gov/vitalsigns/pdf/2014-07-vitalsigns.pdf. Accessed April 20, 2016.

118. Federal Register. Proposed 2016 guideline for prescribing opioids for chronic pain: a notice by the Centers for Disease Control and Prevention on 12/14/2015. https://www.federalregister.gov /documents/2015/12/14/2015-31375/proposed -2016-guideline-for-prescribing-opioids-for-chronic -pain. Accessed September 15, 2016.

119. Centers for Disease Control and Prevention. Guideline for prescribing opioids for chronic pain. http://www.cdc.gov/drugoverdose/pdf/guidelines _factsheet-a.pdf. Accessed April 20, 2016.

120. U.S. Food & Drug Administration. Califf, FDA top officials call for sweeping review of agency

opioids policies. http://www.fda.gov/NewsEvents/Newsroom/PressAnnouncements/ucm484765.htm. Accessed September 15, 2016.

121. U.S. Food and Drug Administration. FDA approves first buprenorphine implant for treatment of opioid dependence. http://www.fda.gov/NewsEvents/Newsroom/PressAnnouncements/ucm503719.htm. Accessed May 27, 2016

122. Demirjian K. Senate passes bill to combat heroin, painkiller abuse. *The Washington Post*. March 10, 2016. https://www.washingtonpost.com/news/powerpost/wp/2016/03/10/senate-set-to-pass-bill-to-combat-opioid-abuse/. Accessed April 20 2016.

123. New York Times Editorial Board. Congress wakes up to the opioid epidemic. *The New York Times*. May 16, 2016. http://www.nytimes.com/2016/05/16/opinion/congress-wakes-up-to-the-opioid-epidemic.html?emc=edit_th_20160516&nl=todaysheadlines&nlid=43782120. Accessed May 19, 2016.

124. Drug Policy Alliance. Republican controlled senate overwhelmingly passes landmark opioid bill—the Comprehensive Addiction and Recovery Act (CARA). http://www.drugpolicy.org/news/2016/03/republican-controlled-senate-overwhelmingly-passes-landmark-opioid-bill-comprehensive-a. Accessed April 20, 2016.

125. National Association for Alcoholism and Drug Abuse Counselors. Comprehensive Addiction and Recovery Act (CARA). http://www.naadac.org/CARA. Accessed April 20, 2016.

126. Coalition to Stop Opioid Overdose. National organizations band together to ensure that Congress passes comprehensive policies to combat the U.S. opioid epidemic May 19, 2016. http://www.stopopioidoverdose.org/2016/05/19/national-organizations-band-together-to-ensure-that-congress-passes-comprehensive-policies-to-combat-the-u-s-opioid-epidemic/. Accessed May 20, 2016.

127. *Healthy People 2020*. Global health. https://www.healthypeople.gov/2020/topics-objectives/topic/global-health. Accessed May 18, 2016.

128. Pike BL, Saylors KE, Fair JN, LeBreton, M. et al. The origin and prevention of pandemics. *CID*. 2010;50:1636-1638. http://cid.oxfordjournals.org/content/50/12/1636.full.pdf±html. Accessed May 19, 2016.

129. Feacham R. Global health in the 21st century: identifying the big priorities. Center for Strategic & International Studies. https://csis-prod.s3.amazonaws.com/s3fs-public/legacy_files/files/attachments/091014_global_health.pdf. Accessed May 19, 2016.

130. Flight Durations. London to Hong Kong flight time. http://www.flight-durations.com/London-to-Hong-Kong. Accessed May 19, 2016.

131. World Health Organization. Ebola virus disease. January 2016. http://www.who.int/mediacentre/factsheets/fs103/en/. Accessed May 19, 2016.

132. World Health Organization. Statement on the 9th meeting of the IHR Emergency Committee regarding the Ebola outbreak in West Africa. March 29, 2016. http://www.who.int/mediacentre/news/statements/2016/end-of-ebola-pheic/en/#. Accessed May 19, 2016.

133. Centers for Disease Control and Prevention. Cost of the Ebola epidemic. http://www.cdc.gov/vhf/ebola/outbreaks/2014-west-africa/cost-of-ebola.html. Accessed May 19, 2016.

134. Centers for Disease Control and Prevention. Cases of Ebola diagnosed in the United States. http://www.cdc.gov/vhf/ebola/outbreaks/2014-west-africa/united-states-imported-case.html. Accessed May 19, 2016.

135. Centers for Disease Control and Prevention. Ebola vaccine trial begins in Sierra Leone. http://www.cdc.gov/media/releases/2015/p0414-ebola-vaccine.html. Accessed May 19, 2016.

136. German Center for Infection Research. Ebola vaccine: promising phase I trials. *Science Daily*. May 3, 2016. https://www.sciencedaily.com/releases/2016/05/160503131401.htm. Accessed May 19, 2016.

137. News Medical. Swine flu—a threatening pandemic or media panic? June 3, 2009. http://www.news-medical.net/news/20090603/Swine-flu-a-threatening-pandemic-or-media-panic.aspx. Accessed May 20, 2016.

138. World Health Organization. Pandemic (H1N1) 2009—update 112. August 6, 2010. http://www.who.int/csr/don/2010_08_06/en/. Accessed May 20, 2016.

139. Department of Health and Human Services. About pandemics. FLU.gov. http://www.flu.gov/pandemic/about/index.html. Accessed May 19, 2016.

140. Roos R. CDC estimate of global H1N1 pandemic deaths: 284,000. June 27, 2012. Center for Infectious Disease Research and Policy. http://www.cidrap.umn.edu/news-perspective/2012/06/cdc-estimate-global-h1n1-pandemic-deaths-284000. Accessed May 20, 2016.

141. Centers for Disease Control and Prevention. CDC estimates of 2009 H1N1 influenza cases, hospitalizations and deaths in the United States. http://www.cdc.gov/h1n1flu/estimates_2009_h1n1.htm. Accessed May 20, 2016.

142. Wong VL. Background paper 6.2: Pandemic influenza in priority medicines for Europe and the world. World Health Organization. http://www.who.int/medicines/areas/priority_medicines/Ch6_2Pandemic.pdf. Accessed May 22, 2016.

143. World Health Organization. Summary table of SARS cases by country. November 1, 2002–August 7,

2003. http://www.who.int/csr/sars/country/country 2003_08_15.pdf?ua=1. Accessed May 18, 2016.

144. Canadian Environmental Health Atlas. SARS outbreak in Canada. http://www.ehatlas.ca/sars -severe-acute-respiratory-syndrome/case-study /sars-outbreak-canada. Accessed May 18, 2016.

145. Frangoul A. Counting the costs of a global epidemic. CNBC. February 5, 2014. http://www.cnbc.com /2014/02/05/counting-the-costs-of-a-global -epidemic.html. Accessed May 19, 2016.

146. Centers for Disease Control and Prevention. About Zika virus diseaseZ. http://www.cdc.gov/zika/about/. Accessed May 18, 2016.

147. World Health Organization. Zika virus key facts. http://www.who.int/mediacentre/factsheets/zika /en/. Accessed May 19, 2016.

148. Henry J. Kaiser Family Foundation. The 2015–2016 Zika outbreak. https://kaiserfamilyfoundation.files .wordpress.com/2016/03/the-2015-2016-zika -outbreak-infographic.pdf. Accessed April 3, 2016.

149. Associated Press. U.S. officials say the more they learn about Zika, the scarier it is. *Mod Healthc*. April 11, 2016. http://www.modernhealthcare.com/article/20160411 /NEWS/160419987. Accessed April 22, 2016.

150. United Nations News Center. Zika: UN health agency launches global response strategy; member states briefed on outbreak. http://www.un.org/apps /news/story.asp?NewsID=53249#.V0237r0uF50. Accessed May 12, 2016.

151. Reuters. Factbox: why the Zika virus is causing alarm. April 26, 2016. http://www.reuters.com /article/us-health-zika-qanda-factbox-idUSKCN0 XN2TQ?mod=related&channelName=healthNews. Accessed May 29, 2016.

152. World Health Organization. WHO director-general summarizes the outcome of the Emergency Committee regarding clusters of microcephaly and Guillain-Barré syndrome. http://www.who.int/mediacentre /news/statements/2016/emergency-committee-zika-microcephaly/en/. Accessed May 12, 2016.

153. Centers for Disease Control and Prevention. Zika virus: case counts in the U.S. as of August 24, 2016. http://www.cdc.gov/zika/geo/united-states.html. Accessed May 31, 2016.

154. Centers for Disease Control and Prevention. Pregnant women with any laboratory evidence of possible Zika virus infection in the United States and territories, 2016. http://www.cdc.gov/zika/geo /pregwomen-uscases.html. Accessed May 26, 2016.

155. Centers for Disease Control and Prevention. About estimated range of *Aedes aegypti* and *Aedes albopictus*

in the United States, 2016 (maps). http://www.cdc .gov/zika/vector/range.html. Accessed May 28, 2016.

156. Monaghan A, Morin C, Steinhoff D, Wilhelmi O, et al. Potential Zika virus risk estimated for 50 U.S. cities. National Center for Atmospheric Research. March 16, 2016. https://www2.ucar.edu/atmosnews /news/19850/potential-zika-virus-risk-estimated -for-50-us-cities. Accessed May 31, 2016.

157. Dennis B. Obama asks Congress for $1.9 billion to combat spread of Zika virus. *The Washington Post*. February 22, 2016. https://www .washingtonpost.com/national/health-science /obama-asks-congress-for-19-billion-to-combat -spread-of-zika-virus/2016/02/22/c5b270c4-d9af -11e5-891a-4ed04f4213e8_story.html. Accessed April 3, 2016.

158. Moe A. House passes Zika bill but funding level is far below Obama's request. NBC News. May 19, 2016. http://www.nbcnews.com/storyline/zika-virus -outbreak/house-passes-zika-bill-funding-level-far -below-obama-s-n576536. Accessed May 26, 2016.

159. Sun LH. Zika funding battle steals states' public health emergency money. *The Washington Post*. April 25, 2016. https://www.washingtonpost.com/news /to-your-health/wp/2016/04/25/zika-funding -battle-steals-states-public-health-emergency -money/. Accessed May 26, 2016.

160. Hamburg R, Segal LM, Martin A. Investing in America's health: a state-by-state look at public health funding and its key facts, 2016. Trust for America's Health. http://healthyamericans.org/assets/files/TFAH -2016-InvestInAmericaRpt-FINAL.pdf. Accessed April 20, 2016

161. Fowler R. Severe acute respiratory syndrome (SARS) lessons learned. World Health Organization. https:// www.nationalacademies.org/hmd/~/media/Files /Activity%20Files/PublicHealth/GHRF%20WS%203 /Presentations/1_Rob%20Fowler.pdf. Accessed May 16, 2016.

162. The White House. Fact sheet: the U.S. commitment to the global health security agenda. November 16, 2015. https://www.whitehouse.gov/the-press -office/2015/11/16/fact-sheet-us-commitment -global-health-security-agenda. Accessed May 28, 2016.

163. Valentine A, Wexler A, Kates J. The Henry J. Kaiser Family Foundation. The U.S. global health budget: analysis of the fiscal year 2017 budget request. http:// files.kff.org/attachment/issue-brief-the-u-s-global -health-budget-analysis-of-the-fiscal-year-2017 -budget-request. Accessed May 11, 2016.

CHAPTER 12

Research: How Health Care Advances

CHAPTER OVERVIEW

This chapter explains the focus of different types of research and how each type contributes to the overall advances in health and medicine. Health services research, a newer field that addresses the study of the healthcare system itself rather than specific problems of disease or disability, is described. The offices and goals of a major funding source for health services research, the federal Agency for Healthcare Research and Quality, are listed. Finally, research into the quality of medical care, the problems being addressed, and the research challenges of the future are discussed.

The last half of the 1900s and the early 2000s have seen remarkable growth of scientifically rigorous research in medicine, dentistry, nursing, and other health professions. The change from dependence on the clinical impressions of individual physicians, tradition, and other healthcare practitioners to reliance on more accurate scientific findings from carefully controlled studies is one of the most important advances in medicine. Readers of peer-reviewed professional journals can now monitor the progress of basic science and clinical and technologic discoveries, more confident that the published findings were based on research studies designed and conducted to yield statistically significant results.

In contrast, volumes of reports of medical developments that appear in the popular media and on the Internet are often premature and, depending on the source, may be cause for skepticism. The imprudent publication of inadequately proved or unproved therapies, the sensationalizing of minor scientific advances, and the promotion of fraudulent devices and treatments create unrealistic patient expectations that often result in disappointment, mistreatment, and costly deceptions. While the Internet can be a valuable tool for patients to learn about healthcare issues, it also often provides bad information, which can lead to confusion, anxiety, and false hopes about fraudulent cures.

Despite the advanced state of the Internet and modern communications technologies, from both professional and public perspectives, the continuing emergence of new technologies and clinical advances creates ongoing challenges of evaluation, interpretation, and potential applications.

▶ Focus of Different Types of Research

FIGURE 12-1 illustrates the focus of different types of healthcare research. There are clear distinctions among researchers in terms of methods and the nature of their subsequent findings. Although the kinds of information derived from each type of research may be different, each knowledge gain is an essential step in the never-ending quest to create a more efficient and effective healthcare system.[1]

Types of Research

Research studies conducted by those in professional disciplines fall into several categories.

Basic Science Research

Basic science research is the work of biochemists, physiologists, biologists, pharmacologists, and others concerned with sciences that are fundamental to understanding the growth, development, structure, and function of the human body. Much of basic science research is at the cellular level and takes place in highly sophisticated laboratories. Other basic research may involve animal or human studies. Whatever its nature, basic science research is an essential antecedent of advances in clinical medicine.

Clinical Research

Clinical research focuses primarily on the various steps in the process of medical care: the early detection, diagnosis, and treatment of disease or injury; the maintenance of optimal physical, mental, and social functioning; the limitation and rehabilitation of disability; and the palliative care of those who are irreversibly ill. Individuals in all the clinical specialties of medicine, nursing, allied health, and related health professions conduct clinical research,

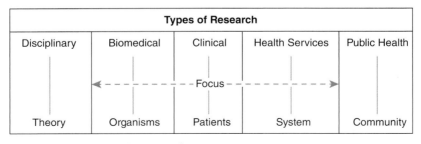

FIGURE 12-1 **Variations in Research Focus**

Republished with permission Health Administration Press. From Aday, Lu Ann, et al.: Evaluating the Healthcare System: Effectiveness, Efficiency and Equity, 3rd edition,© 2004; permission conveyor through Copyright Clearance Center, Inc.

often in collaboration with those in the basic sciences. Much of clinical research is experimental, involving carefully controlled clinical trials of diagnostic or therapeutic procedures, new drugs, or technological developments.

Clinical trials test a new treatment or drug against a prevailing standard of care. If no standard drug exists or if it is too easily identified, a control group receives a placebo or mock drug to minimize subject bias. To reduce bias further, random selection is used to decide which volunteer patients are in the experimental and control groups. In a well-designed study, none of the personnel associated with the study (e.g., patient, physicians, outcomes assessors) know who is receiving the test drug or treatment until the study is completed and the identifying code revealed.

Research studies have a number of safeguards to protect the safety and rights of human and animal subjects. Studies funded by governmental agencies or foundations are subject to scrutiny by peer-review committees or "study sections" that judge the scientific merit of the research design and the potential value of the findings. Next, a hospital- or academically based institutional review board (IRB) insures the safeguarding of human subjects and appraises the use of research animals.

Human subjects must provide an informed consent agreement to participate in research to ensure they appreciate both the risks and potential benefits of their participation. Studies with a very low potential for human harm often require only verbal consent, whereas studies that collect blood or tissue from a subject usually require a more formal written consent agreement. The agreement spells out in plain language the risks, benefits, and possible side effects of participating. Some studies may be potentially harmful just based on the mental anguish the subjects may experience by being contacted by investigators or when the subject of the research may be embarrassing or stigmatizing. Subjects must weigh any potential risks against any potential benefits. Often, there are risks but no direct benefits to the subjects other than the knowledge they are helping to advance science.

The processes for the protection of human subjects in medical research is far too complex a topic to be described in complete detail in this text. There is a multitude of existing references the reader can consult to learn more.[2]

Epidemiological Research

Epidemiology, or population research, is concerned with the distribution and determinants of health, diseases, and injuries in human populations. Much of that research is observational. An observational study is the collection of observed information about natural phenomena, the characteristics and behaviors of people, aspects of their location or environment, and their exposure to certain circumstances or events.

Observational studies may be descriptive or analytical. Descriptive studies use patient records, interview surveys, various databases of existing medical data, and other information sources to identify those factors and conditions that determine the distribution of health and disease among specific populations. They provide the details or characteristics of diseases or biologic phenomena and the prevalence or magnitude of their occurrences. Descriptive studies are relatively fast and inexpensive and often raise questions or suggest hypotheses to be tested. They often are followed by analytic studies, which test hypotheses and try to explain biologic phenomena by seeking statistical associations between factors that may contribute to a subsequent occurrence and the initial occurrence itself.

Some analytic studies attempt, under naturally occurring circumstances, to observe the differences between two or more populations with different characteristics or behaviors. For example, data about smokers and nonsmokers may be collected to determine the relative risk of a related outcome such as lung cancer, or a cohort study may follow a population over time, as in the case of a Framingham, Massachusetts, study.[3] For years, epidemiologists have been studying a cooperating Framingham population to determine associations between variables such as diet, weight, exercise, other behaviors, and characteristics related to heart disease and other outcomes. These observational studies are valuable in explaining patterns of disease or disease processes and providing information about the association of specific activities or agents with health or disease effects.

Experimental Epidemiology. Observational studies are usually followed by experimental studies. In experimental studies, the investigator actively intervenes by manipulating one variable (often called the independent variable) to see what happens with the other (often called the dependent variable or the one that changes when the independent variable is changed). Although they are the best test of cause and effect, such studies are technically difficult to carry out and often raise ethical issues. For example, it would not be ethical to conduct a clinical trial where one group was going to be exposed to a potential toxin to determine if the toxin caused cancer.

Control populations are used to ensure that other non-experimental and usually unknown variables are not affecting the outcome. Like clinical trials, such studies may raise ethical issues when experiments involve the use of a clinical procedure that may expose the subjects to significant or unknown risk. Ethical questions also are raised when experimental studies require the withholding of some potentially beneficial drug or procedure from individuals in the control group to prove decisively the effectiveness of the drug or procedure. For example, it would not be ethical to test a new anti-hypertension medication using a control group of patients with hypertension that would not receive any treatment because the risks of untreated hypertension are known to be harmful. In such a case, the control group may receive their usual care with their current anti-hypertension medication and the intervention group would receive a new drug hypothesized to better treat hypertension.

Other Applications of Epidemiologic Methods. Because the population perspective of epidemiology usually requires the study and analysis of data obtained from or about large-scale population samples, the discipline has developed principles and methods that can be applied to the study of a wide range of problems in several fields. Thus, the concepts and quantitative methods of epidemiology have been used not only to add to the understanding of the etiology of health and disease but also to plan, administer, and evaluate health services. The concepts and methods also are used to forecast the health needs of population groups, to assess the adequacy of the supply of health personnel, and to determine the outcomes of specific treatment modalities in a variety of clinical settings.

Advances in statistical theory and the epidemiology of medical care make it possible to analyze and interpret performance data obtained from the large Medicare and other insurance databases. Many of the research findings of seemingly inexplicable geographic variations in the amount and cost of hospital treatments and in the use of a variety of healthcare services have resulted from the analysis of Medicare claims data and other large health insurance databases.

Health Services Research

Until the 1980s, most medical research was basic science research or research into the biological processes of the human body at the cellular and molecular levels. In the 1980s, the concept of health services research was born. Investigators focused on using established scientific methods in basic medical research to study the healthcare system itself. The goal was to find new and more effective means of diagnosis and treatment and, in effect, to improve the quality and length of life.

For the two decades after World War II, supply-side subsidy programs dominated federal healthcare policy. Like other subsidy programs, Medicare and Medicaid were politically crafted solutions rather than research-based strategies. Nevertheless, these major healthcare subsidy programs were the driving forces behind the rise of health services research. The continuous collection of cost and utilization data from these programs revealed serious deficiencies in the capability of the healthcare system to efficiently and effectively deliver the knowledge and skills already at hand. In addition, evidence was growing that the large variations in the kinds and amounts of care delivered for the same health conditions represented unacceptable volumes of inappropriate or questionable care and too much indecision or confusion among clinicians about the best courses of treatment. Health services research was born of the need to improve the efficiency and effectiveness of the healthcare system and to determine which of the healthcare treatment options for each health condition produces the best outcomes.

▶ Agency for Healthcare Research and Quality

Beginning with John Wennberg's documenting large differences in the use of medical and surgical procedures among physicians in small geographic areas in the late 1980s, a number of similar studies brought the value of increasingly more costly health care into serious question. Wennberg noted that the rate of surgeries correlated with the numbers of surgeons in a geographic area and that the number of available hospital beds rather than differences among patients correlated with the rate of a population's hospitalization.

He found that per-capita expenditures for hospitalization in Boston, Massachusetts, were consistently double those in nearby New Haven, Connecticut.[2,4,5] Widely varying physician practice patterns provided little direction as to the most appropriate use of even the most common clinical procedures. In addition, adequate outcome measures for specific intervention modalities generally were lacking.

The problem did not escape the attention of the 101st Congress. The development of new knowledge through research has long been held as an appropriate and essential role of the federal government, as evidenced by the establishment and proactive role of the National Institutes of Health (NIH). When it became clear that indecision about the most appropriate and effective ways to diagnose and treat specific medical, dental, and other conditions was contributing to unacceptably large variations in the cost, quality, and outcomes of health care, federal legislation was passed to support the development of clinical guidelines. The Agency for Health Care Policy and Research (AHCPR) was established in 1989 as the successor to the National Center for Health Services Research and Health Care Technology. It became one of eight agencies of the Public Health Service within the Department of Health and Human Services.

AHCPR was responsible for updating and promoting the development and review of clinically relevant guidelines to assist healthcare practitioners in the prevention, diagnosis, treatment, and management of clinical conditions. The authorizing legislation directed that AHCPR or public and not-for-profit private organizations convene panels of qualified experts. These panels were charged to review the literature that contained the findings of numerous studies of clinical conditions and, after considering the scientific evidence, to recommend clinical guidelines to assist practitioner and patient decisions about appropriate care for specific clinical conditions.[6]

The agency's priority activities included funding two types of research projects: patient outcome research teams and literature synthesis projects or meta-analyses. Both the patient outcome research teams and the smaller literature synthesis projects identified and analyzed patient outcomes associated with alternative practice patterns and recommended changes where appropriate. During its decade-long existence, the AHCPR supported studies that resulted in a prodigious array of publications focused on patient care and clinical decision making, technology assessment, the quality and costs of care, and treatment outcomes. Although no longer directly involved in producing clinical practice guidelines, the agency currently assists private sector groups by supplying them with the scientific evidence they need to develop their own guidelines.

Significant changes occurred in the mandate of AHCPR since its 1989 inception. The agency narrowly escaped the loss of funding and faced possible elimination in 1996 after incurring the wrath of national organizations of surgeons. In keeping with its original mission, AHCPR had issued clinical guidelines. One such guideline discouraged surgery as a treatment for back pain on the grounds that it provided no better outcomes than more conservative treatments. Organizations of angry surgeons led a lobbying effort that convinced key members of Congress that the agency was exceeding its authority by establishing clinical practice standards without considering the expertise and opinions of the medical specialists involved.[7]

The dispute was resolved when the AHCPR agreed to function as a "science partner" with public and private organizations by assisting in developing knowledge that could be used to improve clinical practice. The agency agreed to produce clinical guidelines that would focus on funding research on medical interventions and analyzing the data that would underlie the development of clinical guidelines.

The Health Care Research and Quality Act of 1999 renamed the AHCPR to the Agency for Healthcare Research and Quality (AHRQ). The mission of AHRQ is to (1) improve the outcomes and quality of healthcare services, (2) reduce its costs, (3) address patient safety, and (4) broaden effective services through the establishment of a broad base of scientific research that promotes improvements in clinical and health systems practices, including prevention of disease.[8]

While clinical practice guidelines subsequently would be generated by medical specialty and other healthcare organizations, the AHRQ's role would be to evaluate recommendations made in the clinical practice guidelines to ensure they were based on a systematic review of the literature (evidence-based) and were revised for currency on a regular basis.

More than 2,000 active, evidence-based clinical practice guidelines that have met the AHRQ evaluation criteria have been collected in a database, organized by searchable topics, and made available online at the AHRQ's National Guideline Clearinghouse (http://www.guideline.gov/). The AHRQ also maintains a searchable database of nearly 5,000 archived guidelines that have been updated or withdrawn.

A top priority of the AHRQ is transmitting its sponsored research results and new health information consumers. In addition to a number of consumer-oriented publications, the agency provides information to the public via the Internet. Its website, http://www.ahrq.gov, offers a robust array of healthcare information. The AHRQ is now a major collaborating organization of the Patient-Centered Outcomes and Research Institute (PCORI) established by the Affordable Care Act (ACA), described later in this chapter.

▶ Health Services Research and Health Policy

Health services research combines the perspectives and methods of epidemiology, sociology, economics, and clinical medicine by applying the basic concepts of epidemiology, biostatistics, process, and outcome measures that reflect the behavioral and economic variables associated with questions of therapeutic effectiveness and cost–benefit. The ability of health services research to address issues of therapeutic effectiveness and cost–benefit during the nation's quest for fiscal exigency has contributed to the field's substantial growth and current value.

The contributions of health services research to health policy are impressive. Major examples include the Wennberg studies of small area variation in medical utilization, the prospective payment system based on diagnosis-related groups,[9,10] research on inappropriate medical procedures,[11] resource-based relative value scale research,[12–14] and the background research that supported the concepts of health maintenance organizations and managed care.

The RAND Health Insurance Experiment,[15,16] one of the largest and longest-running health services research projects ever undertaken, began in 1971 and contributed vast amounts of information on the effects of cost-sharing on the provision and outcomes of health services. Participating families were assigned to one of four different fee-for-service plans or to a prepaid group practice. Individuals in the various plans differed significantly in their rate of healthcare use, with little measurable effect on health outcomes. The Health Insurance Experiment was followed by two large research studies: the Health Services Utilization Study and the Medical Outcomes Study. The findings of both gave impetus to the federal support of outcomes research.[17] Determining the outcomes and effectiveness of different healthcare interventions aids clinical decision making, reduces costs, and benefits patients.

Quality Improvement

Until the 1990s, health care's impressive accomplishments had made it difficult for healthcare researchers, policy makers, and organizational leaders to publicly acknowledge that poor-quality health care is a major problem within the dynamic and productive biomedical enterprise in the United States. In 1990, after two years of study, hearings, and site visits, the Institute of Medicine issued a report that cited widespread overuse of expensive invasive technology, underuse of inexpensive "caring" services, and implementation of error-prone procedures that harmed patients and wasted money.[18,19]

Although these conclusions from this prestigious body were devastating to healthcare reformers, they were hardly news to health service researchers. For decades, practitioners assumed that quality, like beauty, was in the eye of the beholder, and, therefore, was immeasurable except in cases of obvious violation of generally accepted standards. The medical and other healthcare professions had promoted the image of health care as a blend of almost impenetrable, science-based disciplines, leaving the providers of care as the only ones capable of understanding the processes taking place. Thus, only physicians could judge the work of other physicians. Such peer review-based assessment has always been difficult for reviewers and limited in effectiveness. Peer review recognizes that only part of medical care is based on factual knowledge. A substantial component of medical decision making is based on clinical judgment. Clinical judgment requires combining consideration of the potential risks and benefits of each physician's implicit list of alternatives in making diagnostic and treatment decisions with his or her medical intuition regarding the likelihood of success based on the condition of each patient. Under these complex and often inexplicable circumstances, physicians are repelled by the notion of either judging or being judged by their colleagues.

For these reasons, until recently, quality assurance whether in hospitals or by regulatory agencies, was focused on identifying only exceptionally poor care. This practice, popularly known as the "bad apple theory," was based on the presumption that the best way to ensure quality was to identify the poor performers, or "bad apples," and remove or rehabilitate them. Thus, during the 1970s and 1980s, quality-assurance interventions only followed the detection of undesirable occurrences. For example, flagrant violations of professional standards had to be documented before professional review organizations required physicians to begin quality improvement plans. Physicians were guaranteed due process to dispute the evidence.

Focusing on isolated violations required a great deal of review time to uncover a single case that called for remedial action. In addition, it was an unpleasant duty for reviewers to assign blame to a colleague who might soon be on a committee reviewing their records. Most importantly, such quality inspections represented a method that implicitly defined quality as the absence of mishap. Clinician dislike of quality-assurance activities during the 1970s and 1980s was well founded, as these processes were professionally offensive and had little constructive impact.

Specifying and striving for excellent care are very recent quality-assurance phenomena in the healthcare arena. Hospitals and other healthcare organizations that had long focused on peer-review committees, incident reports, and other negative quality-monitoring activities experienced difficulty in transforming to teamwork and higher levels of transparency in quality monitoring and reporting activities.

Health services researchers had known for decades that healthcare quality was measurable and that excellent, as well as poor, care could be identified and quantified. As early as 1966, Avedis Donabedian[20] characterized the concept of health care as divided into the components of structure, process, and outcomes and the research paradigm of their assumed linkages, all of which have guided quality-of-care investigators to this day.

Donabedian suggested that the number, kinds, and skills of the providers, as well as the adequacy of their physical resources and the manner in which they perform appropriate procedures should, in the aggregate, influence the quality of subsequent outcomes. Although today the construct may seem like a statement of the obvious, at the time, attention to structural criteria was the major, if not the only, quality assurance activity in favor. It was generally assumed that properly trained professionals, given adequate resources in properly equipped facilities, performed at acceptable standards of quality. For example, for many years, the then Joint Commission on Accreditation of Hospitals made judgments about the quality of hospitals on the basis of structural standards, such as physical facilities and equipment, ratios of professional staff to patients, and the qualifications of various personnel. Later, it added process components to its structural standards and, most recently, has shifted its evaluation process to focus on care outcomes.

Early landmark quality-of-care studies used implicit and explicit normative or judgmental standards. Implicit quality standards rely on the internalized judgments of the expert individuals involved in the quality assessment. Explicit quality standards are those developed and agreed on in advance of the assessment. Explicit standards minimize the variation and bias that invariably result when judgments are internalized. More recent studies judge the appropriateness of hospital admissions and various procedures and, in general, associate specific structural characteristics of the healthcare system with practice or process variations.

Another method for assessing the quality of healthcare practices is based on empirical quality standards. Derived from distributions, averages, ranges, and other measures of data variability, information collected from a number of similar health service providers is compared to identify practices that deviate from the norms. A current popular use of empirical standards is in the patient severity-adjusted hospital performance data collected by health departments and community-based employer and insurer groups to measure and compare both process activities and outcomes. These performance "report cards" are becoming increasingly valuable to the purchasers of care who rely on an objective method to guide their choices among managed care organizations, healthcare systems, and group practices. The empirical measures of quality include such variables as:

- Timeliness of ambulation
- Compliance with basic nursing care standards
- Average length of stay
- Number of home care referrals
- Number of rehabilitation referrals
- Timeliness of consultation completion
- Timeliness of orders and results
- Patient waiting times by department or area
- Infection rates
- Decubitus rates
- Medication errors
- Patient complaints
- Readmissions within 30 days
- Neonatal and maternal mortalities
- Perioperative mortalities

Both normative and empirical standards are used in studying the quality of health care in the United States. For example, empirical analyses are performed to test or modify normative recommendations. Empirical or actual experience data are collected to confirm performance and outcome improvements after the imposition of clinical guidelines derived from studies using normative standards.

▶ Medical Errors

In 1999, the Institute of Medicine again issued a report on the quality of medical care.[21] Focused on medical errors, the report described mistakes occurring during the course of hospital care as one of the nation's leading causes of death and disability. Citing two major studies estimating that medical errors killed 44,000–98,000 people in U.S. hospitals each year, the Institute of Medicine report was a stunning indictment of the systems of hospital care at that time. The report contained a series of recommendations for improving patient safety in the admittedly high-risk environments of modern hospitals. Among the recommendations was a proposal for establishing a center for patient safety within the AHRQ. The proposed center would establish national safety goals, track progress in improving safety, and invest in research to learn more about preventing mistakes.[21] Congress responded by designating part of the increase in budget for the AHRQ for that purpose.

In 2005, the Patient Safety and Quality Improvement Act was enacted by Congress to establish patient safety organizations (PSOs) to improve the quality and safety of healthcare delivery by encouraging healthcare providers and institutions to identify, analyze, and implement prevention strategies to reduce or eliminate risks and hazards associated with the delivery of care to patients and to voluntarily report and share patient safety data without fear of legal discovery. PSOs are overseen by the AHRQ, which also maintains online access to the latest annotated links to patient safety literature and safety news at the Patient Safety Network (PSNet).[22]

Despite the government reaction to the 1999 Institute of Medicine (IOM) report and the intervening 17 years, a recent analysis published in 2016 indicates that medical errors are likely the third most common cause of death in the United States.[23]

▶ Evidence-Based Medicine

According to Sackett et al., "Evidence-based medicine is the conscientious, explicit, and judicious use of current best evidence in making decisions about the care of individual patients. The practice of evidence-based medicine means integrating individual clinical expertise with the best available external clinical evidence from systematic research. Individual clinical expertise refers to the proficiency and judgment that individual clinicians acquire through clinical experience and clinical practice."[24] A more recent and concise definition from Chilvers et al. is evidence-based medicine (EBM) which "... involves combining the best research evidence with the patient's values to make decisions about medical care."[25] Although these statements may appear to be a description of the way physicians and other healthcare providers have practiced since the inception of scientific medicine, it reflects a concern that the opposite is true. The wide range of variability in clinical practice, the complexity of diagnostic testing and medical decision making, and the difficulty that physicians have in keeping up with the overwhelming volumes of scientific literature suggest that a significant percentage of clinical management decisions are not supported by reliable evidence of effectiveness.

Although everyone generally assumes that physicians are reasonably confident that the treatments they give are beneficial, the reality is that medical practice is fraught with uncertainty. In addition, the ethical basis for clinical decision making allows physicians to exercise their preferences for certain medical theories or practices that may or may not have been evaluated to link treatment to benefits.[26]

Proponents of EBM propose that if all health services are intended to improve the health status and quality of life of the recipients, then the acid test is whether services, programs, and policies improve health beyond what could be achieved by different means or by doing nothing at all. Although evidence is the key to accountability, patient preference is also integrated into the practice of EBM which more recently has become known as evidence-based practice (EBP). The overarching tenet of EBP is that the decisions made by healthcare providers, administrators, policy makers, patients, and the public all should be based on the highest level of evidence currently available and appropriate application to individual patients.[27]

What constitutes "the best evidence" refers to the highest form of evidence available for the particular medical issue or question in the hierarchy of evidence. The following is an abridged summary of the hierarchy of evidence:

1. *Systematic review:* A meta-analysis of several high-quality randomized, controlled clinical trials. An analysis of multiple analyses has more value as its conclusions are based on the larger, combined populations studied in all the individual clinical trials. This usually is considered the highest level of evidence but is also the most expensive and difficult to carry out.

2. *Randomized controlled clinical trial:* A study where patients are randomly assigned to two or more experimental groups where each group is identical to the others with the exception of the treatment they are assigned. Often one of the "treatments" is a placebo or no treatment. Selection of patients is carefully controlled to reduce the potential for any confounder or bias between the experimental groups. Often the study patients, their physicians, and the outcomes assessors are "blinded" to what treatment each patient was randomized to, again to minimize potential bias of the results. After systematic reviews, this is generally considered the highest form of evidence.

3. *Observational study:* An analysis of real-world data. Studies can be either prospective, where one or more groups of patients is followed for a period of time, or retrospective, where existing data representing past clinical events is analyzed.

4. *Case series:* A published summary of a small number of individual cases in the biomedical literature. These usually occur for extremely rare conditions or for new illnesses or syndromes and often when the diagnosis is unknown. Rigorous analyses usually are not performed. The goal is to attempt identification of the similarities between the cases presented and posit a unifying cause or effective treatment. Case series are generally developed by experts and undergo peer review before they are published.

5. *Expert opinion:* Usually expresses the opinion of a medical specialist in an area of interest to a particular patient. This is the lowest or least-rigorous form of evidence but also the most commonly practiced. It can occur formally, with a referral to a specialist by a patient's primary care physician, or informally, when one physician discusses a case or medical issue with a colleague in person, over the phone, or via email.

The goal of EBM is to inform the practice of medicine by providing the practitioner with the ability to determine the highest level of evidence for their clinical questions and then use their clinical judgment along with the patients' preferences and values for its application. This is often called the evidence-based process, or EBP.

Many, if not most, medical decisions are made using the lower levels of evidence (i.e., only expert opinion, case series, or observational evidence). This is not at all a bad thing if the evidence used is indeed the highest level of evidence that exists at the time of the medical decision. There are many reasons why randomized controlled clinical trials cannot be conducted. They are expensive in terms of time and effort, and they often can raise ethical questions. For example, who would volunteer for a randomized trial of radiation exposure by receiving either harmful doses of radiation or placebo? It would be highly unethical to conduct such a study, so the best science can do is perform observational studies on "natural experiments" where people were accidentally exposed to harmful radiation such as in the Chernobyl disaster or the Japanese populations of Hiroshima or Nagasaki after the United States dropped nuclear bombs to end World War II. Similar examples are populations exposed to toxic chemicals in their water, land, or air. In such cases, observational studies compare the groups exposed to the toxic agents with similar populations from other similar areas that were not exposed. While it is difficult to adjust the findings for all possible confounders between the two groups, the evidence produced by such analyses likely will be the highest level researchers will be able to obtain for toxic exposures.

Another reason observational studies are performed is because the data are readily available and the analyses are often relatively inexpensive. With the ever-increasing amount of data as artifact to our daily lives, many observational studies that were only dreamed of a few years ago can now be performed simply due to the depth and breadth of available data. This has produced the unfortunate terms "Big Data" and "Big Data Analytics." These terms refer generally to the potential knowledge that can be gained from the analyses of extremely large data sets. However, this concept is nothing new and the size of the data stores available do not compensate for the well-established limitations of observational studies. Also, the methods of analysis for "Big Data" (i.e., statistics and modeling) are not new.

One of the major problems with observational studies is the existence of unknown confounders between groups or cohorts. A confounder is a variable that explains the difference in outcome between groups that is not known or compensated for in the observational analysis; in effect, association between variables does not prove causation. For example, the rate of drownings correlates with the rate of ice cream consumption. However, it is apparent that eating ice cream does not really put individuals at risk of drowning. The confounding variable in this case is the season, as the rate of ice cream consumption and the rate of drowning both increase during warm weather when more people swim. Even though the rates of drowning and ice cream consumption correlate, obviously, one does not cause the other. Unaware of the seasonal variable, it might indeed be concluded that eating ice cream inexplicably is related to the risk of drowning. This example represents the power of randomization in a controlled clinical trial. The randomization, if truly random, automatically adjusts for all possible confounding variables, known or unknown, between the groups under study. With observational studies, all the confounders must be known and adjusted for in the analysis to ensure accurate results. This is often extremely difficult to do because there are myriad potential confounders in the real world.

A famous example that illustrates the limitations of observational studies and the value of randomized controlled clinical trials is the research on post-menopausal estrogen supplementation. For a time, the highest level of evidence on the benefits of the use of estrogen supplementation in post-menopausal women used only several observational studies.[28-31] These observational studies grouped women of similar age, race, and demographics into two groups—those taking estrogen supplementation those and not taking it. The two groups were followed and the rates of heart attack, stroke, bone loss and other outcomes were documented. Because these studies showed a small but significant benefit for women who took estrogen supplementation in terms of reduced rates of heart attack, stroke, bone loss, and high cholesterol, the studies had enormous influence on the prescribing of supplemental estrogen to post-menopausal women. Eventually, a large, well-designed randomized controlled trial was conducted and, surprisingly, demonstrated that taking estrogen supplementation not only did *not* reduce the rates of heart attack or stroke but actually slightly increased them and increased the rates of invasive breast cancer and pulmonary embolus.[32] What was wrong with all the prior observational studies? It was the fact that women who took supplemental estrogen proactively also were more likely to be generally more health conscious. Further analysis showed that the women in the observational studies who took estrogen also were more likely to see their doctors for preventive checkups, eat more healthfully, and follow preventive instructions from their physicians such as taking estrogen. It was not that the estrogen reduced the rates of heart attack and stroke in the observational studies, it was that the women who would take estrogen were just healthier than the women who did not take estrogen. The unknown confounder in all the observational studies was the participants' overall health practices! Published results of the randomized, controlled, clinical trial resulted in discontinuation of supplemental estrogen prescriptions almost overnight. But, as stated earlier, for many questions in medicine, observational studies will likely be the only ones ever carried out and are therefore the best available evidence. This is why evidence-based practice includes the use of clinical judgment and patient preference and values, as all the available evidence is far from perfect and in some cases, just incorrect.

Despite its common-sense approach, EBM has had many detractors. When EBM started gaining traction in the 1990s, many dismissed it as "cookbook medicine."[33] Others focused on the limitation of outcomes research. "Outcomes research using claims data is an excellent way of finding out what doctors are doing, but it's a terrible way to find out what doctors should be doing," stated Thomas C. Chalmers, MD, of Harvard School of Public Health.[34]

The situation has changed rapidly, however. Articles on evidence-based medicine appear frequently in the medical literature.[36] Cost-control pressures that encourage efforts to ensure that therapies have documented patient benefit, growing interest in the quality of patient care, and increasing sophistication on the part of patients concerning the care they receive have stimulated acceptance of the concepts of EBM.[35]

▶ Outcomes Research and the Patient-Centered Outcomes Research Institute

Given the enormous investment in U.S. health care and the inequitable distribution of its services, do the end effects on the health and well-being of patients and populations justify the costs? Insurance companies, state and federal governments, employers, and consumers all look to outcomes research for information to help them make better decisions about what kinds of health care should be reimbursed, for whom, and when.

Because outcomes research evaluates results of healthcare processes in the real world of physicians' offices, hospitals, clinics, and homes, it contrasts with traditional randomized controlled studies that test the effects of treatments in controlled environments. In addition, the research in usual service settings, or "effectiveness research," differs from controlled clinical trials, or "efficacy research," in the nature of the outcomes measured. Traditionally, studies measured health status, or outcomes, with physiologic measurements—laboratory tests, complication rates, recovery, or survival. To capture health status more adequately, outcomes research also should measure a patient's functional status and well-being. Satisfaction with care also must complement traditional measures.

Functional status includes three components that assess patients' abilities to function in their own environment:

1. Physical functioning
2. Role functioning—the extent to which health interferes with usual daily activities, such as work or school
3. Social functioning—whether health affects normal social activities, such as visiting friends or participating in group activities

Personal well-being measures describe patients' sense of physical and mental well-being—their mental health or general mood, their personal view of their general health, and their general sense about the quality of their lives. Patient satisfaction measures the patients' views about the services received, including access, convenience, communication, financial coverage, and technical quality.

Outcomes research also uses meta-analyses, a technique to summarize comparable findings from multiple studies. More importantly, however, outcomes research goes beyond determining what works in ideal circumstances to assessing which treatments for specific clinical problems work best in different circumstances. Appropriateness studies are conducted to determine the circumstances in which a procedure should and should not be performed. Even though a procedure is proved to be effective, it is not appropriate for every patient in all circumstances. The frequency of inappropriate clinical interventions is one of the major quality-of-care problems in the system, and research is underway to develop the tools to identify patient preferences when treatment options are available. Although most discussions about appropriateness stress potential cost savings that could be achieved by reducing unnecessary care and overuse of services, outcomes research may be just as likely to uncover underuse of appropriate services.

It is important to recognize that the ultimate value of outcomes research can be measured only by its ability to incorporate the results of its efforts into the healthcare process. To be effective, the findings of outcomes research must first reach and then change the behaviors of providers, patients, healthcare institutions, and payers. The endpoint of outcomes research, the clinical practice guidelines intended to assist practitioners and patients in choosing appropriate health care for specific conditions, must be disseminated in acceptable and motivational ways. With the health-care industry in a state of rapid change, the need to make appropriate investments in outcomes research became increasingly apparent with the inescapable conclusion that the United States cannot continue to spend more than 17 percent of its gross domestic product each year on health care without learning more about what that investment is buying.[36,37]

The American Recovery and Reinvestment Act (ARRA) of 2009 included $1.1 billion over a period of two years to expand comparative effectiveness research by the AHRQ and the NIH. The ARRA established a Federal Coordinating Council to recommend research priorities and create a strategic framework for research activities. The IOM recommended 100 priority research areas for funding by the ARRA. Recommendations from the Federal Coordinating Council and the IOM were released in June 2009, and the ARRA required the secretary of the U.S. Department of Health and Human Services to consider these recommendations in directing research funds.[38,39] The goal of comparative effectiveness research is to enhance healthcare treatment decisions by providing information to consumers, providers, and payers to improve health outcomes by developing and disseminating evidence "on the effectiveness, benefits, and harms of different treatment options. The evidence is generated from research studies that compare drugs, medical devices, tests, surgeries, or ways to deliver health care."[39] Historically, clinical research examined the effectiveness of one method, product, or service at a time. Comparative effectiveness research compares two or more different methods for preventing, diagnosing, and treating health conditions, using methods such as practical clinical trials, analyses of insurance claim records, computer modeling, and systematic reviews of literature. Disseminating research findings in a form that is quickly useable by clinicians, patients, policy makers, health plans, and other payers about the effectiveness of treatments relative to other options is key to comparative research effectiveness goals. In addition, "identifying the most effective and efficient interventions has the potential to reduce unnecessary treatments, which may help lower costs."[39,40]

The Patient-Centered Outcomes Research Institute

Empowering the Federal Coordinating Council, the ACA created the Patient-Centered Outcomes Research Institute (PCORI), a not-for-profit, independent agency dedicated to conducting comparative effectiveness research. The PCORI is governed by a board of directors appointed by the U.S. Government Accountability Office and is funded through the Patient-Centered Outcomes Research Trust Fund. The ACA allocated $210 million to PCORI activities for the fiscal years 2010–2012 and a total of $970 million for the years 2013–2019. Support is derived from the general U.S. Treasury fund, and fees are assessed to Medicare, private health insurance, and self-insured plans.[41] The PCORI maintains a strong patient and stakeholder orientation with patient satisfaction recognized as an essential component of quality of care. Although the subjective ratings of health care rendered by patients may be based on markedly different criteria from those considered important by healthcare providers, they capture aspects of care and personal preferences that contribute significantly to perceived quality. The PCORI recognizes that it has become increasingly important in the competitive market climate of health care that the providers' characteristics, organization, and system attributes that are important to patients be identified and monitored. In addition to healthcare providers' technical and interpersonal skills, patient concerns such as waiting times for appointments, emergency responses, helpfulness and communication of staff, and facilities' appearances contribute to patient evaluations of health services delivery programs and subsequent satisfaction with the quality of care received.

As of May 2016, the PCORI has funded a total of 774 research projects with $4.4 billion. The top five areas funded included cancer, mental/behavioral health, cardiovascular health, respiratory diseases, and trauma/injury.[42] They also funded the national Patient-Centered Clinical Research Network (PCORNET), thus far composed of 13 clinical data research networks and 20 patient-powered research networks to increase the efficiency of various comparative effectiveness research project. In the few years that PCORI has been in existence, there are already dozens of papers published on the emerging research findings.[43]

Patient Satisfaction Surveys

Prior to the PCORI's establishment in 2006, a number of instruments were devised to measure patient satisfaction with health care. Most insurance plans, hospitals, and other health service facilities and agencies adopted one or more to regularly assess patient satisfaction. In 2016, the "… first national, standardized, publicly reported survey of patients' perspectives of hospital care" was created by the Department of Health and Human Services. It is known as the Hospital Consumer Assessment of Healthcare Providers and Systems Survey (HCAHPS).[44] "The HCAHPS survey is administered to a random sample of adult patients across medical conditions between 48 hours and six weeks after discharge; the survey is not restricted to Medicare beneficiaries. Hospitals may either use an approved survey vendor, or collect their own HCAHPS data (if approved by CMS to do so). HCAHPS can be implemented in four different survey modes: mail, telephone, mail with telephone follow-up, or interactive voice recognition (IVR)."[45] Results are publicly reported on the "Hospital Compare" website. In addition, beginning in 2008, hospital reporting is required in order to receive full inpatient prospective payment systems reimbursement updates.[46]

Other surveys, such as the Patient Satisfaction Questionnaire developed at Southern Illinois University School of Medicine, are short, self-administered survey forms. Others, such as the popular patient satisfaction instruments of the Picker Institute of Boston, Massachusetts, may be used as self-administered questionnaires mailed to patients after a healthcare experience or completed by interviewers during telephone surveys.[47] Whether by mail, direct contact, or telephone interview, questioning patients after a recent healthcare experience is an effective way both to identify outstanding service personnel and uncover fundamental problems in the quality of care as perceived by patients. These activities help promote humane and effective care and are sound marketing techniques for providers.[48]

Since the 1950s, the federal government has invested heavily in biomedical research. The ensuing public–private partnership in health has produced some of the finest medical research in the world. The growth of medical knowledge is unparalleled, and the United States can take well-deserved pride in its research accomplishments.

However, many, if not most, of the sophisticated new technologies have addressed the need to ameliorate the problems of patients who already have a condition or disease. Both the priorities and the profits intrinsic to U.S. healthcare system have focused on remedial rather than preventive strategies. Only in the cases of frightening epidemics, such as that of polio in the mid-1900s and AIDS in the 1990s, have the requisite moral imperatives prevailed in order to adequately fund research efforts that address public health problems. Much of the funding for medical research has failed to fulfill the generally held belief that the products of taxpayer-supported research should benefit not only the practice of medicine but also the community at large. If its intended goals are achieved, the PCORI will change the research focus to be highly inclusive of all stakeholders with a major voice from healthcare consumers by involving them in research topic priority determination and identifying the best mechanisms for meaningfully translating findings into clinical settings.[49]

▶ **Research Ethics and Conflicts of Interest**

The increasing volume of research funding emanating from pharmaceutical and medical device companies is of serious concern. Pharmaceutical companies that pay researchers to design and interpret drug trials have been accused of misrepresenting the results or suppressing unfavorable findings. The conflicts that arise in the testing of new drugs and medical devices and publishing the results deepen as increasing numbers of studies are shifted from academic institutions to commercial research firms.[50]

For example, in 2009 the attorney general of New Jersey issued subpoenas to five prominent medical device makers for failing to disclose financial conflicts of interest among the physicians researching their products. Physicians who were testing and recommending the use of certain medical devices were found to have been compensated with stock in the companies making those devices.[51]

To compound the problem, since the 1990s, much of the U.S. Food and Drug Administration's (FDA) budget is funded by the user fees the pharmaceutical industry pays the FDA to evaluate and approve new drugs.[52] The funding of the clinical trials required for new drugs as part of the FDA's approval process also are funded by the pharmaceutical companies themselves. The FDA is supposed to oversee the design and outcomes of the trials. However, political and pharmaceutical pressures have caused the FDA to stray from its science-based public health mandate. For example, in 2005, the FDA was sharply criticized for its alleged failure to adequately monitor the risks of widely advertised and commonly used drugs for the treatment of arthritis.[53] The FDA's handling of clinical trial data collected is a major problem. Although the information collected is necessary for FDA approval of a product, once the product is approved, the FDA does not provide the public with a full report of the drug's safety and efficacy. The withheld information falls into the definition of "trade secrets," and the FDA has taken the position that research data are entitled to protection as proprietary information. This explains the number of recent examples of FDA-approved drugs that were later discovered to have major safety risks.[54] Clearly, the FDA must reconsider its position that clinical trial data fall into the classification of trade secrets.

The most egregious violation of professional ethics is found in the growing body of evidence that physicians at some of the most prestigious U.S. medical schools have been attaching their names and reputations to scientific publications ghostwritten by employees of pharmaceutical companies. The publications are intended, of course, to boost the sales of pharmaceutical products.[55] The NIH, which funds much of the nation's medical research, suggests that the universities involved, rather than the government, should address the problem of ghost authorship. Because university administrators find it difficult to censure the prestigious medical faculty at their institutions, the problem remains minimally addressed with no noted measurable decline in frequency in professional biomedical literature. However, in 2010, Section 6002 of the ACA also known as the "Sunshine Act" now "… requires medical product manufacturers to disclose to the Centers for Medicare and Medicaid Services (CMS) any payments or other transfers of value made to physicians or teaching hospitals. It also requires certain manufacturers and group purchasing organizations (GPOs) to disclose any physician ownership or investment interests held in those companies."[56]

The pharmaceutical industry also has had a long history of influence in medical education throughout the United States and Canada by providing medical students with funding for food at medical student conferences, and free medical equipment, books, and office supplies, etc. In large part due to medical student-led investigations and activism, many medical schools are creating policies to significantly limit or curtail this influence by preventing pharmaceutical companies from making such donations.[57]

▶ Future Challenges

The change in emphasis from basic science research toward health services research and population health will likely continue as the federal government moves its Medicare payment model from volume-based to value-based purchasing. This new model under the Medicare Access & CHIP Reauthorization Act (MACRA) will require more health services research on not only how to improve the health of populations, but also what changes to the existing healthcare infrastructure will be required to drive the new system. Research will be needed on what organizational structures and policies new accountable care organizations work best where physicians, hospitals, and other healthcare providers will be working together in new ways and with new goals. Research also will be needed on what changes to the existing health information technology infrastructure are necessary to better support population health, centralized electronic reporting to various government agencies, and information sharing between multiple healthcare institutions, which will be essential for new accountable care organizations to function efficiently.

The advent of ubiquitous advanced genetic testing will require research on how to analyze, summarize, and present unprecedentedly large volumes of genetic sequencing data into meaningful information into a form busy clinicians can use efficiently. Medical education will require updating new skills needed by clinicians in areas of population health, systems-based care, health information technology, and basic outcomes research. Research on what new curricula are needed in the era of MACRA will be essential. Continued pressure to improve the quality and drive down the cost of medical care will fuel more comparative effectiveness research to insure the best and most cost-effective treatments are utilized.

In summary, research that advances science and develops new technologies will be an integral part of healthcare reform for the foreseeable future. This will be true regardless of the method or kind of reform that takes place in the United States.

KEY TERMS FOR REVIEW

Analytic Studies
Basic Science Research
Case Series
Clinical Research
Comparative Effectiveness Research
Descriptive Study
Empirical Quality Standards

Expert Opinion
Explicit Quality Standards
Hospital Consumer Assessment of Healthcare Providers and Systems Survey (HCAHPS)
Health Services Research
Implicit Quality Standards

Institutional Review Board (IRB)
Observational Study
Patient-Center Outcomes Research Institute (PCORI)
Patient Safety Network (PSNet)
Randomized Controlled Clinical Trial
Systematic Review

CHAPTER ACRONYMS

AHCPR Agency for Health Care Policy and Research
AHRQ Agency for Healthcare Research and Quality

ARRA American Recovery and Reinvestment Act
EBM Evidence-based medicine
EBT Evidence-based treatment
FDA U.S. Food and Drug Administration

HCAHPS Hospital Consumer Assessment of Healthcare Providers and Systems Survey
GPO Group purchasing organization
IOM Institute of Medicine
IRB Institutional Review Board
MACRA Medicare Access & CHIP Reauthorization Act

NIH National Institutes of Health
PCORI Patient-Centered Outcomes Research Institute
PCORNET Patient-Centered Clinical Research Network
PSO Patient safety organization
PSNet Patient safety network

References

1. Aday LA, Lairson DR, Balkrishnan R, et al. *Evaluating the Medical Care System: Effectiveness, Efficiency, and Equity.* Ann Arbor, MI: Health Administration Press; 1993.
2. Wennberg JE, Freeman JL, Culp WJ. Are hospital services rationed in New Haven or over-utilised in Boston? *Lancet.* 1987;1:1185-1189.
3. Framingham Heart Study. History of the Framingham heart study. 2016. https://www.framinghamheartstudy.org/about-fhs/history.php. Accessed June 1, 2016.
4. Wennberg J. Which rate is right? *N Engl J Med.* 1986;314:310-311.
5. Wennberg JE, Freeman JL, Shelton RM, Bubolz TA. Hospital use and mortality among Medicare beneficiaries in Boston and New Haven. *N Engl J Med.* 1989;321:1168-1173.
6. United States Department of Health and Human Services Agency for Health Care Policy and Research. *AHCPR Program Note.* Rockville, MD: Public Health Service; 1990.
7. Stephenson J. Revitalized AHCPR pursues research on quality. Agency for health care policy and research. *JAMA.* 1997;278:1557.
8. U.S. Department of Health and Human Services. Agency for Healthcare Research and Quality. http://www.ahrq.gov/cpi/about/index.html. Accessed May 24, 2016.
9. Mills R, Fetter RB, Riedel DC, Averill R. AUTOGRP: an interactive computer system for the analysis of health care data. *Med Care.* 1976;14:603-615.
10. Berki SE. DRGs, incentives, hospitals, and physicians. *Health Aff.* 1985;4:70-76.
11. Chassin MR, Kosecoff J, Park RE, et al. Does inappropriate use explain geographic variations in the use of health care services? A study of three procedures. *JAMA.* 1987;258:2533-2537.
12. Hsiao WC, Stason WB. Toward developing a relative value scale for medical and surgical services. *Health Care Financ Rev.* 1979;1:23-38.
13. Hsiao WC, Braun P, Becker E, et al. *A National Study of Resource-based Relative Value Scale for Physician Services: Final Report to the Health Care Financing Administration.* Boston, MA: Harvard School of Public Health; 1988.
14. Hsiao WC, Braun P, Dunn D, Becker ER, DeNicola M, Ketcham TR. Results and policy implications of the resource-based relative-value study. *N Engl J Med.* 1988;319:881-888.
15. Newhouse JP. A design for a health insurance experiment. *Inquiry.* 1974;11:5-27.
16. Newhouse JP, Manning WG, Duan N, et al. The findings of the RAND health insurance experiment—a response to Welch et al. *Med Care.* 1987;25:157-179.
17. Newhouse J. Controlled experimentation as research policy. In: Ginzberg E, ed. *Health Services Research: Key to Health Policy.* Cambridge, MA: Harvard University Press; 1991:162-194.
18. Lohr KN, The Institute of Medicine. *Medicare: A Strategy for Quality Assurance.* Vol 1. Washington, DC: National Academy Press; 1990.
19. Surver J. Striving for quality in health care: an inquiry into policy and practice. *Health Care Manag Rev.* 1992;17:95-96.
20. Donabedian A. Evaluating the quality of medical care.1966. *Milbank Q.* 2005;83:691-729.
21. Institute of Medicine. To err is human: building a safer health system. 1999. https://psnet.ahrq.gov/resources/resource/1579. Accessed May 27, 2016.
22. United States Department of Health and Human Services Agency for Healthcare Research and Quality. Patient safety organizations. 2012. https://psnet.ahrq.gov/. Accessed May 27, 2016.
23. Makary MA, Daniel M. Medical error-the third leading cause of death in the US. *BMJ.* 2016;353:i2139.
24. Sackett DL, Rosenberg WMC, Gray JAM, Haynes RB, Richardson WS. Evidence based medicine: what it is and what it isn't. *BMJ.* 1996;312:71.
25. Torpy JM, Lynm C, Glass RM. JAMA patient page. Evidence-based medicine. *JAMA.* 2009;301:900.
26. Marwick C. Federal agency focuses on outcomes research. *JAMA.* 1993;270:164-165.
27. Guyatt G, Rennie D, Meade MO, Cook DJ. *Users' Guides to the Medical Literature: A Manual for*

Evidence-Based Clinical Practice. 3rd ed. New York, NY: McGraw-Hill Education; 2014.

28. Chilvers CE, Knibb RC, Armstrong SJ, Woods KL, Logan RF. Post menopausal hormone replacement therapy and risk of acute myocardial infarction—a case control study of women in the East Midlands, UK. *Eur Heart J*. 2003;24:2197-2205.

29. de Vries CS, Bromley SE, Farmer RD. Myocardial infarction risk and hormone replacement: differences between products. *Maturitas*. 2006;53:343-350.

30. Grady D, Rubin SM, Petitti DB, et al. Hormone therapy to prevent disease and prolong life in postmenopausal women. *Ann Intern Med*. 1992;117:1016-1037.

31. Rijpkema AH, van der Sanden AA, Ruijs AH. Effects of post-menopausal oestrogen-progestogen replacement therapy on serum lipids and lipoproteins: a review. *Maturitas*. 1990;12:259-285.

32. Rossouw JE, Anderson GL, Prentice RL, et al. Risks and benefits of estrogen plus progestin in healthy postmenopausal women: principal results from the women's health initiative randomized controlled trial. *JAMA*. 2002;288:321-333.

33. Goodman JC. Cookbook medicine: The right recipe for patients? *Physician Exec*. 2011;37:18-20.

34. Watanabe M. A call for action from the national forum on health. *CMAJ*. 1997. http://www.cmaj.ca/content/156/7/999.full.pdf±html. Accessed May 27, 2016.

35. Hooker RC. The rise and rise of evidence-based medicine. *Lancet*. 1997;349:1329-1330.

36. Keehan SP, Cuckler GA, Sisko AM, et al. National health expenditure projections, 2014–2024: spending growth faster than recent trends. *Health Aff*. 2015; 34:1407-1417.

37. Centers for Medicare & Medicaid Services. Historical National Health Expenditure Accounts. December 12, 2015. https://www.cms.gov/research-statistics-data-and-systems/statistics-trends-and-reports/nationalhealthexpenddata/nationalhealthaccountshistorical.html. Accessed May 27, 2016.

38. Benner JS, Morrison MR, Karnes EK, Kocot SL, McClellan M. An evaluation of recent federal spending on comparative effectiveness research: priorities, gaps, and next steps. *Health Aff*. 2010; 29:1768-1776.

39. Agency for Healthcare Research and Quality. What is comparative effectiveness research? http://effectivehealthcare.ahrq.gov/index.cfm/what-is-comparative-effectiveness-research1/. Accessed May 27, 2016.

40. Henry J. Kaiser Family Foundation. Explaining health care reform: what is comparative effectiveness research? September 29, 2009; http://kff.org/health-costs/issue-brief/explaining-health-care-reform-what-is-comparative/. Accessed May 27, 2016.

41. United States Internal Revenue Service. Patient-Centered Outcomes Research Trust Fund fee (irc 4375, 4376 and 4377): questions and answers. July 10, 2015. https://www.irs.gov/uac/patient-centered-outcomes-research-trust-fund-fee-questions-and-answers. Accessed May 27, 2016.

42. Patient Centered Outcomes Research Institute. Research and results. May 23, 2016; http://www.pcori.org/research-results. Accessed June 2, 2016.

43. Patient Centered Outcomes Research Institute. Papers resulting from PCORI-funded research studies. 2016. http://www.pcori.org/research-results/pcori-literature/papers-resulting-pcori-funded-research-studies. Accessed June 2, 2016.

44. Centers for Medicare & Medicaid Services. HCAHPS: Patients' perspectives of care survey. September 25, 2014. https://www.cms.gov/Medicare/Quality-Initiatives-Patient-Assessment-instruments/HospitalQualityInits/HospitalHCAHPS.html. Accessed June 2, 2016.

45. Centers for Medicare & Medicaid Services. The HCAHPS survey: frequently asked questions. https://www.cms.gov/medicare/quality-initiatives-patient-assessment-instruments/hospitalqualityinits/downloads/hospitalhcahpsfactsheet201007.pdf. Accessed June 2, 2016.

46. Centers for Medicare & Medicaid Services. Details for title: CMS-1632-F and IFC, CMS-1632-CN2 and changes due to the consolidated appropriations act of 2016. August 17, 2015. https://www.cms.gov/Medicare/Medicare-Fee-for-Service-Payment/AcuteInpatientPPS/FY2016-IPPS-Final-Rule-Home-Page-Items/FY2016-IPPS-Final-Rule-Regulations.html. Accessed June 2, 2016.

47. Stanford Hospital and Clinics Medical Staff Update Online. New patient satisfaction survey will help improve service. March 2003. http://med.stanford.edu/shs/update/archives/MAR2003/survey.html. Accessed June 1, 2016.

48. WISL Health. Doctor's empathy boosts patient satisfaction. March 11, 1016. http://www.wsiltv.com/story/31445888/doctors-empathy-boosts-patient-satisfaction. Accessed June 2, 2016.

49. Dubois RW, Graff JS. Setting priorities for comparative effectiveness research: from assessing public health benefits to being open with the public. *Health Aff*. 2011;30:2235-2242.

50. United States Department of Health and Human Services. Office of Inspector General. The Food and Drug Administration's oversight of clinical investigators' financial information. 2009. http://oig.hhs.gov/oei/reports/oei-05-07-00730.pdf. Accessed May 28, 2016.

51. State of New Jersey Office of the Attorney General. Landmark settlement reached with medical device maker synthes. 2009. http://www.nj.gov/oag/newsreleases09/pr20090505a.html. Accessed May 28, 2016.

52. Mercola JM. FDA Wants More Money, Claims They Are a "Bargain." 2013. http://articles.mercola

.com/sites/articles/archive/2013/05/01/fda-budget -increase.aspx. Accessed September 9, 2016.

53. UCONN Health. FDA hearing to determine arthritis drugs' safety. February 16, 2005. http://today.uchc .edu/headlines/2005/feb05/arthritisdrug.html. Accessed May 28, 2016.

54. Bodenheimer T. Uneasy alliance—clinical investigators and the pharmaceutical industry. *N Engl J Med*. 2000;342:1539-1544.

55. Singer N. Senator moves to block medical ghostwriting. *New York Times*, August 18, 2009.

http://www.nytimes.com/2009/08/19/health /research/19ethics.html?_r=2&scp=1&sq=Ghosts %20in%20the%20Journals&st=cse. Accessed June 2, 2016.

56. Health Policy Briefs. The physician payments Sunshine Act. *Health Aff*. October 2, 2014. http:// www.healthaffairs.org/healthpolicybriefs/brief .php?brief_id=127. Accessed June 2, 2016.

57. Holloway K. Uneasy subjects: medical students' conflicts over the pharmaceutical industry. *Soc Sci Med*. 2014;114:113-120.

CHAPTER 13

Future of Health Care

CHAPTER OVERVIEW

This chapter recaps and summarizes selected topics in a future-oriented context. It outlines ongoing changes and tentatively forecasts future developments in institutional components and processes of the U.S. healthcare system. The chapter concludes with a summary of predictions and future questions.

The enactment of the Patient Protection and Affordable Care Act of 2010 (the ACA) was an historic achievement that expanded Americans' access to health insurance and embedded the population health perspective into federal cost control and quality-improvement policies. The ACA reaches into virtually every dimension of the healthcare system with monumental changes unprecedented in the healthcare system's history.

Predicting the future of the U.S. healthcare system in these times of change is difficult as the system continues its evolution and reforms continue. The discussions that follow represent only educated conjecture about the directions the healthcare system will take in the coming years. Even the most thoughtful forecasts, founded on carefully studied trends and expert projections, undoubtedly will be affected by unforeseeable developments in the healthcare environment. Trend extrapolation in the policy arena is most reliable under stable conditions.[1] The policy arena of the foreseeable future will be anything but stable as reforms continue. In fact, the Congressional Budget Office has pointed out that the scope and complexities of the ACA legislation make accurate predictions of fiscal and many other future outcomes extremely difficult or impossible.[2]

According to chaos theory, "A small change in input can quickly translate into overwhelming differences in output," and as history has demonstrated, the healthcare system is particularly sensitive to input changes.[3] In the past, virtually every effort to address one of the three basic problems of the healthcare system—cost, quality, and access—resulted in significant changes in one of the others. For example, improving access to health care for low-income populations and older adults through Medicaid and Medicare had major inflationary effects on costs. Attempts to control costs through managed care resulted in professional and consumer pushback regarding access and quality. Thus, it is important to recognize that policy changes, no matter how well-intentioned, may have unintended consequences. Only experience reveals those consequences.

▶ Paradox of U.S. Health Care

The extraordinary successes and technologic accomplishments of the U.S. healthcare system have brought worldwide acclaim to U.S. scientists and clinicians. However, successes and accomplishments often have been offset by the system's evident deficiencies of limited access, high costs, and variations in quality. The policy decisions of government and healthcare leadership of the past six decades are duly credited with medicine's impressive advances, its prestige, and its wealth. Those healthcare policies led the National Institutes of Health and other federal funding agencies to invest heavily in the potential of the nation's universities and medical schools to develop basic and applied research and to dedicate federal and state funds to the expansion of academic medical centers. The burgeoning healthcare industry prompted the initiation of federal programs that significantly expanded the number and size of U.S. hospitals and led to an exponential increase in the size of the healthcare workforce. The policies that produced the financial incentives in the healthcare reimbursement system encouraged specialization among physicians and other healthcare practitioners. However, those policies also contributed to the longstanding problems of inequitable access, variable quality, and seemingly uncontrollable growth in costs. The success of the healthcare industry, with the growth of its workforce, astounding physical and technologic infrastructure, its impressive outcomes, and its unfettered revenues must be weighed against its failure to recognize a social mission broader than only addressing the individual needs of those able to access its services. The technology-oriented, can-do culture that pervaded health care mesmerized healthcare providers and patients with the belief that more dramatic technological marvels would improve Americans' health status. American policymakers and the public supported the rising costs of health care with ascending expectations for what medicine could accomplish. Historically, a population perspective was absent from these assumptions. As medical technology advanced, virtually no recognition was given to the facts that a significant proportion of medical conditions arise from "non-clinical" social and behavioral factors.[4]

The passage of the ACA represented discontent with a system that could not ensure a basic level of health care to a significant proportion of the American public, that could not control costs that increased well above the rate of other services, and that provided many services of doubtful necessity and therapeutic benefit.[5]

▶ Accountability for Quality and Costs

The healthcare system, apart from advances in clinical practice, has demonstrated an inherent resistance to change. Entrenched interests among many professions, employers, and financial and educational institutions have repeatedly demonstrated the power to maintain the status quo. As a consequence, the longstanding and escalating problems of healthcare costs and clinical quality have remained unabated for decades. Because there are no single solutions to these complex problems and little likelihood that all or most of the vested interests would support a set of simultaneously applied solutions, problems continued.

Failed attempts to address the variable quality of clinical care illustrate one facet of the problem. Concerns about the quality of health care, both anecdotally and empirically, have been expressed for decades. In 1999, the widely publicized assessment of the problem by the Institute of Medicine (IOM) entitled "To Err Is Human: Building a Safer Health System"[6] produced a brief flurry of discussion in Congress late in the Clinton administration and then moved far down on the list of U.S. concerns.

More than 15 years after the IOM report, new research estimated the number of premature deaths associated with preventable harm in hospitals at more than 400,000 per year.[7] A 2016 report cited medical errors as the third-leading cause of death in the United States.[8] When 3,000 people died in the terrorist attacks on September 11, 2001, the United States went to war. With estimates of more than 1,000 people dying every day as a result of medical errors, the silence and inaction are astounding.

In fairness, physicians and other providers are beset by so many professional challenges, of necessity, the vast majority leave the more global problems of clinical practice to their organizational leadership. Physicians and other providers are caught between patient demands, their own challenges as to the best course of treatment, and the need to manage costs. In addition, the steady production of new drugs, devices, and procedures makes current knowledge quickly obsolete. The time and effort required to remain current with clinical developments places a significant burden on busy practitioners.[9]

Continuing efforts to achieve system-wide improvements in healthcare quality are taking many forms. The Agency for Healthcare Research and Quality (AHRQ) is helping to pierce the culture of silence that surrounds medical errors by operating a peer-reviewed, Web-based medical journal, *Morbidity and Mortality Rounds on the Web*, to stimulate discussion of medical errors in a blame-free environment.[10] The AHRQ encourages physicians and other health professionals to submit medical error cases to the website for interactive discussion and analysis. Contributors may remain anonymous. The Department of Health and Human Services (DHHS) is participating in the Hospital Quality Information Initiative, a joint effort with the leadership of the nation's hospitals, to provide the public with information on the quality of care.[11] Also, the ACA contains several provisions that directly affect patient safety by establishing, for example, a system to track hospital medical errors and incentives to financially reward hospitals that have improved their medical error rates.[12] Over the past several years, the Centers for Medicare & Medicaid Services (CMS) have enforced non-payment rules for several types of hospital-acquired conditions (HACs).[13,14] A 2016 CMS report noted that a cumulative total of 1.3 million fewer HACs were experienced by hospital patients over the three years from 2011 to 2013 relative to the number of HACs that would have occurred if rates had remained steady at the 2010 level. The CMS estimates that approximately 50,000 fewer patients died in the hospital as a result of the reduction in HACs, and approximately $12 billion in healthcare costs were saved from 2010 to 2013.[15]

However, in 2013, the Leapfrog Group, an organization of Fortune 500 corporations that promotes hospital safety and quality, released findings from an analysis of six years of hospital data. This discouraging report noted that "little progress was observed" and concluded: "Our study highlights the complexity of improving the quality and safety of health care in the United States through reliance on purchaser pressure and public disclosure, both of which feature prominently in the Affordable Care Act."[16] Whether or not some combination of financial penalties and incentives, more public disclosure, and other activities will have material effects to significantly reduce overall medical error rates will remain an open question for the future.

Like the longstanding problems with the quality of care, the problem of escalating healthcare costs has continued for decades. The evolution of U.S. healthcare insurance through managed care principles in the 1980s and 1990s had a temporary impact on the rate of national healthcare spending growth.[17] However, as a share of the nation's economy, healthcare expenditures have continued their upward trajectory with growing concerns about waste and variations in outcomes. Rising costs coupled with concerns about quality are reflected in core provisions of the ACA. The ACA's investments in Medicare-funded delivery system reforms such as patient-centered medical homes, accountable care organizations (ACOs), value-based purchasing, bundled payments for care, and other initiatives all tie provider reimbursement to the quality of population health outcomes. The CMS has set aggressive goals for value-based payments within the Medicare fee-for-service system such that 30 percent of Medicare payments will be tied to quality or value through alternative payment models by the end of 2016, and 50 percent of Medicare payments will be tied to quality or value by the end of 2018.[15] Reforms are incorporating proven interventions to address behavioral, social, and environmental determinants of health and generating findings for application to learning and further system refinements.[15] The Medicare Access and CHIP Reauthorization Act of 2015 (MACRA) builds upon the foundations of the ACA in transforming the delivery system to reward value over volume by restructuring the way that Medicare reimburses physicians. The MACRA replaces a former patchwork of cost and quality monitoring programs with one program to streamline reporting and monitoring processes, as discussed in detail in other chapters. It also repeals a highly flawed Medicare physician-reimbursement method.[18] The MACRA also requires the CMS to undertake standardization of quality measurements through a "Quality Measure Development Plan" that will address known measurement and performance gaps and align measures with other federal programs and the private sector.[19] Standardization of quality measures will be a critical element in the future of the MACRA's payment systems' integrity. The required federal rulemaking process to implement the new law was ongoing in June, 2016. As proposed rules were released for public comment, physician advocacy groups responded with voluminous requests to delay the law's implementation and leveled specific criticisms about costs of compliance by physician practices and criteria for participation.[20] A report of a physician survey noted major concerns about whether physicians in solo and small group practices will be able to economically survive the transition to MACRA payment parameters. The report noted that MACRA compliance will be difficult for small physician practices, which struggle with managing patient data. Resulting predictions suggest that many solo and small group practices will either merge into larger groups or abandon Medicare participation entirely.[21] Nonetheless, the core principles of the MACRA that tie payment to the quality of patient outcomes likely will remain intact. The MACRA will be the most significant development since the implementation of the ACA as it adds more refined ways of delivering, coordinating, and paying for healthcare services.[22] The future holds opportunities for much learning from the ongoing evaluation and research about the nature and sustainability of both the ACA and the MACRA. It is clear that under current laws, the federal government and Congressional momentum to achieve improved quality at reduced cost will continue.

▶ **Health Information Technology**

There is a growing level of evidence supporting the value of electronic health records (EHRs) that facilitate computerized physician order entry and computerized decision support systems, as discussed in Chapter 3. This is particularly true in areas such as improving delivery of preventive care. However, there is wide agreement that the imposition of health information technology (HIT) on delivery systems can be disruptive to work processes and work cultures.[23] Many other factors can be expected to make the continuing implementation of HIT complex and challenging, including achievement of secure data portability, cost containment, and training. An additional challenge will be the future sustainability of health information exchange (HIE) organizations' infrastructure when federal subsidies for their operations expire. The regional health information organizations (RHIOs) that administer HIEs are seeking alternative sources of funding and developing ways to generate revenue, but most have not yet developed a standard business model that would be broadly applicable and professionally acceptable across all communities. While the benefits of HIEs are documented and desirable, finding solutions to cultural and business model issues will be essential to achieve the goal of a nationwide network of regional exchanges. Nevertheless, progress in the adoption of EHRs has continued. The percentage of office-based physicians with basic EHR capability increased 336 percent between 2006 and 2013, from 11 to 48 percent.[24] In the future, the addition of a physician criterion for Medicare payment under the MACRA intends to further incentivize EHR use.[25]

In 2011, hospital adoption of at least a basic EHR system was above 20 percent in 32 states and above 40 percent in 7 states. By 2014, hospital adoption of at least a basic EHR system was above 60 percent in all but two states and above 80 percent in 17 states.[26]

To achieve the overall HIT goals of improving quality and managing costs, much work remains in the areas of research and implementation.

▶ Hospitals

Hospitals will remain critically important entities in the U.S. healthcare system, and as reforms progress, they will continue to assume new roles as major components of integrated systems of care. Hospitals also will continue to be the sites of technologically advanced medical care, education, and training for physicians and other health professionals as well as clinical research. Hospitals' service constellations will continue changing as privately operated ambulatory surgery centers, urgent and immediate care facilities, and diagnostic facilities increasingly displace services that once were their province. Hospital emergency departments and inpatient services will remain mainstays of communities' safety nets for needy populations.

Hospital consolidations through mergers and acquisitions are predicted to continue at the frenetic pace witnessed in the past several years. All signs point toward more consolidations in order to gain market share and leverage the population-based reimbursement and quality improvement mandates of major government and private payers.[27] This trend goes hand-in-hand with hospitals' acquisitions of physician private practices.[28] Acquiring physician practices assures hospitals of a flow of inpatients as well as revenue from diagnostic and other outpatient services.

There are reasons for optimism in the prospect of ACOs partnering with hospitals as major participants. Such partnerships hold promise for successfully addressing the negative hallmarks of the healthcare system—fragmentation, duplication, medical errors, and excessive costs. Observers are expressing concern, however, that the newly established ACOs are joining healthcare organizations that otherwise would compete with each other, thus creating networks with potential monopoly power.[29] Healthcare market analysts also have pointed out that hospital mergers can actually increase the amounts hospitals can bill payers and the costs to patients.[30] In addition, concerns are rising about the absence of regulatory controls on mergers and acquisitions that have the potential to reduce or eliminate services that may not be deemed profitable but meet important needs in specific communities. A 2016 report by *MergerWatch*, which analyzes the hospital industry, noted that only 10 states require government review before hospital facilities and services may be shut down.[31]

Debates and analyses will continue regarding hospitals' roles in the reformed system and healthcare marketplace. Results of government and private-entity experiments with the reconfigured roles of hospitals in a new population-focused, value-driven delivery system will yield numerous opportunities for continued refinements that affect both the quality and costs of care.

▶ Changing Population Composition

The U.S. population is not only growing older, but increasing numbers of older adults are surviving to a very advanced age.[32] In addition, the number of intact families capable of housing and caring for aged relatives has diminished as women work outside the home, the number of single-parenting families increases, and divorce rates hover at approximately 50 percent. Families raise fewer children, and those children often migrate to other locations making direct care of their parents impossible. Consequently, the healthcare needs of the growing population of frail, older adults is expected to place increasing demands on the healthcare system. Those demands will focus particularly on the chronic-care component of U.S. system, a sector that has not been particularly attractive to healthcare providers in the past. In addition, much of the long-term care capability in the United States is in the hands of the private, for-profit sector, which has an uneven record of service quality.[33]

The healthcare needs of this older adult population also will be influenced by its changing racial and ethnic diversity. Minority groups and Hispanics in particular will become larger proportions of the elderly population.[34] These changes have important implications for the healthcare system. There are significant differences in mortality rates, chronic conditions, service preferences, and use, as well as attitudes toward medical care across racial/ethnic groups. For example, Hispanics have lower rates of diseases such as hypertension and arthritis and higher rates of conditions such as diabetes than Caucasians. Blacks are more likely to require treatment for hypertension, cerebrovascular disease, diabetes, and obesity, and they have persistently higher mortality rates than whites.[35] Increased demands on the healthcare system posed by population changes are coupled with the problems of healthcare workforce supply. Growth in demand for nurses, nursing assistants, and various types of therapists in the acute-care sector and the relative unattractiveness of long-term facilities as employment sites for those service personnel have left many long-term care facilities dangerously understaffed. The long-term care industry's ability to develop innovative approaches to attracting and retaining staff will have important implications as service demands swell with the aging of the baby-boom generation. Identifying solutions to the staffing crises in long-term care has been the subject of ongoing research at academic and policy development institutions throughout the country.[36,37] With an amendment to the Federal Fair Labor Standards Act effective in 2016, the nation's 2 million home care workers will be entitled to the federal minimum wage, time-and-a-half pay for overtime, and pay for time spent traveling between client homes.[38] Advocates believe these new federal wage protections may make home care employment more attractive in the future and help ease the ongoing recruitment and retention challenges in the long-term care industry.[38]

Until recently, the needs of the informal caregiver system were virtually ignored. Legislative action at the federal level only recently began to recognize these needs. In a hopeful future sign, a Congressional proposal now has partially paid family medical leave under consideration.[39]

In the future, the chronically ill who do not require long-term care facility placement will continue to have difficulties interacting with a healthcare system that has an historical focus on acute illness and has not dealt effectively with the aged population's physical disabilities, psychosocial issues, and lifestyle adjustments. Emerging service delivery models may help address these issues by providing a continuum of care that focuses on service coordination and maintenance of optimal functionality.[40] ACOs, patient-centered medical homes, and ACA-supported Medicaid programs, such as the Community-based Care Transitions Program to support older Americans to maintain residence in their homes, are just some examples of emerging models. However, the pervasive system changes required to move from an episodic and disjointed care model to one that encompasses a holistic approach to older patients' needs will continue to present significant future challenges.

▶ Growth in Home Care and Ambulatory Care Services

Home Care Services

Changes occurring in hospital care that promote shortened lengths-of-stay and growth in the aging population have resulted in rapid growth of home healthcare services. Between 1997 and 2013, the number of Medicare-certified home health agencies increased by 1700 to 12,613.[41] Between 2001 and 2013 the number of home healthcare episodes rose from 3.9 million to 6.7 million.[41] Beginning in 2010 and continuing until 2030, approximately 10,000 Americans will reach the of age 65 each day.[42] As the population of older Americans rapidly increases, home healthcare services can be expected to experience corresponding expansion.

Ambulatory Care Services

Many factors are responsible for the extraordinary growth in the use of ambulatory versus hospital-based services. Ambulatory or "same-day" surgical procedures are growing in number due to continuing advances in diagnostic technology, anesthesiology, and surgical techniques and instrumentation. Also, payers exert pressure to avoid expensive hospitalization whenever possible. The number of ambulatory surgery centers (ASCs) has grown from approximately 1,000 in 1988 to more than 6,000 in 2013.[43] The number of centers continues growing at a rate of approximately 3 percent each year as the CMS approves more procedures for reimbursement in the ASC setting.[44] Growth in the number of these facilities is expected to continue.

Continued proliferation of urgent care centers and retail clinics also is expected in the future. These ambulatory facilities have gained widespread acceptance among consumers for their general user-friendliness and convenience. In addition, payers reimburse for their services as a much less expensive alternative to hospital emergency department care. A 2015 survey reported that 89 percent of urgent care centers saw increases in visits in 2014, and 91 percent anticipated growth into additional locations in 2015.[45]

Expanding from approximately 300 retail clinic sites in 2007, current projections estimate that the number of retail clinic sites will grow to 2,400 in 2016, with a 14 percent growth annually through 2017.[46] In addition, more than 100 partnerships between retail clinics and health systems have been established where payers are integrating retail clinics into their care delivery networks to reduce emergency department usage and related costs.[47] These partnerships and factors similar to those contributing to the growth in urgent care centers will continue into the future.

During the period between 2000 and 2011, annual emergency department (ED) visits increased 26.2 percent, from 108 million to 136.3 million.[48] The increase in ED visits was attributed to overall population growth, increase in illness-related diagnoses, and lack of private health insurance. The uninsured and Medicaid patients demonstrated the greatest increase in rates of ED use as compared with privately insured patients.[49] In the future, ED visit volume will bear close watching as the ACA's implementation proceeds and new care-delivery models expand their reach. One of the expected effects of enrolling millions more Americans in private insurance and Medicaid was a decrease in expensive ED use as individuals gained improved access to primary care. However, a 2015 report by the American College of Emergency Physicians noted that ED volume actually increased since 2014 when the requirement to have health insurance became effective.[50] Possible explanations for the continuing trend of increasing ED use may be the difficulty of the previously uninsured in breaking from prior habits and/or the difficulty in obtaining primary care appointments. The effect of the more proactive and preventive care focus of primary care may take several years to take effect, especially if the newly insured have a backlog of healthcare problems they need to address.

▶ The Healthcare Workforce

Because physicians and nurses are the primary participants in all dimensions of the healthcare system, the following discussions focus on these professions and their respective future roles and influences.

Health care is one of the nation's largest and most important industries and employs a diverse workforce of 12 million people representing more than 200 occupations and professions.[51] As the healthcare system continues to change and adapt to reforms, the kinds of employees and the sites of their employment will be in transition during upcoming years. Although hospitals remain the major employers, the trend is toward the highest employment growth among health maintenance organizations, ambulatory clinics and services, and home healthcare providers. In addition, according to the U.S. Bureau of Labor Statistics, "Healthcare occupations and industries are expected to have the fastest employment growth and to add the most jobs in the nation between 2014 and 2024."[52] New occupations and professions will continue to develop and require more specialized knowledge and more sophisticated skills to accommodate technological advancements. Such specialization also reduces the flexibility of employers to increase staffing efficiency and adds to costs. As a result, there is increasing deployment of multi-skilled health practitioners, particularly among hospitals, which may, for example, combine the roles of occupational and physical therapy assistants into one position. As hospitals continue to seek efficiencies in personnel deployment, such tactics are likely to continue in the future.

Physician Supply and Distribution

In 2006, the American Association of Medical Colleges (AAMC) set a target for a 30 percent increase in the number of first-year medical students based on 2002 enrollment data. Although not attained by 2015, the projected first-year medical school enrollment for 2019 represents a 29.2 percent increase from 2002.[53] In the period 2002–2014, the number of physician graduates grew at an annual rate of 2.8 percent.[54] However, the AAMC currently estimates that by 2025, there will be a shortage of between 12,500 and 31,100 primary care physicians and between 28,200 and 63,700 specialists.[55] Adding to the shortfall issue, the CMS capped its support for hospitals' physician residency training programs at 1996 levels, and with few minor exceptions, it has not added to these training program slots for 20 years.[54] To help address this issue, the ACA authorized CMS to redistribute available residency training slots from hospitals that have closed or underutilized their slots to hospitals in need of additional residents.[56] The ACA also promotes residency training in outpatient settings and in rural and underserved areas by increasing flexibility in the laws and regulations that govern Medicare's residency program funding.[57] Although ACA provisions will help optimize the use of available CMS-funded residency slots, the gap between U.S. medical school graduates and available U.S. residency slots will increase at a time when projected physician shortages in the United States will become more pronounced.[54] Despite predicted physician shortages, in 2015, U.S. medical schools began graduating more physicians than available residency program training slots.[54] Unless Congress acts quickly to fund support for additional residency program training slots, the future will see a large and growing pool of successful medical school graduates whose careers will end due to lack of residency training opportunities—at a time when physician shortages will be increasing.

In addition to predicted physician shortages, the United States has long-term problems with the distribution of physician supply that can be expected to continue. A persistent problem is the geographic variation in physician practice location. The number of active physicians providing patient care per 100,000 population in each state varies from a high of more than 432.4 per 100,000 population in Massachusetts to a low of 184.7 per 100,000 population in Mississippi.[58] The low supply of physicians in rural and inner-city communities will continue to create a medical care delivery challenge for populations in these underserved areas.

Emerging Physician Roles

Hospitalists

Physicians called "hospitalists" substitute for patients' primary physicians for the duration of the hospital stay and provide and/or coordinate all patient care by staff and specialists. Hospitalists reduce the inherent costs of primary care physicians by eliminating the need for daily primary care physician visits to inpatients. Because it is generally accepted that hospitalists shorten lengths of hospital stays, improve the continuity and quality of hospital care, and are economically advantageous to hospitals, hospitalist medicine is rapidly becoming the preferred model of inpatient care.[59] Given that hospital medicine is the fastest-growing medical specialty in the United States with more than 48,000 practitioners identifying as hospitalists, the hospitalist "movement" will likely continue to evolve rapidly as a mainstay of hospital care.[60] Perhaps most emblematic of their growing importance in the healthcare system is the creation of a set of dedicated billing codes for hospitalists by the CMS in 2016.[60]

Physicians as Hospital Employees (Not Hospitalists)

Increasing employment of primary care and specialist physicians by hospitals has been one response to the changing healthcare system environment. The number of physicians directly employed by hospitals grew by 34 percent between 2000 and 2010. In one year from 2013 and 2014 alone, physicians directly employed by hospitals increased from 10 to 21 percent.[61] This trend is expected to continue. Physicians view hospital employment as freeing them from flat reimbursement rates, complex insurance and health information technology (HIT) requirements, high malpractice premiums, and work–life balance challenges. Hospitals view physician employment as opportunities to gain market share for admissions, increased use of diagnostic testing and other outpatient services, and referrals to high-revenue specialty services.[62] In addition, hospital executives cite physician–hospital integration as an important strategy to prepare for payment reforms such as accountable care organizations and penalties for hospital readmissions.[63]

Physicians as Managers

Another emerging role for physicians is that of medical manager or administrator. Physicians, many with additional management or administration training, are entering the medical management field in leadership roles with ACOs. The emergence of ACOs as not-for-profit entities requiring executive leadership are offering new career paths for physicians interested in healthcare system management as an alternative to direct patient care.[64]

Whether or not ACA provisions will succeed in attenuating imbalances in both the medical specialty and primary care workforces to meet American society's medical care needs will remain an open question. As in so many other aspects of health care, it is likely that market forces combined with policy decisions will determine the outcomes.

Nurses

The latest available survey of the RN population indicated that in 2012, 2.9 million RNs were in active practice in the United States. Assuming RNs continue to train at current levels, and accounting for new entrants and attrition, the RN supply is expected to reach 3.8 million in 2025—a 33 percent increase. However, the nationwide demand for RNs is projected to grow slower than the supply, such that by 2025, the projected demand will be 3.5 million—a 21 percent increase over 2012 numbers.[65] The national projection of a surplus of RNs masks the projected imbalance of RNs at the state level. Sixteen states are projected to have RN shortages where state supply of RNs is not expected to meet state-specific demands.[65] Another reason for the projected national level surplus is the increasing number of nursing school graduates. There was a 108 percent increase in the number of nurses passing the national licensure examination for RNs during the 2001–2011 period.[66] While experts agree that the next decade will see significant growth in the number of RNs, it remains uncertain as to whether the distribution of nursing supply will meet actual future needs.

National Health Care Workforce Planning

The United States has never planned comprehensively or strategically for the development and deployment of its healthcare workforce.[67] Complex supply and demand factors influence workforce requirements, and the prediction of future requirements is severely confounded by the lack of uniform data at national and state levels across the professions.[68] Current workforce shortages in professions such as generalist physicians, nurses, and mental health workers; the disproportionate geographic distribution of many types of providers in urban and rural areas; and underrepresentation by minorities in the health professions were focal points to be addressed by the ACA's National Health Care Workforce Commission (NHCWC). For the first time in U.S. history, the NHCWC intended to comprehensively address national workforce planning, development, and deployment issues. However, to date, the NHCWC has not convened due to Congress' unwillingness to provide required funding.[69] The aging population, the shifting nature of diseases, healthcare delivery and reimbursement reforms, new technology, and economic factors will continue to change consumer demands and provider expectations, all lending more complexity to the challenges of planning for future workforce requirements.

The continued influx of previously uninsured individuals as a result of the ACA alone will put unprecedented stresses on healthcare system personnel. In fact, there is mounting evidence that since implementation of the ACA, there has been an increase in the stress and burnout levels of primary care physicians.[70] In the future it will be necessary to modify the roles and scope of practice of many of the healthcare professions to adapt to changing service patterns. The centrality of the healthcare workforce to the quality, costs, and accessibility of the healthcare system makes attention to resolving workforce issues essential to the future of healthcare delivery in the United States.

▶ Employer-Sponsored Health Insurance

In 2015, employer-sponsored health insurance covered 147 million people, 57 percent of the U.S. population under 65 years of age.[71] It is the predominant form of health insurance coverage in the United States. Therefore, it was not surprising that in the wake of the ACA's implementation, concerns arose about the law's effects on employers. The law did not require employers to provide health insurance coverage. However, if an employer did so, by 2015, the law mandated those firms with 100 or more full-time equivalent (FTE) employees to provide health coverage to at least 95 percent of their full-time employees and dependents up to age 26, or pay a penalty of $2,000 per full-time employee (in excess of 30 employees).[72] The primary concern about the law's effects was that employers would cease offering health insurance coverage rather than face what could prove to be substantial penalties. In addition, in the decade prior to the ACA employer mandate taking effect, average total health insurance premiums had increased 69 percent, potentially creating even stronger rationale for employers to drop health insurance coverage all together.[73]

To date, following implementation of the employer mandate, concerns about employers dropping health insurance coverage have not materialized and the percentage of employers offering coverage has remained essentially unchanged.[71,74] And, in spite of onerous predictions that the employer mandate would cause employers to decrease hiring of full time workers, to change full-time workers to part-time status, or to increase new employee waiting periods to obtain health insurance coverage, only small percentages of employers made such changes.[71]

However, trends in employer-sponsored health insurance coverage are emerging in the form of employees' adoption of high-deductible health plans (HDHPs). Today, almost one-fourth of workers have such plans, and since 2009, the percent of employees covered by HDHPs has tripled.[71] This trend is important because HDHPs substantially increase employees' financial risk for their healthcare costs. While HDHP up-front premium costs are lower than other types of plans, 46 percent of HDHP subscribers have annual deductibles of more than $1,000.[75] The deductible is the amount individuals must pay out-of-pocket before insurance coverage begins. While in theory, requiring out-of-pocket spending should promote consumers' prudent choices for care, expert observations and preliminary research are raising many concerns. Only a few of the concerns include: consumer ignorance about how plans actually work, especially about provision of no-or-low cost deductibles for preventive services; evidence that consumers are avoiding necessary and appropriate care due to costs; and evidence that out-of-pocket expenses negatively impact consumers' compliance with medically recommended follow-up care including use of prescription drugs.[75] Some studies suggest that HDHPs' dampening effects on appropriate use of health services in the short-term may lead to costly health consequences in the long-term.[75] As adoption of HDHPs continues to accelerate and HDHPs impact ever-larger segments of the population, future longitudinal research findings on the effects of these plans will be central to informing policy decisions.

▶ Medical Technology

In this era of health reform that emphasizes value over volume, debates continue about the ineffective and inefficient uses of medical technology. Following are just two examples of many that could be offered. The first discusses the rapid proliferation of an unproven technology. The second discusses the overuse of an existing technology.

In 2013, *Modern Healthcare* published an editorial entitled "End the Medical Arms Race."[76] The editorial cited Americans' fascination with high-technology medicine and the propensity to embrace even unproven technology when it is offered.[76] Noting that "advanced technology sells," the editorial discussed how competitive healthcare systems influence patient demand through aggressive marketing and advertising.[76] The editorial noted that "the medical evidence that justifies investing in the latest high-tech equipment often isn't there, at least not yet."[76] This is illustrated by the first example, intensity-modulated radiotherapy (IMRT) for prostate cancer. The rapid adoption of IMRT reveals the coercive power of enticing, but as yet unproven, medical technology. IMRT treatment costs $15,000–$20,000 more than other standard therapies and may have potential benefits of improving treatment effectiveness and reducing side effects.[77] However, definitive evidence that IMRT yields better outcomes than other standard therapies will not be available for several years when the results of a National Cancer Institute-funded study are known.[76] Start-up costs for an IMRT installation are approximately $2 million with total hospital costs for an installation ranging as high as $10 million.[76]

University of Michigan researchers who studied more than 125,000 men diagnosed with prostate cancer during a seven-year period, reported limited evidence to justify IMRT as a replacement for a prior therapy that has "high-level evidence" for effectiveness.[77] Nevertheless, in the seven-year study period, the researchers reported a tenfold increase in the use of IMRT and a 90 percent reduction in the use of prior standard therapy.[77] Analyses gave several reasons for the rapid adoption of IMRT in advance of evidence to support its clinical benefits and cost-effectiveness. Reasons included ethical issues about withholding a potentially beneficial treatment, patient demands, economic competition among physicians, and financial incentives created by high Medicare reimbursement.[77] In addition to high reimbursement rates fueling IMRT adoption, researchers also cited physician ownership of treatment facilities and self-referrals as factors contributing to the proliferation of IMRT technology.[77] Discussing policy implications of their findings, researchers suggested that delivery system changes such as shifts from fee-for-service reimbursement to financial risk-sharing arrangements, such as ACOs and bundled payments for care, may help to encourage more efficient care and limit the use of as yet unproven technology such as IMRT. With regard to developing evidence of effectiveness for new technology, they suggest extension of Medicare payment for patients' participation in clinical trials or disease registries to help determine net benefits.[77]

The second example illustrates the overuse of an existing technology. Indiscriminate use of computed tomography (CT) scanning remains an ongoing issue. In use since the 1970s, CT scans were a medical breakthrough and continue to be invaluable diagnostic aids. The number of scans grew from approximately 3 million in 1980 to more than 85 million in 2011. Recently, the Food and Drug Administration reports that 30–50 percent of CT scans are medically unnecessary.[78]

Using radiation doses equivalent to hundreds of x-rays, CT scans are not benign and studies suggest that long-term exposure to their radiation may contribute to the development of cancer.[78] Controversies rage about risks versus benefits with some experts contending that diagnostic benefits outweigh the risks of radiation exposure. Other experts note that while medically necessary scans are beneficial, excessive and indiscriminate use poses clear dangers.[78] There are still other dimensions to the issues with this technology. First, dubbed "incidentalomas" because they are found incidentally in CT scans performed for other purposes, findings include benign tissue abnormalities that often prompt unnecessary and expensive additional diagnostics including invasive biopsies, additional scans over time, or even unnecessary treatment.[78] Second, radiation dosage can vary widely for the same type of scan; with the exception of mammograms, there are no federal regulations governing radiation doses. A study conducted by the University of California-San Francisco found that radiation doses for scans in the same hospital varied as much as 13-fold with doses much higher than required.[78] In addition, many patients are inappropriately subjected to multiple CT scans. Some reasons cited for duplication are physicians refusing to accept scans performed in facilities other than their own, the inability to access scans performed in other facilities, and specialists requiring patients to receive scans prior to a patient's first visit.[78]

Recent initiatives to curb overuse of diagnostic procedures and treatments include the "Choosing Wisely" Campaign (the Campaign) discussed in Chapter 4. Guidelines issued by the Campaign include recommendations on appropriate use of head CT scans for emergency department (ED) patients.[79] A 2013 study of ED visits and imaging procedures from more than 700 hospitals in 45 states encompassing more than 600,000 minor head injury cases, found that almost two-thirds resulted in head CT scans—10 times more than the Campaign guidelines recommend. Other study findings noted that only 20 percent of EDs adhered to Campaign guidelines for patient complaints of fainting and headache.[79] Another study reported in 2015 concluded that most CT scans in the ED are unnecessary.[80] Reasons for excessive use of CT scanning include: technology availability, fears of missed diagnoses (and potential liability), physicians' perceptions of patients' desire for the test, patient expectations, and institutional financial pressure to make use of the equipment.[81]

As the foregoing examples illustrate, the issues of appropriate technology applications are multi-factorial involving matters such as personal and institutional financial incentives, patient expectations and demands, and the availability of the technology itself. As payers continue the direction toward rewarding higher value and more efficient care, there is reason for guarded optimism that appropriate changes will evolve.

▶ ACA and MACRA: Reemergence of Population Health Principles

Historically, the different value systems of population health-oriented public health practitioners and individually centered private health providers have been a great divide in the healthcare system. The scientific advances of the past decades heightened the value differences between practitioners with a population perspective versus those focused on the cure of individual patients. Physician education emphasizing sophisticated technologies and specialization left little opportunity for education on the core topics and concepts of population health. Despite the centrality of public health in providing basic health services and the well-documented economic advantages of prevention as compared with cure, public health has had neither public nor political recognition as an essential and all-encompassing effort to prevent illness and promote health.

However, core tenets of the ACA and the MACRA that focus on achieving improved population health by realigning reimbursement incentives from piecemeal care to care for population groups are forcing change. With delivery system reforms under these laws such as bundled payments for care, ACOs, and other alternative payment models, reimbursement drivers shift from a high-volume individually based orientation to prudent resource use linked with population health outcomes. Over time, these reforms have potential to begin closing the gap between the principles of public health and medicine.

The ACA also created the Prevention and Public Health Fund (the Fund), the nation's first mandatory funding stream dedicated to improving public health.[82] The Fund was intended to eliminate the previously unpredictable federal budget appropriations for public health and prevention programs. The ACA mandates the Fund's use to "improve health and help restrain the rate of growth in private and public sector health care costs," and emphasizes development of "a national prevention, health promotion and public health strategy."[82,83] The ACA originally authorized $18.75 billion for the Fund for fiscal years 2010–2022 and $2 billion in each succeeding year.[82] However, with funding reductions in 2012 and 2016 to accommodate other needs in the federal budget, the Fund was left with slightly less than 50 percent of its intended amount for public health prevention, wellness, and preparedness activities.[82] This outcome is a glaring example of political priorities pre-empting public health resource priorities.

The ACA includes several additional provisions with significant effects on public health. One example is the establishment of National Prevention, Health Promotion and Public Health Council (the Council) chaired by the U.S. Surgeon General to develop and lead a National Prevention Strategy that builds on existing federal programs such as *Healthy People 2020* and to make recommendations to the President and Congress for federal policy changes that support public health goals.[83–85] The Council currently provides leadership to and coordination of public health activities of 20 federal departments, agencies, and consults with outside experts and stakeholders.[84,85] The Council's 2014 report outlined several accomplishments made with community partners across the United States in areas such as tobacco control and promotion of enhanced nutritional supplementation for low-income children.[86] In the area of public health workforce development, the ACA has made significant new resources available to expand the public health workforce in underserved areas and reduce minority underrepresentation in the workforce ranks through scholarship and loan programs.[87–89]

In summary, population health-oriented provisions of the ACA and the MACRA hold promise of a healthcare system that recognizes, and most importantly supports, the centrality of population health concepts, principles, and practices to improving the health status of all Americans. As reforms advance, major challenges will remain to bring about necessary changes in strongly held perceptions and prior patterns of practice.

▶ Ethical Challenges

Physicians practicing in today's healthcare system confront a two-faced ethical challenge in assuring their patients receive the best possible care. The first face of the challenge is insurers' requirements that physicians conform to specific treatment, review, evaluation, reporting, service authorization, and financial criteria for reimbursement. Physician practices typically deal with multiple insurers, which often have differing requirements, creating enormous bureaucratic burdens that subtract substantial time from patient care. As the delivery system moves from volume-driven to value-driven models, it is expected that these burdens will increase. Physicians already admit the need to sometimes exaggerate the severity of a patient's condition to circumvent insurers' criteria in order to assure that patients receive necessary care. Another dimension to this ethical challenge recognizes the lure of traditional fee-for-service reimbursement that fuels overuse, and wasteful and inappropriate services. The core ethical dilemma resides in how to balance legitimate cost and quality concerns with patients' best interests as the primary consideration. Physicians will remain "caught in the middle" for the foreseeable future.

The second face of ethical challenges results from a "success" problem. Medicine's remarkable technologic advancement in the four past decades now enables life prolongation in a range from very premature infants to the terminally ill, to brain-dead individuals with no potential for future functional capacity. In the absence of transparent professional consensus on ethical guidelines to deal with decisions about continuing care in such cases, if a patient's family does not agree with an attending physician's recommendations, physicians are left without the support of professionally developed guidance.

In addition, among the most critical of future ethical issues are those related to advances in the field of molecular biology, gene manipulation, and gene therapy. The advent of inexpensive technology that will allow scientists to sequence an individual's entire DNA in less than 72 hours is on the horizon in the next decade. President Obama's proposed 2017 budget includes $309 million to "continue scaling up the Precision Medicine Initiative which is focused on developing treatments, diagnostics and prevention strategies tailored to the individual genetic characteristics of each patient."[90] As genome sequencing becomes more common, a host of unintended consequences and ethical issues will arise. The professional medical community is only beginning dialogue on the future obligations for the holders of individuals' genome data. Traditionally, laboratory tests are analyzed, reported, acted upon, and then archived. Genomic data is different because as more discoveries are made, periodic reanalysis of patients' genomic data could provide extremely valuable information for predicting future disease states and healthcare decision making. U.S. society has not even begun to approach questions about by whom, under what circumstances, and even whether or not such periodic reanalysis will be performed. These loom as significant future questions. In addition, training of physicians and other healthcare professionals about implications of the use of human genomic data in their practices will be an enormous future challenge. Enveloping all these challenges are concerns about the potential unethical applications of genome technology. In the future, the need for ethical discernment and transparent consensus on professional guidelines for medical practice will be paramount.

Finally, as discussed in Chapter 12, there are many research-related ethical concerns about conflicts of interest and appropriate public disclosure. Some of these have invoked legal actions.[91] Two of these concerns include shifting research funded by pharmaceutical and medical device companies from academic institutions to commercial research firms with obvious vested interests, and the shift of the FDA's funding from the federal government to the same pharmaceutical companies it is intended to monitor.[91,92] A provision of the ACA, the "Sunshine Act" that requires disclosures to the CMS about any payments or other transfers of value made to physicians or teaching hospitals, may help to bring these ethical breaches under control.[93] Another continuing ethical issue is the violation of professional ethics found in the growing body of evidence that physicians at some of the most prestigious U.S. medical schools have been attaching their names and reputations to scientific publications ghostwritten by employees of pharmaceutical companies to boost sales of pharmaceutical products.[93]

▶ Summary of Predictions and Future Questions

Although tensions continue between the advocates of immediate system revisions and those who prefer more limited, incremental changes, the passage of the ACA and the MACRA recognized the need for transformative system reforms.

Throughout the history of U.S. health care, the American public was persuaded to instruct its elected representatives that health care is an inherent "good." Arguments about the system's costs, disorganization, illogical redundancies, and inexplicable variations in quality and access were countered by prevailing beliefs that the healthcare system's scientific and technologic superiority offset its deficiencies.

The need to remedy the deficiencies in the U.S. healthcare system, however, grew to become undeniable concerns. An increasing proportion of American citizens and policymakers believed that the United States must develop a more socially responsible system of health care and end the nation's embarrassing distinction as the only Western world democracy that does not provide universal health insurance coverage for its citizens. Health insurance in the United States evolved from the professional and economic objectives of providers rather than consumer needs and was financed by a convoluted system of private insurance augmented by inadequately managed and inflationary public-sector programs. It is therefore not surprising that the resulting system has been characterized by escalating costs and glaring gaps in coverage. Clearly, the problems could not be satisfactorily solved without major structural revisions. Solutions to the problems of huge variations in costs, treatments, and outcomes; fragmented services; episodic treatment of illness; and poorly distributed over- and under-capacity in the healthcare system are engendered by solutions contained in the principles of the ACA and the MACRA:

- Alter the healthcare focus from diagnosing and treating illness to maintaining wellness and preventing illness
- Expand the healthcare system's accountability from the health status of individual patients to that of defined populations
- Change the health services' emphasis from acute episodic care to continuous comprehensive care and chronic disease management
- Eliminate the financial incentives to provide more services and substitute incentives to provide appropriate care at an appropriate level
- Change from merely coordinating the delivery of services to actively managing the quality of processes and outcomes
- Add a commitment to the resolution of community and public health issues

Healthcare reforms can make the systems of care different but cannot make health care better by themselves. Only healthcare providers working in concert with integrated systems can improve healthcare outcomes.

Reformed systems of reimbursement and accountability for population health outcomes intend to free primary care physicians and other providers from many of the incentives of fee-for-service medicine in order to allow practitioners to emphasize wellness and prevention and reduce unnecessary interventions. Reforms in this regard include a 2015 CMS rule that authorized Medicare payments for non-face-to-face care planning and coordination activities for patients with multiple chronic illnesses.[95] In 2016, CMS proposed another new Medicare payment rule to begin in 2017 that will compensate clinicians for their investment of time and other resources involved in primary care planning and coordination, mental health care, and care for cognitive impairment such as Alzheimer's disease. Announcing the proposed rule, the acting CMS administrator commented, "If this rule is finalized, it will put our nation's money where its mouth is by continuing to recognize the importance of prevention, wellness, and mental health and chronic disease management."[96]

A 2015 report issued by the international accounting firm KPMG noted that to be successful, the reformed, value-based U.S. healthcare system must include:[97]

- Patient engagement, with patients as active participants in healthcare decisions
- Outcome definition and measurement, transparent to providers and patients
- Coordinated care among all involved providers including community participants
- Strong governance earmarked by provider and management involvement
- Contracts that commit providers to an outcomes-oriented approach to patient care

The relationship of hospitals with physicians will take on increasing importance as more physicians join hospitals as employees and prior hospital–physician relationships continue to undergo profound change in new integrated models of care delivery.

The changing demographics of an aging U.S. population will require major expansions of long-term care facilities and services. Long-term care will become an increasingly complex array of services integrated into vertical care systems. Of all the problems facing the future healthcare system, the aging population, with its attendant burdens of chronic disease and disability, presents a most formidable organizational and economic challenge. Long-term care facilities and services will be confronted with developing long-range plans to cope with burgeoning future demands.

The growing demand for support of chronic care will continue, driving changes in the national healthcare system structure. As increasing numbers of middle-aged Americans find themselves faced with the care of aged and functionally limited relatives, the demand for expanded support of chronic-care services will increase. Public awareness of the deficiencies of the current system will grow and likely bring considerable pressure for policy changes in care-giving systems and supports.

Although the healthcare system is in considerable turmoil in this reform era, it is certain that the healthcare sciences will continue to make progress. Clinicians and researchers will adopt advances such as devices for minimally invasive surgery, gene mapping and therapy, new vaccines, and other advances that will continue to transform the practice of medicine.

These dramatic advances, however, will be accompanied by new and vexing problems of cost, accessibility, training, and professional ethics. The availability of new knowledge also vastly exceeds the capacity of the institutions that deliver and finance health care to access and use it. The enormous potential for good that the U.S. healthcare system enjoys comes with deep concerns. How will the recipients of new technology be chosen? Who will address the ethical dilemmas that accompany genetic manipulation? When will the need to set stricter standards of competence when people's lives are at stake be faced by the medical profession? When will the government reign in the unlimited profits of pharmaceutical firms that price their drugs beyond the means of those who need them the most? These and many other issues are central to a future constructive reformation of U.S. healthcare system.

The ACA and the MACRA represent new and pragmatic approaches to addressing longstanding problems in the U.S. healthcare system. No matter how successful these laws turn out, the facts will remain that the laws represent historic landmarks after the nation's long history of other attempts and failures made to enact much-needed healthcare reforms.

These are exciting times for students of health care. Never have large changes in an essential industry held the potential to intimately affect so many people. It is a time for introspection regarding values, circumspection regarding advocacy for positions, and careful review of ongoing experimental changes. Will healthcare system reforms achieve the long-sought balance among the key issues of access, cost, and quality? Can the United States achieve a more optimal health policy scenario marked by fiscal and clinical accountability for defined populations, equitable resource allocations, and transparent reporting on costs and quality? Answers to the foregoing and other questions will await actual experience and rigorous research over the next several years.

KEY TERMS FOR REVIEW

Employer Mandate
Hospitalist
Medicare Access and CHIP
  Reauthorization Act of 2015
  (MACRA)

National Health Care
  Workforce Commission
  (NHCWC)

Patient Protection and
  Affordable Care Act of 2010
  (ACA)

CHAPTER ACRONYMS

AAMC American Association of Medical
  Colleges
ACO Accountable care organization
AHRQ Agency for Healthcare Research and
  Quality
ASC Ambulatory surgery center
CMS Centers for Medicare & Medicaid
  Services
CT Computed tomography

DHHS Department of Health and Human
  Services
ED Emergency department
EHR Electronic health record
IOM Institute of Medicine
HDHP High-deductible health plan
HIT Health information technology
IMRT Intensity-modulated radiotherapy
RHIO Regional health information organization

References

1. Longest BB. *Health Policymaking in the United States*. Chicago, IL: Health Administration Press; 2016:307.
2. Congressional Budget Office. Updated estimates of the insurance coverage provisions of the Affordable Care Act. March 2016. Available from https://www.cbo.gov/sites/default/files/114th-congress-2015-2016/reports/49892/49892-breakout-AppendixB.pdf. Accessed May 25, 2016.
3. Gleick J. Chaos: making a new science. In: Sifonis JG, Goldberg B, eds. *Corporation on a Tightrope: Balancing Leadership, Governance, and Technology in an Age of Complexity*. New York: Viking; 1987:9.
4. DeVoe JE, Bazemore AW, Cottrell EK, et al. A conceptual framework and path for integrating social determinants of health into primary care practice. *Ann Fam Med*. 2016;14:104-108. http://www.annfammed.org/content/14/2/104.full. Accessed June 11, 2016.
5. Health Policy Brief. Reducing waste in health care. December 13, 2012. *Health Aff*. http://healthaffairs.org/healthpolicybriefs/brief_pdfs/healthpolicybrief_82.pdf. Accessed June 11, 2016.
6. Committee on Quality of Health Care in America, Institute of Medicine, Kohn LT, Corrigan JM, Donaldson MS, eds. *To Err Is Human: Building a Safer Health System*. Washington, DC: National Academy Press; 2000.
7. James JT. A new evidence-based estimate of patient harms associated with hospital care. *J Patient Saf*. 2013;9:122-128. http://journals.lww.com/journalpatientsafety/Fulltext/2013/09000/A_New,_Evidence_based_Estimate_of_Patient_Harms.2.aspx?TB_iframe=true&width=288&height=432. Accessed June 11, 2016.
8. Makary MA, Daniel M. Medical error—the third leading cause of death in the US. *BMJ*. 2016;353:i2139-2141. http://www.bmj.com/content/bmj/353/bmj.i2139.full.pdf. Accessed May 17, 2016.
9. Alper BS, Hand JA, Elliott SG, et al. How much effort is needed to keep up with the literature relevant for primary care? *J Med Libr Assoc*. 2004;92:429-437.
10. Agency for Healthcare Research and Quality Patient Safety Network. WebM&M cases and commentaries. https://psnet.ahrq.gov/webmm. Accessed June 13, 2016.
11. Centers for Medicare & Medicaid Services. Hospital quality initiative. July 2008. https://www.cms.gov/Medicare/Quality-Initiatives-Patient-Assessment-Instruments/HospitalQualityInits/downloads/HospitalOverview.pdf. Accessed June 16, 2016.

12. Centers for Medicare & Medicaid Services. The Affordable Care Act: helping providers help patients. https://www.cms.gov/Medicare/Medicare-Fee-for-Service-Payment/ACO/Downloads/ACO-Menu-Of-Options.pdf. Accessed May 16, 2016.

13. Centers for Medicare & Medicaid Services. Hospital-acquired conditions. https://www.cms.gov/Medicare/Medicare-Fee-for-Service-Payment/HospitalAcqCond/Hospital-Acquired_Conditions.html. Accessed May 21, 2016.

14. Agency for Healthcare Research and Quality. Patient Safety Network. Patient safety primer: never events. https://psnet.ahrq.gov/primers/primer/3/never-events. Accessed May 21, 2016.

15. Centers for Medicare & Medicaid Services. CMS quality strategy 2016. https://www.cms.gov/medicare/quality-initiatives-patient-assessment-instruments/qualityinitiativesgeninfo/downloads/cms-quality-strategy.pdf. Accessed June 11, 2016.

16. Moran J, Scanlon D. Slow progress on meeting hospital safety standards: learning from the Leapfrog Group's efforts. *Health Aff.* 2013;32:27-34. http://content.healthaffairs.org/content/32/1/27.full.html. Accessed June 13, 2016.

17. Smith S, Heffler S, Freeland M. The next decade of health care spending: a new outlook. *Health Aff.* 1999;18:89-90.

18. Centers for Medicare & Medicaid. Medicare Access and CHIP Reauthorization Act of 2015: Quality Payment Program. https://www.cms.gov/Medicare/Quality-Initiatives-Patient-Assessment-Instruments/Value-Based-Programs/MACRA-MIPS-and-APMs/NPRM-QPP-Fact-Sheet.pdf. Accessed June 14, 2016.

19. Centers for Medicare & Medicaid Services. *CMS Quality Measure Development Plan: Supporting the Transition to the Merit-based Incentive Payment System (MIPS) and Alternative Payment Models (APMs).* Baltimore, MD: Centers for Medicare & Medicaid Services;2016.https://www.cms.gov/Medicare/Quality-Initiatives-Patient-Assessment-Instruments/Value-Based-Programs/MACRA-MIPS-and-APMs/MACRA-MIPS-and-APMs.html. Accessed June 16, 2016.

20. Lowes R. Delay MACRA, organized medicine tells CMS. *Medscape Medical News.* June 28, 2016. http://www.medscape.com/viewarticle/865464. Accessed June 30, 2016.

21. Lowes, R. Many physicians predict mass exodus from Medicare over MACRA. Medscape Medical News. June 28, 2016. http://www.medscape.com/viewarticle/865288?nlid=107587_2048&src=WNL_mdplsnews_160701_mscpedit_imed&uac=28608SZ&spon=18&impID=1144337&faf=1#vp_2. Accessed June 30, 2016.

22. Kutscher B. Docs face stark choices under new Medicare pay proposal. *Mod Healthc.* April 30, 2016.

http://www.modernhealthcare.com/article/20160430/MAGAZINE/304309988. Accessed May 18, 2016.

23. Sittig DF, Ash JS, Zhang J, Osheroff JA, Shabot MM. Lessons from "unexpected increased mortality after implementation of a commercially sold computerized physician order entry system." *Pediatrics.* 2006;118:797-801.

24. Hsiao CJ, Hing E. Use and characteristics of electronic health record systems among office-based physician practices: United States, 2001–2013, NCHS data brief no. 143. 2015. http://www.cdc.gov/nchs/data/databriefs/db143.htm. Accessed March 9, 2016.

25. Conway PH, Gronniger T, Pham H, et al. MACRA: new opportunities for Medicare providers through innovative payment systems (updated). Health Affairs Blog. September 28, 2015. http://healthaffairs.org/blog/2015/09/28/macra-new-opportunities-for-medicare-providers-through-innovative-payment-systems-3/. Accessed March 8, 2016.

26. Charles D, Gabriel M, Searcy T. Adoption of electronic health record systems among U.S. nonfederal acute care hospitals: 2008–2014, ONC data brief no. 23. https://www.healthit.gov/sites/default/files/data-brief/2014HospitalAdoptionDataBrief.pdf. Accessed March 9, 2016.

27. Daly R. Hospital deal uptick continues. Healthcare Financial Management Association. October 21, 2015. http://www.hfma.org/Content.aspx?id=42986. Accessed September 15, 2016.

28. Gunderman R. Should doctors work for hospitals? *The Atlantic.* May 27, 2014. http://www.theatlantic.com/health/archive/2014/05/should-doctors-work-for-hospitals/371638/. Accessed April 8, 2016.

29. Richman BD, Schulman KA. A cautious path forward on accountable care organizations. *JAMA.* 2011;305:602-603.

30. Melnick GA, Fonkych K. Hospital prices increase in California, especially among hospitals in the largest multi-hospital systems. *Inquiry.* 2016;53:1-7. http://inq.sagepub.com/content/53/0046958016651555.full.pdf±html. Accessed June 18, 2016.

31. Lee PG. Who makes sure hospital mergers do no harm? Almost nobody. *Health Leaders' Media.* June 10, 2016. http://www.healthleadersmedia.com/leadership/who-makes-sure-hospital-mergers-do-no-harm-almost-nobody. Accessed June 18, 2016.

32. U.S. Department of Health and Human Services, Administration on Aging, Administration for Community Living. Projected future growth of the older population by age 1900–2050, persons 65 and older. http://www.aoa.acl.gov/aging_statistics/future_growth/future_growth.aspx#. Accessed February 4, 2016.

33. Center for Medicare Advocacy. Non-profit vs. for-profit nursing homes: is there a difference in care? 2012. http://www.medicareadvocacy.org/non-profit-vs-for-profit-nursing-homes-is-there-a-difference-in-care/. Accessed February 5, 2016.

34. U.S. Department of Commerce. U.S. Census Bureau. An aging nation: the older population in the United States. May 2014. https://www.census.gov/prod/2014pubs/p25-1140.pdf. Accessed April 7, 2016.

35. Wolf DA. Population change: friend or foe of the chronic care system? *Health Aff.* 2001;20:64-78. http://content.healthaffairs.org/content/20/6/28. Accessed April 9, 2016.

36. Merlis M. *Financing Long Term Care in the Twenty-first Century: The Public and Private Roles*. Institute for Health Policy Solutions. New York, NY: The Commonwealth Fund; 1999:20. http://www.commonwealthfund.org/~/media/files/publications/fund-report/1999/sep/long-term-care-financing-in-the-twenty-first-century--the-public-and-private-roles/merlis343-pdf.pdf. Accessed March 20, 2016.

37. Stone R, Harahan MF. Improving the long-term care workforce serving older adults. *Health Aff.* 2010;29:109-115. http://content.healthaffairs.org/content/29/1/109.full.pdf±html. Accessed March 20, 2016.

38. Paraprofessional Healthcare Institute. Home care workers deserve minimum wage & overtime. http://phinational.org/campaigns/home-care-workers-deserve-minimum-wage-protection. Accessed March 20, 2016.

39. National Partnership for Women & Families. Family and Medical Insurance Act (FAMILY Act). March 2015. http://www.nationalpartnership.org/issues/work-family/family-act.html. Accessed June 21, 2016.

40. Medicaid.gov. Improving care transitions. https://www.medicaid.gov/medicaid-chip-program-information/by-topics/quality-of-care/care-transitions.html. Accessed June 21, 2016.

41. Medicare Payment Advisory Commission. Report to the Congress. Chapter 9. March 2015. http://www.medpac.gov/docs/default-source/reports/mar2015_entirereport_revised.pdf?sfvrsn=0. Accessed September 15, 2016.

42. Pew Research Center. Baby boomers retire. December 29, 2010. http://www.pewresearch.org/daily-number/baby-boomers-retire/. Accessed June 21, 2016.

43. Pallardy C, Becker S. 50 things to know about the ambulatory surgery center industry. Becker's ASC Review. http://www.beckersasc.com/lists/50-things-to-know-about-the-ambulatory-surgery-center-industry.html. Accessed February 23, 2016.

44. Fields R. Number of ambulatory surgery centers approaches number of hospitals nationwide. Becker's ASC Review. http://www.beckersasc.com/asc-transactions-and-valuation-issues/number-of-ambulatory-surgery-centers-approaches-number-of-hospitals-nationwide.html. Accessed February 23, 2016.

45. Becker's Hospital Review. 20 things to know about urgent care. http://www.ucaoa.org/blogpost/1190415/239114/20-Things-to-Know-About-Urgent-Care--2016. Accessed February 16, 2016.

46. Accenture. Number of U.S. retail health clinics will surpass 2,800 by 2017, Accenture forecasts. https://newsroom.accenture.com/news/number-of-us-retail-health-clinics-will-surpass-2800-by-2017-accenture-forecasts.htm. Accessed February 14, 2016.

47. Bachrach D, Frohlic J, Garcimonde A, Nevitt K. Building a culture of health: the value proposition of retail clinics. April 2015. The Robert Wood Johnson Foundation. http://www.rwjf.org/content/dam/farm/reports/issue_briefs/2015/rwjf419415. Accessed February 14, 2016.

48. National Center for Health Statistics. Health, United States, 2014: With Special Feature on Adults Aged 55-64. Hyattsville, MD. 2015. Table 82 (page 2 of 3). Visits to physician offices, hospital outpatient departments, and hospital emergency departments, by age, sex and race: United States, selected years 1995–2011. http://www.cdc.gov/nchs/data/hus/hus14.pdf#082. Accessed January 14, 2016.

49. Hernandez-Boussard T, Burns CS, Wang NE, Baker LC, Goldstein BA. The Affordable Care Act reduces emergency department use by young adults: evidence from three states. *Health Aff.* 2014;33:1648-1654. http://www.ncbi.nlm.nih.gov/pmc/articles/PMC4453768/. Accessed September 15, 2016.

50. American College of Emergency Physicians. ER visits continue to rise since implementation of the Affordable Care Act. May 4, 2015. http://newsroom.acep.org/2015-05-04-ER-Visits-Continue-to-Rise-Since-Implementation-of-Affordable-Care-Act. Accessed June 19, 2016.

51. United States Bureau of Labor Statistics. Occupational employment and wages summary. March 30, 2016. http://www.bls.gov/news.release/ocwage.nr0.htm. Accessed May 14, 2016.

52. United States Bureau of Labor Statistics. Employment projections: 2014–24 summary. December 8, 2015. http://www.bls.gov/news.release/ecopro.nr0.htm. Accessed April 5, 2016.

53. American Association of Medical Colleges. Results of the 2014 medical school enrollment survey. April 2015. https://members.aamc.org/eweb/upload/Results%20of%20the%202014%20Medical%20School%20Enrollment%20Survey.pdf. Accessed April 20, 2016.

54. Grover A, Orlowski JM, Erikson CE. The nations physician workforce and future. *Am J Med Sci*. 2016;351:11-19.

55. American Association of Medical Colleges. Physician supply and demand through 2025: key findings. March 2015. https://www.aamc.org/download/426260/data/physiciansupplyanddemandthrough2025keyfindings.pdf. Accessed April 3, 2016.

56. American Association of Medical Colleges. AAMC summaries of DGME and IME sections of the Health Reform Bill and CMS proposed rules implementing these provisions. July 28, 2010. https://www.aamc.org/download/163590/data/summaries_of_gme

_sections_of_health_reform_bill_.pdf. Accessed March 25, 2016.

57. Henry J. Kaiser Family Foundation. Summary of the Affordable Care Act. April 25, 2013. http://kff.org/health-reform/fact-sheet/summary-of-the-affordable-care-act/. Accessed March 25, 2016.

58. Association of American Medical Colleges. 2015 state physician workforce data book. November 2015. http://members.aamc.org/eweb/upload/2015 StateDataBook%20(revised).pdf. Accessed March 30, 2016.

59. Glabman M. Hospitalists: The next big thing? *Trustee*. 2005;58:6-11.

60. Society of Hospital Medicine. Centers for Medicare & Medicaid Services grants billing code for hospitalists. February 26, 2016. http://www.hospitalmedicine.org /Web/Media_Center/Press_Release/2016/medicaid -code-feb25.aspx?utm_source=Web_banner&utm _medium=web&utm_content=2.25_Bill%20 Code&utm_campaign=Advocacy_16. Accessed March 8, 2016.

61. Becker's Hospital Review. 8 statistics on physician employment. July 14, 2014. http://www.becker shospitalreview.com/hospital-physician-relationships /8-statistics-on-physician-employment.html. Accessed April 9, 2016.

62. Singleton T, Miller P. The physician employment trend: What you need to know. *Fam Pract Manag*. 2015;22:11-15.

63. Gunderman R. Should doctors work for hospitals? *The Atlantic*. May 27, 2014. http://www.theatlantic .com/health/archive/2014/05/should-doctors-work -for-hospitals/371638/. Accessed April 8, 2016.

64. Colla C, Lewis VA, Shortell SA, Fisher ES. First national survey of ACOs finds that physicians are playing strong leadership and ownership roles. *Health Aff*. 2014;33:964-971. http://content.healthaffairs.org /content/33/6/964.full.pdf±html. Accessed June 19, 2016.

65. Auerbach DI, Buerhaus PI, Staiger DO. Registered nurses are delaying retirement, a shift that has contributed to recent growth in the nurse workforce. *Health Aff*. July 16, 2014;33:1-7. http://content .healthaffairs.org/content/33/8/1474. Accessed June 19, 2016.

66. United States Department of Health and Human Services. Health Resources and Services Administration. *The U.S. Nursing Workforce: Trends in Supply and Education*. April 2013. http://bhpr .hrsa.gov/healthworkforce/reports/nursing workforce/nursingworkforcefullreport.pdf. Accessed April 28, 2016.

67. Hahn A, Sussman J. Foundations and Health Care Reform 2010. Policy brief: improving workforce efficiency. Brandeis University: The Heller School for Social and Policy Management; July 14, 2010. http://

sillermancenter.brandeis.edu/PDFs/Workforce%20 Policy%20Brief%20in%20conf%20template%20v2 .pdf. Accessed May 14, 2016.

68. Bipartisan Policy Center. The complexities of national health care workforce planning: executive summary. October 18, 2011. http://bipartisanpolicy.org/sites /default/files/Workforce%20study_Public%20 Release%20040912.pdf. Accessed May 14, 2016.

69. Buerhaus PJ, Retchin S. The dormant National Health Care Workforce Commission needs Congressional funding to fulfill its mission. *Health Aff*. 2013; 32:2021-2024. http://content.healthaffairs.org/content /32/11/2021.full.pdf±html?sid=0a59ca29-9f68-4451 -839d-767ae642cc9a. Accessed June 19, 2016.

70. Shanafelt TD, Hasan O, Dyrbye LN, et al. Changes in burnout and satisfaction with work-life balance in physicians and the general US working population between 2011 and 2014. *Mayo Clin Proc*. 2015;90:1600-1613.

71. The Henry J. Kaiser Family Foundation and Health Research & Educational Trust. 2015 employer health benefits survey: summary of findings. September 22, 2015. http://kff.org/report-section/ehbs-2015-summary -of-findings/. Accessed May 17, 2016.

72. Obamacare Facts. Obamacare employer mandate. http://obamacarefacts.com/obamacare-employer -mandate/. Accessed May 24, 2016.

73. Inama M. Will your employer still pay for your health insurance in five years? *Leavitt Partners*. May 28, 2015. http://leavittpartners.com/2015/05/will-your -employer-still-pay-for-your-health-insurance-in -five-years/. Accessed June 26, 2016.

74. Claxton G, Rae M, Panchal N, et al. Health benefits in 2015: stable trends in the employer market. *Health Aff*. 2015;34:1779-1788. http://content.healthaffairs .org/content/34/10/1779. Accessed June 26, 2016.

75. Islam I. Trouble ahead for high deductible health plans? Health Affairs Blog. October 7, 2015. http:// healthaffairs.org/blog/2015/10/07/trouble-ahead-for -high-deductible-health-plans/. Accessed May 17, 2016.

76. Goozner M. End the medical arms race. *Mod Healthc*. June 29, 2013. http://www.modernhealthcare.com /article/20130629/MAGAZINE/306299988. Accessed June 4, 2016.

77. Jacobs BL, Zhang Y, Skolarus TA, Hollenbeck BK. Growth of high-cost intensity-modulated radiotherapy for prostate cancer raises concerns about overuse. *Health Aff*. 2012;31:750-759. http://content .healthaffairs.org/content/31/4/750.full.pdf±html. Accessed June 11, 2016.

78. Boodman SG. Heavy use of CT scans raises concerns about patients' exposure to radiation. *Kaiser Health News*. January 6, 2016. http://khn.org/news/heavy -use-of-ct-scans-raises-concerns-about-patients -exposure-to-radiation/. Accessed June 18, 2016.

79. Koppenheffer M. New evidence of head CT scan overuse in the ED. Advisory Board. February 20, 2015. https://www.advisory.com/research/physician-executive-council/prescription-for-change/2015/02/head-ct-scan-overuse. Accessed June 18, 2016.

80. Mitsunaga MM, Yoon HC. Journal club: head CT scans in the emergency department for syncope and dizziness. *Am J Roentgenol.* 2015;204:24-28. http://www.ncbi.nlm.nih.gov/pubmed/25539233. Accessed June 18, 2016.

81. Galewitz P. ER use of CT scans rises sharply, raising questions about costs and benefits. *Kaiser Health News.* August 10, 2011. http://khn.org/news/er-use-of-ct-scans-rises-sharply-raising-questions-about-costs-and-benefits/. Accessed June 20, 2016.

82. American Public Health Association. Prevention and Public Health Fund fact sheet 2016. https://www.apha.org/~/media/files/pdf/factsheets/160127_pphf.ashx. Accessed April 26, 2016.

83. Staff of the Washington Post. *Landmark: The Inside Story of America's New Health-Care Law and What It Means for All of Us.* New York: Perseus Books Group; 2002:224.

84. The Institute for Healthcare Consumerism. Obama administration releases national prevention strategy. http://www.theihcc.com/en/communities/policy_legislation/obama-administration-releases-national-prevention-_gozwz678.html. Accessed May 18, 2016.

85. Majette GR. PPACA and public health: creating a framework to focus on prevention and wellness and improve the public's health. *J Law Med Ethics.* 2011;39:373-374. http://www2.law.csuohio.edu/newsevents/images/39JLME366.pdf. Accessed May 18, 2016.

86. National Prevention Council. Annual status report. Washington, DC: U.S. Department of Health and Human Services, Office of the Surgeon General; 2014. http://www.surgeongeneral.gov/priorities/prevention/2014-npc-status-report.pdf. Accessed May 19, 2016.

87. Health Resources and Services Administration. Implementing our strategic plan: activities and accomplishments in fiscal year 2013. http://www.hrsa.gov/about/strategicplanimplementation2013.pdf. Accessed May 18, 2016.

88. Democratic Policy and Communications Center. The Patient Protection and Affordable Care Act. http://dpc.senate.gov/healthreformbill/healthbill52.pdf. Accessed May 18, 2016.

89. American Nurses Association. Health care transformation: the Affordable Care Act and more, June 18, 2014. http://nursingworld.org/MainMenuCategories/Policy-Advocacy/HealthSystemReform/AffordableCareAct.pdf. Accessed May 18, 2016.

90. Department of Health and Human Services. Fiscal year 2017 budget in brief. Strengthening health and opportunity for all Americans. http://www.hhs.gov/sites/default/files/fy2017-budget-in-brief.pdf. Accessed April 9, 2016.

91. State of New Jersey Office of the Attorney General. Landmark settlement reached with medical device maker synthes. 2009. http://www.nj.gov/oag/newsreleases09/pr20090505a.html. Accessed September 15, 2016.

92. United States Department of Health and Human Services. Office of Inspector General. The Food and Drug Administration's oversight of clinical investigators' financial information. January 2009. http://oig.hhs.gov/oei/reports/oei-05-07-00730.pdf. Accessed May 28, 2016.

93. The physician payments Sunshine Act. October 2, 2014. *Health Aff.* http://www.healthaffairs.org/healthpolicybriefs/brief.php?brief_id=127. Accessed June 2, 2016.

94. Singer N. Senator moves to block medical ghostwriting. *New York Times.* August 18, 2009. http://www.nytimes.com/2009/08/19/health/research/19ethics.html?_r=2&scp=1&sq=Ghosts%20in%20the%20Journals&st=cse. Accessed June 12, 2016.

95. Centers for Medicare & Medicaid Services. Chronic care management services. May 2015. https://www.cms.gov/Outreach-and-Education/Medicare-Learning-Network-MLN/MLNProducts/Downloads/ChronicCareManagement.pdf. Accessed June 25, 2016.

96. Centers for Medicare & Medicaid Services. Medicare proposes substantial improvements to paying for care coordination and planning, primary care, and mental health in doctor payment rule. July 7, 2016. https://www.cms.gov/Newsroom/MediaReleaseDatabase/Press-releases/2016-Press-releases-items/2016-07-07.html. Accessed July 8, 2016.

97. PR Newswire. Value-based healthcare puts focus on patient outcomes. March 25, 2015. http://www.prnewswire.com/news-releases/value-based-healthcare-puts-focus-on-patient-outcomes-300055550.html. Accessed June 21, 2016.

Appendix A

Websites

▶ U.S. Government

Administration for Children and Families:
http://www.acf.hhs.gov/

Administration for Community Living:
http://www.acl.gov/

Administration on Aging:
http://www.aoa.gov/

Agency for Healthcare Research and Quality:
http://www.ahrq.gov/

Agency for Toxic Substances and Disease Registry:
http://www.atsdr.cdc.gov/

American Recovery and Reinvestment Act of 2009:
https://www.gpo.gov/fdsys/pkg/BILLS
-111hr1enr/pdf/BILLS-111hr1enr.pdf

Bureau of Labor Statistics:
http://bls.gov/

Centers for Disease Control and Prevention:
http://www.cdc.gov/

Centers for Medicare & Medicaid Services:
http://www.cms.gov/

Children's Health Insurance Program (CHIP):
https://www.medicaid.gov/chip/chip
-program-information.html

Congressional Budget Office:
http://www.cbo.gov/

Congressional Research Service Careers:
https://www.loc.gov/crsinfo/

Department of Health and Human Services:
http://www.hhs.gov/

Department of Veterans Affairs:
http://www.va.gov

Federal Trade Commission:
http://www.FTC.gov

Food and Drug Administration:
http://www.fda.gov/

Health Resources and Services Administration:
http://www.hrsa.gov/

Indian Health Service:
http://www.ihs.gov/

Medicare Payment Advisory Commission:
http://medpac.gov/

National Center for Complementary and Integrative Health:
http://www.nccih.nih.gov/

National Center for Health Statistics:
http://www.cdc.gov/nchs/

National Guideline Clearinghouse:
http://guideline.gov/

National Institute on Drug Abuse:
https://www.drugabuse.gov/

National Institutes of Health:
http://www.nih.gov/

National Library of Medicine Databases:
http://clinicaltrials.gov/ and http://www
.nlm.nih.gov/medlineplus/

National Institute on Drug Abuse:
https://www.drugabuse.gov/

Office of Disease Prevention and Health
Promotion:
https://health.gov/

Office of the National Coordinator for
Health Information Technology:
http://www.healthit.gov/

Patient Protection and Affordable Care Act
of 2010:
https://www.gpo.gov/fdsys/pkg/PLAW
-111publ148/pdf/PLAW-111publ148.pdf

Substance Abuse and Mental Health
Services Administration:
http://www.samhsa.gov/

Veterans Health Administration:
http://www.va.gov/health/

▶ Non-governmental Organizations

AARP (formerly American Association of
Retired Persons)
http://www.aarp.org

Accreditation Council for Graduate Medical
Education:
www.acgme.org

Ambulatory Surgery Center Association:
http://www.ascassociation.org/home

American Association for Homecare:
https://www.aahomecare.org

American Association of Colleges of
Osteopathic Medicine:
www.aacom.org

American Academy of Family Physicians:
http://www.aafp.org/home.html

American Academy of Urgent Care
Medicine:
http://aaucm.org/

American Association of Medical Colleges:
http://www.aamc.org

American Board of Emergency Medicine:
https://www.abem.org/public/

American College of Physicians:
https://www.acponline.org/

American Hospital Association:
http://www.aha.org

American Board of Medical Specialties:
http://www.abms.org/

American Board of Internal Medicine:
www.abim.org

American Health Care Association:
http://www.ahcancal.org/Pages/Default
.aspx

American Health Information Management
Association:
http://www.ahima.org/

America's Health Insurance Plans:
http://www.ahip.org/

American Medical Association:
http://www.ama-assn.org/ama

American Medical Informatics Association:
https://www.amia.org/

American Nurses Association:
http://nursingworld.org/

American Public Health Association:
http://www.apha.org

Association of Academic Health Centers:
http://www.aahcdc.org/

Association of American Medical Colleges:
http://www.aamc.org

Association of State and Territorial Health
Officials:
http://www.astho.org/

Commonwealth Fund:
http://www.commonwealthfund.org/

Families USA:
http://www.familiesusa.org/

Healthcare Information and Management
Systems Society:
http://www.himss.org/

Henry J. Kaiser Family Foundation:
http://www.kff.org/

Institute for Healthcare Improvement:
www.ihi.org

Joint Commission:
http://www.jointcommission.org/

Medscape:
http://www.medscape.com/

Modern Healthcare:
http://www.modernhealthcare.com/

National Academy of Medicine (formerly
Institute of Medicine):
https://nam.edu/

National Alliance for Caregiving:
http://www.caregiving.org/

National Alliance on Mental Illness:
http://www.nami.org/

National Association for Home Care &
Hospice:
http://www.nahc.org/

National Association of Community Health
Centers:
http://nachc.org/

National Association of County & City
Health Officials:
http://www.naccho.org

National Center for Assisted Living:
https://www.ahcancal.org/ncal/Pages
/index.aspx

National Committee for Quality
Assurance:
http://www.ncqa.org/

National Council on Aging:
http://www.ncoa.org/

National Institute of Mental Health:
http://nimh.gov/index.shtml

National Prevention Strategy:
http://www.surgeongeneral.gov
/priorities/prevention/strategy/

Robert Wood Johnson Foundation:
https://www.rwjf.org/

Urgent Care Association of America:
http://www.ucaoa.org/

U.S. Government Accountability Office:
www.gao.gov

World Bank (World Development
Indicators)
http://databank.worldbank.org/data
/download/GDP.pdf

World Health Organization:
http://www.who.int/en/

Glossary

A

Academic health center: A university-affiliated complex of professional, academic, and clinical care facilities such as medicine, nursing, pharmacy, dentistry, and allied health professions that are the principal places of education and training for physicians and other healthcare personnel, the sites for most basic medical research, and the settings for clinical trials. Academic health center teaching hospitals are major providers of highly sophisticated patient care required by trauma centers; burn centers; neonatal intensive care centers; and the technologically advanced treatment of cancer, heart disease, and neurologic and other acute and chronic conditions. Academic health center teaching hospitals also provide much of the primary care for the economically disadvantaged populations in their geographical area.

Accountable care organization (ACO): A group of providers and suppliers of health care, health-related services, and others involved in caring for Medicare patients that voluntarily work together to coordinate care for the patients they serve under the original Medicare (not Medicare Advantage managed care) program. The ACA enables ACOs to share in savings to the federal government based on performance in improving quality and reducing healthcare costs.

Accreditation: A process whereby a professional organization or non-governmental agency grants recognition to a school, educational program, or healthcare institution for demonstrated ability to meet predetermined criteria for established standards. Accreditation contrasts with certification, which is a process through which a state or professional organization attests to an individual's advanced training and performance abilities in a field of healthcare practice.

Accreditation Council for Graduate Medical Education (ACGME): The independent, not-for-profit professional organization that accredits 3–7 year programs of advanced education and clinical practice required by physicians to provide direct patient care in a recognized medical specialty.

Agency for Healthcare Research and Quality (AHRQ): The federal agency charged with research to develop and disseminate evidence-based practice guidelines. The AHRQ's National Guideline Clearinghouse maintains an online database organized by searchable topics for more than 2000 evidence-based clinical practice guidelines that have met AHRQ evaluation criteria.

Aging in place: A healthcare system that brings together a variety of health and other supportive services to enable older, frail adults to live independently in their own residences for as long as is safely possible.

Alternative medicine: The practice of using non-mainstream treatment approaches in place of conventional medicine.

Alternative payment model (APM): A model through which physicians and other healthcare providers accept a measure of financial risk and are reimbursed based upon prudent resource use and the quality of patient outcomes rather than on a piecemeal fee-for-service basis. Examples of APMs include bundled payments for care and accountable care organizations.

Ambulatory care: Services that do not require an overnight hospital stay.

Ambulatory surgery center (ASC): A facility performing surgical and nonsurgical procedures on an ambulatory (outpatient) basis in a hospital or freestanding center's general operating rooms, dedicated ambulatory surgery rooms, and other specialized rooms such as endoscopy units and cardiac catheterization labs.

American Board of Medical Specialties (ABMS): An independent, not-for-profit organization, the ABMS assists its 24 specialty member boards to develop and utilize professional and educational standards that apply to the certification of physician specialists in the United States and internationally.

Analytic studies: Test hypotheses and try to explain biologic phenomena by seeking statistical associations between factors that may contribute to a subsequent occurrence and the initial occurrence itself.

Assessment (as a core function of public health): Collecting and analyzing data to define population health status and quantify existing or emerging health problems.

Assisted living: A program that provides and/or arranges for daily meals, personal and other supportive services, health care, and 24-hour oversight to persons residing in a group residential facility who need assistance with the activities of daily living.

Assurance (as a core function of public health): Governmental public health agency responsibility to ensure that basic components of the healthcare delivery system are in place.

B

Balanced Budget Act of 1997 (BBA): The Act contained significant changes to Medicare and Medicaid. It extended healthcare coverage to uninsured children with a major funding allocation to a new Children's Health Insurance Program (CHIP). The Act also proposed to reduce growth in Medicare and Medicaid spending by $125.2 billion in five years. It increased beneficiary premiums for Medicare Part B and required new prospective payment systems for hospital outpatient services, skilled nursing facilities, home health agencies, and rehabilitation hospitals. One of its most significant effects was opening the Medicare program to private insurers through the Medicare+Choice Program, by allowing financial risk sharing for the Medicare program with the private sector through managed care plans.

Basic science research: Conducted by biochemists, physiologists, biologists, pharmacologists, and others concerned with sciences that are fundamental to understanding the growth, development, structure, and functions of the human body and its responses to external stimuli. Much basic science research is conducted at the cellular level.

Behavioral scientist: Behavioral scientists include professionals in social work, health education, community mental health, alcoholism and drug abuse services, and other health and human service areas. Bachelor's or master's level degree professionals in these fields counsel and support individuals and families in addressing the personal, economic, and social problems associated with illness, addictions, employment challenges, and disabilities.

Block grants: Mechanism to shift the federal government's direct support and administration of healthcare programs to state and local governments.

Bundled payment for care initiative (BPCI): Developed by the CMS Center for Medicare & Medicaid Innovation (CMMI) that was created by the ACA; the BPCI recognizes that separate Medicare fee-for-service payments for individual services provided during a beneficiary's single illness result in fragmented care with minimal coordination across providers and settings, rewarding service quantity rather than quality. The BPCI is testing whether, as prior research has shown, payments for bundled "episodes of care" can align incentives for hospitals, post–acute care providers, physicians, and other healthcare personnel to collaborate across many settings to achieve improved patient outcomes at lower cost.

C

Capitation: A managed care reimbursement method that prepays providers for services on a per-member per-month basis whether or not services are used. If providers exceed the predetermined capitation amount, they may incur a financial penalty. If providers use fewer resources than predicted, they may retain the excess as profit.

Case series: A published summary of a small number of individual cases in the biomedical literature that usually occur for extremely rare conditions or for new illnesses or syndromes and often when the diagnosis is unknown, typically without rigorous analyses. Case series generally are developed by experts and undergo peer review before they are published.

Carve-out: A process through which insurers outsource subscribers' mental illness care oversight to firms specializing in managing service use for mental health diagnoses.

Certification: A regulatory process, much less stringent than licensure, under which a state or professional organization attests to an individual's advanced training and performance abilities in a field of healthcare practice. Specific professions set certification standards for approval by their respective state or professional organizations.

Children's Health Insurance Program (CHIP): Established by the Balanced Budget Act of 1997, the CHIP targets uninsured, eligible children for Medicaid enrollment. It has successfully enrolled millions of children in Medicaid and has been re-funded continuously since its inception, including for two additional years through the Medicare Access and CHIP Reauthorization Act of 2015 (MACRA).

Clinical Observation Unit (COU): Dedicated locations adjacent to hospital EDs or as beds located in other areas of the hospital, COUs use a period of 6-24 hours to triage, diagnose, treat and monitor patient responses while common complaints such as chest pain, abdominal pain, cardiac arrhythmias, and congestive heart failure are assessed.

Clinical research: Primarily focuses on steps in the process of medical care such as the early detection, diagnosis, and treatment of disease or injury; the maintenance of optimal, physical, mental, and social functioning; the limitation and rehabilitation of disability; and the palliative care of those who are irreversibly ill. Clinical research is conducted by a variety of professionals in medicine, nursing, and allied health, often in collaboration with basic scientists.

Community-rated insurance: Insurance plans in which all individuals in a defined group pay premiums without regard to age, gender, occupation, or health status. Community ratings help ensure nondiscrimination against groups with varying risk characteristics to provide coverage at reasonable rates for the community as a whole.

Co-morbidity: When two disorders or illnesses occur in the same person, simultaneously, or one after another.

Comparative effectiveness research: Research designed to inform healthcare decisions by providing evidence on the effectiveness, benefits, and harms of different treatment options. Evidence is generated from research studies that compare drugs, medical devices, tests, surgeries, or ways to deliver health care.

Complementary medicine: Treatment that is not mainstream medicine but is used together with mainstream medicine. An example of complementary medicine would be using acupuncture to treat allergies in addition to obtaining conventional allergy medication prescribed by an allergist.

Computerized decision support system (CDSS): An electronic information-based system in which individual patient data is matched with a computerized knowledge base such as evidence-based clinical practice guidelines, to assist healthcare providers in formulating accurate diagnoses, recommendations, and treatment plans. A CDSS may generate "hard stops" to prevent a disallowed practice or severe errors or "soft stops" that warn of less severe errors and allow physicians to choose to ignore or follow the warning.

Computerized physician order entry (CPOE): Process in which a physician enters patient treatment orders into an individual patient's electronic health record.

Continuing care retirement community (CCRC): Residences on a retirement campus, typically in apartment complexes designed for functional older adults. Unlike ordinary retirement communities that offer only specialized housing, CCRCs offer a comprehensive program of social services, meals, and access to contractual medical services in addition to housing.

Continuing life care community (CLCC): The most expensive of CCRC options. CLCCs offer unlimited assisted living, medical treatment, and skilled nursing care without any additional charges as residents' needs change over time.

D

Deinstitutionalization: The mental health movement beginning in the 1960s through which severely mentally ill patients previously confined to large state or county psychiatric hospitals were discharged to community boarding or nursing homes. The movement marked a major shift of mental health service provision from primarily inpatient settings to community-based facilities.

Department of Health and Human Services (DHHS): The federal government's principal agency concerned with health protection and promotion and provision of health and other human services to vulnerable populations. In addition to administering the Medicare and Medicaid programs, DHHS includes 11 operating divisions.

Descriptive studies: Identify factors and conditions that determine the distribution of health and disease among specific populations using patient records, interview surveys, various databases, and other information sources to provide the details or characteristics of diseases or biologic phenomena and the prevalence or magnitude of their occurrence. Descriptive studies are relatively fast and inexpensive and often raise questions or suggest hypotheses to be tested by analytic studies.

Diagnosis-related groups (DRGs): A case payment system that radically changed hospital reimbursement, shifting hospital reimbursement from the retrospective to a prospective basis. The DRG system provided incentives for the hospital to spend only what was needed to achieve optimal patient outcomes. If outcomes could be achieved at a cost lower than the preset payment, the hospital retained an excess payment for those cases. If the hospital spent more to treat cases than allowed, it absorbed the excess costs. This payment system was widely adopted by non-governmental health insurers.

Disability-adjusted life years (DALYs): The total number of years of life lost to illness, disability, or premature death within a given population.

Disease management programs: MCO programs that attempt to control costs and improve care quality for individuals with chronic and costly conditions through methods such as the use of evidence-based clinical guidelines, patient self-management education, telemedicine, disease registries, risk stratification, proactive patient outreach, and performance feedback to providers. Programs may also use clinical specialists who provide monitoring and support to patients with disease management issues.

Disproportionate share hospital (DSH) payment: Federal law requires these Medicaid payments to states for hospitals serving large numbers of Medicaid and low-income, uninsured individuals. The law establishes an annual DSH allotment for each state. DSH payments provide critical financial supplements to hospitals serving the neediest populations.

E

Ecological models: Models that identify causes of public health problems rooted in the physical and/or social environment and behavior related to an individual. Ecological models take into account the vast number of determinants that affect the health status of groups of people and facilitate decisions about the most expeditious path to developing effective interventions.

Electronic health record (EHR): Computerized patient records that essentially replace paper charts.

Emergency Medical Treatment and Labor Act (EMTALA): Enacted in the 1995 federal budget because of concerns about inappropriate patient transfers between hospitals prompted by payment considerations. EMTALA requires hospitals to treat everyone who presents in their emergency departments regardless of ability to pay. Stiff financial penalties and risk of Medicare decertification by hospitals inappropriately transferring patients, accompanies the EMTALA legal provisions.

Empirical quality standards: Derived from distributions, averages, ranges, and other measures of data variability, empirical quality standards compare information collected from a number of similar health service providers to identify practices that deviate from norms.

Employer mandate: Under the ACA, it requires all businesses with 50 or more full-time equivalent employees to provide health insurance to at least 95 percent of their full-time employees and dependents up to age 26, or pay a fee by 2016. Employers are subject to a $2,000 fee per full-time employee (in excess of 30 employees). The mandate does not apply to businesses with 49 or fewer employees.

Evidence-based clinical practice guidelines: Systematically developed protocols based on extensive research that are considered the most objective and least biased clinical practice guidelines. They serve as a means to assist in preventing the use of unnecessary treatment modalities and in avoiding negligent events, with patient safety and the delivery of consistent high-quality care as foremost priorities.

Experience-rated insurance: Insurance plans that use historically documented patterns of healthcare service utilization for defined populations of subscribers to determine premium charges.

Experimental studies: In experimental studies, the investigator actively intervenes by manipulating one variable to see what happens with the other. Although they are the best test of cause and effect, such studies are technically difficult to carry out and often raise ethical issues. Control populations are used to ensure that other non-experimental variables are not affecting the outcome.

Expert opinion: The lowest or least rigorous form of evidence, but also the most commonly practiced; usually expresses the opinion of a medical specialist in an area of interest to a particular patient; it can occur formally, with a referral to a specialist by a patient's primary care physician, or informally when physicians discuss a case or medical issue with a colleague via phone, email, or face-to-face in an informal setting.

Explicit quality standards: Standards that are professionally developed and agreed on in advance of a quality assessment. Explicit standards minimize the variation and bias that result when judgments are internalized.

F

Federally qualified health center (FQHC): Community-based primary care center staffed by a multidisciplinary team of health care and related support personnel, with fees adjusted based on ability to pay. FQHCs also provide services to link patients with other community resources. Funded by the Health Resources and Services Administration to serve the neediest populations, FQHCs must meet specific operating parameters and may be organized as part of a local health department, a larger human services organization, or a stand-alone, not-for-profit agency.

Federated model of health information exchange: An HIE design in which member institutions maintain their own data at their respective sites in the standardized format used by an HIE. In this model, individual, trans-institutional patient records are assembled in real time by searching all institutions' databases only when requested by authorized users for a particular episode of care.

Focused Practice in Hospital Medicine (FPHM): The American Board of Internal Medicine educational program through which physicians already certified in the internal medicine specialty obtain certification as hospitalists.

Financial risk-sharing: A practice that transfers some measure of financial risk from insurers to providers and beneficiaries. Such transfers of financial risk to beneficiaries commonly take the form of co-payments and deductibles. Co-payments require that beneficiaries pay a set fee each time they receive a covered service, such as a co-payment for each physician office visit. Deductibles require beneficiaries to meet predetermined, out-of-pocket expenditure levels before an insurer assumes payment responsibility. Financial risk-sharing by providers bases their reimbursement levels on insurer-determined parameters related to costs, patient treatment outcomes, and other factors for defined population groups.

Flexner Report: The landmark report resulting from a comprehensive review of the quality of education in U.S. and Canadian medical schools, funded by the Carnegie Foundation. Issued in 1910, the report was a searing indictment of most medical schools of the time. The report gave increased leverage to medical education reformers and stimulated financial support from foundations and wealthy individuals which enabled university-affiliated medical schools to gain significant influence over the direction of medical education.

G

Graduate medical education consortia: Formal associations of medical schools, teaching hospitals, and other organizations involved in the training of medical residents. The consortia provide centralized coordination and direction that encourages the members to function collectively with major aims to improve the structure and governance of residency programs, to increase residents' ambulatory care training experiences, and to address imbalances in physician specialty and location.

H

Healthcare effectiveness data and information set (HEDIS): A data collection and aggregation system that provides a standardized method for MCOs to collect, calculate, and report information about their performance to allow employers, other purchasers, and consumers to compare different health insurance plans. The HEDIS has evolved through several stages of development and continuously refines its measurements through rigorous reviews and independent audits.

Health information administrator: Health information administrators are responsible for the activities of the medical records departments of hospitals, skilled nursing facilities, managed care organizations, rehabilitation centers, ambulatory care facilities, and other licensed healthcare entities. They maintain information systems to permit patient data to be received, recorded, stored, and retrieved to assist in diagnosis and treatment and supply research data for tracking disease patterns, evaluating the quality of patient care, verifying insurance claims, and maintaining patient record confidentiality. A bachelor's degree in health information administration is the entry-level credential.

Health information exchange (HIE): Networks that enable exchange among basic levels of interoperability of patient information among electronic health records maintained by individual physicians and healthcare organizations. HIEs are organized and governed by regional health information organizations (RHIOs).

Health Information Technology for Economic and Clinical Health Act (HITECH Act): A component of the American Recovery and Reinvestment Act of 2009 dedicated to promoting nationwide adoption and use of electronic health records.

Health insurance marketplace (HIM): The ACA required states to establish health benefit exchanges (now known as health insurance marketplaces, or HIMs) to facilitate individuals' and small employers' choices among health plans. With participation by insurance companies in each state, HIMs created a competitive health insurance market by providing web-based, easily understandable, comparative information for consumers on plan choices and standardized rules regarding health plan offers and pricing.

Health services research: A research field combining perspectives and methods of epidemiology, sociology, economics, and clinical medicine. Health services research also uses process and outcome measures reflecting behavioral and economic variables associated with questions of treatment effectiveness and cost-benefit.

Health systems agency (HSA): An organization created by the National Health Planning and Resources Development Act of 1974 that included broad representation of healthcare providers and consumers on governing boards and committees to deliberate and recommend healthcare resource allocations to their respective federal and state governing bodies.

High-deductible health plan (HDHP): First dubbed "consumer-driven health plan," the plans are now known as high deductible health plans (HDHPs). HDHP's goals are to entice employees with lower premium costs in exchange for agreeing to make out-of-pocket up-front payments for health services. The HDHP intends to encourage cost-consciousness about the use of healthcare services. Today, HDHPs are the second most common type of plan offered by employers with 24 percent of U.S. workers selecting this option.

Hill–Burton Act: The 1946 federal law that provided funding to construct new and expand existing U.S. hospitals.

HMO Act of 1973: Federal legislation enacted by the Nixon administration that provided loans and grants for the planning, development, and implementation of combined insurance and healthcare delivery organizations and required that a comprehensive array of preventive and primary care services be included in the HMO arrangement. By linking the payment for services with the quality of care, the HMO Act paved the way for the proliferation of managed care principles that became the foundation of U.S. health insurance reform in the succeeding three decades.

Horizontal integration: Consolidation of two or more hospitals or other entities under one owner through merger or acquisition.

Hospice: A philosophy supporting a coordinated program of care for the terminally ill that focuses on maintaining comfort and quality of life. The most common criterion for admission into hospice is a diagnosis of a terminal illness with a limited life expectancy of six months or less.

Hospital Consumer Assessment of Healthcare Providers and Systems Survey (HCAHPS): The first national, standardized, publicly reported survey of patients' perspectives of hospital care created by the Department of Health and Human Services. Results are publicly reported on the CMS "Hospital Compare" website.

Hospitalist: A physician, typically board certified in internal medicine, who specializes in the care of hospital patients. A hospitalist may be an employee of one or more hospitals or an employee of one or more companies that contract with hospitals to provide services.

I

Implicit quality standards: Standards that rely on the internalized judgments of expert individuals conducting a quality assessment and as such are subject to variation and bias.

Indemnity insurance: A form of insurance in which the insurance company sets allowable charges for services that it will reimburse after services are delivered and allows providers to bill patients for any uncovered excess costs.

Information blocking: A practice by some electronic health record providers and developers that actively blocks transfer of electronic information between institutions with different electronic systems..

Individual mandate: Under the ACA, the requirement that all American citizens (with specific exclusions) obtain health insurance coverage or pay a penalty.

Informed consent: Legally recognized patient right, formalized in a document for a patient's signature, to ensure patients' understanding of the risks and benefits of a medical intervention.

Institutional review board (IRB): Professionally constituted expert groups of individuals who judge the merit of research studies and ensure appropriate and ethical participant safeguards are provided to protect research subjects' safety. A primary function of an IRB is to ensure fully informed consent and research subjects' understanding of risks and benefits of participation.

International medical graduates (IMGs): Physicians trained in medical schools outside the United States who fill the annual shortfall in U.S. medical school graduates required to staff hospitals. Responsibility for evaluating credentials of IMGs entering the United States' residency programs lies with the Educational Commission for Foreign Medical Graduates.

Integrative medicine: A treatment approach that brings conventional medicine and complementary medicine together in a coordinated manner.

L

Laboratory technologists and technicians: Clinical laboratory personnel who analyze body fluids, tissues, and cells checking for bacteria and other micro organisms; analyze chemical content of body fluids; test drug levels in blood to monitor the effectiveness of treatment; and match blood for transfusion. Technologists have a bachelor's or higher degree; technicians may hold associate's degrees or certificates.

Licensure: The most restrictive form of health professional regulation administered by individual states. It defines a professional's scope of practice and educational and testing requirements to engage legally in the practice of a profession.

Long-term care facility (LTCF): An institution such as a nursing home, skilled nursing facility (SNF), or assisted living facility that provides health care to people who are unable to manage independently in the community. Care may represent custodial or chronic care management or short-term rehabilitative services.

M

Maintenance of Certification (MOC): An American Board of Medical Specialties (ABMS) requirement of ongoing, educational programs and recertification examinations every 10 years in each of the specialties and subspecialties in which a physician is certified. The requirements culminate in an ABMS-sponsored board recertification examination 10 years after first receiving certification and every ten years thereafter.

Managed behavioral healthcare organization (MBHO): A corporate entity to which a health plan may outsource the management of mental health services for its subscribers. The MBHO assumes the financial risks and benefits of managing treatment budgets and authorization for access to mental health services.

Meaningful use: The criterion defined by the ONC in collaboration with the Centers for Medicare and Medicaid Services that entails meeting a set of time-delineated requirements for eligible professionals and hospitals to qualify for incentive payments under the HITECH Act. In 2015 this criterion was redefined under the Medicare Access and CHIP Reauthorization Act.

Medicaid: Title XIX amendment to the Social Security Act of 1935, Medicaid is a joint federal/state program providing insurance coverage for a prescribed scope of basic healthcare services to Americans who qualify based on income parameters, established on a state-by-state basis. Medicaid is principally funded from federal general funds with matching dollars to the states and state general funds. Unlike Medicare, which reimburses providers through intermediaries such as Blue Cross, Medicaid directly reimburses providers. Rate-setting formulas, procedures, and policies vary widely among states.

Medicare: Title XVIII amendment to the Social Security Act of 1935, Medicare guarantees a minimum level of health insurance benefits to all Americans beginning at age 65 (and other special needs groups without regard to age). Medicare has four parts: A, B, C, and D, which cover (A) physician and outpatient services, (B) hospital care, (C) participation in managed care plans, and (D) prescription drugs. Most Medicare parts require beneficiary cost-sharing. Medicare funds derive largely from payroll taxes levied on all American workers that are matched by their employers in equal amounts.

Medicare Access and CHIP Reauthorization Act of 2015 (MACRA): Extends funding for Medicaid's Children's Health Insurance Program (CHIP) for two years and establishes a physician payment schedule that predictably specifies the inflation rate for Medicare physician reimbursement. The MACRA also promotes paying for value and quality of care rather than quantity through programs streamlining physicians' participation in quality reporting and payment incentives using the merit-based incentive payment system (MIPS) and alternative payment models (APMs).

Medicare Advantage: A program through which Medicare beneficiaries may have their benefits administered by managed healthcare organizations (MCOs).

Medicare Modernization and Prescription Drug Act of 2003 (MMA): In addition to adding prescription drug coverage for Medicare beneficiaries, the Act established Medicare Advantage plans with new parameters to replace the Medicare+Choice option created by the Balanced Budget Act of 1997.

Merit-based incentive payment system (MIPS): Under the MACRA, combines three previous quality reporting programs into one reporting system, scoring eligible professionals (EPs) on quality, resource use, clinical practice improvement activities, and meaningful use of certified EHR technology. The composite MIPS performance score determines whether EPs will receive an annual upward, downward, or no payment adjustment.

Monolithic model of health information exchange: An HIE design in which all member institutions send clinical data to one central repository where all data reside together in one universal and standardized format. In this model, authorized users may access individual, trans-institutional patient records from the central repository.

N

National Center for Complementary and Integrative Health (NCCIH): A center of the National Institutes of Health devoted to defining, through rigorous scientific investigation, the usefulness and safety of complementary and integrative interventions and providing the public with research-based information to guide health care decision making.

National Committee for Quality Assurance (NCQA): The most influential managed care quality assurance organization, formed in 1979. NCQA primary functions are accreditation for MCOs, PPOs, managed behavioral healthcare organizations, new health plans, and disease-management programs; certifying organizations that verify provider credentials and consultation on physician organizations; and utilization management for organizations, patient-centered medical homes, and disease-management organizations and programs.

National Health Care Workforce Commission (NHCWC): Established by the ACA, the NHCWC was mandated to evaluate and make recommendations for the nation's healthcare workforce including education and training support for existing and potential new workers at all levels, efficient workforce deployment, professional compensation, and coordination among different types of providers. Congress has withheld funding, so the NHCWC has never commenced work.

National Prevention, Health Promotion, and Public Health Council: Established by the ACA and chaired by the U.S. Surgeon General, an organization charged with developing and leading a national prevention strategy and making recommendations to the President and Congress for federal policy changes that support public health goals. The Council provides leadership to and coordination of public health activities of 17 federal departments, agencies, and offices and receives input from a 22 nonfederal member, presidentially appointed Prevention Advisory Group.

Natural history of disease: A matrix used by epidemiologists and health services planners that places everything known about a particular disease or condition in the sequence of its origin and progression when untreated. The matrix identifies causes and stages of a particular disease or condition and facilitates matching of causes and stages with appropriate types of interventions intended to prevent the condition's occurrence or to arrest its progress after onset.

Naturally occurring retirement community (NORC): Apartment complexes, neighborhoods, or sections of communities where residents have opted to remain in their homes as they age.

Never events: Egregious medical errors occurring in hospitals, such as wrong-sided surgery, the treatment for which the DHHS will not provide reimbursement.

NIH Public Access Policy: Mandated by Congress, it requires authors of all scientific papers on NIH-funded research that are published in the peer-reviewed biomedical journals to deposit their accepted manuscripts in a repository maintained by the National Library of Medicine that is freely searchable on the Internet. Since the NIH policy was implemented, several additional federal agencies adopted the policy including the CDC, Department of Defense, Department of Agriculture, and the AHRQ.

Non-parity: Refers to reimbursement for psychiatric services on bases that are not on par with reimbursement for non-psychiatric illnesses. Examples include imposition of lifetime limits on eligibility for psychiatric services and selective insurer fee discounts for psychiatric care.

Non-quantitative treatment limitations (NQTLs): Limitations or restrictions of covered insurance benefits which, though not numerically expressed, otherwise limit the scope or duration of benefits for treatment. In assuring parity of mental health with medical/surgical benefits, insurance plans must apply NQTLs in a comparable and no more stringent manner to mental health as compared and medical/surgical benefits.

Nurse practitioner: A registered nurse, typically with a master's degree, who may specialize in a particular area of nursing practice such as primary care, geriatrics, psychiatry, emergency medicine, or other medical fields. Nurse practitioners function under the supervision of physicians and provide diagnostic, preventive, and therapeutic healthcare services and may prescribe medications as allowed by law as delegated by physicians.

O

Observational studies: May be descriptive or analytical; descriptive studies use patient records, interview surveys, existing medical databases, and other information sources to identify factors and conditions that determine the distribution of health and disease among specific populations; descriptive studies are relatively fast and inexpensive and often raise questions or suggest hypotheses to be tested; they are often followed by analytic studies, which test hypotheses that try to explain biologic phenomena by seeking statistical associations between factors that may contribute to a subsequent occurrence and the initial occurrence itself.

Office of the National Coordinator for Health Information Technology (ONC): The federal agency created to coordinate nationwide efforts to implement health information technology and exchange of health information.

Oregon Death with Dignity Act of 1994: Also known as the Oregon Physician-Assisted Suicide Act, it legalized allowing "an adult resident of Oregon, who is terminally ill to voluntarily request a prescription for medication to take his or her life."

Osteopathic medicine: A philosophy of medical education with particular focus on the musculoskeletal system. Graduates receive a DO rather than MD degree and are considered as rigorously trained and qualified as their MD degree counterparts.

P

Palliative care: Treatment given to relieve the symptoms of a disease rather than attempting to cure the disease.

Patient-centered medical home (PCMH): A team-based model of care led by a personal physician who provides continuous and coordinated care throughout a patient's lifetime to maximize health outcomes, including appropriately arranging patients' care with other qualified professionals for preventive services, treatment of acute and chronic illness, and assistance with end-of-life issues.

Patient-Centered Outcomes Research Institute (PCORI): Created by the ACA as a not-for-profit, independent agency dedicated to conducting comparative effectiveness research, the PCORI is governed by a board of directors appointed by the U.S. Government Accountability Office. The PCORI maintains a strong patient and stakeholder orientation with patient satisfaction recognized as an essential component of quality of care.

Patient Safety Network (PSNET): An AHRQ online access system providing annotated links to the latest patient safety literature and safety news.

Personal health record (PHR): Offered by proprietary companies, a platform on which individual patients create their own records in standardized format to enable them to physically carry records to providers or make them available to providers via the Internet.

Physician assistant (PA): Provides healthcare services under the supervision of a physician. Most hold master's degrees. PAs are trained to provide diagnostic, preventive, and therapeutic healthcare services as delegated by physicians and prescribe medications as allowed by law. PAs are employed in specialties such as internal medicine, pediatrics, family medicine, orthopedics, emergency medicine, and surgery.

Physician Compare: The CMS website, mandated by the ACA, to provide basic contact, practice characteristics, and clinical quality data on Medicare participating physicians and other healthcare professionals. As of 2016, quality data is available only at the physician group, not individual physician level.

Point-of-service (POS) plan: A POS plan is a hybrid of HMO and PPO plans; called "point-of-service" because beneficiaries can select whether to use a provider in a POS approved network or seek care outside the POS plan network when a particular medical need arises. Selecting an out-of-network provider without a primary care referral can incur significant out-of-pocket costs.

Policy development (as a core function of public health): Generating recommendations

from available data to address public health problems, analyzing options for solutions, and mobilizing public and community organizations through implementation plans.

Population health focus: A healthcare system orientation to providing medical care and health-related services that shifts emphasis from individual medical interventions with piecemeal reimbursement to providers' accountability for the outcomes of medical care and overall health status of a defined population group.

Preferred provider organization (PPO): Formed by physicians and hospitals to serve the needs of private, third-party payers and self-insured companies, PPOs guarantee a volume of business to hospitals and physicians in return for negotiated fee discounts. PPOs offer attractive features to both physicians and hospitals. Currently, PPOs are the most popular managed care plans.

Prescription drug monitoring program (PDMP): A state-operated program using an electronic database which tracks prescribing and dispensing controlled prescription drugs to give pharmacists and prescribers patients' history and identify individuals at high-risk who could benefit from intervention.

Prospective payment system (PPS): PPS is the catch-all term for the case payment system of diagnosis-related groups (DRGs) that Medicare required beginning in 1984. PPS shifted hospital reimbursement from a fee-for-service retrospective mode to a pre-paid prospective mode. The PPS provides incentives for hospitals to spend only what is needed to achieve optimal patient outcomes. If outcomes are achieved at a cost lower than the preset payment, hospitals retain the balance.

Prevention and Public Health Fund: Established by the ACA, the nation's first mandatory funding stream dedicated to improving public health. The Fund is intended to eliminate the prior shortcomings of unpredictable federal budget appropriations for public health and prevention programs. The ACA mandates the Fund's use to improve health and help restrain the rate of growth in private and public sector healthcare costs through programs at the local, state, and federal levels to "curb tobacco use, increase access to primary preventive care services, and help state and local governments respond to public health threats and outbreaks."

Primary prevention: Measures designed to promote health and prevent disease or other adverse health occurrences (e.g., health education to encourage good nutrition, exercise, and genetic counseling) and specific protections (e.g., immunization and the use of seat belts).

PubMed Central: The National Library of Medicine repository of all scientific papers on NIH-funded research and scientific papers funded by other federal agencies such as the CDC.

Q

Quality payment program (QPP): Established by the Medicare and CHIP Reauthorization Act of 2015 (MACRA), the QPP allows physicians to select participation in one of two CMS system options that define the way in which they will be reimbursed for services under Medicare: either the Medicare incentive payment program (MIPS) or the alternative payment model (APM).

R

Randomized controlled clinical trial: A study where patients are randomly assigned to two or more experimental groups where each group is identical to each other with the exception of the assigned treatment; often one of the "treatments" is a placebo or no treatment. Patient selection is controlled to reduce potential for any confounder or bias between the experimental groups. Study patients, their physicians, and the outcomes assessors are "blinded" to treatment each patient received, randomized to minimize potential bias of results. After systematic reviews, this is generally considered the highest form of evidence.

Readmissions reduction program: Mandated by the ACA, a Medicare program through which payments to hospitals are reduced based on the readmission of patients with specified diagnoses within 30 days of a prior hospitalization. Penalty determinations are based on three prior years' hospital discharge data.

Recovery-oriented systems of care (ROSC): A holistic, integrated, person-centered and strength-based approach to mental health interventions. ROSC views recovery as a process of pursuing a fulfilling life and seeks to enhance a person's positive self-image and identity through linking their strengths with family and community resources. The ROSC shifts care from the old episodic care model to one that emphasizes continuity and provides choice through the treatment planning process.

Regional health information organization (RHIO): Organizations that create systems agreements, processes, and technology to manage and facilitate exchange of health information between institutions and across different vendor platforms within specific geographic areas. RHIOs administer HIEs.

Respite care: Temporary surrogate care given to a patient when that patient's primary caregiver must be absent. It includes any family managed care program that helps to avoid or forestall the placement of a patient in a full-time institutionalized environment by providing planned, intermittent caregiver relief.

Retail clinic: Operated at retail sites such as pharmacies and supermarkets under consumer-friendly names, such as "MinuteClinic" and "TakeCare." Staffed by nurse practitioners or physician assistants; a physician is not required on site; clinics have physician consultation available by phone.

Registration: Begun as a method to facilitate contacts among professionals and potential employers, registration is the least restrictive form of health professional regulation. Most registration programs are voluntary and range from listings of individuals offering a specific service to professional or occupational groups requiring educational qualifications and testing.

Rural health networks: To address challenges of providing a continuum of care with scarce resources, networks join rural healthcare providers in formal, not-for-profit corporations or through informal linkages to achieve a defined set of mutually beneficial purposes. Networks may advocate at local and state levels on rural healthcare issues, cooperate in joint community outreach activities, and seek opportunities to negotiate with insurers to cover services for their communities' populations.

S

Secondary prevention: Early detection and prompt treatment of a disease or condition to achieve an early cure, if possible, or to slow progression, prevent complications, and limit disability. Most preventive health care is currently focused on this level.

Skilled nursing facility (SNF): A facility, or distinct part of one, primarily engaged in providing skilled nursing care and related services for people requiring medical or nursing care, or rehabilitation services. Skilled nursing care is provided by or under the direct supervision of licensed nursing personnel and provides 24-hour nursing care and other types of services.

Self-funded health insurance: An arrangement through which an employer (or other group, such as a union or trade association) collects and pools premiums into a fund or account used to pay for medical benefit claims instead of using a commercial carrier. Self-funded plans often use the services of an actuarial firm to set premium rates and a third-party administrator to administer benefits, pay claims, and collect data on utilization. Self-funded plans offer advantages to employers, such as avoiding additional administrative and other charges made by commercial carriers, avoiding premium taxes, and enabling interest accrual on cash reserves held in the benefit accounts.

Social Security Act of 1935: The most significant social initiative ever passed by Congress with the core feature of providing monthly retirement benefits to virtually all working Americans. It was the legislative basis for many major health and welfare programs, including the Medicare and Medicaid programs.

Serious mental illness: Mental illness resulting in profound functional impairment which substantially interferes with or limits one or more major life activities.

Systematic review: A meta-analysis of several high-quality randomized, controlled clinical trials. An analysis of multiple analyses has more value as its conclusions are based on the larger, combined populations studied in all the individual clinical trials. This is usually considered the highest level of evidence but is also the most expensive and difficult to carry out.

T

Teaching hospital: A hospital affiliated with a medical school that provides accredited clinical education programs for medical students, medical and dental residents, and other health professionals.

Telehealth: A collection of means or methods for enhancing health care, public health, and health education delivery and support using telecommunications technologies.

Tertiary prevention: Rehabilitation and maximizing remaining functional capacity when a disease or condition has occurred with residual comprise to physical functionality.

Third-party administrator (TPA): A firm contracted by an employer which self-funds employee health insurance to administer benefits, pay claims, and collect data on utilization. Many TPAs also provide case management services for potentially expensive cases to help coordinate care and control employer risk of catastrophic expenses.

Therapeutic science practitioner: Therapeutic sciences practitioners include physical therapists, occupational therapists, speech language pathology and audiology therapists, radiation therapists, and respiratory therapists, representing some of the allied health disciplines in this category. Depending on their field, therapeutic science practitioners' require credentials ranging from bachelor's degrees to doctoral-level educational preparation.

Two-midnight rule: A CMS policy that defines hospital stays of less than two-midnights' duration as outpatient visits billable under Medicare Part B, rather than more highly reimbursed inpatient care under Medicare Part A. Exceptions to the rule may be granted only on a case-by-case basis per judgment of the attending physician and supporting documentation. The rule also moved hospital Medicare audits from Recovery Audit Contractors who were paid contingency fees, to independent not-for-profit Quality Improvement Organizations.

U

Urgent care center: A facility that provides walk-in, extended-hour access for acute illness and injury care that is either beyond the scope or the availability of the typical primary care practice or retail clinic. Urgent care centers also may provide other health services such as occupational medicine, travel medicine, and sports and school physicals.

V

Value-based purchasing (VBP): Mandated by the ACA; a Medicare program through which participating hospitals may earn incentive payments based on clinical outcomes and patient satisfaction or incur reductions in Medicare payments based on compliance with Medicare-determined criteria for "clinical processes of care" and "patient experience of care measures."

Vertical integration: A process through which one entity unites related and complementary organizations to create a system that provides a continuum of care. In its most complete form, a vertically integrated system encompasses medical and health-related services required throughout an individual's life span.

Voluntary ambulatory healthcare agency: Governed by a volunteer board of directors, a community-based, not-for-profit agency that may provide direct medical care, education, advocacy, or a combination of these services. Many voluntary agencies were established by interest groups to address unmet health or health-related needs of specific population groups. Financial support includes government grants, fees for services, third-party reimbursement, and private contributions.

Index

A

AACN. *See* American Association of Colleges of Nursing (AACN)
AAFP. *See* American Academy of Family Physicians (AAFP)
AAMC. *See* American Association of Medical Colleges (AAMC)
ABIM. *See* American Board of Internal Medicine (ABIM) Foundation
ABMS. *See* American Board of Medical Specialties (ABMS)
ACA implementation provisions
  goals, 37
  improving quality and lowering costs, 38–39
  increasing access to affordable care, 40
  new consumer protections, 38
  public health, 331–332
ACA. *See* Affordable Care Act (ACA); Patient Protection and Affordable Care Act (ACA)
academic health centers, 30, 76–77, 82–84, 144–145, 153, 155. *See also* medical schools
academic medical centers. *See* academic health centers
accountable care organizations (ACOs), 96–98, 103, 111, 119, 226–227, 374–375
accreditation, 150–151, 179, 181, 214–215, 218, 256, 261, 264, 318, 320
Accreditation Council for Graduate Medical Education (ACGME), 146–147, 150–151, 153, 159

ACF. *See* Administration for Children and Families (ACF)
ACGME. *See* Accreditation Council for Graduate Medical Education (ACGME)
ACL. *See* Administration for Community Living (ACL)
ACP. *See* American College of Physicians (ACP)
active, evidence-based clinical practice guidelines, 157
acupuncture, 11, 190
acute care hospitals, 12, 62, 74–75, 83, 101, 191, 225. *See also* hospitals
acute-care not-for-profit hospitals, 120
Adams, John, 304
Administration for Children and Families (ACF), 307
Administration for Community Living (ACL), 307
Administration on Aging (AoA), 263
Administrative Simplification provisions, 33
Adolescents. *See also* children
  mental health services needs, 285–286
adult and family nurse practitioners, 178
adult care facilities, 12
adult day care, 263–264
adult homes, 253
adult immunizations, 316
advanced primary care (APC), 115–117
Affordable Care Act (ACA), 71, 96, 100, 180–181, 184, 186, 190, 193–194, 255. *See also*

Patient Protection and Affordable Care Act (ACA)
agencies
  charitable, 247
  federal, 86, 162, 208, 289
  healthcare, 132, 221, 224–225, 250, 254, 256–257, 261, 267
  home health, 253–254, 257, 377
  hospice, 260–261
  local health, 321, 323
  not-for-profit, 132, 261
  public health, 50, 131–132, 305–306, 320, 326–328
  regulatory, 252, 266, 357
  social service, 288
  state health, 310–311, 313–315
  voluntary facilities and, 12, 132, 262, 306
Agency for Health Care Policy and Research (AHCPR), 355–356
Agency for Health Research and Quality (AHRQ), 115, 119, 157, 162, 308, 356, 359, 364, 373
Agency for Toxic Substances and Disease Registry (ATSDR), 308
aging
  of baby-boom generation, 270, 376
  care complexity, 12
  changing demographics, 387
  chiropractic care, 183
  dental care, 181
  healthcare access, 16–17
  healthcare expenditure, 208–209
  healthcare workforce and, 184–186, 191
  homecare services, 377
  natural history, 10
  psychiatric disorders, 287
  RN population, 177

aging in place, 264–265
AHA. *See* American Hospital
    Association (AHA)
AHCPR. *See* Agency for Health
    Care Policy and Research
    (AHCPR)
AHRQ. *See* Agency for Health
    Research and Quality
    (AHRQ)
ALFs. *See* assisted-living facilities
    (ALFs)
allied health personnel, 184
alternative medicine, 189
alternative payment models (APMs),
    102, 227–228, 230
Alzheimer's disease, 262–264,
    336, 386
AMA. *See* American Medical
    Association (AMA)
ambulatory care. *See also*
    accountable care
    organizations (ACOs)
    continuing advances, 133
    federally qualified health
        centers (FQHCs), 128–130
    growth in, 377–378
    history, 120–121
    hospital emergency services,
        122–123
    not-for-profit agencies, 132
    other practitioners, 120
    patient-centered medical homes,
        115–119
    private medical practice,
        111–114
    public services, 130–132
    retail clinics, 126–127
    surgery centers, 127–128
    telehealth, 133
    trends, 109–111
    urgent care centers, 124–126
ambulatory surgery center,
    127–128
American Academy of Family
    Physicians (AAFP), 115
American Association of Colleges
    of Nursing (AACN),
    175, 177
American Association of Medical
    Colleges (AAMC),
    172–173, 378
American Board of Internal
    Medicine (ABIM)
    Foundation, 93, 171

American Board of Medical
    Specialties (ABMS),
    149–151, 159, 163
American College of Emergency
    Physicians, 124, 378
American College of Nurse
    Midwives, 178
American College of Physicians
    (ACP), 115, 127
American Hospital Association
    (AHA), 73
American Journal of Managed Care,
    256
American Medical Association
    (AMA), 23–24, 31,
    112, 142
American Public Health
    Association (APHA), 330,
    333–334
American Recovery and
    Reinvestment Act
    (ARRA), 46, 48–49, 52,
    61, 130, 364
analytic studies, 353
AoA. *See* Administration on Aging
    (AoA)
APC. *See* advanced primary care
    (APC)
APHA. *See* American Public Health
    Association (APHA)
ARRA. *See* American Recovery
    and Reinvestment Act
    (ARRA)
assessment, 308, 316, 318, 321–322,
    334, 337
assisted living, 250–253, 260, 266,
    268
assisted-living facilities (ALFs),
    252–253
Association of American Medical
    Colleges (AAMC),
    143, 150, 153
    Medical School Objectives
        Project, 159
Association of State and Territorial
    Health Officials (ASTHO),
    310–315
assurance, 321, 322, 335
ASTHO. *See* Association of State and
    Territorial Health Officials
    (ASTHO)
ATSDR. *See* Agency for Toxic
    Substances and Disease
    Registry (ATSDR)

B

baby boomers, 173. *See also* older
    Americans
bad apple theory, 357
Balanced Budget Act of 1997 (BBA),
    14–15, 34, 223–224
Balanced Budget Refinement Act of
    1999, 224
Baltimore College of Dental Surgery,
    180
basic science research, 352, 354, 367
BBA. *See* Balanced Budget Act of
    1997 (BBA)
behavioral health services
    barriers to care, 285–287
    financing, 291–295
    future of, 295–296
    historical overview, 278–281
    organization, 287–289
    primary care integration, 289–290
    recipients, 281–284
    recovery oriented systems, 289
    treatment, 285
Behavioral Risk Factor Surveillance
    System (BRFSS), 333
behavioral scientists, 184, 187–188
Benefits Protection and
    Improvement Act, 224
Best Pharmaceuticals for Children
    Act (BPCA), 286
biomedical advances
    ethical dilemmas, 29–30
    high-technology medicine, 29
block grants, 26, 28
Blue Cross, 24–25
BPCI. *See* Bundled Payments for
    Care Improvement Initiative
    (BPCI)
BRFSS. *See* Behavioral Risk Factor
    Surveillance System (BRFSS)
Bundled Payments for Care
    Improvement Initiative
    (BPCI), 101, 225–227
Burton, Harold, 73
Bush, George, W., 35, 46, 289

C

CAH. *See* critical access hospital
    (CAH) model
CAHIIM. *See* Commission on
    Certification for Health

Informatics and Information Management (CAHIIM)

CAN. *See* Caregiver Action Network (CAN), 263

CAP. *See* College of American Pathologists (CAP)

capitation, 211, 214

CAPTE. *See* Commission on Accreditation in Physical Therapy Education (CAPTE)

CARA. *See* Comprehensive Addiction and Recovery Act (CARA)

Caregiver Action Network (CAN), 263

carve-outs, 279

case series, 361

CCRCs. *See* continuing care retirement communities (CCRCs)

CDC. *See* Centers for Disease Control and Prevention (CDC)

CDSS. *See* computerized decision support system (CDSS)

CE. *See* continuing education (CE)

Cedars-Sinai Medical Center, 49

Center for Medicare and Medicaid Innovation (CMMI), 101, 117

Centers for Medicare & Medicaid Services (CMS), 50–53, 60–61, 248, 250, 308, 373–374, 378–379, 385–386

Centers for Disease Control and Prevention (CDC), 301, 308, 323–324, 334

CEO. *See* chief executive officer (CEO)

certification, 171, 173, 178–179, 181, 186–189

certificate of need, 221

certified nurse midwife (CNM), 179

CFO. *See* chief financial officer (CFO)

Chadwick, Edwin, 303–304

Chalmers, C. Thomas, 362

chaos theory, 371

chief executive officer (CEO), 82

chief financial officer (CFO), 82

chief information officers (CIOs), 82

chief medical information officers (CMIOs), 82

chief nursing officer (CNO), 80, 82

Children's Health Insurance Program (CHIP), 34, 38, 102, 118, 122, 227–230, 234

Children
mental health services needs, 285–286

CHIP. *See* Children's Health Insurance Program (CHIP)

chronic brain disease, 285

chronic-care component, U.S. system, 376

chronic care services, future of, 387

chronic illness, 291, 386

CIOs. *See* chief information officers (CIOs)

Citizens Committee on Graduate Medical Education, 148

CLASS Act. *See* Community Living Assistance Services and Supports Act (CLASS Act)

CLCC. *See* continuing life care community (CLCC)

clinical interventions, 4, 27, 77, 333, 363

clinical judgment, 357, 361–362

clinical laboratory scientists, 185

clinical observation units (COUs), 124

clinical practice guidelines, 156–157, 215, 356, 363

Clinical Quality Measures (CQM), 53

clinical research, 352–353, 364–365

Clinton Health Security Act of 1993, 31

Clinton, Bill, 213, 224

CMIOs. *See* chief medical information officers (CMIOs)

CMMI. *See* Center for Medicare and Medicaid Innovation (CMMI)

CMS. *See* Centers for Medicare & Medicaid Services (CMS)

CNM. *See* certified nurse midwife (CNM)

CNO. *See* chief nursing officer (CNO)

comorbidity, 284–285, 288

Coalition to Stop Opioid Overdose, 338

CoDA. *See* Commission on Dental Accreditation (CoDA)

College of American Pathologists (CAP), 58

College of Philadelphia, 142

Commission on Accreditation in Physical Therapy Education (CAPTE), 186–187

Commission on Accreditation of Rehabilitation Facilities, 264

Commission on Certification for Health Informatics and Information Management (CAHIIM), 189

Commission on Dental Accreditation (CoDA), 181

Commission on Rehabilitation Counselor Certification, 188

Committee on the Costs of Medical Care, 25

Community Care Transitions Program, 38, 257

Community Health Accreditation Program, 256

Community Living Assistance Services and Supports Act (CLASS Act), 268–270

community-rated insurance, 210

comparative effectiveness research, 364–365, 367

complaint–response system, 154

complementary medicine, 189

Comprehensive Addiction and Recovery Act (CARA), 338

Comprehensive Health Planning Act of 1966, 27, 221

Comprehensive Primary Care (CPC) Initiative, 117

computed tomography (CT), 80, 382–383

computerized decision support system (CDSS), 54–56, 62, 65

Computerized Physician Order Entry (CPOE), 48, 53

continuing care retirement communities (CCRCs), 265

continuing education (CE), 171

continuing life care community (CLCC), 266

Index

costs. *See also* financing, health care
    of assisted livings, 253
    Ebola virus disease, 339
    insurance coverage and, 234
    quality improvement and, 38–39, 372–374
    malpractice insurance, 160
    psychiatric disability treatment, 288
COUs. *See* clinical observation units (COUs)
CPC. *See* Comprehensive Primary Care (CPC) Initiative
CPOE. *See* Computerized Physician Order Entry (CPOE)
CQM. *See* Clinical Quality Measures (CQM)
critical access hospital (CAH) model, 14
CT. *See* computed tomography (CT)

D

DALYs. *See* disability-adjusted life years (DALYs)
Dartmouth College, 142
DDM. *See* Doctor of Dental Medicine (DDM)
DDS. *See* Doctor of Dental Surgery (DDS)
deinstitutionalization, 261, 280
dementia, 262–263, 287
Department of Defense Military Health System, 309–310
Department of Health and Human Services (DHHS), 202, 305–309, 321, 373
descriptive studies, 353
DHHS. *See* Department of Health and Human Services (DHHS)
diagnosis-related groups (DRGs), 28, 86, 109, 221–222, 267
disability-adjusted life years (DALYs), 281, 283
disease-management programs (DMP), 215
disproportionate share hospital (DSH) payments, 232
DMD. *See* Doctor of Medical Dentistry (DMD)
DMP. *See* disease-management programs (DMP)

DNP. *See* Doctor of Nursing Practice (DNP)
DO. *See* doctor of osteopathic medicine (DO)
Doctor of Dental Medicine (DDM), 181
Doctor of Dental Surgery (DDS), 181
Doctor of Medical Dentistry (DMD), 181
Doctor of Medicine (MD), 172
Doctor of Nursing Practice (DNP), 175
Doctor of Osteopathic Medicine (DO), 145, 172
Doctor of Pharmacy (Pharm.D.), 182
Doctor of Physical Therapy (DPT), 186
Donut hole, 220
DPT. *See* Doctor of Physical Therapy (DPT)
DRGs. *See* diagnosis-related groups (DRGs)
DSH. *See* disproportionate share hospital (DSH)
dual eligible, 229

E

EBM. *See* evidence-based medicine (EBM)
Ebola virus disease (EVD), 339
ecological model, 302
Economic Opportunity Act, 26
ED. *See* emergency department (ED)
EHRs. *See* electronic health records (EHRs)
electronic health records (EHRs), 46–50, 53–58, 62–65, 82–83, 103, 149, 159, 374–375
eligible professionals (EPs), 102
emergency department (ED), 109, 118, 120, 122–123, 377–378, 383
Emergency Economic Stabilization Act, 291
emergency medical services (EMS), 65
Emergency Medical Treatment and Labor Act (EMTALA), 222
Emergency Severity Index (ESI), 123

empirical quality standards, 358
employer mandate, 234, 381
EMS. *See* emergency medical services (EMS)
EMTALA. *See* Emergency Medical Treatment and Labor Act (EMTALA)
end-of-life legislation, 34–35. *See* Oregon Death with Dignity Ac
End-of-Life Option Act, 35
Environmental Protection Agency (EPA), 335
EPA. *See* Environmental Protection Agency (EPA)
EPs. *See* eligible professionals (EPs)
eRx incentive program, 64
ESI. *See* Emergency Severity Index (ESI)
EVD. *See* Ebola virus disease (EVD)
evidence-based clinical practice guidelines, 156–157
evidence-based medicine (EBM), 360–362
experience-rated insurance, 210
experimental studies, 354
expert opinion, 361
explicit quality standards, 358

F

Family Medical Leave Act (FMLA), 257
FDA. *See* U.S. Food and Drug Administration (FDA)
Federal Budget Reconciliation Act of 1980, 221
Federal Emergency Relief Act, 305
Federal Fair Labor Standards Act of 2016, 270, 376
federal government
    behavioral health services, 278–280
    biomedical research, 365
    disease management programs, 215
    assistance, family caregivers, 257
    healthcare concerns, 26–27
    healthcare service payments, 218, 222
    health information technology and, 35, 50–53

long-term care insurance, 268
Medicaid program guidelines, 228
medical school funding, 151
public health responsibilities, 304, 306–309
quality control and planning efforts, 27–28
Federal Medical Assistance Percentage (FMAP), 228
federally qualified health centers (FQHCs), 128–131
federated model of health information exchange, 58
financial risk sharing, 211
financing, health care
  behavioral health services, 291–295
  health insurance, 209–217
  influencing factors, 208–209
  local government and, 217–228
  self-funded health insurance, 217
  waste, fraud and abuse, 207–208
firearm violence, 334–335
Flexner Report, 143–144, 148
FMAP. *See* Federal Medical Assistance Percentage (FMAP)
FMLA. *See* Family Medical Leave Act (FMLA)
focused practice in hospital medicine (FPHM), 95, 151
Food and Drug Administration (FDA), 305, 308
FPHM. *See* focused practice in hospital medicine (FPHM)
FQHCs. *See* federally qualified health centers (FQHCs)

G

germ theory of diseases, 254
global health issues, 338–341
graduate medical education, 145–147
Great Depression of 1929, 24–25
gross domestic product (GDP), 202, 220
group purchasing organizations (GPOs), 366
Guillain-Barré Syndrome (GBS), 340

H

HACs. *See* hospital-acquired conditions (HACs), 225
Harvard University, 142
HCAHPS. *See* Hospital Consumer Assessment of Healthcare Providers and Systems Survey (HCAHPS)
HDHPs. *See* High-Deductible Health Plans (HDHPs)
health care
  access, 17–18
  aging population, 16–17
  conflicts of interest, 18–19
  disease history and prevention levels, 4–9, 5–8
  ethical dilemmas, 19
  health and disease index, 3–4
  Internet's role, 36
  looming challenges, 20
  priorities, 15
  problems, 2
  quality of care, 18
  rural networks, 14–15
  social choices, 16
  stakeholders, 9–13
  technologic ingenuity, 15–16
Health Care Research and Quality Act of 1999, 356
healthcare workforce
  allied health personnel, 184
  behavioral scientists, 187–188
  chiropractors, 183
  clinical nurse specialists, 180
  dentistry, 180–182
  future of care delivery, 193–194
  healthcare administrators, 184
  influencing factors, 191–192
  licensed practical nurse (LPN), 177–178
  nurse practitioners (NPs), 173–174, 178–179
  optometry, 183–184
  pharmacy, 182
  physician assistants (PAs), 179–180
  physicians, 172–173
  podiatric medicine, 182–183
  registered nurses, 174–177
  support services, 188–190
  technicians and technologists, 185–186
  therapeutic science practitioners, 186–187
  workforce issues, 192–193
health information administrators, 188–189
health information exchange (HIE), 49, 56–61
health information technology (HIT), 149, 156, 159, 374–375, 379
Health Information Technology for Economic and Clinical Health Act (HITECH), 35, 46, 50, 103, 159, 163
health insurance
  age requirement, 181
  children's, 229–230
  effects on hospital industry, 73–74
  employer sponsored, 234, 381
  enrollees, 92
  individual mandate, 96, 233
  managed care, 210–214
  mental health, 291–295
  payment system, 201–206, 209
  private, 122, 183, 209–210, 216, 377
  self-funded, 217
  state government's role, 310
health insurance marketplaces (HIM), 202, 233
Health Insurance Portability and Accountability Act (HIPAA), 33–34, 56, 58, 60, 268
Health Maintenance Organization Act of 1973, 28, 210–211
health maintenance organizations (HMOs), 28, 99, 211–212, 214
Health Planning Resources and Development Act, 221
health professions, 169–170
  credential and regulation, 170–172
Health Professions Educational Assistance Act of 1963, 26
Health Resources and Services Administration (HRSA), 129, 308, 331
health savings account option (HSA), 213

health services research, 354–355
    future challenges, 367
    healthcare quality and, 357–358
    health policy and, 356–357
Healthcare Effectiveness Data and
    Information (HEDIS), 215
Healthy People 2000, 321, 323
Healthy People 2010, 323
Healthy People 2020, 323, 331, 333, 336
HEDIS. *See* Healthcare Effectiveness
    Data and Information
    (HEDIS)
HHAs. *See* home health agencies
    (HHAs)
HIE. *See* health information
    exchange (HIE)
High-Deductible Health Plans
    (HDHPs), 213–214, 381
Hill–Burton Act, 74
HIM. *See* health insurance
    marketplaces (HIM)
HIPAA. *See* Health Insurance
    Portability and
    Accountability Act (HIPAA)
HIT. *See* health information
    technology (HIT)
HITECH. *See* Health Information
    Technology for Economic
    and Clinical Health Act
    (HITECH)
HMO Act of 1973, 211
HMOs. *See* health maintenance
    organizations (HMOs)
H1N1 influenza pandemic, 339
home health agencies (HHAs),
    254, 257
horizontal integration, 88
hospices, 35, 219, 229, 250–251, 253,
    258–262, 327
Hospital Consumer Assessment
    of Healthcare Providers
    and Systems Survey
    (HCAHPS), 365
hospitalists, 95–96, 151, 156, 379
hospitals. *See also* Accountable
    Care Organizations(ACOs);
    Affordable Care Act (ACA)
    administrative departments, 82
    allied health professionals, 80
    Bundled Payments for Care
        Improvement Initiative, 101
    communication challenges, 83
    continuing change, 103–104
    diagnostic services, 80–81
    discharge planning, 87

governing boards, role, 93–95
group reimbursement system, 86
growth and decline, 74
health insurance, 73
historical perspectives, 72–73
horizontal integration, 88
hospitalists and, 95–96
hotel services, 82
information technology's impact
    on, 82–83
market reforms, 87–88
medical care hazards, 89–91
medical care variations, 92
medical division, 78–79
Medicaid, 73–74
Medicare, 73–74
Medicare Access & CHIP
    Reauthorization Act of 2015
    (MACRA), 102–103
mergers and acquisition
    (M&A), 97
nursing division, 79–80
nutritional services, 81–82
other patient support
    services, 81
patients, types and roles, 83
population focus, 96–97
Readmissions Reduction
    Program, 99–101
rehabilitation services, 81
research efforts in quality
    improvement, 93
rights and responsibilities of
    hospitalized patients, 84–85
staffing shortages, 92
teaching, 76–77
Two-Midnight Rule, 101–102
types, 75–76
value-based purchasing (VBP)
    program, 99
vertical integration, 89
Veterans Health Administration
    (VHA), 77–78
HRSA. *See* Health Resources and
    Services Administration
    (HRSA)

I

IHI. *See* Institute for Healthcare
    Improvement (IHI)
IMGs. *See* international medical
    graduates (IMGs)
implicit quality standards, 358

IMRT. *See* intensity-modulated
    radiotherapy (IMRT)
indemnity insurance, 209
Indian Health Services (IHS),
    308–309
Indirect Medical Education (IME)
    adjustment, 145
individual mandate, 232–233
information blocking, 56–57
Information Technology (IT), 77,
    82–83. *See also* Internet
informed consent, 85, 353
Institute for Healthcare
    Improvement (IHI), 91
Institute of Medicine (IOM), 207,
    320–321, 326, 357, 359, 373
Institutional Review Board
    (IRB), 353
integrative medicine, 189–190
integrative medicine practitioners,
    189–190
intensity-modulated radiotherapy
    (IMRT), 382
interest groups
    American Medical
        Association, 31
    businesses, 32
    consumers, 32
    insurance companies, 31–32
    labor unions, 32
    pharmaceutical industry,
        32–33
    public health lobby, 32–33
Internal Medicine Board
    Certification, 95
international medical graduates
    (IMGs), 152, 173
Internet
    health care and, 36
    physicians and, 161
intraocular lens implants, 29
IOM. *See* Institute of Medicine
    (IOM)
IRB. *See* Institutional Review
    Board (IRB)
isolation hospitals, 72

J

Johnson, Lyndon, 26–27
Joint Commission, The (TJC), 91,
    128, 218–219, 222, 249, 252,
    256, 279, 337, 358

Joint Review Committee on
        Education in Radiology, 185
*Journal of the American Geriatrics
        Society*, 256
*Journal of the American Medical
        Association*, 143
Judeo-Christian concept, 19

K

Kaiser Family Foundation, 13, 37
Kennedy, Edward, 36
Kennedy, John, F, 45
King's College, 142
knowledge gaps, 3

L

laboratory technologists and
        technicians, 184–185, 188
lead poisoning, 335–336
licensed practical nurse (LPN),
        177–178
licensed vocational nurse
        (LVN), 177
licensure, 170–171, 175, 177, 180,
        183, 187–188, 193
Lifespan Respite Care Act, 263
Lifespan Respite Care
        Reauthorization Act of
        2015, 263
Logical Observations Indexes
        Names and Codes (LOINC),
        57–58, 60
LOINC. *See* Logical Observations
        Indexes Names and Codes
        (LOINC)
long-term care
        adult day care, 263–264
        aging in place, 265
        assisted-living facilities (ALFs),
                252–253
        congressional hearings, 249–250
        continuing care retirement
                communities (CCRCs),
                265–266
        early models, 246–248
        future, 268–271
        high-technology home care, 267
        home care, 254–258
        hospice care, 258–261
        insurance, 267–268

naturally occurring retirement
        community (NORC), 267
respite care, 261–263
skilled nursing facility (SNF),
        250–252
long-term care facilities (LTCFs),
        250, 270
long-term care financing
        collaborative (LTCFC), 270
long-term care insurance (LTCI),
        253, 267–268, 270
LPN. *See* licensed practical nurse
        (LPN)
LTCFC. *See* long-term care
        financing collaborative
        (LTCFC)
LTCFs. *See* long-term care facilities
        (LTCFs)
LVN. *See* licensed vocational nurse
        (LVN)

M

MACRA. *See* Medicare Access and
        CHIP Reauthorization Act
        of 2015 (MACRA)
magnetic resonance imaging (MRI),
        80, 185
maintenance of certification
        (MOC) program, 95, 150,
        170–171
managed behavioral healthcare
        organization (MBHO),
        214, 294
managed care
        cost control, 293–294
        healthcare expenditure, 208–210
        health insurance as, 210–215,
                373–374
        Medicaid, 230
        post-DRG, 87–88
managed care organizations
        (MCOs), 2, 28, 212, 230
MAPCP. *See* Multi-payer Advanced
        Primary Care Practice
        (MAPCP)
master patient index (MPI),
        58–60
MBHO. *See* Managed Behavioral
        Healthcare Organization
        (MBHO)
MD. *See* Doctor of Medicine (MD)
Meaningful Use Program, 50–53, 51,
        60–61, 64

Medicaid
        ACA expansion, 231–232, 234
        additional reforms, 118
        after 2016, 52
        behavioral health care,
                280–281, 291
        benchmark development, 25–28,
                30–31, 33–34, 37–40
        beneficiaries, 117
        certification standards, 256
        creation, 73–74
        EHR Incentive Program,
                50–52
        expansion by 2020, 293
        healthcare expenditure,
                202–206, 214–215, 218,
                220–223, 226–232, 234
        incentive programs,
                comparison, 50–52, 64
        legislation in 1965, 25
        long-term care, 261–264, 268
        managed care, 230
        meaningful use program, 64
        nursing care facilities,
                250–252
        PAC reform plan, 255
        population perspective, 3, 11,
                17, 19
        quality initiatives, 230–231
        reimbursement, 132–133
        retail clinics, 126
Medicaid Money Follows the Person
        (MFP), 17
medical doctor (MD), 145, 180
medical education
        in colonial America to 1880s,
                141–143
        dental, 180
        future perspectives, 162–163
        graduate, 145–147, 173
        pharmaceutical industry, 365
        specialization, 30, 76–77
        Veterans Administration, 309
medical errors, 18, 21, 56, 89–90,
        103, 224, 309, 359, 373, 375
medical schools, 30–31
        affiliations, 121
        clinical education, 75
        in colonial America to 1880s,
                141–143
        enrollees, 172–173
        HIT training, 159
        liability insurance, 160
        reforms, 143–144
        research, 144–145, 372

training programs, 122, 146, 153, 379
Veterans Affairs, 77, 309
medical specialties
certification, 149–150
deficient training, 148
delineation and growth, 147
graduate medical education, 145
nursing division, 79
medical training
certification of physicians, 149–150
graduate, 173
Medicare
additional reforms, 118
behavioral health care, 280–281, 291
benchmark development, 25–28, 30–31, 33–34, 37–40
beneficiaries, 117
certification standards, 256
Community First Choice Option, 256
creation, 73–74
EHR Incentive Program, 50–52
expanded coverage eligibility, 116
healthcare expenditure, 202–208, 210, 214–215, 217–229
in 2015, 52
incentive programs, 50–52, 64
long-term care, 261–264, 268
meaningful use program, 64
nursing care facilities, 250–252
PAC reform plan, 255
population perspective, 3, 11, 14–15, 17, 19
reimbursement services, 132–133, 264
retail clinics, 126
Medicare Access and CHIP Reauthorization Act of 2015 (MACRA), 1, 71, 96, 102–103, 118, 159, 163, 201, 225, 227–228, 230, 235, 367, 374–375, 383–387
Medicare Advantage, 214, 219–220, 226
Medicare and Medicaid Electronic Health Record Incentive Program, 50
Medicare Improvements for Patients and Providers Act, 64

Medicare Modernization and Prescription Drug Act of 2003 (MMA), 219–220
Medicare Shared Savings Program (MSSP), 97
Mental Health Parity Act of 1996, 291
Mental Health Parity and Addiction Equity Act of 2008 (MHPAEA), 291–292, 294
Mental Retardation Facilities and Community Mental Health Centers Construction Act of 1963, 279
merit-based incentive payment system (MIPS), 102–103, 118, 227–228
MFP. See Medicaid Money Follows the Person (MFP)
MHPAEA. See Mental Health Parity and Addiction Equity Act of 2008 (MHPAEA)
MIPS. See merit-based incentive payment system (MIPS)
MMA. See Medicare Modernization and Prescription Drug Act of 2003 (MMA)
MOC. See maintenance of certification (MOC) program
monolithic model of health-information exchange, 58–59
MRI. See magnetic resonance imaging (MRI)
Multi-payer Advanced Primary Care Practice (MAPCP), 117

N

NACCHO. See National Association of County & City Health Officials (NACCHO)
National Adult Day Services Association, 264
National Association of County & City Health Officials (NACCHO), 131, 315–316, 318
National Center for Complementary and Integrative Health (NCCIH), 12, 189

National Center for Health Statistics (NCHS), 62–63, 111, 250
National Committee for Quality Assurance (NCQA), 118–119, 214–215
National Council Licensure Examination for RNs (NCLEX-RN), 175
National Health Care Workforce Commission (NHCWC), 193–194, 380
National health expenditures (NHEs), 202–205
National Health Interview Survey (NHIS), 189
National Health Planning and Resources Development Act of 1974, 27
National Health Security Act, 223
National Health Service Corps (NHSC), 331
National Hospice and Palliative Care Organization (NHPCO), 260
National Institute of Mental Health (NIMH), 279, 281, 285
National Institutes of Health (NIH), 162, 305, 309, 355, 364, 366
National Library of Medicine (NLM), 58
National Mental Health Act of 1946, 278
National Prevention Strategy, 9, 15, 331, 384
National Prevention, Health Promotion and Public Health Council (the Council), 331
National Quality Forum (NQF), 225
National Study of Long-Term Care Providers (NSLTCP), 250
natural history of disease, 4, 9
naturally occurring retirement community (NORC), 267
NCCIH. See National Center for Complementary and Integrative Health (NCCIH)
NCDs. See non-communicable diseases (NCDs)
NCHS. See National Center for Health Statistics (NCHS)

NCLEX-RN. *See* National Council Licensure Examination for RNs (NCLEX-RN)
NCQA. *See* National Committee for Quality Assurance (NCQA)
never events, 225
Next generation accountable care organization (NGACO), 119
NGACO. *See* Next generation accountable care organization (NGACO)
NHCWC. *See* National Health Care Workforce Commission (NHCWC)
NHEs. *See* National health expenditures (NHEs)
NHIS. *See* National Health Interview Survey (NHIS)
NHPCO. *See* National Hospice and Palliative Care Organization (NHPCO)
NHSC. *See* National Health Service Corps (NHSC)
NIH public access policy, 162
NIH. *See* National Institutes of Health (NIH)
NIMH. *See* National Institute of Mental Health (NIMH)
NLM. *See* National Library of Medicine (NLM)
non-communicable diseases (NCDs), 332
non-parity, 280, 290–291
non-quantitative treatment limitations (NQTLs), 292
NORC. *See* naturally occurring retirement community (NORC)
not-for-profit agency ambulatory services, 132
NP. *See* nurse practitioner (NP)
NQF. *See* National Quality Forum (NQF)
NQTLs. *See* non-quantitative treatment limitations (NQTLs)
NSLTCP. *See* National Study of Long-Term Care Providers (NSLTCP)
nurse practitioner (NP), 178–179
Nurse Training Act, 26

O

Obama, Barack
American Recovery and Reinvestment Act (ARRA), signing, 35, 46, 130
epidemic budget, 338–339, 341
gun violence prevention, 334
health budget 2016, 117
healthcare reform, 31–32
MACRA law, 102
paid leave legislation, 257
political climate 2017, 277
proposed 2017 budget, 385
observational studies, 353–354, 361–362
Occupational Safety and Health Act of 1970, 32
OECD. *See* Organization for Economic Cooperation and Development (OECD)
Office of the National Coordinator for Health Information Technology (ONCHIT or "the ONC"), 46, 52
older Americans, 17, 26, 35, 38, 133, 229, 246, 248–249, 251, 264–265, 267, 269–270, 280, 287, 377
Omnibus Budget Reconciliation Act of 1987, 250, 252
ONCHIT (or "the ONC"). *See* Office of the National Coordinator for Health Information Technology (ONCHIT or "the ONC")
opioid epidemic, 336–338
Oregon Death with Dignity Act of 1994, 34–35
Organization for Economic Cooperation and Development (OECD), 2
osteopathic medicine, 172
outcomes research, 363–364

P

PA. *See* physician assistant (PA)
PA-C. *See* physician Assistant-Certified (PA-C)
PACE. *See* program for all-inclusive care for the elderly (PACE)
PAHO. *See* Pan American Health Organization (PAHO)
palliative care, 256, 258, 259–261
Pan American Health Organization (PAHO), 340
Patient's Bill of Rights, 84
Patient Choice and Control at End-of-Life Act, 35
Patient Protection and Affordable Care Act (ACA), 1, 36–37, 111, 252, 371–374, 377–381, 383–387. *See also* Affordable Care Act (ACA)
accountable care organization (ACO) model, 226–227
employer requirements, 216–217
financing mandates, 232–234
implementation provisions, 37–40, 201–204, 207, 209
insurance coverage, 234–235
judicial challenges, 37
Medicaid expansion, 231
Medicare costs, 224–225
value-based purchasing (VBP) program, 227
Patient Safety Network (PSNet), 359
patient safety organizations (PSOs), 359
patient satisfaction surveys, 365
Patient-Centered Clinical Research Network (PCORNET), 365
patient-centered medical homes (PCMHs), 111, 115–119, 227
Patient-Centered Outcomes and Research Institute (PCORI), 356, 364–365
Patient-Centered Primary Care Collaborative (PCPCC), 116
PCMH. *See* patient-centered medical home (PCMH)
PCORI. *See* Patient-Centered Outcomes and Research Institute (PCORI)
PCORNET. *See* Patient-Centered Clinical Research Network (PCORNET)
PCPCC. *See* Patient-centered Primary Care Collaborative (PCPCC)
PDMPs. *See* Prescription drug monitoring programs (PDMPs)

Pediatric Research Equity Act (PREA) of 2003, 286
personal health records (PHRs), 65
PET. *See* positron emission tomography (PET)
PHAB. *See* Public Health Accreditation Board (PHAB)
Pharm.D. *See* Doctor of Pharmacy (Pharm.D.)
PHNCI. *See* Public Health National Center for Innovations (PHNCI)
PHRs. *See* personal health records (PHRs)
physician assistant (PA), 179
Physician Assistant-Certified (PA-C), 179
Physician Compare (website), 157–158
physicians
    changing hospital relationship, 155–156
    ethical issues, 160–161
    generalist to specialist ratio, 152–154
    health information technology (HIT) and, 159
    Internet and, 161
    malpractice insurance, concerns, 160
    report cards, 157–158
    supply and distribution, 151–152
point-of-service (POS), 212, 214
policy development, 318, 321, 334
Poor Law Amendment Act of 1834, 303
population health focus, 77
POS. *See* point-of-service (POS)
positron emission tomography (PET), 80
PPOs. *See* preferred provider organizations (PPOs)
PPS. *See* prospective payment system (PPS)
preferred provider organizations (PPOs), 212, 214
Prescription drug monitoring programs (PDMPs), 338
President's Science Advisory Committee, 45
Prevention and Public Health Fund (the Fund), 326

preventive medicine, 154–155
primary prevention, 4, 15
privacy rule, 33
program for all-inclusive care for the elderly (PACE), 265
prospective payment system (PPS), 221–223
PSNet. *See* Patient Safety Network (PSNet)
PSOs. *See* patient safety organizations (PSOs)
public funding, behavioral health care, 292–293
Public Health Accreditation Board (PHAB), 320
Public Health Act of 1848, 303
Public Health National Center for Innovations (PHNCI), 320
Public Health Service Act of 1965, 27
PubMed Central, 162

Q

QIO. *See* quality improvement organization (QIO)
QPP. *See* quality payment program (QPP)
quality improvement organization (QIO), 87, 102
quality payment program (QPP), 227

R

randomized controlled clinical trial, 360–363
RBRVS. *See* resource-based relative value scale (RBRVS)
Readmissions Reduction Program, 97, 99–100
Recovery Oriented Systems of Care (ROSC), 289
regional health information organizations (RHIOs), 57, 60, 375
Regional Medical Programs and Comprehensive Health Planning Act, 27
Registered Nurses, 174–177
registration, 170, 172, 186

research
    basic science research, 352
    clinical research, 352–353
    ethics, 366
    epidemiological research, 353–354
    health services research, 354–355
residency review committee (RRC), 148
resource-based relative value scale (RBRVS), 223
respite care, 256, 260–263
retail clinics, 124, 126–127
RHIOs. *See* regional health information organizations (RHIOs)
rights and responsibilities of hospitalized patients
    informed consent, 85
    second opinions, 85
Robert Wood Johnson Foundation (RWJF), 13, 92, 177, 320
ROSC. *See* Recovery Oriented Systems of Care (ROSC)
rural health networks, 14–15
RWJF. *See* Robert Wood Johnson Foundation (RWJF)

S

SAMHSA. *See* Substance Abuse and Mental Health Services Administration (SAMHSA)
SARS. *See* Severe Acute Respiratory Syndrome (SARS)
secondary prevention, 9
security rule, 33
self-funded health insurance, 217
Serious Mental Illness (SMI), 281, 284, 285, 288–289, 293–295
Severe Acute Respiratory Syndrome (SARS), 338, 340
Sierra Leone College of Medicine and Allied Health Sciences, 339
Sierra Leone Ministry of Health and Sanitation, 339
SIM. *See* State Innovation Models (SIM)
skilled nursing facility (SNF), 250–252

SNOMED Clinical Terms (SNOMED-CT), 58
SNOMED. *See* Systematic Nomenclature of Medicine (SNOMED)
Social Security Act of 1935, 2, 26, 73–74, 218, 220, 228, 248, 305. *See also* Medicaid; Medicare
Social Security Administration, 218
Social Security and Disability Insurance, 279
social workers
    ambulatory care practitioners, 120, 131
    emergency department (ED) services, 122
    FQHC model, 129
    in healthcare workforce, 188
    home care, 254
    hospices, 260
    psychiatric, 287
    rehabilitation services, 81
SSI. *See* Security Income (SSI)
stakeholders, U.S. healthcare industry
    care facilities, 11
    complementary and alternative therapists, 11–12
    employers, 9, 11
    government, 11
    health insurers, 12
    health professionals, 11
    health professions education and training institutions, 13
    hospitals, 11
    long-term care industry, 12
    organizations, 13
    professional associations, 13
    public, 9
    research communities, 13
    voluntary facilities and agencies, 12
State Innovation Models (SIM), 117
substance abuse, 75, 124, 130, 187–188, 280–288, 291–292, 309
Substance Abuse and Mental Health Services Administration (SAMHSA), 280, 309
Sunshine Act, 366, 385
Supplemental Security Income (SSI), 279

Systematic Nomenclature of Medicine (SNOMED), 58
systematic review, 356, 360, 364

T

teaching hospitals, 75–76, 79
technology. *See also* Information Technology
    biomedical advances, 29–30
    diagnostic services, 80–81
    healthcare expenditures, 208–210, 220–221, 223, 227, 231
    health information, 45–65, 159
    health personnel and, 191–194
    home care innovations, 254, 258, 264, 267, 269
    Information Technology's Impact on Hospitals, 82–83
    Internet, 161
    nuclear medicine, 185
    telehealth, 133
    unanswered questions, 15–16
Technology Assessment Act of 1972, 30
telehealth, 133
terminal illness, 188, 258
tertiary prevention, 9
therapeutic science practitioners, 184, 186–187
third-party administrator (TPA), 217
TPA. *See* third-party administrator (TPA)
trauma centers, 75, 144
TRICARE program, 310
Truman, Harry, S., 31, 36
tuberculosis, 131, 174, 249, 304–305, 324, 329
Two-Midnight Rule, 101–102
type 2 diabetes, 185

U

U.S. Army, 148
U.S. Chamber of Commerce, 32
U.S. Council of Economic Advisors 2014, 231
U.S. Department of Justice, 207, 258

U.S. Food and Drug Administration (FDA), 366
U.S. Government Accountability Office, 364
U.S. public health services. *See also* agencies
    ACA provisions, 331–332
    challenges and responses, 321–327
    clinical medicine and, 327–329
    definition, 301–302
    early history, 302–303
    Ebola virus disease (EVD), 339
    enduring and emerging challenges, 332–334
    ethics, 330
    firearm violence, 334–335
    future of, 341–342
    global issues, 338–339
    government's responsibility, 306–309
    H1N1 influenza pandemic, 339
    health department relationship (state and local), 319–320
    lead poisoning, 335–336
    local government's role, 315–319
    opioid epidemic, 336–338
    severe acute respiratory syndrome (SARS), 340
    state's role, 310–315
    voluntary national accreditation program, 320
    voluntary organizations, 327
    Zika virus, 340–341
U.S. residency programs, 146–147, 154, 173, 184
UCAOA. *See* Urgent Care Association of America (UCAOA)
ultrasonography, 80–81, 185
UMLS. *See* Unified Medical Language System (UMLS)
unemployment, 92, 288
Unified Medical Language System (UMLS), 58
uninsured/underinsured Americans, 9, 17–18, 32
    ACA provisions, 154, 194, 202, 232, 234, 277–278, 280–281
    access to affordable care, 39–40
    children, 34, 229–230
    dental care, 182
    DSH payments, 232

uninsured/underinsured Americans
(*continued*)
emergency department (ED)
visits, 377–378
firearm violence, 335
healthcare expenditure,
208, 218
hospital emergency services,
122
local health departments
and, 319
Medicaid expansion, 231
not-for-profit ambulatory
services, 132
public funding, 292
types of hospitals, 75
United States
aging population, 16
ambulatory care, 111–112, 123,
127, 132–133
behavioral health services, 277,
280–281, 293
biomedical advances, 29
EHR adoption progress,
62–64
health expenditure, 201,
206–210, 226, 228, 230
health professionals, 170,
172–176, 179–183, 185–188,
190, 193
HIT goals, 53
long-term care, 246, 249, 258,
262–263, 266, 268
medical education, 141–144,
148, 153–154, 159,
162-163
number of hospitals, 73

public medical care, 304–306,
309, 315, 321, 324–327,
331–341
quality of clinical care, 373–374,
376, 379–381, 386–387
United States Department of
Veterans Affairs (VA), 56,
62, 75, 77–78, 309
Urgent Care Association of America
(UCAOA), 124–126
urgent care center, 124–126
utilization review committees, 86

V

VA. *See* United States Department of
Veterans Affairs (VA)
vaccine trials, EVD, 339
Valium, emotional ills, 29
Value-Based Purchasing (VBP),
99, 227
VBP. *See* Value-Based Purchasing
(VBP)
vertical integration, 89
veterans administration health
information, 62
Veterans Health Administration
(VHA), 77–78, 309
VHA. *See* Veterans Health
Administration (VHA)
Visiting Nurses Association, 249
voluntary ambulatory healthcare
agencies, 132
voluntary facilities and agencies, 12
voluntary national accreditation
program, 320

W

websites, 36–37, 101, 393
Wellstone–Domenici Parity Act of
2008, 280
WHO. *See* World Health
Organization (WHO)
withholds, 211
women
ambulatory care facilities,
110
in nursing, 73, 92, 173
Medicaid programs and, 229
observational studies, 362
physicians, 172
working, 376
Zika infection, 340
World Bank, 339–340
World Health Organization (WHO),
332, 339–341
World War I, 24, 174, 278
World War II, 25, 27, 30, 73, 175,
180, 209, 246, 278, 305,
355, 361

Y

yellow fever, 29, 304
yoga, 11, 190

Z

Zika virus, 340–341